Essentials of Cultural Anthropology

Essentials of Cultural Anthropology

A Toolkit for a Global Age

Kenneth J. Guest

**Baruch College
The City University of New York**

W. W. Norton & Company
New York • London

W. W. Norton & Company has been independent since its founding in 1923, when William Warder Norton and Mary D. Herter Norton first published lectures delivered at the People's Institute, the adult education division of New York City's Cooper Union. The firm soon expanded its program beyond the Institute, publishing books by celebrated academics from America and abroad. By midcentury, the two major pillars of Norton's publishing program—trade books and college texts—were firmly established. In the 1950s, the Norton family transferred control of the company to its employees, and today—with a staff of four hundred and a comparable number of trade, college, and professional titles published each year—W. W. Norton & Company stands as the largest and oldest publishing house owned wholly by its employees.

Editor: Peter Lesser
Project Editor: Linda Feldman
Assistant Editor: Samantha Held
Manuscript Editor: Alice Vigliani
Managing Editor, College: Marian Johnson
Managing Editor, College Digital Media: Kim Yi
Production Manager: Ashley Horna
Media Editor: Eileen Connell
Media Editorial Assistant: Ava Bramson
Marketing Manager: Julia Hall
Design Director: Hope Miller Goodell
Book Design: Kiss Me I'm Polish LLC
Photo Editor: Trish Marx
Permissions Manager: Megan Jackson
Composition: Jouve
Manufacturing: RR Donnelley Kendallville

Permission to use copyrighted material is included on p. A29.

Library of Congress Cataloging-in-Publication Data

Guest, Kenneth J.
  Essentials of cultural anthropology : a toolkit for a global age / Kenneth J. Guest, Baruch
College, The City University of New York.
      pages cm
  Includes bibliographical references and index.
  ISBN 978-0-393-26501-9 (pbk.)
  1. Ethnology.   2. Applied anthropology.   3. Globalization. I. Title.
  GN316.G845 2016
  305.8—dc23   2015023572

W. W. Norton & Company, Inc., 500 Fifth Avenue, New York, NY 10010-0017
wwnorton.com

W. W. Norton & Company Ltd., Castle House, 75/76 Wells Street, London W1T 3QT
1 2 3 4 5 6 7 8 9 0

About the Author

Kenneth J. Guest is professor of anthropology at Baruch College, The City University of New York, and author of *God in Chinatown: Religion and Survival in New York's Evolving Immigrant Community* (NYU Press, 2003). His research focuses on immigration, religion, globalization, ethnicity, and entrepreneurialism.

Professor Guest's ethnographic research in China and the United States traces the immigration journey of recent Chinese immigrants from Fuzhou, southeast China, who, drawn by restaurant, garment shop, and construction jobs and facilitated by a vast human smuggling network, have revitalized New York's Chinatown. His writing explores the role of Fuzhounese religious communities in China and the United States; the religious revival sweeping coastal China; the Fuzhounese role in the rapidly expanding U.S. network of all-you-can-eat buffets and take-out restaurants; and the higher-education experiences of the Fuzhounese second generation.

A native of Florida, Professor Guest studied Chinese at Beijing University and Middlebury College. He received his B.A. from Columbia University (East Asian Languages and Cultures), an M.A. from Union Theological Seminary (Religious Studies), and the M.A., M.Phil., and Ph.D. from The City University of New York Graduate Center (Anthropology).

Brief Contents

Part 1: Anthropology for the 21st Century

Chapter 1: Anthropology in a Global Age   4
Chapter 2: Culture   30
Chapter 3: Fieldwork and Ethnography   62
Chapter 4: Language   92

Part 2: Unmasking the Structures of Power

Chapter 5: Race and Racism   120
Chapter 6: Ethnicity and Nationalism   152
Chapter 7: Gender   176
Chapter 8: Sexuality   204
Chapter 9: Kinship, Family, and Marriage   234
Chapter 10: Class and Inequality   262

Part 3: Change in the Modern World

Chapter 11: The Global Economy   296
Chapter 12: Politics and Power   332
Chapter 13: Religion   360
Chapter 14: Health and Illness   392

Contents

Preface   xxi

Part 1: Anthropology for the 21st Century

Chapter 1: Anthropology in a Global Age   4
Coke, Water, and the Women of Plachimada   5

What is Anthropology?   8
Brief Background   8
Anthropology's Unique Approach   9

**Through What Lenses Do Anthropologists Gain a
Comprehensive View of Human Cultures?**   12
Physical Anthropology   13
Archaeology   15
Linguistic Anthropology   17
Cultural Anthropology   18

**What is Globalization, and Why Is It Important
for Anthropology?**   18
Globalization and Anthropology   19
Globalization: Key Dynamics   20

How is Globalization Transforming Anthropology?   24
Changing Communities   24
Changing Research Strategies   25

Toolkit   28
Thinking Like an Anthropologist: Living in a Global Age   28
Key Terms   29

Chapter 2: Culture 30

The Kiss: Richard Gere and Shilpa Shetty in India 31

What is Culture? 33
Culture Is Learned and Taught 34
Culture Is Shared Yet Contested 35
Culture Is Symbolic and Material 35

How Has the Culture Concept Developed in Anthropology? 42
Early Evolutionary Frameworks 42
American Historical Particularism 43
British Structural Functionalism 44
Culture and Meaning 44

How Are Culture and Power Related? 46
Power and Cultural Institutions 46
Hegemony 48
Human Agency 48
Jena High School: Connecting Meaning and Power 50

How Much of Who You Are Is Determined by Biology and How Much by Culture? 52
Biological Needs versus Cultural Patterns 52
Nature versus Nurture 53

How Is Culture Created? 55
Manufacturing the Desire to Consume 55

How Is Globalization Transforming Culture? 56
A Homogenizing Effect 57
Migration and the Two-Way Transference of Culture 57
Increasing Cosmopolitanism 58

Toolkit 60
Thinking Like an Anthropologist: The Kiss as a Cultural Act 60
Key Terms 61

Chapter 3: Fieldwork and Ethnography 62

Death without Weeping: Fieldwork in a Brazilian Shantytown 63

What Is Unique about Ethnographic Fieldwork, and Why Do Anthropologists Conduct This Kind of Research? 65

Fieldwork Begins with People 66

Fieldwork Shapes the Anthropologist 66

Fieldwork as Social Science and as Art 68

Fieldwork Informs Daily Life 69

How Did the Idea of Fieldwork Develop? 69

Early Accounts of Encounters with Others 69

Nineteenth-Century Anthropology and the Colonial Encounter 70

The Professionalization of Social Scientific Data-Gathering and Analysis 70

How Do Anthropologists Get Started Conducting Fieldwork? 76

Preparation 76

Strategies 77

Mapping 78

Skills and Perspectives 79

Analysis 80

How Do Anthropologists Write Ethnography? 82

Polyvocality 82

Reflexivity 83

Ethnographic Authority 83

What Moral and Ethical Concerns Guide Anthropologists in Their Research and Writing? 83

Do No Harm 84

Obtain Informed Consent 85

Ensure Anonymity 86

How Are Fieldwork Strategies Changing in Response to Globalization? 86

Changes in Process 86

Changes in Content 87

Toolkit 90

Thinking Like an Anthropologist: Applying Aspects of Fieldwork to Your Own Life 90

Key Terms 91

Chapter 4: Language 92

Language and Immigration Debates in Arizona 93

What Is Language and Where Does It Come From? 95

The Origins of Human Language   95

Descriptive Linguistics   98

Kinesics and Paralanguage   99

Can Language Shape Our Ways of Thinking?   100

Language, Thought, and Culture   100

The Role of Focal Vocabulary   101

**How Do Systems of Power Intersect with Language
and Communication?**   102

The "N-Word"   103

Language and Gender   104

Language and Dialect   106

Language Variation in the United States   107

Historical Linguistics   109

What Are the Effects of Globalization on Language?   111

Diminishing Language Diversity   111

Hastening Language Loss   112

Toolkit   116

Thinking Like an Anthropologist: Language, Immigration,
and U.S. Culture   116

Key Terms   117

Part 2: Unmasking the Structures of Power

Chapter 5: Race and Racism

Chapter 5: Race and Racism   120

Hurricane Katrina   121

Do Biologically Separate Races Exist?   124

Fuzzy Boundaries in a Well-Integrated Gene Pool   125

The Wild Goose Chase: Linking Phenotype to Genotype   126

How Is Race Constructed around the World?   128

Race and the Legacy of Colonialism   128

How Is Race Constructed in the United States?   131

Race and the U.S. Census 132

History of U.S. Racial Categories: Constructing Whiteness 133

The Rule of Hypodescent 135

Race and Immigration 136

What Is Racism? 140

Types of Racism 140

Resisting Racism 143

Race, Racism, and Whiteness 146

Toolkit 150

Thinking Like an Anthropologist: Shifting Our Perspectives
on Race and Racism 150

Key Terms 151

Chapter 6: Ethnicity and Nationalism

Chapter 6: Ethnicity and Nationalism 152

The Soccer World Cup 153

What Does "Ethnicity" Mean to Anthropologists? 156

Ethnicity as Identity 156

Creating Ethnic Identity 157

How Is Ethnicity Created and Put in Motion? 161

Ethnicity as a Source of Conflict 161

Ethnicity as a Source of Opportunity 165

Ethnic Interaction in the United States:
Assimilation versus Multiculturalism 168

What Is the Relationship of Ethnicity to the Nation? 169

Imagined Communities and Invented Traditions 169

Anticolonialism and Nationalism 171

The Challenges of Developing a Sense of Nationhood 172

Toolkit 174

Thinking Like an Anthropologist: Who Is an American? 174

Key Terms 175

Chapter 7: Gender

Chapter 7: Gender 176

Gender Discrimination in Silicon Valley 177

Are Men and Women Born or Made? 179

Distinguishing between Sex and Gender 179

The Cultural Construction of Gender 181

The Performance of Gender 185

Are There More Than Two Sexes? 186

A Theory of Five Sexes 187

Alternate Sexes, Alternate Genders 188

How Do Anthropologists Explore the Relationship between Gender and Power? 190

Revisiting Early Research on Male Dominance 191

Gender Stereotypes, Gender Ideology, and Gender Stratification 193

Challenging Gender Ideologies and Stratification 196

How Is Globalization Transforming Women's Lives? 199

Impacts on Women in the Labor Force 199

Toolkit 202

Thinking Like an Anthropologist: Broadening Your View of the Cultural Construction of Gender 202

Key Terms 203

Chapter 8: Sexuality 204

Sexuality Everywhere 205

What Is "Natural" about Human Sexuality? 207

The Intersection of Sexuality and Biology 208

Sexuality and Culture 211

What Does a Global Perspective Tell Us about Human Sexuality? 212

Same-Gender "*Mati* Work" in Suriname 212

Machismo and Sexuality in Nicaragua 214

How Has Sexuality Been Constructed in the United States? 215

The Invention of Heterosexuality 216

"White Weddings" 219

Lesbian and Gay Commitment Ceremonies 221

Federal Law and Public Opinion 223

How Is Sexuality an Arena for Working Out Relations of Power? 224

Intersections of Race and Sexuality for Black Gay Women 224

Sexuality and Power on U.S. College Campuses 226

How Does Globalization Influence Local Expressions of Sexuality? 228

Sexuality, Language, and the Effects of Globalization in Nigeria 229

Toolkit 232

Thinking Like an Anthropologist: Sexuality in Your Life 232

Key Terms 233

Chapter 9: Kinship, Family, and Marriage 234

Sperm Donor 150 Meets His Children 235

How Are We Related to One Another? 237

Descent 238

Marriage and Affinal Ties 246

Are Biology and Marriage the Only Bases for Kinship? 251

Houses, Hearths, and Kinship: The Langkawi of Malaysia 251

Creating Kin to Survive Poverty: Black Networks near Chicago, Illinois 252

Is a Country Like One Big Family? 253

Reproducing Jews: Issues of Artificial Insemination in Israel 253

How Is Kinship Changing in the United States? 255

The Nuclear Family: The Ideal versus the Reality 255

Chosen Families 256

The Impact of Assisted Reproductive Technologies 257

Families of Same-Sex Partners 258

Toolkit 260

Thinking Like an Anthropologist: Kinship in Personal and Global Perspective 260

Key Terms 261

Chapter 10: Class and Inequality 262

Class at a Baltimore Orioles Baseball Game 263

Is Inequality a Natural Part of Human Culture? 266

Egalitarian Societies 266

Ranked Societies 267

How Do Anthropologists Analyze Class and Inequality? 269

Theories of Class 269

How Are Class and Inequality Constructed in the United States? 275

A Look at the Numbers 276

Ethnographic Portraits of Class in the United States 278

What Are the Roots of Poverty in the United States? 283

The "Culture of Poverty": Poverty as Pathology 284

Poverty as a Structural Economic Problem 285

Why Are Class and Inequality Largely Invisible in U.S. Culture? 286

The Role of the Media 287

The Consumer Culture 287

What Are the Effects of Global Inequality? 289

Toolkit 292

Thinking Like an Anthropologist: Observing the Dynamics of Class through Baseball and Beyond 292

Key Terms 293

Part 3: Change in the Modern World

Chapter 11: The Global Economy 296

Chocolate and Civil War in Côte d'Ivoire 297

What Is an Economy, and What Is Its Purpose? 299

From Foraging to Industrial Agriculture: A Brief Survey of Food Production 300

Distribution and Exchange 302

What Are the Roots of Today's Global Economy? 304

Early Long-Distance Trade Routes 304

Colonialism 305

Anticolonial Struggles 308

The Modern World Economic System 309

From Fordism to Flexible Accumulation 312

What Are the Dominant Organizing Principles of the Modern World Economic System? 314

Capitalism, Economic Liberalism, and the Free Market 314

Neoliberalism 315

How Does Today's Global Economy Link Workers with Consumers Worldwide? 316

Tsukiji: Fish Market at the Center of the World 317

How Is Today's Global Economy Reshaping Migration? 318

Pushes and Pulls 319

Bridges and Barriers 319

Global Migration Patterns 322

Types of Immigrants 323

Is Today's Global Economic System Sustainable? 326

Successes and Failures 326

The Human Ecological Footprint 327

World on the Edge 329

Toolkit 330

Thinking Like an Anthropologist: Situating Yourself within the Global Economy 330

Key Terms 331

Chapter 12: Politics and Power 332

Arab Spring 333

How Have Anthropologists Viewed the Origins of Human Political History? 336

Bands 337

Tribes 338

Chiefdoms 339

Putting Typologies in Perspective 340

What Is the State? 341

The Modern Western-Style State 341

Aspects of State Power 343

How Is Globalization Affecting the State? 344

International Nonstate Actors Challenge State Sovereignty 344

Civil Society Organizations Gain a Global Reach 345

What Is the Relationship among Politics, the State, Violence, and War? 346

Are Humans Naturally Violent or Peaceful? 346

The State and War 348

Anthropology on the Front Lines of War and Globalization 349

How Do People Mobilize Power outside the State's Control? 351

Social Movements 352

Alternative Legal Structures 355

Toolkit 358

Thinking Like an Anthropologist: Applying Politics to Daily Life and Beyond 358

Key Terms 359

Chapter 13: Religion 360

Buddhist Monks Protest in Myanmar 361

What Is Religion? 364

Seeking a Working Definition 364

Local Expressions and Universal Definitions 365

What Tools Do Anthropologists Use to Understand How Religion Works? 368

Émile Durkheim: The Sacred and the Profane 369

Religion and Ritual 370

Karl Marx: Religion as "the Opiate of the Masses" 372

Max Weber: The Protestant Ethic and Secularization 375

Shamanism 376

Religion and Magic 377

In What Ways Is Religion Both a System of Meaning and a System of Power? 382

Religion and Meaning 382

Religion and Power 383

Blurring the Boundaries between Meaning and Power 384

How Is Globalization Changing Religion? 386

Relocating Rituals and Deities from the Home Country 387

Toolkit 390

Thinking Like an Anthropologist: Religion in the
    Twenty-First Century 390
Key Terms 391

Chapter 14: Health and Illness 392
Hundred-Year-Old Twin Sisters 393

How Does Culture Shape Our Ideas of Health and Illness? 395
The Anthropology of Childbirth 396
Ethnomedicine 400
Biomedicine 402
Are There Other Global Health Systems? 404

How Can Anthropologists Help Solve Health Care Problems? 407
Creating a Public Health System in Rural Haiti 407

Why Does the Distribution of Health and Illness Mirror That of Wealth and Power? 409
Health Transition and Critical Medical Anthropology 409
Staff Attitudes Affect Health Care Delivery in a
    New York Women's Clinic 411

How Is Globalization Changing the Experience of Health and Illness and the Practice of Medicine? 413
Medical Migration 413
Multiple Systems of Healing 413

Toolkit 418
Thinking Like an Anthropologist: Health in the
    Individual and in the Global Population 418
Key Terms 419

Glossary A1
References A11
Credits A29
Index A33

Preface

Anthropology may be the most important course you take in college. That may seem like a bold statement. But here's what I mean.

CULTURAL ANTHROPOLOGY: A TOOLKIT

The world in the twenty-first century is changing at a remarkable pace. We are experiencing an interaction with people, ideas, and systems that is intensifying at breathtaking speed. Communication technologies link people instantaneously across the globe. Economic activities challenge national boundaries. People are on the move within countries and between them. As a result, today we increasingly encounter the diversity of humanity, not on the other side of the world but in our schools, workplaces, neighborhoods, religious communities, and families. How will we develop the skills and strategies for engaging and navigating the complex, multicultural, global, and rapidly changing reality of the world around us?

Anthropology is the toolkit you are looking for. Cultural anthropology is the study of humans, particularly the many ways people around the world today and throughout human history have organized themselves to live together: to get along, to survive, to thrive, and to have meaningful lives. *Essentials of Cultural Anthropology: A Toolkit for a Global Age* will introduce you to the fascinating work of anthropologists and the research strategies and analytical perspectives that anthropologists have developed—our tools of the trade—that can help you better understand and engage today's world as you move through it.

I teach Introduction to Cultural Anthropology to hundreds of students every year at Baruch College, a senior college of The City University of New York. Baruch has an incredibly diverse student body, with immigrants from more than a hundred countries, speaking dozens of languages and thinking about culture, race, gender, and family in as many different ways. Some of my students will become anthropology majors. More will become anthropology minors. But at Baruch, in fact, most students will become business majors.

This book emerges from my efforts to make anthropology relevant to all of my students as they navigate their everyday lives, think about the world as it is and as it is becoming, and consider tackling the crucial issues of our times. On a practical level, we all employ the skills of anthropology on a daily basis. Every time you walk into a room and try to figure out how to fit into a new group of people—in your classroom, in a student club, at the office, at a party, in your religious community, when your new love interest takes you home to meet the family—how in the world do you deduce what the rules are? Where you fit in? What you're supposed to do? What the power dynamics are? What you can contribute to the group? *Essentials of Cultural Anthropology: A Toolkit for a Global Age* is designed to help you develop those skills—to think more deeply and analyze more carefully—and to prepare you to use them in a diversity of settings at home or around the world.

WHY A NEW TEXTBOOK?

The world has changed dramatically in the past forty years and so has the field of anthropology. *Essentials of Cultural Anthropology: A Toolkit for a Global Age*—like the parent version, *Cultural Anthropology*—presents the theoretical, methodological, and pedagogical innovations that are transforming anthropology and highlights both historical and contemporary research that can provide students with insight into the ways in which anthropologists approach the crucial challenges and questions of our times. *Essentials* contains 14 concise chapters that I hope will easily fit into most courses—either as a stand-alone text or paired with additional primary readings and assignments. My goal with *Essentials* is to place at students' fingertips a lively, compelling presentation of the key concepts and debates at the heart of anthropology today in a shorter text—written without boxes and special features—that allows faculty increased flexibility in course development and design.

Globalization. As the world is changing, so too are the people anthropologists study. Even the way anthropologists conduct research is changing. In the contemporary period of rapid globalization, the movement, connection, and interrelatedness that have always been a part of human reality have intensified and become more explicit, reminding us that our actions have consequences for the whole world, not just for our own lives and those of our families and friends. This book integrates globalization into every chapter, analyzing its effects throughout the text rather than in a series of boxes, icons, or the occasional extra chapter so commonly seen in contemporary textbooks. The introductory chapter, "Anthropology in a Global Age," establishes an analytical framework of globalization that is developed in every succeeding chapter—whether the topic is fieldwork, language, ethnicity, economics, or kinship—and gives students the tools to understand its impact on people's lives as they encounter them in ethnographic examples throughout the book.

Reframing the Culture Concept. The concept of culture has been central to anthropological analysis since the beginning of our field. But anthropologists have significantly reframed our thinking about culture over the past forty years. In the 1960s, Clifford Geertz synthesized anthropological thinking about culture as a system of meaning—shared norms, values, symbols, and categories. In the ensuing years, anthropologists have paid increasing attention to the relationship of power to culture, building on the work of Antonio Gramsci, Michel Foucault, and Eric Wolf to examine the ways cultural meanings are created, learned, taught, enforced, negotiated, and contested. *Essentials of Cultural Anthropology: A Toolkit for a Global Age* integrates this holistic and complex concept of culture into every chapter, exploring both meaning and power in human culture. Chapter 5, for example, is titled "Race and Racism," acknowledging that not only is race a social construction of ideas but also that ideas of race can be expressed and made real through cultural processes, institutions, and systems of power—racism—in ways that create patterns of stratification and inequality in U.S. culture and in cultures around the world.

Anthropology for the Twenty-First Century. *Essentials of Cultural Anthropology: A Toolkit for a Global Age* reflects the field of anthropology as it is developing in the twenty-first century. While carefully covering the foundational work of early anthropologists, every chapter has been designed to introduce the cutting-edge research and theory that make anthropology relevant to today's world. Chapters on classic anthropological topics such as language, religion, and kinship incorporate contemporary research and help students understand why anthropological thinking matters in day-to-day life. Chapters on sexuality, the global economy, class and inequality, and health and illness give students a sense of historical and contemporary research in the field and bring the presentation of anthropology fully into the twenty-first century.

Ethnography. Anthropologists conduct fascinating research about the lives of people all over the world. In many ways ethnography is at the heart of anthropology, reflecting our unique research strategies, our analytical methodologies, and our deep commitment to the project of cross-cultural understanding and engagement in our attempts to make the world a better place. But ethnographies often get lost in introductory textbooks. *Essentials of Cultural Anthropology: A Toolkit for a Global Age* introduces scores of ethnographic studies set in dozens of different countries, presenting both new research and classic studies in ways that are accessible to undergraduates so that the rich work of anthropologists comes alive over the course of the semester.

Relevance. *Essentials of Cultural Anthropology* responds to my students' request for relevance in a textbook. Each chapter opens with a recent event that raises central questions about the workings of human culture. Key questions throughout the chapter guide students through an introduction to the anthropological strategies and analytical frameworks that can enable them to think more deeply about the chapter-opening event and the underlying issues they may confront in their own lives. "Thinking Like an Anthropologist" sections wrap up each chapter and challenge students to apply what they have learned.

Additional Resources
Learn more at wwnorton.com/instructors

CULTURAL ANTHROPOLOGY FIELDWORK JOURNAL

Ethnographic fieldwork is one of the most fundamental (and for students sometimes daunting) tools for anthropological study. Ken Guest's *Cultural Anthropology Fieldwork Journal* provides 17 step-by-step exercises to help students apply the concepts they are learning in class while out in the real world. Designed to complement *Essentials of Cultural Anthropology: A Toolkit for a Global Age*, every activity in the *Fieldwork Journal* enhances students' understanding of the concepts covered in the parent textbook. Compact and easy to use, the *Fieldwork Journal* includes space to write notes and record data.

The media package for *Essentials of Cultural Anthropology: A Toolkit for a Global Age* provides additional pedagogical tools that inspire students to *do* anthropology and apply it to their own lives. Instructors have everything they need to make traditional and online classes easier to manage: a DVD of clips that will enliven lectures and spark discussion; illustrated PowerPoints that include instructor-view lecture notes; and a fully customizable coursepack for Blackboard and other course-management systems.

EBOOK
Available at nortonebooks.com

Essentials of Cultural Anthropology is also available as an ebook. An affordable and convenient alternative, the ebook retains the content of the print book and allows students to highlight and take notes with ease.

POWERPOINTS
David Anderson, Radford University/Roanoke College

Downloadable from wwnorton.com/instructors and perfect for classroom presentation, these resources include:

- **Lecture PowerPoints:** Illustrated with images from the text, these lecture PowerPoint slides feature a suggested classroom lecture outline in the notes field that will be particularly helpful to first-time teachers.

- **Art PowerPoints and JPEGs:** All of the art from the book and from the coursepack is sized for classroom display.

INSTRUCTOR DVD

Russell Sharman

The Instructor DVD features documentary and ethnographic film clips for initiating classroom discussion and showing students how anthropology is relevant to their lives. Filmmaker and anthropologist Russell Sharman has selected clips that are both engaging and pedagogically useful. The clips are also offered in streaming versions in the coursepack. Each streamed clip is accompanied by a quiz, exercise, or activity.

COURSEPACK

David Anderson, Radford University/Roanoke College; Chad T. Morris, Roanoke College; and David Houston; University of Vermont

Essentials of Cultural Anthropology's coursepack offers assessment and review materials for instructors who use Blackboard, Moodle, Canvas, and other learning-management systems. In addition to chapter-based assignments, test banks and quizzes, and an optional ebook, the coursepack includes interactive learning tools that will enliven hybrid, online, or traditional classrooms. Features include:

- Review and key-term quizzes for each chapter
- A variety of question types, including ranking and matching questions
- "Thinking Like an Anthropologist" and "Your Turn: Fieldwork" exercises and activities
- Streaming film clips from the Instructor DVD, each supported by a quiz or exercise
- The test bank

TEST BANK

Jennifer Cardinal, University of New Mexico; Andrew Carey, University of New Mexico; Shirley Heying, University of New Mexico; Jayne Howell, California State University, Long Beach; Michelle Raisor, Blinn College; Nicholas Rattray, Butler University; David Houston, University of Vermont

The test bank for *Essentials of Cultural Anthropology* is designed to help instructors prepare exams. Devised according to Bloom's taxonomy, the test bank includes 50–60 multiple-choice questions per chapter. In addition to Bloom's, each question is tagged with metadata that place it in the context of the chapter, as well as difficulty level, making it easy to construct tests that are meaningful and diagnostic.

INTERACTIVE INSTRUCTOR'S GUIDE

The Interactive Instructor's Guide makes lecture development easy with an array of teaching resources that can be searched and browsed according to a number of criteria. Resources include chapter outlines and summaries; lecture ideas; discussion questions, recommended readings, videos, and websites; video exercises with streaming video; and activities with downloadable handouts. Instructors can subscribe to a mailing list to be notified of periodic updates and new content.

Acknowledgments

Writing a book of this scope is a humbling experience. I have been awed by the remarkable work of the anthropologists I have encountered, whether through written texts, films, or one-on-one conversations. And I have been inspired by the commitment of my fellow anthropologists to deep understanding of people and cultures, to the search for insights into how the world really works, and to engagement with the world and its people in ways that may help make the world a better place. I have learned a great deal, personally and professionally, on this journey. Along the way it has been my privilege to have the support and encouragement of a remarkable array of people.

First, I would like to thank those colleagues whose invaluable feedback at many stages of the revision process led to the creation of this book. I have adopted many of the recommendations that they made.

Kathleen Adams, Loyola University Chicago

Sabrina Adleman, Lansing Community College

Mark Allen, California State Polytechnic University, Pomona

Peter Allen, Rhode Island College

Myrdene Anderson, Purdue University

Tracy J. Andrews, Central Washington University

Kristi Arford, Northern Essex Community College

James D. Armstrong, College at Plattsburgh, State University of New York

Elizabeth Arnold, Grand Valley State University

Christine B. Avenarius, East Carolina University

Bridget Balint, Indiana University

Diane Baxter, University of Oregon

AnnMarie Beasley, Cosumnes River College

O. Hugo Benavides, Fordham University

David Beriss, University of New Orleans

Ethan Bertrando, Cuesta College

Brad Biglow, Florida State College at Jacksonville

Krista Billingsley, University of Tennessee

Maggie Bodemer, California Polytechnic State University

Deborah A. Boehm, University of Nevada, Reno

Laurian Bowles, Davidson College

Angela Bratton, Georgia Regents University

Elise Brenner, Bridgewater State University

Mary Jill Brody, Louisiana State University

Boyd Brown III, Nichols College

Susan Brownell, University of Missouri, St. Louis

Ronda Brulotte, University of New Mexico

Jan Brunson, University of Hawai'i at Manoa

Kathleen Bubinas, University of Wisconsin – Waukesha

Liam Buckley, James Madison University

Anne Buddenhagen, John Jay College of Criminal Justice

Jennie Burnet, University of Louisville

Noah Butler, Loyola University Chicago

Maria Leonor Cadena, Fullerton College

Walter Calgaro, Prairie State College

Jennifer Chase, University of North Texas

Kristen Check, University of South Carolina

Aldo Civico, Rutgers University

Paula Clarke, Columbia College

Kimberley Coles, University of Redlands

Elizabeth E. Cooper, University of Alabama

Mark Cozin, Raritan Valley Community College

Mary Lou Curran, Mount Wachusett Community College

Joanna Davidson, Boston University

Christina Davis, Western Illinois University

Dona Davis, University of South Dakota

Allan Dawson, Drew University

Jeanne de Grasse, Butler Community College

Jeffrey Debies-Carl, University of New Haven

Teresa Delfin, Whittier College

Rene M. Descartes, State University of New York at Cobleskill

Rosemary Diaz, Southern Connecticut State University

William Doonan, Sacramento City College

Haley Duschinski, Ohio University

Paulla Ebron, Stanford University

Terilee Edwards-Hewitt, Montgomery College

Kenneth Ehrensal, Kutztown University

Tracy Evans, Fullerton College

Jason Fancher, Mt. Hood Community College

Derick Fay, University of California, Riverside

Rick Feinberg, Kent State University

Doug Feldman, The College at Brockport, State University of New York

Elena Filios, Charter Oak State College

Mike Folan, New Hampshire Technical Institute

Allison Foley, Indiana University, South Bend

Ben Ford, Indiana University of Pennsylvania

Todd French, Depauw University

John Fritz, Salt Lake Community College

Cynthia Gabriel, Eastern Michigan University

Sue-Je Gage, Ithaca College

Ismael García Colón, College of Staten Island

Carlos Garcia-Quijano, University of Rhode Island

Peter M. Gardner, University of Missouri

Laura Gonzalez, San Diego Miramar College

Julie Goodman, California Baptist University

Henri Gooren, Oakland University

Mark Gordon, Pasadena City College

Thomas Gordon, Monroe College

Alexis Gray, Norco College

Peter B. Gray, University of Nevada, Las Vegas

Thomas Gregor, Vanderbilt University

Joyce D. Hammond, Western Washington University

Melissa D. Hargrove, University of North Florida

Adam Harr, St. Lawrence University

Tina Harris, University of Amsterdam

Kimberly Hart, Buffalo State, State University of New York

Gary Heidinger, Roane State Community College

Deanna Heikkinen, Los Angeles Valley College

Nicole Hess, Washington State University, Vancouver

Jude Higgins, Salt Lake Community College

Servando Z. Hinojosa, University of Texas – Pan American

Dorothy L. Hodgson, Rutgers University

David Hoffman, Mississippi State University

Derek Honeyman, University of Arizona

Sherman Horn, Tulane University

Kendall House, Boise State University

Brian Howell, Wheaton College

Jayne Howell, California State University, Long Beach

Arianne Ishaya, De Anza College

Alice James, Shippensburg University

Paul James, Western Washington University

Alana Jolley, Saddleback College

Carla Jones, University of Colorado

Barbara Jones, Brookdale Community College

Jessica Jones-Coggins, Madison Area Technical College

Hannah Jopling, Fordham University

Ingrid Jordt, University of Wisconsin – Milwaukee

Karen Kapusta-Pofahl, Washburn University

Peta Katz, University of North Carolina at Charlotte

Neal B. Keating, College at Brockport, State University of New York

Grace Keyes, St. Mary's University

Melissa King, San Bernardino Valley College

Alice Kingsnorth, American River College

Ashley Kistler, Rollins College

Christine Kitchin, Ocean County College

Chhaya Kolavalli, University of Kentucky

Kathryn Kozaitis, Georgia State University

Kathy Koziol, University of Arkansas

Ruth Laird, Mission College

Gabriel Lataianu, Bergen Community College

Ida Leggett, Middle Tennessee State University

Elinor Levy, Raritan Valley Commmunity College

Pierre Liénard, University of Nevada, Las Vegas

Pamela Lindell, Sacramento City College

David M. Lipset, University of Minnesota

Chris Loeffler, Irvine Valley College

Aurolyn Luykx, University of Texas at El Paso

Pamela Maack, San Jacinto College

Yvette Madison, Pennsylvania Highlands Community College

Valentina Martinez, Florida Atlantic University

Scott Matter, University of Vermont

Michael Mauer, College of the Canyons

Kathryn Maurer, Foothill College

Siobhan McCollum, Buffalo State, State University of New York

Jack McCoy, Monmouth University

Reece McGee, Texas State University

Bettie Kay McGowan, Eastern Michigan University

Karletty Medina, Northern Essex Community College

Arion Melidonis, Oxnard College

Seth Messinger, University of Maryland, Baltimore County

Jim Mielke, University of Kansas

Ryan Moore, Florida Atlantic University

Scotty Moore, Houston Community College

Juliet Morrow, Arkansas State University

Joylin Namie, Utah Valley University

Chris Nelson, University of North Carolina at Chapel Hill

Neil Nevins, New Hampshire Technical Institute

Rachel Newcomb, Rollins College

Evelyn Newman Phillips, Central Connecticut State University

Carol Nickolai, Community College of Philadelphia

Jeremy Nienow, Inver Hills Community College

Jennifer Oksenhorn, Suffolk County Community College

Michael O'Neal, St. Louis Community College

Erik Ozolins, Mount San Jacinto College

Liana Padilla-Wilson, Los Medanos College

Eric Paison, Golden West College

Craig Palmer, University of Missouri

Amanda Paskey, Cosumnes River College

Phyllis Passariello, Centre College

Crystal Patil, University of Illinois at Chicago

Mike Pavlik, Joliet Junior College

Linda Pelon, McLennan Community College

Ramona Pérez, San Diego State University

Dana Pertermann, Blinn College

Holly Peters-Golden, University of Michigan

Wayne Politsch, Lewis and Clark Community College

Lin Poyer, University of Wyoming

Marla Prochnow, College of the Sequoias

Erica Prussing, University of Iowa

Sharon Rachele, California State Polytechnic University, Pomona

Michelle Raisor, Blinn College

Amanda Reinke, University of Tennessee, Knoxville

Daniel Robinson, University of Florida

Monica Rothschild-Boros, Orange Coast College

Frances Rothstein, Montclair State University

Stephanie Sadre-Orafai, University of Cincinnati

Kristin Safi, Washington State University

Maureen Salsitz, Cypress College

Bruce Sanchez, Lane Community College

Keri Sansevere, Monmouth University

Antonia Santangelo, York College, City University of New York

Richard Sattler, University of Montana

Jennifer Schlegel, Kutztown University

Scott Schnell, University of Iowa

Kathy Seibold, The College of Idaho

Frank Shih, Suffolk County Community College

Gregory Simon, Pierce College

Suzanne Simon, University of North Florida

Michael Simonton, University of Cincinnati

Nancy Smith, South Plains College

Sarah Smith, Delta College

Brian Spooner, University of Pennsylvania

Chelsea Starr, University of Phoenix

Erin Stiles, University of Nevada, Reno

Karen Stocker, California State University, Fullerton

Michelle Stokely, Indiana University Northwest

Richard Stuart, University of North Carolina at Greensboro

Circe Sturm, University of Texas at Austin

Noelle Sullivan, Northwestern University

Patricia Taber, Ventura College

Orit Tamir, New Mexico Highlands University

Arthur Tolley, Indiana University East

Patricia Tovar, John Jay College of Criminal Justice

Mark Tracy, Minneapolis Community and Technical College

Monica Udvardy, University of Kentucky

Lisa Valkenier, Merritt College

Jay VanderVeen, Indiana University South Bend

Katherine Wahlberg, Florida Gulf Coast University

Salena Wakim, Mount San Jacinto College

Renee Walker, State University of New York at Oneonta

Deana Weibel, Grand Valley State University

Nicole Weigel, State University of New York College at Oneonta

Margaret Weinberger, Bowling Green State University

Jill Wenrick, California State Polytechnic University, Pomona

Max White, Piedmont College

Cassandra White, Georgia State University

Jennifer Wies, Eastern Kentucky University

Rebecca Wiewel, University of Arkansas, Fort Smith

Laura Wilhelm, University of Nevada, Reno

Benjamin Wilreker, College of Southern Nevada

Scott Wilson, California State University, Long Beach

Paul C. Winther, Eastern Kentucky University

Katrina Worley, American River College

Aníbal Yáñez-Chávez, California State University, San Marcos

Laura Zeeman, Red Rocks Community College

I would also like to thank the editors and staff at W. W. Norton who took a chance on this project to rethink the way anthropology is learned and taught. Julia Reidhead years ago encouraged me to keep my lecture notes in case I might write a textbook someday. Peter Lesser, my first editor, embraced the vision of the original book, signed me, brought me into the Norton fold and, with assistant editor Samantha Held, has guided the creation of *Essentials*. Karl Bakeman advised me throughout the writing and production of the Full book, and has been integral to its continued success among my colleagues and students. Alice Vigliani has been an excellent copyeditor. Ted Szczepanski, Trish Marx, and the Norton photo research department have worked hard to find engaging and beautiful illustrations. Linda Feldman and Ashley Horna handled every part of the manuscript and managed to keep the many pieces of the book moving through production. Norton's cultural anthropology marketing and sales team, Julia Hall, Natasha Zabohonski, Julie Sindel, Jonathan Mason, and Roy McClymont have advocated for the book with enthusiasm and boundless energy. Eileen Connell, Ava Bramson, and Alice Garrard put together all of the media resources that accompany the textbook. When it comes to creating new digital resources to help anthropologists teach in the classroom or teach online, I couldn't ask for a better team of people. Thanks to you all.

Heartfelt thanks to my many colleagues who have helped me think more deeply about anthropology, including members of the Sociology and Anthropology Department at Baruch College, especially Glenn Petersen, Robin Root, Carla Bellamy, Barbara Katz-Rothman, Angie Beeman, Myrna Chase, and Shelley Watson, as well as Jane Schneider, Louise Lennihan, Ida Susser, Peter Kwong, Michael Blim, Jonathan Shannon, Christa Salamandra, Russell Sharman, Dana Davis, Jeff Maskovsky, Rudi Gaudio, Charlene Floyd, and Zoë Sheehan Saldana. Members of the New York Academy of Sciences Anthropology Section helped me think more deeply about the relationship of culture and power. Leslie Aiello and the staff of the Wenner-Gren Foundation provided a vibrant venue to engage the cutting edges of anthropological research. The board of the American Ethnological Society allowed me to explore the theme of anthropologists engaging the world through their spring 2012 conference. My research assistants Alessandro Angelini, Andrew Hernann, Chris Grove, Suzanna Goldblatt, Lynn Horridge, and Chris Baum continually introduced me to the richness of contemporary scholarship and creative strategies for teaching and learning. Thanks also to a wonderful group of friends and family who have supported and encouraged me during this fascinating and challenging journey: K and Charlene, Douglas, Marybeth, Julia, Asher, Dayna, Zoë, Sally and Steve, Marty and Linda, the guys at the Metro Diner—Nick, Marco, and Antonio—the SPSA community, the Ajax soccer family, Shari, Vicki, Frances Helen, and Thomas Luke.

Finally, I would like to thank my students at Baruch College who every class ask to be introduced to an anthropology that is relevant to their daily lives, that tackles significant contemporary issues, and that provides them the tools of analysis and empowerment to live awake, conscious, and engaged. This book is dedicated to you and your potential to make the world a better place.

Perhaps the quintessential human task is to pass to the next generation the accumulated insights, understandings, and knowledge that will empower them to live life fully and meaningfully and to meet the challenges confronting humanity and the planet. I hope this book might contribute to that existential endeavor.

Essentials of Cultural Anthropology

Part 1

Anthropologists in the twenty-first century engage a world that is experiencing an unprecedented interaction of people, ideas, images, and things that continues to intensify. Communication technologies link people instantaneously across the globe. Economic activities challenge national boundaries. People are on the move between countries and within them. Here, young Afghan women work at the first women-only Internet café in Kabul, 2012. How can *you* use the tools of anthropology to engage this world on the move?

Anthropology
for the
21st Century

Chapter 1
Anthropology in a Global Age

Every morning the women of Plachimada, a rural area in southern India, begin a five-kilometer (three-mile) trek in search of fresh water. The morning journey for water is a common task for many women across the world, for one-third of the planet's population lives with water scarcity. But such scarcity is new for the people of Plachimada, an area of typically rich agricultural harvests.

Local residents trace the changes to March 2000, when the Coca-Cola Company opened a bottling plant in the village. The plant is capable of producing 1.2 million bottles of Coke, Sprite, and Fanta every day. Nine liters of fresh water are needed to make one liter of Coke, so Plachimada's large underground aquifer was an attractive resource for the company. But according to local officials, when the company began to drill more wells and install high-powered pumps to extract groundwater for the factory, the local water table fell dramatically—from

Indian village women protest the Coca-Cola Company's exploitation of underground water supplies.

45 meters (147.5 feet) below the surface to 150 meters (492 feet), far more than could be explained by periods of limited rainfall. Hundreds of local non-Coca-Cola wells ran dry, and harvests became much less productive. Local residents also claimed that Coca-Cola workers were dumping chemical wastes on land near the factory and that the runoff was polluting the groundwater. Local women organized protests and a sit-in at the factory gates.

With the assistance of local media and international human rights networks, the protestors' activism drew national and international attention. It even spurred solidarity actions, including support from university students in the United States, Canada, the United Kingdom, and Norway. As a result, the local village council withdrew the Coca-Cola factory's license. But the state government maintained its support. The case finally reached the highest state court, which ruled that Coca-Cola must cease illegal extraction of groundwater in Plachimada (Shiva 2006; Aiyer 2007).

For those of us who often enjoy a Coke with lunch or dinner—or breakfast—the story of the women of Plachimada offers a challenge to consider how our lives connect to theirs. It is a challenge to explore how a simple soft drink, made by a U.S. corporation with global operations, may link people halfway around the world in ways both simple and profound. This is also the challenge of anthropology today: to understand the rich diversity of human life and to see how our particular life experiences connect to those of others. By bringing these perspectives together, we can grasp more fully the totality and potential of human life.

At the same time, the world is changing before our eyes. Whether we call it a global village or a world without borders, we in the twenty-first century are experiencing a level of interaction among people, ideas, and systems that is intensifying at a breathtaking pace. Communication technologies link people instantaneously across the globe. Economic activities challenge national boundaries. People are on the move within countries and among them. Violence and terrorism disrupt lives. Humans have had remarkable success at feeding a growing world population, yet income inequality continues to increase—among nations and also within them. And increasing human diversity on our doorstep opens possibilities, both for deeper understanding and for greater misunderstanding. Clearly, the human community in the twenty-first century is being drawn further into a global web of interaction.

For today's college student, every day can be a cross-cultural experience. This may manifest itself in the most familiar places: the news you see on television, the music you listen to, the foods and beverages you consume, the women or men you date, the classmates you study with, the religious communities you attend. Today you can realistically imagine contacting any of our 7.2 billion co-inhabitants

MAP 1.1
Plachimada

In the twenty-first century, people are experiencing unprecedented levels of interaction, encounter, movement, and exchange. Here, passengers board an overcrowded train in Dhaka, Bangladesh, returning home to celebrate the Muslim holy day of Eid al-Fitr.

on the planet. You can read their posts on Facebook and watch their videos on YouTube. You can visit them. You wear clothes that they make. You make movies that they view. You can learn from them. You can affect their lives. How do you meet this challenge of deepening interaction and interdependence?

Anthropology provides a unique set of tools, including strategies and perspectives, for understanding our rapidly changing, globalizing world. Most of you are already budding cultural anthropologists without realizing it. Wherever you may live or go to school, you are probably experiencing a deepening encounter with the world's diversity. This phenomenon leads to broad questions such as, How do we approach human diversity in our universities, businesses, families, and religious communities? How do we understand the impact of global transformations on our lives?

Whether our field is business or education, medicine or politics, we all need a skill set for analyzing and engaging a multicultural and increasingly interconnected world and workplace. *Cultural Anthropology: A Toolkit for a Global Age* introduces the anthropologist's tools of the trade to help you to better understand and engage the world as you move through it, and if you so choose, to apply those strategies to the challenges confronting us and our neighbors around the world. To begin our exploration of anthropology, we'll consider four key questions:

- **What is anthropology?**
- **Through what lenses do anthropologists gain a comprehensive view of human cultures?**
- **What is globalization, and why is it important for anthropology?**
- **How is globalization transforming anthropology?**

What Is Anthropology?

anthropology

The study of the full scope of human diversity, past and present, and the application of that knowledge to help people of different backgrounds better understand one another.

Anthropology is the study of the full scope of human diversity and the application of that knowledge to help people of different backgrounds better understand one another. The word *anthropology* derives from the Greek words *anthropos* ("human") and *logos* ("thought," "reason," or "study"). The roots of anthropology lie in the eighteenth and nineteenth centuries, as Europeans' economic and colonial expansion increased that continent's contact with people worldwide.

BRIEF BACKGROUND

Technological breakthroughs in transportation and communication during the eighteenth and nineteenth centuries—shipbuilding, the steam engine, railroads, the telegraph—rapidly transformed the long-distance movement of people, goods, and information, in terms of both speed and quantity. As colonization, communication, trade, and travel expanded, groups of merchants, missionaries, and government officials traveled the world and returned to Europe with reports and artifacts of what seemed to them to be "exotic" people and practices. More than ever before, Europeans encountered the incredible diversity of human cultures and appearances. *Who are these people?* they asked themselves. *Where did they come from? Why do they appear so different from us?*

From the field's inception in the mid-1800s, anthropologists have conducted research to answer specific questions confronting humanity. And they have applied their knowledge and insights to practical problems facing the world.

Franz Boas (1858–1942), one of the founders of American anthropology, became deeply involved in early twentieth-century debates on immigration, serving for a term on a presidential commission examining U.S. immigration policies. In an era when many scholars and government officials considered the different people of Europe to be of distinct biological races, U.S. immigration policies privileged immigrants from northern and western Europe over those from southern and eastern Europe. Boas worked to undermine these racialized views of immigrants. He conducted studies that showed the wide variation of physical forms within groups of the same national origin, as well as the marked physical changes in the children and grandchildren of immigrants as they adapted to the environmental conditions in their new country (Baker 2004; Boas 1912).

Audrey Richards (1899–1984), studying the Bemba people in the 1930s in what is now Zambia, focused on issues of health and nutrition among women and children, bringing concerns for nutrition to the forefront of anthropology. Her ethnography, *Chisungu* (1956), featured a rigorous and detailed study of the coming-of-age rituals of young Bemba women and established new standards for the conduct of anthropological research. Richards's research is often credited with opening a pathway for the study of nutritional issues and women's and children's health in anthropology.

Today anthropologists apply their knowledge and research strategies to a wide range of social issues. For example, they study HIV/AIDS in Africa, immigrant farm workers in the United States, ethnic conflict in the former Yugoslavia, street children in Brazil, and Muslim judicial courts in Egypt. Anthropologists trace the spread of disease, promote economic development in underdeveloped countries, conduct market research, and lead diversity-training programs in schools, corporations, and community organizations. Anthropologists also study our human origins, excavating and analyzing the bones, artifacts, and DNA of our ancestors from millions of years ago to gain an understanding of who we are and where we've come from.

Sixty percent of anthropologists today work in *applied anthropology*—that is, they work outside of academic settings to apply the strategies and insights of anthropology directly to current world problems. Even many of us who work full time in a college or university are deeply involved in public applied anthropology.

ANTHROPOLOGY'S UNIQUE APPROACH

Anthropology today retains its core commitment to understanding the richness of human diversity. Specifically, anthropology challenges us to move beyond **ethnocentrism**—the strong human tendency to believe that one's own culture or way of life is normal, natural, and superior to the beliefs and practices of others. Instead, as we will explore throughout this book, the anthropologist's toolkit of research strategies and analytical concepts enables us to appreciate, understand, and engage the diversity of human cultures in an increasingly global age. To that end, anthropology has built upon the key concerns of early generations to develop a set of characteristics unique among the social sciences.

ethnocentrism

The belief that one's own culture or way of life is normal and natural; using one's own culture to evaluate and judge the practices and ideals of others.

Anthropology Is Global in Scope. Our work covers the whole world and is not constrained by geographic boundaries. Anthropology was once noted for the study of faraway, seemingly exotic villages in developing countries. But from the beginning, anthropologists have been studying not only in the islands of the South Pacific, in the rural villages of Africa, and among indigenous peoples in Australia and North America, but also (though to a lesser degree) among factory workers in Britain and France, among immigrants in New York, and in other communities in the industrializing world. Over the last thirty years, anthropology has turned significant attention to urban communities in industrialized nations. With the increase of studies in North America and Europe, it is fair to say that anthropologists now embrace the full scope of humanity—across geography and through time.

Anthropologists' Perspectives Start with People and Their Local Communities.

Although the whole world is our field, anthropologists are committed to understanding the local, everyday lives of the people we study. Our unique perspective focuses on the details and patterns of human life in the local community and then examines how particular cultures connect with the rest of humanity. Sociologists, economists, and political scientists primarily analyze broad trends, official organizations, and national policies, but anthropologists—particularly cultural anthropologists—adopt **ethnographic fieldwork** as their primary research strategy (see Chapter 3). They live with a community of people over an extended period to understand their lives by "walking in their shoes."

Anthropologists have constantly worked to bring often-ignored voices into the global conversation. As a result, the field has a history of focusing on the cultures and struggles of non-Western and nonelite people. In recent years, some anthropologists have conducted research on elites—"studying up," as some have called it—by examining financial institutions, aid and development agencies, medical laboratories, and doctors. But the vast majority of our work has addressed the marginalized segments of society.

Anthropologists Study People and the Structures of Power.

Human communities are full of people, the institutions they have created for managing life in organized groups, and the systems of meaning they have built to make sense of it all. Anthropology maintains a commitment to studying both the people and the larger structures of power around them. These include families, governments, economic systems, educational institutions, militaries, the media, and religions, as well as ideas of race, ethnicity, gender, class, and sexuality.

ethnographic fieldwork

A primary research strategy in cultural anthropology involving living with a community of people over an extended period to better understand their lives.

Once noted for the study of seemingly far away and "exotic" people and places, anthropologists today increasingly study the complex interaction of diverse communities in global cities like London.

To comprehensively examine people's lives, anthropologists consider the structures that empower and constrain those people, both locally and globally. At the same time, anthropologists seek to understand the "agency" of local people—in other words, the central role of individuals and groups in determining their own lives, even in the face of overwhelming structures of power.

Anthropologists Believe That All Humans Are Connected.

Anthropologists believe that all humans share connections that are biological, cultural, economic, and ecological. Despite fanciful stories about the "discovery" of isolated, seemingly lost tribes of "stone-age" people, anthropologists suggest that there are no truly isolated people in the world today and that there rarely, if ever, were any in the past. Clearly, some groups of people are less integrated than others into the global system under construction today. But none are completely isolated. And for some, their seeming isolation may be of recent historical origins. In fact, when we look more closely at the history of so-called primitive tribes in Africa and the Americas (more recently called *indigenous*), we find that many were complex state societies before colonialism and the slave trade led to their collapse.

This map shows the King of Mali, West Africa, in 1375, seated at the center of his vast kingdom—a key point along trade routes stretching across Africa and into the Middle East and beyond.

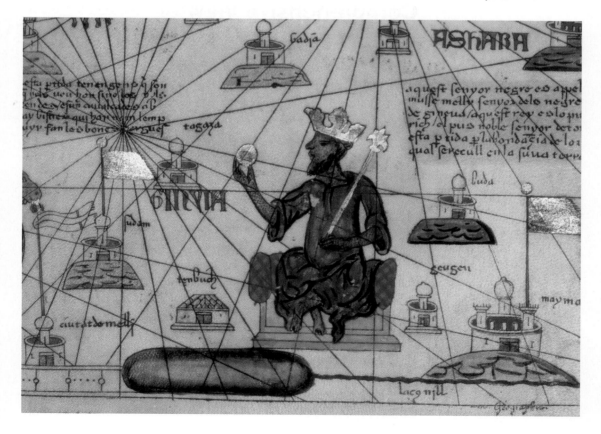

Although some anthropology textbooks show "tribal"-looking people in brightly colored, seemingly exotic clothing holding cell phones, which suggests the rapid integration of isolated people into a high-tech, global world, anthropological research indicates that this imagined isolation never really existed. Despite the world's incredible cultural diversity, human history is the story of movement and interaction, not of isolation and disconnection. Yes, today's period of rapid globalization is intensifying the interactions among people and the flow of goods, technology, money, and ideas within and across national boundaries, but interaction and connection are not new phenomena. They have been central to human history. Our increasing connection today reminds us that our actions have consequences for the whole world, not just for our own lives and those of our families and friends.

Through What Lenses Do Anthropologists Gain a Comprehensive View of Human Cultures?

four-field approach

The use of four interrelated disciplines to study humanity: physical anthropology, archaeology, linguistic anthropology, and cultural anthropology.

holism

The anthropological commitment to consider the full scope of human life, including culture, biology, history, and language, across space and time.

One of the unique characteristics of anthropology in the United States is that it has developed four "lenses" for examining humanity. Constituting the **four-field approach**, these interrelated fields are physical anthropology, archaeology, linguistic anthropology, and cultural anthropology. In Europe, the four fields are quite separate, but the history of anthropology in the United States (see Chapter 3) has fostered a holistic approach for examining the complexity of human origins and human culture, past and present.

Holism refers to anthropology's commitment to look at the whole picture of human life—culture, biology, history, and language—across space and time. The field's cross-cultural and comparative approach considers the life experiences of people in every part of the world, comparing and contrasting cultural beliefs and practices to understand human similarities and differences on a global scale. Anthropologists conduct research on the contemporary world and also look deep into human history.

Because we analyze both human culture and biology, anthropologists are in a unique position to offer insights into debates about the role of "nature" versus "nurture." How do biology, culture, and the environment interact to shape who we are as humans, individually and as groups? The four-field approach is key to implementing this holistic perspective within anthropology.

PHYSICAL ANTHROPOLOGY

Physical anthropology, sometimes called *biological anthropology*, is the study of humans from a biological perspective—in particular, how they have evolved over time and have adapted to their environments. Most scholars agree that modern humans share a common ancestor with other primates such as chimpanzees, apes, and monkeys. In fact, genetic studies reveal that humans share 97.7 percent of DNA with gorillas and 98.7 percent with chimpanzees. Both the fossil record and the genetic evidence suggest that the evolutionary line leading to modern humans split from the one leading to modern African apes between five and six million years ago. Through a complex evolutionary process that we are learning more about every day, *Homo sapiens* (the group of modern humans to which you and I belong) evolved in Africa fairly recently in the grand scheme of things—probably less than 200,000 years ago—and gradually spread across the planet (Larsen 2014).

Physical anthropology has several areas of specialization. **Paleoanthropology** traces the history of human evolution by reconstructing the human fossil record. Thus, paleoanthropologists excavate the teeth, skulls, and other bones of our human ancestors and analyze them to track changes in human physical form over time. From these fossils they map changes in key categories such as overall body size, cranial capacity, hand structure, head shape, and pelvic position. Such changes reveal developments in walking, diet, intelligence, and capacity for cultural adaptation. Since the late 1970s, paleoanthropologists have also used molecular genetics to trace changes in human ancestors over time. The sequencing of DNA allows us to measure how closely humans are related to other primates and

physical anthropology
The study of humans from a biological perspective, particularly focused on human evolution.

paleoanthropology
The study of the history of human evolution through the fossil record.

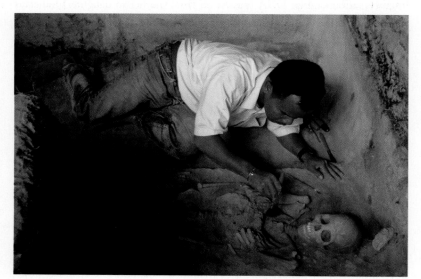

Paleoanthropologists trace the history of human evolution by reconstructing the human fossil record. Here, Ketut Wiradyana unearths a fossilized human skeleton buried in a cave in Indonesia's Aceh province.

Primatologist Jane Goodall studies chimpanzee behavior in an African nature preserve.

primatology

The study of living nonhuman primates as well as primate fossils to better understand human evolution and early human behavior.

even to follow the movement of groups of people through the flow of genes. For instance, mitochondrial DNA (passed on from mother to daughter) indicates that modern *Homo sapiens* first appeared in Africa around 150,000 years ago and migrated out of Africa 100,000 years ago. This DNA evidence generally matches the findings of the archaeological record.

Primatology is another specialization within physical anthropology. Primatologists study living, nonhuman primates and primate fossils—including monkeys, apes, chimpanzees, and gorillas—to see what clues their biology, evolution, behavior, and social life might provide about our own, particularly our early human behavior. Careful observation of primates in their natural habitats and in captivity has offered significant insights into sexuality, parenting, male/female differences, cooperation, intergroup conflict, aggression, and problem solving.

Physical anthropologists also study the diversity of human physical forms that have evolved over time. Humans come in all shapes and sizes. Our differences range from body size and facial shape to skin color, height, blood chemistry, and susceptibility to certain diseases. Physical anthropologists attribute general patterns of human physical variation to adaptation to different physical environments as humans spread from Africa across the other continents.

Variations in skin color, for instance, can be traced to the need to adapt to different levels of ultraviolet light as humans migrated away from the equator (see Chapter 5).

However, studies of human biology show that the physical similarities among the world's people far outweigh the differences. In fact, there is more variation *within* what are assumed to be "groups" than *between* groups. This is clearly evident in terms of the thorny concept of race (see Chapter 5). A biologically distinct race would include people in a group who share a greater statistical frequency of genes and physical traits than do people outside the group. Physical anthropologists find no evidence of distinct, fixed, biological races. Rather, there is only one human race. Attempts to identify distinct biological races are flawed and arbitrary, as no clear biological lines exist to define different races. Racial categories, which vary significantly from culture to culture, are loosely based on a few visible physical characteristics such as skin color, but they have no firm basis in genetics (Larsen 2014; Mukhopadhyay, Henze, and Moses 2007). We will return to this discussion of the biological and social dimensions of race in Chapter 5.

ARCHAEOLOGY

Archaeology involves the investigation of the human past by means of excavating and analyzing material remains (artifacts). The goal is not to recover buried treasure, but to understand past human life. Some archaeologists study the emergence of early states in places such as Egypt, India, China, and Mexico. They have unearthed grand sites such as the pyramids of Egypt and Mexico and the terra-cotta warriors guarding the tomb of China's Qin Dynasty emperor. Others focus on the histories of less spectacular sites that shed light on the everyday lives of people in local villages and households.

Archaeology is our only source of information about human societies before writing began (around 5,500 years ago). Because we are unable to travel back through time to observe human behavior, **prehistoric archaeology** seeks to reconstruct human behavior from artifacts that give significant clues about our ancestors' lives. Campsites, hunting grounds, buildings, burials, and especially garbage dumps are rich sources of material. There archaeologists find tools, weapons, pottery, human and animal bones, jewelry, seeds, charcoal, ritual items, building foundations, and even coprolites (fossilized fecal matter). Through excavation and analysis of these material remains, archaeologists reconstruct family and work life. What animals did the people eat? What seeds did they plant? What tools and crafts did they make? Coprolites reveal a great deal about the local diet. Burial sites provide significant data about how people treated their elders and their dead, what rituals they may have practiced, and their ideas about the afterlife. Archaeological evidence can suggest trade patterns, consumption habits, gender roles, and power stratification.

archaeology
The investigation of the human past by means of excavating and analyzing artifacts.

prehistoric archaeology
The reconstruction of human behavior in the distant past (before written records) through the examination of artifacts.

Historic archaeology explores the more recent past and often combines the examination of physical remains and artifacts with that of written or oral records. Historic archaeologists excavate houses, stores, factories, sunken slave ships, even polar ice caps to better understand recent human history and the impact of humans on the environment. For example, recent excavations of former slave plantations in the southern United States, combined with historical records such as deeds, census forms, personal letters, and diaries, have provided rich insight into the lives of African slaves in the seventeenth and eighteenth centuries. Students in the North Atlantic Biocultural Organisation international field school conduct excavations in Iceland that reveal not only historical information about the settling of the North Atlantic but also data on major changes in the contemporary global climate. Core samples from borings drilled through the glaciers reveal sediments deposited from the air over thousands of years as the glaciers formed; such samples allow archaeologists to track global warming and the impact of greenhouse gases on climate change.

In a contemporary example of applied archaeology, since 1973 archaeologist William Rathje, a "garbologist" at the University of Arizona, has been learning about contemporary culture by examining what people throw away. Although many studies of consumption, waste disposal, and eating and drinking habits focus on surveys and interviews, Rathje's Garbage Project has involved analyzing huge quantities of garbage in Tucson (by hand). He has found that what people actually do and what they say they do can be completely different. In this case, only 15 percent of households responding to a survey reported drinking some beer and none reported drinking more than eight cans a week, but analysis of the

Prehistoric garbage dumps provide rich sources of material for understanding the cultural practices of human ancestors. Today, "garbologists" also learn about contemporary culture by examining what people throw away, including in large trash landfills like the one pictured here.

garbage from the same neighborhood showed that 80 percent drank some beer and 50 percent drank more than eight cans a week.

In 1987 the Garbage Project began investigating landfills across the United States and Canada to uncover what is thrown away and what happens to it once it reaches the landfills. Like the earlier project in Tucson, expectations did not match reality. Landfills were not overwhelmed by dirty diapers and fast food containers but by paper that could have been easily recycled, including newspapers that, when buried deep within the landfills, took far longer to biodegrade than anticipated. The surprising data developed from the Garbage Project excavations has helped shape waste disposal practices and landfill management and has provided further impetus to the movement for comprehensive recycling programs that are now commonplace in many parts of the country (Rathje and Murphy 2001).

LINGUISTIC ANTHROPOLOGY

Linguistic anthropology involves the study of human language in the past and the present. Languages are complex, vibrant, and constantly changing systems of symbols through which people communicate with one another. (Think about how hard it is to get your ideas across in your college papers, in text messages, or even in conversation with your parents.) Languages are very flexible and inventive. (Consider how English has adapted to the rise of the Internet to include such new words and concepts as spam, instant messages, texts, Googling, and Skyping.) A language clearly reflects a people's ideas of and experiences with the world. But linguistic anthropologists suggest that language may also limit and constrain a people's views of the world. In other words, can we think clearly about something if we don't have an adequately sophisticated language?

Language is perhaps the most distinctive feature of being human. It is the key to our ability to learn and share culture from generation to generation, to cooperate in groups, and to adapt to our environment. While some animals—including dolphins and whales, bees, and ravens—have a limited range of communication, human language is more complex, creative, and extensively used.

Linguistic anthropology includes three main areas of specialization. **Descriptive linguists** work to carefully describe spoken languages and preserve them as written languages. For example, some descriptive linguists spend years in rural areas helping local people construct a written language from their spoken language. **Historic linguists** study how language changes over time within a culture and as it moves across cultures. **Sociolinguists** study language in its social and cultural contexts. They examine how different speakers use language in different situations or with different people. They explore how language is affected by factors such as race, gender, age, and class. Consider the so-called "N-word"—a very controversial word in the United States today. Sociolinguists

linguistic anthropology
The study of human language in the past and the present.

descriptive linguists
Those who analyze languages and their component parts.

historic linguists
Those who study how language changes over time within a culture and how languages travel across cultures.

sociolinguists
Those who study language in its social and cultural contexts.

would explore the word's usage in American English: Where did it come from? Who uses it, and in what situations? How does its meaning change according to the speaker and the context? When is it a term of racial hatred? When is it a term of camaraderie? We will explore these issues further in Chapter 4.

CULTURAL ANTHROPOLOGY

cultural anthropology
The study of people's communities, behaviors, beliefs, and institutions, including how people make meaning as they live, work, and play together.

Cultural anthropology is the study of people's everyday lives and their communities—their behaviors, beliefs, and institutions. Cultural anthropologists explore all aspects of human culture, such as war and violence, love and sexuality, child rearing and death. They examine what people do and how they live, work, and play together. But they also search for patterns of meaning embedded within each culture, and they develop theories about how cultures work. Cultural anthropologists examine the ways in which local communities interact with global forces.

participant observation
A key anthropological research strategy involving both participation in and observation of the daily life of the people being studied.

Ethnographic fieldwork is at the heart of cultural anthropology. Through **participant observation**—living and working with people on a daily basis, often for a year or more—the cultural anthropologist strives to see the world through the eyes of others. Intensive fieldwork has the power to educate the anthropologist by (1) making what may at first seem very unfamiliar into something that ultimately seems quite familiar, and (2) taking what has seemed very familiar and making it seem very strange. Through fieldwork, anthropologists look beyond the taken-for-granted, everyday experience of life to discover the complex systems of power and meaning that all people construct. These include the many systems we will cover throughout this book: gender, sexuality, race, ethnicity, religion, kinship, and economic and political systems.

ethnology
The analysis and comparison of ethnographic data across cultures.

Cultural anthropologists analyze and compare ethnographic data across cultures in a process called **ethnology**. This process looks beyond specific local realities to see more general patterns of human behavior and to explore how local experiences intersect with global dynamics. Ultimately, through intensive ethnographic fieldwork and cross-cultural comparison, cultural anthropologists seek to help people better understand one another and the way the world works.

What Is Globalization, and Why Is It Important for Anthropology?

globalization
The worldwide intensification of interactions and increased movement of money, people, goods, and ideas within and across national borders.

The term **globalization** refers to the worldwide intensification of interactions and the increased movement of money, people, goods, and ideas within and across national borders. Growing integration of the global economy has driven the intense globalization of the past forty years. Corporations are relocating factories halfway around the world. People are crossing borders legally and illegally

Increasing movement of people within and between countries, often under precarious circumstances, is one key characteristic of globalization. Here, Italian Coast Guard divers rescue African immigrants whose boat has run aground off the Italian coast.

in search of work. Goods, services, and ideas are flowing along high-speed transportation and communication networks. People, organizations, and nations are being drawn into closer connection.

Globalization is not an entirely new phenomenon. Intensification of global interaction occurred in earlier eras as breakthroughs in communication and transportation brought the world's people into closer contact. The present period of globalization, however, has reached a level of intensity previously unknown.

Although globalization is often portrayed in a positive light in the media and popular discourse, the realities are much more complicated. The new technologies associated with globalization may indeed allow more and more people to interact and communicate, but billions of other people are being left out of these advances. Moreover, along with the economic expansion and growth associated with globalization, there are equally significant global economic inequalities.

GLOBALIZATION AND ANTHROPOLOGY

Globalization and anthropology are intricately intertwined, both in history and in the contemporary world. As we have noted, the field of anthropology emerged in the mid-nineteenth century during a time of intense globalization. At that time, technological inventions in transportation and communication were consolidating a period of colonial encounter, the slave trade, and the emerging capitalist economic system and were enabling deeper interactions of people across cultures. Early anthropologists sought to organize the vast quantity of information that was emerging about people across the globe, though, unlike most contemporary anthropologists, who conduct research in the field, they did so primarily from the comfort of their own homes and meeting halls.

Today another era of even more intense globalization is transforming the lives of the people whom anthropologists study in every part of the world. And, as we will see throughout this book, it is also transforming the ways anthropologists conduct research and communicate their findings. To understand these sweeping changes, we must understand the key dynamics of globalization at play in the world today (Inda and Rosaldo 2002; Lewellen 2002).

GLOBALIZATION: KEY DYNAMICS

Globalization today is characterized by several key dynamics. These are time-space compression, flexible accumulation, increasing migration, uneven development, and rapid change. These dynamics are reshaping the ways humans adapt to the natural world, and the ways the natural world is adapting to us.

time-space compression

The rapid innovation of communication and transportation technologies associated with globalization that transforms the way people think about space and time.

Time-Space Compression. According to the theory of **time-space compression**, the rapid innovation of communication and transportation technologies has transformed the way we think about space (distances) and time. Jet travel, supertankers, superhighways, high-speed railways, telephones, fax machines, computers, the Internet, digital cameras, and cell phones have compressed time and space, changing our sense of how long it takes to do something and how far away someplace or someone is. The world is no longer as big as it used to be.

Consider these examples of a changing sense of time. Today we can fly from New York to Paris in eight hours or from Los Angeles to Hong Kong in twelve. A letter that once took ten days to send from Texas to Kenya now can be attached as a PDF and e-mailed with a few clicks of a mouse. We instant message, text message, Skype, and videoconference. The order placed at a McDonald's drive-through may be taken by a phone operator in California, entered in a computer, and come out as a Quarter Pounder with Cheese at the pickup window in Hawaii (Richtel 2006). These kinds of changes have transformed not only how long it takes us to do something, but also how quickly we expect other people to do things. For example, how much time do you have to respond to an e-mail or text message before someone thinks you are rude or irresponsible?

flexible accumulation

The increasingly flexible strategies that corporations use to accumulate profits in an era of globalization, enabled by innovative communication and transportation technologies.

Flexible Accumulation. A second characteristic of today's globalization, **flexible accumulation**, reflects the fact that advances in transportation and communication have enabled companies to move their production facilities and activities around the world in search of cheaper labor, lower taxes, and fewer environmental regulations—in other words, to be completely flexible about the way they accumulate profits (see Chapter 11). Companies in developed countries move their factories to export-processing zones in the developing world, a process called "offshoring." Other corporations shift part of their work to employees in other parts of the world, a process called "outsourcing." For example, General Motors used to make all of its automobiles in Flint, Michigan. But now the company has factories in Mexico, Brazil, China, and Thailand. Walmart, once known for its advertising campaign "Made in America," now has five thousand factories in China.

Other examples span the globe as well: Phone and computer companies hire English-speaking operators and technicians in Bangalore, India, to answer customers' questions called in on 800 numbers. A company based in Sierre Leone, West Africa, processes traffic tickets issued in New York City. X-rays, CT scans, and MRIs taken in Colorado may be read and interpreted by doctors in Manila, the Philippines. Clearly, flexible accumulation allows corporations to maximize profits, while time-space compression enables the efficient management of global networks and distribution systems (Harvey 1990).

Increasing Migration. A third characteristic of globalization is **increasing migration**, in terms of the movement of people both within countries and between countries. In fact, recent globalization has spurred the international migration of more than 200 million people, 38 million of them to the United States alone (see Chapter 11). Perhaps 400 million more are internal migrants within their own countries, usually moving from rural to urban areas in search of work. The Chinese government counts nearly 230 million internal migrants floating in China's cities, drawn by construction projects, service jobs, and export-oriented factories.

In countries from Pakistan to Kenya to Peru, rural workers migrate to urban areas seeking to improve their lives and the lives of their families back home. This movement of people within and across national borders is stretching out human relationships and interactions across space and time. Immigrants send money home, call and e-mail friends and family, and sometimes even travel back and forth. Migration is building connections between distant parts of the world, replacing face-to-face interactions with more remote encounters and potentially reducing the hold of the local environment over people's lives and imaginations.

increasing migration
The accelerated movement of people within and between countries.

Uneven Development. Globalization is also characterized by **uneven development**. Although many people associate globalization with rapid economic development and progress, globalization has not brought equal benefits to the world's people. Some travel the globe for business or pleasure; others have absolutely no access to any form of transportation. Although 50 percent of the world's people now have cell phones, the distribution is uneven. Europe, North America, and Asia account for well more than 50 percent of such high-tech consumption, while areas of Africa are marginalized and excluded from

uneven development
The unequal distribution of the benefits of globalization.

the globalization process. Such uneven development and uneven access to the benefits of globalization reflect the negative side of changes in the world today.

Although the global economy is creating extreme wealth, it is also creating extreme poverty. Excluding China (which has experienced rapid economic growth), global poverty has increased over the past twenty years. Fully 40 percent of the world's population lives in poverty, defined as income of less than $2 per day. Just over 1 billion people live in extreme poverty, surviving on less than $1 each day (United Nations Development Programme 2013b). Even in the United States, the wealthiest country in the world, some full-time workers earning minimum wage make so little money that they must rely on state welfare programs for food stamps and medical care for themselves and their children. In Chapter 11, we will explore the possibility that the rapid growth seen in globalization actually *depends on* uneven development—extracting the resources of some to fuel the success of others.

rapid change

The dramatic transformations of economics, politics, and culture characteristic of contemporary globalization.

Rapid Change. Globalization is driving **rapid change** in human activities and in the physical world. Although change has been a constant in human history, the pace of change in the modern era—particularly the rate of technological innovation and development—is unlike anything humans experienced in the past. Our economic, social, and political institutions and practices would be nearly unrecognizable to people living even two to three hundred years ago.

Adapting to the Natural World. Of course, modern humans and our ancestors have been adapting to changes for millions of years. In fact, perhaps our most unique characteristic is our ability to adapt—to figure out how to survive and thrive in a world that is rapidly changing. Although change has been a constant, so has human adaptation, both biological and cultural.

Our species has successfully adapted genetically to changes in the natural environment over millions of years. We walk upright on two legs. We have binocular vision and see in color. We have opposable thumbs for grasping. Our bodies also adapt temporarily to changes in the environment on a daily basis. We sweat to keep cool in the heat, tan to block out the sun's ultraviolet rays, shiver to generate warmth in the cold, and breathe rapidly to take in more oxygen at high altitudes.

As our ancestors evolved and developed greater brain capacity, they invented cultural adaptations—tools, the controlled use of fire, and weapons—to navigate the natural environment. Today our use of culture to adapt to the world around us is incredibly sophisticated. In the United States, we like our air conditioners on a hot July afternoon and our radiators in the winter. Oxygen masks deploy for us in sky-high airplanes, and sunscreen protects us against sunburn and skin cancer. These are just a few familiar examples of adaptations our culture has made. Looking more broadly, the worldwide diversity of human culture itself is a testimony to human flexibility and adaptability to particular environments.

Shaping the Natural World. To say that humans adapt to the natural world is only part of the story, for humans actively shape the natural world as well. Humans have planted, grazed, paved, excavated, and built on at least 40 percent of Earth's surface. Our activities have caused profound changes in the atmosphere, soil, and oceans. Whereas our ancestors struggled to adapt to the uncertainties of heat, cold, solar radiation, disease, natural disasters, famines, and droughts, today we confront changes and social forces that we ourselves have set in motion. These changes include climate change, water scarcity, overpopulation, extreme poverty, biological weapons, and nuclear missiles. As globalization intensifies, it escalates the human impact on the planet and on other humans, further accelerating the pace of change.

Human activity already threatens the world's ecological balance. We do not need to wait to see the effects. For instance, population growth and consumption patterns have placed incredible stress on Earth's water resources, both freshwater and saltwater. As the opening story of Plachimada, India, reveals, the struggle to gain access to the freshwater in lakes, rivers, and aquifers can be a source of conflict. Private companies are buying up rights to water in many countries, and bottled water sales have grown to a $50 billion global business today. The seemingly vast oceans are also experiencing significant distress. In the middle of the Pacific Ocean sits a floating island of plastic the size of Texas, caught in an intersection of ocean currents. The plastic originates mainly from consumers in Asia and North America. Pollution from garbage, sewage, and agricultural fertilizer runoff, combined with overfishing and spills from offshore oil drilling, may

Actual stomach contents of a baby albatross on the remote north Pacific Midway Atoll, two thousand miles from the nearest continent. Thousands die as their parents feed them lethal quantities of floating plastic trash that they mistake for food as they forage over the polluted Pacific Ocean. © Chris Jordan, courtesy of Kopeikin Gallery, Los Angeles.

kill off edible sea life completely by 2048. These sobering realities are characteristic of today's global age and the impacts of increasing globalization.

Humans and Climate Change. Human activity is also producing rapid **climate change**. Driven by the increase of greenhouse gases in the atmosphere, largely from the burning of fossil fuels, global warming is already reshaping the physical world and threatening to radically change much of modern human civilization. Scientists predict a rise in average global temperatures of between 2.5 and 10 degrees Fahrenheit by 2100. Changing weather patterns have already begun to alter agricultural patterns and crop yields. Global warming has spurred rapid melting of polar ice and glaciers, well before most scientists had predicted, and the pace is increasing.

Melting glaciers mean rising sea levels. Given the current speed of melting, a one- to two-foot sea-level rise in the coming decades is entirely possible. Half of the world's population lives within fifty miles of the coast, so the implications are enormous—especially in low-lying delta regions. Bangladesh, home to more than 150 million people, will be largely underwater. Miami will have an ocean on both sides. Should all the glacier ice on Greenland melt, sea levels would rise an estimated twenty-three feet.

How will the planet cope with the growth of the human population from 7.2 billion in 2015 to more than nine billion in 2050? Our ancestors have successfully adapted to the natural world around us for millions of years, but human activity and technological innovation now threaten to overwhelm the natural world beyond its ability to adapt to us.

How Is Globalization Transforming Anthropology?

The field of anthropology has changed significantly in the past thirty years as the world has been transformed by globalization. Just as the local cultures and communities we study are changing in response to these forces, our focus and strategies must also change.

CHANGING COMMUNITIES

As time and space compress, the world gets smaller. Migration, economic activity, and flows of money, ideas, media images, and the elements of popular culture such as music, movies, and television have created a new diversity of experiences that reach every corner of the world. As they do so, they mingle with and

---

climate change

Changes to Earth's climate, including global warming produced primarily by increasing concentrations of greenhouse gases created by human activity such as burning fossil fuels and deforestation.

influence local cultures and challenge traditions and customs. As a result, many local cultural patterns are being forced to shift and adapt.

Debates over the effects of globalization on local cultures and communities are intense. Vulnerable people and cultures are encountering powerful economic forces. Many communities are seeing the redefinition of aspects of personal lives and cultural beliefs—in terms of family, gender roles, ethnicity, sexuality, love, and work patterns. Critics of globalization warn of the dangers of homogenization and the loss of traditional local cultures as products marketed by global companies flood into local communities. (Many of these brands originate in Western countries: for example, Coca-Cola, Microsoft, McDonald's, Levi's, Disney, Walmart, CNN, and Hollywood.) Yet proponents note the new exposure to diversity that is now available to people worldwide, opening possibilities for personal choice that were previously unimaginable. As in the case of Plachimada, India, although global forces are increasingly affecting local communities, local communities are also actively resisting these forces, fighting detrimental changes, negotiating better terms of engagement, and embracing new opportunities.

CHANGING RESEARCH STRATEGIES

Globalization is transforming not only the communities that we study, but also the strategies we use to study them (see Chapter 3). Today it is impossible to study a local community without considering the global forces that affect it. Thus, anthropologists are engaging in more multi-sited ethnographies, comparing communities linked, for instance, by migration, production, or communication. My own research is a case in point.

Multi-sited Ethnography: China and New York. When I began my fieldwork in New York City's Chinatown in 1997, I anticipated conducting a year-long study of Chinese immigrant religious communities—Christian, Buddhist, and Daoist—and their role in the lives of new immigrants. I soon realized, however, that I did not understand why tens of thousands of immigrants from Fuzhou, China, were taking such great risks—some hiring human smugglers at enormous cost—to come and work in low-paying jobs in restaurants, garment shops, construction trades, and nail salons. To figure out why so many were leaving China, one summer I followed their immigrant journey back home.

MAP 1.2
Fuzhou/New York

I boarded a plane from New York to Hong Kong and on to Fuzhou, the capital of Fujian Province on China's southeast coast. From Fuzhou, I took a local bus to a small town at the end of the line. A ferry carried me across a river to a three-wheeled motor taxi that transported me across dirt roads to the main square of a rural fishing village at the foot of a small mountain. I began to hike up the slope and finally caught a ride on a motorcycle to my destination.

Rural Fuzhou villagers worship at a Chinese temple constructed with funds sent home by community members working in the United States.

Back in New York, I had met the master of a temple, an immigrant from Fuzhou who was raising money from other immigrant workers to rebuild their temple in China. He had invited me to visit their hometown and participate in a temple festival. Now, finally arriving at the temple after a transcontinental journey, I was greeted by hundreds of pilgrims from neighboring towns and villages. "What are you doing here?" one asked. When I told them that I was an anthropologist from the United States, that I had met some of their fellow villagers in New York, and that I had come to learn about their village, they began to laugh. "Go back to New York!" they said. "Most of our village is there already, not here in this little place." Then we all laughed together, acknowledging the irony of my traveling to China when they wanted to go to New York—but also marveling at the remarkable connection built across the ten thousand miles between this little village and one of the most urban metropolises in the world.

Over the years I have made many trips back to the villages around Fuzhou. My research experiences have brought alive the ways in which globalization is transforming the world and the practice of anthropology. Today 70 percent of the village population resides in the United States, but the villagers live out time-space compression as they continue to build strong ties between New York and China. They travel back and forth. They build temples, roads, and schools back home. They transfer money by wire. They call, text, Skype, and post videos online. They send children back to China to be raised by grandparents in the village. Parents in New York watch their children play in the village using webcams and the Internet.

Back home, local factories built by global corporations produce toys for Disney and McDonald's and Mardi Gras beads for the city of New Orleans. The local jobs provide employment alternatives, but they have not replaced migration out of China as the best option for improving local lives.

These changes are happening incredibly rapidly, transforming people's lives and communities on opposite sides of the world. But globalization brings uneven benefits that break down along lines of ethnicity, gender, age, language, legal status, kinship, and class. These disparities give rise to issues that we will address in depth throughout this book. Such changes mean that I as an anthropologist have to adjust my own fieldwork to span my subjects' entire reality, a reality that now encompasses a village in China, the metropolis of New York City, and many people and places in between (Guest 2003). And as you will discover throughout this book, other anthropologists are likewise adapting their strategies to meet the challenges of globalization. Learning to think like an anthropologist will enable you to better navigate our increasingly interconnected world.

Toolkit

Thinking Like an Anthropologist:
Living in a Global Age

As you begin your exploration of anthropology, the women of Plachimada discussed in the chapter opening may provide you with a powerful image to keep in mind and challenge you to think more anthropologically about the world and its people. *Essentials of Cultural Anthropology: A Toolkit for a Global Age* is designed to help you explore the richness of human diversity, uncover your conscious and subconscious ideas of how the world works (or should work), and develop some strategies for living, working, and learning in an environment where diversity is a part of daily life.

Solving the challenges that face the human race in your lifetime will require greater engagement, interaction, and cooperation—not more isolation and ignorance. The future of the planet requires everyone to develop the skills of an anthropologist if our species is to thrive and, perhaps, even to survive. These skills include cross-cultural knowledge and sensitivity; perceptiveness of other people; understanding of systems of meaning and systems of power; and consciousness of one's own culture, assumptions, beliefs, and power. By the end of this book, you will have many of the skills needed to think carefully about these questions.

- **What is anthropology?**
- **Through what lenses do anthropologists gain a comprehensive view of human cultures?**
- **What is globalization, and why is it important for anthropology?**
- **How is globalization transforming anthropology?**

You also will discover that the study of anthropology helps you rethink many of your assumptions about the world and how it works. For the magic of anthropology lies in unmasking the underlying structures of life, in spurring the analytical imagination, and in providing the skills to be alert, aware, sensitive, and successful in a rapidly changing—and often confusing—multicultural and global world.

Key Terms

anthropology (p. 8)

ethnocentrism (p. 9)

ethnographic fieldwork (p. 10)

four-field approach (p. 12)

holism (p. 12)

physical anthropology (p. 13)

paleoanthropology (p. 13)

primatology (p. 14)

archaeology (p. 15)

prehistoric archaeology (p. 15)

historic archaeology (p. 16)

linguistic anthropology (p. 17)

descriptive linguists (p. 17)

historic linguists (p. 17)

sociolinguists (p. 17)

cultural anthropology (p. 18)

participant observation (p. 18)

ethnology (p. 18)

globalization (p. 18)

time-space compression (p. 20)

flexible accumulation (p. 20)

increasing migration (p. 21)

uneven development (p. 21)

rapid change (p. 22)

climate change (p. 24)

Chapter 2
Culture

In April 2007, U.S. movie star Richard Gere stood on a stage near Delhi, India, and led thousands of truck drivers in a Hindi-language chant of "No condoms, no sex! No condoms, no sex!" HIV/AIDS has become an epidemic among Indian truck drivers, who transport millions of tons of goods and produce around the country as India's economy grows. Gere and other movie stars have lent their celebrity to raise awareness about the need for HIV/AIDS prevention in the Indian trucking community. At the end of the chant, Gere reached across the stage to Indian movie star Shilpa Shetty, dipped her backward, and kissed her on both cheeks as the crowd roared.

Video images of this kiss spread like wildfire across India, replayed on television and published on the front pages of newspapers. Although many Indians ignored it, the kiss drew violent protests from others—particularly religious fundamentalists and Hindu nationalists.

When is a kiss more than a kiss? Richard Gere kisses Shilpa Shetty during an AIDS awareness program for truck drivers in New Delhi, India.

From left to right: A kiss in Brazil. A greeting in Laos, South Asia. A kiss in France.

A spokesperson for the Hindu nationalist Bharatiya Janata Party condemned the kiss, saying, "Such a public display is not part of Indian tradition." Demonstrators in Mumbai (Bombay) burned images of Gere and Shetty in effigy and set fire to glamour shots of Shetty. They deplored the public display of sexuality, especially because the pair is not married and Gere is a foreigner. In the northern city of Meerut, crowds of hundreds of thousands chanted, "Down with Shilpa Shetty!" A court in Rajasthan issued warrants for the arrest of Gere and Shetty. Said Shetty, "I understand this [kissing] is his [Gere's] culture, not ours. But this was not such a big thing or so obscene for people to overreact in such a manner."

Have you kissed someone lately? Perhaps your kiss didn't inspire nationwide protests. But kissing can be tricky, even in your own culture. Whom can you kiss? How should you kiss them? How do you know? What if you read the signals wrong? What if you kiss the wrong person? What if you do it in the wrong place?

Although Americans may consider kissing as "doing what comes naturally," as an instinctive or biological impulse to show affection or sexuality, the world's cultures have remarkably different ideas about kissing and touching, about love and sex. Ten percent of the people in the world don't kiss at all. In Tahiti, kissing was unknown until European colonialists introduced the practice. Brazilians kiss and hug with gusto. Faithful Catholics may kiss the Pope's ring to show reverence. Parents kiss their children's foreheads as a sign of blessing. In much of Europe, where kissing is the primary greeting, practices vary by country and even within countries. In Paris, four kisses is standard, starting with the left cheek, while in most of the rest of France two kisses suffice. In the Netherlands, kisses begin and end on the right cheek, with three at least, and more to show affection to a close relative or the elderly. In the United Kingdom, there is very little kissing. Handshakes and nods are the normal greetings there.

Kissing is a powerful symbolic action that arouses intense personal feelings and expresses complicated social meanings. It might be easier if someone handed us a kissing manual. Instead we have culture. Culture is our manual for understanding and interacting with the people and the world around us. It includes shared meanings, belief systems, and cultural knowledge—in other words, shared ways of seeing and understanding the world. It shapes every aspect of our human experience. But culture is not fixed in stone or accepted by everyone, even those living in a particular place or time. So culture also provides the arena where our ideas about how to behave—even what we ought to say and think—are debated, challenged, and enforced.

In this chapter, we will apply an anthropologist's viewpoint to culture and consider its crucial role in shaping how we behave and what we think. In particular, we will consider:

- **What is culture?**
- **How has the culture concept developed in anthropology?**
- **How are culture and power related?**
- **How much of who you are is determined by biology and how much by culture?**
- **How is culture created?**
- **How is globalization transforming culture?**

By the end of the chapter you should have a clear sense of how anthropologists think about culture and use culture to analyze human life. By exploring this seemingly familiar concept, you can become conscious of the many unconscious patterns of belief and action that you accept as normal and natural. You can also begin to see how such patterns shape your everyday choices and even your basic conceptions of what is real and what isn't.

What Is Culture?

When people hear the word *culture,* they often think about the material goods or artistic forms produced by distinct groups of people—Chinese food, Middle Eastern music, Indian clothing, Greek architecture, African dances. Sometimes people assume that culture means elite art forms such as those displayed in museums, operas, or ballets. But for anthropologists, culture is much more: it encompasses people's entire way of life.

Culture is a system of knowledge, beliefs, patterns of behavior, artifacts, and institutions that are created, learned, and shared by a group of people. Culture includes shared norms, values, symbols, mental maps of reality, and material objects as well as structures of power—including the media, education, religion, and politics—in which our understanding of the world is shaped, reinforced, and challenged. Ultimately, the culture that we learn shapes our ideas of what is normal and natural, what we can say and do, and even what we can think.

culture

A system of knowledge, beliefs, patterns of behavior, artifacts, and institutions that are created, learned, and shared by a group of people.

CULTURE IS LEARNED AND TAUGHT

enculturation

The process of learning culture.

Humans do not genetically inherit culture. We learn culture throughout our lives from the people and cultural institutions that surround us. Anthropologists call the process of learning culture **enculturation**. Some aspects of culture we learn through formal instruction: English classes in school, religious instruction, visits to the doctor, history lessons, dance classes. Other processes of enculturation are informal and even unconscious as we absorb culture from family, friends, and the media. All humans are equally capable of learning culture and of learning any culture they are exposed to.

The process of enculturation, passing cultural information within populations and across generations, is not unique to humans. Many animals learn social behavior from their immediate group: Wolves learn hunting strategies from the wolf pack. Whales learn to produce and distinguish the unique calls of their pod. Among monkeys and apes, our closest biological relatives, learned behaviors are even more common. Chimpanzees have been observed teaching their young to create rudimentary tools, stripping bark from a twig that they then insert into an anthill to extract a tasty and nutritious treat. But the human capacity to learn culture is unparalleled.

Culture is taught as well as learned. Humans establish cultural institutions as mechanisms for enculturating their members. Schools, medical systems, media, and religious institutions promote the ideas and concepts that are considered central to the culture. Rules, regulations, laws, teachers, doctors, religious leaders, police officers, and sometimes militaries promote and enforce what is considered appropriate behavior and thinking.

How is culture learned and taught? Here, kindergartners learn Mandarin Chinese at the New York Chinese School.

CULTURE IS SHARED YET CONTESTED

Enculturation occurs as part of a group. No individual has his or her own culture. Culture is a shared experience developed as a result of living as a member of a group. Through enculturation, humans learn how to communicate and establish patterns of behavior that allow life in community, often in close proximity and sometimes with limited resources. Cultures may be shared by groups, large and small. For example, anthropologists may speak of Indian culture (one billion people) as well as the culture of the Yanomami tribe (several thousand people) living in the Amazonian rainforest. Your college classroom has a culture, one that you must learn in order to succeed academically. A classroom culture includes shared understandings of what to wear, how to sit, when to arrive or leave, how to communicate with classmates and the instructor, and how to challenge authority, as well as formal and informal processes of enculturation.

Although culture is shared by members of groups, it is also constantly contested, negotiated, and changing. Culture is never static. Just as cultural institutions serve as structures for promoting enculturation, they also serve as arenas for challenging, debating, and changing core cultural beliefs and behaviors. Intense debates erupt over school curriculums, medical practices, media content, religious practices, and government policies as members of a culture engage in sometimes dramatic confrontations about their collective purpose and direction.

CULTURE IS SYMBOLIC AND MATERIAL

Through enculturation, over time the members of a culture develop a shared body of cultural knowledge and patterns of behavior. Though anthropologists no longer think of culture as a completely separate, unique possession of a specific group of people, most argue that a common cultural core exists, at least among the dominant segments of the culture. Norms, values, symbols, and mental maps of reality are four elements that an anthropologist may consider in attempting to understand the complex workings of a culture. These are not universal; they vary from culture to culture. Even within a culture not everyone shares equally in that cultural knowledge, nor does everyone agree completely on it. But the elements of a culture powerfully frame what its participants can say, what they can do, and even what they think is possible and impossible, real or unreal.

Norms. **Norms** are ideas or rules about how people should behave in particular situations or toward certain other people—what is considered "normal" and appropriate behavior. Norms may include what to wear on certain occasions such as weddings, funerals, work, and school; what you can say in polite company; how younger people should treat older people; and who you can date or, as the opening anecdote demonstrated, who you can kiss. Many norms are assumed, not written down. We learn them over time—consciously and

norms
Ideas or rules about how people should behave in particular situations or toward certain other people.

unconsciously—and incorporate them into our patterns of daily living. Other norms are formalized in writing and made publicly available, such as a country's laws, a system of medical or business ethics, or the code of academic integrity in your college or university. Norms may vary for segments of the population, imposing different expectations on men and women, for instance, or children and adults. Cultural norms may be widely accepted, but they also may be debated, challenged, and changed.

Consider the question of who you can marry. You may consider the decision to be a matter of personal choice, but in many cultures the decision is not left to the whims of young people. The results are too important. Often it is two families who arrange the marriage, not two individuals, although these patterns are under pressure from the globalization of Western cultural practices.

Cultures have clear norms, based on ideas of age, kinship, sexuality, race, religion, class, and legal status, that specify what is normal and what is not. Let's consider some extreme cases. In Nazi Germany, the Nuremburg Laws passed in 1935 banned marriage between whites and nonwhites, particularly Jews. From 1949 to 1985, South Africa's apartheid government, dominated by white lawmakers, declared marriage and sex between whites and "coloreds" (people of mixed race), Asians, and blacks to be a crime under the Prohibition of Mixed Marriages Act and the Immorality Act. In the history of the United States, as many as forty states passed antimiscegenation laws—that is, laws barring interracial marriage and sex. Such laws targeted marriages between whites and nonwhites—primarily blacks, but also Asians and Native Americans. Only in 1967 did the U.S. Supreme Court unanimously rule (in *Loving v. Virginia*) that these laws were unconstitutional, thereby striking down statutes still on the books in sixteen states (all the former slave states plus Oklahoma).

Cultural norms may discourage *exogamy* (marriage outside one's "group") and encourage *endogamy* (marriage within one's "group"). Think about your own family. Who could you bring home to your parents? Could you cross boundaries of race, ethnicity, nationality, religion, class, or gender? Although U.S. culture has very few formal rules about whom one can marry—with some exclusions around age, sexuality, and certain kinship relations—cultural norms still powerfully inform and enforce our behavior.

Most people, though not all, accept and follow a culture's norms. If they choose to challenge the norms, other members of the culture have means for enforcing its standards, whether through shunning, institutionalized punishment such as fines or imprisonment, or in more extreme cases, violence and threats of violence. Protestors in India certainly took steps to enforce perceived cultural norms about public sexuality and nationalism in the case of Richard Gere and Shilpa Shetty.

Values. Cultures promote and cultivate a core set of **values**—fundamental beliefs about what is important, what makes a good life, and what is true, right, and beautiful. Values reflect shared ultimate standards that should guide people's behavior, as well as goals that people feel are important for themselves, their families, and their community. What would you identify as the core values of U.S. culture? Individualism? Independence? Care for the most vulnerable? Freedom of speech, press, and religion? Equal access to social mobility?

As with all elements of culture, cultural values are not fixed. They can be debated and contested. And they may have varying degrees of influence. For example, if you pick up a newspaper in any country you will find a deep debate about cultural values. Perhaps the debate focuses on modesty versus public displays of affection in India, economic growth versus environmental pollution in China, or land settlement versus peace in the Middle East. A hot global topic is the proper balance of security and privacy. Stand in line to board an airplane anywhere in the world, and you will experience the changing landscape in this debate. In the United States after the attacks of September 11, 2001, on the World Trade Center in New York and the Pentagon in Washington, D.C., the country has hotly debated these competing values. In 2002 and 2007, the U.S. Congress passed the USA PATRIOT Acts to reduce the danger of terrorism by easing restrictions on government eavesdropping on telephone calls and e-mails, surveillance of noncitizens, and indefinite detention of suspected terrorists. Civil rights groups have protested the unchecked invasion of privacy, warning that the legislation undermines the most highly valued aspects of our culture. This debate continues today.

Ultimately, values are not simply platitudes about people's ideals about the good life. Values are powerful cultural tools for clarifying cultural goals and motivating people to action. Values can be so potent that some people are willing to kill or die for them.

Symbols. Cultures include complex systems of symbols and symbolic actions—in realms such as language, art, religion, politics, and economics—that convey meaning to other participants. In essence, a **symbol** is something that stands for something else. For example, language enables humans to communicate abstract ideas through symbols—written and spoken words, as well as unspoken sounds and gestures (see Chapter 4). People shake hands, wave, whistle, nod, smile, give two thumbs up, give thumbs down, give someone the middle finger. These symbols are not universal, but within their particular cultural context they convey certain meanings.

Much symbolic communication is nonverbal, action-based, and unconscious. Religions include powerful systems of symbols that represent deeper meanings

values
Fundamental beliefs about what is important, true, or beautiful, and what makes a good life.

symbol
Anything that signifies something else.

to their adherents. Consider mandalas, the Koran, the Torah, the Christian cross, holy water, statues of the Buddha—all carry greater meanings and value than the physical material they are constructed of. National flags, which are mere pieces of colored cloth, are symbols that stir deep political emotions. Even money is simply a symbolic representation of value guaranteed by the sponsoring government. It has no value, except in its symbolism. Estimates suggest that only about 10 percent of money today exists in physical form. The rest moves electronically through banks, stock markets, and credit accounts (Graeber 2011).

Symbols change in meaning over time and from culture to culture. Not understanding another culture's collective understandings—sets of symbolic actions—can lead to embarrassing misunderstandings and cross-cultural miscues. As an undergraduate student in Beijing, I was approached on a public bus by a Chinese man who wanted to practice his English. Standing within a foot of me, he began to pepper me with questions. I backed away, uncomfortable with how close he was. He simply continued to move toward me, closing any gap I attempted to open and being clearly puzzled by my attempts to move away. From my cultural perspective, he was rudely invading "my space." From his perspective, he was moving into appropriate conversational distance and I was acting strangely by repeatedly backing up.

I was comforted later to find that studies reveal four spatial comfort zones specific to U.S. culture that differ from those in other cultures. For example, our *public zone* of 12 feet or more is the comfortable amount of space in a public forum between a speaker and an audience, such as a classroom or lecture hall. The *social zone* of 4 to 12 feet is appropriate for people who do not know each

How close is too close? Passengers crowd onto a long-distance bus in Chengdu in Southwest China's Sichuan province. Collective understandings about personal space vary across cultures.

other well but need to communicate directly, as in an interview or professional meeting. The *personal zone*, from 1.5 to 4 feet, is appropriate for casual friends sitting together or chatting. Finally, the *intimate zone*, from 1.5 feet to contact, you can imagine for yourself (Hall 1966). In some instances, we cannot maintain these distances and so adjust our behavior to compensate for awkwardness and discomfort. In a crowded elevator everyone stops talking, balances out the space between them, and stares at the moving floor number lights. On a crowded bus, train, or subway, people avoid eye contact, limit physical contact even with people inches away, and stop talking. Men look up at the ceiling when standing at urinals in crowded bathrooms. Our collective understandings of space are largely unconscious but very powerful. Compliance or noncompliance with these notions symbolically communicates significant information.

Mental Maps of Reality. Along with norms, values, and symbols, another key component of culture is **mental maps of reality**. These are "maps" that humans construct of what kinds of people and what kinds of things exist. Because the world presents overwhelming quantities of data to our senses, our brains create shortcuts—maps—to navigate our experience and organize all the data that comes our way. A roadmap condenses a large world into a manageable format (one that you can hold in your hands or view on your portable GPS system) and helps us navigate the territory. Likewise, our mental maps organize the world into categories that help us sort out our experiences and what they mean. We do not want all the details all the time. We could not handle them anyway. From our general mental maps we can then dig deeper as required.

Our mental maps are shaped through enculturation, but they are not fixed. Like other elements of culture, they can be challenged and redrawn. Today globalization continues to put pressure on mental maps of reality as people on the planet are drawn into closer contact with the world's diversity. We will examine these transformations throughout this book, especially in chapters on language, race, ethnicity, gender, sexuality, and kinship.

Mental maps have two important functions. *First, mental maps classify reality.* Starting in the eighteenth century, European naturalists such as Carolus Linnaeus (1707–1778) began creating systems of classification for the natural world. These systems included five kingdoms subdivided into phylum, class, order, family, genus, and species. Through observation (this was before genetics), these naturalists sought to organize a logical framework to divide up the world into kinds of things and kinds of people. In a similar way, our cultures' mental maps seek to classify reality—though often a culture's mental maps are drawn from the distinct vantage point of those in power.

A culture creates a concept such as time. Then we arbitrarily divide it into millennia, centuries, decades, years, seasons, months, weeks, hours, morning,

mental maps of reality
Cultural classifications of what kinds of people and things exist, and the assignment of meaning to those classifications.

afternoon, evening, minutes, seconds. Categories of time are assumed to be scientific, universal, and "natural." But mostly they are cultural constructs. The current Gregorian calendar, which is used in much of the world, was introduced in 1582 by the Catholic Church, but its adoption occurred gradually; it was accepted in the United States two hundred years later in 1756, and in China in 1949. Until 1949 and still today, much of China relies on a lunar calendar in which months and days align with the waxing and waning of the moon. New Year's Day shifts each year. So do Chinese holidays and festivals. Even in the Gregorian calendar, the length of the year is modified to fit into a neat mental map of reality. A year (how long it takes Earth to orbit the sun) is approximately 365.2425 days long, so every four years the Gregorian calendar must add a day, creating a leap year of 366 days.

Now check your watch. Even the question of what time it is depends on accepting a global system of time zones centered at the Greenwich meridian in England. But countries regularly modify the system according to their needs. The mainland United States has four time zones. China, approximately the same physical size, uses only one time zone. Russia has eleven. There is a time change of three and a half hours when you cross the border between China and Afghanistan. As these examples demonstrate, categories that seem completely fixed and "natural" are in reality flexible and variable, showing the potential role of culture in defining our fundamental notions of reality.

Mental maps of reality become problematic when people treat cultural notions of difference as being scientifically or biologically "natural." Race is a key example. As we will see in Chapter 5, the notion of race is assumed in popular culture and conversation to have a biological basis. There is, however, no scientific basis for this assumption. The particular racial categories in any given culture do not correlate directly to any biological differences. Although most people in the United States would name whites, blacks, Hispanics, Asians, and perhaps Native Americans as distinct races, no genetic line marks clear differences among these categories. The classifications are created by our culture and are specific to our culture. Other cultures draw different mental maps of the reality of human physical variation. The Japanese use different racial categories than the United States. Brazilians have more than five hundred racial classifications.

Second, mental maps assign meaning to what has been classified. Not only do people in a culture develop mental maps of things and people, but they also place values and meanings upon those maps. For example, we divide the life span into categories—infants, children, adolescents, teenagers, young adults, adults, and seniors, for example—but then we give different values to different ages. Some carry more respect, more protection, and more rights, privileges, and responsibilities. In the United States, these categories determine at what age you can marry, have sex, drink alcohol, drive, vote, go to war, stand trial, retire, or collect Social Security and Medicare benefits.

In considering the earlier discussion of time, we can see how these classifications gain value and meaning. U.S. culture puts a premium on time, discourages idle leisure, and encourages people to work hard and stay busy. "Time is money!" we often hear, and so it should not be wasted. Assuming that our mental maps of reality are natural can cause us to disregard the cultural values of others. For instance, we may see as lazy those whose cultures value a midday nap. This effect of our mental maps is important for anthropologists to understand (Wolf-Meyer 2012).

As our opening story illustrated, the study of culture can be extremely complicated. Richard Gere's kiss of Shilpa Shetty was a symbolic act that communicated certain information to people across India—most likely, information that Gere, as a foreigner, had not intended. The kiss and its interpretation represent one prominent concept of culture as a system of meaning: a shared set of ideas, norms, and values learned over time and embodied in objects and behavior that become symbolic—something that stands for or means something else. Gere's kiss also sparked an intense debate over cultural ideas and patterns of behavior, including ideas about sexuality, religion, nationalism, and even globalization. This reaction reveals that culture is also an arena where relationships of power among people are worked out and worked on. To fully grasp the anthropological understanding of culture, we will examine the historical development of the culture concept before turning our attention to more recent notions of culture as a system of meaning and as a system of power.

What does it mean to be a child laborer in your culture? A child laborer at a Baltimore, Maryland, packing company, 1909.

British anthropologist Edward Burnett Tylor.

How Has the Culture Concept Developed in Anthropology?

The concept of culture has been central to anthropology ever since the English anthropologist Edward Burnett Tylor (1832–1917) crafted his definition in the opening paragraph of his book *Primitive Culture* in 1871: "Culture or Civilization, taken in its wide ethnographic sense, is that complex whole which includes knowledge, belief, art, morals, law, custom and any other capabilities and habits acquired by man as a member of society."

Tylor understood culture to be a unified and complex system of ideas and behavior learned over time, passed down from generation to generation, and shared by members of a particular group. Over the past century and a half, culture has become more than a definition; it is now a key theoretical framework for anthropologists attempting to understand humans and their interactions.

EARLY EVOLUTIONARY FRAMEWORKS

Edward Burnett Tylor and James Frazer (1854–1941) of England and Lewis Henry Morgan (1818–1881) of the United States were among the leading early anthropologists. They sought to organize the vast quantities of data about the diversity of cultures worldwide that were being accumulated through colonial and missionary enterprises during the nineteenth century. These anthropologists were influenced by Charles Darwin's theory of biological evolution, which maintains that the diversity of biological species resulted from gradual change over time in response to environmental pressures. Thus they suggested that the vast diversity of cultures represented different stages in the evolution of human culture.

unilineal cultural evolution

The theory proposed by nineteenth-century anthropologists that all cultures naturally evolve through the same sequence of stages from simple to complex.

The early anthropologists suggested that all cultures would naturally evolve through the same sequence of stages, a concept known as **unilineal cultural evolution.** They set about plotting the world's cultures along a continuum from most simple to most complex, using the terms *savage*, *barbarian*, and *civilized*. Western cultures were, perhaps too predictably, considered the most evolved or civilized. By arranging all of the world cultures along this continuum, the early anthropologists believed that they could trace the path of human cultural evolution, understand where some cultures had come from, and predict where other cultures were headed.

Succeeding generations of anthropologists rejected unilineal cultural evolution as being too Eurocentric, too hierarchical, and lacking adequate data to support its grand claims. Franz Boas, the founder of American anthropology, and Bronislaw Malinowski, a Polish anthropologist who spent most of his life teaching in England, represent two main schools of anthropology that moved beyond the evolutionary framework for viewing cultural differences.

AMERICAN HISTORICAL PARTICULARISM

Franz Boas (1858–1942) conducted fieldwork among the Kwakiutl indigenous people of the Pacific Northwest of the United States and Canada before becoming a professor of anthropology at Columbia University in New York and a curator of the American Museum of Natural History. Boas rejected unilineal cultural evolution, its generalizations, and its comparative method. Instead he advocated for an approach called **historical particularism**. He claimed that cultures arise from different causes, not uniform processes. According to Boas, anthropologists could not rely on an evolutionary formula to explain differences among cultures but must study the particular history of each culture to see how it developed. Evolutionists such as Tylor, Frazer, and Morgan argued that similarities among cultures emerged through independent invention as different cultures independently arrived at similar solutions to similar problems. Boas, in contrast, while not ruling out some independent invention, turned to the idea of *diffusion*—the borrowing of cultural traits and patterns from other cultures—to explain apparent similarities.

Boas's belief in the powerful role of culture in shaping human life exhibited itself in his early twentieth-century studies of immigrants. His research with the children of immigrants from Europe revealed the remarkable effects of culture and environment on their physical forms, challenging the role of biology as a tool for discrimination. As a Jewish immigrant himself, Boas was particularly sensitive to the dangers of racial stereotyping, and his work throughout his career served to challenge white supremacy, the inferior ranking of non-European people, and other expressions of racism.

Boas's students Ruth Benedict (1887–1948) and Margaret Mead (1901–1979) continued his emphasis on the powerful role of culture in shaping human life and the need to explore the unique development of each culture. Benedict's popular studies, *Patterns of Culture* (1934) and *The Chrysanthemum and the Sword* (1946), explored the ways in which cultural traits and entire cultures are uniquely patterned and integrated. Mead conducted research in Samoa, Bali, and Papua New Guinea and became perhaps the most famous anthropologist of the twentieth century, promoting her findings and the unique tools of anthropology to the general American public.

Mead turned her attention particularly to enculturation and its powerful effects on cultural patterns and personality types. In her book *Coming of Age in Samoa* (1928), she explored the seeming sexual freedom and experimentation of young Samoan women and compared it with the repressed sexuality of young women in the United States, suggesting the important role of enculturation in shaping behavior—even behavior that is imagined to have powerful biological origins. Mead's controversial research and findings over her career challenged biological assumptions about women and contributed to heated debates about the role of women in U.S. culture in the twentieth century.

historical particularism
The idea, attributed to Franz Boas, that cultures develop in specific ways because of their unique histories.

American anthropologist Ruth Benedict.

BRITISH STRUCTURAL FUNCTIONALISM

Between the 1920s and 1960s, in a rejection of unilineal cultural evolution, many British social anthropologists viewed anthropology more as a science and fieldwork more as a science experiment that could focus on the specific details of a local society. These anthropologists viewed human societies as living organisms, and through fieldwork they sought to analyze each part of the "body." Each part of society—including the kinship, religious, political, and economic structures—fit together and had its unique function within the larger structure. Like a living organism, a society worked to maintain an internal balance, or equilibrium, that kept the system working. Under this conceptual framework, called **structural functionalism**, British social anthropologists employed a synchronic approach to control their science experiments—analyzing contemporary societies at a fixed point in time without regard to historical context. By isolating as many variables as possible, especially by excluding history and outside influences such as neighboring groups or larger national or global dynamics, these anthropologists sought to focus narrowly on the culture at hand.

Early practitioners of this approach included Bronislaw Malinowski (1884–1942), who employed an early form of functionalism in his ethnography of the Trobriand Islands, *Argonauts of the Western Pacific* (1922), discussed in more detail in Chapter 3; and E. E. Evans-Pritchard (1902–1973) in his classic ethnography of the Sudan, *The Nuer* (1940), which we will consider further in Chapters 3 and 9. Later, British anthropologists, including Max Gluckman (1911–1975), in his work on rituals of rebellion, and Victor Turner (1920–1983), in his work on religious symbols and rituals, critiqued earlier structural functionalists for ignoring the dynamics of conflict, tension, and change within the cultures they studied. Their intervention marked a significant turn in the study of culture by British anthropologists.

CULTURE AND MEANING

One predominant view within anthropology in recent decades sees culture primarily as a set of ideas or knowledge shared by a group of people that provides a common body of information about how to behave, why to behave that way, and what that behavior means. The anthropologist Clifford Geertz (1926–2006), a key figure in this **interpretivist approach**, urged anthropologists to explore culture primarily as a symbolic system in which even simple, seemingly straightforward actions can convey deep meanings.

In a classic example, Geertz examines the difference between a wink and a twitch of the eye. Both involve the same movement of the eye muscles, but the wink carries a meaning, which can change depending on the context in which it occurs. A wink can imply flirting, including a friend in a secret, or slyly

structural functionalism

A conceptual framework positing that each element of society serves a particular function to keep the entire system in equilibrium.

MAP 2.1
Trobriand Islands

interpretivist approach

A conceptual framework that sees culture primarily as a symbolic system of deep meaning.

Preparations for a cockfight outside a Hindu temple in Bali. How do you analyze the deep webs of meaning at play in any cultural event?

signaling agreement. Deciphering the meaning requires a complex, collective (shared) understanding of unspoken communication in a specific cultural context. Collective understandings of symbols and symbolic actions enable people to interact with one another in subtle yet complex ways without constantly stopping to explain themselves.

Geertz's essay "Deep Play: Notes on a Balinese Cockfight" (1973a) describes in intricate detail a cockfight—a common activity even today in local communities across Bali, a small island in the South Pacific. Geertz describes the elaborate breeding, raising, and training of the roosters; the scene of bedlam at the fight; the careful selection of the birds; the rituals of the knife man, who provides the razors for the birds' feet; the fight itself; the raucous betting before and during the fight; and the aftermath, with the cutting up of the losing cock and the dividing of its parts among participants in the fight.

Geertz argues that such careful description of cultural activity is an essential part of understanding Balinese culture. But it is not enough. He claims that we must engage in **thick description**, looking beneath the surface activities to see the layers of deep cultural meaning in which those activities are embedded. The cockfight is not simply a cockfight. It also represents generations of competition among the village families for prestige, power, and resources within the community. It symbolizes the negotiation of those families' prestige status and standing within the larger groups. For Geertz, all activities of the cockfight reflect these deeper webs of meaning, and their analysis requires extensive description that uncovers those deeper meanings. Indeed, according to Geertz, every cultural action is more than the action itself; it is also a symbol of deeper meaning. (Even a simple kiss, as Richard Gere found out, carries a deeper cultural meaning.)

MAP 2.2
Bali

thick description

A research strategy that combines detailed description of cultural activity with an analysis of the layers of deep cultural meaning in which those activities are embedded.

How Are Culture and Power Related?

Anthropologists have often separated culture from power. The field has focused primarily on culture as a system of ideas, as represented in the section you have just read. But more recent scholarship has pushed anthropology to consider the deep interconnections between culture and power (Gramsci 1971; Foucault 1977; Wolf 1982), and the chapters of this book take this challenge seriously.

Power is often described as the ability or potential to bring about change through action or influence, either one's own or that of a group or institution. This may include the ability to influence through force or the threat of force. Power is embedded in many kinds of social relations, from interpersonal relations, to institutions, to structural frameworks of whole societies. Throughout this book we will work to unmask the dynamics of power embedded in culture, including systems of power such as race and racism, ethnicity and nationalism, gender, human sexuality, economics, and family.

The anthropologist Eric Wolf (1923–1999) urged anthropologists to see power as an aspect of all human relationships. Consider the relationships in your own life: teacher/student, parent/child, employer/employee, landlord/tenant, lender/borrower, boyfriend/girlfriend. Wolf (1990; 1999) argued that all such human relationships have a power dynamic. Though cultures are often assumed to be composed of groups of similar people who uniformly share norms and values, in reality people in a given culture are usually diverse and their relationships are complicated.

Power in a culture reflects **stratification**—uneven distribution of resources and privileges—among participants. Some people are drawn into the center of the culture. Others are ignored, marginalized, or even annihilated. Power may be stratified along lines of gender, racial or ethnic group, class, age, family, religion, sexuality, or legal status. These structures of power organize relationships among people and create a framework through which access to cultural resources is distributed. As a result, some people are able to participate more fully in the culture than others. This balance of power is not fixed; it fluctuates over time. By examining the way access to the resources, privileges, and opportunities of a culture are shared unevenly and unequally, we can begin to use culture as a conceptual guide to power and its workings.

POWER AND CULTURAL INSTITUTIONS

One key to understanding the relationship between culture and power is to recognize that a culture is more than a set of ideas or patterns of behavior shared among a collection of individuals. A culture also includes the powerful institutions that these people create to promote and maintain their core values. Ethnographic

power

The ability or potential to bring about change through action or influence.

stratification

The uneven distribution of resources and privileges among participants in a group or culture.

A young Muslim woman with two French flags pulled over her head covering marches in Paris against a French ban on religious symbols, including head coverings, in public schools.

research must consider a wide range of institutions that play central roles in the enculturation process. For example, schools teach a shared history, language, patterns of social interaction, notions of health, and scientific ideas of what exists in the world and how the world works. Religious institutions promote moral and ethical codes of behavior. The various media convey images of what is considered normal, natural, and valued. Other prominent cultural institutions that reflect and shape core norms and values include the family, medicine, government, courts, police, and the military.

These cultural institutions are also locations where people can debate and contest cultural norms and values. In 2003, an intense debate erupted in France about Muslim girls wearing headscarves to public schools. Although few girls actually wore headscarves, the controversy took on particular intensity in the aftermath of the events of September 11, 2001, the invasions of Afghanistan and Iraq, and terrorist incidents in Europe. For many people in France, the wearing of head coverings represented a grave danger to French society, particularly its commitment to equality for women, its history of ethnic assimilation, and its tradition of the separation of church and state. Passage of a law banning the headscarf from public schools was intended as a signal (to people both inside and outside France) of the country's commitment to these principles.

Despite legal challenges, strikes by students, and street demonstrations in opposition to the law, in 2004 the French government banned any clothing in public schools that indicates particular religious beliefs. Although the language of the law was broadly stated to include all religions, everyone understood that the headscarves of Muslim girls were the target. France's public schools had become the venue for debating, contesting, and enforcing key French cultural norms and values (Bowen 2006). As we will see, cultural institutions such as schools are not only places where norms are enforced, but also places where powerful ideas of what is normal and natural are shaped.

HEGEMONY

The Italian political philosopher Antonio Gramsci (1891–1937) described two aspects of power. Material power, the first component, includes political, economic, or military power. It exerts itself through coercion or brute force. The second aspect of power involves the ability to create consent and agreement within a population, a condition that Gramsci called **hegemony** (1971).

hegemony

The ability of a dominant group to create consent and agreement within a population without the use or threat of force.

Gramsci recognized the tremendous power of culture—particularly the cultural institutions of media, schools, and religion—to shape, often unconsciously, what people think is normal, natural, and possible, and thereby directly influence the scope of human action and interaction. Cultures, which develop slowly over time, include a shared belief system of what is right and what is wrong, and what is normal and appropriate. In this hegemony of ideas, some thoughts and actions become unthinkable, and group members develop a set of "beliefs" about what is normal and appropriate that come to be seen as natural "truths." The French sociologist Michel Foucault (1926–1984), in *Discipline and Punish* (1977), described this hegemonic aspect of power as the ability to make people discipline their own behavior so that they believe and act in certain "normal" ways—often against their own interests, even without a tangible threat of punishment for misbehavior.

Earlier in this chapter we discussed antimiscegenation laws in the history of the United States. These laws drew upon cultural beliefs in "natural" biological differences among races and the seemingly unnatural, deviant practice of intermarriage. Despite the elimination of these formal laws, a certain hegemony of thought remains: many in U.S. culture still see interracial marriage as unthinkable and undoable. As evidence, consider current intermarriage rates in the United States (Figure 2.1). According to the U.S. Census Bureau (2010), there were 5,303,000 interracial marriages in 2010, only 8.78 percent of all marriages in the United States. Clearly, although U.S. culture has very few formal rules about whom one can marry, cultural norms still powerfully inform and enforce our behavior. As this example shows, views against interracial marriage do not require legal sanction to remain dominant, hegemonic norms.

HUMAN AGENCY

Although hegemony can be very powerful, it does not completely dominate people's thinking. Individuals and groups have the power to contest cultural norms,

FIGURE 2.1
Interracial Marriage Patterns in the United States, 2010

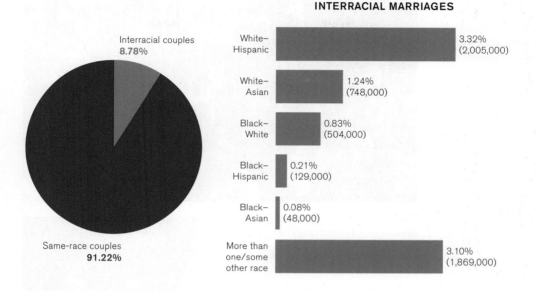

INTERRACIAL MARRIAGES

Interracial couples
8.78%

Same-race couples
91.22%

White–Hispanic 3.32% (2,005,000)

White–Asian 1.24% (748,000)

Black–White 0.83% (504,000)

Black–Hispanic 0.21% (129,000)

Black–Asian 0.08% (48,000)

More than one/some other race 3.10% (1,869,000)

Source: U.S. Census Bureau. 2010. America's Families and Living Arrangements: 2010, Table FG3. www.census.gov/hhes/families/files/cps2010/tabFG4-all.xls (accessed 4/27/15).

values, mental maps of reality, symbols, institutions, and structures of power—a potential known as **agency**. Cultural beliefs and practices are not timeless; they change and can be changed. Cultures are not biologically determined; they are created over time by particular groups of people. By examining human agency, we see how culture serves as a realm in which battles over power take place—where people debate, negotiate, contest, and enforce what is considered normal, what people can say, do, and even think.

Although a dominant group may have greater access to power, resources, rights, or privileges, the systems of power they create are never absolute, and their dominance is never complete. Individuals and groups with less power or no power may contest the dominant power relationships and structures, whether through political, economic, religious, or military means. At times these forms of resistance are visible, public, and well organized, including negotiations, protests, strikes, or rebellions. At other times the resistance may be more subtle, discreet, and diffuse. For example, James Scott's book *Weapons of the Weak: Everyday Forms of Peasant Resistance* (1985) identifies strategies—such as foot-dragging, slowdowns, theft, sabotage, trickery, arson, and false compliance with regulations—that people in very weak positions use to express their agency and to resist the dominant group.

agency

The potential power of individuals and groups to contest cultural norms, values, mental maps of reality, symbols, institutions, and structures of power.

Resistance to unfair conditions takes many forms. *Top*: Egyptian protestors in Tahrir Square, Cairo, demonstrate against their government. *Bottom*: Malaysian farmers conduct a slowdown to protest working conditions.

JENA HIGH SCHOOL: CONNECTING MEANING AND POWER

In the central courtyard of Jena High School in Jena, Louisiana, stood a "white tree" where the white students liked to gather during breaks. At a school assembly in September 2006, Kenneth Purvis, a black student, asked the principal if he could sit under the tree and was told that he could sit wherever he wanted. The next day, Purvis and a cousin went to stand under the tree. The following morning, three nooses were found swinging from the tree.

Three white students, members of the rodeo team, were identified as the perpetrators. The principal recommended their expulsion, but the superintendent and the mostly white school board imposed three days of in-school suspension instead. "Adolescents play pranks," the superintendent told the *Chicago Tribune*. "I don't think it was a threat against anyone."

Was this really a harmless, meaningless prank? Why were the nooses hung in *that* tree at *that* time? Having thought about the cultural intersection of meaning and power in this chapter, how do we begin to understand these events from an anthropological perspective?

To someone from another culture, perhaps a noose is simply a piece of rope twisted and threaded into an elaborate knot. But to those who know U.S. cultural history, this manipulated rope holds deep meaning and expresses stark relationships of power. Historically, nooses are closely associated in U.S. culture with the practice of whites lynching blacks that began after the Civil War. Nooses and lynchings were intended to terrorize. They signaled to the African American population that although they may have won certain legal rights and protections, they should not consider themselves safe: not everyone in the society would obey the law, and some would take violent action outside the law to enforce the cultural norms that they considered appropriate. Although lynchings ended in the United States by the 1940s, the image of the noose is deeply embedded in the culture and its symbolism remains chillingly clear. In this historical context, perhaps we can begin to see that the hanging of three nooses from a tree in the Jena

MAP 2.3
Louisiana

Marchers gather in Jena, Louisiana, to protest the treatment of black teenagers in the aftermath of a fight sparked by several nooses being hung from a tree in the courtyard of Jena High School.

school courtyard was not a random act but one that employed the deep symbolic meaning of the twisted and knotted rope to send a message about what some students thought were the proper relations of power in their school and community. As we consider the intersection of symbols and power in culture, and in this case in a key cultural institution—a school—from an anthropological perspective, how do we understand the role of the actors in the incident, including the students, principal, school board, superintendent, and community?

How Much of Who You Are Is Determined by Biology and How Much by Culture?

Biology is important. We live in our bodies, after all. We feel, smell, taste, hear, and see the world around us through our bodies. We communicate with and through our bodies. And, yes, we have certain biological drives that are essential for survival. All humans must eat, drink, and sleep. But no matter how strong our biological needs or our hormones, odors, and appetites might be, culture exerts an overwhelming influence on what we think, on how we behave, and even on the shape and functions of our bodies.

BIOLOGICAL NEEDS VERSUS CULTURAL PATTERNS

Although popular discourse often assigns biology the primary role in determining who we are and establishing the framework of culture, anthropological research consistently reveals the powerful role culture plays in shaping our lives. Human genetic codes are 99.9 percent identical, so if behavior were entirely biologically driven, we should expect to find very similar behavioral responses to biological influences. Instead we find remarkable variety across cultures. Even the most basic human activities, such as eating, drinking, sleeping, and defecating, are carried out in remarkably distinct ways. All humans must do these things. But shared biological needs do not ensure shared cultural patterns.

Of course, food and liquid enter the body through the mouth and get digested in the stomach and intestines. But what goes in and how it goes in are other stories. Perhaps you find dog or snake or pony to be inedible, although these are delicacies in other cultures. Many Chinese dislike cheese, a staple of North American and European diets. Even how and where you eat and drink, or how many times a day, varies from culture to culture. You may use forks, knives, spoons, chopsticks, or hands. You may eat once a day, three times a day, or—like many Americans—six times a day (breakfast, "coffee break," lunch, afternoon snack, dinner, midnight snack).

Everyone sleeps each day, but some people sleep six hours a night, others eight. Americans nap, Argentinians take a siesta, and Chinese *xiu-xi*. Many college students average six hours of sleep a night during the week and ten on the weekend. Who you sleep with also varies by culture, with variations including husbands and wives, parents and children, siblings, mothers and children, grandparents and grandchildren. All these patterns vary by culture, and even within a culture they may vary by age, gender, and class.

What about defecation? Surely this is simple enough that we all do it in the same way. But in China, men and women squat to defecate. In North America, they sit on toilets and use toilet paper. In India, instead of toilet paper, many people use water from a brass bowl applied by splashing with their left hand. In cities, this may take place in a bathroom; in rural areas, it takes place in the fields or on the beach.

NATURE VERSUS NURTURE

Many popular debates claim that basic patterns of human behavior, intellectual capacity, and psychological tendencies are determined by biology. In a speech in the fall of 2005, economist Lawrence Summers, then president of Harvard University, wondered aloud whether one of the reasons his school and others like it had more men than women on the science and math faculties related to different biological endowments—that men's brains were better suited for success in these areas. Summers's comments plunged him into the middle of an intense worldwide debate about what determines humans' fundamental character—our biology or our culture, our nature or our nurture (Pollitt 2005). Whether the debate involves issues of gender difference, racial categories, ethnic divisions, or sexuality, impassioned and often uninformed opinions find voice on all sides.

Connecting Culture and Behavior. Although contemporary genetic discoveries are opening new realms of understanding about human biology, we are not close to linking certain genes or groups of genes with particular behaviors or characteristics. At best, we can imagine these connections based on perceived patterns of behavior. We do have, however, much clearer indications of the ways cultural patterns and beliefs shape human behavior. In the debate over the origins of gender inequality in the upper echelons of math and science careers, we might look instead to gender stereotyping in the classroom, enculturation of girls, and conscious and unconscious gender bias in hiring and promotion practices. It may feel more comfortable to trace inequality to innate biological differences; a link might enable us to dismiss or excuse the inequality as "natural."

But there is no biological evidence of this link. The current evidence is that these patterns of inequality and stratification are culturally constructed and completely changeable (Hopkins 1999; Pollitt 2005).

Culture is learned from the people around us. It is not written into our DNA. Instead we are born with the ability to learn any culture that we might be born into or move into. We have the ability to learn any language and master any set of beliefs, practices, norms, or values. This may seem obvious, but it is a crucial principle to understand as we examine the many cultural patterns in our own experience that we regard as normal, even natural. Such cultural practices are not universal to all humans. Rather, they are uniquely created in each culture. Recognition of this fact allows us to consider how learned patterns of belief and practice have been created and how they might be changed.

Questioning the Biological Basis of Behavior. Anthropologists' comparisons of diverse cultures allow us to question the biological basis for most if not all of human behavior. As you saw in the opening anecdote about the kiss, what may seem natural, biological, or universal is actually deeply embedded in the particular culture around us. Consider the smile. Evidence suggests that most people worldwide agree on the meaning of certain facial expressions. But even a smile can be complicated to interpret when combined with certain subtle physical or facial gestures—especially for people not born into that culture. Although there may be general agreement about the core role of the smile, its complex meanings are not fixed in the body or brain. Instead culture gives meaning to the biology of the smile (Lancaster 2003). Later in this book, in the chapters on race, ethnicity, gender, family, and human sexuality, we will explore the nature versus nurture debates in further detail.

It is impossible to separate human nature from human culture. As popular as it may be to think that nature has driven our development as humans, even our long evolutionary process has been deeply influenced by culture. Ultimately, it is culture that has made us human, enabling us to evolve physically and in our patterns of relationship with others. For example, with the development of simple stone tools as early as 2.5 million years ago, culture allowed our ancestors to adapt to the world around them. Stone tools (in particular, hand axes and choppers) enabled our ancestors to butcher meat more quickly and efficiently, thereby providing higher quantities of protein for the developing brain and influencing the direction of our physical adaptation. In cases such as these, the power of culture to direct and modify biological instincts is indisputable. Over time, cultural adaptations—from the control of fire, to the development of language, to the invention of condoms and birth control pills—have replaced genetic adaptations as the primary way humans adapt to and manipulate their physical and social environments.

How Is Culture Created?

Culture does not emerge out of the blue. It is created over time, shaped by people and the institutions they establish. Culture is not fixed. It is changed, contested, and negotiated. Just as we have examined the relationship between culture and power, we can analyze the processes through which culture is created by considering the origins of a consumer culture as part of twentieth-century capitalism.

MANUFACTURING THE DESIRE TO CONSUME

As capitalism has grown and shifted over the centuries into its present global form, so has the culture that supports and shapes it. Twentieth- and early twenty-first-century global capitalism is deeply tied to a culture of consumerism that has emerged with the support and promotion of corporations, governments, and financial institutions. The culture of consumerism includes norms, values, beliefs, practices, and institutions that have become commonplace and accepted as normal, and that cultivate the desire to acquire consumer goods to enhance one's lifestyle (McCracken 1991; 2005).

Advertising, marketing, and financial services industries work to transform the cultural values of frugality, modesty, and self-denial of the old Protestant ethic into patterns of spending and consumption associated with acquiring the material goods of a middle-class lifestyle. The culture of consumerism promotes spending and consumption even when people don't have money. Today, through global marketing and media advertising campaigns, increased trade, and rising migration, the desire for this lifestyle is being promoted around the world. Over the last few decades, following economic and political reforms in India, China, Russia, and the Middle East, hundreds of millions more people are now seeking that middle-class lifestyle seen on television and advertised on the Internet. This trend is placing incredible stress on the planet's natural resources and environment.

In many parts of the world, consumerism has become more than an economic activity. It is a way of life, a way of looking at the world—a culture. In fact, many key cultural rituals now focus on consumption. In the United States, holidays such as Christmas, Valentine's Day, Mother's Day, and Father's Day all promote the purchase of gifts, as do birthdays, weddings, and anniversaries.

And consumption metaphors infiltrate our daily speech: "Let's have a beer" means "perhaps we can be better friends." "Let's have lunch" means "let's get to know each other better." "Can I buy you a drink?" means "I find you attractive." Even romance has become associated with conspicuous consumption. How else to show love and affection than by splurging on a fancy dinner and buying expensive gifts of flowers and jewelry?

Advertising. The advertising industry is key in arousing our desires for goods and services. Consider that children in the United States watch up to forty thousand television commercials a year (American Academy of Pediatrics 2006). Many children's television programs are themselves thinly disguised advertisements for products featuring their characters, from lunch boxes to clothing to action figures. Advertising appears before and during movies in the theater, at sporting events, in department stores and shopping malls, on billboards, and in store windows. Your favorite websites and social media are covered with advertisements. So are your clothes. Even your classroom is full of advertisements that you most likely do not notice: all the labels and tags on computers, pens, notebooks, backpacks, food packaging, and soda cans.

Advertising is a powerful tool of enculturation, teaching us how to be "successful" in consumer culture, how to be cool and normal. If only we could dress like people in the advertisements and imitate their lifestyles, then we would be more desirable. The culture of consumerism tells us that having these things will bring us better friends, better sex, stronger families, higher-paying jobs, fancier houses, faster cars, sharper picture definition, and truer sound quality. Do you find yourself believing this is true?

Financial Services and Credit Cards. The financial services industry makes sure that once our desires are aroused, we have access to money to make our dreams a reality—at a small price. In 2012, the average American carried ten credit cards, and U.S. credit card debt was $793 billion, an average of $15,799 per household (StatisticBrain.com 2014).

College students are a key target of the credit industry, which promotes credit cards on campus and through the mail regardless of students' ability to repay. Credit cards grease the wheels of consumer culture. And so contemporary capitalism invests heavily to arouse our desire and promote the expansion of the culture of consumerism.

What stirs your desire to consume? Shopping on Black Friday in the Lenox Square Mall in Atlanta, Georgia. Black Friday, the day after Thanksgiving, marks the start of the U.S. holiday shopping season.

How Is Globalization Transforming Culture?

Cultures have never been comprised of completely isolated or bounded groups of people located in a particular place. As we discussed in Chapter 1, anthropologists resist the myths of isolated and "primitive" groups who have lived on their own without contact. Encounter, interaction, movement, and exchange have been much more fundamental aspects of humanity. Cultures have always been influenced by the flow of people, ideas, and goods, whether through migration, trade, or invasion. Today's flows of globalization are intensifying the exchange and diffusion of people, ideas, and goods, creating more interaction and engagement among cultures. Let's consider three key interrelated effects of globalization on local cultures: homogenization, a two-way transference of culture through migration, and increased cosmopolitanism.

A HOMOGENIZING EFFECT

The development of global corporations, products, and markets has produced what some anthropologists consider a homogenized, global culture of McDonald's, Levi's, Coca-Cola, CNN, Hollywood, and U.S. cultural values. Anthropologists and other cultural activists worry that the spread of this culture—fueled by goods, images, and ideas from Western cultures—is creating a homogenizing process that will diminish the diversity of the world's cultures as foreign influences inundate local practices, products, and ways of thinking.

At the same time, the elements of global culture symbolically represent to many people in developing countries the opportunity for economic advancement and participation in the idealized middle-class lifestyle of consumption associated with these consumer products. In *Golden Arches East: McDonald's in East Asia* (1998), James Watson suggests that East Asians in Tokyo, Japan; Seoul, Korea; Hong Kong; Beijing, China; and Taipei, Taiwan, go to McDonald's not so much for the food but to participate in what they view as a middle-class activity. By eating out and eating Western fast food, they hope to align themselves with the Western middle-class norms and values to which they aspire.

MIGRATION AND THE TWO-WAY TRANSFERENCE OF CULTURE

The movement of people in large numbers within and across national boundaries associated with contemporary globalization reveals that cultures are not necessarily bound to a particular geographic location. People migrate with their cultural beliefs and practices. They incorporate the cultural practices of their homelands into their new communities. They build links to their homelands through which culture continues to be exchanged.

Robert Smith's book *Mexican New York* (2006) reveals one example of the deep transnational connections—links across national borders—that have become increasingly common in today's globalizing world. Direct flights physically link immigrants living in the suburbs of New York City to their hometowns in Mexico in five hours. Telephone calls, e-mails, and videoconferences connect families and communities. The Mexican town of Tihuateca relies heavily on money sent back from villagers in New York City to build roads, water systems,

A McDonald's restaurant in downtown Manila, capital of the Philippines, advertises the McDo Rice Burger, a local product added to McDonald's standard global menu.

and schools. Community leaders travel between countries to strengthen relationships, promote projects, and raise funds. These stories and many others reveal how global flows of people are transforming local cultures in both the sending and the receiving countries (see Chapter 11).

INCREASING COSMOPOLITANISM

A third significant effect of globalization on culture is that the increasing flow of people, ideas, and products has allowed worldwide access to cultural patterns that are new, innovative, and stimulating. Local cultures are exposed to a greater range of cultural ideas and products—such as agricultural strategies and medicines, to name just two. Globalization means that communities in the most remote parts of the world increasingly participate in experiences that bridge and link cultural practices, norms, and values across great distances, leading to what some scholars have called a new cosmopolitanism.

Cosmopolitanism is a very broad, sometimes global, outlook, rather than a limited, local one—an outlook that combines both universality and difference (Appiah 2006). The term is usually used to describe sophisticated urban professionals who travel and feel at home in different parts of the world. But anthropologist Lila Abu-Lughod's study *Dramas of Nationhood: The Politics of Television in Egypt* (2005) explores the emergence of cosmopolitanism even among Egypt's rural poor. Her book explores the role of television dramas—much like American soap operas, but more in tune with political and social issues—in creating ideas

MAP 2.4
Egypt

cosmopolitanism
A global outlook emerging in response to increasing globalization.

In a globalizing age, local cultures are increasingly exposed to a vast array of people, ideas, and products. Here, a montage of images from a day on Egyptian television, with channels from Egypt and across the Middle East, including comedy and music from Lebanon, old Egyptian films, American entertainment, and news and religious discussion programs.

of a national culture, even among rural Egyptians, and crafting the identity of the new Egyptian citizen.

Abu-Lughod's ethnography of television pushes us to move beyond notions of single cultures sharing a set of ideas and meanings distinct from other cultures in an era of mass media, migration, and globalization. Television, she argues, "is an extraordinary technology for breaking the boundaries and intensifying and multiplying encounters among life-worlds, sensibilities and ideas" (2005, 45). By the 1990s, there were six million television sets in Egypt, and more than 90 percent of the population had access. In this reality, television provides material—produced somewhere else—that is consumed locally; it is inserted into, mixed up with, and interpreted by local knowledge and systems of meaning.

Even though poverty prevents the people in Abu-Lughod's study from fully participating in the consumer culture of commodities promoted by television programming and commercials, they are not untouched by these features of cosmopolitanism.

The influences of globalization ensure that even in rural Egyptian peasant culture, the knowledge of other worlds comes not only from television but also from foreign friends, tourists, visiting scholars/anthropologists, relatives migrating to find work in cities, imported movies and electronics, and even teachers trained by the Egyptian state and their approved textbooks. This is just one example of the powerful effects of the intersection of culture and globalization. No matter where you look in the twenty-first century, you are sure to find some elements of this intersection.

Toolkit

Thinking Like an Anthropologist:
The Kiss as a Cultural Act

Every day, culture is all around us. It informs our thoughts and actions; guides us through complex interactions in our families, schools, jobs, and other personal relationships; and even shapes the way we perceive reality. Thinking like an anthropologist can help you to better understand yourself and those around you, and to analyze your own culture and other cultures you encounter in this globalizing world.

In thinking about the kiss between Richard Gere and Shilpa Shetty, consider the questions we have raised about culture.

- **What is culture?**

- **How has the culture concept developed in anthropology?**

- **How are culture and power related?**

- **How much of who you are is determined by biology and how much by culture?**

- **How is culture created?**

- **How is globalization transforming culture?**

After putting these questions into anthropological perspective, think about how your culture's norms, values, symbols, and mental maps of reality affect your understanding of Gere's kiss of Shetty.

We see the kisses of others symbolically—as deeply entwined in webs of meaning. We "read" differences in how they kiss—on the cheek, forehead, or lips; short or long; lips puckered or deeply enmeshed. We differentiate kisses of affection, social greeting, ceremony, and eroticism. We see kisses between lovers of opposite genders, between lovers of the same gender, between parents and children, between young and old, and we "understand" each one differently through the lens of culture. Perhaps you believe that much is revealed through a first kiss. Is the person strong, sensitive, hot, reserved, passionate, a good lover, a good mother for your children, a frog or a prince? This chapter has demonstrated how all these "instincts" are filtered through and constructed by our enculturation—what we have been taught through agents such as family, school, friends, religion, and the media.

Beyond symbolism, we see how culture and power are connected. We know there may be physical consequences if we break the norms. We know that kisses can be expressions of physical dominance and aggression, expressions of the power of one person over another. Being kissed against one's will is associated with rape or adult/child incest and sexual abuse in which cultural notions of sexuality intersect with notions of gender, age, and kinship. Erotic kissing between relatives is shunned. And public kissing between same-sex couples may put them in physical danger. A kiss, Gere's kiss of Shetty, may also be an opportunity to explore relationships of power—perhaps in terms of gender, sexuality, nationalism, or religion. Gere did not think carefully about what his kiss would mean. But now that you are thinking like an anthropologist, you can.

Key Terms

culture (p. 33)

enculturation (p. 34)

norms (p. 35)

values (p. 37)

symbol (p. 37)

mental maps of reality (p. 39)

unilineal cultural evolution (p. 42)

historical particularism (p. 43)

structural functionalism (p. 44)

interpretivist approach (p. 44)

thick description (p. 45)

power (p. 46)

stratification (p. 46)

hegemony (p. 48)

agency (p. 49)

cosmopolitanism (p. 58)

Chapter 3
Fieldwork and Ethnography

Over many years, Nancy Scheper-Hughes, now a professor of cultural anthropology at the University of California, Berkeley, invested herself in trying to understand the lives of the women and children of one particular shantytown in Brazil. Her research resulted in numerous articles and an award-winning ethnography, *Death without Weeping: The Violence of Everyday Life in Brazil* (1992). Scheper-Hughes's efforts reflect the deep commitment of anthropologists to *ethnographic fieldwork*—a research strategy for understanding the world through intense interaction with a local community of people over an extended period.

Scheper-Hughes first arrived in Brazil's Alto do Cruzeiro (Crucifix Hill) in 1965 as a Peace Corps volunteer to assist in community development and health promotion. That year, a severe drought had created food and water shortages and a military coup had spread political and economic chaos throughout the country. In the Alto, more than 350 babies died out of a total population

Mother and child in a Rio de Janeiro favela, Brazil.

MAP 3.1
Brazil

ethnographic fieldwork

A primary research strategy in cultural anthropology involving living with a community of people over an extended period to better understand their lives.

Burial of an infant in the Alto do Cruzeiro favela in northeast Brazil. How did anthropologist Nancy Scheper-Hughes make sense of the "death without weeping" that she found in this poor community?

of a little more than 5,000. Scheper-Hughes later wrote, "There were reasons enough for the deaths in the miserable conditions of shanty-town life. What puzzled me was the seeming indifference of Alto women to the death of their infants and their willingness to attribute to their own tiny offspring an aversion to life that made their deaths seem wholly natural, indeed all but anticipated" (1989, 10).

This puzzle crystallized her research agenda as she returned to the Alto many times over the ensuing years to conduct **ethnographic fieldwork**. Scheper-Hughes found it was possible to reduce diarrhea and dehydration-induced death among infants and toddlers in the shantytown with a simple solution of sugar, salt, and water. But it was more difficult to convince a mother to rescue a child she perceived as likely to die, a baby she already thought of as "an angel rather than a son or daughter." The high expectancy of death led mothers to differentiate between infants whom they saw as "thrivers and survivors" and those seen as born already "wanting to die." Scheper-Hughes found that in this environment, part of learning to be a mother was learning which babies to let go of and which ones it was safe to love. This led her to a rethinking of "mother love." What does the idea of mother love mean in the impoverished context of Alto do Cruzeiro?

Scheper-Hughes suggests that Alto women are doing what must be done, given their context where the real dangers were "poverty, deprivation, sexism, chronic hunger, and economic exploitation." Reflecting on this high-risk environment, she asks, "If mother love is, as many psychologists and some feminists believe, a seemingly natural and universal maternal script, what does it mean to women for whom scarcity, loss, sickness, and deprivation have made that love frantic and robbed them of their grief, seeming to turn hearts to stone?" (1989, 14).

Their experience, suggests Scheper-Hughes, compares more aptly to a battlefield or an overcrowded emergency room where actions are guided by the practice of triage—prioritizing the treatment of those who can be saved. "In their slowness to anthropomorphize and personalize their infants, everything is mobilized so as to prevent maternal over-attachment and, therefore, grief at death. The bereaved mother is told not to cry, that her tears will dampen the wings of her little angel so that she cannot fly up to her heavenly home" (16). Scheper-Hughes suggests that in these difficult conditions, Alto women are left with no choice but to find the best way to carry on with their lives and nurture those children who have the best chance of survival.

What can you learn about fieldwork by reading about Nancy Scheper-Hughes's research? A middle-class woman from the United States, she traveled to one of the poorest places in the world, learned the language, lived in the community, built relationships of trust, accompanied local people through the births and deaths of their children, and searched for meaning in the midst of the pain.

As you might imagine, the fieldwork experience can become more than a strategy for understanding human culture. Fieldwork has the potential to radically transform the anthropologist. Can you imagine making the same commitment Scheper-Hughes did?

The term *fieldwork* implies going out to "the field" to do extensive research. Although in the history of anthropology this may have meant going a long way from home, as Scheper-Hughes did, contemporary anthropologists also study human culture and activities in their own countries and communities. By exploring the practice of fieldwork, you will gain a deeper understanding of how anthropologists go about their work. In particular, in this chapter we will consider:

- **What is unique about ethnographic fieldwork, and why do anthropologists conduct this kind of research?**
- **How did the idea of fieldwork develop?**
- **How do anthropologists get started conducting fieldwork?**
- **How do anthropologists write ethnography?**
- **What moral and ethical concerns guide anthropologists in their research and writing?**
- **How are fieldwork strategies changing in response to globalization?**

By the end of the chapter you will see both how professional anthropologists employ fieldwork strategies and how fieldwork can provide a valuable toolkit for gathering information to make decisions in your own life. Fieldwork skills and strategies can help you navigate the many unfamiliar or cross-cultural experiences you will encounter at work or school, in your community, or in your family. And hopefully you will see how key fieldwork strategies can help you become a more engaged and responsible citizen of the world.

What Is Unique about Ethnographic Fieldwork, and Why Do Anthropologists Conduct This Kind of Research?

Ethnographic fieldwork is the unique strategy that anthropologists—particularly cultural anthropologists—have developed to put people first as we analyze how human societies work. Chemists conduct experiments in laboratories. Economists analyze financial trends. Demographers crunch census data. Historians pore over records and library archives. Sociologists, economists, and political scientists analyze trends, quantifiable data, official organizations, and national policies. But anthropologists start with people and their local communities. Even though the whole world is our field, our unique perspective first focuses on the details and patterns of human life in the local setting.

FIELDWORK BEGINS WITH PEOPLE

Through fieldwork, we try to understand people's everyday lives, to see what they do and to understand why. By living with others over an extended period, we seek to understand their experience through their eyes. We participate in their activities, take careful notes, conduct interviews, take photographs, and record music. We make maps of communities, both of the physical environment and of family and social relationships. Although careful observation of the details of daily life is the first step, through intensive fieldwork anthropologists look beyond the taken-for-granted, everyday experience of life to discover the complex systems of power and meaning that people construct to shape their existence. These include the many systems discussed throughout this book: gender, sexuality, race, ethnicity, religion, kinship, and economic and political systems. As we extend our analysis as anthropologists, we try to see how local lives compare to others and fit into larger human patterns and global contexts.

FIELDWORK SHAPES THE ANTHROPOLOGIST

Fieldwork experience is considered an essential part of an anthropologist's training. It is the activity through which we learn the basic tools of our trade, earn credibility as effective observers of culture, and establish our reputation as full members of the discipline. Through the process, we learn the basic research strategies of our discipline and hone those skills—careful listening and observation, engagement with strangers, cross-cultural interaction, and deep analysis of human interactions and systems of power and privilege. Through fieldwork we learn empathy for those around us, develop a more global consciousness, and uncover our own ethnocentrism. Indeed, fieldwork is a rite of passage, an initiation into our discipline, and a common bond among anthropologists who have been through the experience.

Fieldwork transforms us. In fact, it is quite common for anthropologists entering the field to experience culture shock—a sense of disorientation caused by the overwhelmingly new and unfamiliar people and experiences encountered every day. Over time, the disorientation may fade as the unfamiliar becomes familiar. But then, many anthropologists feel culture shock again when returning home, where their new perspective causes previously familiar people and customs to seem very strange.

The Nacirema. In a now-famous article, "Body Ritual among the Nacirema" (1956), anthropologist Horace Miner helps readers understand the dichotomy between familiar and strange that anthropologists face when studying other cultures. Miner's article examines the cultural beliefs and practices of a group in North America who he finds has developed elaborate and unique practices focusing on care of the human body. He labels this group "the Nacirema."

Miner hypothesizes that underlying the extensive rituals he has documented lies a belief that the human body is essentially ugly, is constantly endangered by forces of disease and decay, and must be treated with great care. Thus the Nacirema have established extensive daily rituals and ceremonies, rigorously taught to their children, to avoid these dangers. For example, Miner describes the typical household shrine—the primary venue for Nacirema body rituals:

A healing specialist conducts an elaborate ceremony, the facial treatment, a key body ritual among the Nacirema.

> While each family has at least one shrine, the rituals associated with it are not family ceremonies but are private and secret. . . . The focal point of the shrine is a box or chest which is built into the wall. In this chest are kept the many charms and magical potions without which no native believes he could live. . . . Beneath the charm-box is a small font. Each day every member of the family, in succession, enters the shrine room, bows his head before the charm-box, mingles different sorts of holy water in the font, and proceeds with a brief rite of ablution. (Miner 1956, 503–4)

In addition, the Nacirema regularly visit medicine men and "holy-mouth men." These individuals are specialists who provide ritual advice and magical potions.

> The Nacirema have an almost pathological horror of and fascination with the mouth, the condition of which is believed to have a super-natural influence on all social relationships. Were it not for the rituals of the mouth, they believe that their teeth would fall out, their gums bleed, their jaws shrink, their friends desert them and their lovers reject them. The daily body ritual performed by everyone includes a mouth-rite. It was reported to me that the ritual consists of inserting a small bundle of hog hairs into the mouth, along with certain magical powders, and then moving the bundle in a highly formalized series of gestures. (504)

Do these exotic rituals of a seemingly distant tribe sound completely strange to you, or are they vaguely familiar? Miner's descriptions of the Nacirema are intended to make the strange seem familiar and the familiar strange. "Nacirema" is actually "American" spelled backward. Miner's passages describe the typical American bathroom and personal hygiene habits: "Holy water" pours into the sink. The "charm-box" is a medicine cabinet. The Nacirema medicine men are doctors, and the "holy-mouth men" are dentists. The "mouth-rite" is toothbrushing.

Development of the anthropological perspective through fieldwork, in which we investigate the beliefs and practices of other cultures, enables us to perceive our own cultural activities in a new light. Even the most familiar aspects of our lives may then appear exotic, bizarre, or strange when viewed through the lens of anthropology. Through this cross-cultural training, anthropology offers the opportunity to unlock our ability to imagine, see, and analyze the incredible diversity of human cultures. It also enables us to avoid the tendencies of ethnocentrism, in which we often view our own cultural practices as "normal" and against which we are inclined to judge the cultural beliefs and practices of others.

FIELDWORK AS SOCIAL SCIENCE AND AS ART

Fieldwork is simultaneously a social scientific method and an art form. It is a strategy for gathering data about the human condition, particularly through the life experiences of local people in local situations. Fieldwork is an experiment for testing hypotheses and building theories about the diversity of human behavior and the interaction of people with systems of power—a scientific method for examining how the social world really works. As such, anthropologists have developed techniques such as participant observation, field notes, interviews, kinship and social network analysis, life histories, and mapping—all of which we will discuss in this chapter.

But fieldwork is also an art. Its success depends on the anthropologist's more intuitive ability to negotiate complex interactions, usually in an unfamiliar cultural environment, to build relationships of trust, to make sense of patterns of behavior, to be conscious of one's own biases and particular vantage point. Ethnographic fieldwork depends on the ability of an outsider—the anthropologist—to develop close personal relationships over time in a local community and to understand the everyday experiences of often-unfamiliar people. It requires the anthropologist to risk being changed in the process—the risk of mutual transformation. Successful ethnographic fieldwork also depends on the anthropologist's ability to tell the subjects' stories to an audience that has no knowledge of them and in ways that accurately reflect the subjects' lives and shed light on the general human condition. This is also an art.

FIELDWORK INFORMS DAILY LIFE

Anthropologist Brackette Williams suggests that fieldwork can even be a kind of "homework"—a strategy for gathering information that will help the anthropologist to make informed decisions in order to act morally and to weigh in advance the likely consequences of her or his actions. Williams studied homelessness and begging in New York City and Tucson, Arizona, over a period of several years. She began with some very practical questions about whether to give money to homeless people begging on the subway she took to work in New York City every day.

Her research started with careful observation of all the people involved, including homeless individuals and all the others on the subway. She continued with informal and formal interviews, careful note taking, and background reading. In the process she began to identify a clear set of stories and begging styles, and to examine the complicated set of responses made by people on the subway who were being asked for money.

Williams suggests that this approach to her daily dilemma was not only an interesting use of her ethnographic fieldwork skills and training, but also "socially required homework" for anyone who confronts complex problems in daily life, whether with family, friends, school, work, or politics (Williams 1995). Can you imagine using this strategy to explore a problem, puzzle, or question in your life?

MAP 3.2
Tucson/New York

Early anthropologists encountered a world of people already in motion. The 1375 Catalan Atlas shows the world as it was then known. It depicts the location of continents and islands as well as information on ancient and medieval tales, regional politics, astronomy, and astrology.

How Did the Idea of Fieldwork Develop?

EARLY ACCOUNTS OF ENCOUNTERS WITH OTHERS

Descriptive accounts of other cultures existed long before anthropologists came on the scene. For centuries, explorers, missionaries, traders, government bureaucrats, and travelers recorded descriptions of the people they encountered. For example, nearly 2,500 years ago, the Greek historian Herodotus wrote about his travels in Egypt, Persia, and the area now known as Ukraine. In the thirteenth century, the Venetian explorer Marco Polo chronicled his travels from Italy across the silk route to

China. And the Chinese admiral Zheng He reported on his extended voyages to India, the Middle East, and East Africa in the fifteenth century, seventy years before Columbus arrived in the Americas. These are just a few of the many early accounts of encounters with other peoples across the globe.

NINETEENTH-CENTURY ANTHROPOLOGY AND THE COLONIAL ENCOUNTER

The roots of anthropology and of fieldwork lie in the intense globalization of the late nineteenth century. At that time, the increased international movement of Europeans—particularly merchants, colonial administrators, and missionaries—generated a broad set of data that stimulated scientists and philosophers of the day to make sense of the emerging picture of humanity's incredible diversity (Stocking 1983). They asked questions like these: Who are these other people? Why are their foods, clothing, architecture, rituals, family structures, and political and economic systems so different from ours and from one another's? Are they related to us biologically and culturally? If so, how?

Fieldwork was not a common practice at the beginning of our discipline. In fact, many early anthropologists, such as Edward Burnett Tylor (1832–1917), are now considered "armchair anthropologists" because they did not conduct their own research; instead they worked at home in their armchairs analyzing the reports of others. One early exception was Louis Henry Morgan (1818–1881), who conducted fieldwork among Native Americans in the United States. As we discussed in Chapter 2, Tylor and Morgan were leading figures in attempts to organize the data that was accumulating, to catalogue human diversity, and to make sense of the many questions it stimulated. These men applied the theory of unilineal cultural evolution—the idea that all cultures would naturally evolve through the same sequence of stages from simple to complex, and that the diversity of human cultural expressions represented different stages in the evolution of human culture, which could be classified in comparison to one another.

THE PROFESSIONALIZATION OF SOCIAL SCIENTIFIC DATA-GATHERING AND ANALYSIS

Succeeding generations of anthropologists in Europe and North America rejected unilineal cultural evolution as being too Eurocentric, too ethnocentric, too hierarchical, and lacking adequate data to support its grand claims. Anthropologists in the early twentieth century developed more sophisticated research methods—particularly ethnographic fieldwork—to professionalize social scientific data-gathering.

Franz Boas: Fieldwork and the Four-Field Approach. In the United States, Franz Boas (1858–1942) and his students focused on developing a

four-field approach to anthropological research, which included gathering cultural, linguistic, archaeological, and biological data. Boas's early work among the indigenous Kwakiutl people of the Pacific Northwest of the United States and Canada firmly grounded him in the fieldwork process, as he learned about others' culture through extensive participation in their daily lives, religious rituals, and economic activities. After settling in New York City in the early twentieth century as a professor of anthropology at Columbia University and curator of the American Museum of Natural History, Boas (and his students) embarked on a massive project to document Native American cultures being devastated by the westward expansion of settlers across the continent.

Often called **salvage ethnography** because of the speed at which it was conducted, Boas's approach required the rapid gathering of all available material, including historical artifacts, photographs, recordings of spoken languages, songs, and detailed information about cultural beliefs and practices—from religious rituals to family patterns, from gender roles to political structures. Pressed for time (because the Native cultures were rapidly disappearing) and having limited financial resources, these ethnographers often met with a small number of elderly informants and focused on conducting oral interviews rather than observing actual behavior. Despite the limitations of this emerging fieldwork, these early projects built upon Boas's commitment to historical particularism when investigating local cultures (see Chapter 2) and defined a continuing characteristic of American anthropology: a combined focus on culture, biology, artifacts, and language that today we call the "four-field approach" (see Chapter 1).

Another key contribution of Boas and his students was a commitment to the development of **cultural relativism** as a basic fieldwork perspective: to see each culture on its own merits; to understand it first from the inside, according to its own logic and structure. This rejection of ethnocentrism became a cornerstone of anthropology for generations to come (Stocking 1989).

Bronislaw Malinowski: The Father of Fieldwork.
Across the Pacific Ocean, Bronislaw Malinowski (1884–1942), considered by many to be the "father of fieldwork," went even further than Boas in developing cultural anthropology's research methods. Malinowski, a Polish citizen who later became a leading figure in British anthropology, found himself stuck for a year on the Trobriand Islands as a result of World War I. His classic ethnography, *Argonauts of the Western Pacific* (1922), has become most famous for its examination of the

American anthropologist Franz Boas in Inuit clothing during fieldwork in the Pacific Northwest of North America, 1883.

salvage ethnography

Fieldwork strategy developed by Franz Boas to rapidly collect cultural, material, linguistic, and biological information about U.S. Native populations being devastated by westward expansion.

cultural relativism

Understanding a group's beliefs and practices within their own cultural context, without making judgments.

British anthropologist Bronislaw Malinowski at a bachelor's house in Kasanai, Trobriand Islands, ca. 1915–18.

Kula ring, an elaborate system of exchange. The ring involved thousands of individuals across many islands, some of whom traveled hundreds of miles by canoe to exchange Kula valuables (in particular, shell necklaces and armbands).

Argonauts also set new standards for fieldwork. In the opening chapter, Malinowski proposes a set of guidelines for conducting fieldwork based on his own experience. He urges fellow anthropologists to stay for a long period in their field sites, learn the local language, get off the veranda (that is, leave the safety of their front porch to mingle with the local people), engage in participant observation, and explore the "mundane imponderabilia"—the seemingly commonplace, everyday items and activities of local life.

Although some of these suggestions may seem obvious to us nearly a century later, Malinowski's formulation of a comprehensive strategy for understanding local culture was groundbreaking and has withstood the test of time. Of particular importance has been his conceptualization of **participant observation** as the cornerstone of fieldwork. For anthropologists, it is not enough to observe from a distance. We must learn about people by participating in their daily activities, walking in their shoes, seeing through their eyes. Participant observation gives depth to our observations and helps guard against mistaken assumptions based on observation from a distance (Kuper 1983).

E. E. Evans-Pritchard and British Social Anthropology.
Between the 1920s and 1960s, many British social anthropologists viewed anthropology more as a science designed to discover the component elements and patterns of society (see Chapter 2). Fieldwork was their key methodology for conducting their scientific experiments. Adopting a *synchronic approach*, they sought to control their experiments by limiting consideration of the larger historical and social context in order to isolate as many variables as possible.

participant observation

A key anthropological research strategy involving both participation in and observation of the daily life of the people being studied.

British anthropologist E. E. Evans-Pritchard seated among Nuer men and boys in southern Sudan, ca. 1930.

E. E. Evans-Pritchard (1902–1973), one of the leading figures during this period, wrote a classic ethnography in this style. In *The Nuer* (1940), based on his research with a Sudanese "tribe" over eleven months between 1930 and 1936, Evans-Pritchard systematically documents the group's social structure—political, economic, and kinship, capturing the intricate details of community life. But later anthropologists have criticized his failure to consider the historical context and larger social world. Indeed, the Nuer in Evans-Pritchard's study lived under British occupation in the Sudan, and many Nuer participated in resistance to British occupation despite an intensive British pacification campaign against the Sudanese during the time of Evans-Pritchard's research. Later anthropologists have questioned how he could have omitted such important details and ignored his status as a British subject when it had such potential for undermining his research success.

MAP 3.3
The Nuer Region of East Africa

American anthropologist Margaret
Mead with a mother and child
in the Admiralty Islands, South
Pacific, 1953.

MAP 3.4
Samoa

Margaret Mead: Fieldwork and Public Anthropology. Margaret
Mead conducted pioneering fieldwork in the 1920s, famously examining teen
sexuality in *Coming of Age in Samoa* (1928) and, later, gender roles in Papua
New Guinea. Perhaps most significant, however, Mead mobilized her fieldwork findings to engage in crucial scholarly and public debates at home in the
United States. At a time when many in the United States argued that gender roles
were biologically determined, Mead's fieldwork testified to the fact that U.S. cultural norms were not found cross-culturally but were culturally specific. Mead's
unique blending of fieldwork and dynamic writing provided her with the authority and opportunity to engage a broad public audience and made her a powerful
figure in the roiling cultural debates of her generation.

The People of Puerto Rico: **A Turn to the Global.** During the
1950s a team of anthropologists headed by Julian Steward, and including Sydney
Mintz and Eric Wolf, engaged in a collaborative fieldwork project at multiple
sites on the island of Puerto Rico. Steward's resulting ethnography, *The People
of Puerto Rico* (1956), marked the beginning of a significant anthropological

turn away from studies of seemingly isolated, small-scale, nonindustrial societies toward studies that examined the integration of local communities into a modern world system. In particular, the new focus explored the impact of colonialism and the spread of capitalism on local people. Mintz, in *Sweetness and Power* (1985), later expanded his fieldwork interests in Puerto Rican sugar production to consider the intersections of local histories and local production of sugar with global flows of colonialism and capitalism. Wolf, in *Europe and the People without History* (1982), continued a lifetime commitment to reassert forgotten local histories—or the stories of people ignored by history—into the story of the modern world economic system.

Annette Weiner: Feminism and Reflexivity.

In the 1980s, anthropologist Annette Weiner retraced Malinowski's footsteps to conduct a new study of the Trobriand Islands sixty years later. Weiner quickly noticed aspects of Trobriand culture that had not surfaced in Malinowski's writings. In particular, she took careful note of the substantial role women played in the island economy. Whereas Malinowski had focused attention on the elaborate male-dominated system of economic exchange among islands, Weiner found that women had equally important economic roles and equally valuable accumulations of wealth.

In the course of her fieldwork, Weiner came to believe that Malinowski's conclusions were not necessarily wrong but were incomplete. By the time of Weiner's study (1988), anthropologists were carefully considering the need for **reflexivity** in conducting fieldwork—that is, a critical self-examination of the role of the anthropologist and an awareness that who one is affects what one finds out. Malinowski's age and gender influenced what he saw and what others were comfortable telling him. By the 1980s, feminist anthropologists such as Weiner and Kathleen Gough, who revisited Evans-Pritchard's work with the Nuer ([1971] 2001), were pushing anthropologists to be more critically aware of how their own position in relationship to those they studied affected their scope of vision.

reflexivity
A critical self-examination of the role the anthropologist plays and an awareness that one's identity affects one's fieldwork and theoretical analyses.

Barbara Myerhoff: A Turn to Home.

Barbara Myerhoff's first book, *Peyote Hunt* (1974), traces the pilgrimage of the Huichol Indians across the Sierra Madre of Mexico as they retell, reclaim, and reinvigorate their religious myths, rituals, and symbols. In her second book, *Number Our Days* (1978), Myerhoff turns her attention closer to home. Her fieldwork as described in the 1978 book focuses on the struggles of older Jewish immigrants in a southern California community and the Aliyah senior citizens center through which they create and remember ritual life and community as a means of keeping control of their daily activities and faculties as they age. Their words pour off the pages of her book as she allows them to tell their life stories. Myerhoff becomes a character in her own book, tracing her interactions and engagements with the members of the center and reflecting poignantly on the process of self-reflection and transformation that she experiences as a younger Jewish woman studying a community of older Jews.

Number Our Days marks a turn in anthropology from the study of the "other" to the study of the self—what Victor Turner calls in his foreword to Myerhoff's book "being thrice-born." The first birth is in our own culture. The second birth immerses the anthropologist in the depths of another culture through fieldwork. Finally, the return home is like a third birth as the anthropologist rediscovers his or her own culture, now strange and unfamiliar in a global context.

How Do Anthropologists Get Started Conducting Fieldwork?

Today cultural anthropologists call on a set of techniques designed to assess the complexity of human interactions and social organizations. You probably use some variation of these techniques as you go about daily life and make decisions for yourself and others. For a moment, imagine yourself doing fieldwork with Nancy Scheper-Hughes in the Brazilian shantytown of Alto do Cruzeiro. How would you prepare yourself? What strategies would you use? How would you analyze your data?

PREPARATION

literature review

The process of reading all the available published material about a research site and/or research issues, usually done before fieldwork begins.

Prior to beginning fieldwork, anthropologists go through an intense process of preparation. We start by reading everything we can find about our research site and the particular issues we will be examining. This **literature review** provides a crucial background for the experiences to come. Following Malinowski's recommendation, anthropologists also learn the language of their field site. The ability to speak the local language eliminates the need to work through interpreters and allows us to participate in the community's everyday activities and conversations, which richly reflect local culture.

Before going to the field, anthropologists search out possible contacts: other scholars who have worked there, community leaders, government officials, perhaps even a host family. A specific research question or problem is defined and a research design created. Grant applications are submitted to seek financial support for the research. Permission to conduct the study is sought ahead of time from the local community and, where necessary, from appropriate government agencies. Protocols are developed to protect those who will be the focus of research. Anthropologists attend to many of these logistical matters following a preliminary visit to the intended field site before fully engaging the fieldwork process.

Finally, we assemble the **anthropologist's toolkit**—all the equipment needed to conduct our research. What tools would Nancy Scheper-Hughes have needed to conduct her research on a daily basis in Brazil? Today this toolkit—most likely a backpack—might include a notebook, pens, camera, voice recorder (and batteries!), maps, cell phone, dictionary, watch, and identification.

anthropologist's toolkit
The tools needed to conduct fieldwork, including a notebook, pen, camera, voice recorder, and dictionary.

STRATEGIES

Once in the field, anthropologists apply a variety of research strategies for gathering quantitative and qualitative data. **Quantitative data** include statistical information about a community—data that can be measured and compared, including details of population demographics and economic activity. **Qualitative data** include information that cannot be counted but may be even more significant for understanding the dynamics of a community. Qualitative data consist of personal stories and interviews, life histories, and general observations about daily life drawn from participant observation. Qualitative data enable the ethnographer to connect the dots and answer the questions of why people behave in certain ways or organize their lives in particular patterns.

quantitative data
Statistical information about a community that can be measured and compared.

qualitative data
Descriptive data drawn from nonstatistical sources, including participant observation, personal stories, interviews, and life histories.

Central to a cultural anthropologist's research is participant observation. By participating in our subjects' daily activities, we experience their lives from the perspective of an insider. Through participant observation over time, we establish **rapport**—relationships of trust and familiarity with members of the community we study. The deepening of that rapport through intense engagement enables the anthropologist to move from being an outsider toward being an insider. Over time in a community, anthropologists seek out people who will be our advisors, teachers, and guides—sometimes called **key informants** or cultural consultants. Key informants may suggest issues to explore, introduce community members to interview, provide feedback on research insights, and warn against cultural miscues.

rapport
The relationships of trust and familiarity developed with members of the community being studied.

key informant
A community member who advises the anthropologist on community issues, provides feedback, and warns against cultural miscues. Also called "cultural consultant."

interview

A research strategy of gathering data through formal or informal conversation with informants.

life history

A form of interview that traces the biography of a person over time, examining changes and illuminating the interlocking network of relationships in the community.

survey

An information-gathering tool for quantitative data analysis.

kinship analysis

A traditional strategy of examining genealogies to uncover the relationships built upon structures such as marriage and family ties.

social network analysis

A method for examining relationships in a community, often conducted by identifying who people turn to in times of need.

field notes

The anthropologist's written observations and reflections on places, practices, events, and interviews.

mapping

The analysis of the physical and/or geographic space where fieldwork is being conducted.

Another key research strategy is the **interview**. Anthropologists are constantly conducting interviews while in the field. Some interviews are very informal, essentially involving a form of data-gathering through everyday conversation. Other interviews are highly structured, closely following a set of questions. Semi-structured interviews use those questions as a framework but leave room for the interviewee to guide the conversation. One particular form of interview, a **life history**, traces the life story of a key informant as a means of understanding change over time in that person's life and illuminating the interlocking network of relationships in the community. Life histories provide insights into the frameworks of meaning that individuals build around their life experiences. **Surveys** can also be developed and administered to gather quantitative data and reach a broader sample of participants around key issues, but rarely do they substitute for participant observation and face-to-face interviews as the anthropologist's primary strategy for data collection.

We also map human relations. **Kinship analysis**, a traditional strategy, enables anthropologists to explore the interlocking relationships of power built on family and marriage. In more urban areas where family networks are diffuse, a **social network analysis** may prove illuminating. One of the simplest ways to analyze a social network is to identify who people turn to in times of need.

Central to our data-gathering strategy, anthropologists write detailed **field notes** of our observations and reflections. These field notes take various forms. Some are elaborate descriptions of people, places, events, sounds, and smells. Others are reflections on patterns and themes that emerge, questions to be asked, and issues to be pursued. Some field notes are personal reflections on the experience of doing fieldwork—how it feels physically and emotionally to be engaged in the process. Although the rigorous recording of field notes may sometimes seem tedious, the collection of data over time allows the anthropologist to revisit details of earlier experiences, to compare information and impressions over time, and to analyze changes, trends, patterns, and themes.

Sophisticated computer programs can assist in the organization and categorization of data about people, places, and institutions. But in the final analysis, the ability to recognize key themes and patterns relies on the instincts and insights of the ethnographer.

MAPPING

Often one of the first steps an anthropologist takes upon entering a new community is to map the surroundings. **Mapping** takes many forms and produces many different products. While walking the streets of the field site, the ethnographer develops a spatial awareness of where people live, work, worship, play, and eat, and of the space through which they move. After all, human culture exists in real physical space. And culture shapes the way space is constructed and used.

Likewise, physical surroundings influence human culture, shaping the boundaries of behavior and imagination. Careful observation and description, recorded in maps and field notes, provide the material for deeper analysis of these community dynamics.

Urban ethnographers describe the power of the **built environment** to shape human life. Most humans live in a built environment, not one made up solely or primarily of nature. By focusing on the built environment—what we have built around us—scholars can analyze the intentional development of human settlements, neighborhoods, towns, and cities. Growth of the built environment is rarely random. Rather, it is guided by political and economic choices that determine funding for roads, public transportation, parks, schools, lighting, sewers, water systems, electrical grids, hospitals, police and fire stations, and other public services and infrastructure. Local governments establish and enforce tax and zoning regulations to control the construction of buildings and approved uses. Mapping the components of this built environment may shed light on key dynamics of power and influence in a community.

Anthropologists turn to quantitative data to map who is present in a community, including characteristics such as age, gender, family type, and employment status. This demographic data may be available through the local or national census, or the anthropologist may choose to gather the data directly by surveying the community if the sample size is manageable. To map historical change over time in an area and discern its causes, anthropologists also turn to archives, newspaper databases, minutes and records of local organizations, historical photos, and personal descriptions, in addition to census data.

Mapping today may be aided by online tools such as satellite imagery, geographic information system (GIS) devices and data, online archives, and electronic databases. All can be extremely helpful in establishing location, orientation, and in the case of photo archives, change over time. On their own, however, these tools do not provide the deep immersion sought by anthropologists conducting fieldwork. Instead anthropologists place primary emphasis on careful, first-hand observation and documentation of physical space as a valuable strategy for understanding the day-to-day dynamics of cultural life.

built environment

The intentionally designed features of human settlement, including buildings, transportation and public service infrastructure, and public spaces.

SKILLS AND PERSPECTIVES

Successful fieldwork requires a unique set of skills and perspectives that are hard to teach in the classroom. Ethnographers must begin with open-mindedness about the people and places they study. We must be wary of any prejudices we might have formed before our arrival, and we must be reluctant to judge once we are in the field. Boas's notion of cultural relativism is an essential starting point: Can we see the world through the eyes of those we are studying? Can we understand their systems of meaning and internal logic? The tradition of anthropology suggests that cultural relativism must be the starting point if we are to accurately hear and retell the stories of others.

A successful ethnographer must also be a skilled listener. We spend a lot of time in conversation, but much of that time involves listening, not talking. The ability to ask good questions and listen carefully to the responses is essential. A skilled listener hears both what is said and what is not said—something we refer to as zeros. **Zeros** are the elements of a story or a picture that are not told or seen, key details omitted from the conversation. Who or what is missing from it? Zeros offer key insights into issues and topics that may be too sensitive to discuss or display publicly.

A good ethnographer must be patient, flexible, and open to the unexpected. Sometimes sitting still in one place is the best research strategy because it offers opportunities to observe and experience unplanned events and unexpected people. For instance, I have a favorite tea shop in one Chinese village where I like to sit and wait to see what happens. The overscheduled fieldworker can easily miss the "mundane imponderabilia" that constitute the richness of everyday life.

At times the most important, illuminating conversations and interviews are not planned and scheduled ahead of time. Patience and a commitment to conduct research over an extended period allow the ethnographic experience to come to us on its own terms, not on the schedule we assign to it. This is one of the significant differences between anthropology and journalism. It is also a hard lesson to learn and a hard skill to develop.

A final perspective essential for a successful ethnographer is openness to the possibility of **mutual transformation** in the fieldwork process. This is risky business because it exposes the personal component of anthropological research. It is clear that by participating in fieldwork, anthropologists alter—in ways large and small—the character of the community being studied. But if you ask them about their fieldwork experience, they will acknowledge that in the process they become transformed on a very personal level—their self-understanding, their empathy for others, their worldviews. The practice of participant observation over time entails building deep relationships with people from another culture and directly engages the ethnographer in the life of the community.

ANALYSIS

As the fieldwork experience proceeds, anthropologists regularly reflect on and analyze the trends, issues, themes, and patterns that emerge from their carefully collected data. One framework for analysis that we will examine in this book is power: Who has it? How do they get it and keep it? Who uses it, and why? Where is the money, and who controls it? The anthropologist Eric Wolf thought of culture as a mechanism for facilitating relationships of power—among

zeros

Elements of a story or a picture that are not told or seen and yet offer key insights into issues that might be too sensitive to discuss or display publicly.

mutual transformation

The potential for both the anthropologist and the members of the community being studied to be transformed by the interactions of fieldwork.

families, between genders, and among religions, classes, and political entities (1999). Good ethnographers constantly assess the relations of power in the communities they study.

Whereas earlier anthropologists such as Evans-Pritchard focused narrowly on the local culture being studied, today's anthropologists explore and analyze global connections as well—relationships between the local community and the global processes that affect it. For example, in the 2005 film *Mardi Gras: Made in China*, the ethnographic filmmakers David Redmon and Ashley Sabin trace the connection between (1) the beads used in New Orleans Mardi Gras festivities to entice women to bare their breasts, and (2) the sweatshop factories in China where the beads are made by young teenage girls who work twelve-hour days, six days a week. As globalization intensifies in the twenty-first century, anthropologists who conduct fieldwork in local communities are paying increasing attention to these kinds of local–global links.

Ethnographers also submit their local data and analysis to cross-cultural comparisons. We endeavor to begin from an **emic** perspective—that is, understanding the local community on its own terms. But the anthropological commitment to understanding human diversity and the complexity of human cultures also requires taking an **etic** perspective—viewing the local community from the anthropologist's perspective as an outsider. This provides a foundation for comparison with other relevant case studies. The overarching process of comparison and assessment, called **ethnology**, uses the wealth of anthropological studies to compare the activities, trends, and patterns of power across cultures. The process enables us to better see what is unique in a particular community and how it contributes to identifying larger patterns of cultural beliefs and practices. Perhaps the largest effort to facilitate worldwide comparative studies is the Human Relations Area Files at Yale University (www.yale.edu.hraf), which has been building a database of ethnographic material since 1949 to encourage cross-cultural analysis.

What is the global journey of Mardi Gras beads? *Left:* Hands of a Chinese woman burned, cracked, and stained from making Mardi Gras beads in sweatshop conditions. The beads are exported for sale in the United States at the annual Mardi Gras festival in New Orleans, Louisiana. *Right:* Young American women exchange nudity for the beads in New Orleans's French Quarter during Mardi Gras.

emic

Involving an approach to gathering data that investigates how local people think and how they understand the world.

etic

Involving description of local behavior and beliefs from the anthropologist's perspective in ways that can be compared across cultures.

ethnology

The analysis and comparison of ethnographic data across cultures.

How Do Anthropologists Write Ethnography?

After gathering data through fieldwork, anthropologists must decide how to tell the stories of the people they study. Although ethnographic films are a vibrant part of our field, most anthropologists make their contributions through ethnographic writing—either articles or books. The art of ethnographic writing has been a particularly hot topic within anthropology for the past twenty-five years, and both style and content have changed dramatically since Malinowski and Evans-Pritchard published their books in the early twentieth century.

Ethnography has changed as anthropology has changed. More women and people of color are writing, bringing their unique perspectives into the anthropological discourse. More people from non-Western countries are writing, challenging the position of Western writers as unquestioned authorities on other cultures. And with better communication systems, people are reading what we write about them, even when we write it halfway around the world. This has had a profound effect on the conversations between author and subject and on the ethnographer's final product.

It is unavoidable that what we write will in some way provide only a limited view of the lives of those we study. The process of collecting, organizing, and analyzing our data presumes not only that we present facts, but also that we choose which facts to present, which people to highlight, and which stories to tell. As authors, we have the power to interpret the people and their experiences to our audience. This is an awesome and sometimes overwhelming responsibility, which often leaves the ethnographer at a loss for how to proceed. In researching my book, *God in Chinatown*, for instance, I conducted more than one hundred interviews, each lasting one hour or more. The process of selecting certain stories and specific quotations was arduous.

POLYVOCALITY

Changes in ethnographic fieldwork and writing over recent decades have sought to make the process more participatory and transparent. Today most ethnographic projects involve people from the community in the research process and include their voices more directly in the written product.

polyvocality

The practice of using many different voices in ethnographic writing and research question development, allowing the reader to hear more directly from the people in the study.

Polyvocality—the use of many voices in ethnographic writing—allows the reader to hear directly from the people in the study and, by bringing their stories to life, makes them more vibrant and available to the reader. Anthropologists also increase polyvocality in their research by inviting key informants to help design the research, including interview and survey questions. Others may be invited to read sections of the manuscript as it is being drafted. In contemporary ethnographic writing, the author's voice also comes out more clearly as ethnographies have moved from the style of Evans-Pritchard (1940) toward that of Geertz (1973a)—from being a scientific report toward being thick description and an interpretation of what is observed.

REFLEXIVITY

In recent years, the practice of reflexivity—self-reflection on the experience of doing fieldwork—has become more prevalent in written ethnographies. Contemporary writers make an effort to reveal their own position in relationship to their study so that readers can assess what biases, strengths, or handicaps the author may have. The ethnographer's age, gender, race/ethnicity, nationality, sexuality, and religious background may have a direct impact on (1) the ease with which he or she establishes rapport or gains access to the research community, and (2) the successful analysis of his or her findings. A careful ethnographer must address these issues in the research design and implementation and may choose to reflect on them in the written report.

ETHNOGRAPHIC AUTHORITY

Ultimately, the ethnographer must wrestle with the question of ethnographic authority: What right does he or she have to present certain material, make certain claims, and draw certain conclusions? That authority is not automatically given, so authors make efforts, often early on in the ethnography, to establish their credentials and identify the grounds on which readers should trust them and the decisions they made during fieldwork and writing. These attempts to establish ethnographic authority include discussions of the length of time engaged in the study, language skills, special training and preparation, research design and implementation, and the quality of the relationship with subjects in the study. The quality and persuasiveness of the writing can also be significant in establishing the ethnographer's credibility. The inclusion of direct quotes can confirm the author's conclusions, provide more direct access to the fieldworker's data, and enable the reader to better assess the author's conclusions.

What Moral and Ethical Concerns Guide Anthropologists in Their Research and Writing?

Anthropologists often face moral and ethical dilemmas while conducting fieldwork. These dilemmas require us to make choices that may affect the quality of our research and the people we study. Indeed, the moral and ethical implications of anthropological research and writing are of deep concern within the discipline and have been particularly hot topics at various times in its history. As a result, the American Anthropological Association (AAA) has developed an extensive set of ethical guidelines, which you can view at www.aaanet.org.

DO NO HARM

At the core of our ethics code is the mandate to do no harm. Even though as anthropologists we seek to contribute to general human knowledge, and perhaps shed light on a specific cultural, economic, or political problem, we must not do so at the expense of the people we study. In fact, this issue spurred the creation of the AAA's code of ethics. The organization's website presents a great variety of advice about the anthropologist's responsibility to the people being studied.

Several key examples in the history of anthropology demonstrate the importance of the "Do no harm" mandate. In the 1960s and 1970s, anthropologists came under heavy criticism for their role in colonialism, particularly for intentionally and unintentionally providing information on local cultures to colonial administrators and military agents. After World War II, anthropology as a discipline was criticized for aiding the European colonial encounter, assisting colonial administrators by providing detailed descriptions and analysis of local populations, many of which were actively engaged in struggles against colonial rule. Anthropology was criticized for helping to create an image of colonial subjects as unable to govern themselves and in need of Western guidance and rule (Asad 1973). During the Vietnam War in the 1960s, some anthropologists were criticized for collaborating with the U.S. military occupation and counterinsurgency efforts. In the 1970s, the AAA experienced internal political turmoil as it addressed accusations of covert research conducted in Southeast Asia by anthropologists (Wakin 1992).

More recently, the ethical practices of two American researchers, anthropologist Napolean Chagnon and geneticist-physician James Neel, who worked among Brazil's indigenous Yanomami people (Chagnon 1968) in the 1960s and following, have come under question. In his book *Darkness in El Dorado* (2000), journalist Patrick Tierney has claimed, among other things, that Chagnon and Neel compromised their subjects' health to see how unprotected indigenous populations would respond to the introduction of infectious disease. Later investigations did not support Tierney's most serious charges, and the original findings of the AAA against Chagnon and Neel were rescinded. The controversy, however, stimulated a significant debate within anthropology about the code of ethics expected of all members.

Recently the U.S. military has actively recruited anthropologists for service as cross-cultural experts in Iraq and Afghanistan, renewing impassioned debates within the discipline about the proper role of anthropologists in military and covert operations. Through the Human Terrain Systems program, the U.S. military recruits, trains, and deploys anthropologists to be embedded with combat units and to advise military commanders on building local community relationships. The role of anthropologists in military-sponsored "nation-building" projects has been supported by some (McFate 2005) but criticized by many others who have warned of the "weaponizing of anthropology"—turning anthropological research strategies and knowledge into a tool of war (Price 2011).

OBTAIN INFORMED CONSENT

One of the key principles for protecting research subjects involves obtaining **informed consent**. It is imperative that those whom we study agree to participate in the project. To do so, they must understand clearly what the project involves and the fact that they have the right to refuse to participate. After all, anthropological research is not undercover investigation using covert means and deception. The anthropologist's hallmark research strategy is participant observation, which requires establishing rapport—that is, building relationships of trust over time. To develop rapport, the subjects of our studies must be clearly informed about the goals and scope of our projects and must willingly consent to being a part of them.

U.S. federal regulations protect human subjects involved in any research, and proposals to conduct research on humans, including anthropological research,

Left: An American soldier in rural Vietnam, 1967. *Right:* U.S. Marines in Marjah, Afghanistan, 2012. The relationship of anthropology to colonialism and war has been complicated. During the Vietnam War, for instance, some anthropologists were criticized for collaborating with the U.S. military occupation and counterinsurgency efforts. Today the controversy continues as the U.S. military's Human Terrain Systems program recruits anthropologists to help troops understand local culture and make better decisions in the field.

informed consent

A key strategy for protecting those being studied by ensuring that they are fully informed of the goals of the project and have clearly indicated their consent to participate.

must be reviewed by the sponsoring organization. Such regulations were originally designed to cover medical research, but anthropologists—whether students or professionals—now participate in these institutional reviews before conducting research.

ENSURE ANONYMITY

Anthropologists take precautions to ensure the privacy and safety of those they study by providing anonymity in research notes and in publications. We frequently change the names and disguise the identities of individuals or, at times, whole communities. For example, Nancy Scheper-Hughes disguises the identities of people and places in Brazil to protect the community and individuals she worked with (for example, "the market town that I call Bom Jesus da Mata"). **Anonymity** provides protection for the people in our studies who may be quite vulnerable and whose lives we describe in intimate detail. This consideration becomes particularly important and sometimes controversial in situations in which research involves illegal activities—for instance, Claire Sterk's ethnography about prostitution (2000) or Philippe Bourgois's work with drug dealers in New York City (2003).

anonymity

Protection of the identities of the people involved in a study by changing or omitting their names or other identifying characteristics.

How Are Fieldwork Strategies Changing in Response to Globalization?

The increased movement of people, information, money, and goods associated with globalization has transformed ethnographic fieldwork in terms of both its process and its content.

CHANGES IN PROCESS

Changes in communication and transportation have altered the ongoing relationship between the anthropologist and the community being studied. Global communication allows the fieldworker and the community to maintain contact long after the anthropologist has left the field, facilitating a flow of data, discussions, and interpretation that in the past would have been very difficult to continue. The expansion of global transportation networks means that an anthropologist may find someone from the researched community showing up on his or her doorstep from another part of the world.

CHANGES IN CONTENT

Globalization has also deeply affected fieldwork content. No longer can an anthropologist study a local community in isolation from global processes. As even the most remote areas are affected by intensifying globalization—whether through media, tourism, investment, migration, or global warming—ethnographers are increasingly integrating the local with the global in their studies. In some cases, particularly in studies of migration, ethnographic fieldwork is now multi-sited, encompassing research in two or more locations to represent more fully the scope of the issue under study.

Nancy Scheper-Hughes's career reflects many recent changes in ethnographic fieldwork. Her earliest research, introduced in the chapter opener, focused on local life in the Brazilian shantytown Alto do Cruzerio. She has carefully monitored changes in the community in the ensuing years, including dramatic recent improvements in infant mortality rates stemming from Brazilian economic growth combined with direct government promotion of local health care services (Scheper-Hughes 2013).

Scheper-Hughes's other recent work places Alto do Cruzeiro in the middle of an illicit global trade in harvested human organs (Scheper-Hughes 2002). While she continues to explore the richness of local life in Brazil, she has expanded her research scope to examine how the experiences of the poor in one community are mirrored in the lives of poor people in many other countries and are linked by a gruesome global trade driven by demand from the world's economic elite. Scheper-Hughes first began hearing rumors while working in northeast Brazil, rumors of the abduction and murder of poor children, whose bodies—minus heart, lungs, liver, kidneys, and eyes—would later be found on roadsides, in sugarcane fields, or in hospital dumpsters. Later, as she began writing articles about these organ-stealing rumors, other anthropologists reported similar stories of organ theft in Central and South America, India, Korea, Eastern Europe, and many parts of Africa.

Reflecting on the meaning of these stories, Scheper-Hughes writes, "To the anthropologist . . . working closely with the urban poor, the rumors spoke to the ontological insecurity of people 'to whom almost anything could be done.' They reflected everyday threats to bodily security, urban violence, police terror, social anarchy, theft, loss, and fragmentation. Many of the poor imagined, with some reason as it turns out, that autopsies were performed to harvest usable tissues and body parts from those whose bodies had reverted to the state" (Scheper-Hughes 2002, 36).

As an engaged medical anthropologist, Scheper-Hughes has spent countless hours investigating the extensive illegal international trade in smuggled human organs. Contemporary globalization, especially the time-space compression of

A middleman and two young Filipino men with scars; each of the two men has sold a kidney as part of the global trade in human organs.

transportation and communication, enables trafficking networks to spread across national boundaries and around the world. These same cornerstones of globalization have allowed Scheper-Hughes and her organization, Organs Watch, based at the University of California, to develop an extensive global network of anthropologists, human rights activists, transplant surgeons, journalists, and government agencies that have collaborated to address issues of human organ trafficking in India, Pakistan, Israel, South Africa, Turkey, Moldova, Brazil, the Philippines, and the United States.

As a member of two World Health Organization panels on transplant trafficking and transplant safety, Scheper-Hughes has seen firsthand the global search for kidneys: the often-poor kidney sellers; the kidney hunters who track them down; and the kidney buyers willing to cross borders, break laws, and pay as much as $150,000 in advance to the organ brokers for a chance at a new kidney and a new life. In 2009 the U.S. Federal Bureau of Investigation arrested a Brooklyn rabbi who had been arranging kidney sales, highlighting the deep integration of illegal international organ trafficking into developed-country markets where, for example, 80,000 Americans linger on a kidney waiting list, struggling through dialysis to stay alive, and where the wait times for a donor in some parts of the country are as long as nine years.

The trajectory of Scheper-Hughes's career from fieldwork in a small favela in Brazil to fieldwork in international organ-trafficking networks reflects many of the transformations shaping anthropological fieldwork over the last forty years. No local community can be viewed as isolated. Anthropologists must consider each local fieldwork site in light of the myriad ways in which local dynamics link to the world beyond. Today fieldwork includes attention to global flows, networks, and processes as anthropologists trace patterns across national and cultural boundaries while keeping one foot grounded in the lives of people in local communities.

Toolkit

Thinking Like an Anthropologist:
Applying Aspects of Fieldwork to Your Own Life

You don't have to go to Brazil to use the skills of an anthropologist. Maybe you will be inspired by this book to explore a culture in another part of the world, perhaps by a language you study, a professor whose class you take, or a new friend you meet. Or maybe you will apply these skills nearer to home. In Chapter 1 you were asked to begin seeing yourself as a budding anthropologist, one who is already working hard to understand the complicated, globalizing world and how you fit into it. Fieldwork skills are the key to navigating what lies ahead of you.

As you think back to the fieldwork of Nancy Scheper-Hughes, remember the questions we asked at the beginning of the chapter:

- **What is unique about ethnographic fieldwork, and why do anthropologists conduct this kind of research?**

- **How did the idea of fieldwork develop?**

- **How do anthropologists get started conducting fieldwork?**

- **How do anthropologists write ethnography?**

- **What moral and ethical concerns guide anthropologists in their research and writing?**

- **How are fieldwork strategies changing in response to globalization?**

Consider how the concepts we have discussed can be applied not only by a professional anthropologist but also by each one of us in our daily lives.

You already use many of the strategies, skills, and perspectives of ethnographic fieldwork to navigate your daily journey through life. Whether in your family, your workplace, or your school, you have to understand the people with whom you interact. You participate and observe, establish rapport, listen, interview, gather life histories, and map out family and social networks. If you keep a journal or diary, you already have started taking field notes about the people and cultural patterns around you. You are constantly assessing who has power, how they got it, and how they use it. While you may already use many of these tools, the goal of this chapter has been to show the rigor with which they can be applied if you take fieldwork seriously, and to enable you to apply them in a more systematic and self-conscious way in your daily life.

Key Terms

ethnographic fieldwork (p. 64)

salvage ethnography (p. 71)

cultural relativism (p. 71)

participant observation (p. 72)

reflexivity (p. 75)

literature review (p. 76)

anthropologist's toolkit (p. 77)

quantitative data (p. 77)

qualitative data (p. 77)

rapport (p. 77)

key informant (p. 77)

interview (p. 78)

life history (p. 78)

survey (p. 78)

kinship analysis (p. 78)

social network analysis (p. 78)

field notes (p. 78)

mapping (p. 78)

built environment (p. 79)

zeros (p. 80)

mutual transformation (p. 80)

emic (p. 81)

etic (p. 81)

ethnology (p. 81)

polyvocality (p. 82)

informed consent (p. 85)

anonymity (p. 86)

Chapter 4
Language

Everything you and I have worked for is being wiped out before our eyes. Our borders, our language, and our culture are under siege.

—Michael Savage, author and radio talk show host, 2003

In April 2010, the state of Arizona passed a law mandating police to arrest anyone who gives a reasonable suspicion of being an undocumented immigrant. If that person cannot prove his or her legal status, he or she must be detained immediately. The law treats a very contentious issue. Arizona lawmakers argue that the law responds to the federal government's failure to monitor borders and protect U.S. citizens from foreigners who they fear will take their jobs and endanger their neighborhoods. The statement quoted above echoes this sentiment, revealing the way many people closely link language change to social upheaval. Civil rights activists, however, ask how police will determine "a reasonable suspicion of being

Could language use have marked you with "a reasonable suspicion of being undocumented" under a 2010 Arizona law? A billboard in Phoenix, Arizona, warns of uncertainty ahead.

undocumented." They fear that law enforcement officers will rely on how the person looks (skin color), dresses, or speaks. Will someone who speaks Spanish or who speaks English with a Spanish accent be more likely to be arrested and detained? Is language an effective screen for legal status or citizenship?

Debates about language have been raging in the United States over the past twenty years. Thirty states have passed English-only laws limiting classroom instruction, driver's license exams, road signs, and even health warnings to one language. The U.S. House of Representatives has passed legislation several times declaring English to be the national language of the United States, although these bills have never been signed into law. The United States, historically, has been a country of many languages: Dutch, French, Spanish, German, Italian, Chinese, not to mention hundreds of Native American languages and hundreds of others spoken by contemporary immigrants. Spanish has been spoken in what is now the U.S. South and Southwest since the 1500s, when the Spanish conquistadors Francisco Vásquez de Coronado and Hernando Cortéz explored and colonized the area on behalf of the Spanish Crown. How has language come to be such a hot-button issue in the United States today?

Nearly seven thousand languages are currently in use in the world. Through linguistic anthropology, one of the four fields of anthropology, we explore not only the details of a language's vocabulary and grammar but also the role of language in people's lives—both as individuals and as communities. Languages are not abstract concepts with ideal forms perfectly displayed in a dictionary or a textbook. Languages are dynamic and alive. Communication is a social act. Words are part of actions. We call a friend, text a classmate, tell a story, say a prayer, ask a favor. Human language uses an infinite number of forms to communicate a vast array of information. We communicate through poetry, prose, gestures, signs, touch, text messaging—even anthropology textbooks. Not only can we communicate content in great detail, but we also have the wondrous capacity to share the content of our imaginations, our anger, fear, joy, and the deepest longings of our souls.

Humans are born with the ability to learn language—not a particular language, but whatever one they are exposed to as they grow up. Exactly what we learn and the context in which we learn it vary widely. Languages change and grow, constantly adapting to the needs and circumstances of the people who speak them. Although the number of languages shrinks every year under the pressures of globalization, the remarkable diversity of human language reflects humans' dramatically different ways of perceiving, thinking about, and engaging with the world. Because languages are deeply embedded in culture—languages are culture—they also become arenas where norms and values are created, enforced, and contested, where group identity is negotiated, and where systems of power and status are taught and challenged.

In this chapter we will consider how anthropologists study human language and communication. In particular, we will ask:

- **What is language and where does it come from?**
- **Can language shape our ways of thinking?**
- **How do systems of power intersect with language and communication?**
- **What are the effects of globalization on language?**

By the end of the chapter you will have a better understanding of how language works, have the conceptual tools to analyze the role of language in your personal life and within your language community, and comprehend the forces that will shape language and communication in our increasingly global future.

What Is Language and Where Does It Come From?

Language is a system of communication that uses symbols—such as words, sounds, and gestures—organized according to certain rules to convey any kind of information. All animals communicate in some fashion, often relying on a *call system* of sounds and gestures that are prompted by environmental stimuli. Ants share information through chemical trails and pheromones; bees dance to communicate distance and direction to flower petals and nectar. Dogs growl or bark to express hostility or warning. And a border collie named Betsy, featured on the cover of *National Geographic* magazine, could recognize more than 340 distinct words and commands (Morrell 2008). Dolphins produce complicated vocal signals—clicks, whistles, squeaks, trills. Whales have been found to "sing"—to create a vocalization that appears to have a unique tune or accent for each clan or pod of whales.

Although these are all examples of communication—providing information by a sender to a receiver—they are not symbolic language as humans use it. In comparison, human language is a complex system that involves the combination of many small, meaningful elements into larger syllables, words, and sentences following certain rules but with infinite variations. Human language involves sounds and gestures along with myriad symbols with deep historical and cultural meaning. It is remarkably flexible and creative, rapidly adapting to changes in human life and the environment.

THE ORIGINS OF HUMAN LANGUAGE

In searching for the evolutionary origins of human language, anthropologists, particularly primatologists, have investigated language use and communication

language

A system of communication organized by rules that uses symbols such as words, sounds, and gestures to convey information.

All animals communicate in some fashion. A border collie named Betsy could recognize more than 340 distinct words and commands.

among our nearest primate relatives—chimpanzees, orangutans, and other great apes—with some surprising results. In their natural habitats, primates produce an astonishing array of vocalizations to communicate information about food, sex, and potential predators. These calls are passed along genetically through the generations. Nonhuman primates lack the physical apparatus to create human sounds and human speech. Specifically, their ability to manipulate their vocal cords, tongue, and lips is far more limited than that of humans. But do they have the mental capacity to create human language? In recent years, a set of studies has explored nonhuman primate language capabilities.

Chantek, an orangutan born at a primate research center in Georgia in 1977, was raised much like a human child from nine months of age by anthropologist Lyn Miles at the University of Tennessee at Chattanooga. Now living at Zoo Atlanta in a special habitat, Chantek has mastered several hundred signs and can also understand some spoken English. Reports on the language development of Chantek and other primates who have been taught a form of language suggest that they have the ability to move beyond rote memorization of certain signs, and indicate a more humanlike capacity to lie, swear, tell jokes, invent new words by combining signs, and even try to teach language to others (Fouts 1997; Miles 1993).

Do nonhuman primates have the capacity to create human language? Koko, a gorilla, with Francine Patterson, learned over 400 signs in sign language.

Scholars disagree about the final implications of research on nonhuman primate language capacity. Some have suggested that although this capacity is not as complex as human language, these nonhuman primates can develop language skills at the level of a two- or three-year-old human child (Miles 1993). Others argue that their behavior is mostly imitative—imitating their caregivers rather than using language creatively (Sebeok and Umiker-Sebeok 1980; Terrace et al. 1979). Certainly chimpanzees, gorillas, and orangutans can master rudimentary language signs and can even, at times, exhibit key aspects of human language skills. Their language use reflects **productivity**, meaning that they can use known words to invent new word combinations. Their language can also exhibit **displacement**—that is, the ability to use words to refer to objects not immediately present or events happening in the past or future. But, fundamentally, these primates do not use language in the human sense. They do not create and use basic language elements in their natural habitats. They cannot achieve the extremely complex human language system that is perhaps the most distinct aspect of human culture and that enables us to store and pass on huge quantities of information not embedded in our genes.

If our most immediate primate relatives do not approach the physical or mental language capacity of humans, then how did human language capacity evolve? Recent genetic information and archaeological evidence provide strong clues. Let's consider the genetic information first. Around 1990, a family in Britain (now known only as KE to protect their privacy) was discovered to have a rare mutation of the *FOXP2* gene. The same variant of *FOXP2* is found in chimpanzees. More than half of the members of the KE family inherited severe speech problems that made them unintelligible even to their own relatives (Trivedi 2001). Not only were affected family members unable to physically form words because of a limited ability to make fine lip and tongue movements, but cognitive differences also led them to have difficulty in recognizing and using grammar. As children, these family members were taught to use certain hand gestures to compensate. Genetic analysis indicates that the presence of the particular *FOXP2* gene variant may be crucial for activating and inactivating key human speech capacities, an evolutionary development that appears to be essential to human speech. Such analysis also traces the emergence of human language to within the past 150,000 years.

Archaeological evidence provides further clues to the origins of human language. Fossilized brain casts from archaic *Homo sapiens* known as Neandertals (who lived from about 120,000 to about 35,000 years ago) and even earlier *Homo* species reveal the neurological and anatomical features necessary for speech. Our early human ancestors' capacity to cooperate in hunting and tool making also suggests that some language ability existed before the evolution of *Homo sapiens*. Cultural evidence supporting extensive language use appears around 50,000 years

productivity
The linguistic ability to use known words to invent new word combinations.

displacement
The ability to use words to refer to objects not immediately present or events occurring in the past or future.

ago, including art, tool making, and other technologies that required language to facilitate their transmission from generation to generation. Language as it has developed among modern humans would have enhanced the capacity for group cooperation and the transmission of cultural knowledge; in this way, it conveyed a significant advantage in adapting to less hospitable natural environments and increasing the potential for survival.

DESCRIPTIVE LINGUISTICS

Language is a system of symbols. It is a system of otherwise meaningless sounds, marks (writing), and gestures that are made meaningful by a group of people through the collective history and tradition of their culture. Think of the English word *pig*. Say it out loud. Now create a mental image of a pig. Why do those three letters and that particular sound represent a pig? They don't look like a pig or sound like any of the noises that a pig makes. But when you say the word, an image is transferred from your brain into sound, which travels through the air into another person's ears and to that person's brain, where an image appears that is similar to yours—if not precisely the same. **Descriptive linguistics** is the study of the construction of those sounds, their meanings, and their combination into forms that communicate meaning.

Through descriptive linguistics, anthropologists work to describe the elements and rules of a particular language. Imagine that you went to do ethnographic fieldwork in a village in the mountains of the Philippines where the residents had no writing system for their local language. Your task would be to learn that language and to create a system for writing it down, perhaps using the English alphabet. Where would you begin? After identifying a person or a few people from the village who would be your teachers, perhaps you would work your way from the most simple aspects of the language to the most complex. A language has a limited number of **phonemes**—the smallest units of sound that can make a difference in meaning. For instance, the English letters *b* and *p* sound very similar, but they make a significant difference in meaning. If you failed to carefully distinguish the different phoneme use in the village where you were working, you might mistakenly switch one for the other in a word followed by the sound *ig* when describing your host's home. In that case, you would end up with *pig* instead of *big*. The study of what sounds exist and which ones are important in a particular language is called **phonology**.

Extending your linguistic analysis, you would know that **morphemes** are the smallest units of sound that carry meaning on their own. (Phonemes, in contrast, have no meaning of their own.) So, for instance, the morphemes *cow* and *horse* can convey meaning without needing additional sounds. The study of the patterns and rules of how sounds combine to make morphemes is called **morphology**. In human languages, we combine morphemes to form phrases

descriptive linguistics

The study of the sounds, symbols, and gestures of a language, and their combination into forms that communicate meaning.

phonemes

The smallest units of sound that can make a difference in meaning.

phonology

The study of what sounds exist and which ones are important for a particular language.

morphemes

The smallest units of sound that carry meaning on their own.

morphology

The study of patterns and rules of how sounds combine to make morphemes.

and sentences, relying on specific patterns and rules called **syntax**. So, following Standard American English syntax, we would place a possessive pronoun before the noun, not afterward. We would say or write *my pig,* not *pig my*—although the latter pattern might be linguistically appropriate in another language. **Grammar** encompasses the combined set of observations about the rules governing the formation of morphemes and syntax that guide language use.

KINESICS AND PARALANGUAGE

To fully describe and understand another language, the linguist must master more than its spoken and written elements. Human language is accompanied by and embedded in a gesture–call system—made up of body movements, noises, and tone of voice—that also conveys significant amounts of information. **Kinesics**, the study of the relationship between body movements and communication, explores all the facial expressions, gestures, and postures that convey messages with or without words. For example, nods, handshakes, bows, and arms folded tightly across the chest all communicate information, although their meanings are not universal; they vary from culture to culture. The thumbs-up and the "okay" hand signals used in North America are considered rude gestures in certain other cultures. North Americans point with their fingers, but Filipinos point with their lips. Have you ever had the experience of making a motion or gesture that someone else misunderstood? If so, what was the cultural context?

Human language is also accompanied by **paralanguage**—an extensive set of noises (such as laughs, cries, sighs, yells) and tones of voice that convey significant information about the speaker. Paralanguage indicates whether the speaker is (for example) happy, sad, angry, tired, scared, disgusted, or enthusiastic. Try saying the sentence *The exam is on Thursday* using each of these tones of voice. The effect on communication is really quite stunning.

Humans have been communicating in writing for thousands of years. *Left:* Ancient Egyptian stele with hieroglyphs, ca. twenty-seventh to twenty-fifth century B.C.E. *Right:* Rune stone on Adelsö Island near Stockholm, Sweden, eleventh century C.E.

syntax

The specific patterns and rules for constructing phrases and sentences.

grammar

The combined set of observations about the rules governing the formation of morphemes and syntax that guide language use.

kinesics

The study of the relationship between body movements and communication.

paralanguage

An extensive set of noises (such as cries) and tones of voice that convey significant information about the speaker.

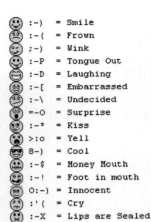

:-)	= Smile
:-(	= Frown
;-)	= Wink
:-P	= Tongue Out
:-D	= Laughing
:-[	= Embarrassed
:-\	= Undecided
=-O	= Surprise
:-*	= Kiss
>:o	= Yell
8-)	= Cool
:-$	= Money Mouth
:-!	= Foot in mouth
O:-)	= Innocent
:'(	= Cry
:-X	= Lips are Sealed

Did you ever wonder why emoticons developed in e-mails and text messages?

As much as 90 percent of emotional information is communicated through body movements and paralanguage. No wonder that e-mail and text messaging have developed an extensive set of "emoticons" and "emojis"—symbols that indicate the emotional content intended by the sender. E-mails and text messaging are beneficial developments in that they allow rapid response over distances great and small in our globalizing world, and they are increasingly used in the business world and personal life. But because they are devoid of the kinesics and paralanguage that play such key roles in face-to-face human communication, they significantly increase the potential for misunderstandings. Do you trust e-mail or text messaging to communicate your most intimate thoughts?

Can Language Shape Our Ways of Thinking?

The power of language to shape human thought and culture has been a hot topic in linguistic anthropology for many generations. Linguistic anthropologists have considered questions such as: Is there an underlying, genetically structured grammar to all languages? Do languages evolve in response to local environments? Do vocabularies and classifications of reality embedded in a language affect the way its speakers think and see the world? In this section we will look at research on the relationships among language, thought, and culture, as well as a culturally specific phenomenon known as *focal vocabulary*.

LANGUAGE, THOUGHT, AND CULTURE

In the nineteenth and twentieth centuries, a number of linguists, including Ferdinand de Saussure and Claude Levi-Strauss, proposed theories of language that assumed an underlying structure to all the world's languages. In the 1950s Noam Chomsky, a linguist and philosopher, suggested that the human brain is hardwired with a basic framework for organizing language that creates a universal grammar—a similar structure in all languages (1957). In Chomsky's view, all humans share a similar language ability and ways of thinking. He felt that this proposition explains our ability to learn other languages and to translate fluidly from one language to another.

Sapir-Whorf hypothesis

The idea that different languages create different ways of thinking.

The work of Edward Sapir and his student Benjamin Lee Whorf—later given the name **Sapir-Whorf hypothesis**—took a different direction, suggesting that different languages create different ways of thinking (Sapir and Swadesh 1946). Their hypothesis proposed that languages establish certain mental categories, or classifications of reality, almost like a grammar for organizing the worldview that shapes peoples' ways of perceiving the world. Whorf's linguistic research with the Hopi, a Native American group in the southwestern United States, suggested that the Hopi language differs from English both in vocabulary and in basic grammatical categories that are key to conceptualizing how the world works. For instance, rather than using separate verb tenses expressing past, present, and future, the Hopi language combines past and present into one. Whorf suggested that this pattern reflects a different conceptualization of time and a unique worldview in which past and present reflect lived reality whereas the future is hypothetical or potential (Carroll 1956).

"Shakespeare in the Bush": A Nigerian (Mis)interpretation of _Hamlet._ Laura Bohannan explores the challenges that different vocabulary and conceptualizations of the world pose for translation between languages and cultures. She relates her discoveries in the article "Shakespeare in the Bush: An American Anthropologist Set Out to Study the Tiv of West Africa and Was Taught the True Meaning of _Hamlet_" (1966). While Bohannan was conducting fieldwork in a small village in Nigeria, Tiv elders asked her to tell them a story from her own culture. She attempted to explain _Hamlet_, one of the classic stories of English literature, but time and again was unable to translate directly from English to Tiv. Words such as _chief_ and _leader_ hold distinctly different meanings and roles in the two cultures; they do not translate. The "dead" in Hamlet do not translate because the Tiv have no concept of ghosts. Instead, they imagined Shakespeare's characters as beset by witchcraft.

MAP 4.1
Nigeria

As Bohannan attempted to use Tiv words to tell Shakespeare's story, the original meanings of the English words became blurred, and the standard message of _Hamlet_ was lost in translation. Bohannan's insights as related in "Shakespeare in the Bush" reveal both the power of our environment to shape our language and the power of our language to shape the way we see the world.

THE ROLE OF FOCAL VOCABULARY

Contemporary studies in linguistic anthropology suggest that although the vocabulary and grammar of the language we learn may influence the way we see the world, language does not control or restrict our thinking. Languages are dynamic. They change and adapt as the natural and cultural worlds shift. Humans creatively invent new words and concepts to describe and discuss the changing world as they experience it. Evidence of this adaptability can be found in a language's **lexicon**—all the words for names, ideas, and events that make up a language's dictionary.

Of particular interest to linguistic anthropologists is a language's **focal vocabulary**—that is, words and terminology that develop with particular sophistication to describe the unique cultural realities experienced by a group of people.

lexicon

All the words for names, ideas, and events that make up a language's dictionary.

focal vocabulary

The words and terminology that develop with particular sophistication to describe the unique cultural realities experienced by a group of people.

Thus the Bolivian Aymar Indians have two hundred names for potatoes, reflecting the potato's role as a major source of food in their diet. The Nuer of Sudan, studied by E. E. Evans-Pritchard (1940), relied on cattle in their economy, political system, and kinship structures; thus they developed more than four hundred words to distinguish different types of cattle. In today's globalizing world, a focal vocabulary has emerged to describe and engage in digital communication. Words such as *mouse, modem, download,* and *attachment*—even *e-mail, text,* and *tweet*—are very recent creations designed to facilitate communication among those working in the digital communication age.

Even the human description and perception of the color spectrum varies across and within cultures, seemingly according to need. Anthropologist Robin Lakoff (2004) examined how color terms in American English have expanded over the last fifty years, being promoted by the fashion and cosmetics industries. An extensive color vocabulary is not uniform among Americans; it varies primarily by gender. Women are far more likely than men, for instance, to be able to distinguish between salmon and peach, teal and mauve, or cranberry and dusky orange. A similar gender-based focal vocabulary exists in American sports language. This highly specialized set of terms and distinctions, used primarily by men, allows complex communication about complicated human activity but is applicable in extremely limited scenarios.

Clearly, language, including vocabulary, provides categories for recognizing and organizing the world; but language also reflects reality. Language is not rigidly structured or controlling. It is remarkably flexible and fluid, responding to changes in the surrounding culture and enabling us to describe and analyze our world with remarkable specificity.

How Do Systems of Power Intersect with Language and Communication?

sociolinguistics

The study of the ways culture shapes language and language shapes culture, particularly the intersection of language with cultural categories and systems of power such as race, gender, class, and age.

Language comes alive when people communicate with one another. But languages are deeply embedded in the patterns of particular cultures. What people actually say and how they say it are intricately connected to the cultural context, to the speakers' social position, and to the larger systems of power within which the language operates. Linguistic anthropologists, especially sociolinguists, study these connections. **Sociolinguistics**, which we will consider in this section, is the study of the ways in which culture shapes language and language shapes culture— particularly the intersection of language with cultural categories and systems of power such as age, race, ethnicity, sexuality, gender, and class (Wardhaugh 2009).

THE "N-WORD"

Words can be very powerful. They can hurt. They can heal. Some do so more than others. Words also are symbols. They can carry profound meanings based on the history of their use in a culture. As we explore the intersection of language and culture, particularly the intersection of language and systems of power, a consideration of the history and contemporary usage of the "N-word" provides rich insights. In U.S. culture, the "N-word" carries such powerful connotations that many people are reluctant to say it out loud or put it in print. Television stations censor it from their broadcasts. Politicians shy away from controversy over its usage. It is so powerful that most people only refer to it as the "N-word."

Nigger has been used as a derogatory term for African Americans throughout much of U.S. history—as a symbol of white power, slavery, and the threat of violence. In the twentieth century, the use of the "N-word" in public discourse was replaced successively by the use of *Negro, colored, black,* and *African American.* In 1962, the U.S. federal government legally changed the offending name on all public properties under its control, replacing it with *Negro* (Severson 2011). The "N-word," however, has not disappeared. It continues to hold tremendous symbolic power as its use invokes the history of racism, inequality, and the threat to make those dangers real in the present.

Despite its sordid history, today the use of the "N-word" has been revived among African American youth and in hip-hop and rap music. As a result, a debate has raged even within the African American community about its appropriateness. Many older African Americans reject its use because of its long-standing association with U.S. systems of race and racism. In contrast, younger

How would sociolinguists analyze the history and contemporary usage of the "N-word" so commonly deployed by U.S. rappers, including Jay-Z (*left*) and Kanye West (*right*), here performing in concert?

generations often articulate their desire to appropriate the term for their own generation and rob it of its historical power.

My students remind me that some young people today quite commonly use the "N-word" to express friendship and camaraderie, not anger and hostility. At the same time, they recognize distinct rules about this usage—rules that factor in race, gender, age, and status and that attempt to mitigate against the former role of the "N-word" in this country's systems of race and racism. These young people carefully say "niggah," not "nigger," perhaps taking a slight edge off the word's powerful meaning. They only use it among friends. White people rarely address a person of color with the greeting. Boys never call girls "niggah." Girls rarely use it among themselves. Young people never use it in reference to older people. And students never use it in addressing a professor.

Think about how you feel when you hear the "N-word" spoken aloud. Is your reaction affected by your race, gender, age, or status, or by those of the speaker? Do you feel comfortable using the "N-word" in daily speech? If so, where, when, and with whom? If not, what is the source of your discomfort? Sociolinguists study language in this way. They examine the use of language in its specific contexts and the way language shapes and is shaped by other dynamics of power.

LANGUAGE AND GENDER

Ethnic and racial dynamics are not the only sources of tension in communication. Have you ever walked away from a conversation with someone of the opposite sex and thought to yourself, s/he has no idea what I'm talking about! You are not alone. Bookstores are full of titles that promise to help you figure it out: *Men Are from Mars, Women Are from Venus* (Gray 2004); *The 5 Love Languages: The Secret to Love That Lasts* (Chapman 2010); *You Just Don't Understand: Women and Men in Conversation* (Tannen 2001). Clearly, women and men are developing different patterns of language use. How and why?

There is no hard evidence that the brains of men and women are wired differently, leading to gender differences in language and other behavior. But linguistic anthropologists have examined the powerful role of culture in shaping language. In this instance, language and gender are intricately intertwined in personal and public conversations, among groups of men or groups of women, and in mixed-sex talk. In particular, linguists use two main theoretical frameworks for analyzing these patterns. The frameworks are sometimes known as the *difference model* and the *dominance model*.

Linguistic anthropologist Deborah Tannen's popular book *You Just Don't Understand: Women and Men in Conversation* (2001) is built on the difference model. Tannen suggests that conversations between men and women are basically a form of cross-cultural communication. Between the ages of five and

fifteen, boys and girls grow up in different linguistic worlds. At the time when most children are developing and perfecting their communication skills, boys and girls are operating in largely segregated gender groups. Girls mostly hang out in small groups, indoors in more intimate conversations. Boys tend to play in larger groups, often outdoors, and compete with one another for group status, often through verbal jokes, stories, and challenges. These patterns, according to Tannen, are reinforced in later years through socializing, sports, and work. No wonder that boys and girls have a difficult time communicating with one another when they finally begin to look for relationships. It is as if they have grown up in two different cultures, two different worlds.

But is miscommunication always rooted in misunderstanding? Or are there real, underlying conflicts between the genders that lead to the miscommunication (Cameron 2007)? Other linguistic anthropologists, working from the dominance model, examine how the cultures of communication learned by boys and girls intertwine with gender dynamics throughout the larger culture: at home, school, work, and play, and even through religion. According to these scholars, if gender stratification and hierarchy are prevalent in the larger culture (see Chapter 7), and if men are generally in positions of superiority, then language will reflect men's dominance and may play a key role in enabling it (West 1998; Lakoff 2004).

Research on mixed-sex communication over the past thirty years consistently shows that many men adopt linguistic strategies that allow them to establish and maintain dominance in conversation and in social interaction. Men are more likely to use dominant speech acts such as commands, explanations, contradictions, criticisms, challenges, and accusations. Women are more likely to ask, request, agree, support, accommodate, accept, and apologize. Men are more likely to interrupt other speakers to insert their ideas or concerns, express doubts, or offer advice.

Did you ever wonder why men and women struggle to communicate? Are their brains wired differently for language, or have they grown up in different social worlds learning different communication skills?

Despite stereotypes to the contrary, men also tend to dominate conversations through the amount of talking they do. Men claim more "air time" than women in meetings, seminars, board rooms, and classrooms—especially in public forums where they see some possibility of maintaining or increasing their power and status. Working from the dominance model of mixed-sex communication, many linguistic anthropologists suggest that language and gender, as reflected in male and female communication patterns, are intricately connected to patterns of stratification in the culture at large (Holmes 1998).

LANGUAGE AND DIALECT

Politics and power can play key roles in how we evaluate a system of communication. For instance, how do we distinguish between a language and a dialect? Is it purely on a linguistic basis? A language is commonly described as a complete system of communication, while a **dialect** is considered a nonstandard variation of a language. Naming something a dialect generally places it in a subordinate relationship to the language. However, from a linguistic anthropologist's perspective, the distinction is not always simple. Human languages vary widely in spoken and written form and in accent, pronunciation, vocabulary, and grammar. Yet, from a linguistic perspective, all languages serve as effective communication tools for the people who speak them.

The categorization and evaluation of certain ways of speaking as a dialect and others as a language can frequently be traced to the exertion of power—political power of the nation, the state, the media, and even the stratification among racial and ethnic groups. Yiddish linguist Max Weinreich reputedly once said that a dialect is a language without an army or a navy. In other words, the elevated status associated with a language derives not from its superior linguistic form or communication capacity, but from its ability to establish—perhaps impose—a particular form as the norm by which to judge other ways of speaking. A particular language variation or way of speaking may be elevated in a culture as the **prestige language**, associated with wealth, success, education, and power.

French sociologist Pierre Bourdieu proposes that language skills serve as a type of cultural capital—a resource or asset available to language users that can be converted into financial capital, such as wages and benefits. Mastery over it brings a set of resources that enable the individual to be more successful. Bourdieu notes that linguistic standards are established and reinforced by a culture's educational institutions, government, media, and religious organizations. They may be taught in schools, used in national media broadcasts such as radio and television, or selected as a sign of competence in business hiring practices. Other language variations are then judged against the norm of the prestige language, and their speakers—often said to be speaking a dialect—are associated with inferior positions within the culture (Bourdieu 1982, 1984).

dialect

A nonstandard variation of a language.

prestige language

A particular way of speaking, or language variation, that is associated with wealth, success, education, and power.

LANGUAGE VARIATION IN THE UNITED STATES

Although globally the English language varies widely in pronunciation, vocabulary, and grammar, in the United States—through national television, radio, and the educational system—the midwestern accent and grammatical usage have become the prestige language variation. This is sometimes called Standard Spoken American English (SSAE) or simply Standard English, against which all other variations are judged. As we explored in this chapter's opening story, judgments about language can have consequences well beyond the realm of communication. We turn first to consider issues of cultural context and race as they intersect with Standard English.

Code Switching in Academia.
In cultures with distinct language variations, dialects, and accents, individuals may become skilled at **code switching**—that is, switching back and forth between one variation and another according to cultural context. Code switching takes many different forms, as speakers may switch from language to language and from linguistic style to style.

Educational systems tend to resist acknowledging speech variations as equally effective, instead choosing to promote a prestigious version as inherently better. (For instance, think about the linguistic standards your instructor used to grade your last English paper.) In educational environments, as a result, students, teachers, and administrators all learn to switch frequently from informal to formal styles of speaking and writing as required. Talking with friends in the hallway may assume a very different form than responding to a professor's query in class. Writing a text message or a posting on Facebook elicits a distinctly different writing style compared with polishing a research paper for a class assignment.

Recently I received the following e-mail from a student who appears to have struggled to understand when to switch codes:

> Hi, how r u? this is xxxx from ur class which is on monday n wednesday @ 9:30. i just wanted to ask u that about the book critique. I know what i as suppose to do in terms of writing about the book however i am lost n not sure wht i should do abt the articles and how u want us to relate it to our paper. I mean am i suppose to write abt the book n then relate it to da article n den offer my own opinion on it? plz let me know how i should b doing dis or if this is how i should be doing it. . . . . . Thank you

While this use of language may serve perfectly well in a text or e-mail with a friend or peer, the failure to code switch in a communication with a professor runs the risk of sending the wrong signals. What evaluations might a professor make of a communication like this one written by a student in text-speak?

code switching

Switching back and forth between one linguistic variant and another depending on the cultural context.

Black English: "Spoken Soul." Linguistic anthropologists and other scholars of language have extensively studied one particular form of English that is spoken by millions of African Americans in the United States. At times, this variation has been referred to as Black English, Black English Vernacular, or African American Vernacular English.

Black English is perhaps the most stigmatized variation of American English, mistakenly criticized as broken or flawed English and associated with urban African American youth. But from a linguistic perspective, Black English is a complete, consistent, and logical variation of the English language with a unique history and a distinct and coherent pronunciation, vocabulary, and grammar. Studies by Labov (1972) and other scholars have carefully demonstrated that Black English is not an ungrammatical jumble but a sophisticated linguistic system with clear rules and patterns (Table 4.1).

Scholars disagree about the exact origins of Black English. Some trace its vocabulary and grammar to the West African linguistic roots of slaves who were forcibly brought to work in the American colonies. Others trace its heritage to nonstandard English used by poor English immigrants who interacted with African slave workers in the plantation system of the American South. The creole languages—blends between the indigenous language and the colonial language—found in Jamaica, Trinidad, Barbados, and Guyana that developed during and after the slave trade may also have been potential sources for the unique forms that Black English has taken (Rickford and Rickford 2000).

Despite its stigmatization within certain parts of American society and the intense cultural pressure to assimilate to Standard English, Black English not only has survived and developed but has become a symbol of identity and solidarity for many within the African American community. Rickford and Rickford (2000) document how this "Spoken Soul"—spoken by African Americans of all ages across the United States and closely associated with African American identity and culture—comes alive in the African American community. Indeed,

TABLE 4.1
Contrasts between Standard English Vernacular and Black English

STANDARD ENGLISH	STANDARD ENGLISH CONTRACTION	BLACK ENGLISH VERNACULAR
You are ready	You're ready	You ready
He is ready	He's ready	He ready
We are ready	We're ready	We ready
They are ready	They're ready	They ready

Source: William Labov. 1972. *Language in the Inner City: Studies in the Black English Vernacular.* Philadelphia: University of Pennsylvania Press.

it is vibrant in homes, schools, streets, and churches and on the airwaves. It is representative of a culture, history, and worldview that are distinct from white culture and ways of speaking.

The linguistic status of Black English entered prominently into the U.S. national debate in 1996. At that time, the Oakland Unified School District in California recommended recognizing it, under the name Ebonics—from *ebony* ("black") + *phonics* ("sounds")—as a distinct language and supporting student speakers of Black English as if they were learning Standard English as a second language in school. The ensuing controversy obscured the Oakland school district's efforts to address a local problem with national implications—the struggles of African American children to succeed in school. Critics warned that the "teaching of Ebonics" in U.S. public schools (which was never the stated goal of the Oakland school district) would undermine the use of Standard English, which they considered central to U.S. national identity, unity, and progress.

Although the school district revised its plan and the controversy subsided, traces of the resistance to recognizing Black English have lingered. They have created negative stereotypes for efforts to understand the unique linguistic character of Black English and the struggles that young Black English speakers may have in educational settings dominated by Standard English. In fact, the debate about English language diversity and the place of Standard English in U.S. culture continues through efforts at the local, state, and national levels.

HISTORICAL LINGUISTICS

Historical linguistics is the study of the development of language over time, including its changes and variations. By analyzing vocabulary and linguistic patterns, historical linguists trace the connections between languages and identify

historical linguistics
The study of the development of language over time, including its changes and variations.

their origins. For example, through comparative analysis of vocabulary, syntax, and grammar, we know that Spanish and French historically developed from their parent language, Latin. English, German, Dutch, and other Scandinavian languages evolved from an earlier proto-Germanic language. Both Latin and proto-Germanic branched out from an even earlier language called Proto-Indo-European; it was spoken more than six thousand years ago and also gave birth to the languages spoken today in Greece, India, Iran, and Eastern Europe (Mallory and Adams 2006; McWhorter 2001).

Over thousands of years of adaptation, growth, and change, human language developed more along the lines of a **language continuum** rather than into distinct languages. In a language continuum, people who live near one another speak in a way that is mutually intelligible. The farther one travels, the more the language varies, but it tends to be at least partially mutually intelligible to those living nearby—if not 100 percent, then substantially. Although disrupted to some extent over centuries by migration and the strengthening of nation-states, language continuums still exist in many parts of the world. For instance, a strong language continuum has existed between Italy and France. If you were to walk from village to village beginning at the southern tip of Italy, travel northward, and then head northwest into France, you would find that people at either end of the journey would not be able to communicate with one another—their languages would be mutually unintelligible. But along the journey, the local residents of each village you pass through would be able to understand their neighbors in the nearby villages. Changes would be evident from location to location, but communication would be mutually intelligible.

An extensive language continuum exists in China as well. Though written Chinese is essentially the same throughout the country, there are thousands of local variations of spoken Chinese, most of which are mutually unintelligible. For example, speakers of Mandarin, Cantonese, Shanghainese, Fuzhounese, and Sichuanese cannot understand one another. Linguistically none is considered superior or inferior to another, but they do vary in prestige. Mandarin is the most widely spoken Chinese language variation. Called *Putonghua* ("the common language") or *Guoyu* ("the national language"), Mandarin is based on the local version of Chinese spoken in and around the national capital, Beijing. For centuries, imperial administrators who governed areas across China on behalf of the emperor in Beijing adopted Mandarin, so it became the norm associated with China's economic and political elite. After the Chinese civil war in 1949, the new government established *Putonghua* as the national standard for all media broadcasts as well as for instruction in all schools. As a result, regardless of the local variations of the Chinese language, today everyone learns *Putonghua* as a second language. But this is a political decision, not a statement of its linguistic superiority.

language continuum

The idea that variation in languages appears gradually over distance so that groups of people who live near one another speak in a way that is mutually intelligible.

Clearly, languages evolve as human groups use them, adapt them, or surrender them to more prevalent forms. The current age of globalization will provide even more opportunities for languages to meet and either mix or remain largely unchanged. This means that the field of historical linguistics will continue to trace dynamic aspects of language variation and change well into the future.

What Are the Effects of Globalization on Language?

The movement of people throughout human history has played a role in the way that languages change and develop. As people move, elements of vocabulary and grammar are loaned to and imposed on populations that come into contact. Languages are full of loanwords that have been adopted from others. The encounter of linguistic communities occurs with increasing rapidity in the contemporary era of globalization. Still, approximately seven thousand languages resound around the world today. A few have hundreds of millions of speakers. Most have a few thousand. However, globalization is consolidating language use among a small group of languages while threatening the extinction of thousands of others (Table 4.2).

DIMINISHING LANGUAGE DIVERSITY

The current pattern of increasing global interconnection threatens to diminish language diversity worldwide. In an earlier era of globalization, colonialism spread English, Spanish, Portuguese, French, Dutch, German, and Russian beyond Europe to people around the globe. Because these former colonial languages provide points of access to the current global economic and political system, many of them continue to expand today. In addition, increasing migration to urban centers often leads speakers of less widely used languages to assimilate and adopt the more widely used language. The more prominent languages—including the former colonial languages and other regional or national languages—dominate global media, including television, radio, print, and digital media. Through this dominance they are crowding out the less widely used languages and their speakers.

As a result of these dynamics, today the ten most prominent languages are spoken by more than 50 percent of the world's population. The top eighty-three languages account for 80 percent of humanity. The 3,500 least widely used languages, in total, account for only 0.2 percent of the world's language users (Harrison 2007). English has a unique position in the world at the moment, with as many as two billion speakers. Many of these are nonnative speakers who learn English as a second language because of its central role in universities, medicine,

TABLE 4.2
Top Twenty World Languages, 2014

LANGUAGE	NUMBER OF NATIVE SPEAKERS
1. Chinese	1.197 billion
2. Spanish	414 million
3. English	335 million
4. Hindi	260 million
5. Arabic	237 million
6. Portuguese	203 million
7. Bengali	193 million
8. Russian	167 million
9. Japanese	122 million
10. Javanese	84.3 million
11. Lahnda	82.6 million
12. German	78.2 million
13. Korean	77.2 million
14. French	75.0 million
15. Telugu	74.0 million
16. Marathi	71.8 million
17. Turkish	70.8 million
18. Tamil	68.8 million
19. Vietnamese	67.8 million
20. Urdu	63.9 million

Source: M. Paul Lewis, Gary F. Simons, and Charles D. Fennig (eds.). 2014. *Ethnologue: Languages of the World, Seventeenth edition.* Dallas, Texas: SIL International. Online version: www.ethnologue .com/17/ (accessed 4/17/15).

computing, entertainment, and intergovernmental relationships. English is currently a prestige language that provides effective access to international economic activity and political engagement.

HASTENING LANGUAGE LOSS

Linguistic anthropologists warn that as many as half of the seven thousand languages in the world today could be lost by the end of the twenty-first century. In 2005, 204 languages had fewer than ten speakers. Another 344 had fewer than one hundred speakers. Together, these 548 languages represent almost 10 percent of the world's languages. They have very little chance of survival and face almost certain language death. This is the outcome of **language loss**. On average, one

language loss

The extinction of languages that have very few speakers.

language is lost every ten days (Harrison 2007). The most rapid disappearances are in northern Australia, central South America, the Pacific Northwest of North America, and eastern Siberia; this group also includes the Native American languages spoken in Oklahoma and the southwestern United States.

Languages develop over time to enable human groups to adapt to a particular environment and to share with one another information that is essential to their local culture. When a language is lost, when it is crowded out by more widely used languages, we lose all of the bodies of information and local knowledge that had been developed—perhaps over thousands of years—by that community. Within a language is embedded rich knowledge about plants, animals, and medicines. Within a language is embedded a particular group's unique way of knowing the world and thinking and talking about human experience.

Language Revitalization. Most languages have never been written down. Does this surprise you? If you are a speaker of one of the more prominent languages, such as English, perhaps it does. As many of the less widely used languages face extinction, some groups are undertaking efforts to preserve them in written form.

Documenting a local language may involve years of work in a detailed and painstaking process that draws on all the basic skills of fieldwork and descriptive linguistics. One of the most extensive efforts to create written records of small languages is the work of a group called the Summer Institute of Linguistics (SIL). Formerly known as the Wycliff Bible Translators, SIL sends missionaries to the field, often to remote areas, to live with a community and create a written language in order to translate the Christian Bible into the local language.

Some linguistic anthropologists consider SIL's work to be controversial. They are concerned that the Christian nature of the project means that certain aspects of local culture—including indigenous religious beliefs, ritual language, songs, and art connected to local religion—are at risk of being ignored and extinguished. Other scholars acknowledge the significant data that would be lost if SIL translators were not doing the detailed work of documenting hundreds of local languages that are threatened with extinction in small communities worldwide. Despite this controversy, SIL has succeeded in producing a widely used compendium of all the world's languages called *Ethnologue*. Although it started with only forty entries in 1951 as a language guide for Christian missionaries, in 2014 *Ethnologue*'s seventeenth edition catalogued 7,106 languages (Lewis 2014).

Preserving Endangered Languages. Information technology is beginning to transform the ways in which linguistic anthropologists document and preserve endangered languages, creating new opportunities for revitalization. Consider the Native American Lakota language. Its approximately fifty

Globalization threatens the loss of many smaller local languages, and with them their local knowledge and ways of understanding the world. Ramona Dick is an elder in the Washoe tribe, which is based mainly in California and Oregon. As a child, she refused to be sent to a school where students were required to speak only English.

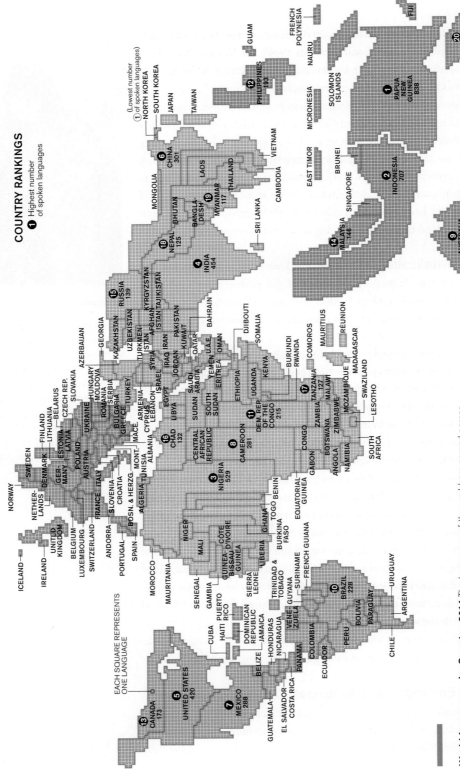

COUNTRY RANKINGS

① Highest number of spoken languages

① (Lowest number) of spoken languages

EACH SQUARE REPRESENTS ONE LANGUAGE

Country Rankings (from map labels):

- **①** PAPUA NEW GUINEA 838
- **②** INDONESIA 707
- **③** NIGERIA 529
- **④** INDIA 454
- **⑤** UNITED STATES 420
- **⑥** CHINA 301
- **⑦** MEXICO 288
- **⑧** CAMEROON 281
- **⑨** AUSTRALIA 244
- **⑩** BRAZIL 228
- **⑪** DEM. REP. OF THE CONGO 215
- **⑫** PHILIPPINES 193
- **⑬** CANADA 173
- **⑭** MALAYSIA 146
- **⑮** RUSSIA 139
- **⑯** CHAD 132
- **⑰** TANZANIA 127
- **⑱** NEPAL 125
- **⑲** MYANMAR 117
- **⑳** VANUATU 116

World Languages by Country, 2014 The languages of the world are spread across countries in ways that may surprise you. Take a moment to identify the twenty countries with the most language diversity and the country with the least language diversity.

Source: M. Paul Lewis, Gary F. Simons, and Charles D. Fennig (eds.). 2014. *Ethnologue: Languages of the World, Seventeenth edition*. Dallas, Texas: SIL International. Online version: www.ethnologue.com/17/ (accessed 4/17/15).

thousand speakers live primarily in tribal areas scattered across North and South Dakota, as well as in cities, towns, and rural areas across the United States. Their tribally owned lands are in some of the poorest U.S. counties. Few children learn Lakota today, threatening the language with eventual extinction. So the Lakota have placed a high priority on preserving their language and culture and increasing Lakota language use among young people. Linguists have been working to document the Lakota language by collecting and preserving language samples, cultural knowledge, and artifacts. Some have even done intensive immersion in the Lakota language. But limited resources, combined with the geographic dispersion of Lakota speakers, have inhibited these efforts.

Recently, a small local company, LiveAndTell, has been building an online digital platform for Lakota language preservation and instruction. Using participatory social media technology similar to that of YouTube and Flickr, LiveAndTell has been creating opportunities for Lakota speakers to collaborate, create, and share digital artifacts. Families are writing family stories and posting photos, audio recordings, videos, and online annotations. School research projects are being uploaded to community sites. In these ways, the dispersed Lakota language community is creating an online archive of the living language. For instance, one contributor posted a picture of a car and then tagged each part—steering wheel, mirror, tire, and so on—with the Lakota name and an audio file of its pronunciation. Entries like these provide detailed linguistic information that is not available in standard dictionaries and may never come to light in formal oral interviews with professional linguists (Arobba et al. 2010).

Humans are born with the ability to learn language. But exactly what we learn and the context in which we learn it vary widely. Languages change and grow, they are taught, debated, and contested. Humans are constantly adapting language to meet the needs of local communities and global interactions. And while today local languages are under increasing stress, the continuing diversity of human languages provides a vivid portrait of the dramatically different ways humans perceive, consider, and engage the world. As we have seen throughout this chapter, linguistic anthropologists are deeply engaged in the analysis and understanding of the role language plays in human life and in understanding the transitions and changes that are facing the human linguistic landscape in an era of increasing globalization.

Toolkit

Thinking Like an Anthropologist:
Language, Immigration, and U.S. Culture

As you encounter the complexities of language in daily life—communicating with a boyfriend or girlfriend, collaborating with classmates from other places, studying abroad, working with people in multinational corporations, debating immigration policy, or understanding gender in classroom dynamics—thinking like an anthropologist can help you better understand your own experiences and those of others. First, take a moment to review the questions we asked at the beginning of this chapter:

- **What is language and where does it come from?**
- **Can language shape our ways of thinking?**
- **How do systems of power intersect with language and communication?**
- **What are the effects of globalization on language?**

In our opening story, we considered how language has entered the immigration debates in Arizona. Now that you have been studying anthropology—and in this chapter, linguistic anthropology—how would you analyze the underlying issues at play in this debate? Why has language become such a hot-button issue in U.S. politics? How is English intertwined with notions of American identity, class, and belonging? The long-held model of incorporating new immigrants into U.S. culture—the melting pot that blends everyone's diversity into one big stew—now competes with a salad bowl metaphor in which immigrants don't blend in completely but contribute their unique diversity to a multicultural salad. This new model has encountered resistance, particularly from people who fear a fragmentation of U.S. culture.

Language use has become symbolic of these larger debates. Studies consistently show that the children of immigrants grow up speaking English as their first language, not the language of their parents' country of origin (Portes, Fernandez-Kelly, and Haller 2009). Yet the debate over language instruction in education continues. Along with Arizona's new immigration law, the Arizona Department of Education has instituted new policies for bilingual education programs. In 2010, fully 150,000 of the state's 1.2 million public school students were categorized as English Language Learners—a long-term pattern. How to best educate those students has been a topic of heated debate for years. In the 1990s, Arizona recruited thousands of bilingual teachers to lead bilingual classes for students who may have grown up speaking Spanish at home. Many of the new teachers were recruited from Latin America, and their first language was Spanish. Then, in 2000, Arizona voters passed a referendum mandating that instruction of nonnative English speakers be in English only. The 2010 policy changes adopted new fluency standards for teachers, focusing on pronunciation and writing. Teachers who were unable to meet the new standards were removed from the classrooms of nonnative English speakers (Jordan 2010).

The Arizona education debates reveal the way that language functions as more than a system of symbols that enable people to communicate. Language is also a key cultural arena in which norms are established, values are promoted, and relationships of power are negotiated.

Key Terms

language (p. 95)

productivity (p. 97)

displacement (p. 97)

descriptive linguistics (p. 98)

phonemes (p. 98)

phonology (p. 98)

morphemes (p. 98)

morphology (p. 98)

syntax (p. 99)

grammar (p. 99)

kinesics (p. 99)

paralanguage (p. 99)

Sapir-Whorf hypothesis (p. 100)

lexicon (p. 101)

focal vocabulary (p. 101)

sociolinguistics (p. 102)

dialect (p. 106)

prestige language (p. 106)

code switching (p. 107)

historical linguistics (p. 109)

language continuum (p. 110)

language loss (p. 112)

Part 2

What lies beneath the surface of any beautiful scene? The project of anthropology includes unmasking the structures of power—the deep complexities of how humans organize themselves in groups. In Part 2 we will explore structures of race, ethnicity, gender, sexuality, and kinship in order to help you develop the analytical tools to see more deeply, navigate more carefully, and engage more fully the world around you. Here, children ↓ play soccer in the street at La Boca, Buenos Aires, Argentina.

Unmasking the Structures of Power

Chapter 5
Race and Racism

On August 29, 2005, Hurricane Katrina slammed into the Louisiana coast. The U.S. population watched their television sets in horror as the storm surge breached the New Orleans levee system and water flooded into the city's urban center, engulfing homes, businesses, and churches. Following the storm, news broadcasts showed residents wading through fetid water to find food, Coast Guard helicopters rescuing stranded residents from rooftops, and tens of thousands of desperate people—including children, the elderly, and the disabled—begging to be rescued from the Superdome and Convention Center, which had been designated the shelter of last resort but lacked food, water, and working bathrooms. The U.S. government, apparently crippled in its disaster response, took days to deliver emergency aid. More than one hundred countries offered assistance as the world watched, stunned by scenes more commonly associated with a developing country in Africa or Asia.

Is there really any such thing as a "natural disaster"? New Orleans neighborhood devastated by flooding after Hurricane Katrina.

When Katrina struck the coast, the storm center actually missed New Orleans. Yet heavy rain and storm surge overwhelmed the city's aged pumping system, and 80 percent of the city flooded when the levees broke. The city's poor—overwhelmingly African American—were the most severely affected and largely had to fend for themselves. Because the government was unprepared and slow to respond, more than half the population was displaced from New Orleans. The city's population of 454,000 in 2005 plummeted to 210,000 a year later (Elliot 2009), and the proportion of African American residents, 68 percent before Katrina, only rebounded to 60 percent by 2010. By mid-2011 the total population had only recovered to 360,740 (U.S. Census Bureau 2013).

Anthropologist and geographer Neil Smith makes the point that "there is no such thing as a natural disaster." Hurricanes, tsunamis, earthquakes, droughts, and volcanic eruptions are all natural events. Whether they become a disaster, however, depends on social factors: location, vulnerability of the population, government preparedness, effectiveness of the response, and sustained reconstruction efforts. The difference between who lives and who dies in a natural event is largely determined by social inequality. For instance, rising sea levels related to climate change are making cities such as Venice, Dacca (Bangladesh), and New Orleans especially vulnerable to floods; but the impact on certain people in those places will be determined by racial hierarchies and income stratification (Smith 2006).

Is it possible to view the events around Hurricane Katrina and New Orleans through the lens of race? Race and racism are incredibly difficult topics of conversation in U.S. culture, whether we are in a classroom, a religious community, a hospital, or the halls of Congress. How do we create opportunities to explore ideas of race and the way those ideas shape our lives and culture? In a country that likes to think of itself as color-blind, how do we as anthropologists make sense of the continuing inequality in income, wealth, education, access to health care, and incarceration rates that breaks so clearly along color lines (Shanklin 1998)?

Anthropologists view race as a framework of categories created to divide the human population. Western Europeans originally developed this framework as part of their global expansion beginning in the 1400s (Sanjek 1994). As they encountered, mapped, and colonized people in Africa, Asia, the Pacific, and the Americas, Europeans placed them into an "international hierarchy of races, colors, religions and cultures" (Trouillot 1994, 146). The exact labels and expressions have varied over time and place as colonial powers engaged with local cultures and confronted local resistance. But the underlying project—to stratify people into groups based on assumptions of natural differences in intelligence, attractiveness, capacity for civilization, and fundamental worth in relation to people of European descent—has been remarkably consistent (Mullings 2005a).

As we will explore in this chapter, today anthropologists find no scientific basis for classifications of race. Genetically there is only one race—the human race, with all its apparent diversity. Yet despite consistent efforts over the last century by anthropologists and others to counter the inaccurate belief that races are biologically real, race has remained a powerful framework through which many people see human diversity and through which those in power organize the distribution of privileges and resources. Race—which is scientifically not real—has become culturally real in the pervasive racism found in many parts of the globe, including the United States.

Over the past five hundred years, race as a way of organizing the world has been put to destructive use, wreaking an enormous toll on both its victims and its proponents. Race and racism have justified the conquest, enslavement, forced transportation, and economic and political domination of some humans by others for more than five centuries. Today race and racism have become so integral to patterns of human relations in many parts of the world that inherited racial categories may seem to be natural and the inequality built on racism may seem to represent "real" differences among "real" races.

In this chapter we will critique arguments for the existence of discrete biological human groups called "races." We will consider the roots of race and racism in the European colonial past and their expression in various places today. We will examine the construction of race in the United States over the past four hundred years and the way race and racism continue to shape U.S. culture. In particular, we will consider the following questions:

- **Do biologically separate races exist?**
- **How is race constructed around the world?**
- **How is race constructed in the United States?**
- **What is racism?**

We will examine **race** as a flawed system of classification, created and re-created over time, that uses certain physical characteristics (such as skin color, hair texture, eye shape, and eye color) to divide the human population into a few supposedly discrete biological groups and attribute to them unique combinations of physical ability, mental capacity, personality traits, cultural patterns, and capacity for civilization. Drawing on anthropological research, we will see, however, that racial categories have no biological basis. We might even say that races, as a biological concept, do not exist. The danger in this statement about biological race is that it may lead us to the mistaken conclusion that race does not exist. On the contrary, race has very real consequences.

Race is a deeply influential system of thinking that affects people and institutions. Over time, imagined categories of race have shaped our cultural institutions—schools, places of worship, media, political parties, economic practices—and have organized the allocation of wealth, power, and privilege at

race
A flawed system of classification, with no biological basis, that uses certain physical characteristics to divide the human population into supposedly discrete groups.

all levels of society. Race has served to create and justify patterns of power and inequality within cultures worldwide, and many people have learned to see those patterns as normal and reasonable. So in this chapter we will also examine **racism**: individuals' thoughts and actions, as well as institutional patterns and policies, that create or reproduce unequal access to power, privilege, resources, and opportunities based on imagined differences among groups (Omi and Winant 1994).

By the end of the chapter you will have the anthropological tools to understand not only the flaws in arguments for biologically discrete races, but also the history and current expressions of race and racism globally and in the United States. You will be prepared to apply those tools, if you so choose, to engaging in efforts against racism on your college campus, in your community, and throughout the world.

Do Biologically Separate Races Exist?

Many of us were enculturated to believe that "race" refers to distinct physical characteristics that mark individuals as clearly belonging in one group and not in another. However, anthropologists see race very differently. Contemporary studies of human genetics reveal no biologically distinct human groups. We can state this with certainty despite centuries of scientific effort to prove the existence

of distinct biological races, and despite widespread popular belief that different races exist. In fact, humans are almost identical, sharing more than 99.9 percent of our DNA. The small differences that do exist are not distributed in any way that would correspond with popular or scientific notions of separate races. Race is not fixed in nature but, as we will explore later in this chapter, is created, perpetuated, and changed by people through individual and collective action.

First, however, let's explore some of the science behind race.

FUZZY BOUNDARIES IN A WELL-INTEGRATED GENE POOL

Some physical anthropologists have compared modern humans to a little village that has grown very quickly. Throughout the short 200,000-year history of modern humans, we have basically been functioning as one enormous, interconnected gene pool, swapping genetic material back and forth (by interbreeding) quite freely within the village. Over the years, our family trees have intersected again and again.

If you trace your own family back for thirty generations—parents to grandparents to great-grandparents, and so on—you will find that in just over a thousand years you have accumulated one billion relatives. So it is not hard to imagine the myriad and unpredictable exchanges of genetic material among that large a group. Now extend your family tree back one hundred thousand years—the time it has taken for a few small groups of humans to migrate out of Africa and populate the entire planet. It is easy to imagine the billions of times this growing population has exchanged genetic material. Such deep integration of the human

What can you know about a person's genetic makeup based on her (or his) outward appearance? Variations of skin color or other visible characteristics often associated with race are shaped by less than 0.1 percent of our genetic code. Contrary to certain stereotypes, they do not predict anything else about a person's genetic makeup, physical or mental capabilities, culture, or personality.

Do Biologically Separate Races Exist? **125**

gene pool means that no clear and absolute genetic lines can be drawn to separate people into distinct, biologically discrete, "racial" populations.

As a result of this gene flow, human variation changes gradually over geographic space in a continuum (what physical anthropologists refer to as a cline), not by abrupt shifts or clearly marked groups. Even skin color, perhaps most frequently imagined to demarcate separate races, in fact varies so gradually over geographic space that there are no clear boundaries between one population and another, nor color groupings that distinguish one population from another. If you flew from western Africa to Russia, you would notice distinct variations in physical human form between the population where you boarded the plane and the population where you disembarked. But if you walked from western Africa to Russia, there would never be a point along the way where you would be able to stop and say that the people on one side of the road are of one race and the people on the other side are of a different race.

Perhaps more surprising, a person who starts walking in western Africa may have more in common genetically with someone at the end of her trek in Russia than she does with a neighbor at home. This seems hard to imagine because we have been enculturated to believe that a very small number of traits—including skin color, hair texture, and eye color and shape—can serve to categorize people into distinct groups and predict larger genetic patterns. This is a flawed assumption. The human gene pool continues to be highly integrated. Genetic variations such as skin color, expressed in an individual's external appearance, are only 0.1 percent of that person's genetic code; they do not predict anything else about his or her genetic makeup. People in a particular region of the world whose ancestors inhabited that area for an extended period may have some increased probability of genetic similarity because of the greater probability of swapping genetic material with those geographically closer. But group boundaries are fuzzy and porous. People move and genes flow. Ultimately, group genetic probabilities cannot predict any one individual's reality.

Think about human physical variation as you would the grades you earn in school. Teachers often assign grades on a continuum from 0 to 100. Some teachers use letter grades instead. We may choose to call a 79 a C and an 80 a B. These are decisions based on convenience or the need to differentiate student success. Likewise, dividing people into separate races along the continuum of human genetic diversity is not based in nature but in human choices.

THE WILD GOOSE CHASE: LINKING PHENOTYPE TO GENOTYPE

In considering human physical diversity, physical anthropologists distinguish between genotype and phenotype. **Genotype** refers to the inherited genetic factors that provide a framework for an organism's physical form; these factors

genotype
The inherited genetic factors that provide the framework for an organism's physical form.

constitute the total genetic endowment that the organism, in turn, can pass down to its descendants. In contrast, **phenotype** refers to the way genes are expressed in an organism's physical form (both visible and invisible) as a result of the interaction of genotype with environmental factors, such as nutrition, disease, and stress.

The widespread belief that certain phenotypes such as skin color are linked to physical and mental capabilities, personality types, or cultural patterns is incorrect but deeply ingrained and difficult to reimagine.

As individuals, we may make snap judgments based on phenotypical traits that we erroneously assume indicate a person's "race"; with a quick glance we may think we know something significant about that individual. On the basis of phenotype alone, we may consider someone to be smarter, faster, stronger, safe or dangerous, better at business, better at math, a better dancer or singer, more prone to alcoholism, more artistic, more susceptible to certain diseases, a better lover. You might call this the "White Men Can't Jump" or "Asians Are Better at Math" way of thinking about race and genes. We assume that we can know something significant about a person's genetic makeup just by looking at her phenotype. But can we really tell anything about someone from the way he or she looks?

A relatively small number of genes control the traits frequently used today to distinguish one "race" from another—skin color, eye shape, or hair texture. As a result, in the short history of modern humans these genes have been able to change rapidly in response to the environment. For example, as humans moved out of Africa and across the globe into a wide variety of physical environments, traits such as skin color, shaped by a relatively small cluster of genes, were more susceptible to environmental pressures and adapted more quickly. In contrast, traits such as intelligence, athletic or artistic ability, and social skills appear to be shaped by complex combinations of thousands or tens of thousands of genes, so they have been much less susceptible to environmental pressures. Adaptations in skin color were not accompanied by adaptations in, say, intelligence, musical ability, or physical ability. It is important to note that genetic research consistently shows that the genes that influence skin color, eye shape, or hair texture are not linked to any other genes and cannot predict anything about the rest of a person's underlying genotype (Mukhopadhyay, Henze, and Moses 2007).

Jonathan Marks, a leading physical anthropologist, compares the problem of sorting people into races with the problem children might have in sorting blocks into categories. Imagine that you start with a pile of blocks and ask a group of children to sort them into "large" and "small." They might agree on some—the largest and the smallest. But others in between might be harder to classify. "The fact that the blocks can be sorted into the categories given, however, does not imply that there are two kinds of blocks in the universe, large and small—and

phenotype

The way genes are expressed in an organism's physical form as a result of genotype interaction with environmental factors.

that the child has uncovered a transcendent pattern in the sizing of the blocks. It simply means that if categories are given, they can be imposed upon the blocks" (Marks 1995, 159).

What if you asked the children to sort instead by color or to distinguish among wooden, metal, and plastic blocks? What about blocks with smooth sides or grooved sides? The children could sort the blocks into any of these categories. But if you didn't link the multiple characteristics of the blocks—all the red blocks wooden, or all the plastic blocks grooved—then the children would end up with a completely different arrangement of blocks depending on whatever categories they arbitrarily decided to sort for.

The same is true for humans and the concept of race. If you give people a limited range of categories for skin color groups, they will be able to place many people into these categories. Some individuals who lie in the boundaries may be more difficult to categorize. But would this exercise uncover some deep, intrinsic pattern about humans? No, because traits like skin color are not linked to any other particular set of genes and cannot serve to predict anything else about the underlying genotype.

How Is Race Constructed around the World?

Racial categories are human constructs; they are not found in nature. Yet they have become so deeply internalized that they feel natural and provide one of the most powerful frameworks through which we experience the world (Mukhopadhyay, Henze, and Moses 2007). Anthropologists examine race and racism on a global scale and thus from different angles, identifying their similarities and variations and, in the process, revealing the ways those concepts have evolved and might be changed through individual and collective action.

RACE AND THE LEGACY OF COLONIALISM

colonialism

The practice by which a nation-state extends political, economic, and military power beyond its own borders over an extended period of time to secure access to raw materials, cheap labor, and markets in other countries or regions.

Contemporary global expressions of race and racism are deeply rooted in the systems of classification that western Europeans created as they expanded their colonial empires into Africa, Asia, the Pacific, and the Americas beginning in the 1400s. **Colonialism** became the centerpiece of European global economic activity, combining economic, military, and political control of people and places to fuel Europe's economic expansion and enhance the European position in the emerging global economy (see Chapter 11). The classification of people based on phenotype, particularly skin color, became the key framework for creating a hierarchy of races—with Europeans at the top—that linked people's looks with assumptions about their intelligence, physical abilities, capacity for culture, and basic worth. Eventually this framework served to justify colonial conquests, the trans-Atlantic slave trade, and the eradication of much of the indigenous population of the Americas (Gregory and Sanjek 1994).

Taking a global perspective, anthropologists often refer to "racisms" in the plural, reflecting the varieties of ways race has been constructed among people in different places. Locally, racisms and systems of racial classification are complex frameworks built out of the encounter of colonialism with local cultural patterns, global migration, and specific movements of resistance.

Racial frameworks and systems of racism have changed significantly over the last century. After World War II, colonial-era racisms shifted as national liberation movements struggled to end occupations by foreign powers. In addition, in this postcolonial period, key internal struggles challenged long-term patterns of race and racial discrimination. Notably, the antiapartheid movement in South Africa resisted dominant white rule, eventually reversing decades of legal structural discrimination and violence. The civil rights movement challenged more than three hundred years of race-based inequality in the United States. Today globalization has brought about new experiences of race and racism.

Indeed, in today's global world, flexible accumulation produces new relationships between corporations and workers; the migration of workers within countries and across national borders yields new racial formations; and time-space compression enhances communication tools that can be employed to resist old hierarchies while also perpetuating old racial frameworks on a global scale. Racisms today, though rooted in similar historic realities, are shifting as they intersect with other systems of power, whether those are ethnicity, gender, sexuality, kinship, or class (Mullings 2005b). The exact expression of these constructs varies from culture to culture and place to place.

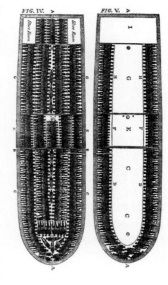

Diagram of a slave ship from the Atlantic slave trade.

Race, Class, and Gender, and Hundreds of Races in Brazil.

Brazil provides a good location to explore the cultural construction of race and the application of ideas of race to the creation of stratification. The United States and Brazil are today the two largest multiracial countries in the Western Hemisphere, although they have traveled two very different paths in framing racial identities and hierarchies. By the time Brazil outlawed slavery in 1888, the country had the largest African population in the New World. This situation reflected the grim fact that during and after Brazil's time as a colony of Portugal (1500–1815), 40 percent of all Africans in the Atlantic slave trade were brought to Brazil to work on Portuguese plantations and mines. Brazil was the last country in the Americas to outlaw slavery—a full generation after the U.S. Emancipation Proclamation in 1863.

Today Brazilians describe the human physical diversity called "race" in great detail. Although Brazil's system of racial classification is color-coded, its color

MAP 5.1
Brazil

miscegenation
A demeaning historical term for interracial marriage.

terminology is far more expansive, encompassing hundreds of categories (Freyre 1933; Harris 1964, 1970). Terms include *alva* (pure white), *alva-escuro* (off-white), *alva-rosada* (pinkish white), *branca* (white), *clara* (light), *branca morena* (darkish white), *branca suja* (dirty white), *café* (coffee colored), *café com leite* (coffee with milk), *canela* (cinnamon), *preta* (black), and *pretinha* (lighter black) (Fluehr-Lobban 2006). Race categories follow along a nuanced continuum of appearance rather than a few rigid categories such as those used in the United States.

Brazil's population of Europeans, Africans, and indigenous people has had a long history of interracial mixing. The Portuguese colonial government promoted assimilation and did not bar **miscegenation**—that is, interracial marriage. As a result, many single Portuguese men who settled in Brazil chose to intermarry. Nor has Brazil applied the rule of hypodescent—the "one drop of blood" rule—that in the United States meant that having even one black ancestor out of many could mark an individual as black (see "The Rule of Hypodescent" below). As a result, a family may include children who are categorized as various shades of white, brown, and black.

Race in Brazil is not solely a function of skin color. In fact, race intersects closely with class—including land ownership, wealth, and education—in determining social status. Because of the power of class, a Brazilian's racial position can be modified by his or her level of affluence. Affluence can shift a Brazilian's racial identity in spite of skin color and other supposedly "racial" markers (Walker 2002).

Some scholars refer to Brazil as a "racial democracy" and extol the nation as an exceptional example of racial harmony (Freyre [1933] 1944; Harris 1964; and Kottak 2006). Brazil's government abolished the use of racial categories in the 1930s and constitutionally banned racism in 1951. The complex and fluid color classifications—the absence of a clear color line between black and white—are seen as a sign of tolerance. In addition, the incorporation of key African cultural practices (including carnival, samba, Candomblé religious practices, capoeira, and specific cuisine) as symbols of the Brazilian nation is often cited as supporting evidence for the racial democracy thesis (Downey 2005).

Other scholars have noted that despite the appearance of racial democracy, inequality exists in almost every area of Brazilian life and is directly linked to color. Darker-skinned Brazilians face higher levels of exclusion and injustice, including a systemic correlation between color and economics. Most of the poor are Afro-Brazilians. Most of the rich are white. Racial democracy may instead be simply a myth that serves as a cornerstone of Brazil's national denial of the existence of racism (Harrison 2002b, 160).

In *Laughter Out of Place* (2003), anthropologist Donna Goldstein writes about working poor women from the bleak favela (shantytown), ironically named Felicidade Eterna ("eternal happiness"), who support their families as domestic workers in the homes of middle-class Brazilian families in the affluent sections of

Rio de Janeiro. Gloria, poor and dark skinned, raising fourteen children, including nine of her own, works as a domestic servant, shopping, cooking, and cleaning. She earns five dollars a day—just enough to feed herself and her family. The pay is off the books, so she has no legal labor protections, no insurance, and no pension. Goldstein links the contemporary culture of domestic work, particularly the employer–domestic servant relationships, to the historic institution of slavery in Brazil. Middle-class families enjoy a kind of learned helplessness similar to that of the slave owner—allowing their workers to do the dirty, manual chores. The employer–domestic servant relationship, like the owner–slave relationship, is characterized by domination, strict rules, and social separation.

How do Brazil's marginalized and oppressed people make sense of their lives—lives overburdened with poverty, violence, and work at the bottom of a global hierarchy of race, class, and gender; yet lives that also display dignity and resilience? Goldstein explores the role of laughter and humor as means to cope with persistent brutality. She particularly notes a humor that recognizes life's absurdities and ironies and provides perspective to a sense of injustice. She recalls, for instance, the awkwardness of "laughter out of place," as domestic workers and employers laugh at different times and for different reasons when they watch the local soap operas that dramatize middle-class Brazilian life. The distinctive life experiences of worker and employer create vastly different viewing experiences, casting the televised dramas and traumas of the Brazilian middle class in sharp contrast to the survival needs of the domestic workers living in the favela—a contrast so absurd as to evoke laughter out of place.

How Is Race Constructed in the United States?

Race is perhaps the most significant means used to mark difference in U.S. culture. References to it can be found on census forms, school applications, and birth certificates, as well as in the media and casual conversation. Race is also a key framework that shapes the allocation of power, privilege, rewards, and status, and infuses all of our political, economic, religious, recreational, educational, and cultural institutions (Smedley 1993). Yet it is one of the least discussed topics in U.S. culture and one of most difficult to explore, even in anthropology. How do we begin to engage this difficult dialogue?

How can anthropology help make sense of race as you experience it in the classroom, your workplace, your family, and today's rapidly globalizing world? Because race is not biologically fixed, we must instead examine the process through which race has been—and still is being—constructed in the United States.

RACE AND THE U.S. CENSUS

The U.S. Census, taken every ten years since 1790, provides a fascinating window into the changing conception of "race." The 1850 census had three categories: White, Black, and Mulatto. Mulatto referred to people of mixed race. The 1870 census expanded to five categories to incorporate new immigrants from China and to count the Native American population: White, Black, Mulatto, Chinese, and Indian (Native American). Respondents did not identify their own race; instead, census workers assigned them to a racial category based on their appearance.

By 1940, the census form had eight categories, eliminating the option for mixed race and adding more categories from Asia, including Hindu, a religion: White, Negro, Indian, Chinese, Japanese, Filipino, Hindu, and Korean. The 2010 census form included fourteen separate "race" boxes. Respondents could check one, many, or all of them.

This brief look at changes in the census form provides clear indications that race has been and still is an evolving human construction. The changing race categories do not reflect a change in human genotype or phenotype, but in how the government organizes the diversity of people within its borders. The census construction of race reflects the U.S. government's power to establish certain categories and apply those categories to make decisions about government resources.

Borderlands where racial categories are under debate provide a glimpse of the nation's changing racial past and future. For instance, increased immigration

What can changes in the U.S. census form tell us about shifting concepts of race? Here, comparable parts of the United States Census Questionnaire, 1870, and the United States Census Questionnaire, 2010.

from Latin America, Asia, the Pacific Islands, and the Middle East has complicated the census form and discussions about race in the United States. Note the rapid expansion of options in the census for people from Asia.

The position of Hispanics is also in flux. Beginning with the 2000 census, for instance, "Hispanic" was removed from the race question. In effect, Spanish/Hispanic/Latino became a unique ethnic group with its own separate question. Unlike others—for example, Irish, Welsh, Italians, or Greeks—the census form now suggests that Hispanics are the only U.S. ethnic group that could be of any race. It remains to be determined whether U.S. culture will move beyond the underlying black/white dichotomy, or whether the current flux is simply a reorganizing of new immigrants into that dichotomy (Rodriguez 2000).

HISTORY OF U.S. RACIAL CATEGORIES: CONSTRUCTING WHITENESS

The U.S. racial system developed in the vortex of slavery and the European conquest of indigenous people of the North American continent. From its origins, American colonial life was built on the importation of indentured workers from Europe and slaves from Africa, along with the expropriation of land from Native Americans. Intensive agricultural work, particularly in the U.S. South, required a reliable and plentiful labor supply. Native Americans suffered quick and brutal extermination in other parts of the Americas through forced labor, violence, and disease, but they largely resisted forced labor in the North American colonies. European indentured laborers were in short supply. So imported African slaves

Left: An advertisement for a slave auction, June 23, 1768. *Right:* A slave family picking cotton in the fields near Savannah, Georgia, ca. 1860s.

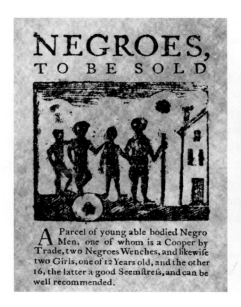

became the preferred workforce. Over three hundred years, millions were forcibly transported to the Americas through the trans-Atlantic slave trade.

The unique slave system that emerged relied not only on the legal right of landholders to enslave but also on the widespread acceptance of **white supremacy**—the belief that nonwhites were biologically different, intellectually inferior, and not fully human in a spiritual sense. Reflecting these ideas, the U.S. Census from 1790 to 1860 counted slaves as only three-fifths of a person. Only in 1868 did the Fourteenth Amendment to the U.S. Constitution put an end to this practice. Subsequently, the 1870 census was the first to count all people as whole people.

The term *white* was itself a construction, first appearing in a public document in reference to a separate race only in 1691 in Virginia. Colonial laws created and rigidly regulated **whiteness**, establishing sharp boundaries of who was white and who was not. Intermarriage was outlawed—a practice that the U.S. Supreme Court did not overturn until 1967. Mixing was punished by the loss of white status.

Anthropologist Pem Buck's *Worked to the Bone* (2001) documents the ways in which white privilege was invented in early 1700s Virginia to prevent rebellion among poor landless whites who were beginning to join with enslaved African workers against the European economic elite. Elites introduced a set of privileges reserved for whites—the right to own a gun, livestock, and land; the right to obtain freedom at the end of indenture; the right to discipline blacks; and eventually the right to vote. These legal privileges were designed to ensure the cooperation of poor working whites and white indentured servants, who together constituted a majority of the early colonial populations, and to drive a wedge between the European and African laborers who had much in common.

Efforts to eliminate slavery spread rapidly but unevenly after the American Revolution (1775–83), culminating in the Civil War (1861–65) and President Abraham Lincoln's 1863 Emancipation Proclamation. Yet long-established patterns of unequal treatment and entrenched ideas of white racial superiority persisted, providing the foundation for continuing inequality, discrimination, and white dominance. **Jim Crow** segregation laws throughout the South legally enforced the boundaries between whites and blacks in housing, education, voting rights, property ownership, and access to public services such as transportation, bathrooms, and water fountains. Vigilante white-supremacist groups such as the Ku Klux Klan, founded in 1866, emerged to enforce through violence and terror what they considered to be the natural racial order. Especially in the South, lynchings became a widespread means to intimidate blacks, enforce segregation, and ensure behavior that whites considered normal and appropriate. Between 1870 and the 1940s, thousands of African American men and women were tortured and brutally murdered (Brundage 1993).

white supremacy

The belief that whites are biologically different from and superior to people of other races.

whiteness

A culturally constructed concept originating in 1691 Virginia designed to establish clear boundaries of who is white and who is not, a process central to the formation of U.S. racial stratification.

Jim Crow

Laws implemented after the U.S. Civil War to legally enforce segregation, particularly in the South, after the end of slavery.

A segregated summer social event—an annual barbecue—on an Alabama plantation, ca. 1935.

THE RULE OF HYPODESCENT

Imposition of the rule of hypodescent has been key to drawing and maintaining boundaries between the races since the days of slavery, when one single drop of "black blood"—that is, one African ancestor—constituted blackness. *Hypo* literally means "lower." Through **hypodescent** the race of children of mixed marriages is assigned to the lower or subordinate category of the two parents—or, in many cases, the subordinate category of any one of many ancestors.

Hypodescent rules were enshrined in the laws of many U.S. states and backed by the U.S. Supreme Court. Consider the 1982 court case of Susie Phipps. Born looking "white," Phipps grew up assuming she was white. But when she requested a copy of her birth certificate in 1977, she found herself listed as "colored." A 1970 Louisiana law mandated that a person be designated black if his or her ancestry was one-thirty-second black—referring to any one of the thirty-two most recent ancestors. (This was an improvement over previous state hypodescent law, which set the threshold at one in sixty-four.) Phipps lost a court challenge to this categorization because the state produced evidence that she was three-thirty-seconds black—more than enough to satisfy the 1970 legal standard. Both the Louisiana Supreme Court and the U.S. Supreme Court refused to review the lower court's ruling and allowed the decision to stand (Jaynes 1982; Fluehr-Lobban 2006). Phipps's case reveals the process through which U.S. categories of race have been created and the tortured logic employed to assign individuals to particular racial categories. Also on full display are (1) the central role of the state in establishing and maintaining boundaries between the races it has constructed, and (2) the

hypodescent

Sometimes called the "one drop of blood rule"; the assignment of children of racially "mixed" unions to the subordinate group.

powerful influence of the legacies of slavery and past discrimination on the present (Omi and Winant 1994).

Although hypodescent is no longer enforced in law, it is still widely practiced in U.S. culture. A prominent contemporary example would be U.S. president Barack Obama. His mother was a white woman from Kansas (she was also an anthropologist). His father was from Kenya in East Africa. They met as students in Hawaii, where Obama was born. Though 50 percent of his genes came from his father and 50 percent from his mother, the concept of hypodescent still shapes the way some people regard Obama's race.

RACE AND IMMIGRATION

For more than four centuries, the boundaries of whiteness in the United States have been carefully guarded, and a group's admission to that category has been rare and difficult. When the nation encountered diverse immigration from Asia and eastern and southern Europe beginning in the nineteenth century, debate raged about where the newcomers fit: Were the Chinese white? Were the Irish, Germans, Greeks, Italians, eastern Europeans, Jews, and Catholics really white, or were they biologically distinct from earlier immigrants from England, France, and the Nordic countries?

nativism

The favoring of certain long-term inhabitants over new immigrants.

eugenics

A pseudoscience attempting to scientifically prove the existence of separate human races to improve the population's genetic composition by favoring some races over others.

The struggle to guard the boundaries of whiteness has been particularly intense at certain times, generating passionate debate and sparking a sentiment of **nativism**—that is, the desire to favor native inhabitants over new immigrants. Nativists in the nineteenth century fought particularly hard to preserve the so-called racial purity of the nation's Anglo-Saxon origins. Riots, violence, discrimination, and anti-immigrant sentiment were commonplace. In the 1800s a pseudoscience arose, called **eugenics**, that attempted to use scientific methodologies to prove the existence of separate races and, in particular, the superiority of the white "race" and the inferiority of all nonwhites.

Chinese, Irish, and Other Immigrants: What Race?

Chinese immigrants first arrived in large numbers in the 1850s to work in California's gold mines, on its farms, and in railroad construction. Because they constituted the first group of Asians to come to this country, other residents struggled to place them in the U.S. racial hierarchy. European immigrant laborers saw the Chinese as competitors for jobs and branded them the Yellow Peril—a "race" that could not be trusted. Federal and state governments treated the Chinese immigrants ambivalently at best and often with great hostility.

Today most people consider Irish, Italians, Greeks, and eastern Europeans to be white, but none of these groups were received as white when they first came to the United States. They initially faced discrimination, prejudice, and exclusion because they were not Anglo-Saxon Protestants. When the Irish immigrants

arrived in the 1840s and 1850s, they were poor, rural, Catholic, landless, and fleeing intense poverty and disease as a result of the Irish potato famine. Thus, they were seen as an inferior race (Ignatiev 1995).

Confronted with increasing immigration and diversity in the nineteenth and early twentieth centuries, the U.S. legal and political systems struggled for consistent definitions of who was white and who was not. Consider the 1923 U.S. Supreme Court case in which Bhagat Singh Thind, an upper-class Sikh immigrant from India, applied for U.S. citizenship. Despite the 1790 U.S. law limiting the right to naturalization (that is, becoming a citizen) to whites, Thind argued that as a part of the original "Aryan" or Caucasian race, he was white. Even though the justices agreed with his claim of Aryan or Caucasian ancestry, the Court found that Thind was not white as used in "common speech, to be interpreted in accordance with the understanding of the common man" (Lopez 2006, 66). Popular anti-immigrant and nativist sentiment had overcome even the pseudoscience of race prevalent at the time.

How exactly did the Irish, the Italians, and the eastern European Jews become "white"? Their increasing numbers, their intermarriage with members of other white groups, and their upward class mobility created conditions for inclusion in the white category. Karen Brodkin's book *How the Jews Became White Folks* (1998) offers additional insights into the whitening process of immigrants after World War II. At that time, the U.S. economy was emerging virtually unscathed

A 1903 cartoon from the magazine *Judge* illustrates anti-immigrant sentiment at the turn of the twentieth century. A tide of newcomers—Riff Raff Immigration—representing the criminal element of other countries washes up on American shores, to the displeasure of Uncle Sam, presenting a "danger" to American ideas and institutions.

from the war's destruction, unlike its competitors in Europe and Japan. And rapid growth in the U.S. economy was supporting an unparalleled expansion of the nation's middle class. Brodkin suggests that an extensive government program to reintegrate soldiers after the war paved the road to upward mobility for many U.S. citizens.

Indeed, the GI Bill of Rights provided a wide array of programs to sixteen million soldiers, who were primarily white and male. The benefits included preferential hiring, financial support during the job search, small business loans, subsidized home mortgages, and educational benefits that included college tuition and living expenses. Newly trained and educated veterans quickly filled the needs of the growing U.S. economy for professionals, technicians, and managers—jobs that offered opportunities for upward mobility and, thus, racial mobility. These educational opportunities, the dramatic rise in home ownership, and the expansion of new corporate jobs dramatically enlarged the U.S. middle class. The simultaneous elevation of living standards and financial assets of both native whites and new European immigrants softened earlier boundaries of whiteness and allowed the status of many immigrants to shift from racially nonwhite to ethnic white.

Middle Easterners. Racial categories continue to be created and contested in the United States today. Where, for example, do people from the Middle East fit? Are Saudis, Iranians, Afghanis, Kurds, Syrians, Turks, and Egyptians "white," African American, or Asian? The shifting characterization of people from the Middle East—especially after the terrorist attacks of September 11, 2001—reveals another border region in the race debate and demonstrates how conceptions of race in the United States are constantly changing.

In a study of fourth graders in Brooklyn, New York, after the September 11 attacks, Maria Kromidas (2004) explores the way nine-year-old children engage issues of race, religion, and region to create racial categories, assign certain people (both children and adults) to them, and enforce those boundaries through language, humor, and social interaction.

Using the common U.S. Census categories, the school that Kromidas studied could be described as 28 percent black, 1 percent white, 46 percent Hispanic, and 25 percent Asian. But these four categories do not reveal the diversity of the school and its neighborhood—a diversity that makes the students' formulations of race all the more complicated. Although the students and the surrounding community are predominantly African American and second- and third-generation Latino, a significant part of the population is composed of new immigrants from Nigeria, Bangladesh, Guyana, Jamaica, and the Dominican Republic.

In light of the events of September 11, students in the elementary school seem preoccupied with the potential danger from a perceived enemy—one they see racially as "brown, foreign, strange, and Muslim" (Kromidas 2004, 29). Though the children do not consider their Muslim classmates to be "evil" or "terrorists," they do take note of these classmates' identities as never before. Kromidas ("MK" in the dialogues below) notes in particular the equation of enemies with Indians, Pakistanis, or Afghanis, and eventually all Arabic ("Araback") people. Here we see a racial construction, a lumping together of unrelated people based on a general phenotype—in this case, skin color.

Consider the following small-group student discussions:

EXAMPLE 1

SHERI:	We were talking about who started it first, and if they kill a lot of white people. . . . I mean a lot of people we got to go to war right then.
MK:	Who are they?
SHERI:	The Indians.
MK:	The Indians?
SHERI:	I don't know—that's what I call them.
JONATHAN:	The Pakistans!
MK:	The Pakistans?
SODIQ:	The Afghanistans!
MK:	The Afghanistans?
JOSEPH:	The terrorists.

Later that afternoon:

EXAMPLE 2

SHERI:	I feel sorry for the Afghanistan people.
SUSANNA:	Why do you feel sorry after what they did?
SHERI:	Because they gonna die! (*Most of the class breaks up with laughter.*)
LATISHA:	(*standing up*) I feel happy! (*laughter*)
LATISHA:	No, no, no . . . because they want to kill our people, they're going to die too. They want to have a party when we die, so we should celebrate! [*referring to news clips of street celebrations in the Middle East after September 11*]
ANUPA:	If they die, it will be better for us.
MK:	Who are they?
ANUPA:	The Araback people.
MARISELA:	The Afghanistans have always hated the Americans. I know because I always watch the news.

EXAMPLE 3

LATISHA: The Indians, I call them Indians ...

MK: Who?

LATISHA: The people that was in the airplane. They said that God told
             them to do this. (*throwing up her hands and moving her head in
             mock frustration*) Why would he tell them ... ?

TEACHER: (*Interrupting*) You see, they had certain beliefs, but ...
             (Kromidas 2004, 18–19)

These conversations yield some interesting observations. First, the students have taken on images presented in the media and from the conversations of adults around them; second, the students manipulate those images to create patterns of exclusion in their own context. Through their conversations, language groups, social interactions, and friendship networks, the students seek to clarify boundaries and to include and exclude newcomers according to what they see as racial characteristics. In the racial maps of the United States, South-Asian Americans and Arab Americans do not have a clear place. Kromidas suggests that in the classroom, as in U.S. culture at large, the fourth graders of New York City are creating a new racial category and placing people in it. The category is generally defined as not white, not black, but brown; foreign, strange, Muslim, and possibly enemy.

Before September 11, "Middle Eastern" was not considered a separate race in the United States. Officially, the government's Office of Management and Budget includes people of Middle Eastern descent as whites, along with people of European and North African descent. But the **racialization** (that is, giving a racial character) of Middle Easterners in U.S. culture after September 11 suggests a movement away from whiteness as reflected in Kromidas's study of fourth graders in Brooklyn.

racialization

The process of categorizing, differentiating, and attributing a particular racial character to a person or group of people.

What Is Racism?

Racism is a complex system of power that draws on the culturally constructed categories of race to rank people as superior or inferior, and to differentially allocate access to power, privilege, resources, and opportunities.

TYPES OF RACISM

Racism has multiple aspects that include individual and institutional components as well as the set of ideas—the ideology—that acts like glue to hold them together.

Individual Racism. **Individual racism** is expressed through prejudiced beliefs and discriminatory actions. Being prejudiced involves making negative assumptions about a person's abilities or intentions based on the person's perceived race. Discriminating involves taking negative actions toward a person on the basis of his or her perceived race. Individual racism may be expressed through a lack of respect or through suspicion, scapegoating, and violence ranging from police brutality to hate crimes (Jones 2000). Individual, personally mediated acts of racism may be intentional or unintentional. They may be acts of commission (things that are done) or acts of omission (things that are left undone).

Institutional Racism. Racism is more than individual prejudiced beliefs or discriminatory acts. Racism also includes **institutional racism**, sometimes called *structural racism*—patterns by which racial inequality is structured through key cultural institutions, policies, and systems. These include education, health, housing, employment, the legal system (legislatures, courts, and prison systems), law enforcement, and the media. Institutional racism originates in historical events and legal sanctions. But, even when outlawed, it can persist through contemporary patterns of institutional behavior that perpetuate the historical injustices (Jones 2000; Cazenave 2011; Feagin and Feagin 2011; Neubeck and Cazenave 2001).

In the United States, stratification along racial lines is a legacy of discrete historical events that include slavery, Jim Crow legal segregation, expropriation of indigenous lands, and immigration restrictions. Through these legal forms of institutional racism, the political, economic, and educational systems were organized to privilege whiteness. Today, despite the elimination of legal racial discrimination and segregation, patterns of inequality still break along color lines as a result of continuing individual and institutional racism. Such racism is evident in employment rates, income and wealth differentials, home ownership, residential patterns, criminal sentencing patterns, incarceration rates, application of the death penalty, infant mortality, access to health care, life expectancy, investments in public education, college enrollments, and access to the vote.

For example, the U.S. educational system has been a site for intense contestation over race and racism. In 1896—three decades after the end of slavery—the Supreme Court ruled in *Plessy v. Ferguson* that state-sponsored segregation, including in public schools, was constitutional as long as the separate facilities for separate races were equal. Across the South, individual white school administrators often refused, on overtly racist grounds, to allow children of color—black, Hispanic, Asian American—entrance to school buildings. But these individual actions alone did not constitute the total system of racism at work. They were systematically supported and enforced by government institutions: local boards of education, legislators, local police with guns and dogs, and court systems—including the U.S. Supreme Court.

A racially segregated classroom in Monroe Elementary School, Topeka, Kansas, March 1953. Students Linda Brown (*front right*) and her sister Terry Lynn (*far left, second back*), along with their parents, initiated the landmark civil rights lawsuit *Brown v. Board of Education.*

Only in 1954 did the Supreme Court reverse itself in the case of *Brown v. Board of Education*, declaring unanimously that state laws establishing separate public schools for black and white students were unconstitutional and that separate educational facilities were inherently unequal. At the time, seventeen states, primarily across the South, required racial segregation. Sixteen prohibited it.

Contemporary racial disparities in school funding reveal how historical patterns of institutional racism can continue long after discrimination has been declared illegal (Miller and Epstein 2011). In 2003, the New York Court of Appeals, the state's highest court, found a long-standing disparity in state funding of public schools in New York City and suburban areas. New York City public schools, with high proportions of students of color, received an average of $10,469 per student, whereas schools in more affluent, predominantly white New York suburbs received $13,760 per student. The courts ordered New York State to increase its annual education budget by up to $5.6 billion to cover the costs of redressing this inequality while also providing $9.2 billion for capital improvement of New York City school buildings. The State of New York has yet to fully comply with these requirements.

Racial Ideology. Racism relies on a third component—a set of popular ideas about race, or a **racial ideology**—that allows the discriminatory behaviors of individuals and institutions to seem reasonable, rational, and normal. Ideas about the superiority of one race over another—shaped and reinforced in the school system, religious institutions, government, and the media—caused people in the United States to believe that slavery was natural, that the European settlers

racial ideology

A set of popular ideas about race that allows the discriminatory behaviors of individuals and institutions to seem reasonable, rational, and normal.

had a God-given right to "civilize" and "tame" the American West, and that seg-regated schools were a reasonable approach to providing public education. As these ideas became ingrained in day-to-day relationships and institutional pat-terns of behavior, they ultimately provided the ideological glue that held racial stratification in place.

Today social scientists note that contemporary racial ideologies are much more subtle, often drawing on core U.S. values of individualism, social mobility, meritocracy, and color-blindness to make their case. So, for instance, in his book *Racism without Racists* (2010), sociologist Eduardo Bonilla-Silva critiques the contemporary calls in U.S. culture for color blindness—the elimination of race as a consideration in a wide range of institutional processes from college admissions to the reporting of arrests by police. The ideology of color blindness suggests that the best way to end discrimination in the post–civil rights era is to treat individuals as equally as possible without regard to race. Bonilla-Silva warns that while the desire to transcend race by adopting a stance of color blindness appears reasonable and fair, the approach ignores the uneven playing field created by centuries of legal racism in areas such as wealth, property ownership, education, health, and employment. A color-blind ideology, Bonilla-Silva suggests, may actually perpetuate racial inequality by obscuring the historical effects of racism, the continuing legacy of racial discrimination, and the entrenched patterns of institutional behavior that undergird racism today.

In a country like the United States, which prides itself on being a meritocracy (a system that views people as a product of their own efforts and in which equal opportunity is available to all), the continuing existence of racism and skin-color privilege in the twenty-first century is difficult for many people to acknowledge. When the dominant culture celebrates the ideals of individualism and equal access to social mobility, it is ironic that for many people, success depends not only on hard work, intelligence, and creativity but also on the often unrecognized and unearned assets—cultural, political, and economic—that have accrued over hundreds of years of discrimination and unequal opportunity based on race.

RESISTING RACISM

Along with the history of individual and institutional racism, it is important to also acknowledge the long tradition of work against racism that continues today. Anthropologist Steven Gregory's ethnography *Black Corona* (1998) tells the story of the organized political resistance by a predominantly African American com-munity in Corona, Queens, in New York City, when confronted by attitudes and policy expressions of racial discrimination. The African American community in Corona dates back to the 1820s, and it expanded under an influx of middle-class residents from Harlem in the first half of the twentieth century. By the 1970s, however, Corona, like many other urban U.S. communities, began to feel the

MAP 5.2
Queens

devastating impact of globalization, particularly flexible accumulation, as New York City's economy deindustrialized. At this time, the city's economy moved from an industrial and manufacturing base to one driven by finance, information, and services (Baker 1995; Harvey 1990). As New York lost thousands of manufacturing jobs and billions of dollars in tax revenue and federal funds, residents of Corona struggled during the transition.

In the face of drastic government cutbacks to basic community services such as housing, education, and public safety, residents of Corona's LeFrak City—a public housing complex containing six thousand rental apartments—mobilized to demand sustained public investment in the maintenance and security of the property from their landlord, the City of New York. Confronting stereotypes of the apartment complex as a site of crime, welfare dependency, and family disorganization, African American parents in LeFrak City founded Concerned Community Adults (CCA), a community-based civic association, to engage in neighborhood improvement projects and strengthen relationships with the city's politicians and agencies. The CCA's Youth Forum organized neighborhood young people for social activities and leadership formation; together with the CCA, it worked to improve relations with the local police, who regularly harassed youth in the area. Through community-based action, LeFrak City residents worked with churches, community groups, and informal associations to establish their position as political actors, assert control over the neighborhood's physical condition, and insist on self-definition rather than accept the stereotypes held by surrounding communities and city leaders.

In the early 1990s, the Port Authority of New York and New Jersey—which controls the area's airports, bridges, and port facilities—announced plans to build an elevated light rail train between Manhattan's central business district and LaGuardia Airport that would cut directly through the heart of Corona's African American community. Residents had had extensive negative experiences battling the city over earlier plans to expand LaGuardia, which abuts Corona, that involved the loss of waterfront properties to the construction of runways, highway access, and exposure to the pollution of adjacent Flushing Bay. In its new plan, the Port Authority, representing the City of New York, argued that the city needed improved public transportation between Manhattan and LaGuardia to compete in the global economy and in the burgeoning global financial services industry. The elevated rail line through Corona, the argument went, would be good for the city's economy.

Corona residents warned that construction of this major infrastructure project through their community would not have any local benefit but instead would generate severe environmental consequences, lower the quality of life in the neighborhood, and divide and isolate portions of the community. They demanded that the rail line be built underground on property already owned by New York City

between Corona and the airport that had been carved out to build the Grand Central Parkway years earlier. Local residents formed neighborhood committees and alliances with existing civic organizations, community groups, and churches. They engaged the city's public planning process and established alternative political forums outside the government's control to press for their case. They also created multicultural alliances with concerned groups in neighboring communities. Eventually the Port Authority abandoned the planned elevated train.

Gregory's ethnographic study of Corona's African American community reveals the power of local communities of color to mobilize and engage in political activism. It also demonstrates how such groups can contest the stereotypes of urban black communities and the practices of racial discrimination and exclusion, whether those involve housing, policing, or the environmental and community impacts of public infrastructure projects.

RACE, RACISM, AND WHITENESS

Popular conversations about race and racism tend to focus on the experiences of people of color. Whiteness is typically ignored, perhaps taken for granted. But analyzing race in the United States requires a careful look at whiteness. Anthropologists refer to "white" as an unmarked category—one with tremendous power, but one that typically defies analysis and is rarely discussed. Recent scholarship has been moving whiteness into the mainstream debates about race in the United States (Hargrove 2009; Harrison 1998, 2002a; Hartigan 1999; Marable 2002; Mullings 2005a; Roediger 1992).

Although the events of the U.S. civil rights movement occurred well before most of today's college students were born, the media images of police blocking African Americans from attending white schools, riding in the front of the bus, sitting at department store lunch counters, or drinking from "whites-only" water fountains remain etched in our collective cultural memory. Although the overt signs declaring access for "whites only" have been outlawed and removed, many patterns of interpersonal and institutional behavior have resisted change (McIntosh 1989).

"White Privilege." In her article "White Privilege: Unpacking the Invisible Knapsack" (1989), anthropologist Peggy McIntosh writes of "an invisible package of unearned assets" that are a legacy of generations of racial discrimination. Through these assets, whites have become the beneficiaries of cultural norms, values, mental maps of reality, and institutions. Unearned advantages and unearned power are conferred systematically and differentially on one group over others, whether those benefits lie in health, education, housing, employment, banking and mortgages, or the criminal justice system.

McIntosh articulates an extensive list of these privileges, ranging from the mundane to the profound. They include: (1) going shopping without being followed or harassed by store security; (2) using checks, credit cards, or cash and counting on skin color to not work against the appearance of financial responsibility; (3) seeing people of your "race" widely represented in the news, social media, and educational curricula; (4) swearing, dressing in second-hand clothes, or not answering letters or e-mails without having people attribute these choices to bad morals, poverty, or the illiteracy of your "race"; (5) feeling confident that you have not been singled out by race when a police officer pulls you over or an airport security guard decides to conduct a full-body scan; (6) criticizing the government and its policies without being considered an outsider.

As we have discussed in this chapter, since the early European settlement of North America, the boundaries of whiteness have been carefully constructed and guarded. Today the skin-color privileges associated with whiteness still pass down from generation to generation. They are simply harder to see. Acknowledging this fact enables us to analyze the functioning and effects of race and racism as a complete system.

As McIntosh writes, "For me white privilege has turned out to be an elusive and fugitive subject. The pressure to avoid it is great, for in facing it I must give up the myth of meritocracy. If these things are true, this is not such a free country, one's life is not what one makes it; many doors open for certain people through no virtues of their own" (1989, 12). Moving forward, McIntosh urges students to distinguish between (1) the positive advantages that we wish everyone could have and that we can all work to spread, and (2) the negative types of advantages that, unless challenged and corrected, will always reinforce current racial hierarchies.

Intersections of Whiteness and Class. It is important to note the powerful intersection of race and class. **Intersectionality** provides a framework for analyzing the many factors—especially class and gender—that determine how race is lived and how all three systems of power and stratification build on and shape one another. In *Living with Racism: The Black Middle-Class Experience* (1994), sociologist Joe Feagin and psychologist Melvin Sikes write about middle-class African Americans who, despite their class status, continue to face racial discrimination. Though reflecting a privileged class status in comparison to other African Americans, the class advantages of middle-class African Americans still are limited by racial disadvantage. Because race and class intersect so deeply, improved class status cannot be assumed to bring a decrease in the experience of racial discrimination.

Whiteness is also stratified along deep, intersecting lines of class and region, gender and sexuality so that not all people of European descent benefit equally from the system of white privilege. In a study of a town she calls Shellcracker Haven, southwest of Gainesville, Florida, anthropologist Jane Gibson (1996) explored the process through which a community of poor whites has been systematically cut off from their local means of making a living. By imposing restrictions on fishing, gaming, and trapping as well as on agricultural activities—all of which benefit large-scale businesses—the Florida state government and its agencies have gradually prevented Shellcracker Haven's residents from making a living on the land or nearby water.

Gibson argues that these policies of disenfranchisement have been rationalized by stereotypes that state authorities promote. Such stereotypes portray the local people as "white trash," "swamp trash," and "crackers"; as dirty, skinny, shoeless, toothless, illiterate, and unintelligent. The stereotypes deflect attention from the skewed distribution of wealth and power and the uneven investments in

intersectionality

An analytic framework for assessing how factors such as race, gender, and class interact to shape individual life chances and societal patterns of stratification.

MAP 5.3
Florida

Anthropologists of race in the United States have studied the often "unmarked" category of whiteness. The privileges of whiteness in the United States are not experienced uniformly, but are stratified along deep lines of class, region, gender, and sexuality.

roads, education, and health care that result from state policies. Poor whites are a subordinated group, distinct from successful middle- and upper-class whites in the state.

Gibson's study reveals that whiteness is not monolithic. Indeed, people who place themselves in this racial group experience a wide range of life chances. Poor whites in the United States comprise a mix of 22.3 million people, both urban and rural, who do not necessarily reflect the advantages of whiteness (Wray and Newitz 1996). The worst stereotypes portray poor whites as backward, inbred, lazy, illiterate, unintelligent, and uncultured. Epithets such as "redneck," "hillbilly," and "white trash" distance these whites from the middle-class social norms and economic success stereotypically associated with their whiteness (Hartigan 2005). Although the historical development, regional particularities, and current circumstances vary among groups of poor whites, their poverty and social ostracism mark an extreme end of the U.S. class spectrum. In the current age of globalization, economic restructuring and global competition are further undermining the white privilege for many poor and working-class whites as manufacturing jobs leave the United States.

In this chapter we have begun our work as budding anthropologists to unmask the structures of power, starting with race and racism. We have seen how flawed ideas of "race" serve as a rationale for very real systems of power built around racial stratification both in the United States and around the world. As globalization, particularly global migration, brings cultural systems of meaning and stratification into closer contact, your ability to analyze and engage dynamics of race and racism will prove to be increasingly important. In the following chapters we will consider other systems of power—including ethnicity, gender, sexuality, kinship, and class—and their points of mutual intersection with race.

Toolkit

Thinking Like an Anthropologist:
Shifting Our Perspectives on Race and Racism

As you encounter race and racism in your life—on campus, in the classroom, at the workplace, in the news, or in your family—thinking like an anthropologist can help you to better understand these experiences. As you untangle this knotty problem, remember to think about the big questions we addressed in this chapter:

- **Do biologically separate races exist?**
- **How is race constructed around the world?**
- **How is race constructed in the United States?**
- **What is racism?**

After reading this chapter, you should be better equipped to engage the challenges of race and racism. As you think back on the chapter-opening story about the impact of Hurricane Katrina on the population of New Orleans, how would you apply the ideas of this chapter to assist your analysis and inform your responses?

Hurricane Katrina was a dangerous storm, but its effects were a social disaster that disproportionately affected people along lines of race and class. Few would say that U.S. government leaders allowed the effects of Hurricane Katrina to occur because of individual prejudice or bigotry. But even though a catastrophic hurricane had been anticipated for New Orleans since 2001, the city, state, and federal governments had no effective evacuation plan. Why? In a city stratified by race and class, some residents had cars by which to leave the city and credit cards with which to pay for gas and hotel rooms. Others had to wait for the government to send buses, which arrived nearly a week later. Moreover, protective wetlands had been sold to developers, and the budget for maintaining and improving levees and pumps had been cut by 80 percent (Smith 2006; Marable 2006).

How do we make sense of what happened? Neil Smith (2006) suggests that there is no such thing as a natural disaster. Rather, he says, natural events become disasters for some people because of social factors, including race and social inequality. Can we imagine that the effects of Hurricane Katrina might reflect a type of structural racism buried in the practices and policies of our social institutions (which developed over hundreds of years of overt racial prejudice) that continue to affect where people live, how public infrastructure is funded, how government prepares for and responds to events, and how public needs are addressed?

Key Terms

race (p. 123)

racism (p. 124)

genotype (p. 126)

phenotype (p. 127)

colonialism (p. 128)

miscegenation (p. 130)

white supremacy (p. 134)

whiteness (p. 134)

Jim Crow (p. 134)

hypodescent (p. 135)

nativism (p. 136)

eugenics (p. 136)

racialization (p. 140)

individual racism (p. 141)

institutional racism (p. 141)

racial ideology (p. 142)

intersectionality (p. 147)

Chapter 6
Ethnicity and Nationalism

When the World Cup soccer tournament opened in June 2010 in South Africa, teams from thirty-two nations carried the hopes and dreams of their supporters into the competition. Soccer stadiums filled up with fans painted in national colors, draped in national flags, and singing national songs and anthems. Other fans tuned in to television and radio broadcasts around the world, exulting and suffering along with the fates of their national teams. Over three years, 205 teams had battled through 848 matches to reach South Africa—the most extensive global tournament in history. At the time of the World Cup final, more than 700 million people gathered worldwide in pubs, restaurants, and crowded town squares to watch Spain play the Netherlands. What can we learn about ethnicity and nationalism from the World Cup?

What can soccer teach us about ethnicity and nationalism? Here Germany's Jerome Boateng *(left)* challenges for the ball against his half-brother, Ghana's Kevin-Prince Boateng, during a 2010 World Cup soccer match in Johannesburg, South Africa.

Jerome Boateng and Kevin-Prince Boateng, two half-brothers born in Germany to a Ghanaian father and German mothers, both played in the World Cup—but for different national teams. Jerome played for Germany, the country of his birth. Kevin-Prince played for the Ghanaian national team, representing the country of his father's birth. What makes someone a member of a certain nation? The simple answer, it seems, should be birth. But in today's age of globalization, nationality is not so simple. The rules of FIFA, the world soccer federation, state that to play for a national team, a player must either be born in that country or have a parent or grandparent from that country. A player can also establish a new nationality by living in a new country for five years. But once a choice of nationality is made, it is irrevocable. As the son of an immigrant from Ghana, but born in Germany, Kevin-Prince could choose his nationality. In the World Cup, we see the complications of identity for children of immigrants and the changing rules of nationality on the international stage.

But what exactly is a nation? When Germany knocked England out of the World Cup, commentators in the United Kingdom lamented the death of the "ninety-minute nation" (Younge 2010). What did this mean? First, consider that England no longer exists as a separate nation. It is now part of the United Kingdom—along with Scotland, Wales, and Northern Ireland. In fact, the disappearance of England within the United Kingdom is a sore point for many of English descent. Their rival ethnic groups have gained political recognition in recent years. Scotland has a parliament; Wales and Northern Ireland have national assemblies. But politically, England has been subsumed into the United Kingdom.

The soccer pitch is one of the few places where English ethnic identity and nationalism can still be expressed. The game was born in England. In consideration of this, FIFA allows the English to continue fielding a World Cup team even without a nation. When the England team takes the field, English ethnicity and nationalism reemerge. The flag of England's patron saint, St. George, flies high over the prime minister's residence, temporarily replacing the Union Jack. Period costumes emerge on the streets of London. Traditional English songs resound in pubs. Through sports, the nation exists as long as England is playing. But at the end of a ninety-minute game, the "ninety-minute nation" returns to its place within the United Kingdom.

Let's consider another example. Midway through the World Cup, the French national team imploded as the world and the French nation watched. The whole team went on strike, refusing to practice before a crucial match that resulted in a humiliating, early exit from the tournament. What had happened? During the competition, a vitriolic rant by one of the team's stars, laced with ethnic comments, set off intense conflicts within the diverse French team—whose racial and ethnic composition reflects the country's colonial past and recent immigration.

What makes someone French? Here, French national soccer team players train prior to a World Cup match in South Africa, 2010.

Indeed, immigration, nationality, and race are red-hot topics in France. With a long colonial past in Africa and Asia and significant recent immigration from these former colonies, France seethes with conflict over who is really French. Riots have erupted in immigrant neighborhoods. The national government recently banned Muslim women from wearing the veil in public. Thus one must ask: Is it possible to "become" French? How long does it take? The difficult French national debates over ethnicity and nationalism were on display and under negotiation at the World Cup.

The World Cup is more than a series of soccer matches. As anthropologists, we know that sports are more than just a game. Yes, games happen in real time with dirt and sweat, tactics and strategies, wins and losses and ties. But games are also symbolic, both for the players and for their fans. Victory and defeat, disappointment and heroism are wrapped up in a drama larger than life. Sports are a venue for the creation and negotiation of personal and national identity. They are sites of moral education about sportsmanship, leadership, the value of compromise, how to cope with victory and defeat, and how to work together with diverse people (MacClancy 1996). Wrapped up in an international competition like the World Cup are emotionally fraught matters: national identity and citizenship, the national and ethnic imaginations of people worldwide, the history of colonialism and independence, old rivalries, national pride, the expression of national character, and the negotiation of a people's place on the modern world stage. Moreover, the spectacle of the World Cup illustrates how the promotion of nationalism by the media, corporations, and national leaders has direct benefits for viewership, profit, and political power.

In this chapter we will explore ethnicity and nationalism from an anthropological perspective. In particular, we will ask three key questions:

- **What does "ethnicity" mean to anthropologists?**
- **How is ethnicity created and put in motion?**
- **What is the relationship of ethnicity to the nation?**

After reading this chapter you will be able to understand and analyze the role of ethnicity and nationalism in your own life and in communities and countries worldwide.

What Does "Ethnicity" Mean to Anthropologists?

We hear the word *ethnicity* all the time. The press reports on "long-held ethnic conflicts" that shatter the peace in Ireland, Rwanda, Iraq, and Sri Lanka. We check boxes on college applications and U.S. census forms to identify our ethnicity or race. We shop in the "ethnic foods" aisle of our supersized grocery store to find refried beans, soy sauce, pita, and wasabi. Our use of *ethnicity* is not particularly consistent or terribly clear. In recent years in the United States, *ethnicity* has been increasingly substituted for *race* when describing group differences. *Ethnic* is often paired with *minority*, a term signifying a smaller group that differs from the dominant, majority culture in language, food, dress, immigrant history, national origin, or religion. But this usage ignores the ethnic identity of the majority. The same lack of clarity is true for our use of the terms *nation*, *nationalism*, and *nation-state*, all of which often blur together and at times seem indistinguishable from *ethnicity*.

ETHNICITY AS IDENTITY

Over a lifetime, humans develop complex identities that connect to many people in many ways. We build a sense of relationship, belonging, and shared identity through connections to family, religion, hometown, language, shared history, citizenship, sports, age, gender, sexuality, education, and profession. These powerful identities influence what we eat, who we date, where we work, how we live, and even how we die. **Ethnicity** is one of the most powerful identities that humans develop: it is a sense of connection to a group of people who we believe share a common history, culture, and (sometimes) ancestry and who are distinct from others outside the group (Jenkins 1996; Ericksen 2010). Ethnicity can be seen as a more expansive version of kinship—the culturally specific creation of

ethnicity

A sense of historical, cultural, and sometimes ancestral connection to a group of people who are imagined to be distinct from those outside the group.

relatives—only including a much larger group and extending further in space and time. As we will see in this chapter, the construction of ethnicity, like kinship, is quite complicated, moving well beyond easy equation with biological ancestry. Ethnic identification beyond our immediate associations is primarily perceived, felt, and imagined rather than clearly documentable.

With the intensification of globalization and the increasing flows of people, goods, and ideas across borders, one might anticipate that the power of ethnicity to frame people's actions and to influence world events would diminish. Instead, ethnicity seems to be flourishing—rising in prominence in both local and global affairs. Why is it so powerful? When threatened or challenged, people often turn to local alliances for support, safety, and protection. Ethnicity is one of the strongest sources of solidarity available.

As the effects of globalization intersect with systems of power at the local level, many people turn to ethnic networks and expressions of ethnic identity to protect their local way of life in the face of intense pressures of homogenization. As we will consider later in this chapter, ethnicity also can serve political purposes on the national and local levels as political elites and other ethno-entrepreneurs use calls for ethnic solidarity to mobilize support against perceived enemies inside and outside the nation-state. Rather than diminishing in the face of globalization, ethnicity emerges even more powerfully in specific situations of conflict, tension, and opportunity.

CREATING ETHNIC IDENTITY

Anthropologists see ethnicity as a cultural construction, not as a natural formation based on biology or inherent human nature. Fredrik Barth (1969) describes ethnicity as the "social organization of cultural difference"; in other words, people construct a sense of ethnicity as they organize themselves in relation to others whom they perceive as either culturally similar or culturally different. Ethnic identity starts with what people believe about themselves and how others see them. Identity formation begins early and continues throughout our lives. People learn, practice, and teach ethnicity. Anthropologists who study it seek to understand how it is created and reinforced, how boundaries are constructed, how group identity is shaped, and how differences with others are perpetuated (Jenkins 2008). Who do you consider to be in your ethnic group? Who belongs to a different group?

Ethnic identity is taught and reinforced in a number of ways. One key method is the creation and telling of **origin myths**. By myth, we do not mean falsehood but rather a story with meaning. In the United States, the "American" origin myth includes stories of historical events—such as the landing of the *Mayflower*, the first Thanksgiving, the Boston Tea Party, the American Revolution, the Civil War, the settling of the West—that are retold to emphasize a shared destiny as

origin myth

A story told about the founding and history of a particular group to reinforce a sense of common identity.

well as shared values of freedom, exploration, individualism, and multiculturalism. The American origin myth of the first Thanksgiving is ritually enacted each year with a national holiday. Schoolchildren produce dramas and artwork based on textbook stories. Families gather to feast, usually eating certain traditional foods. Nationally televised parades and sporting events add to the ritual's celebratory character. However, origin myths—like all elements of culture—are continuously promoted, revised, and negotiated. For example, recent years have seen more open discussion of the brutal conquest of Native Americans and, in books such as Howard Zinn's *A People's History of the United States* (2005), more challenges to classic textbook representations of the American origin myth.

People create and promote certain **ethnic boundary markers** in an attempt to signify who is in the group and who is not. These may include a collective name; shared cultural practices such as food, clothing, and architecture; a belief in common ancestors; association with a particular territory; a shared language or religion; and an imagination of shared physical characteristics. But ethnic boundaries are usually not clearly fixed and defined. Our social worlds rarely have distinct groups with clear boundaries. Not everyone imagined to be inside the group is the same; not everyone imagined to be outside the group is noticeably different. No group is completely homogeneous.

Identity, including ethnic identity, can be fluid and flexible, reflecting shifting alliances and strength over time and according to need (Ericksen 2010). People move between groups through marriage, migration, and adoption. Groups may vanish in situations of war or **genocide** (the deliberate and systematic destruction of an ethnic or religious group). New ethnic groups may come into existence—a process called *ethnogenesis*—when part of an existing group splits off or two groups form a new one.

Because ethnicity is not biologically fixed, self-identification with a particular ethnic group can change according to one's social location. This occurs

In what ways do stories, paintings, and even Thanksgiving turkey floats help create an American ethnic identity? *Left:* A 1914 depiction of the first Thanksgiving at Plymouth, Massachusetts. *Right:* The Tom Turkey float moves through Times Square during the Macy's Thanksgiving Day Parade, in New York City.

ethnic boundary marker
A practice or belief, such as food, clothing, language, shared name, or religion, used to signify who is in a group and who is not.

genocide
The deliberate and systematic destruction of an ethnic or religious group.

through a process called **situational negotiation of identity**. For example, Kevin-Prince Boateng in our chapter-opening story could have chosen to be German, German-Ghanaian, Ghanaian, African, Afro-European, perhaps even a member of his father's local ethnic group in Ghana. At points during his life he may choose to identify himself with any of these, depending on the situation. Have you ever had the experience of identifying with a different aspect of your identity as you moved between groups or locations?

situational negotiation of identity

An individual's self-identification with a particular group that can shift according to social location.

Constructing Indian Identity in the United States. The immigration experience profoundly affects ethnicity and ethnic identification. New immigrants reshape their home-country ethnic identification to build alliances and solidarity in their new host country. In her book *From the Ganges to the Hudson* (1995), anthropologist Johanna Lessinger explores the process by which a new Indian ethnic identity is created and publicly demonstrated through consumption, public festivals, and Indian immigrant media. Indian immigrants arrive in New York from all corners of their homeland, speaking different languages, following diverse cultural practices and religions, and reflecting class and caste stratifications. In India, a country of more than 1.2 billion people, these individuals would identify themselves as representing different ethnicities. But after arriving in New York as immigrants from India, they all begin the process of becoming Indian American.

Little India, a bustling shopping district in Jackson Heights, Queens, has become the symbolic center of Indian immigrant life and a key to the construction of Indian ethnic identity in the United States. Vibrant with the sights, sounds, and smells of India, the streets are lined with Indian grocery and spice shops, Indian restaurants, clothing and jewelry stores, travel agencies, music and video distributors, and electronics stores. Indian immigrants come from all parts of New York City and the metropolitan region to walk the streets of Little India and shop, eat, and take in the many symbols of "home."

India is home to people of many different ethnicities, shaped by geography, language, food, and cultural practices. But in New York City, Indian immigrants have created a wide-ranging ethnic infrastructure that supports and promotes the construction of a unified Indian ethnic identity in their new homeland. The infrastructure includes ethnic associations, religious temples, cultural societies, newspapers, television programming, and major public festivals. One of the largest festivals is the India Day Parade held in late August to mark India's nationhood and independence from British colonialism. Like the dozens of ethnic parade celebrations in New York each year, Indian immigrant community organizations, business owners, and hometown associations sponsor marching bands, singers, dancers, banners, and a vast array of colorful floats. In 2009, Shilpa Shetty (the Indian actress mentioned in the opening anecdote of

MAP 6.1
New York/India

Indian actress Preity Zinta and Kamla Persad-Bissessar, prime minister of Trinidad and Tobago (home to many Indian immigrants), lead the 2010 India Day Parade in New York City.

Chapter 2) was the India Day Parade's grand marshal. In 2010, the parade featured the prime minister of Trinidad and Tobago, a Caribbean country to which many Indians were sent as laborers in the nineteenth century and from which many have migrated to New York. By including Indians of Caribbean descent, the parade organizers demonstrate their intention to unify the diverse diaspora of Indians now residing in New York City. Holding a public festival like the India Day Parade is a powerful way to stake a claim to a place in the multiethnic mosaic that is New York—to send a clear signal to all New Yorkers, including the political establishment, that Indians are here, are organized, and want to be taken seriously.

Ethnic boundaries are often fluid, messy, and contested. For example, exactly who is Indian American? Each year since 1994, the South Asian Lesbian and Gay Alliance (SALGA) has requested permission to march in the India Day Parade, only to be denied by parade organizers. Does this mean that gay men and lesbians of Indian ancestry are not Indian? Members of SALGA hold demonstrations each year along the parade route, holding signs that read "We are also Indians!" Despite the parade organizers' desire to build a broad-based Indian American identity and coalition, they are willing to declare SALGA not Indian enough to participate in the event. In this situation, sexuality becomes a more powerful boundary marker than country of origin. The rift over the India Day Parade is a very public and symbolic representation of the contestation of ethnic boundary markers—a struggle that reveals deep disagreements among Indian immigrants and many of their children—and the debate involved in defining who is Indian in the United States.

How Is Ethnicity Created and Put in Motion?

For most of the world's people, ethnicity is not a pressing matter in daily life. But it can be activated when power relationships undergo negotiation in a community or a nation. Then people call on shared ideas of ethnicity to rally others to participate in their causes, whether those causes involve ensuring self-protection, building alliances, constructing economic networks, or establishing a country. Ethnicity can also be activated by charismatic entrepreneurs of ethnicity who seek support from co-ethnics in their fight for political, economic, or military power against real or perceived enemies. The sections that follow illustrate how ethnicity can be harnessed for either harmful or beneficial outcomes.

ETHNICITY AS A SOURCE OF CONFLICT

The anthropological study of ethnicity requires an open-mindedness to new ideas of how ethnicity is formed and how it works—ideas that may be at odds with our everyday usage of the terms *ethnicity* and *ethnic groups*. Rogers Brubaker, in his book *Ethnicity without Groups* (2004), warns against "groupism" when studying ethnicity. Anthropologists may anticipate that we will work with clearly defined groups having fixed boundaries and homogenous membership who will act in a unified fashion. But this is not what we find on the ground as we explore ethnicity on the local level. Ethnicity is much more complicated, involving people with many perspectives, disagreements, and at times competing loyalties. The strong bonds of ethnicity that we associate with ethnic groups may wax and wane.

Why do the power and intensity of ethnicity harden and crystallize at certain times? When studying ethnic conflict, as in the cases of Rwanda and the former Yugoslavia that follow, Brubaker encourages paying attention to ethnic group–making projects. Such projects occur when ethno-political entrepreneurs—political, military, and religious leaders—promote a worldview through the lens of ethnicity. They use war, propaganda, and state power to mobilize people against those whom they perceive as a danger. Ethnicity may not even be the problem. Rather, the struggle for wealth and power uses the convenient narrative of ethnicity to galvanize a population to collective action. Once the wedge of ethnic difference has been driven into a population and used to achieve power, it can be self-perpetuating and extremely difficult to break (Ericksen 2010).

Mobilizing Ethnic Differences in Rwanda. In 1994, the East African country of Rwanda was shattered by a horrific genocide involving two main groups, Hutu and Tutsi. Over a few months, as many as one million Tutsi and an unknown number of moderate Hutus died in a slaughter perpetrated by extremist

Hutu death squads. In a country of only seven million people before the geno-cide, where Hutu made up 85 percent of the population and Tutsi 15 percent, how did this tragedy occur? How do Tutsi and Hutu, who have lived together in the region for generations and centuries, tell each other apart?

Before German and Belgian colonial rule in the early twentieth century, Hutu and Tutsi were distinguished mainly by occupation and social status. Hutu were primarily farmers; Tutsi were cattle owners. The two groups share a com-mon language and religious affiliations. Intermarriage has been quite common. Children of mixed marriages inherited their fathers' identity. Although Tutsi were later stereotyped as taller and thinner than Hutu, it is not possible to distin-guish between members of the two groups by looks alone.

In a common colonial practice used in countries worldwide, colonial gov-ernments chose one native group to serve as educated and privileged intermedi-aries between the local population and the colonial administration. The Belgian colonial government (1919–62) elevated Tutsi to the most influential positions in Rwandan society, to the exclusion of Hutu leaders. In an attempt to rational-ize its prejudicial behavior, in the 1920s the Belgian colonial government hired scientists to measure Hutu and Tutsi anatomy—including skull size—so as to physically differentiate between the two groups. These flawed studies, based on the pseudoscience of eugenics (see Chapter 5) that developed in Europe and the United States, declared that Tutsi were taller, bigger brained, and lighter skinned—closer in physical form to Europeans and thus "naturally" suited to the role assigned to them by the Belgian colonial government.

To maintain and enforce this segregation, in 1933 the Belgian colonial gov-ernment established a national identity card that included the category "eth-nicity." Even after independence in 1962, Rwandan officials continued to use the identity card, forcing all citizens to be labeled as Hutu, Tutsi, Twa (a small minority population), or naturalized (born outside Rwanda). The cards were dis-continued only in 1996 after the genocide.

Many Hutu resented the Belgians' decision to elevate Tutsi to power in the colonial government. Periodic protests in the early years of colonial occupation were followed by a major uprising against Tutsi elites in 1956. In 1959, the Hutu seized power and forced many Tutsi into exile in neighboring countries. At inde-pendence in 1962, the Hutu consolidated full power and implemented repressive policies toward the Tutsi. A full-blown civil war erupted in 1990. Subsequently, a 1993 United Nations–backed cease-fire collapsed when the plane of the Rwandan president, a Hutu, was shot down in April 1994.

What followed was an extensive genocide campaign by Hutu extremists who blamed Tutsi for the death of their president. Rwandan radio broadcast instructions to kill all Tutsi, including spouses and family members, as well as any Hutu moderates who were unwilling to cooperate. Hutu civilian death squads

MAP 6.2
Rwanda

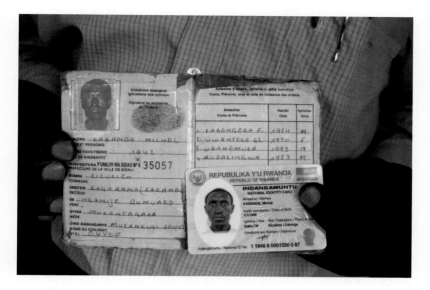

Rwandan identity cards listing each citizen's ethnic identity were discontinued only in 1996 after the genocide of as many as one million Tutsi.

implemented the "Hutu Power" genocide program, a deliberate and seemingly long-planned extermination of Tutsi. As a result, Tutsi and moderate Hutu were killed largely by hand with machetes and clubs after local officials gathered them up into schools and churches. Hutu death squads used the Rwandan identity cards to identify Tutsi victims for extermination.

What role did ethnicity play in the Rwandan genocide? Western press and government reports referred to the extermination as "tribal violence," the result of "ancient ethnic hatreds" and a failed nation-state. However, we can see how colonial European policies constructed and enforced notions of difference between Hutu and Tutsi—including notions of physical and mental difference—that were not deep-rooted historical patterns but that nonetheless later served to rationalize genocide (Mamdani 2002). Indeed, the twentieth-century history of Rwanda reveals the ways in which local ethnic relationships can be broken down and reconstituted in long-lasting ways by a foreign superpower that uses ethnicity as a weapon to divide and rule and how those new patterns of ethnicity can be mobilized to fuel a struggle for economic, political, and military power.

Orchestrating Ethnic Conflict in the Former Yugoslavia. The

disintegration of the former Yugoslavia in the late 1980s and early 1990s led to a devastating civil war that harnessed ethnicity as a powerful weapon of conflict and hatred. The war began in 1992 among Catholic Croats, Orthodox Christian Serbs, and Bosnian Muslims as national political leaders scrambled for control over land and power. In direct contrast to journalistic accounts of the war, which traced its origins to ancient ethnic hatreds that condemned the country's people to an endless cycle of violence, Norwegian anthropologist Tone Bringa has offered a different perspective. In her ethnography *Being Muslim the Bosnian Way* (1995), she declares, "The war was not created by those villagers. . . . The war has been orchestrated from places where the people I lived and worked among were not represented and where their voices were not heard" (5).

Beginning in 1987, Bringa conducted fieldwork in a diverse, Muslim–Catholic village in central Bosnia. She carefully describes the integrated social structures of daily village life—including the role of women, religion, and the family—and pays particular attention to the way Muslims practiced their faith. Bringa did not find a village populated with people who had always hated one another. They spoke the same language, went to school together, traded in the same local market, and shared village life as friends and neighbors. Bringa pointedly notes that despite the usual tensions any small community would face, these people of different faiths had lived together peacefully for five hundred years.

Significant change occurred in the community during the short time of Bringa's fieldwork. When she began her research, local Muslims based their identity on differences in religious practices from those of their Catholic neighbors. The emphasis was on practices such as scheduling of worship, prayer, and holiday celebrations, not on religious beliefs and convictions. However, these perceptions of self and others changed as war broke out and state leaders imposed new ethnic and cultural policies. Gradually, local Muslims were forced to identify less with their local community and more with the religious beliefs of other Bosnian Muslims, and they had to turn to the outside Muslim world as a source of solidarity and support.

When Bringa returned to the village in the spring of 1993—revealed in riveting scenes from her documentary film *Bosnia: We Are All Neighbors* (1993)—to her horror she found that almost every Muslim home had been destroyed by Croat forces, with assistance from local Croat men of the village. All four hundred Muslims in the village (two-thirds of its population) had fled, been killed, or been placed in concentration camps. **Ethnic cleansing**—efforts of one ethnic or religious group to remove or destroy another in a particular geographic area—had destroyed the dynamic and peaceful fabric of village life that Bringa recalled from only a few years earlier. As she writes in the preface to her book, "my anthropological training had not prepared me to deal with the very rapid and total disintegration of the community. . . . [T]his war has made sense neither to the anthropologist nor to the people who taught her about their way of life" (Bringa 1995, xviii). Her second documentary, *Returning Home: Revival of a Bosnian Village* (Bringa and Loizos 2002), examines the return of some of the Muslim refugees and the attempt to reconstruct the village life that was destroyed during the civil war. In Bringa's account of Bosnian village life we can see the vulnerability of local ethnic identities to manipulation by outside political and military forces.

MAP 6.3
Bosnia

ethnic cleansing

Efforts by representatives of one ethnic or religious group to remove or destroy another group in a particular geographic area.

ETHNICITY AS A SOURCE OF OPPORTUNITY

Ethnicity is not only mobilized to rally support in times of conflict. Ethnicity also can be mobilized to create opportunities, including engagement in everyday economics. Today ethnicity is being packaged and produced for a multibillion-dollar market: food, clothing, music, fashion, and cultural artifacts. People eat at ethnic restaurants, buy ethnic music, and decorate their homes and offices with ethnic furnishings. Perhaps you have some "ethnic" items in your dorm room or at home. John and Jean Comaroff, in their book *Ethnicity, Inc.* (2009), examine how the purposeful creation of ethnicity facilitates big business. The Comaroffs pay particular attention to the way ethnically defined populations are branding themselves and becoming ethno-corporations in order to capitalize on their ethnicity. Ethno–theme parks, cultural villages, and ecotourism all promote the ethnic experience to attract investors and customers. These are just a few pieces of the "Ethnicity, Inc." puzzle. (In contrast, for an example of a majority group's marketing of minority theme parks, see the group of images on p. 167.)

Bafokeng, Inc., in South Africa. For a look at ethnicity being mobilized for economic benefits, the story of one group in South Africa is remarkable for its corporate success. The Bafokeng, a Tswana nation in South Africa's North West province, trace their history in the area to the twelfth century. Between 1840

MAP 6.4
South Africa

and the mid-1860s, their land was taken by white colonial settlers. Thereafter the Bafokeng, who could not own land under the new regime, went to work as laborers on the farms that had once been theirs; later they toiled in diamond mines to the south. Ultimately, though, to recover their land, the Bafokeng decided to try to buy it back. Pooling portions of their wage labor under the auspices of the Tswana king, and with a white German missionary serving as their proxy, the Bafokeng began a long-term strategy to repurchase their farms. Eventually, they reacquired thirty-three farms by the early twentieth century. To protect their land rights, the natives registered these farms under the name of the Royal Bafokeng Nation, Inc.—a private, corporate owner—not in the names of individuals.

Throughout much of the twentieth century, the Bafokeng engaged in complicated legal battles with the South African state to keep control over their land. Tensions rose dramatically when, in 1924, surveyors discovered that the Merensky Reef geologic formation that lay directly under Bafokeng land was the world's largest source of platinum metals and held significant deposits of chromite and graphite as well. Battles with the state and corporations over mining rights continued until the 1960s, when a deal was reached with a private company to provide the Bafokeng with royalties on all minerals extracted from their land. Once again, the Bafokeng placed their revenues into a communal trust. Since that time, they have invested their assets aggressively, transforming the Royal Bafokeng Nation (RBN) into a massive ethno-corporation.

The extent of this corporation's scope is remarkable. Its rapidly diversifying array of businesses now includes mining and construction companies (by 2004, mining contracts alone produced more than $65 million in profits), investment companies, and even a premier soccer team—all held in the name of the Royal Bafokeng Nation. At home, it has invested heavily in jobs programs by establishing mid-size companies such as Bafokeng Civil Works, Bafokeng Brick and Tile, Bafokeng Chrome, Bafokeng Bakery, and a Bafokeng shopping center. The RBN has also invested in infrastructure such as roads, bridges, reservoirs, electricity, schools, and health clinics, and it has established a fund for Bafokeng individuals who are pursuing professional training or higher education. Over time, the ethnic group has become an ethno-enterprise—built, branded, packaged, and advertised on the Bafokeng ethnic name and identity.

Many scholars, politicians, and economists expected the RBN to wither away in the face of globalization, modernity, and the homogenizing influence of the capitalist economy. However, the RBN ethno-corporation has flourished. It provides a remarkable example of the ways in which ethnicity can be mobilized by stakeholders in identity-based businesses to create alternative strategies for survival and success in the global marketplace.

Despite their corporate success, all is not well within the Bafokeng nation itself. Questions regularly arise about who benefits from this version of "Ethnicity, Inc." Individual Bafokeng do not own shares in RBN, Inc. Its money is not distributed among members but is reinvested in the corporation. Despite investments in job programs, infrastructure, and education in the homeland, recent studies show that the Bafokeng have a 39 percent unemployment rate, 95 percent use pit latrines for toilets, and less than 13 percent have electricity. With extreme poverty rates, some observers refer to the Bafokeng as "a rich nation of poor people" (Comaroff and Comaroff 2009, 109). How would you assess the effectiveness of this mobilization of ethnicity by the Bafokeng?

Each year, half a million tourists visit the Dai Minority Park in China's southwestern Yunnan Province. This is one of many ethno-parks owned and operated by members of China's Han majority (96 percent of the population), who market the nation's fifty-five ethnic minorities to a primarily middle-class Han clientele (Chio 2014). Here, tourists can live in Dai-style houses, eat ethnic meals, and participate in reenactments of ritual celebrations such as the water festival, pictured here, originally an annual three-day festival but now performed every day for the entertainment of visitors. How might ethno–theme parks benefit the Chinese government's goal of national unity? How do you think they affect the local communities?

ETHNIC INTERACTION IN THE UNITED STATES: ASSIMILATION VERSUS MULTICULTURALISM

The United States has an extremely complicated history of dealing with people of different ethnic backgrounds. The relationship of "ethnic" and "American" (as applied to the United States) remains controversial today. From the outset, several factors made the United States one of the most ethnically diverse countries in the world: immigration from various regions in Europe, the importation of African slaves, and the conquest of Native American peoples. But this diverse population has experienced extremely different paths to incorporation into U.S. culture. In fact, these paths have often followed color lines that divide people of lighter and darker complexions.

melting pot

A metaphor used to describe the process of immigrant assimilation into U.S. dominant culture.

assimilation

The process through which minorities accept the patterns and norms of the dominant culture and cease to exist as separate groups.

Scholars have often used the **melting pot** metaphor to describe the standard path into U.S. culture. In the melting pot, minorities adopt the patterns and norms of the dominant culture and eventually cease to exist as separate groups—a process scholars call **assimilation**. Eventually all cooked in the same pot, diverse groups become assimilated into one big stew. According to this metaphor, tens of millions of European immigrants from dozens of countries with myriad languages, cultures, and religious practices have been transformed into ethnic whites through marriage, work, education, and the use of English.

But in reality the melting pot has never been completely successful in the United States. Even the creation of whiteness, as we saw in Chapter 5, was often contentious and difficult, marked by intense rivalries and violence. Nathan Glazer and Daniel Patrick Moynihan's landmark study *Beyond the Melting Pot* (1970) found a failure to reach complete assimilation among European immigrants and their descendants as late as the third generation. For Africans, Native Americans, Latinos, and many Asian immigrants, the United States has been resistant to their assimilation into the dominant culture, regardless of their educational level or socioeconomic status.

The incredibly diverse flows of immigration to the United States since 1965 have made earlier familiar categories inadequate to capture the rapidly shifting ethnic character of the nation's population today. As discussed in Chapters 5 and 11 (on race and migration, respectively), immigrants and their children are creating new ethnic identities and new ways of becoming American. Today a multiculturalist narrative competes with the melting pot metaphor to represent the role of ethnicity in U.S. culture. **Multiculturalism** refers to the process through which new immigrants and their children enculturate into the dominant national culture and yet retain an ethnic culture. In multiculturalism, both identities may be held at the same time.

multiculturalism

A pattern of ethnic relations in which new immigrants and their children enculturate into the dominant national culture and yet retain an ethnic culture.

Tensions over which model will be dominant in the U.S. ethnicity story—assimilation or multiculturalism—are constantly rising to the surface. For example, attempts to establish English as the official language of towns, states, and even the U.S. federal government can be seen as (1) an effort to mandate language assimilation into the melting pot, and (2) a reassertion of the dominant culture's centrality against the rising trend toward multiculturalism (Rumbaut and Portes 2001).

What Is the Relationship of Ethnicity to the Nation?

Almost all people today imagine themselves as part of a nation-state. But this has not always been the case. **States**—regional structures of political, economic, and military rule—have existed for thousands of years, beginning in the regions now known as modern-day Iraq, China, and India. But the nation-state is a relatively new development. The term signifies more than a geographic territory with borders enforced by a central government. **Nation-state** assumes a distinct political entity whose population shares a sense of culture, ancestry, and destiny as a people. Though the term **nation** once was used to describe a group of people who shared a place of origin, today the word *nation* is often used interchangeably with *nation-state*. **Nationalism** emerges when a sense of ethnic community combines with a desire to create and maintain a nation-state in a location where that sense of common destiny can be lived out (Gellner 1983; Wolf 2001; Hearn 2006).

IMAGINED COMMUNITIES AND INVENTED TRADITIONS

Across the world over the past two hundred years, people have shifted their primary associations and identifications from family, village, town, and city to an almost universal identification with a nation or the desire to create a nation. Yet despite our contemporary assumptions that identification with an ethnic group or a nation has deep history, anthropological research reveals that most ethnic groups and nations are recent historical creations, our connection to people within these groups recently imagined, and our shared traditions recently invented.

Benedict Anderson (1983) conceived of the nation as an **imagined community**. He called it "imagined" because almost all of the people within it have never met and most likely will never meet. They may be separated by sharp divisions of class, politics, or religion and yet imagine themselves to have a common heritage and collective responsibility to one another and their nation. This sense of membership in an imagined national community can be strong enough to lead people into battle to protect their shared interests.

Anderson traces the imagined communities in Europe to the development of print communication in the capitalist economies that emerged in the eighteenth

state

An autonomous regional structure of political, economic, and military rule with a central government authorized to make laws and use force to maintain order and defend its territory.

nation-state

A political entity, located within a geographic territory with enforced borders, where the population shares a sense of culture, ancestry, and destiny as a people.

nation

A term once used to describe a group of people who shared a place of origin; now used interchangeably with *nation-state*.

nationalism

The desire of an ethnic community to create and/or maintain a nation-state.

imagined community

The invented sense of connection and shared traditions that underlies identification with a particular ethnic group or nation whose members likely will never all meet.

and nineteenth centuries. As people shared communication and information through newspapers and books published in a common language, Anderson suggests, they began to define themselves—to imagine themselves—as part of the same nation, the same community. Anderson's conception of imagined communities has become an essential analytical tool for thinking about nations and nationalisms.

Another view suggests that nations are invented. According to Eric Hobsbawm and Terence Ranger (1983), nations are not ancient configurations but instead are recent constructions with invented traditions. They may evoke a sense of deep history and inspire a broad sense of unity, but these nations are relatively new. For example, we imagine the French nation-state to have a deep and unitary history, but prior to the 1800s the French were a scattered collection of urban and rural people who spoke different languages, celebrated different holidays and festivals, practiced different religions, and held primary loyalty not to the French state but to their city, town, village, or extended family. It was two national infrastructure projects, launched in the early 1800s, that ultimately played key roles in inventing a French nation.

What did these infrastructure projects involve? First, a new education system was introduced on a national scale. Its textbooks promoted a shared sense of French history, and perhaps most important, all schools used the Paris dialect of French as the medium of instruction. This created a standard national language—a lingua franca—that facilitated communication among the population. Second, the construction of an extensive network of roads and railways

MAP 6.5
France

French classroom, 1829. What role can education play in creating a sense of common nationality?

integrated rural areas into a national market economy. This new transportation infrastructure promoted the rapid flow of goods between agricultural and industrial sectors and allowed the regular movement of workers between countryside and city, thereby providing a national labor pool for France's growing economy. These national infrastructure projects proved crucial to transforming the diverse people living within the territorial boundaries of what is now modern-day France into a French people with a common sense of identity, history, language, and tradition (Weber 1976).

ANTICOLONIALISM AND NATIONALISM

At times, efforts to imagine a national identity among a diverse group of people gain strength through the need—perceived or real—to join together against the threat of a common enemy. The outsiders—"others" who do not belong to the group—may be stereotyped along lines of religion, race, language, ethnicity, or political beliefs. War is the most dramatic strategy for evoking nationalism and mobilizing a population for the project of nation-building.

Through much of the nineteenth and twentieth centuries, colonialism effectively constructed "the other" in the minds of people at home. Colonial governments, merchants, and missionaries represented those whom they were colonizing as backward, tribal, heathen, and violent—in other words, needing to be civilized, Christianized, and modernized. Through their colonial conquests, the emerging nation-states of Europe redrew the political borders of much of the world to suit their own economic needs: they mapped out territorial boundaries without regard to local ethnic, political, economic, or religious realities.

Subsequently, the destruction of European economies during World War II (1939–45) weakened the colonial powers' ability to control their colonies. National independence movements that had been gaining strength in colonies throughout Asia, Africa, the Middle East, Latin America, and the Caribbean before World War II were able to develop military capabilities and guerrilla fighting tactics during the war and, subsequently, turned their efforts more fully toward liberating their countries from the colonial occupiers. The anticolonialist efforts led to a rise of nationalism in former colonies as disparate populations banded together to reassert local control.

As mentioned above, the territorial boundaries created by European colonial powers ignored local realities in favor of colonial economic and political interests. As a result, by the end of the colonial era few of the newly formed countries had homogeneous populations. Most now encompassed multiple ethnicities and identities within state borders that previously had not existed. Such disparities caused thorny problems for nationalist movements and for the nation-states that formed after independence (Robbins 2013).

THE CHALLENGES OF DEVELOPING A SENSE OF NATIONHOOD

The following case study from Iraq will expand your understanding of nation, nationalism, nation building, and the modern nation-state. Can you identify in this example the key concepts introduced in this chapter?

MAP 6.6

Iraq

Are There Any Iraqis in Iraq? Since the U.S. invasion and occupation of Iraq in 2003, news reports have featured stories of ethnic violence among Sunni, Shia, and Kurds—violence that the media portrays as the true obstacle to democracy and peace. The front pages of newspapers and the leads on evening news tell stories of seemingly endless and senseless suicide bombings, roadside explosives, armed militias, kidnappings, and assassinations. Elections are held, but the elected officials, torn by intense ethnic, religious, and political differences, are unable to form a functioning government. In the same way that the Western press typically reports what it describes as ethnic conflicts around the world—whether in Rwanda, Sudan, Sri Lanka, India, or the former Yugoslavia—deep and long-standing ethnic and religious cleavages in Iraq are blamed for an environment in which civil war and government collapse are almost inevitable. The same narrative has been used to explain Iraq's inability to protect its borders and defend its citizens against the invading forces of ISIL (the Islamic State in Iraq and the Levant—sometimes called ISIS) which, beginning in 2014, occupied the key western Iraqi cities of Fallujah, Mosul, Tikrit, and other territories.

Why, after so many years of nation building with U.S. economic and military support, have the Iraqi people been unable to form a strong government and military and stop the violence? Aren't there any Iraqis in Iraq—people who would put the country first, ahead of other ethnic or religious differences?

Iraq does not have an ancient history as a nation. Although cities such as Baghdad have an ancient history in the region of Mesopotamia, sometimes called the "cradle of civilization," the country of Iraq did not exist before World War I. Even then, Iraq was not formed through local initiative. A secret treaty between France and Great Britain (the Sykes-Picot Agreement), signed during World War I, carved up their opponent, the Ottoman Empire, to form many of the countries we find in the Middle East today. The two European powers, with Russia's consent, drew national borders—including those of present-day Iraq—to meet their needs for economic access, trade routes, and political control. The powers mapped out these borders with little regard for the history, politics, religions, and ethnic makeup of the local populations.

With a mandate from the new League of Nations in 1920, the British established a monarchical government in the new state of Iraq and recruited and empowered leaders from the minority Sunni population to run the government. Members of the Shia and Kurd populations, excluded from leadership roles in the government, actively fought for independence from British colonial occupation. Britain subsequently granted full independence to Iraq in 1932 (with the exception of another brief military occupation during World War II), but the Sunni minority retained control of the government until the fall of Saddam Hussein in 2003.

After the U.S. military occupied Iraq in 2003, the people of Iraq inherited a collapsed state structure and confronted the prospects of "nation building" in a country under foreign occupation that had experienced decades of state-sponsored violence. Yet media representations of Iraq consistently traced its problems to the roots of ethnic conflict. Social scientists from many fields question these simple storylines that portray deep ethnic and religious hatreds as the cause of Iraq's current difficulties (Ericksen 2010). Ethnicity, they warn, should never be seen that simply or monolithically. A more careful examination may find that (1) ethnic and religious lines are not drawn so clearly, and (2) other identities based on factors such as region, family, and class—even international relations—may also play key roles in the unfolding of events. With a weak state unable to provide security to its population, people turn to other strategies for mobilizing support, safety, and the means for achieving a livelihood (Eller 1999).

As globalization creates flows of people, ideas, goods, and images across borders and builds linkages among local communities worldwide, we might anticipate that ethnicity and nationalism—which are associated with local and national identities—would have less capacity to shape people's lives and influence the way people make decisions. Instead, in many parts of the world we see an intensification of ethnic and national identities and related conflicts. Understanding the processes through which ethnicity and nationalism are imagined and mobilized and their traditions invented, often over relatively short periods, can provide a set of tools for analyzing the role of ethnicity in our world today.

Toolkit

Thinking Like an Anthropologist:
Who Is an American?

In the opening story of the World Cup—one of the most global of all sporting events—and in the ethnographic examples throughout the chapter, we have seen how ethnic identity and nationalism continue to be imagined, built, nurtured, taught, learned, promoted, negotiated, and contested. And we have explored an anthropological perspective on three questions that connect the concepts of ethnicity and nationalism:

- **What does "ethnicity" mean to anthropologists?**
- **How is ethnicity created and put in motion?**
- **What is the relationship of ethnicity to the nation?**

Few of us are aware of the role of ethnicity and nationalism in our lives or how our culture works to promote them. As you learn to think like an anthropologist yourself, can you begin to see the process of ethnic identity construction at work in your own life and in the major debates of the culture that surrounds you? Consider these recent debates about who is and who is not an American:

- Despite an official "certificate of live birth" and other clear evidence that President Obama was born in the state of Hawaii on August 4, 1961, more than 25 percent of Americans surveyed in an August 2010 poll by the Pew Research Center claim that he is not a U.S. citizen. How is that possible?

- Some leading politicians want to change the Fourteenth Amendment of the U.S. Constitution. The amendment was passed after the Civil War to protect African Americans by ensuring that anyone born in the United States is granted full rights of citizenship. "Anchor babies," children born in the United States to Hispanic parents who are undocumented immigrants, are the target of these recent suggested changes to the Constitution. Some people fear that these babies are being "dropped as an anchor" so their parents can become citizens when their child attains the age of twenty-one. Do you think the U.S. Constitution should be amended to address this issue? Or is this debate simply a substitute for a larger struggle over who belongs to U.S. culture and who does not? How should a child's nationality and citizenship be defined?

- Plans to build an Islamic community center in lower Manhattan burst into the national awareness in August 2010. The center's organizers intended it as a place for healing and reconciliation after the tragedy of September 11 and as a symbol of American Muslims' determination to overcome the image of Islam as a violent religion. But certain enraged politicians denounced what they called the "Ground Zero mosque," demanding that it be stopped or moved away from Ground Zero. What role do ethno-political entrepreneurs play in an attempt to define Muslims as ethnic outsiders in the United States?

After reading this chapter, you should be better prepared with the anthropological tools to understand the ways ethnicity and nationalism work in your life and in your imagined communities—whether they are built around family, religion, hometown, ethnic group, or nation-state.

Key Terms

ethnicity (p. 156)

origin myth (p. 157)

ethnic boundary marker (p. 158)

genocide (p. 158)

situational negotiation of identity (p. 159)

ethnic cleansing (p. 164)

melting pot (p. 168)

assimilation (p. 168)

multiculturalism (p. 168)

state (p. 169)

nation-state (p. 169)

nation (p. 169)

nationalism (p. 169)

imagined community (p. 169)

Chapter 7
Gender

In May 2012, Ellen Pao filed a sexual harassment and discrimination lawsuit against Kleiner Perkins Caufield & Byers (KPCB), a leading Silicon Valley venture capital firm where she had been a partner since 2005. Pao, a graduate of Princeton University, Harvard Business School, and Harvard Law School, claimed that in addition to experiencing unwanted sexual advances (followed by retaliation when she complained), she and other women at KPCB were consistently passed over for promotions and given a smaller share of corporate profits in comparison to the firm's male partners. Rather than highlighting an isolated incident, Pao's lawsuit illuminates patterns in gender dynamics in Silicon Valley and in the information technology industry as a whole. Despite KPCB's reputation for promoting women's corporate leadership, of thirty-eight investment partners in 2012, only nine were women. Only six of the top one hundred technology company chief executives were women. Nationally, only 25 percent of software engineers were women (Perlroth 2012).

Why are women underrepresented in the U.S. information technology field? The nonprofit group Girls Who Code wants to address the imbalance by teaching teenage girls to write computer code.

The National Center for Women and Information Technology (2015) reports that women are underrepresented throughout the U.S. information technology field. Although 57 percent of all U.S. college graduates in 2013 were women, they held only 18 percent of degrees in computer and information sciences, down from 37 percent in 1985. Overall, women constituted only 26 percent of the computing workforce in 2014. These numbers are more striking when correlated with race: only 3 percent of the computing workforce comprised African American women; 5 percent Asian American women; and 1 percent Hispanic women.

Why are women underrepresented in jobs related to computers and information technology? How have these patterns in employment, pay, and promotion in Silicon Valley come about? What are the implications of these patterns for the lives and work of women and men? Attention to these questions of gender—that is, the characteristics associated with being a woman or man in a particular culture—is central to the practice of anthropology.

Since the pioneering work of Margaret Mead challenged U.S. cultural assumptions about human sexuality and gender roles (see Chapter 3), anthropologists, especially feminist anthropologists, have been at the forefront of attempts to bring the tools and analysis of anthropology to bear on crucial contemporary debates, social movements, and political struggles. Over the last forty years, **gender studies**—research into understanding who we are as men and women—has become one of the most significant subfields of anthropology. Indeed, anthropologists consider the ways in which gender is constructed as a central element in every aspect of human culture, including sexuality, health, family, religion, economics, politics, sports, and individual identity formation.

As we have seen throughout this book, people create diverse cultures with fluid categories to define complex aspects of the human experience. The same holds true for gender. Even biological sex is far more fluid and complex than people are taught. As we will see later in this chapter, nature creates diversity, not rigid categories. As globalization transforms gender roles and gender relations on both the local level and a global scale, anthropologists play an essential role in mapping the changing gender terrain of the modern world. In this chapter we will explore these issues in more detail:

- **Are men and women born or made?**
- **Are there more than two sexes?**
- **How do anthropologists explore the relationship between gender and power?**
- **How is globalization transforming women's lives?**

By the end of this chapter you will be better prepared to understand the role that sex and gender play in the culture around you, including in the classroom, family,

gender studies
Research into masculinity and femininity as flexible, complex, and historically and culturally constructed categories.

workplace, place of worship, and at the ballot box. You will also be able to apply anthropological insights into gender issues as they emerge in your own life—insights that will serve you well as boyfriends or girlfriends, spouses, parents, students, teachers, workers, managers, and community leaders in our increasingly global world.

Are Men and Women Born or Made?

"That's just the way guys are," some women sigh when a man says or does some stereotypical "man" thing. "Women!" a man may exclaim, hands in the air, as if all the other guys in the room know exactly what he means. But what *do* they mean? Is there some essential male or female nature that differentially shapes the personalities, emotions, patterns of personal relationships, career choices, leadership styles, and economic and political engagements of women and men?

DISTINGUISHING BETWEEN SEX AND GENDER

Much of what we stereotypically consider to be "natural" male or female behavior—driven by biology—might turn out, upon more careful inspection, to be imposed by cultural expectations of how men and women should behave. To help explore the relationship between the biological and cultural aspects of being men and women, anthropologists distinguish between sex and gender. **Sex**, from an anthropological viewpoint, refers to the observable physical differences between male and female human beings, especially the biological differences related to human reproduction. **Gender** is composed of the expectations of thought and behavior that each culture assigns to people of different sexes.

Historically, biological science has tended to create distinct mental maps of reality for male and female anatomy. Three primary factors have generally been considered in determining biological sex: (1) genitalia, (2) gonads (testes and ovaries, which produce different hormones), and (3) chromosome patterns (women have two X chromosomes; men have one X and one Y). Within this context, human males and females are said to display **sexual dimorphism**—that is, they differ physically in primary sexual characteristics as well as in secondary sexual characteristics such as breast size, hair distribution, and pitch of voice. Men and women on average also differ in weight, height, and strength. An average man is heavier, taller, and stronger than an average woman. Women on average have more long-term physical endurance and live longer.

sex

The observable physical differences between male and female, especially biological differences related to human reproduction.

gender

The expectations of thought and behavior that each culture assigns to people of different sexes.

sexual dimorphism

The phenotypic differences between males and females of the same species.

Gender roles, even those stereo-typically associated with male strength and aggression, are in flux across the globe. Here, two women in the U.S. military patrol the front lines in Helmand Province, Afghanistan.

It is important to note, however, that in comparison to other animal species, human sexual dimorphism, particularly with regard to body size and voice timbre, is relatively modest (Fedigan 1982). On average, human males (U.S. average, 190 pounds) weigh about 15 percent more than females (U.S. average, 163 pounds) (Ogden et al. 2004). In comparison, male gorillas on average are double the size of female gorillas (Cawthon Lang 2005). In an extreme case of sexual dimorphism, among deep-sea anglerfish (*Cryptopasaras couesi*), the female can weigh as much as 10 kilograms (or 10,000 grams), whereas the male weighs only about 150 grams—1.5 percent the size of the females. Male anglerfish fuse their mouths to a female's skin and then gradually atrophy: they lose their digestive organs, brain, heart, and eyes, eventually becoming nothing more than a pair of gonads that release sperm in response to the female's egg release (Pietsch 1975).

Sexual dimorphism among humans is far from absolute. In fact, human male and female bodies are much more similar than different. Many biological characteristics associated with human sexual dimorphism fall along a continuum—a range—in which men and women overlap significantly. Not all men are taller than all women, though many are. Not all women live longer than all men, though most do. And as we will see later in this chapter, even primary characteristics of biological sex do not always fit into the two assumed categories of male and female.

Cross-cultural anthropological research challenges the assumed links between biology and behavior. Knowing a person's biological sex does not enable us to predict what roles that person will play in a given culture. In some cultures, people with two X chromosomes do most of the cooking, farming, public speaking, and ritual activity; in others, people with one X and one Y chromosome fill those roles. Alternatively, the tasks may be done by both but stratified by power and prestige. In many Western cultures, for instance, both XX and XY cook. But women tend to cook in the home, while men predominate as restaurant chefs. Clearly, this is not a biologically driven division of labor. What could be the cultural reasons?

Even roles stereotypically associated with male strength and aggression are in flux today. Women do heavy labor—like the women of Plachimada in this book's opening chapter who rise early to carry water drums miles from the well to their homes. In addition, the predominance of men in violence and warfare is shifting as militaries in many parts of the world rely on women soldiers to fly remote-controlled predator drones, launch missiles, and engage in firefights on the front lines of battle. Because biology cannot predict the roles that men and women play in a given culture, anthropologists consider how gender is constructed culture by culture, and they explore the implications of those constructions for the men and women in each context.

THE CULTURAL CONSTRUCTION OF GENDER

Humans are born with biological sex, but we learn to be women and men. From the moment of birth we begin to learn culture, including how to walk, talk, eat, dress, think, practice religion, raise children, respond to violence, and express our emotions like a man or a woman (Mauss 1979). We learn what kinds of behavior are perceived as masculine or feminine. Thus, anthropologists refer to the **cultural construction of gender**.

Family, friends, the media, doctors, educational institutions, religious communities, sports, and law all enculturate us with a sense of gender that becomes normative and seems natural. For example, parents "do gender" with their children. They assign them boy or girl names; dress them in appropriately gendered clothing, colors, and jewelry; and give them the "right" haircuts. Parents even speak to their boy and girl children in different tones of voice. As we see gender being performed all around us, we learn to perform it in our turn. In these ways gender is taught, learned, and enforced.

Over a lifetime, gender becomes a powerful, and mostly invisible, framework that shapes the way we see ourselves and others (Bern 1981, 1983). Our relationships with others become an elaborate gendered dance of playing, dating, mating, parenting, and loving that reinforces our learned ideas of masculinity and femininity and establishes differing roles and expectations. Gender is also a potent cultural system through which we organize our collective lives, not necessarily on the basis of merit or skill but on the constructed categories of what it means to be a man or a woman (Rubin 1975; Lorber 1994; Bonvillain 2007; Brettell and Sargent 2009).

cultural construction of gender The ways humans learn to behave as a man or woman and to recognize behaviors as masculine or feminine within their cultural context.

How is gender taught and learned through youth sports like this T-ball game?

Teaching Gender in the United States: Boys, Girls, and Youth Sports.

Sports is a key cultural arena in which individuals learn gender roles. A study of young boys and girls playing co-ed T-ball provides insights into how gender in the United States is subtly and not-so-subtly taught, learned, and enforced through youth sports (Landers and Fine 1996). T-ball is the precursor to baseball in which kids hit a ball off a stationary, upright plastic stick (a tee) rather than a ball thrown from a pitcher.

Landers and Fine found that T-ball coaches established a hierarchy of opportunity, training, and encouragement that favored boys over girls. Boys consistently received more playing time than girls, played positions (such as shortstop or first base) that provided more opportunities to touch the ball and develop their skills, and had more opportunities to practice hitting the ball at the plate. Boys frequently received coaching advice, while girls' mistakes went uncorrected. Parents and other players supported this hierarchy of training and opportunity and, along with the coaches, offered less or more encouragement along gender lines. For example, boys received more words of praise for their successes. These hierarchies were apparent not only between boys and girls, but within gendered groups as well. Among the boys, praise and opportunity were unequally distributed: those who were already stronger, faster, better coordinated, or more advanced in baseball skills were favored over those who were not as advanced. Moving beyond the T-ball experience, the researchers noted that ideal forms of masculinity and manliness are taught, learned, and enforced on the baseball field as well, promoting aggressiveness, assertiveness, competitiveness, physical strength and skill, and a drive to succeed and win (Landers and Fine 1996).

Did you ever participate in youth sports, either in the United States or in another country? If so, what was your experience like? Did your parents sign you up for certain sports—basketball, soccer, lacrosse, football, wrestling, ice hockey, dance, gymnastics, figure skating, cheerleading? If so, what role might their ideas of gender have played in their choice? Landers and Fine's study suggests that attributes stereotypically associated with boys such as athleticism, assertiveness, aggression, strength, and competitiveness are actively constructed along gender lines through a wide variety of youth sports. In considering their study, can you see the ramifications of such gender training on individuals' attitudes and behaviors as they become adults with responsible roles in family, work, and politics?

While recognizing the physical differences between men and women—modest as they are when considering the diversity of the whole human population—how do we factor in the role of culture in something like sports and athleticism? Gender enculturation in sports and physical play begins early and happens in varied settings. I remember taking my toddler son to the playground and watching as other parents encouraged their little boys to run, climb, and jump while urging their little girls to play nicely in the sandbox. Starting in everyday settings like this, perhaps we can begin to imagine the cumulative effects of parental expectations, peer pressure, and media images on girls' motivation to engage in intense physical activity and competition. As a result, sports may reflect less about real physical differences in speed, endurance, and strength and more about how a given culture constructs and maintains gender and sex norms. Perhaps becoming a world-class athlete depends more on opportunity, encouragement, coaching, nutrition, training facilities, and wealth than on being a man or a woman.

Today, as training and opportunities increase, women are closing the performance gap with men in many sports. But the persistence of inequality throughout sports culture precludes an accurate comparison between women and men athletes at the current time.

Constructing Masculinity in a U.S. High School. Since the 1970s, gender studies have focused primarily on women. Recent studies, however, have begun to explore the gender construction of male identity as well as the broader construction of masculinity. The ethnography described here touches on several key aspects of this complex process.

C. J. Pascoe's ethnography *Dude, You're a Fag* (2007) explores the construction of gender—and particularly masculinity—in a suburban, working-class, racially diverse high school in north-central California. Calling someone a fag, what Pascoe calls "fag discourse," occurred almost exclusively among white male students in a daily banter of teasing, bullying, and harassment. Basing her conclusions on interviews with students, Pascoe found that calling someone a fag was not about whether someone was or was not gay; instead, it was directed at guys who danced like girls, cared about their clothing, seemed too emotional, or did something incompetent. In other words, white male students directed the epithet at other males who were not considered sufficiently masculine. Gay guys were tolerated as long as they were not effeminate, as long as they could throw a football around. Among the teenagers in Pascoe's study, fag discourse became a powerful tool for enforcing the boundaries of masculinity—a disciplinary mechanism for making sure "boys are boys" through the fear of abuse or violence.

Moreover, Pascoe points out that masculinity is not always associated with men. Girls can act masculine as well. She describes a group of "masculine" girls who play on the girls' basketball team and "perform masculinity" by the way they dress, display their sexuality, and dominate public spaces around the school. Jessie, a lesbian, is also president of the student council and homecoming queen. Her popularity appears to be related to her performance of masculinity. In these contexts, masculinity and dominance are linked to women's bodies, not to men's. Pascoe thus points out the ways in which both guys and girls can perform masculinity and girls can adopt masculinity to gain status (Bridges 2007; Calderwood 2008; Wilkins 2008).

MAP 7.1
Mexico City

Machismo in Mexico. The construction of male identity does not necessarily yield a rigid result, as the following study reveals. In *The Meanings of Macho* (2007), Matthew Gutmann examines what it means to be a man, *ser hombre*, for the men and women of a small neighborhood in Mexico City. Common conceptions of *machismo* as the concept has spread around the world feature stereotypes of self-centered, sexist, tough guys. When macho is applied to men in Latin America, especially working-class Mexican men, these stereotypes can also include insinuations of violence, drug use, infidelity, and gambling. However, Gutmann's research in a working-class community reveals a complex male world of fathers, husbands, friends, and lovers that does not fit the common stereotypes.

For the men whom Gutmann studied, machismo and masculinity constitute a shifting landscape. What it means to be a man (or a woman) in the community can depend on the particular man or woman or the particular circumstance. One of Gutmann's key informants, the elderly Don Timo, rails against effeminate men but has himself crossed stereotypical gender boundaries by actively helping to raise his children. Two other informants, Tono and Gabriel, who are tough young men, argue about a father's proper role in buying children's Christmas presents. These examples illustrate the fluidity of male identity in the population that Gutmann studied, and the quote below underscores his conclusions:

When analyzing changing male identities in *colonias populares* in
Mexico City, for example, categories that posit static differences in
the male and female populations—the drunks, the loving mothers,
the wife beaters, the machos, the sober family men, the submissive
women—hinder one's efforts more than they assist them. Gender
identities, roles and relations do not remain frozen in place, either for
individuals or for groups. There is continuous contest and confusion
over what constitutes male identity; it means different things to different people at different times. And sometimes different things to
the same person at the same time. (Gutmann 2007, 27)

Ultimately, Guttmann discovered such complex male identities that he
found it impossible to use any simple formula to describe a typical Mexican man,
a Mexican urban working-class man, or a macho Mexican. Instead he found the
men in the community he studied to be working out their roles together with
women, debating and deciding about household chores, child rearing, sex, the use
of money, work outside the home, and the use of alcohol (Limon 1997; Parker
1999). How do these processes take place in your own family?

THE PERFORMANCE OF GENDER

Recently, anthropologists have moved from focusing on gender roles toward
examining **gender performance**. Gender roles can mistakenly be seen as
reflecting stable, fixed identities that fall in one of two opposite extremes—
male or female. But anthropologists increasingly see gender as a continuum
of behaviors that range between masculine and feminine. Rather than being

gender performance
The way gender identity is
expressed through action.

something fixed in the psyche, gender is an identity that is expressed through action (Butler 1990).

My students, when identifying stereotypical masculine and feminine characteristics, often create something similar to the following list:

- *Masculine*: aggressive, physical, tough, competitive, sports oriented, testosterone driven, strong, unemotional
- *Feminine*: gentle, kind, loving, nurturing, smart, persuasive, talkative, enticing, emotional

But we know that both women and men can display any of these characteristics. And any individual may choose to display various characteristics at different times depending on the setting. A man may perform his masculinity—his gender—differently when watching football with his buddies than while out on a date.

Indeed, people regularly make choices about how they will express their gender identity, for whom, and in what context. This is why we say that gender is performed. A man may drive a truck to make a living but also gently change his baby's diapers and take her in a stroller to play in the park. A woman may enjoy sewing dresses for her daughters but also dominate boardroom discussions as CEO of a company.

Viewing gender as performance enables us to broaden our thinking beyond easy dichotomies and universal characteristics of "man" and "woman." Anthropological research suggests that rather than looking for some essential male or female nature rooted in biology that shapes everything from personality to economic activity, a more fruitful exploration must consider the ways in which ideas of gender are constructed and performed in response to each culture's gender norms and expectations. In so doing, gender can be seen less as a naturally limiting framework and more as a set of fluid constructs and flexible choices. By taking this approach, we can more easily see that stratification based on gender is not fixed and natural; rather, it emerges as a result of decisions to arrange access to power, privilege, and resources in particular ways.

Are There More Than Two Sexes?

As our earlier discussion of sexual dimorphism indicated, primary characteristics of biological sex do not always fit neatly into the two assumed categories of male and female. Moreover, even when we can identify a person's biological sex, we cannot predict what roles that person will play in a given culture. The sections that follow make these points abundantly clear.

A THEORY OF FIVE SEXES

Biologist Anne Fausto-Sterling (1993) has proposed a theory that sheds light on the issue of fluidity versus rigidity in conceptualizing categories of biological sex and how they relate to gender identity. In her article "The Five Sexes: Why Male and Female Are Not Enough," Fausto-Sterling describes the middle ground between these two absolute categories. This middle ground encompasses a diversity of physical expressions along the continuum between male and female that once were labeled "hermaphrodite" and now are described as "intersex."

A review of medical data from 1955 to 2000 suggests that "approximately 1.7% of all live births do not conform to [the] ideal of absolute sex chromosome, gonadal, genital and hormonal dimorphism" (Blackless et al. 2000, 151). Using these statistics, we may estimate that millions of people are born as **intersexuals**—that is, as individuals who have some combination of male and female genitalia, gonads, and chromosomes. Fausto-Sterling identifies at least three major groups of intersexuals: Some have a balance of female and male sexual characteristics—for instance, one testis and one ovary. Others have female genitalia but testes rather than ovaries. Still others have male genitalia with ovaries rather than testes.

intersexual
An individual who is born with a combination of male and female genitalia, gonads, and/or chromosomes.

Most Western societies ignore the existence of middle sexes. More commonly, they legally require a determination between male and female at birth. Furthermore, since the 1960s, Western medicine has taken the extreme steps of attempting to "manage" intersexuality through surgery and hormonal treatments. According to the 2000 American Academy of Pediatrics policy statement on intersex surgery, "the birth of a child with ambiguous genitalia constitutes a social emergency" (American Academy of Pediatrics 2000, 138). Medical procedures—most performed before a child comes of age and can decide for him- or herself—aim to return intersex infants to the cultural norm for heterosexual males and females, although about 90 percent of the surgeries make ambiguous male anatomy into female. Decisions are often based on the size of the penis: the smaller the phallus, the more likely the surgery will reassign the person as female. These interventions represent what French social scientist Michel Foucault ([1976] 1990) has referred to as *biopower*—the disciplining of the body through control of biological sex characteristics to meet a cultural need for clear distinctions between the sexes.

These medical interventions have faced increasing criticism both within the medical profession and among advocacy and support groups such as the Intersex Society of North America (www.isna.org) and Accord Alliance (www.accordalliance.org). Such groups have worked to educate the public and the medical community about the experiences of intersex people, particularly about their right to control decisions about their sexual and gender identities.

In 2006, *Pediatrics,* the journal of the American Academy of Pediatrics, published new guidelines that urge practicing greater patient-centered care, avoiding "elective" surgery until the person is old enough to make his or her own decision, and eliminating misleading and outdated language (such as *hermaphrodite*) that distracts from treating the whole person.

The presence of middle sexes suggests that we must reconceptualize one of our most rigid mental maps of reality—the one separating male and female. In the process, perhaps we will recognize that just as gender is culturally constructed, even our ideas of human biology have been culturally constructed as well. Acknowledgement of a diversity of physical expressions along the continuum between male and female may, in turn, allow for a less dualistic and more holistic approach to understanding the complex relationship between biology and gender.

ALTERNATE SEXES, ALTERNATE GENDERS

Cross-cultural studies show that not every culture fixes sexuality and gender in two distinct categories. Many cultures allow room for diversity. For example, even though India's dominant system for mapping sex and gender strongly emphasizes two opposite but complementary roles (male and female), Indian culture also recognizes many alternative constructions. Hindu religion acknowledges these variations in myth, art, and ritual. Hindu myths feature androgynous and intersex figures, and Hindu art depicts a blending of sexes and genders, including males with wombs, breasts, or pregnant bellies. In terms of Hindu ritual, the discussion below explores the role of one alternative group, known as *hijras,* in expressing gender diversity in India.

The Role of *Hijras* in Hindu Ritual. *Hijras* are religious followers of the Hindu Mother Goddess, Bahuchara Mata, who is often depicted and

transgender

A gender identity or performance that does not fit with cultural norms related to one's assigned sex at birth.

described as transgender. (The term **transgender** refers to individuals whose gender identities or performances do not fit with cultural norms related to their assigned sex at birth.) Most *hijras* are born as men, though some may be intersex. In *Neither Man nor Woman: The Hijras of India* (1998) and subsequent writing, Serena Nanda has analyzed these individuals and their role in demonstrating gender diversity.

Through ritual initiation and, for some, extensive ritual surgery to remove penis and testicles (an operation now outlawed in India), *hijras* become an alternative sex and gender. Culturally they are viewed as neither man nor woman, although they tend to adopt many characteristics of the woman's role. They dress, walk, and talk like women and may have sex with men. Because of their transgression of cultural and religious boundaries, they are at once both feared and revered. Many live in *hijra* religious communities on the margins of Hindu

Hindu religious myth, art, and ritual acknowledge alternative gender constructions like this depiction of Ardhanari, an androgynous deity composed of Shiva and his consort Shakti.

society. *Hijras* often face extreme discrimination in employment, housing, health, and education. Many support themselves through begging, ritual performances, and sex work. Violence against them is not uncommon, particularly against *hijra* sex workers.

At the same time, *hijras* are revered as auspicious and powerful ritual figures. They perform at weddings and at birth celebrations—particularly at the birth of a son. Not only do they bless the child and family, but they also entertain the celebrants and guests with burlesque and sexually suggestive songs, dance, and comedy. Their life in the middle ground between strong cultural norms of male and female contributes to their ritual power (Nanda 1998).

These insights underscore the potential for more complex understandings of sex and gender that move beyond assumptions of two discrete categories of male and female, masculine and feminine. As stated throughout this chapter, nature creates diversity. And humans create diverse cultures. Thus, as the topics here have illustrated, biology does not fix in place gender roles, norms, performances, and patterns of interaction and stratification. Being cultural constructs, they all can change. These anthropological findings may challenge you to ask, "How might I work to expose and dismantle stereotypes and unequal structures of power related to gender in my personal life, at school and in the workplace, and in U.S. culture more broadly?"

How Do Anthropologists Explore the Relationship between Gender and Power?

Although gender may often be regarded as affecting individuals on a personal basis—for instance, how you negotiate relationships with people you date, study with, or work for—anthropologists also explore how gender structures relationships of power that have far-reaching effects. Understanding these processes becomes increasingly important as individuals and cultures experience heightened interaction in today's global age (Mascia-Lees 2009).

Meeting in 2000, the member states of the United Nations adopted eight Millennial Development Goals designed to eliminate the most extreme forms of global poverty and inequality:

1. Eradicate extreme poverty and hunger.

2. Achieve universal primary education.

3. Promote gender equality and empower women.

4. Reduce child mortality.

5. Improve maternal health.

6. Combat HIV / AIDS, malaria, and other diseases.

7. Ensure environmental sustainability.

8. Develop a global partnership for development.

As several of the United Nations goals indicate, improving the conditions of women held particular importance. Even though each goal included specific targets, more than a decade later the United Nations Development Programme reported that women's struggles for equality are far from complete.

A quick look at some statistics reveals the current contours of women's struggles worldwide: Sixty percent of the world's poorest people are women and girls. Two-thirds of all children unable to attend school are girls. The chance of dying because of pregnancy in sub-Saharan Africa is 1 in 16, but in the developed world it is only 1 in 3,800. Young women age 15 to 25 are being infected with HIV / AIDS three times faster than men in the same age group. Women are disproportionally affected by environmental degradation. And less than 16 percent of the world's parliamentarians are women (United Nations Development Programme 2013b). It is not hard to conclude from these facts that gender plays a key role in power relationships on many levels and in many arenas.

REVISITING EARLY RESEARCH ON MALE DOMINANCE

As gender studies emerged in anthropology in the 1970s, one of the first targets of research was the apparent universality of male dominance across cultures. In searching for an explanation for what appeared to be women's universally low status, anthropologist Sherri Ortner (1974) proposed the existence of a pervasive, symbolic association of women with nature and men with culture (which was more highly valued). Ortner argued that the biological functions of reproduction, breast-feeding, and child rearing associated women with nature and placed them at a consistent disadvantage in negotiating relationships of power.

At the same time, Michelle Rosaldo (1974) saw the gender roles of men and women across cultures as being split between public and private spheres. Women, constrained by their role in reproduction, were confined to the private, or domestic, sphere—including the home, family, and childbearing. Men tended to dominate the public sphere—politics, economic exchange, and religious rit-ual. Because wealth and social status accrued to activities in the public sphere, men gained and maintained more power, privilege, and prestige than women did. Some scholars speculated that these patterns were rooted in the human evolutionary past—a proposition we will challenge later in this chapter. Others suggested that they might derive from men's superior physical strength. (See also Chodorow 1974.)

As scholars looked more carefully at women's lives in particular cultures, however, the picture became even more complicated. Previous assumptions about universal male dominance, including the gendered division of labor and uni-formly separate spheres of activity and power, were revealed to be historically inaccurate, overly simplistic in their reading of contemporary cultures, and prone to overlook the specific contexts of stratification and inequality (Leacock 1981). This was true not only for women's lives but for men's as well, where wealth,

MAP 7.2
Trobriand Islands

In contrast to Malinowski's earlier study (1922), why did feminist anthropologist Annette Weiner's research (1976) find Trobriand Island women engaged in significant economic activity, including the elaborate exchange of banana leaf bundles and banana fiber skirts (*left*), as well as participation in the yam harvest festival (*right*)?

power, and prestige were stratified both within and between gender groups (Quinn 1977; Rosaldo 1980).

Feminist scholars also began to revisit earlier anthropological research. Perhaps not surprisingly, these scholars discovered the significant role of women in cultures that earlier anthropologists had reported to be uniformly dominated by men. In one important reconsideration of a classic anthropological text, Annette Weiner (1976) revisited Bronislaw Malinowski's (1922) research on the Trobriand Islands, an archipelago of coral atolls just east of Papua New Guinea in the South Pacific. When Weiner reexamined the economic practices of the Trobriand Islands in the 1970s with an eye to the role of gender in shaping economic activity, she found that Malinowski's research was incomplete. Women in fact engaged in an elaborate economic activity that Malinowski had failed to recognize.

The emerging anthropological scholarship of gender in the 1970s provided new tools for Weiner to overcome gender blindness and, instead, see the fullness of Trobriand culture. She wrote:

> Any study that does not include the role of women—as seen by women—as part of the way the society is structured remains only a partial study of that society. Whether women are publicly valued or privately secluded, whether they control politics, a range of economic commodities, or merely magic spells, they function within that society, not as objects, but as individuals with some measure of control. (Weiner 1976, 228)

Weiner's example and admonition resonate throughout anthropology today.

GENDER STEREOTYPES, GENDER IDEOLOGY, AND GENDER STRATIFICATION

The emphasis in gender studies on the cultural construction of gender challenges anthropologists to explore the dynamics of specific cultures to understand what processes serve to construct gender in each society. Today anthropologists are asking questions like these: What are the processes that create **gender stratification**—an unequal distribution of power in which gender shapes who has access to a group's resources, opportunities, rights, and privileges? What are the gender stereotypes and gender ideologies that support a gendered system of power (Brodkin 2007)?

Gender stereotypes are widely held and powerful, preconceived notions about the attributes of, differences between, and proper roles for women and men in a culture. Men, for instance, may be stereotyped as more aggressive, whereas women might be expected to be more nurturing. These stereotypes create important assumptions about what men and women might expect from one another. **Gender ideology** is a set of cultural ideas—usually stereotypical—about men's and women's essential character, capabilities, and value that consciously or unconsciously promote and justify gender stratification. Gender stereotypes and ideologies vary from culture to culture, though their effects may appear similar when viewed through a global lens.

We now consider two examples of the ways in which gender ideologies have influenced thinking in U.S. culture.

The Egg and the Sperm. Emily Martin (1991) has explored the ways in which cultural ideas about gender—that is, gender ideologies—have influenced the way biologists have understood, described, and taught human reproduction. In particular, Martin discusses what she calls the fairy tale of the egg and sperm. By examining the most widely used college biology textbooks at the time of her research, Martin found that the distinct roles of eggs and sperm were described in stereotypical ways, even if those descriptions did not match up with more recent scientific findings. The textbooks described the aggressive sperm as being propelled by strongly beating tails searching for the egg in competition with fellow ejaculates attacking and penetrating the protective barriers of the egg to fertilize the passive, waiting, receiving egg.

Yet Martin cites biology research that reveals a very different dynamic. The tail of the sperm actually beats quite weakly and does not propel the sperm forward. Instead the tail serves only to move the head from side to side enough to keep it from getting stuck on all surfaces except the egg. When the egg and the sperm do connect, the sperm is not the assertive aggressor. Rather, adhesive molecules on both create a chemical bond that keeps them attached. Then the sperm and egg work in tandem. The sperm secretes a dissolving fluid that allows

gender stratification

An unequal distribution of power and access to a group's resources, opportunities, rights, and privileges based on gender.

gender stereotype

A preconceived notion about the attributes of, differences between, and proper roles for men and women in a culture.

gender ideology

A set of cultural ideas, usually stereotypical, about the essential character of different genders that functions to promote and justify gender stratification.

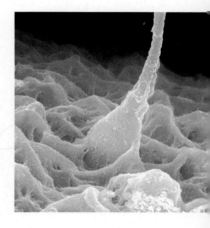

Are the stories you have been told about the meeting of the sperm (blue) and egg drawn from biological research or cultural gender stereotypes?

it to move toward the egg's nucleus. At the same time, the egg draws the sperm in and actually moves its own nucleus to meet the sperm and better enable fertilization. Thus, rather than displaying active and passive roles, the egg and the sperm appear to be mutually active partners in an egalitarian relationship.

According to Martin, writing in the early 1990s, images of the egg and sperm found in popular and scientific writing have been commonly based on cultural stereotypes of male and female. Moreover, the scientific language of biology has promoted these gender stereotypes. Men are considered more active, vigorous, adventurous, and important than women, who are seen as passive, receptive, nurturing, and less valuable and significant. Martin warns that by reading stereotypical feminine and masculine behavior into our accounts of eggs and sperm, we enshrine these gender roles in nature—we make them seem natural. In turn, when this narrative becomes a common description of nature, it reinforces culturally constructed gender patterns, roles, and hierarchies. It is possible to express the effect of such a process of misinformation in this (mistaken) way: "Of course those characteristics of men and women are natural and normal—they show up at the very beginning with the behavior of the sperm and the egg!"

Martin also warns of the social risks of attributing human personalities to eggs and sperm—for instance, describing them like a human couple engaged in deliberate human activity to make a baby. U.S. culture continues to debate when "life" begins—at fertilization, at viability, or at birth. Describing the egg and sperm as engaged in intentional action—a key criterion for personhood—risks opening the door to more scrutiny of pregnant women and restriction of their health choices, from amniocentesis to abortion to fetal surgeries.

Man the Hunter, Woman the Gatherer. Another familiar story that lies at the heart of U.S. gender ideologies is the tale of Man the Hunter, Woman the Gatherer. This fiction is frequently invoked to explain contemporary differences in gender roles by referencing the effects of human evolution. In our deep past, the story goes, human males—being larger and stronger than females—hunted to sustain themselves, their sexual partners, and their offspring (Lee and Devore 1968). Hunting required aggression, inventiveness, dominant behavior, male bonding, mobility, time away from the home, and less time with offspring—all patterns that we imagine have become hardwired into the human brain or imprinted on the human DNA. The ancient pleasure of killing animals supposedly shaped the human male psyche for aggression and violence and continues to drive men today. Women, in contrast, were gatherers (Dahlberg 1981). They collected fruits, seeds, and nuts and were more sedentary, home oriented, child centered, nurturing, cooperative, talkative, and passive.

This story, closely associated today with the field of evolutionary psychology, underlies much contemporary thinking about the origins and "naturalness" of gender relations. Contemporary gender roles, division of labor, and stratification of power, resources, rights, and privileges are assumed to have emerged directly from physical or mental differences that developed during human evolution. So, for instance, because early human males were hunters two million years ago, today modern human men prefer to go off to work, compete in the marketplace, and leave child rearing and housecleaning to the women. Quite simple, really—or is it?

Despite the popularity of this scenario in explaining contemporary male and female behavior, anthropological evidence does not support it. Yes, food foraging—hunting, scavenging, and gathering—was our ancestors' primary survival strategy for millions of years before the introduction of agriculture ten thousand years ago. Hundreds of thousands of people still live in societies where food foraging is a significant means of making a living. But no contemporary foraging societies or nonhuman primate groups display the division of labor described in the Man the Hunter, Woman the Gatherer story. In known foraging societies, women are not sedentary or passive members of the group (Stange 1997).

Though men appear to have done 70 percent of the hunting, it is not even clear that hunting was the foundational activity of early human groups. In fact, human patterns of group interaction more likely developed through the gathering and sharing of plant and seed resources. Archaeological evidence reveals that early hominid teeth were adapted to an omnivorous diet—most likely of plants, seeds, and meat, depending on what food was available in a particular season or area. Hunting would have contributed to this foundation when available, rather than the reverse. Meat may have been a part of the diet, but there is no conclusive evidence that our earliest human ancestors hunted prey

Ancient petroglyphs (rock carvings) discovered in the mountains north of the Saudi Arabian city of Hael appear to depict a hunting party. Were they men, as the hunter-gatherer stereotype would suggest?

themselves. Just as likely, they scavenged meat left behind by other predators (Fedigan 1986).

Anthropologists find no evidence to prove the existence of historical patterns of male dominance, including the protection of dependent women and children. Instead contemporary food-foraging cultures and the archaeological record on gender roles reveal a highly flexible division of labor that enabled human groups to quickly adapt to changing conditions. In fact, a flexibility of roles rather than a clear division of labor may more properly define the key characteristic of male–female relationships over human evolutionary history. Based on the evidence currently available, Man the Hunter, Woman the Gatherer—such as Martin's description of the fairy tale of the egg and the sperm—appears to be a modern-day cultural myth about gender projected back onto human evolutionary history that serves to imbue contemporary gender patterns with an appearance of inevitability and "naturalness" (Fedigan 1986).

Despite the archaeological, physical, and cultural evidence that anthropologists have accumulated to debunk the Man the Hunter, Woman the Gatherer myth, still it is a daunting task to shake free of the popular idea in U.S. culture that men and women have some essential—and essentially different—nature that was shaped in our deep past. The stereotypical "boys will be boys" and "that's just a girl thing" approach to gender differences has become a powerful gender ideology, deeply ingrained in the day-to-day conversations, expectations, relationships, work patterns, pay packages, promotions, and political activities of contemporary life.

Perhaps it is simpler to believe that our genetic blueprint predetermines who we are as men and women. Perhaps this belief in the inevitability of gendered cultural patterns makes us feel better about the gender inequality structured into our cultural practices and institutions. Why try to change what is "inevitable and natural"? But if these cultural ways of thinking about gender mask the essential changeability of gender, then the burden lies more heavily on the individual, the community, and the body politic to challenge patterns of power, privilege, and prestige drawn along gender lines.

CHALLENGING GENDER IDEOLOGIES AND STRATIFICATION

Women challenge and resist gender stereotypes, ideologies, inequalities, and violence directly and indirectly through creative local strategies, often building movements from the bottom up. Although lacking the global media attention or global solidarity afforded to international social movements, these local initiatives begin with women's culture-specific experiences (Abu-Lughod 2000). The following example provides a dramatic illustration of women challenging gender ideology, stratification, and violence.

Mothers of "The Disappeared" in El Salvador. Between 1977 and 1992, the Central American country of El Salvador was torn by a brutal civil war. Threatened by calls for economic equality and political openness, the government unleashed military and military-related death squads in a campaign of violence and terror that targeted students, peasants, union leaders, and anyone else critical of its policies. All who expressed opposition to government policies were labeled subversive and subject to reprisal.

Over the course of the civil war the military assassinated, imprisoned, tortured, raped, and "disappeared" tens of thousands of El Salvadorans. One in every one hundred was murdered or disappeared. The late 1970s were marked by particularly brutal campaigns. Every morning, residents of the capital city awoke to the sight of dead bodies—visibly tortured—left lying in the streets or dumped on the outskirts of town by the death squads. Many were disappeared—that is, detained and never seen again.

The grassroots women's organization CO-MADRES (The Committee of Mothers and Relatives of Political Prisoners, Disappeared, and Assassinated of El Salvador) emerged against this backdrop. The committee was one of a number of "motherist" groups across Central America in which the mothers of victims mobilized for human rights and against violence. Originally founded in 1977 by nine mothers, CO-MADRES quickly grew to include teachers, workers, students, lawyers, housewives, and shopkeepers—still mostly mothers, but with a few fathers as well. CO-MADRES became one of the first groups in El Salvador to challenge the brutal actions of the government and the military.

Initially, the women of CO-MADRES focused on demanding information from government, military, and paramilitary groups about family members who had been incarcerated, assassinated, or disappeared. The women occupied

MAP 7.3
El Salvador

The Mothers of "The Disappeared" march in El Salvador to protest the military's practices of assassination, imprisonment, torture, rape, and "disappearance."

government buildings, demonstrated in public parks and plazas, and held hunger strikes to exert pressure on the state. Searching for their missing relatives, they demanded access to prisons and prisoner lists, uncovered clandestine cemeteries, and formed alliances with international human rights groups to publicize the El Salvadoran government's atrocities.

As they became better organized, the women of CO-MADRES began to participate in movements for greater democratization, particularly demanding the inclusion of women at all levels of El Salvador's political decision-making bodies. Eventually, along with other feminist movements emerging globally, CO-MADRES began to address concerns about the prevalence of gender-based violence and rape and the absence of sex education and sexual autonomy for women in El Salvador.

CO-MADRES continued to work throughout the period of the El Salvadoran civil war despite attacks on the organization and its leaders by the government and its allies. CO-MADRES offices were bombed on multiple occasions. A majority of active CO-MADRES members and all of its leaders were detained, tortured, and raped: forty-eight were detained, five assassinated, and three disappeared. In El Salvador, rape became a common experience for the women activists of CO-MADRES and for urban and rural Salvadoran women whether they participated in a social movement or not.

CO-MADRES activist Alicia Panameno de Garcia, in an interview with anthropologist Lynn Stephen, shared how rape had become a widely used weapon of state-sponsored torture and how psychologically difficult it was to talk about it openly, even with other women victims.

ALICIA: Rape was one of those things we didn't really think about. We weren't really prepared for it happening to us. We didn't think that the military would systematically be using these practices. So the first few women were detained and they were raped and because we are taught that women are supposed to be pure, they didn't talk about that. They didn't say, "They did this to me."

L.S: They didn't talk about it?

ALICIA: Yes. But little by little we discovered it. The women started talking about it. They had to because it had consequences for their health. They needed medical assistance and when we would give people medical aid we started discovering that every one of the women had been raped. (Stephen 1995, 818)

Over time, the CO-MADRES members found that detained men were also being raped as part of their torture. The men were even more reluctant to talk about it than the women.

Eventually, CO-MADRES created a space for women to publicly discuss their experiences, to bring the sexual brutality of the military out into the open, and to talk about their fears—particularly that their husbands would abandon them. Working with other human rights organizations, the group began a process to hold the state accountable for these violations and call into question discriminatory legal codes that provided no rights to rape victims.

The story of CO-MADRES is just one example of the determined, creative, and often risk-filled efforts that women undertake across the globe to address gendered expressions of inequality, stratification, and violence. In an evolving response to their experiences in the midst of El Salvador's civil war, the women of CO-MADRES created a social movement that integrated traditional cultural expressions of femininity—ideas of motherhood, child rearing, and sacrifice for one's children—with direct confrontation of military death squads and government authorities as they demanded equality for women and sought to protect their families and their communities (Stephen 1995; Martin 1999; Molyneux 1999).

How Is Globalization Transforming Women's Lives?

Beginning in the 1980s, anthropologists turned their attention to the impact of globalization and flexible accumulation (see Chapter 11) on women and gender dynamics in local economies. At that time, women in many parts of the world were starting to migrate from rural areas to work in urban, coastal, export-oriented factories established by foreign corporations searching for cheap labor, low taxes, and few environmental regulations. As both local and national economies have continued to undergo rapid transitions, these women have had to negotiate between traditional gender expectations and the pressure to engage in wage labor to support themselves and their families (Mills 2003).

IMPACTS ON WOMEN IN THE LABOR FORCE

Anthropological research spanning the 1980s through the early 2000s reveals that working women in various parts of the globe have experienced similar challenges at the volatile intersection of globalization and local realities (Mills 2003).

Carla Freeman's *High Tech, High Heels* (2000) explores the gendered production processes in export factories on the Caribbean island of Barbados. Women there work in the informatics industry: they do computer data entry of airline tickets and insurance claims, and they key in manuscripts for everything from romance novels to academic journals. Instead of toiling in garment or electronics sweatshops, these women enjoy working in cool, air-conditioned, modern

Globalization is reshaping the lives of working women as corporations search the world for cheap labor, low taxes, and fewer environmental restrictions. But are women reshaping globalization? Here, an international call center in Barbados.

MAP 7.4
Barbados

offices. Freeman asks whether the comfortable conditions in the data-processing factories establish an improved position in the global economy for Barbadian women, or whether this new factory formation is simply another expression of women's exploitation through flexible accumulation.

Key distinctions separate the Barbadian informatics workers from women working in export-processing factories in other countries. They enjoy improved work conditions. As wives, mothers, and heads of households, rather than young, single, temporary sweatshop workers, they have won concessions from the company that include transportation, higher levels of job security, and more flexible work hours to care for their families. Freeman labels these women "pink-collar" workers because they fall between the blue-collar work done on the sweatshop factory floor and the white-collar work carried out in the higher-wage environment of the front office.

Despite the improved working conditions and social status for Barbadian women working in informatics, the company owners strive to extract maximum efficiency from them. Supervisors walk the floor and observe through glass windows to ensure continual surveillance. Managers calculate the keystrokes of each computer terminal. Wages are no higher than those of the typical sweatshop worker and in some cases are lower. The skills of data entry are not transferable to higher-wage clerical work. Women often need to take on additional work sewing, selling in the market, or working in beauty salons to support their families.

Freeman explores the ways in which the Barbadian women express their agency in the face of the informatics factory controls. These women use their status working with computers in air-conditioned offices to negotiate a different class status in the local community. They use clothing to fashion their local identities as well. Indeed, the women workers are preoccupied with fashion: they wear colorful, tailored skirt-suits with jewelry, high heels, and the latest hairstyles. With their clothes, these women perform a professional and modern gender identity that enhances their local reputations and distinguishes them from other low-wage workers in garment and textile factories.

Freeman's research adds to scholarly findings that women factory workers are not simply victims of the exploitative practices of flexible accumulation. Instead, by engaging these capitalist practices directly, women assert their own desires and goals in ways that transform the interaction between the local and the global (Richman 2001; England 2002).

Anthropologists, whether studying gender, sexuality, kinship, race, ethnicity, religion, or any other cultural construct, seek to understand the rich diversity of human bodies and human lives, both past and present, to unlock the presuppositions that reside in mental maps of reality. As we analyze gender, we strive to unmask the structures of power that create unequal opportunities and unequal access to rights and resources along gender lines. These inequalities are far from natural, essential aspects of human life and human community. Rather, they are cultural constructs established in specific historical moments and cultural contexts. Through a careful analysis and exposure of gender as a culturally constructed system of power—not fixed and natural patterns of human relationship—anthropologists hope to participate in opening possibilities for all humans to live to their full potential.

Toolkit

Thinking Like an Anthropologist:
Broadening Your View of the
Cultural Construction of Gender

In the chapter opener, we considered the underrepresentation of women in the U.S. technology industry. Why, if 57 percent of all U.S. college graduates are women, do they hold only 18 percent of the degrees in computer and information sciences, a 50 percent decline from thirty years ago? How have gendered patterns in employment, pay, and promotion in Silicon Valley come about? As you reflect on this story, consider how the big questions that have organized this chapter may help you analyze the situation more deeply:

- **Are men and women born or made?**

- **Are there more than two sexes?**

- **How do anthropologists explore the relationship between gender and power?**

- **How is globalization transforming women's lives?**

Anthropologists consider gender to be a central element in every aspect of human culture, including education, the workplace, sexuality, health, family, religion, politics, sports, and individual identity formation. Throughout this chapter we have explored how anthropologists examine the complex role of gender in crucial contemporary debates, social movements, and political struggles around the world.

Having read this chapter, are you able to take a fresh look at gender in your own life? Perhaps you can begin to see how unique cultural expectations of femininity and masculinity have shaped your ways of thinking and behaving—your interactions with family, friends, romantic interests, classmates, and coworkers. Perhaps you can see how culturally constructed notions of gender have been replicated in patterns of inequality in cultural institutions ranging from education to the workplace. And perhaps you can imagine how stereotypes and gender ideologies like the sperm and the egg or Man the Hunter, Woman the Gatherer provide the rationale for maintaining patterns of inequality and stratification. Try to go through the next week with these tools in your anthropological toolkit and see how your view of the world, particularly the gendered world, might be transformed.

Key Terms

gender studies (p. 178)

sex (p. 179)

gender (p. 179)

sexual dimorphism (p. 179)

cultural construction
of gender (p. 181)

gender performance (p. 185)

intersexual (p. 187)

transgender (p. 188)

gender stratification (p. 193)

gender stereotype (p. 193)

gender ideology (p. 193)

Chapter 8
Sexuality

Sexuality is all around us in U.S. culture.

- People "do it."

- Scientists study it.

- Governments try to regulate it.

- Public school boards battle over sex education curriculums for teenagers.

- Commercials use sex to sell cars, beer, cosmetics, diamonds, and clothes.

- Pornography is the top Internet destination, constituting 25 percent of all search engine requests.

- Reality shows and daytime soap operas test the cultural boundaries of sexual innuendo, overt sex talk, and explicit sex scenes.

- Movies show glamorized young people conducting fanciful sexual relationships with little concern for the dangers of pregnancy, violence, or sexually transmitted diseases.

- Politicians battle over same-sex marriage while the courts consider its constitutional merits.

A Calvin Klein billboard uses sexuality to sell underwear.

- Religious groups debate whether gay men and lesbians should be consecrated as ministers or rabbis.

- The U.S. military struggles to address the growing incidence of rape within its ranks as more women are assigned to active duty in combat zones.

- Public debates rage and anxieties soar about contraception, sexting, abortion, oral sex among teenagers, premarital sex, extramarital sex, and even whether the goal of sexuality should be procreation or pleasure.

- Erectile dysfunction drugs such as Viagra and Cialis promise sex whenever the mood strikes. (Just be sure to call your doctor if your erection lasts more than four hours!)

Sexuality is a profound aspect of human life, one that stirs intense emotions, deep anxieties, and rigorous debate. The U.S. population holds widely varying views of where sexuality originates, what constitutes appropriate expressions of sexuality, and what its fundamental purpose is. It is fair to say that our cultural norms and mental maps of reality are in great flux, and have been for several generations, in response to theological shifts, medical advances, and powerful social movements promoting the equality of women and gay, lesbian, bisexual, and transgender individuals.

Sexuality involves more than personal choices about who our sexual partners are and what we do with them. It is also a cultural arena within which people debate ideas of what is moral, appropriate, and "natural" and use those ideas to create unequal access to society's power, privileges, and resources. Indeed, conflicts about sexuality often reveal the intersections of multiple systems of power, including those based on gender, religion, race, class, and kinship.

Anthropologists have a long but uneven history of studying human sexuality. Bronislaw Malinowski (1927, 1929) and Margaret Mead (1928, 1935), like other early anthropologists writing in the 1920s and 1930s, considered human sexuality a key to understanding the cultures they studied, so they wrote extensively about their research findings of human sexuality across cultures. Mead's work in the islands of the western Pacific challenged the assumption that U.S. attitudes about women, their gender roles, and expressions of sexuality were universal traits immutably fixed in human nature. After World War II, however, anthropological interest turned away from explicit attention to sexuality and focused instead on related issues of marriage, kinship, and the family. Since the 1970s, sexuality has reemerged as a key concern in anthropology, paralleling a rise of interest in the wider academic community spurred by the successes of the U.S. women's movement and the emergence of gay and lesbian studies (Weston 1993). Recently, anthropological scholarship has more intently considered the diverse expressions of sexuality in cultures worldwide, including Western cultures.

In this chapter we will examine the extensive body of work that anthropologists have compiled primarily in this latter period. In particular, we will consider the following questions:

- **What is "natural" about human sexuality?**
- **What does a global perspective tell us about human sexuality?**
- **How has sexuality been constructed in the United States?**
- **How is sexuality an arena for working out relations of power?**
- **How does globalization influence local expressions of sexuality?**

Despite all the sexuality in the air, Americans often struggle to find a common language with which to discuss it (whether in their personal lives, their families, their communities, the political arena, or the classroom) and often lack the theoretical and analytical frameworks to add depth to emotionally heated conversations. By the end of this chapter you should be able to discuss the role of nature and culture in shaping human sexuality. You should be able to recognize how norms of sexuality are created and used to organize the way cultures work. Furthermore, you should have a broader understanding of the vast diversity of human sexuality across cultures. And you should be able to incorporate anthropological insights as you seek to better understand the role of sexuality in your own life and in your relations with others.

What Is "Natural" about Human Sexuality?

Text three friends and ask them to define sexuality. You will most likely get three very different responses. Perhaps this is not surprising in a culture where sexuality is omnipresent but rarely discussed carefully. In 1998, U.S. president Bill Clinton famously said of his liaison with White House intern Monica Lewinsky, "I did not have sexual relations with that woman." He chose those words presumably because he and Lewinsky had not had intercourse. But did they have sex? Such careful word choice by a sitting president giving testimony under oath reveals the challenges of defining behavior that is not only a physiological process but also a cultural construction whose meaning can vary widely.

Consider the following data. A survey of college students in a large midwestern university, with results published in 2006, asked: "Would you say you 'had sex' with someone if the most intimate behavior you engaged in was . . . ?" The survey results showed that even college students do not agree about what "having sex" means. Kissing (2 percent) and petting (3 percent) clearly did not constitute having sex for almost all respondents. Oral "sex" (40 percent) constituted sex for many but not most. For 20 percent of respondents, anal penetration did not constitute having sex. Fully 99.5 percent of respondents indicated that vaginal intercourse did constitute having sex (Sanders and Reinisch 2006). As this study makes evident, even within one population group—college students at one university—there is disagreement over the meaning of the most physical aspects of sexual relations.

For the purposes of this chapter, we will define **sexuality** from two key perspectives. First, sexuality is the complex range of desires, beliefs, and behaviors that are related to erotic physical contact, intimacy, and pleasure. Second, sexuality is the cultural arena within which people debate ideas of what kinds of physical desires and behaviors are morally right, appropriate, and "natural" and use those ideas to create unequal access to status, power, privileges, and resources.

THE INTERSECTION OF SEXUALITY AND BIOLOGY

Clearly, biology plays a key role in shaping sexuality, for sexuality includes distinct physiological processes. But how much of human sexuality is shaped by our nature? As we will see, exactly how our genetic inheritance shapes our desires, attractions, identities, practices, and beliefs is quite complicated and subject to heated debate.

People sometimes think that sexuality is the most "natural" thing in the world. After all, every species must reproduce or face extinction, right? Therefore, many assume that the sexual instincts and behaviors of other animals provide an indication of the natural state of human sexuality unencumbered by the overlays of culture.

Yet research reveals that human sexuality is actually a distinct outlier in the animal kingdom. In his article "The Animal with the Weirdest Sex Life" (1997), scientist and author Jared Diamond suggested that human sexuality is completely abnormal by the standards of the world's 30 million animal species and 4,300 mammal species. Diamond identified many ways in which humans differ from most other mammals, including the following examples:

- Most other mammals live individually, not in pairs, and meet only to have sex. They do not raise children together, and usually the males do not recognize their offspring or provide paternal care. In contrast, most humans engage in long-term sexual partnerships and often co-parent the couple's joint offspring.

- Most mammals engage in public sex, whereas humans, as a rule, have sex in private.

- Most mammals have sex only when the females of the species ovulate, at which time they advertise their fertility through visual signals, smells, sounds, and other changes in their behavior. Human women, however,

sexuality

The complex range of desires, beliefs, and behaviors that are related to erotic physical contact and the cultural arena within which people debate about what kinds of physical desires and behaviors are right, appropriate, and natural.

Bonobos, dolphins, and humans are the only mammals that have sex for fun rather than exclusively for procreation.

may be receptive to sex not only during ovulation but also at other times during their menstrual cycle.

- Possibly most intriguing, humans, dolphins, and bonobos—a variety of ape—are the only mammals that have sex for fun rather than exclusively for reproduction. In fact, in contemporary U.S. culture, humans seem to do it mostly for fun.

By the standards of most mammals (including great apes, to whom we are most closely related), we humans are the sexual outliers. Despite the common belief that clues to the essentials of human sex drives and behaviors may be

What Is "Natural" about Human Sexuality?   **209**

found in "nature," Diamond makes clear that humans have developed a sex life that lies far outside the natural framework of that of our mammal relatives. If other animals' sex lives do not provide clues to the roots of our sexuality, what can human biology tell us about the genetic and hormonal roots of sexual desire and sexual behavior?

One school of thought, which draws heavily on evolutionary biology, focuses on the ways in which human evolution has created biological drives that are embedded in the genes that shape the human brain and control the body's hormones. These drives work automatically—instinctively—to ensure the reproduction of the species. Human sexuality is thought to rely heavily on the expression of these biological drives.

Physical anthropologist Helen Fisher explores the complex biological roots of human sexuality in her book *Why We Love: The Nature and Chemistry of Romantic Love* (2004), in which she analyzes the relationship of body chemistry to human sensations of love. Fisher suggests that through evolution humans have developed a set of neurochemicals that drive an "evolutionary trajectory of loving" (93). These neurochemicals guide us through three distinct phases of falling in love: finding the right sexual partner, building a relationship, and forming an emotional attachment that will last long enough to raise a child. First, testosterone—found both in women and men—triggers the sense of excitement, desire, arousal, and craving for sexual gratification that we call "lust." Then our bodies release the stimulant dopamine, and possibly norepinephrine and serotonin, to promote the feelings of romance that develop as relationships deepen. Eventually the hormones ocytocin and vasopressin generate the feelings of calm and security that are associated with a long-term partnership; Fisher calls these feelings "attachment." These phases, she suggests, are built into our biological systems to ensure the reproduction of the human species, and they play key roles in shaping human sexuality.

Genetic science, despite remarkable developments that include the ability to map the human genome (the whole human genetic structure), still has limitations as a predictor of individual human sexual behavior. Yes, the frequency of certain behaviors in the human population may suggest an underlying biological component. But it is extremely difficult to directly trace links between specific genes and specific behaviors. So, for instance, despite widespread popular discussion of the topic, geneticists have not been able to identify a "straight" gene or a "gay" gene or any cluster of genes that determines sexual orientation.

Furthermore, we know that genes do not work in isolation from the environment. Our bodies and minds, which are not fully formed at birth, bear the imprint of both gene and environment. Beginning in the womb, our genes interact with the environment—the nutrients, sounds, emotions, and diseases that surround and infuse us. The exact effects of the interaction of biology and

environment are extremely difficult to measure. Even within the parameters of Fisher's study, we cannot predict a particular man's level of sexual desire for a particular partner by measuring his level of testosterone. Attraction, desire, and even disinterest are not only biologically driven but also triggered by a vast array of cultural factors; these may include responses to the potential partner's age, religion, class, race, education, and employment prospects. So, although biology clearly plays a role in human sexuality, exactly how it manifests itself in each individual and how it interacts with the environment and culture is not as clear as many popular descriptions of sexuality suggest.

SEXUALITY AND CULTURE

A second school of thought, one we will consider in more detail throughout the rest of this chapter, focuses on the ways in which the people, events, and cultural environment around us shape—or construct—our sexual desires and behaviors. These feelings and actions may have roots in human evolution, but the constructionist perspective focuses on the process through which humans are enculturated from birth to channel these feelings and desires into a limited number of

How do people, events, and the cultural environment around us shape our sexual desires and behaviors? *Clockwise from top left:* Advertisements featuring sex and love. Lawmakers congratulate Minnesota state senator Scott Dibble (*front left*), lead sponsor of Minnesota's gay marriage bill, after its passage, May 13, 2013. A sex education class at Kealing Junior High School, Austin, Texas.

acceptable expressions. Culture shapes what people think is natural and normal. Parents, family, friends, doctors, religious communities, sex education classes, the media, and many other individual and institutional actors all play a role in shaping the way we express our sexuality and what those expressions mean to others. Thus culture both guides and limits our sexual imaginations.

Constructionists also trace the ways in which, through culture, human groups arrange the diversity of human sexuality into a limited number of categories that are imagined to be discrete (such as homosexual and heterosexual, gay and straight), thereby masking the actual diversity of human expressions of sexuality. Where an individual is assigned within these categories has direct consequences for his or her life chances. Depending on the particular cultural construction of meaning surrounding human sexuality, not all sexual desires and behaviors may be considered equally acceptable. The meaning they acquire in a particular culture has the potential to affect access to social networks, social benefits, jobs, health care, and other resources (Harding 1998; Ore 2010).

It is important to note that the perspectives of evolutionary biology and cultural constructionism discussed in this section need not be mutually exclusive. Rather, they reflect different research emphases into the roots and contemporary expressions of human sexuality.

What Does a Global Perspective Tell Us about Human Sexuality?

A look at human sexuality over time and across cultures reveals significant diversity in (1) how, where, when, and with whom humans have sex, and (2) what certain sexual behaviors mean. This diversity challenges Western culture-bound notions and suggests alternative options for reinterpreting assumed cultural categories of sexuality. The discussions that follow offer examples of alternative constructions of sexuality in Suriname and Nicaragua.

SAME-GENDER "*MATI* WORK" IN SURINAME

In the *Politics of Passion* (2006), cultural anthropologist Gloria Wekker explores the lives of black, working-class Creole women in the port city of Paramaribo, Suriname, a former Dutch colony on the northern coast of South America. Writing about the sexual choices Surinamese women make, Wekker (like Roger Lancaster's study described below) challenges the dominant thinking about sexual identity in Western scholarship and social movements by describing a much more flexible and inclusive approach specific to the local Paramaribo context.

Suriname

South America

MAP 8.1
Suriname

Wekker's study focuses on *mati*—women who form intimate spiritual, emotional, and sexual relationships with other women. Wekker estimates that three out of four working-class black women in Paramaribo engage in "*mati* work" at some point in their lives, establishing relationships of mutual support, obligation, and responsibility with other women—sometimes living in the same household, sometimes separately, and often sharing in child rearing. In contrast to Western notions of fixed, "either/or" sexual identities, *mati* may engage in sexual relationships with both women and men—sometimes simultaneously, sometimes consecutively. Their relationships with men may center on having children or receiving economic support, but frequently *mati* choose a "visiting" relationship with men rather than marriage in order to maintain their independence.

Women join a parade in the port city of Paramaribo, Suriname, on the northern coast of South America.

Born in Suriname and trained as an anthropologist in the United States and the Netherlands, Wekker also writes about the transfer of *mati* work to the Netherlands. In recent decades, young Surinamese women have emigrated from the former colony to its former colonizer in search of economic opportunities. There, *mati* work has often developed in relationships between young immigrants and older black women of Surinamese parentage who have established Dutch citizenship. Wekker describes these relationships as often fraught with complicated power dynamics involving differential age, class, and citizenship status. Yet she notes that this *mati* work does not parallel European ideas of lesbianism.

Wekker pursues this distinction between conceptualizations of sexuality in Suriname and Europe in greater detail as she develops her analysis of *mati* work in Paramaribo. What steps, she asks, must anthropologists take to understand sexual relationships between people of the same gender cross-culturally without distorting what these relationships mean in their actual lives? Wekker argues that Western scholarship mistakenly links all sexual acts between individuals of the same gender to a notion of "homosexual identity"—a permanent, stable, fixed sexual core or essence, whether inborn or learned, that is counterposed to an equally fixed and opposite heterosexual identity. In the Western framework, a person is "either/or." The *mati* of Paramaribo, Wekker argues, approach their sexual choices very differently, regarding sexuality as flexible behavior rather than fixed identity. Their behavior is dynamic, malleable, and inclusive—"both/and"—rather than exclusive.

Wekker urges students of sexuality to not impose Western views about sexuality—what she considers "Western folk knowledge"—on the rest of the world but to understand sexuality in its local reality with the goal of rethinking same-gender behavior in cross-cultural perspective. Rather than thinking of one uniform expression of same-gender sexual behavior, she recommends focusing attention on the variation of people's behaviors. Furthermore, thinking cross-culturally, she argues that research and analysis of same-gender sexuality must recognize that the identical physical sexual acts between same-gendered people may be understood in multiple ways and have vastly different social significance in different cultures and historical periods (Wekker 2006, 1999; Brown 2007; Stone 2007).

MACHISMO AND SEXUALITY IN NICARAGUA

Cultural anthropologist Roger Lancaster explores similar themes in *Life Is Hard: Machismo, Danger and the Intimacy of Power in Nicaragua* (1994), in which he considers expressions of sexuality in a working-class neighborhood in Managua, Nicaragua, during the 1980s. In particular, he examined the concept of machismo—which can be defined as a strong, sometimes exaggerated performance of masculinity. This concept, which Lancaster sees as central to the Nicaraguan national imagination, shapes relationships not only between men and women but also between men and other men. Machismo creates a strong contrast between aggression and passivity. "Real" men—masculine men—are aggressive. But a real man's macho status is always at risk. Machismo must be constantly performed to retain one's social status.

MAP 8.2
Nicaragua

Lancaster was particularly intrigued by the way machismo affects the sexual relations between men. Generally, in U.S. culture, any man who engages in a same-gender sexual behavior is considered gay. But in the Nicaraguan community that Lancaster studied, only the men who passively receive anal intercourse are pejoratively called *cochon*—"queer, faggot, gay." The *machista*, the penetrator, is still considered a manly man—an *hombre-hombres*—under the rules of machismo. For it is the *machista*'s role to achieve sexual conquest whenever possible with whoever is available. The active partner acts out machismo, enhancing his status by dominating a weaker person. Among Nicaraguan men, the intersection of sexuality and power creates a culturally constructed system of arbitrary and unequal value for male bodies in which machismo privileges the aggressive, assertive *machista* penetrator over the passive, receptive, penetrated *cochon*.

Lancaster points out that in Nicaragua the same acts that in the United States would be seen to reveal one's "essential" homosexuality—desire for and sexual activity with someone of the same sex—are interpreted differently. In fact, active, aggressive men enhance their masculinity and macho status, even if they engage in same-gender sexual activity (Lewin 1995; Rouse 1994; Perez-Aleman 1994).

The studies in Suriname and Nicaragua are representative of the vast array of cross-cultural research that cumulatively has been called "the ethnocartography of human sexuality" (Weston 1993), mapping the global scope of diverse human sexual beliefs and behaviors. This ethnocartography marks a period in the anthropology of sexuality that built on the premises that (1) cross-cultural attention to the practices and beliefs of others can yield a deeper analysis of one's own culture, and (2) awareness of the broad panorama of human life offers opportunities for reexamining what seems normal and natural in one's own cultural practices. After reading about the previous studies, in what ways are you challenged to rethink your own conceptions of human sexuality?

We turn now to consider the unique construction of human sexuality in the United States.

How Has Sexuality Been Constructed in the United States?

In many of the studies discussed throughout this chapter, we see expressions of sexuality that do not fit the dominant Western model that limits discussion to two categories: **heterosexuality**, or attraction to and sexual relations between individuals of the opposite sex; and **homosexuality**, or attraction to and sexual relations with members of the same sex. At times in Western cultures this heterosexual-homosexual binary may be supplemented by discussions of **bisexuality**, or attraction to and sexual relations with members of both sexes, and **asexuality**, or lack of erotic attraction to others. The term *transgender* has emerged in recent decades to describe people whose gender identity or gender expression differs from the sex they were assigned at birth (Valentine 2007). But these latter categories are less frequently considered. As we will see, historical and

heterosexuality
Attraction to and sexual relations between individuals of the opposite sex.

homosexuality
Attraction to and sexual relations between individuals of the same sex.

bisexuality
Attraction to and sexual relations with members of both sexes.

asexuality
A lack of erotic attraction to others.

cross-cultural research suggests that the dual-category system of heterosexuality and homosexuality has a uniquely Western cultural history.

THE INVENTION OF HETEROSEXUALITY

Popular conversations about sexuality in the United States often focus on same-gender sexuality. This may not come as a surprise. As discussed in Chapter 5, contemporary conversations about race tend to center on the experiences of being black, Hispanic, or Asian and avoid discussing being white, even though whiteness is the central racial category around which all others have been organized. Likewise, in popular discussions and academic studies of sexuality, talk of different-gender eroticism (heterosexuality) often is overwhelmed by discussions of same-gender eroticism (homosexuality). This emphasis has left heterosexuality largely forgotten and unmarked. In recent years, the anthropology of sexuality has worked to shift scholarly attention to focus on the norm (heterosexuality) and the process by which the particular expression of heterosexuality prevalent in U.S. culture today became the norm (D'Emilio and Freedman 1998).

Historian Jonathan Katz (2007) argues that heterosexuality as it is practiced and understood in contemporary U.S. culture is a fairly recent invention. The respected *Oxford English Dictionary Supplement* lists the first U.S. usage only in 1892. Because words provide clues to cultural concepts, Katz suggests that the lack of earlier citations in popular or scientific venues in the United States indicates that heterosexuality had not achieved widespread cultural currency in the nineteenth century.

Does this mean that women and men in the United States were not engaging in opposite-gender sexual activity prior to the invention of this word? Katz suggests instead that heterosexuality as we think of it is not the same as reproductive intercourse between a man and a woman. Instead what we call "heterosexuality" today is a particular arrangement between the sexes that although not excluding reproductive intercourse, also involves ideas about the practice and purpose of sex that have not always been socially authorized. So, for instance, the early references to heterosexuality often referred to it as a perversion of the natural order because of its association with sex for pleasure rather than for procreation. The Victorian ideal of sexuality, heavily influenced by Christian teachings, considered sex to be for procreation alone. (The Victorian era generally corresponds with the life of the British monarch Queen Victoria [1837–1901].) In this view, sex for pleasure represented a danger to the purposes of God. Masturbation—clearly nonprocreative—was considered a life-threatening, depleting form of self-abuse.

Only in 1892 did the translation of German psychiatrist Richard von Krafft-Ebings's influential work *Psychopathia Sexualis* first introduce to the U.S. scene the modern sense of "heterosexuality" as erotic feelings for the opposite sex and "homosexuality" as erotic feelings for the same sex. This marked a significant shift in the scientific community, supported by a growing number of medical doctors, toward the new idea of sexuality for pleasure rather than exclusively for procreation. The rapidly expanding number of newspapers, books, plays, films, restaurants, bars, and baths associated with the rising consumer culture in the early twentieth century reinforced the gradual shift toward the sex-for-pleasure concept.

Sexology. A scientific study of sexuality, called *sexology*, began to emerge in the United States in the late nineteenth century. This activity played a central role in the establishment of heterosexuality as the dominant erotic ideal and in the gradual process of dividing the U.S. population into distinct heterosexual and homosexual groups. Sexology sought to understand the essence of human sexuality as it was expressed naturally through sexual behavior. Sexologists trusted that this scientific knowledge of human sexual behavior would enable them to look beyond cultural variations in sexual practices to perceive the underlying nature of sexuality across cultures. In the twentieth century, elaborate scientific studies led by prominent scholars of sex such as Alfred Kinsey, Shere Hite, and William Masters and Virginia Johnson used interviews, questionnaires, observation, and participation to explore the sexual lives of thousands of primarily white U.S. residents. Their studies produced surprising results.

Alfred Kinsey (1894–1956), a Harvard-trained biologist and zoologist, produced two of the most famous studies, *Sexual Behavior in the Human Male* (Kinsey, Pomeroy, and Martin 1948) and *Sexual Behavior in the Human Female* (1953). Based on data gathered from thousands of subjects, Kinsey and his collaborators suggested that human sexuality was much more diverse than was commonly assumed. In fact, rather than finding a sharp dichotomy between heterosexuality and homosexuality, his studies revealed a continuum of sexual behavior. Taking into account his respondents' experiences—including the frequency of certain sexual activities, sexual responsiveness to same and opposite genders, fantasies, dreams, and feelings—Kinsey's team placed people along a continuum of sexual feelings and behaviors. This so-called Kinsey Scale plotted exclusively heterosexual behavior on one end of the spectrum and exclusively homosexual behavior on the other, with various points in between.

Kinsey and later sexologists found that human sexuality does not fit into simplistic categories. Rather, it is marked by diversity, flexibility, and fluidity. In a break with earlier sexologists and widespread public opinion at the time, Kinsey rejected the claims that humans represent two discrete populations, heterosexual and homosexual. "Only the human mind invents categories and tries to force facts into separated pigeon-holes. The living world is a continuum" (Kinsey, Pomeroy, and Martin 1948, 639). Kinsey noted that his studies showed same-gendered attraction, fantasies, and experiences to be much more common than previously thought. Furthermore, he found that sexual behaviors could shift over the course of a lifetime, spanning both heterosexual and homosexual activity (Hubbard 1990).

Despite their arguments for the recognition of diversity and flexibility in human sexual behavior, Kinsey's reports contributed in two ways to the establishment of heterosexuality as the dominant erotic ideal in U.S. culture. First, by placing heterosexuality and homosexuality on opposite ends of his scale, Kinsey reinforced the cultural assumptions that these were opposite and irreconcilable categories. Additionally, his studies' reliance on quantitative results reinforced the emerging popular and scientific consensus that because it was the sex most people were having, heterosexuality was the functional norm for human sexuality (Katz 2007; Hubbard 1990).

Over the course of a century, heterosexuality gradually came to be seen as the norm—the presumed "natural" state—against which to judge all other expressions of sexuality in U.S. culture. Today cultural notions of sexuality are in flux, yet a particular version of heterosexuality continues to be constructed and contested. Within this context, we now consider the role of weddings in shaping contemporary conceptions of human sexuality in the United States.

Studies by sexologist Dr. Alfred C. Kinsey (*right*), pictured with his research staff in 1953, challenged common assumptions about U.S. sexual practices.

"WHITE WEDDINGS"

White Weddings: Romancing Heterosexuality in Popular Culture (2008), a study by sociologist Chrys Ingraham, is not a book about wedding ceremonies. It is about wedding culture and what the author calls the "wedding industry"—the vast network of commercial activities and social institutions that market 2.3 million weddings a year in the United States. The wedding industry and the wedding culture, Ingraham argues, provide insights into how U.S. culture gives meaning to marriage and, in the process, constructs contemporary understandings of heterosexuality.

Constructing Heterosexuality. It's hard to turn on the television, log on to the Internet, or check out at the local grocery store without encountering some reminder of U.S. society's fascination with weddings. Bridal magazines, popular tabloids, television shows, and commercials in every medium saturate the culture with images of a spectacle of excess that will, they promise, lead to everyone's fairy-tale ending of "happily ever after." Wedding consultants push wedding announcements, bridal showers, wedding halls, floral arrangements, diamond rings, rehearsal dinners, reception halls, gifts and favors, caterers, photographers, bands, limousines, and glamorous honeymoons to romantic destinations. Wedding registries orchestrate the delivery of just the right gifts of kitchenware, china, household furnishings, and every appliance imaginable. The average bridal gown (mostly made in third world garment shops by women who will never have a white wedding), including alterations, headpiece, and veil, will cost $1,811 (2008 figures). The average U.S. couple will spend more than $27,852 (in 2008) on their "big day." Altogether, the annual $80 billion wedding industry wields enormous social and economic power.

Ingraham reminds her readers that brides are not born. They are made. Every girl in U.S. culture, almost from birth, is bombarded with cultural symbols and messages about what it will take to have her very own white wedding. Barbie dolls and other toy-industry favorites model the perfect bride, complete with accessories (including Ken?) for the perfect white wedding. Disney movies, feature films, and television shows celebrate weddings as key life moments (and central plot devices) and essential cultural symbols. Every broadcast season features a spate of elaborate made-for-television weddings, especially on shows struggling in the ratings.

From childhood, girls are tutored in preparation for the "you may kiss the bride" moment, learning to apply makeup, wear high heels, send valentines, go on dates, and select a prom dress. Boys learn to buy flowers and corsages, wear tuxedos, pay for dates, lead during the first dance, buy an engagement ring, and initiate sex. But no matter where you think human sexuality originates, it is clear that these behaviors do not occur in nature. They are constructed in culture. The wedding industry and wedding culture—the romantic idealization of the wedding ritual—enculturate boys and girls, men and women, about what to do, when, and with whom, in order to lead up to that perfect day. Weddings, Ingraham suggests, and the elaborate rituals that lead up to them over a lifetime, are not only exuberant public celebrations of romantic love. Weddings are also key cultural institutions through which we learn what it means to be heterosexual.

Inequality and Unequal Access. What do weddings tell us about the construction of heterosexuality in U.S. culture? Building on recent feminist scholarship, Ingraham suggests that white weddings, and the marriages that result, offer insights into the gendered power dynamics embedded in the normative patterns of heterosexuality that have developed since the late nineteenth century. These power dynamics disadvantage women while being largely obscured by the idealism and romance that U.S. culture wraps around these institutions. Historically, the institution of heterosexual marriage included legal stipulations that effectively made women the economic and sexual property of their husbands. This assumption continues to be ritualized in contemporary U.S. weddings by the father "giving away" the bride to her soon-to-be husband, exchanging the woman between two men.

Today patterns of inequality are less visible but no less significant. Although not legally sanctioned, assumptions about the proper role and relative value of men and women within the context of heterosexuality promote inequalities in the home. There, the gendered division of labor means that frequently the woman carries a double workload as a wage earner while simultaneously bearing primary responsibility for domestic work and child rearing. In the workplace, usually still dominated by male leadership, women receive unequal pay for equal work, are promoted less often than men, and are targets of sexual harassment.

Ingraham selected the book title *White Weddings* to highlight the issues of class and race that also are embedded in the workings of the wedding industry and the fairy tale of the wedding ritual. White weddings are not available to all. The women sewing wedding dresses, the young men mining diamonds, and the staff serving dinner on the Caribbean honeymoon island cannot afford a white wedding. Nor does the industry depict a diverse population in its advertising, insinuating that white weddings are primarily for white folks. Actually, most Americans cannot afford the average U.S. wedding; they incur significant debt for the ceremony and honeymoon to launch their marriage.

Weddings are often romanticized as rituals of love and commitment, but the question of who can or cannot marry has consequences under the law. In the United States, legally sanctioned marriages convey a wide assortment of federal and state entitlements that are unavailable to those who are unmarried—another example of the use of heterosexuality to organize social life. Advantages are

What is your idea of a perfect wedding? Here, a woman adjusts a bridal gown at a wedding fair in Bucharest, Romania, where the wedding industry has grown despite an economic crisis.

extended in areas as wide-ranging as inheritance rights, tax benefits, health care access, Social Security and other retirement benefits, hospital visitation rights and health care decisions, housing benefits, and insurance coverage. In this context, heated debates about who should be able to marry have implications beyond the realm of moral disagreements. These debates signal profound challenges to an underlying system of power and privilege based on the assumption that heterosexuality, and a particular version of it, is the cultural norm.

In the second edition of her book, Ingraham reflects on the wrenching and at times risky process of evaluating the sacred, valued rituals and institutions of weddings. Her writing elicited responses of appreciation along with expressions of anger, resistance, and dismissal. Clearly, the critique of the dynamics underlying U.S. weddings and marriages caused discomfort for many, and for some the attack felt quite personal. These responses, Ingraham offers, may signify the crucial need to analyze one of the most powerful rituals in U.S. culture and one of the most significant locations for constructing relationships and patterns of power (Ingraham 2008; Milkie 2000; Siebel 2000).

LESBIAN AND GAY COMMITMENT CEREMONIES

The debate about same-sex weddings is one arena where the contestation of U.S. norms of sexuality is thoroughly engaged. In *Recognizing Ourselves* (1998), anthropologist Ellen Lewin opens a window into both the personal and the political dynamics of gay and lesbian commitment ceremonies. Drawing on interviews with more than fifty couples and on her own attendance at dozens of ceremonies, Lewin recounts the stories of U.S. couples wrestling with what it meant to get "married" in a 1990s culture that legally restricted same-sex marriage in all fifty states. Focusing on the actual rituals designed by couples, Lewin unveils the ways these invented rituals foster both continuity and creativity in a culture by integrating themes of love, tradition, kinship, community, authenticity, and resistance (Lewin 1998; Kennedy 1999).

Rituals of Resistance and Acceptance. Lewin reflects on the multiple roles that commitment ceremonies play in the gay and lesbian community, serving as rituals of resistance and as rituals of acceptance. For some in the study, commitment ceremonies, holy unions, and weddings were a form of resistance against the cultural norms and legal standards that denied gay men and lesbians the recognition of their lives and loves in ways readily provided to heterosexuals. Their public performances allowed them a chance to speak of their anger and sorrow, to refuse to be marginalized and mistreated, and to challenge the dominant patterns of heterosexuality and gender stratification in mainstream U.S. culture. Many also saw their ceremonies as part of efforts to legalize same-sex marriage and advocate for the legal, health, and economic benefits associated with heterosexual marriages.

For others, their commitment ceremonies expressed more personal and intimate feelings, including their wish to formalize their bonds of love in sacred and special ways, acknowledge their intensifying personal connections, and make their commitments public. Here Lewin discovered a distinct sense that commitment ceremonies were rituals of acceptance and conformity. By participating in public ceremonies long reserved for heterosexual couples, gay men and lesbians claimed their place in the wider society, acknowledging that they were already part of local communities, schools, families, and workplaces—that they belonged. For these couples, commitment ceremonies became a statement and celebration of their inclusion in mainstream U.S. culture.

Lewin states that for the couples she interviewed, the ritual performances of both resistance and acceptance were not always consciously done or carefully thought through. Nor were the dynamics of resistance and acceptance always mutually exclusive. Instead she reflects on a subtle process of cultural change present in the planning and celebration of commitment ceremonies that embodied multiple meanings reflecting the diverse individuals, unique couples, and complex emotions involved.

As we noted earlier in the chapter, human sexuality encompasses not only desires, beliefs, and behaviors related to erotic physical contact, intimacy, and pleasure, but also a cultural arena in which people promote and contest ideas of what kinds of physical desires and behaviors are morally right, appropriate, and "natural." The studies by Ingraham and Lewin challenge us to consider the ways in which contemporary understandings of sexuality—as expressed through the

highly symbolic ritual of marriage—continue to be shaped, invented, and contested in U.S. culture.

FEDERAL LAW AND PUBLIC OPINION

Indeed, intense debates about marriage equality and same-sex marriage continue today, both in the United States and around the world. Public opinion of same-sex marriage has shifted dramatically in U.S. culture, especially among younger generations. Federal and state laws have also changed over the past decade, as a series of U.S. states have legalized same-sex marriage even as others passed legal restrictions.

Then on June 26, 2015, the U.S. Supreme Court, in a closely divided 5-4 decision, ruled in *Obergefell v. Hodges* that same-sex marriage is a fundamental right guaranteed under the U.S. Constitution. The ruling required all U.S. states to issue marriage licenses to couples regardless of sexual orientation and to recognize those marriages conducted in other states.

Placed in historical perspective and in light of our anthropological perspectives on the fluidity and malleability of human sexuality, perhaps we can view these shifts not as some new and surprising contestation of age-old "natural" patterns of sexuality, but as the most recent rethinking of human sexuality in U.S. culture. If so, we might then be better prepared to analyze the underlying intersections of sexuality and power in our own personal and political lives.

How Is Sexuality an Arena for Working Out Relations of Power?

As we have noted, sexuality is more than an expression of individual desires and identities. French social scientist Michel Foucault (1978, 103) described sexuality as "an especially dense transfer point for relations of power." By this he meant that in every culture, sexuality—like race, ethnicity, class, and gender—is also an arena in which appropriate behavior is defined, relations of power are worked out, and inequality and stratification are created, enforced, and contested.

Indeed, cultural institutions ranging from governments to religious bodies attempt to regulate many aspects of sexuality. These aspects include marriage and divorce; monogamy and polygamy; age of consent; definition of incest; reproductive rights; and the rights of gay men, lesbians, bisexuals, and transgender persons; as well as pornography, sex trafficking, and prostitution. A consideration of "who is allowed to do what with whom and when" exposes the intersections of sexuality and power in a culture. Attention to intersectionality—the way systems of power interconnect to affect individual lives and group experiences—offers a fundamental shift in the way social scientists study inequality and stratification, including the way we think about sexuality. In this section we consider case studies that reflect on these intersections.

INTERSECTIONS OF RACE AND SEXUALITY FOR BLACK GAY WOMEN

Sociologist Mignon Moore's book *Invisible Families* (2011) explores the impact of the intersection of race and sexuality on the identities, relationships, and families of black gay women in the United States. Moore notes that, historically, race has framed black women's political, economic, and religious identities (see also Higgenbotham 1992; Dill 1983). And whereas many middle-class white lesbian couples experience sexuality as the primary framework that shapes their identity, many in the black lesbian community (including African American, Afro-Caribbean, and African immigrant women) find that race—perhaps as much as, if not more than, sexuality—is the primary framework that shapes their identity.

In an interview with Moore, Zoe Ferron (a pseudonym), an African American woman born in 1960 in Brooklyn, New York, reflected on how the identities of race, gender, and sexuality described her:

> If I had to number them one, two, three? Probably Black and lesbian—real close, to be honest with you. I don't know which would come up as one. Probably Black. Woman last. . . . Because that is just what it is. People see your Blackness, and the world has affected me

by my Blackness since the very inception of my life.... My sexuality is something that developed later on, or I became aware of later on, [because] I think *it's always been what it's been*, but I think that it was just something that developed in my psyche. But being Black is something that I've always had to deal with: racism since day one and recognizing how to navigate through this world as a Black person, and even as a Black woman. (Moore 2012, 33)

The intersection of race and sexuality becomes particularly meaningful as black gay women participate in black or gay communities that define themselves around just one of these statuses.

Moore notes that prior to the 1980s, gay sexuality in racial minority communities was rarely articulated in public settings. And only infrequently was it recognized as a component of the community's larger experiences of discrimination and struggle. Instead, openly gay sexuality was perceived to flout notions of "respectability"—virtue, modesty, discipline, responsibility—that had developed within the black middle class and that its leadership promoted as important tools to combat racist stereotypes in the workplace, political arena, and family life (Shaw 1996; Wolcott 2001). Moore points to a strong reluctance during that period by gay blacks to challenge community expectations about respectability by creating families together.

In the intervening years, same-gender sexuality has become an increasingly public issue in U.S. culture through prominent debates about same-sex marriage, the rights of gay men and lesbian adults to adopt children, and the rights of lesbians and gay men to serve openly in the military. At the same time, recognition of same-sex relationships and families has increased in the black community, and black political and religious leaders have begun to address issues related to gay sexuality as matters of civil rights and fairness. Relationships once hidden from families and communities have gradually moved into the public sphere, where the participants can be celebrated as gay women and men and can openly form unions and raise families.

How do the women in Moore's study navigate the black middle-class politics of respectability in order to both live their sexuality openly and maintain strong community connections? Moore suggests that by risking the disruption of this particular version of respectability, black women who live openly as lesbians—forming families, getting married, becoming mothers, and raising children—offer an alternative manifestation of respectability at the intersection of sexuality and race.

Can you see how the intersection of race and sexuality may differentially affect one's life choices and opportunities? In your own life, how is your sexuality shaped by its intersection with other systems of power—perhaps age, gender, race, class, or religion?

SEXUALITY AND POWER ON U.S. COLLEGE CAMPUSES

In what ways do sexuality and power intersect on your college campus? If, as anthropologist Eric Wolf argues (see Chapter 2), every relationship is embedded in complex dynamics of power, how do you personally navigate intersections of sexuality with gender, age, class, race, or religion? Has your college or university created opportunities to discuss matters of sexuality?

sexual violence

Violence perpetuated through sexually related physical assaults such as rape.

Certainly, attention to **sexual violence** on college campuses has increased. Terms such as *date rape* and *domestic violence* have become part of the national conversation, and many colleges and universities have implemented policies on sexual harassment and sexual conduct. Still, many women experience sexual harassment, violence, and rape while in college (Sanday 1990; Fisher, Daigle, and Cullen 2010). While these policies attempt to address extreme expressions of the intersection of power with sexuality, conversations about sexuality can be far more wide-ranging.

Antioch College: From "*No* Means *No*" to "*Yes* Means *Yes*." In the early 1990s, when many colleges were beginning to articulate sexual offense policies, a small liberal arts college in the U.S. Midwest gained national attention for its unusual policy. Most sexual offense policies start with the assumption that "*No* means *no*." Most legal definitions of rape assume that if a woman does not consent or is incapable of consent for any reason, then any sexual activity with

her is considered rape. However, Antioch College in Ohio developed a different type of policy. It was initiated by students; developed by a task force of students, faculty, and administrators; and promoted in mandatory training workshops for all students. The policy went beyond "*No* means *no*" to mandate that participants must receive an explicit "yes" at every step of the encounter. Both participants must negotiate and agree to everything.

According to the policy, "Obtaining consent is an on-going process in any sexual interaction. Verbal consent should be obtained with each new level of physical and/or sexual contact/conduct in any given interaction, regardless of who initiates it. Asking 'Do you want to have sex with me?' is not enough. The request for consent must be specific to each act." Among the policy's specific provisions are the following:

MAP 8.3
Ohio

- The person with whom sexual contact/conduct is initiated is responsible to express verbally and or physically her/his willingness or lack of willingness when reasonably possible.

- If someone has initially consented but then stops consenting during a sexual interaction, she/he should communicate withdrawal verbally and/or through physical resistance. The other individual(s) must stop immediately.

- To knowingly take advantage of someone who is under the influence of alcohol, drugs, and/or prescribed medication is not acceptable behavior.

- If someone verbally agrees to engage in specific contact or conduct, but it is not of her/his own free will due to any of the circumstances stated below, then the person initiating shall be considered in violation of this policy:

- The person submitting is incapacitated by alcohol, drugs, and/or prescribed medication;
- The person submitting is asleep or unconscious;
- The person initiating has forced, threatened, coerced, or intimidated the other individual(s) into engaging in sexual contact and/or sexual conduct. (cited in Cameron 1994)

Antioch's policy drew criticism from many people who considered it excessively intrusive. But linguistic anthropologist Deborah Cameron, who studied the effects of the policy on campus (1994), found that rather than creating awkwardness and uncertainty, for many students the new policy promoted a more elaborate language for talking and thinking about sex. The policy also appeared to have improved some students' sex lives in the process.

The Antioch policy presents a challenge that requires a dramatic shift in thinking about intimate sexual encounters. It also commands a new attention to shifting the power dynamics that underlie current patterns of gender and sexuality in the culture at large. Imagine if all forms of coercion—physical and psychological coercion; the pressure of norms, obligations, and expectations; and the fear of ridicule or abandonment—were removed from the equation, enabling people to engage in sexual intimacy only when they really wanted to. What if "yes" really meant "yes" (Friedman and Valenti 2008)?

How Does Globalization Influence Local Expressions of Sexuality?

Globalization has significantly influenced local expressions of sexuality, and this effect is evident in many arenas. For example, time-space compression (see Chapter 1) is facilitating the movement of people—particularly men—within countries and across national borders in search of sexual pleasure. In addition, disruptions of local economies are pushing women to find wage labor to support themselves and their families. And international campaigns for gay and lesbian rights, often initiated in Western countries, are shaping a global conversation about sexuality and the human rights of sexual minorities worldwide. At the same time, groups opposing gay and lesbian sexuality are promoting their own agendas on a global platform. These transformations suggest that individual expressions of sexuality and local understandings of sexuality are undergoing dramatic shifts as they intersect with economic policies, immigration practices, and political movements at the national, regional, and international levels influenced by processes of globalization (see Curtis 2009).

SEXUALITY, LANGUAGE, AND THE EFFECTS OF GLOBALIZATION IN NIGERIA

The tendency of globalization to intensify connections across national boundaries may generate opportunities for greater cooperation on issues of mutual concern affecting people in disparate parts of the world. But this capacity to bridge barriers also has the potential to homogenize—to shape global discourses that blur distinctions and smooth over differences—in a way that may put local indigenous expressions at risk.

In *Allah Made Us: Sexual Outlaws in an Islamic African City* (2009), linguistic anthropologist Rudolf Gaudio presents an ethnographic study of the language practices of *'yan daudu*, feminine men in the northern Nigerian (Hausa-speaking) city of Kano. *'Yan daudu* are one group of *masu harka*, a code term for "people who do the deed"—that is, men who have sex with other men. *'Yan daudu* are men who act like women: they cook, serve food, sing, dance, or work as prostitutes. Over the years, their role has been publicly recognized in northern Nigerian culture. But with the introduction of strict Islamic sharia law, which forbids same-gender sexuality, in recent years *'yan daudu* have faced increased persecution, harassment, and marginalization on account of their gender and sexual nonconformity. As international campaigns for gay rights intersect with Nigerian culture, the resulting conversations risk drawing local expressions of human sexuality into a national and international debate that links them to so-called Western decadence and new forms of colonialism considered unacceptable by the Nigerian government.

Unlike most Western conceptions of sexuality, *masu harka* and *'yan daudu* do not see homosexual behavior as incompatible with marrying women, forming families, and having children. Nor do they necessarily consider their sexuality incompatible with their Muslim faith. Gaudio met many who are observant Muslims and some who have taken the *hajj,* a pilgrimage to the Muslim holy city of Mecca that is required of every believer who can manage the journey. For some of these men, the pilgrimage to Mecca may enable them to establish status and respectability in the international arena that they could not achieve on their own at home, where many other Nigerians consider them to be outlaws and deviants.

Globalization's Homogenizing Influence. *'Yan daudu* sexual practices in northern Nigeria are complicated by the effects of globalization. Most African countries achieved their independence from European colonial powers in the 1960s and 1970s, and memories of those incursions are still fresh in Africans' collective memory. Moreover, the awareness of new forms of economic,

MAP 8.4
Nigeria

Have international debates about human sexuality put local expressions at risk? Here 'yan daudu dance at a party in Kano, Nigeria. The men's faces have been disguised to conceal their identities.

military, political, and cultural domination that have emerged since the end of colonialism are ever present. Like many Africans, many Nigerians regard homosexuality as part of the wave of Western influences that have been flooding their country and continent for well more than a hundred years.

Most national governments in Africa do not consider the practice of homosexuality as authentically African—certainly not the way homosexuality is framed in international scholarly and activist discourse. These governments see the push for recognizing gay sexual rights as a human right as simply a new front of Western imperial domination. One exception to this perspective is South Africa, where gay rights were included in the new constitution of 1994.

Gaudio's ethnography of *masu harka* shows diverse expressions of sexuality on the local level. The presence of *'yan daudu*, for example, challenges the notion that Africa is devoid of indigenous sexual minorities. But the emergence of an international movement for gay rights threatens to undermine the diversity of local expressions of human sexuality. Gaudio notes that Western scholars and international activists often presume that the international movement's categories can be applied with relative ease from one linguistic and cultural setting to another. However, forcing the conversation into restrictive, binary categories of heterosexuality and homosexuality endangers the continued existence of local sexual expression by placing those indigenous expressions into a debate about foreign influence, imperialism, and so-called Western decadence.

The emerging antigay rhetoric unifies Muslim fundamentalist, Christian orthodox, and evangelical groups. It threatens to close off the possibility of recognizing the diversity of sexual desires, practices, and identities of individuals and local communities that may have previously operated outside the Western-oriented, homosexual-heterosexual framework. In so doing, it reveals the power of globalization to introduce narrower, homogenizing perspectives on the many and varied expressions of human sexuality found in cultures around the globe (Gaudio 2009; Harris 2009; Leap 2010).

As we have seen throughout this chapter, human sexuality is more than the personal choices we make about our sexual partners and how we express our erotic desires. The anthropological lens and a global perspective have enabled us to see that sexuality is a complex relationship between individuals as well as between individuals and the larger culture. We have examined how elements of human sexuality are culturally constructed—formed in relationship to particular people, cultural norms, and expectations. Rather than representing sharply drawn, fixed, and oppositional identities representing two discrete categories, sexuality is diverse, flexible, and fluid.

But we have also seen that the construction of human sexuality—how it is perceived and valued—is a highly contested process. Debates rage and decisions are made about human sexuality that affect people's life chances and access to power, privileges, rights, and resources. Certain rights or benefits may be granted or restricted based on assumptions about sexual preferences or sexual behavior. Given this reality, within anthropology sexuality has become a key cultural location for analyzing, understanding, and contesting stratification and inequality, including the ways sexuality intersects with other systems of power, such as race, gender, ethnicity, nationality, religion, kinship, and class.

Toolkit

Thinking Like an Anthropologist:
Sexuality in Your Life

Sexuality is all around us. Turn on the television, search the Internet, check out at the grocery store, or drive down an interstate highway, and you will find sexuality all around you in reality shows, websites, magazines, and billboard advertisements. At times in U.S. culture, the presence of sexuality is so pervasive as to be overwhelming. In such an environment, how do you begin to make sense of what sexuality means for you on a personal level and for U.S. culture on a political level? Remember to consider the big questions that have organized this chapter:

- **What is "natural" about human sexuality?**

- **What does a global perspective tell us about human sexuality?**

- **How has sexuality been constructed in the United States?**

- **How is sexuality an arena for working out relations of power?**

- **How does globalization influence local expressions of sexuality?**

Although anthropology may not be able to help you decide whom to date or when to do what and where, it does offer a set of tools—perspectives and insights—that may help you think more clearly about what it all means, what the cultural frameworks are within which you negotiate your desires and decisions, and what your full range of options may be when you consider your sexuality within a global perspective. Questions of sexuality run deep in U.S. cultural conversations. Having thought through key issues of sexuality from an anthropological perspective, are you better prepared to engage in the debates and advance the conversation?

Key Terms

sexuality (p. 208)

heterosexuality (p. 215)

homosexuality (p. 215)

bisexuality (p. 215)

asexuality (p. 215)

sexual violence (p. 226)

Chapter 9
Kinship, Family, and Marriage

In November 2005, the *New York Times* published a story about Danielle of Seaford, New York, and JoEllen of Russell, Pennsylvania, titled "Hello, I'm Your Sister. Our Father is Donor 150." These two teenagers, whose mothers conceived them through artificial insemination, had recently found each other through the Donor Sibling Registry: a website that facilitates connections between "donor-conceived" offspring and their donor-parents. Meanwhile, in Venice, California, Jeffrey Harrison read the same *New York Times* story. In the late 1980s, Harrison had earned $400 a month donating sperm to the California Cryobank. He was Donor 150. By agreement, the Cryobank had kept his identity anonymous over the ensuing years. Now he was surprised to be reading a story about these two young women conceived with his sperm. Fifteen months later, on Valentine's Day, Mr. Harrison contacted Danielle and JoEllen to reveal his identity.

———

Jeffrey Harrison, once a highly requested sperm donor, with a biological daughter in Los Angeles, California.

This story exposes key questions about our most important human relations, relations that we sometimes call "family" and that anthropologists have explored under the category of kinship. Who is "related" to whom? Who decides? Is kinship biological, or can family be chosen? Is Jeffrey Harrison indeed the father of Danielle and JoEllen, or is he simply their common donor? How would you interpret the father role of Jeffrey Harrison in comparison to that of the father who raised Danielle, or to that of JoEllen's two mothers? Who actually constitutes "family"?

Humans live in groups. As a species, we rarely live alone or in isolation. Kinship—the creation of relatives—is perhaps the most effective strategy humans have developed to form stable, reliable, separate, and deeply connected groups that can last over time and through generations.

Kinship is the system of meaning and power that cultures create to determine who is related to whom and to define their mutual expectations, rights, and responsibilities. Of course, humans also form groups through work, religion, education, and politics. But none compare to the power of families and kinship networks to provide support and nurture, ensure reproduction of the next generation, protect group assets, and influence social, economic, and political systems.

Kinship groups are often assumed by many in Western cultures to have a biological basis and to arise around the **nuclear family** of mother, father, and children. But when we examine these assumptions in a cross-cultural context, they show themselves to be a Euro-American ideal that not even those cultures have realized. Kinship groups come in a variety of shapes and sizes: We trace our connections through biological ancestors. We create kinship relations through marriage and remarriage. We adopt. We foster. We choose families of people who care about us. Sometimes we even imagine everyone in our nation to be part of one big, related, kinship community.

In the twenty-first century, we are vividly aware of new forms of family life as kinship relations shift, closing off familiar patterns and opening up new ones. The image of a family with mother, father, two kids, and a dog gathered around the dining room table every evening for a home-cooked meal and conversation may be familiar as a cultural icon, but for many people the experience of family is more complicated as families are taken apart, reconstructed, and blended. New reproductive technologies—including artificial insemination, in vitro fertilization, and surrogacy—continue to stretch our ideas of kinship and families by showing how human culture, through science and technology, is shaping biological relationships.

Although the term *kinship* may be unfamiliar to you, the subject material is not. Through kinship studies, anthropologists examine the deepest and most complicated aspects of our everyday lives—our relationships with people closest to us, including our mothers, fathers, brothers, sisters, grandparents, cousins, husbands, wives, and children. These are the people we live with, eat with, count on for support, and promise to take care of when they are in need. We pour our emotions, creative energy, hopes, and dreams into these relationships. Many of the most emotionally vibrant moments of our lives—from joy and love to anger and pain—occur at the intersection of individual and family life: birthdays, holiday celebrations, shared meals, weddings, illnesses, and funerals. Through kinship, we see our lives as part of a continuum. We look back to see the history of the people we come from, and we look ahead to imagine the relatives and families yet to be.

At the same time, kinship is deeply intertwined with forces beyond the everyday activities of family and home. In our families, we also learn basic patterns of human behavior—how to treat one another, how to act in groups, how to navigate differences of age, gender, ethnicity, and sexuality. This enculturation shapes our lives outside the household, including the way we think about gender roles, the division of labor, religious practices, warfare, politics, migration, and nationalism. Because cultural norms, values, and social structures can always be changed, kinship and family also become places of contestation, experimentation, and change that reflect and shape debates within the larger culture.

The study of kinship is one of anthropology's unique innovations for thinking about how culture works. In this chapter, we will explore the following questions about kinship.

- **How are we related to one another?**
- **Are biology and marriage the only bases for kinship?**
- **Is a country like one big family?**
- **How is kinship changing in the United States?**

We will examine the many strategies people use to form kinship groups, and we will consider the implications of kinship's changing expressions in the twenty-first century. By the end of the chapter you should be ready to interpret your own family tree—not simply by creating a list of relatives, but also by considering how those ties are formed and the role that kin play in shaping who you are as an individual and as a member of society. You will also be prepared to understand and analyze the ways debates about kinship shape important aspects of our individual and collective lives locally, nationally, and globally.

How Are We Related to One Another?

Whom are you related to? All humans are closely related genetically, sharing more than 99.9 percent of our DNA. Despite this close biological "kinship" among all humans, closer to home we tend to organize our personal relationships more specifically through systems of common biological descent, marriage, love, and choice. As you will discover throughout this chapter, cultures have a variety of ways of organizing kinship relationships. Some will be familiar to you, and others will not. All are equally valid.

DESCENT

One way that humans construct kinship groups is by tracking genealogical descent. In descent groups, primary relationships are with consanguineal relatives (what U.S. culture refers to as "blood" relatives). These would include your mother, father, sister, brother, grandparents, children, and grandchildren, as well as your uncles and aunts who are your parents' siblings—but not your uncles and aunts who are married to your parents' siblings. **Descent groups** are often imagined as long chains of connections from parents to children that reach back through many generations to a common ancestor or group of ancestors.

Early anthropological studies through the mid-twentieth century assumed the descent group to be central to the social structure of most nonindustrial cultures outside Europe and North America (Malinowski 1929, 1930; Fortes 1949; Radcliffe-Brown 1950; Evans-Pritchard 1951). Anthropologists of that period expected to find extended descent groups that stretched back over many generations and worked together. Such groups were considered key to understanding each culture's economic, political, and religious dynamics because of the way kinship underlies large social networks extending beyond the immediate family into all aspects of cultural life. We will consider one classic example, the Nuer, in the following section.

In contrast, most European and North American cultures do not use descent to organize social groups. Although we may keep track of our ancestors over a few generations, generally we have not constructed large social networks based on kinship connections. In the United States, perhaps the Rockefellers and the Kennedys might loosely qualify. They stretch back over a few generations, tracing roots to a much more recent common ancestor (either John D. Rockefeller or Joseph Kennedy); and although now subdivided into smaller segments, they still maintain strong enough connections to function together at times on common economic, social, political, or ritual activities and projects. But such descent groups are extremely rare in North America.

Anthropologists distinguish two types of descent groups: clans and lineages. **Lineages** can clearly demonstrate genealogical connections through many generations, tracing the family tree to a founding (apical) ancestor. **Clans** likewise claim connection to a founding ancestor, but they do not provide the same genealogical documentation. Descent groups may be *matrilineal*, constructing the group through the mother's side of the family, or *patrilineal*, tracing kinship

descent group

A kinship group in which primary relationships are traced through consanguineous ("blood") relatives.

lineage

A type of descent group that traces genealogical connection through generations by linking persons to a founding ancestor.

clan

A type of descent group based on a claim to a founding ancestor but lacking genealogical documentation.

through the father's side. Both matrilineal and patrilineal patterns reflect *unilineal* descent because they build kinship groups through either one line or the other. In contrast, *ambilineal* descent groups—including Samoans, Maori, Hawaiians, and others in Southeast Asia and the Pacific—trace kinship through both the mother and the father. This alternative pattern is sometimes called *bilateral* or *cognatic*.

Most people in the world practice patrilineal descent as their primary strategy to track kin group membership. At the same time, most people still build kinship networks bilaterally through both parents, even when tracing descent unilineally. Are you aware of how your own family traces descent?

The Nuer of Southern Sudan. The Nuer people of southern Sudan in northeast Africa constitute a classic representation of the descent group. British anthropologist E. E. Evans-Pritchard studied this group in the 1930s (Evans-Pritchard 1951). At the time of his research and until the latter part of the twentieth century, the Nuer were primarily a pastoral, cattle-herding people that moved between settlements throughout the year to adapt to rainy and dry seasons. The Nuer constituted a patrilineal descent group: both boy and girl children were born into the group, but membership could only pass to the next generation through the sons who inherited membership through their fathers. Nuer clans were *exogamous*—meaning that marriages within the group were not permitted. Large clans were divided into lineages, although lineages were extensive enough to spread over several villages.

Cattle were the center of Nuer economic life. They were owned by men, but they were milked by women as well as by boys who had not yet come of age and been initiated into the descent group. A successful marriage proposal often required the groom to provide cattle in exchange for the bride.

What does a descent group look like? *Left:* A chief (*standing*) and his sons, photographed by Bronislaw Malinowski; they represent the core of a patrilineal descent group in the Trobriand Islands. *Right:* A Kennedy family portrait, Hyannis, Massachusetts, 1930s, including, seated second from left, future U.S. attorney general Robert Kennedy; center, future U.S. president John F. Kennedy; second from right, family patriarch Joseph Kennedy Sr.

FIGURE 9.1

Kinship Naming Systems

Early anthropologists identified only six general patterns worldwide for classifying relatives when beginning with the ego's generation: Eskimo, Hawaiian, Sudanese, Omaha, Crow, and Iroquois.

ESKIMO

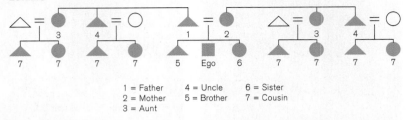

1 = Father	4 = Uncle	6 = Sister
2 = Mother	5 = Brother	7 = Cousin
3 = Aunt		

The Eskimo kinship naming system is the most common in Europe and North America. Only members of the nuclear family are given distinct terms. Aunts and uncles are distinguished from parents but not by side of the family. All cousins are lumped together.

HAWAIIAN

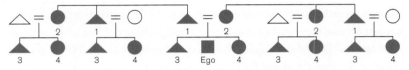

1 = Father and father's brothers   3 = Brothers and male cousins
2 = Mother and mother's sisters   4 = Sisters and female cousins

The Hawaiian system is the least complicated. The nuclear family is deemphasized, and relatives are distinguished only by generation and gender.

SUDANESE

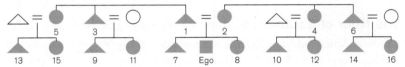

The Sudanese kinship system is the most complex. Each category of relative is given a distinct term based on genealogical distance from ego and the side of the family. There can be eight different cousin terms, all of whom are distinguished from ego's brother and sister.

Source: Dennis O'Neill. 2013. "Kinship: An Introduction to Descent Systems and Family Organization." http://anthro.palomar.edu/kinship (accessed 4/17/15).

The patrilineal kinship structures of clans and lineages provided the primary structure for Nuer political and economic activity. In the villages, the lineages collectively owned land, fisheries, and pastures. Ceremonial leadership of Nuer group life was organized under sacred ritual leaders, but these individuals did not control the social networks built around kinship and cattle, so they were not the driving force in Nuer culture (Stone 2009).

Searching for Kinship Patterns. As early anthropologists gathered kinship data from cultures worldwide, they developed a limited number of

MAP 9.1
The Nuer Region of East Africa

OMAHA

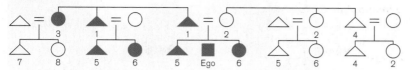

1 = Father and father's brothers
2 = Mother and females on mother's side
3 = Females on father's side
4 = Males on mother's side

5 = Male siblings and parallel cousins
6 = Female siblings and parallel cousins
7 = Male cross cousins
8 = Female cross cousins

The Omaha, Crow, and Iroquois naming systems trace kinship through unilineal descent—either patrilineally or matrilineally—so distinguishing between cousins takes on importance. The Omaha system is typical of kinship patterns traced through patrilineal descent.

CROW

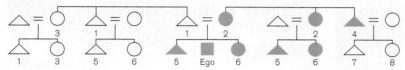

1 = Father and father's brothers
2 = Mother and mother's sisters
3 = Females on father's side
4 = Male on mother's side

5 = Male siblings and parallel cousins
6 = Female siblings and parallel cousins
7 = Male cross cousins
8 = Female cross cousins

The Crow system is typical of kinship patterns traced through matrilineal descent.

IROQUOIS

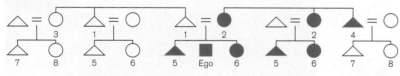

1 = Father and father's brother
2 = Mother and mother's sister
3 = Female on father's side
4 = Male on mother's side

5 = Male parallel cousins
6 = Female parallel cousins
7 = Male cross cousins
8 = Female cross cousins

The Iroquois kinship system can be traced either matrilineally or patrilineally. Note the same term is used for father and father's brother and for mother and mother's sister, reflecting shared membership in lineages.

general categories that facilitated comparison. Despite vast geographic distances and language differences, only four primary systems were identified to classify relatives in the parental generation: *lineal, bifurcate merging, generational,* and *bifurcate collateral.* When beginning with the ego's generation (the ego being the central character and starting point in tracing kinship relationships—for example, you in your own family tree), anthropologists found only six different ways of organizing relatives, in which the variation centered on the classification of siblings and cousins. Each of these six were named after a key group in which the pattern occurred: Eskimo, Hawaiian, Sudanese, Omaha, Crow, and Iroquois (Figure 9.1).

The Nuer, of the Sudan, are a classic representation of a descent group. *Top left:* a Nuer man, his sons, and cattle outside the family homestead, 1930s (photo by E. E. Evans-Pritchard). *Top right:* A Nuer family homestead, 2007. *Bottom left:* Nuer men leaping (beside Evans-Pritchard's tent) in a dance that often took the form of mock battles between village groups. Dances accompanied marriages and provided courtship opportunities for Nuer youth. *Bottom right:* Nuer women dancing in the bride's family homestead at a contemporary Nuer wedding.

Generalized systems of kinship classification can be very useful for identifying and comparing broad patterns of social structure. But anthropologists have found that actual, local kinship patterns do not always match the generalized models. The ways in which human groups trace connections between generations—in other words, how they construct genealogies—can be messy and far from exact. Genealogies are full of gaps, interruptions, disruptions, uncertainties, and imagined or assumed connections. Some groups have extensive genealogies, but even these carefully constructed records may be partly mythical and based on limited recollections or partial history. In contrast, other groups have extremely shallow genealogical memories that span only two or three generations. Segments of these descent groups may no longer live together or act together. Other relatives may have been forgotten or excluded from the main line through conflict. Political, economic, and/or military upheaval may have disrupted collective memory and records. Or kinship patterns may have changed over time as groups adapted to external pressures. As a result, these groups' knowledge of individual ancestors and even whole generations may have been lost.

Once again, the Nuer are an excellent example. Despite representing one of the six key cross-cultural variations in kinship studies (Sudanese), their day-to-day kinship practices did not exactly match the clear patrilineal descent model that might be imagined on a Nuer family tree. Evans-Pritchard determined that the Nuer inherited formal group membership through patrilineal descent, but he and Kathleen Gough (1971), who revisited the study a generation later, found that most Nuer individuals continued to trace kinship relations through both parents. These bilateral kinship relationships created by marriage were often just as important as those created through descent. Specifically, while women married into the Nuer descent group and produced children for that group, they also provided their children with close connections to kin on the mother's side, particularly the mother's brother. This pattern often occurs in patrilineal groups.

When Gough revisited Evans-Pritchard's original study, she suggested that local events in the 1930s may have affected Nuer kinship practices at the time. During the time of Evans-Pritchard's research in the 1930s, the Nuer were resisting British colonial occupation of the Sudan. In addition, they were involved in a conquest of the neighboring Dinka ethnic group. Additional intense conflicts existed among Nuer groups. Gough suggests that these tensions, conflicts, and disruptions may have intensified Nuer attention to kinship and marriage patterns as they attempted to reinforce group identity and assimilate outsiders. Gough also suggests that the particular expressions of kinship recorded by Evans-Pritchard may have been adaptations to political and economic conditions rather than an entrenched, changeless kinship norm (Gough [1971] 2001; see also Stone 2009).

Kinship, Descent, and Change in a Chinese Village. As Gough found in her Nuer study, political factors can shape efforts to construct kinship—a pattern I also uncovered in my own research in a Chinese village. When I conducted fieldwork in the late 1990s, I thought I had found a classic, Nuer-style patrilineal descent group. Ninety percent of the men in the village had the surname Chen and traced their origins back to the founding Chen—the apical ancestor—who they believed had settled in the area more than seven hundred years earlier. The village children, boys and girls, were all named Chen. But the Chen daughters were all to be married out to men in neighboring villages. The Chen men were to marry women from the same neighboring villages who would move in with them at home. The Chen family temple was the largest ancestral hall in the village and served as the center for venerating Chen ancestors. Until the 1960s, village lands, including agricultural plots and fisheries, were held in common by the Chen lineage, which acted like a small corporation. Male elders allocated access to the collectively owned village property to the other males in the descent group during an annual lineage meeting.

The village appeared to be a textbook case of a patrilineal Chinese descent group. But kinship is always a bit more complicated and interesting than anthropologists first imagine. In the late 1960s, family and temple ancestral records were destroyed as part of a national political movement known as the Cultural Revolution—a modernization campaign promoted by the Chinese government to throw out the old and bring in the new. Only in the 1990s did political and economic conditions improve enough for local villagers to consider reconstructing their lost records. An older village member who had become a university professor in the provincial capital accepted the task of writing and publishing a local village history book called a *zhupu* ("gazetteer"). His research included an effort to reconstruct the village genealogy and the Chen line of descent. Funding came from villagers working abroad, particularly in the United States.

When the research was complete, however, the devastating impact of the Cultural Revolution became apparent. Without written records, the reconstructed genealogy relied primarily on oral histories stored in the memories of village elders. Many vividly recalled their parents' and grandparents' generations. Some had heard stories of a few prominent Chen villagers whose earlier travel, business success, or scholarship had made them famous in the villagers' collective memory. Of course, the apical ancestor, his sons, and a few of their immediate descendents had been remembered. Unfortunately, most of the generations prior to 1900 had been left blank. The genealogical details, if they had ever existed, had been destroyed during the Cultural Revolution.

Migration has also challenged the Chen descent group's ability to maintain kinship connections, especially in the context of the current global age. In fact, fully 70 percent of the villagers—most between the ages of eighteen and

MAP 9.2
Fuzhou

Chinese family ancestral hall outside Fuzhou, China, built with money sent by villagers working abroad.

forty—have left China since the early 1980s to seek their fortunes in the United States, Japan, South America, Canada, and Europe. Some return to visit their hometown. Most marry and have children in their new host country. According to the rules of the patrilineal descent group, all children born to villagers working abroad still belong in the descent group, and males can pass on that membership to the next generation. But faced with such a massive out-migration and global diaspora of the lineage, how would they keep track as villagers migrated halfway around the world?

New York is the primary international destination for the village's immigrants. There, with the support of village leaders in China, immigrants have created a village hometown association to rebuild and strengthen hometown kinship ties. The association enables villagers to reconnect, provide mutual support, share information, and use their kinship networks to improve their immigrant experience. Association leaders also keep track of fellow villagers, their marriages, and their offspring. They report these developments back to the Chen family elders in China for proper recording. Through this process, long-held village strategies for kinship formation and group building are adapting to the challenges of wide-scale international migration, spurred by globalization. Modern communication and transportation technologies are enabling Chinese villagers to innovatively extend their notions of patrilineal descent, both spatially beyond China's national boundary and temporally forward into the future.

Certainly the forces of globalization, including migration and time-space compression, are placing stress on kinship systems worldwide. This is occurring as members of kinship groups relocate temporarily or permanently to nearby factories or jobs in other countries to seek improved economic and educational opportunities or to avoid natural disasters and political upheavals. Although generalized kinship categories developed by an earlier generation of anthropologists have provided insights into broad patterns of kinship, anthropologists who study kinship today confront more fluid kinship patterns maintained through flexibility and creativity.

MARRIAGE AND AFFINAL TIES

A second way humans form kinship groups is through marriage—what anthropologists refer to as **affinal relationships**. Unlike the construction of kinship groups through descent, which links direct genealogical ancestors and descendents, marriage builds kinship ties between two people who are (usually) not immediate biological kin. Marriage also creates a relationship between the spouses' respective kinship groups, called "in-laws" in U.S. culture. The new kinship group created through marriage is linked through affinity and alliance, not through shared biology and common descent.

Something like marriage exists in every culture, but its exact form and characteristics vary widely—so widely, in fact, that it is difficult to say that any one characteristic is universal. **Marriages** create socially recognized relationships that may involve physical and emotional intimacy, sexual pleasure, reproduction and raising of children, mutual support and companionship, and shared legal rights to property and inheritance. The bond of marriage may also serve to create connection, communication, and alliance between groups.

Marriages take many forms, including arranged marriages and companionate marriages. **Arranged marriages**, orchestrated by the families of the bride and groom, continue to be prominent in many cultures in Asia, the Pacific, the Middle East, and Africa. Arranged marriages are even common among some religious groups in the United States and, in a sense, among some segments of the upper class who send their children to elite private schools to meet future partners and encourage in-group marriage. These traditional marriages ensure the reproduction and continuation of the kinship group and build alliance with other kin groups. Thus the couple's parents may view the economic and political consequences of marriage alliance as being too important to the larger kinship group to be left to the whims of two young people. In this context, marriage becomes a social obligation and a symbol of commitment to the larger group rather than a mechanism for personal satisfaction and fulfillment. Alliance marriages of this sort require extensive negotiation to balance the needs of the group and the intimate personal feelings of the individuals being married. Bonds of affection may develop in an arranged marriage, but this is not the primary goal.

What about Love? Today marriage patterns are changing rapidly. Younger generations are increasingly thinking of love, intimacy, and personal pleasure—not social obligation—as the foundation on which to build families and kinship relations. Love—and what anthropologists call **companionate marriages**, which are built on love—is the ideal to be achieved.

affinal relationship
A kinship relationship established through marriage and/or alliance, not through biology or common descent.

marriage
A socially recognized relationship that may involve physical and emotional intimacy as well as legal rights to property and inheritance.

arranged marriage
Marriage orchestrated by the families of the involved parties.

companionate marriage
Marriage built on love, intimacy, and personal choice rather than social obligation.

Romantic love appears to be present in cultures worldwide. For decades, many anthropologists and other scholars considered romantic love to be a luxury and a unique product of modern Western cultures or other global elites. You may find it hard to imagine that anthropologists have largely ignored romantic love in their cross-cultural studies, particularly when considering classic love stories like those of Tristan and Isolde in France, China's Jade Goddess, the Indian Kama Sutra, or the Greek love poems of Sappho. A review of 166 ethnographic studies, however, reveals that even though anthropologists have not focused on romantic love, their research has encountered it in many cultures. William Jankowiak and Edward Fisher's (1992) study found references to love in 147 of the 166 studies, an overwhelming 89 percent. And, they claim, the absence of references to love in the others is more likely a result of oversight by the original researchers rather than the absence of romantic love in the cultures.

Ethnographic research has uncovered similar developments in the relationship between love and marriage in many other parts of the world, such as Malaysia (Chan 2006), Papua New Guinea (Wardlow 2006), China (Yan 2003), Egypt (Inhorn 1996), and Brazil (Rebhun 1999; Gregg 2003). In these areas, research reveals diversity in local expressions of companionate marriage but shows that young people increasingly frame marriage in terms of love, in contrast to the marriage patterns of their parents (Hirsch 2007). Consider for a moment how your own views on marriage compare to those of your parents and grandparents.

Monogamy, Polygyny, and Polyandry. Cultural rules, often inscribed in law, may determine who is a legitimate or preferred marriage partner. They may even determine how many people one can marry. Historically, some cultures, such as the Nuer of the Sudan or the Brahmans of Nepal, practiced **polygyny**—several marriages involving one man and two or more women. In a few cultures, including the Nyar of India and the Nyimba of Tibet and Nepal, **polyandry** has been common—marriages between one woman and two or more men. Most marriages in the world demonstrate **monogamy**—marriage (usually) between one man and one woman.

Even where monogamous marriages are the norm, it is common for people to marry more than one person in their lifetime. How does this happen? Marriages may be interrupted by divorce or death. In these cases, individuals who marry again reflect a process called *serial monogamy* in which monogamous marriages follow one after the other.

Incest Taboos. Just as some form of marriage exists in essentially all cultures, likewise all cultures have some form of **incest taboo**, or rules that forbid sexual relations with certain close relatives. Such taboos relate to nuclear family members: parents and children, siblings, and grandparents and grandchildren.

polygyny
Marriage between one man and two or more women.

polyandry
Marriage between one woman and two or more men.

monogamy
A relationship between only two partners.

incest taboo
Cultural rules that forbid sexual relations with certain close relatives.

Incest taboos also affect marriage patterns. A few historical examples of brother-sister marriage exist: among the Inca of Peru, among certain traditional Hawaiian groups, and among ancient Egyptian royalty (perhaps to preserve family control over wealth and power). But these cases are rare. Incest taboos universally prohibit marriage between siblings and between parents and children. But can a person marry a cousin? Let's explore that question more closely.

Beyond the nuclear family, incest taboos vary from culture to culture. In some contemporary cultures, including parts of China, India, the Middle East, and Africa, *cross-cousins* (children of a mother's brother or father's sister) are preferred marriage partners, but *parallel cousins* (children of a father's brother or a mother's sister) are excluded. Even in the United States, incest rules regarding marriage between cousins vary from state to state. Nineteen states allow *first-cousin* marriages (between the children of two siblings). More distant cousins are not excluded from marriage under U.S. law. Former New York City mayor and presidential candidate Rudy Giuliani, for example, was married to his *second cousin* for fourteen years before getting divorced. No other country in the Western world prohibits first-cousin marriage. Moreover, although it is illegal in the United States to marry a *half-sibling* (a brother or sister with whom one shares a parent), this is not illegal in many other cultures. Can you think of anyone in your family or a friend's family who is married to a cousin?

Even though the incest taboo is universal, its origins are unclear. Some scholars have suggested that the taboo arises from an instinctive horror of sex with immediate family members that developed during our evolutionary history (Hobhouse 1915; Lowie [1920] 1961). But studies of primates do not reveal a consistent incest taboo that humans might have inherited (Rodseth et al. 1991). Furthermore, if this instinctive horror existed, then it seems likely that humans would not need to create taboos to restrict incest.

Other theories have addressed the issue from different perspectives. For example, anthropologist Bronislaw Malinowski (1929) and psychologist Sigmund Freud (1952) both suggested that incest taboos might have developed to protect the family unit from sexual competitiveness and jealousy, which would disrupt cooperation. However, neither scholar could substantiate this claim with historical or contemporary ethnographic data. Another theory suggests that incest taboos arose out of concern that inbreeding would promote biological degeneration and genetically abnormal offspring (Morgan [1877] 1964). However, incest taboos predate the development of population science and the understanding of human genetics.

Even using contemporary genetic information, the science does not support the assumptions behind the incest taboo. For instance, incest does not create defective genes. If a harmful trait runs in the family, systematic inbreeding will increase the possibility of the defective gene being passed along and amplified in the gene pool. But long-term systematic inbreeding over many generations has few actual historical human examples. Genetic studies of consanguineous unions (between "blood" relatives) show some increased risk of congenital defects, but only within the studies' margin of error. These risks are actually less than the risk of congenital defects in children whose mothers are over the age of forty; yet this older population is not prohibited from marrying or giving birth (Bennett et al. 2002). Therefore, despite the universal existence of incest taboos, the extent of the taboos varies widely and no consensus exists as to their origins or exact purpose.

Other Marriage Patterns. Beyond explicit incest taboos, all cultures have norms about who is a legitimate or preferred marriage partner. In some groups, including most descent groups, marriage tends to reflect **exogamy**, meaning marriage to someone outside the group. Other groups practice **endogamy**, requiring marriage inside the group. Although kin group exogamy is more prevalent, endogamy exists in numerous cultures. It is practiced, for example, within the Indian caste system and within whole ethnic groups, as evidenced by both historical and contemporary U.S. marriage patterns.

In the United States, we practice *kindred exogamy*: we avoid, either by force of law or by power of tradition, marriage with certain relatives. At the same time, we also follow clear patterns of class and race endogamy. Indeed, most marriages occur between people of the same economic class and within the same "race" (U.S. Census Bureau 2010). As noted in Chapter 2, interracial marriages were outlawed for most of U.S. history, and only in 1967 did the U.S. Supreme Court rule that antimiscegenation laws are unconstitutional. Although interracial marriage is legal today, intense patterns of racial endogamy continue.

Most monogamous marriages occur between one man and one woman, but there are important exceptions, including female marriage among the Nuer of the Sudan and the Nandi of Kenya. Today same-sex marriage has gained increasing acceptance globally, being recognized in the Netherlands (2001), Belgium (2003), Spain (2005), South Africa (2006), Norway (2009), Sweden (2009), Argentina (2010), Iceland (2010), Portugal (2010), Denmark (2012), France (2013), Brazil (2013), Uruguay (2013), New Zealand (2013), and the United Kingdom (2013). In North America, Canada legalized same-sex marriages in 2005. In the United States, as of June 2015 same-sex marriages are legal in all 50 states.

Whether arranged or not, and whether monogamous, polygynous, or polyandrous, marriages may be accompanied by an exchange of gifts—most commonly, bridewealth and dowry—used to formalize and legalize the relationship. Though most contemporary Western cultures view marriage as an individual matter entered into by a couple who are romantically in love, in many non-Western cultures marriages focus on the establishment of strategic alliances, relationships, and obligations between groups—namely, the bride's kin and the groom's kin.

exogamy
Marriage to someone outside the kinship group.

endogamy
Marriage to someone within the kinship group.

While interracial relationships are legal in the United States today, intense patterns of racial endogamy (marriage within the same group) continue. Here, Mildred and Richard Loving embrace at a press conference the day after the U.S. Supreme Court ruled in their favor, June 13, 1967, in *Loving v. Virginia*, overturning Virginia's laws banning interracial marriage. And John Lawrence (*left*) and Tyron Garner (*right*) attend a press conference in Houston, June 26, 2003, after the U.S. Supreme Court in *Lawrence v. Texas* struck down the Texas ban on gay sex as an unconstitutional violation of privacy.

bridewealth

The gift of goods or money from the groom's family to the bride's family as part of the marriage process.

dowry

The gift of goods or money from the bride's family to the groom's family as part of the marriage process.

Bridewealth and dowry gifts formalize and legalize marriages and establish the relationship between these groups.

Bridewealth—common in many parts of Africa, where it often involves the exchange of cattle, cash, or other goods—is a gift from the groom and his kin to the bride's kin. Often thought of as a means to compensate her family for the loss of the bride, bridewealth agreements also establish reciprocal rights and obligations of the husband and wife, give legitimacy to their children, and assign the children to the husband's family. Even with the exchange of bridewealth, though, marriages may not always remain stable. Incompatibility, infertility, and infidelity can threaten the marriage agreement and trigger a return of the bridewealth. In this way, bridewealth can stabilize the marriage by establishing a vested interest for both extended families in the marriage's success (Stone 2009).

Through a **dowry**, the bride's family gives gifts to the husband's family at marriage. Common in India, a dowry may be part of a woman's family inheritance that the woman and her new husband can use to establish their household. In many cases, dowries may be seen as compensation to a husband and his family for taking on the responsibility of a wife, perhaps because of women's relatively low status in India or because upper-class and upper-caste women are not supposed to work. Today gifts often include personal and household items. Compulsory dowries are no longer legal in India (since 1961). But dowries are still quite common as part of the public process of transferring rights and legitimizing alliances. In some unfortunate instances where the dowry is considered insufficient, the bride may become the victim of domestic violence. In extreme cases this may lead to the murder or suicide of the bride, sometimes through bride burning or self-immolation. Such practices have come under severe criticism and are the target of human rights campaigns by groups inside India and in the international community that are committed to protecting the rights and lives of Indian women (Stone 2009).

Are Biology and Marriage the Only Bases for Kinship?

Cross-cultural ethnographic research reveals diverse strategies for constructing kinship ties that do not require direct biological connection or marriage alliances. As you will see, the range of strategies underscores the fluid, socially constructed aspect of kinship in many cultures.

HOUSES, HEARTHS, AND KINSHIP: THE LANGKAWI OF MALAYSIA

Among Malay villagers on the island of Langkawi, studied by Janet Carsten in the 1990s, kinship is not only given at birth but also is acquired throughout life (Carsten 1997). The Langkawi house and its hearth—where people gather to cook and eat—serve as places to construct kinship. In particular, Langkawi kinship is acquired through co-residence and co-feeding. In the local thinking, "blood" and other bodily substances are formed by eating food cooked at home. Other bodily substances, explicitly breast milk and semen, are regarded as forms of blood. Thus a husband and wife gradually become more similar by living and eating together. Sisters and brothers have the closest kinship relationship in childhood because they grow up in the same household eating the same food; but as they marry and move out of the shared home, their "blood" becomes less similar.

The Malay ideal is to marry someone close in terms of genealogy, geography, social status, or disposition. But perhaps because of the Langkawis' history of mobility, as well as the arrival of settlers in their outlying region of the Malay state, local notions of kinship have allowed new people to become close kin by living and eating together. For example, many children in the community have grown up spending significant time in homes with adults other than their birth parents. This fostering has been common for nieces, nephews, grandchildren, and others who are welcomed into the foster family and treated on an equal basis with those born into the family.

MAP 9.3
Langkawi

Among the Langkawi in Malaysia, kinship is created by sharing meals prepared in the family hearth and living together in the same house. *Left:* Langkawi children eat together near the family kitchen. *Right:* A Langkawi child and her maternal great-grandmother sit together, becoming kin, on a house ladder.

In addition, Langkawi understandings of fostering have often included expressions of hospitality in the community, whether one is a short-term or long-term visitor, a visiting student, or a distant relative. Villagers assume that all those who live together and eat together, regardless of their backgrounds, gradually come to resemble one another physically. The ideal guest—successfully fostered—stays for a long time, becomes part of the community, marries a local person, and raises children. In this way, the individual fully enters the kin group. This flexible process has built kinship relations that do not require the connection of biology or marriage. Instead, "[h]ouses and their hearths are the sites of the production of kinship" (Carsten 1997, 128; Carsten 2004; Peletz 1999; Stone 2009).

CREATING KIN TO SURVIVE POVERTY: BLACK NETWORKS NEAR CHICAGO, ILLINOIS

Kinship can even be a means to survive poverty, as Carol Stack's *All Our Kin: Strategies for Survival in a Black Community* (1974) demonstrates. This ethnography is a classic in anthropological kinship studies. Through deep involvement in an impoverished urban African American community called the Flats in a town outside Chicago, Stack uncovered residents' complex survival strategies based on extended kinship networks.

Although the federal government's 1965 Moynihan Report "The Negro Family: The Case for National Action" had branded the black family as disorganized, dysfunctional, and lost in a culture of poverty of its own making, Stack found otherwise. She uncovered a dynamic set of kinship networks based on mutual reciprocity through which residents managed to survive conditions of intense structural poverty and long-term unemployment.

MAP 9.4
Chicago

These kinship networks included biological kin and *fictive kin*—those who became kin. They stretched among households and across generations, extending to include all those willing to participate in a system of mutual support. People provided child care. They loaned money to others in need. They took in children who needed a foster home for a while. They borrowed clothes. They exchanged all kinds of things when asked. They cared for one another's sick or aging family members. Despite survival odds stacked against them in a community with few jobs, dilapidated housing, and chronic poverty, residents of the Flats succeeded in building lifelines for survival through their extended kinship networks (McAdoo 2000; Taylor 2000).

Is a Country Like One Big Family?

References to the nation often invoke metaphors of homeland, motherland, fatherland, and ancestral home. These concepts consolidate political force and build a sense of common nationality and ethnicity. Indeed, Benedict Anderson, in *Imagined Communities* (1983), marvels at the ability of nation-states to inspire a common national or ethnic identity among people who have never met, most likely never will meet, and have little in common socially, politically, or economically. Yet many people feel so connected to their country that they are even willing to die for it. How does this idea of the "nation" gain such emotional power? Janet Carsten (2004) suggests that nationalism draws heavily on ideas of kinship and family to create a sense of connection among very different people.

Like membership in many families, citizenship in the nation generally derives from birth and biology. Citizenship may be conveyed through direct descent from a current citizen. Another key pathway to membership in some nations, available to immigrants and other outsiders, like membership in many other families, is through marriage. Over time, members of the nation come to see themselves as part of an extended family that shares a common ancestry and a deep biological connection. As the boundaries blur among kinship, nationalism, and even religion, these powerful metaphors shape our actions and experiences (Carsten 2004).

REPRODUCING JEWS: ISSUES OF ARTIFICIAL INSEMINATION IN ISRAEL

In Israel, we can see how women serve as key players in defining and maintaining kinship connections. Susan Kahn's (2000) ethnography *Reproducing Jews: A Cultural Account of Assisted Conception in Israel* provides a dramatic contemporary example of the powerful intersection among reproduction, kinship, religion,

MAP 9.5
Israel

What is the relationship between kinship and the nation-state? A lab technician looks through a microscope while fertilizing egg cells at the fertility clinic in Tel Aviv, Israel.

and the state. For historical and religious reasons, Jewish women in Israel feel great pressure to reproduce the family and the nation. Israel's national health policies heavily favor increased reproduction. The national health insurance, for instance, subsidizes all assisted reproductive technologies. It does not promote family planning services to prevent pregnancy. Today the country has more fertility clinics per person than any other nation in the world, and it was the first to legalize surrogate motherhood.

Kahn's study examines a small but growing group of single Jewish mothers who are giving birth through artificial insemination. Because Jewishness passes down matrilineally from mother to child, what happens when a child is conceived through assisted reproductive technologies? These matters are of vital importance to the reproduction of Judaism and the state of Israel and, thus, are subject to intense debate by Jewish rabbis and Israeli state policymakers alike. Some scenarios are straightforward. For instance, in the eyes of the Israeli state any offspring conceived through artificial insemination and born to unmarried Jewish women are legitimate citizens. The line of descent and religious inheritance through the mother is clear. As evidence, the state provides these unmarried mothers with a wide range of support, including housing, child care, and tax breaks.

But other scenarios spur complex disagreements about religion and nationality. What is the effect on citizenship and religious identity when non-Jewish men donate sperm to Jewish women? Who is considered to be the father—the sperm donor or the mother's husband? When Jewish women carry to term eggs from non-Jewish women, who is considered to be the mother—the donor of the egg or the woman who carries the egg to term? The situation is equally complicated if a non-Jewish surrogate mother carries the embryo of a Jewish woman that was fertilized by a Jewish man through in vitro fertilization.

Much is at stake in these arguments for the Jewish religion and for the state of Israel. The decision about kinship in these cases of assisted reproductive technologies intersects with heated debates about how Judaism is reproduced and how Israel is populated. In fact, the decision has implications not only for the Jewish religion but also for notions of ethnic and national belonging and for the pathways to legal citizenship in the state of Israel (Finkler 2002; Nahman 2002; Feldman 2001; Stone 2009).

How Is Kinship Changing in the United States?

Many people see the 1950s-style nuclear family (represented in classic television shows such as *Leave It to Beaver*) as the traditional model of kinship in the United States. The father-husband-breadwinner went to work each day outside the home, while the mother-wife stayed home to take care of the household, raise the children, and be the ideal companion. They owned their own single-family house in the suburbs and functioned as a separate, private family unit. In many ways, this view of the nuclear family has become entrenched as the standard against which to judge other family forms (Schneider 1980).

THE NUCLEAR FAMILY: THE IDEAL VERSUS THE REALITY

The nuclear family concept acquired a particular history in Western industrialized cultures. This occurred as families adapted to an economic system that required increased mobility to follow job opportunities wherever they might lead. Though people are born into a **family of orientation** (in which they grow up and develop life skills), when they reach adulthood they are expected to detach from their nuclear family of orientation, choose a mate, and construct a new nuclear **family of procreation** (in which they reproduce and raise their own children). These "detachable" nuclear family units are extremely well adapted to a culture that prioritizes economic success, independence, and mobility over geographic stability and intergenerational continuity.

Historical studies suggest that the place of the nuclear family as the cornerstone of U.S. culture may be more myth than reality (Coontz 1988, 1992). Although the nuclear family came into prominence during a unique period of economic expansion after World War II, before that time it had not played a major role in the kinship history of the United States. The idealized nuclear

family of orientation
The family group in which one is born, grows up, and develops life skills.

family of procreation
The family group created when one reproduces and within which one rears children.

FIGURE 9.2
Households by Type in the United States, 1970–2010

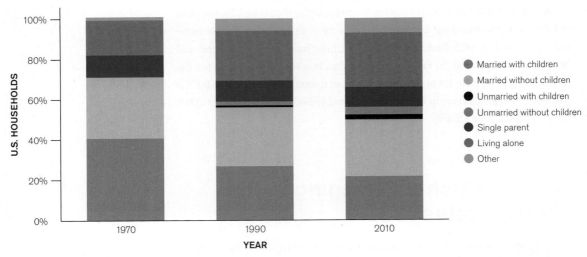

Source: U.S. Census Bureau. 2014. "Families and Living Arrangements." http://www.census.gov/hhes/families/data/families.html (accessed 4/17/15).

family of the twentieth century did not exist for the early colonists and only emerged as a result of industrialization in the nineteenth century. Even at its height in the mid-twentieth century, participation in the nuclear family model was far from universal. It was limited to a minority of Americans, particularly those in the white middle class (Coontz 1988, 1992; Carsten 2004; Stone 2009).

Current kinship patterns in the United States are changing rapidly, just as they are in many other parts of the world. In a wide variety of newly constructed family forms and kinship networks, biology is becoming less central and personal choice is becoming more important (Figure 9.2).

Though the divorce rate has been 50 percent for more than three decades, today in the United States we are creatively renegotiating kinship after divorce. Blended families are constructing new relationships to include step-parents, step-children, step-siblings, multiple sets of grandparents, and extended households of former spouses. Unmarried couples are living together. Same-sex couples are having or adopting children. Families are supplementing biological connections and affinal marriage connections with alternative family forms based on friendship, respect, and mutual support. These patterns reflect new residential and interpersonal relationships that contrast sharply with the imagined privacy and separation associated with the nuclear family ideal.

CHOSEN FAMILIES

People in the United States are increasingly creating kinship through choice. Step-parents, step-children, and step-siblings, as well as families with adopted children, are choosing to construct blended families with deep, enduring bonds. New reproductive technologies are yielding families of choice through in vitro fertilization, artificial insemination, and surrogacy. These patterns cut across all social classes and ethnic groups.

Kath Weston's (1991) ethnographic study of the construction of gay and lesbian families in San Francisco in the 1980s, *Families We Choose*, provides an example of creating kinship through choice. For many gay men and lesbians, "coming out" is a uniquely traumatic experience, especially when the revelation of one's sexuality and life choices generates hostility from close friends and family. When parents, siblings, and other close relatives cut off the kinship ties that U.S. culture suggests should be permanent and enduring, gay men and lesbians have turned to chosen families instead.

Not surprisingly, chosen families come in many shapes and sizes. Gay and straight friends, biological children, children adopted formally and informally, and former lovers all can become kin. Close friends can become family. Support networks and caregivers can take the place of biological kin and become kin themselves. Weston finds this to be a particularly common experience for those who provide care through intense illness, such as AIDS. Love, compassion, and the hard work of care over time make kinship very real in chosen families. This is a crucial development, especially when biological kin ties are inadequate or have failed completely.

Weston's study reminds us not to assume that the natural characteristics of biological kinship ties are better than the actual behavior of chosen families. In the absence of functional, biologically related families, Weston points out, chosen families take on the characteristics of stability, continuity, endurance, and permanence to become "real" (Bolin 1992; Lewin 1992).

Increasingly people are creating kinship through choice. Here, a gay couple in Chengdu, China, share their home with their adopted son, daughter-in-law, and grandson.

THE IMPACT OF ASSISTED REPRODUCTIVE TECHNOLOGIES

Discussions of new technologies that assist in human reproduction have filled the popular media, religious publications, courtrooms, and legislative halls of government. Such technologies include sperm and egg donation, in vitro fertilization, surrogacy, and cloning. Their emergence raises questions about the rights of parents and of children born with this assistance, as well as the impact of these innovations on our ideas and experience of kinship and family. Culture, in the form of medical technology, is now shaping biology. The long-term implications for kinship are unclear but deserve consideration (Franklin 1997).

Reproductive technologies are not new. Most, if not all, cultures have had techniques for promoting or preventing conception or enabling or terminating pregnancy. These have included fertility enhancements, contraceptives, abortion, and cesarean surgeries. Over the last thirty years, technological developments have opened new avenues for scientific intervention in the reproductive process and the formation of kinship. DNA testing can now determine the identity of a child's father with remarkable certainty, erasing uncertainty about paternity. Medical tests can now identify the sex of unborn children, a practice that has become problematic in parts of India and China where a strong cultural preference for male children has led to early termination of many female fetuses (Davis-Floyd 1997). Across the globe, when reproductive technologies become increasingly specialized, the implications for cultural constructs such as family and kinship become progressively more complex.

FAMILIES OF SAME-SEX PARTNERS

Gay and lesbian couples are not new in U.S. culture, but recently they have become more open about their sexual orientation and their relationships. At the same time, many other people are having an increasingly open discussion about gay men, lesbians, and same-sex marriage. Television shows and movies routinely include gay characters. Celebrities like Rosie O'Donnell and Neil Patrick Harris raise children with their same-sex partners. The Episcopal Church ordained the first openly gay bishop, Eugene Robinson. And when a high school in Louisiana canceled its senior prom in 2010 rather than allow a graduating student to bring her girlfriend as her date, a group of parents organized an alternative prom so the girls could attend. These examples demonstrate a growing recognition of same-sex relationships in numerous U.S. cultural arenas.

However, the cultural debate about homosexuality and same-sex marriage in the United States is intense and by no means settled. Within the debate we

Nastassia Heurtelou (*left*) and Luz Heurtelou (*right*) were married at the Brooklyn Clerk's Office, July 24, 2011, when New York became the sixth U.S. state to legalize same-sex marriage.

can see the contestation of cultural norms and values. Opponents raise concerns that these alternative kinship patterns will cause the breakdown of the traditional family and that the acceptance of homosexuality will lead to social disorder. Echoing their concerns, in 1996 the U.S. Congress passed the Defense of Marriage Act, eventually repealed in 2013, which forbade federal government recognition of same-sex marriages. At the same time, as noted earlier, a growing number of states have legalized same-sex marriage, recognized same-sex marriages conducted in other states, and registered civil unions, thereby enabling same-sex couples to qualify for many of the same social benefits that are available to heterosexual couples in those locales.

Drawing on generations of cross-cultural research on kinship, marriage, and the family, in 2004 the American Anthropological Association issued the following statement:

> The results of more than a century of anthropological research on households, kinship relationships, and families, across cultures and through time, provide no support whatsoever for the view that either civilization or viable social orders depend upon marriage as an exclusively heterosexual institution. Rather, anthropological research supports the conclusion that a vast array of family types, including families built upon same-sex partnerships, can contribute to stable and humane societies. (American Anthropological Association 2004)

From an anthropological perspective, these discussions about same-sex marriage illustrate the changing patterns of kinship in the United States. Looking cross-culturally, we see that there is no single definition of marriage, but many. As anthropologist Linda Stone notes, "From a global, cross-cultural perspective, those who seek same-sex marriage are not trying to redefine marriage, but merely to define it for themselves, in their own interests, as people around the world have always done" (Stone 2009, 271).

Today changes in the nuclear family, the rise of families of choice, the increase of same-sex marriages, and advances in assisted reproductive technologies are reshaping views of kinship and family in the United States. These changes do not necessarily indicate a general decline or improvement of family life or moral values. However, they do reveal a shift of kinship patterns away from a biologically defined, nuclear family model toward other models based on choice, flexibility, and fluidity (Stone 2009; Coontz 1992).

While debates will continue over changing marriage and family patterns, from an anthropological perspective one point is undeniable: marriage, family, and kinship are cultural constructs, and as such they are subject to change. You are certain to see even more change in these arenas during your lifetime.

Toolkit

Thinking Like an Anthropologist:
Kinship in Personal and Global Perspective

We experience kinship all the time, although we may not use that term to describe it. Kinship is close to home, for it comes alive in the people we live with, eat with, play with. It is vital as we experience the most dramatic periods of our personal lives. You will continue to make kinship and family relationships—perhaps through marriage, having children, and choosing close friends who ultimately become family. Thinking like an anthropologist can help you to better understand these experiences. And in today's globally interconnected world, having an understanding of the vast diversity of kinship patterns may help you navigate relationships with classmates, friends, family, and colleagues. As you do so, keep in mind the questions that have guided our discussion in this chapter:

- **How are we related to one another?**

- **Are biology and marriage the only bases for kinship?**

- **Is a country like one big family?**

- **How is kinship changing in the United States?**

In thinking about the two teenagers at the beginning of the chapter, how can we apply this chapter's ideas to better understand their situation and, more generally, any future changes in the constructs of kin and family? Who is related to whom? Who decides? Is kinship primarily biological, or can family be chosen? Who constitutes your own family? As you traced your family tree, did you see that kinship is not only about creating a list of relatives, but also about understanding the many ways those ties are formed and the role that kin play in shaping you as an individual and as a member of society? These tools of anthropological analysis will become increasingly important as the concept of kinship continues to change in cultures across the globe during the twenty-first century.

Key Terms

kinship (p. 236)

nuclear family (p. 236)

descent group (p. 238)

lineage (p. 238)

clan (p. 238)

affinal relationship (p. 246)

marriage (p. 246)

arranged marriage (p. 246)

companionate marriage (p. 246)

polygyny (p. 247)

polyandry (p. 247)

monogamy (p. 247)

incest taboo (p. 247)

exogamy (p. 249)

endogamy (p. 249)

bridewealth (p. 250)

dowry (p. 250)

family of orientation (p. 255)

family of procreation (p. 255)

Chapter 10
Class and Inequality

What can you learn about class and inequality in U.S. culture through the lens of professional baseball? Many of us spend hours at ballparks tracking balls and strikes, hits, stolen bases, great fielding plays, batting averages, and earned run averages, or consuming hot dogs, peanuts, popcorn, soda, and beer. But as anthropologists, let's dig deeper and explore the economic and social relationships—which we will refer to as class—of those involved in making the game happen.

Consider a Baltimore Orioles game at Camden Yards Stadium. On the field, the top-paid Orioles player in 2015, center fielder Adam Jones, earned $13 million. That averages out to about $80,000 a game, or $21,700 for each at bat. Numerous lesser-known players made the league minimum of $507,000 for the entire season. Collectively, the Orioles players earned $116 million in 2015. Baltimore manager Buck Showalter earned nearly $3 million for the

An Orioles baseball game at Baltimore's Camden Yards. What can a sporting event tell us about class and inequality?

season. The four umpires each earn between $120,000 and $350,000 per season depending on their years of experience. In contrast, what do you suppose the security guards and grounds crew earn?

From your seat in the stands, you may be able to infer some things about class and inequality from those around you. You may not know the other spectators' average income and wealth, but stadium seating reflects the ability to pay, with the most desirable seats escalating in price as they get closer to the field and home plate. At Camden Yards, the least desirable tickets cost $10 in 2015, while box seats behind home plate cost up to $95. Some people are happy to see one game a year; others buy season tickets. With the average ticket price at $25, a family of four averages $100 to see a game—not to mention parking, refreshments, and souvenirs. If each person gets a hot dog, soda, and popcorn, a family can easily spend $150 to $200 on a trip to the game.

Curiously, the two extreme ends of the class spectrum in Camden Yards are largely invisible.

Peter Angelos, lead owner of the Orioles, is by far the richest man in the stadium. He built his reputation as a lawyer representing labor unions and their members, then amassed a fortune as lead litigator in several high-profile civil lawsuits. Angelos purchased the Orioles with several partners in 1993 for $173 million. By 2015, the franchise was worth $1 billion and had $245 million in operating revenues.

At the opposite extreme are the day laborers who clean the stadium long after the cheering crowds have left. In 2002 these men and women earned $4 an hour, and many lived in homeless shelters near the stadium. Over the next two years they collaborated to form the United Workers Association (UWA), and in 2004 they began a three-year campaign against Angelos and the Maryland Stadium Authority, owner of Camden Yards, seeking a living wage—the minimum hourly wage necessary to meet basic needs such as food, housing, clothing, health care, and transportation. Under pressure from UWA, student groups, and religious communities, Angelos initially agreed to pay the Baltimore City living wage. But by 2005 the workers' hourly wage had increased to only $7, far below what was promised.

Becoming desperate, by summer 2007 eleven stadium cleaners and their supporters announced that on Labor Day they would begin a hunger strike. Rallies at local churches and a statewide educational tour built public support, drew media attention, and ratcheted up pressure for a fair settlement. On the Friday before Labor Day, the governor announced a commitment to pay a state living wage and his expectation that all state agencies and contractors would abide by it. The next day, the Maryland Stadium Authority board voted to guarantee the stadium cleaners the state living wage of $11.30 an hour.

MAP 10.1
Baltimore

Camden Yards stadium cleaners announce a hunger strike for a living wage.

Although this vote signaled a victory for UWA and its supporters, earning $11.30 an hour for the full year in 2009 would still have barely broken the federal poverty line of $22,050 for a family of four. It is hardly enough to live a decent life by typical standards in the United States, where the middle-class dream includes a stable and well-paying job, decent housing, a healthy lifestyle, time for recreation and leisure, and the ability to raise children who will be more prosperous than their parents.

Our brief examination of the baseball game reveals indications of class differences in U.S. culture. Yet of all the systems of stratification and power, class may be the most difficult to see clearly and discuss openly. In previous chapters we have considered stratification along lines of race, ethnicity, gender, and sexuality. In this chapter we will explore the systems of class and inequality that exist in the United States and elsewhere: how they are constructed, how class intersects with race and gender, and how inequality affects individuals' life chances.

By **class** we refer to a system of power based on wealth, income, and status that creates an unequal distribution of the society's resources—usually moving surpluses steadily upward into the hands of an elite. Systems of class stratify individuals' life chances and affect their possibilities for upward social mobility.

In this chapter we will consider the following questions:

- **Is inequality a natural part of human culture?**
- **How do anthropologists analyze class and inequality?**

class

A system of power based on wealth, income, and status that creates an unequal distribution of a society's resources.

- **How are class and inequality constructed in the United States?**
- **What are the roots of poverty in the United States?**
- **Why are class and inequality largely invisible in U.S. culture?**
- **What are the effects of global inequality?**

By the end of the chapter, you will understand how systems of class work and how they affect your life chances and those of others. You may also be motivated to engage in efforts to change systems of inequality if you so choose.

Is Inequality a Natural Part of Human Culture?

Inequality exists in every contemporary culture, though not to the extremes of Peter Angelos and the stadium cleaners in Baltimore. Each society develops its own patterns of stratification that differentiate people into groups or classes. Such categories serve as the basis for unequal access to wealth, power, resources, privileges, and status. As discussed in earlier chapters, these systems of power and stratification may include race, ethnicity, gender, and sexuality. In addition, systems of social class create and maintain patterns of inequality, structuring the relationships between rich and poor, between the privileged and the less well off. But are stratification and inequality intrinsic to human culture?

EGALITARIAN SOCIETIES

As we will consider further in Chapter 11, for thousands of years, until the development of agriculture approximately 10,000 years ago, the primary human economic and social structure has been hunting and gathering. This type of structure has promoted **egalitarian societies** based on the sharing of resources to ensure group success with a relative absence of hierarchy and violence within or among groups. Most modern humans who have ever lived have been hunter-gatherers.

Archaeological evidence suggests that human evolutionary success relied on cooperation and the sharing of food, child rearing, and hunting and gathering responsibilities, not on hierarchy, violence, and aggression. After all, building a system of **reciprocity** in which group members equally share the bounty of the moment has long-term benefits for sustaining the group. Members can then expect the generosity to be reciprocated (Knauft 1991). Although contemporary economic relations tend to be organized around the exchange of money for services, patterns of reciprocity still exist. You may take class notes for someone

egalitarian society

A group based on the sharing of resources to ensure success with a relative absence of hierarchy and violence.

reciprocity

The exchange of resources, goods, and services among people of relatively equal status; meant to create and reinforce social ties.

who returns the favor—reciprocates—at a later date. You may give someone a ride or walk their dog or share your lunch with the understanding that at some point in the future your favor will be reciprocated. In these instances, members of our extended "group" share their resources of time, food, or other amenities for the long-term benefit of sustaining the group. (See Chapter 11 for a longer discussion of reciprocity.)

Reciprocity in action: an Amish community gathers to raise a barn.

Anthropologists have studied egalitarian societies among contemporary hunter-gatherer groups such as the Ju / Hoansi of Africa's Kalahari region (Lee 2003), as well as the Canadian Inuit and the Hadza of Tanzania (Marlowe 2010), among many others. Efforts to establish more egalitarian systems of economic and social relations have also occurred within highly stratified societies. The Amish (Hostetler 1993) and Hutterite (Hostetler 1997) communities in the United States are good examples on a small scale.

RANKED SOCIETIES

Anthropologists also recognize **ranked societies**, where wealth is not stratified but prestige and status are. In these societies, positions of high prestige—such as chief—are largely hereditary. Because only certain individuals can occupy these positions, the social rank of the society is set regardless of the skills, wisdom, or efforts of other members.

ranked society

A group in which wealth is not stratified but prestige and status are.

Chiefs usually do not accumulate great wealth, despite their high prestige. In fact, their lifestyle and standard of living may not vary significantly from those of any other member of the group. Group members offer gifts of tribute to the chief, but these are not kept and hoarded. Instead, the chief redistributes the tribute to group members. This act of gift giving—a form of **redistribution**—ensures his or her prestige while also preserving the well-being of all group members. The chief's rank and status are reinforced not through accumulation of wealth but through reciprocity and generosity (Petersen 2009).

One redistribution ceremony famous in the field of anthropology is the **potlatch** practiced among the Kwakiutl of the Pacific Northwest. Among this Native American group, the chief would establish and reestablish claims to prestige and status by holding an elaborate feast and gift-giving ceremony—a potlatch. He would give guests all of his personal possessions, including extra supplies of food, cooking pots, blankets, weapons, and even boats. What was not given away might

redistribution

A form of exchange in which accumulated wealth is collected from the members of the group and reallocated in a different pattern.

potlatch

Elaborate redistribution ceremony practiced among the Kwakiutl of the Pacific Northwest.

Women of the Makah Nation on the U.S. Pacific Northwest coast prepare salmon steaks for a potlatch, a communitywide redistribution ceremony and feast.

be destroyed as a sign of the chief's great capacity. The more elaborate the gift giving, the more status and rank the chief gained in the community. The chief's generosity also applied pressure on his guests to reciprocate in like manner, or even more elaborately in a later ceremony (Boas 1966). In a practical sense, the potlatch served to distribute key community resources of food and clothing broadly among group members. As a ritual ceremony, it represented a tradition among the Kwakiutl and other ranked societies in which social status is established not by wealth and power, but by the prestige earned via one's capacity for generosity (Boas 1966).

The extreme stratification in today's world is a fairly recent development. Anthropologists trace its roots to the rise of intensive agriculture and populous market towns, where relatively small groups of elite merchants and landholders were able to accumulate wealth. Stratification and inequality became more pronounced in industrialized capitalist economies over recent centuries, and this uneven development appears to be accelerating under the forces of globalization, further concentrating wealth in the hands of the few (Stiglitz 2012).

How Do Anthropologists Analyze Class and Inequality?

We turn now to consider four key theorists of class and inequality. European social philosophers Karl Marx and Max Weber, writing in the nineteenth and early twentieth centuries in the context of the Industrial Revolution, are separated by a century from French sociologist Pierre Bourdieu and U.S. anthropologist Leith Mullings, whose late twentieth-century writings are based in the context of a much more complicated and advanced capitalist economic system.

THEORIES OF CLASS

Each theorist discussed below responds to the unique social and economic challenges of his or her time and offers key analytical insights that allow anthropologists today to more deeply investigate the realities of class and inequality. As you read about each theorist, consider how you might apply their key concepts to understanding the social class relationships and inequality in our opening story about the baseball game.

Karl Marx: Bourgeoisie and Proletariat. Karl Marx (1801–1882), perhaps the most widely read theorist of class, wrote against a background of economic change and social upheaval. During the nineteenth century, rapid

economic changes and new government policies brought massive social upheaval and dislocation to western Europe. As the Industrial Revolution swept through the area, government policies restricted poor rural families' use of common village lands. Deprived of access to land they had depended on for farming, grazing, and gathering, rural people migrated to urban centers to seek jobs in the expanding industrial factories.

Marx's analysis of the increasing inequalities in the emerging capitalist economy of nineteenth-century Europe distinguished between two distinct classes of people. The **bourgeoisie**, or capitalist class, owned the **means of production**—the factories, machines, tools, raw materials, land, and financial capital needed to make things. The **proletariat**, or working class, lacked land to grow their own food, tools to make their own products, and capital to build workshops or factories. Unable to make their own living, they sold their work—their labor—to capitalists in return for wages.

Marx identified labor as the key source of value and profit in the marketplace. Owners sought to constantly increase their income by forcing workers to toil faster, longer, and for lower wages, thereby reducing the cost of production and increasing the difference between the production cost and the sale price. The surplus value created by the workers could then become profit for the owner. In this relationship, capitalists increased their wealth by extracting the surplus labor value from workers. Recognition of these two fundamentally different positions within the economy—two different classes—was essential to Marx's understanding of power relations in a culture.

Today anthropologists apply Marx's ideas to analyze class and power in contemporary society while acknowledging that capitalism has grown much more complex since Marx's time. Intense competition has grown among capitalists, notably between those in the manufacturing and financial sectors. Small business owners and farmers now own the means of production, technically making them part of Marx's bourgeoisie, but they do not possess the same access to capital as others in that class. The working class—the proletariat—is divided, with conflicts along lines of race, gender, and ethnicity. Moreover, increasing global circulation of capital is drawing local cultures and communities into class-based relationships that were not present even a generation ago.

Many contemporary social scientists recognize a middle class of professionals and managers (white-collar workers) that has emerged between capitalists and the working class (blue-collar workers). But others who take a more strict Marxist view of class argue that professionals and managers are still members of the proletariat (Durrenberger and Erem 2010; Buck 2009). They may have more power in the workplace and substantially higher incomes, but they still sell their labor to the bourgeoisie. These managers, government officials, military, police, and even college professors receive special privileges from the bourgeoisie. But it is worth the price to gain the cooperation of this middle class in organizing,

bourgeoisie

Marxist term for the capitalist class that owns the means of production.

means of production

The factories, machines, tools, raw materials, land, and financial capital needed to make things.

proletariat

Marxist term for the class of laborers who own only their labor.

educating, and controlling the working class, thereby maximizing the extraction of profits by the capitalist class.

Along with Friedrich Engels, Marx wrote the *Communist Manifesto* (1848) as a political pamphlet urging workers to recognize their exploited class position and to unite in order to change the relations between proletariat and bourgeoisie emerging in the capitalist system. Marx noted, however, the extreme difficulty for workers to develop a class consciousness—a political awareness of their common position in the economy that would allow them to unite to change the system. Why? Because their continuous struggle simply to make ends meet, as well as the creative means used by the bourgeoisie to keep the proletariat divided, work against a unified challenge to the stratification of society.

Max Weber: Prestige and Life Chances. Max Weber (1864–1920), like Marx, wrote against the backdrop of economic and social upheavals in western Europe caused by the expansion of capitalism during the Industrial Revolution. In analyzing the emerging structures of stratification, Weber added consideration of power and prestige to Marx's concern for economic stratification of wealth and income. By **prestige**, Weber referred to the reputation, influence, and deference bestowed on certain people because of their membership in certain groups (Weber [1920] 1946). Thus certain occupations may hold higher or lower prestige in a culture—for instance, physicians and farm workers. Prestige, like wealth and income, can affect life chances. Prestige rankings affect the way individuals are treated in social situations, their access to influential social networks, and their access to people of wealth and power.

prestige
The reputation, influence, and deference bestowed on certain people because of their membership in certain groups.

life chances

An individual's opportunities to improve quality of life and achieve life goals.

Weber saw classes as groups of people for whom similar sets of factors determine their life chances. By **life chances**, Weber referred to the opportunities that individuals have to improve their quality of life and realize their life goals. Life chances are determined by access not only to financial resources but also to social resources such as education, health care, food, clothing, and shelter. Class position—relative wealth, power, and prestige—determines access to these resources. According to Weber, members of a class share common life chances, experiences, and access to resources, as well as similar exposure and vulnerability to other systems of stratification.

Pierre Bourdieu: Education and Social Reproduction.

Pierre Bourdieu (1930–2002) studied the French educational system to understand the relationship among class, culture, and power ([1970] 1990). Throughout much of the world, education is considered the key to upward social mobility within stratified societies. **Social mobility** refers to the movement of one's class position—upward or downward—in stratified societies. Theoretically, the *meritocracy* of education—whereby students are deemed successful on the basis of their individual talent and motivation—should provide all students an equal opportunity. Instead, Bourdieu's research uncovered a phenomenon of **social reproduction** in the schools: rather than providing opportunities for social class mobility, the educational system helped reproduce the social relations that already exist by passing class position from generation to generation in a family. What factors in schools work against the meritocratic idea and instead serve to limit a person's life chances? First, a family's economic circumstances make a difference. But Bourdieu identified two additional key factors: *habitus* and cultural capital.

social mobility

The movement of one's class position, upward or downward, in stratified societies.

social reproduction

The phenomenon whereby social and class relations of prestige or lack of prestige are passed from one generation to the next.

Bourdieu described ***habitus*** as the self-perceptions and beliefs that develop as part of one's social identity and shape one's conceptions of the world and where one fits into it. *Habitus* is taught and learned at an early age and is culturally reinforced through family, education, and the media. It is not fixed or predetermined, but it is so deeply enculturated that it becomes an almost instinctive sense of one's potential. *Habitus* emerges among a class of people as a set of common perceptions that shape expectations and aspirations and guide the individual in assessing his or her life chances and the potential for social mobility. Life decisions—for instance, the choice of college education or career—are made on the basis of the family's *habitus*.

habitus

Bourdieu's term to describe the self-perceptions and beliefs that develop as part of one's social identity and shape one's conceptions of the world and where one fits into it.

Cultural capital is another key to the social reproduction of class. Bourdieu defined **cultural capital** as the knowledge, habits, and tastes learned from parents and family that individuals can use to gain access to scarce and valuable resources of society. For example, family wealth can create cultural capital for children. With enough money, parents can provide their children with opportunities to travel abroad, learn multiple languages, take music lessons, join sports

cultural capital

The knowledge, habits, and tastes learned from parents and family that individuals can use to gain access to scarce and valuable resources in society.

Children build cultural capital at the Metropolitan Museum of Art in New York City.

clubs, go to concerts and museums, have enriching summer experiences, and build social networks with others who have similar opportunities. These opportunities build the social skills, networks, and sense of power and confidence that are essential for shaping class position and identity in stratified societies. Family wealth enables children to perpetuate cultural capital, including high motivation and a sense of possibilities that are crucial for academic success. Schools reward cultural capital. In the process, schools reproduce social class advantage.

The U.S. public school system is heavily influenced by cultural capital. From an early age, students are split into separate tracks based on standardized test performance and teacher evaluations. Around sixth grade, for example, students are separated into the mathematics track that will lead either to Advanced Placement Calculus their senior year in high school or to remedial or regular math. Selective colleges often screen positively for applicants with AP Calculus credits. As a result, decisions made in sixth grade affect students' college possibilities. Did you know this? Some people with cultural capital do know. A study of middle-school math groups in Boston public schools reveals the way mathematics tracking tends to reproduce class in the classroom. Of the students in the accelerated math track, 56 percent had fathers with a doctorate or other professional degree and 33 percent had fathers with a master's degree. Just 5.6 percent had fathers with only a high school degree. Of the students in remedial math, 48 percent had fathers with a high school diploma or less (Useem 1992).

Leith Mullings: Intersectionality among Race, Gender, and Class.
In recent years, Leith Mullings's work on intersectionality has led anthropologists to reexamine class by analyzing the deep connections among class, race, and gender. Building on the field's long history of holistic ethnographic studies

intersectionality

An analytic framework for
assessing how factors such as
race, gender, and class interact to
shape individual life chances and
societal patterns of stratification.

of local communities, Mullings offers an intersectional approach: she asserts that class, in the United States and many other areas, cannot be studied in isolation but, instead, must be considered together with race and gender as interlocking systems of power. **Intersectionality** provides a framework for analyzing the many factors—especially race and gender—that determine how class is lived and how all three systems of power and stratification build on and shape one another.

In the 1990s Mullings led a study, The Harlem Birth Right Project, on the impact of class, race, and gender on women's health and infant mortality. The study focused on central Harlem, at that time a vibrant, primarily African American community in northern Manhattan, New York City (Mullings 2005; Mullings and Wali 2001). Of particular concern, infant mortality rates in Harlem were twice the rate of New York City's overall. Previous studies (e.g., Schoendorf, Hogue, and Kleinman 1992) had demonstrated that African American women in the United States, at every socioeconomic level, have more problematic birth outcomes than white women regardless of social class. Even college-educated African American women experienced infant mortality at twice the rate of college-educated white women. This observation suggested that factors other than education and social status were at work.

Mullings's research team gathered data through participant observation in community organizations and other sites in Harlem, as well as through surveys, in-depth interviews, and life histories with pregnant women and women with children. On the basis of their data, the team examined how the underlying conditions of housing, employment, child care, and environmental factors, as well as the quality of public spaces, parks, and even grocery and retail stores, might affect the health outcomes being reported in Harlem, where both working-class and middle-class women lived. Since the early 1990s, Harlem has been hard hit by dramatic changes in New York City's economy. Manufacturing jobs with middle-class wages have been lost to flexible accumulation (see Chapters 1 and 11), as New York City–based companies relocate production overseas. Meanwhile, job growth in the metropolitan area has occurred in the high-wage financial sector and in the low-wage service sector. Throughout the 1990s, government social services were cut back while public housing and transportation were allowed to deteriorate.

The effects on working-class and middle-class women in Mullings's study were notable, with increased physical and mental stress, especially for pregnant women. For working-class women, inadequate, overpriced, and poorly maintained private and public housing forced many mothers and their children to be constantly on the move, searching for affordable housing and sharing living spaces with friends and relatives to make ends meet. The need to regularly fight for needed repairs drained time and energy from hard-working women holding multiple low-wage jobs while juggling work and child care. A shortage of steady, well-paying jobs meant that women had very little income security or benefits, so they often pieced

MAP 10.2
Harlem

together a living from multiple sources. Middle-class women, many of whom were employed in the public sector, were also increasingly subject to layoffs as local governments downsized (Mullings 2005; Mullings and Wali 2001).

The Harlem Birth Right Project illustrates a powerful application of the intersectional approach to understanding class and inequality. It reveals how inequality of resources (class), institutional racism, and gender discrimination combine to affect opportunities for employment, housing, and health care in the Harlem community. Mullings's study also points out the determination and creativity women use to overcome interlocking constraints of racism, sexism, and class inequality in order to survive in their chosen community.

Mother and children, Harlem, New York. How do class, race, and gender intersect to affect people's life chances?

How Are Class and Inequality Constructed in the United States?

The United States' national myth tells of a "classless" society with open access to upward social mobility for those who are hardworking and talented, including the potential to rise from rags to riches in a single generation. This is the cultural story we tell, but is it reality? In fact, in the United States one's life chances are heavily influenced by the class position of one's family—the financial and cultural resources passed from generation to generation. What are the chances that a homeless person sweeping the Orioles stadium someday will be able to afford a box seat behind home plate or an apartment near the stadium? What are the chances that her child will become as well educated or as wealthy as Peter Angelos's child?

A LOOK AT THE NUMBERS

Economic statistics provide a sobering picture of inequality in the United States today. They also reveal the increasing concentration of income and wealth at the top rungs of the class ladder. In reviewing statistics related to class, we examine both income and wealth.

income
What people earn from work, plus dividends and interest on investments, along with rents and royalties.

Income. **Income** is what people earn from work, plus dividends and interest on investments along with rents and royalties. (A dividend is a payment by a corporation to its shareholders of a portion of corporate profits. Interest is a fee paid for the use of borrowed money—for example, interest paid on a bank savings account. Rent refers to payment to an owner as compensation for the use of land, a building, an apartment, property, or equipment. Royalties are income based on a percentage of the revenue from the sale of a patent, book, or theatrical work paid to the inventor or author.) Table 10.1a shows a breakdown of average household income in the United States for 2013. Do you know where your family fits in the national income range?

Income patterns reveal the way power is distributed in a society. As Table 10.1b illustrates, income distribution among the U.S. population shows a heavy concentration at the top. These gaps have widened substantially over the past four decades. Furthermore, the gap between people at the top end of the income scale and the average worker has dramatically increased over the past five decades.

wealth
The total value of what someone owns, minus any debt.

Wealth. Wealth is another key indicator of the distribution of power in a society. By **wealth** we mean the total value of what someone owns—including stocks, bonds, and real estate—minus any debt, such as a mortgage or credit card debt. If wealth were evenly distributed, every U.S. household would have had $498,800 in 2010 (Board of Governors of the Federal Reserve System 2012). But wealth is not evenly distributed, as Table 10.2 shows.

Moreover, wealth is even more unevenly distributed than income, and the gap is widening. Since 1976, wealth has increased by 63 percent for the wealthiest 1 percent of the population and by 71 percent for the top 20 percent. Wealth has decreased by 43 percent for the bottom 40 percent of the U.S. population

TABLE 10.1
Income in the United States
A.) Average U.S. Household Income by Percentage of the Population, 2013

PERCENTAGE OF U.S. POPULATION	HOUSEHOLD INCOME RANGE
Top 5%	Above $196,000
Top 20%	Above $105,910
Second 20%	$65,502–$105,910
Middle 20%	$40,188–$65,501
Fourth 20%	$20,901–$40,187
Bottom 20%	Less than $20,900

B.) Distribution of U.S. Household Income, 1967 versus 2013

	TOP 5% OF POPULATION	TOP 20% OF POPULATION	BOTTOM 40% OF POPULATION	BOTTOM 20% OF POPULATION
1967	16.3%	43%	15%	4.1%
2013	22.2%	51%	11.6%	3.2%

Source: U.S. Census Bureau. 2014. Historical Income Tables: Income Inequality, Tables H-1 and H-2 All Races. www.census.gov/hhes/www/income/data/historical/inequality/index .html (accessed 6/9/15).

TABLE 10.2
Distribution of Private Wealth in the United States, 2013

PERCENTAGE OF POPULATION*	PERCENTAGE OF PRIVATE WEALTH
Top 3% of Population	54%
Next 7% of Population	21%
Bottom 90% of Population	25%

*Total U.S. population in 2013 = 310,000,000.
Source: Federal Reserve Board Survey of Consumer Finances. 2014. Cited in http://inequality.org /wealth=inequality (accessed 4/23/15).

(Economic Policy Institute 2011). The widening gap has multiple causes. First, shifts in the U.S. tax code have lowered the top tax rate from 91 percent in the years from 1950 to 1963, to 35 percent from 2003 to 2012, rising to 39.6 percent beginning in 2014, allowing the wealthy to retain far more of their income (Tax Policy Center 2015). Second, wages for most U.S. families have stagnated since the early 1970s. Moreover, credit card, education, and mortgage debt have skyrocketed.

In another surprising statistic about the transfer of wealth from generation to generation, only 1.6 percent of Americans receive $100,000 or more in inheritance. Another 1.1 percent receives $50,000 to $100,000. Ninety-two percent of the population receives no inheritance whatsoever (Domhoff 2012).

Wealth is also stratified by race. Reflecting the devastating long-term effects of slavery and Jim Crow segregation on the African American community, as well as the difficult immigration experiences of most of the U.S. Hispanic population, white households have accumulated fifteen times the net worth of black and Hispanic households.

Most Americans struggle to identify the distribution of income and wealth in the United States and to locate their position within it (Norton and Ariely 2011). After reviewing the quantitative data on income and wealth stratification in the United States, can you identify pieces of information that were particularly surprising to you? Does the statistical picture correspond with the picture of U.S. society that you imagined? Do you have a clearer sense of where you and your family currently stand? Although statistics and quantitative data provide a broad overview, we turn now to several case studies that explore class and income inequality in local contexts and their impact on the life chances of real people in local communities.

ETHNOGRAPHIC PORTRAITS OF CLASS IN THE UNITED STATES

Anthropologists have studied the construction of class and its effects across the spectrum of U.S. culture—in rural, urban, and suburban settings and in relationship to race and gender. Ethnographic portraits like those presented below personalize the numbers we have just seen, putting faces to statistics and bringing real-life stories into the discussion.

MAP 10.3
Kentucky

Poor Whites in Rural Kentucky. In *Worked to the Bone: Race, Class, Power, and Privilege in Kentucky* (2001), anthropologist Pem Davidson Buck provides a dynamic introduction to intersectionality. She analyzes the intersections of class, race, and gender through the history of the poor white population in two rural Kentucky counties. Here, the privileges often associated with whiteness in the United States have been severely limited by class. Buck traces the development of an economic system built on tobacco cultivation, coal mining, and manufacturing that has created a class hierarchy in which "sweat is made to trickle up" (Buck 2001, 13). In other words (reflecting Marx's theory), the surplus value of workers' labor drains upward into the hands of successive layers of elites.

Numerous historical events and processes contributed to this development. The construction of race in Kentucky through slavery, sharecropping, and Jim Crow legislation served to persuade European laborers that they should value their whiteness and attach their primary identities with the white elite rather than build solidarity with laborers of other races. The dispossession of Native Americans from their land consolidated elite control over the territory's natural resources. Later, poor and working-class whites were enticed by the elites with promises of white privilege to view all newcomer groups (such as Jews, Catholics, Irish, and later immigrants) with suspicion as outsiders, ethnic "others," and "white trash," rather than as potential allies in the struggle for fair value, wages, and compensation for their work.

Buck writes about life in central Kentucky from a personal perspective. She and her husband bought land in the rolling farm country, choosing to not pursue careers but to buy land and try to live off of it. They grew food in their garden, raised goats and dairy calves, and took various jobs shoveling corn or stripping tobacco on a large farm to make ends meet. He eventually took a job with a plumbing and heating supply company, and later they started a small plumbing and heating business of their own. All told, they spent twelve years living under the poverty line and producing most of their own food.

> It was while fixing plumbing leaks, lying on my back under kitchen
> counters, soldering pipes while wedged between bottles of cleaning

Miners in Hazard, Kentucky, sit in a "break car" that will carry them down a coal mine shaft for their daily work shift. How does their sweat "trickle up"?

fluids, that I learned about the view from under the sink. I often found myself in fairly wealthy homes, looking up from under the sink at the lady of the house and thinking about her life. She had furniture I could not afford, dressed her children from stores I never entered, and complained about leaking plumbing at a time when what few pipes we had in our own house froze and burst with remarkable regularity. (Buck 2001, 2)

It is this view "from under the sink" that Buck brings to her analysis—the view of the farmhands, handymen, factory workers, and students struggling to make ends meet despite endless hours of back-breaking work. It is the view of people who see clearly how their sweat trickles up to enhance the lives and economic success of others who are already better off.

Buck places Kentucky's economic development within the context of national economic trends and the global economy. Whiteness has been a continuously evolving smokescreen, she claims, adjusted and readjusted to the changing needs of the elites as the drainage system has been reorganized:

We are presently in . . . a period of intense competition, this time between elites around the world struggling to control the global economy. The consequences of that struggle are now filtering into the middle class, although they have been affecting people lower in the drainage system since the late 1970s. Whiteness no longer provides protection from the consequences of policies that make larger and larger portions of the United States into a Third World labor force. Nor does middle-class status provide complete protection. (Buck 2001, 221–22)

Through her analysis, Buck draws connections between class and race in U.S. culture. The construction of class, as she chronicles in her reflections on her community in central Kentucky, has relied on a complex manufacturing of what it means to be white. But as the local economy of the rural United States becomes further integrated into the global economy, and as the sweat of local workers trickles further and further up, even the privileges of whiteness are not enough to protect those who live at or below the poverty line and whose fingers are already "worked to the bone."

Downward Mobility: The Middle Class and the Working Poor.

Wealth and poverty mark the extremes of a fluid class continuum, but the expected trajectory up the ladder—the core of the so-called American dream—often eludes U.S. families. Social mobility does not always involve movement up the class ladder. News stories, television shows, movies, newspapers, and magazines rarely publish articles about the downwardly mobile. Instead, our cultural narrative is a story of a meritocracy where "worthy individuals rise to the top and the undeserving fall by the way side" (Newman 1999, 243).

Katherine S. Newman has written extensively about the vulnerabilities of the U.S. middle class and the obstacles to success for the working poor. In *Falling from Grace: Downward Mobility in the Age of Affluence* ([1988] 1999), Newman explores the economic and psychological struggles of 150 families who strive to maintain their class position in U.S. culture. She interviewed managers, air traffic controllers, factory workers, and displaced homemakers (women and men who have worked primarily in the home but are no longer financially able to continue); she traced their vulnerability to moving down the economic ladder as a result of job losses, relocation of jobs overseas, and divorce (Kingfisher 2001).

What are the effects on the psyche when hard-working, moral individuals spiral downward—that is, when they "fall from grace"? Newman notes that many do not blame the failure of the economic system; instead, they blame their own failure, personal defects, and unworthiness.

In *No Shame in My Game* (1999), Newman asks why, in a nation of great prosperity and wealth, people who work full-time are still poor (Wacquant 2002; Durrenberger 2001). She examines obstacles facing the working poor—those who often work more than full-time to make ends meet and for whom minimum-wage jobs are not enough to pull themselves or their families out of poverty. Many people in the United States believe that urban poverty is a result of lack of motivation, welfare dependency, and a poor work ethic (see "The 'Culture of Poverty': Poverty as Pathology," p. 284); but Newman challenges this vision as a gap in our understanding of urban environments and inner-city economies. In these milieus she has found a broad array of hard-working citizens for whom hard work does not pay off, who struggle to provide for their families, who are one paycheck away from financial disaster. According to Newman, the main determinant of class position and social mobility is not one's work ethic, but structural barriers that have created an increasing gap between the life chances of the well educated and highly skilled and those of high school dropouts (see "Poverty as a Structural Economic Problem," p. 287).

Wealth, Inequality, and Wall Street. Although many anthropologists study the most marginalized members of a culture, a number of research projects have "studied up" (Nader 1972; Savage and Williams 2008): they have investigated power elites and cultural decision makers ranging from elite scientists (Gusterson 1996) and Wall Street executives (Tett 2010) to government officials (Brash 2011). In *Liquidated: An Ethnography of Wall Street* (2008), anthropologist Karen Ho relates how she went to work in a Wall Street investment bank to understand the inner workings of Wall Street in the 1990s during one of its biggest boom periods. Why, she asks, in a time of record corporate profits and soaring stock prices, do we see rapid downsizing, layoffs, and dismantling of the social safety net? She focuses on the surprising fact that when corporations lay off workers and downsize, not only do the companies' stock prices go up but the stock values of the investment banks go up as well.

Ho points to a transformation of the corporate culture of Wall Street: the desire for profits is not new; what is new, she finds, is a disconnect between what is considered best for the corporation and what is best for most of its employees. Today employees seldom benefit from corporate success. Instead the benefits go to stockholders—the top 10 percent of U.S. households own 81 percent of all stocks, while the bottom 90 percent own just 18 percent. Ho suggests that a "new cultural code for doing business" on Wall Street—characterized by a relentless search for unending profits and combined with government deregulation of the financial services industry—rewards efforts to make money, not to make goods and services. Witness in recent years the willingness of commercial banks and investment houses to bundle and resell so-called toxic assets, including the high-risk mortgages that played a key role in the 2008 market meltdown and Wall Street collapse. Ho claims that Wall Street participated in its own dismantling through mergers and liquidations within the financial community itself as large companies consumed smaller ones, downsized, and laid off employees to maximize their own stock values. Ho regards the collapse of Wall Street banks and investment houses in 2008 not so much as a surprise or anomaly, but as a predictable result of Wall Street culture, values, and workplace models.

What is the corporate culture of Wall Street investment banks? Did it contribute to the 2008 financial crash?

Despite the U.S. national myth of a classless society, quantitative and qualitative research studies expose the depth of inequality and stratification as well as the obstacles to social mobility. Although class stratification is not new, historical research suggests it is also not inevitable. Inequality has been shown to not be "essential" in human communities. By examining both statistical and ethnographic material, anthropologists seek to reopen a conversation about the roots of inequality—the obstacles to greater opportunity, social mobility, and improved life chances in a culture that is reluctant to discuss class.

What Are the Roots of Poverty in the United States?

Why do people live in poverty in the United States—one of the wealthiest countries in the world? Anthropologists have actively engaged academic and public policy debates surrounding this conundrum. Policy debates often place responsibility for poverty on the bad habits of the individual or the lack of fair opportunities created by the economic system. The actual roots of poverty must be clearly understood if the experience of poverty is to be eliminated or ameliorated.

The 2013 report of the U.S. Census Bureau found 45.3 million people—14.5 percent of the U.S. population—living in poverty (U.S. Census Bureau 2014). The 46.5 million people living in poverty in 2012 was the largest number in the fifty-three years that poverty statistics have been tracked. Twenty percent of U.S. children live in poverty. The 2013 U.S. government's poverty line for single adults stood at $11,888 in pretax income and $23,834 for a family of four. Many scholars consider the poverty line calculations, developed in 1964, to be unrealistic in today's economy; instead, they calculate a poverty line at 50 percent higher to be a more useful representation of people's standard of living.

Poverty rates vary by race (see Figure 10.1). Our discussions of the history and contemporary expressions of race and racism in the United States in Chapter 5 help shed light on these disparities. Despite prevalent media representations of inner-city poverty among communities of color, and despite the general breakdown by race shown in Figure 10.1, it is important to note that the largest group of the nation's poor are white and live in rural and suburban areas.

What are the root causes of poverty? Anthropologists and other social scientists have articulated numerous theories to explain poverty's origins and persistence. In the United States, two key theories have focused on poverty as pathology and poverty as a structural economic problem.

THE "CULTURE OF POVERTY": POVERTY AS PATHOLOGY

Theories of poverty as pathology trace ongoing poverty to the personal failings of the individual, family, or community. Such theories see these failings as stemming from a combination of dysfunctional behaviors, attitudes, and values that make and keep poor people poor. Anthropologist Oscar Lewis called this a "culture of poverty." His research in Mexico (1959) and the United States (1966) suggested that certain ways of thinking and feeling lead to the perpetuation of poverty among the poor. Lewis argued that children growing up poor in a highly class-stratified economic system were particularly vulnerable to developing feelings of marginality, helplessness, and dependency that would shape their value system, worldviews, aspirations, and character and make it difficult for them to escape poverty.

Lewis's research and theory of a culture of poverty became attractive to policy makers in the United States. Although many scholars, including anthropologists, discredited this theory on the grounds that it blamed the victims of poverty for structural problems beyond their control, the theory formed the basis of key social policies during the latter part of the twentieth century.

Beginning in the 1960s many social scientists, social workers, and government officials adopted the culture of poverty theory. Key among them was Daniel Patrick Moynihan, who in 1965 submitted a report to President Lyndon Johnson titled "The Negro Family: The Case for National Action," commonly

FIGURE 10.1

Percentage of People in Poverty by Race, 2013

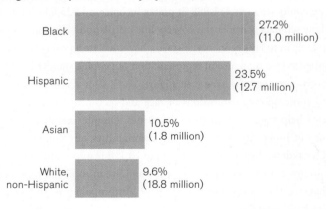

Source: U.S. Census Bureau. 2014. Current Population Survey, 2013 and 2014 Annual Social and Economic Supplements. www.census.gov/hhes/www/poverty/data/incpovhlth/2013/table3.pdf (accessed 6/8/15).

known as the Moynihan Report. Moynihan's report attempted to trace the root causes of poverty in African American communities to cultural patterns despite the evident structural causes of inequality and discrimination built into Jim Crow and segregation laws. By the 1980s and 1990s, debates around the "culture of poverty" transformed into discussions of an urban "underclass." It was suggested that the pathologies displayed by this underclass—including crime, welfare dependency, and female-headed households—continued the cycle of poverty for urban African American communities (Wilson 1987).

POVERTY AS A STRUCTURAL ECONOMIC PROBLEM

Theories of poverty as pathology have been strongly criticized within anthropology. As a distinct counterpoint, proponents of poverty as a structural problem trace its roots to dysfunctional aspects of the economic system. These theories place more responsibility on the failure of government to address fundamental economic patterns that have forced people into poverty and not provided a means out.

Many anthropologists have critiqued the "culture of poverty" theory, beginning with a series of essays edited by Eleanor Burke Leacock (1971). If there are no jobs, inadequate education and health care, and systematic failure to invest in the infrastructure of impoverished neighborhoods and communities, then poverty cannot be changed by changing attitudes and values. What are often considered to be characteristics of a culture of poverty are actually characteristics of poverty itself; they have nothing to do with the attitudes, values, and life choices of those forced to live in poverty. As discussed earlier, Leith Mullings (2005) and others have challenged the depiction of a complacent and ghettoized underclass by pointing to the resilient and determined efforts made by the poor to overcome the dire economic, social, and political conditions that they face.

Anthropologists Judith Goode and Jeff Maskovsky (2001) challenge the culture of poverty argument by questioning its focus on poor communities as isolated spheres. Instead they trace the roots of contemporary poverty in the United States to the impact of global economic processes on the nation's economy, particularly the effects of flexible accumulation and uneven development. The growth of globalization and the expansion of global capitalism, they argue, have launched an economic restructuring in which high-paying, blue-collar manufacturing jobs are shipped overseas as companies search for cheaper labor, lower taxes, and fewer environmental restrictions. The U.S. workforce has become more polarized between highly educated, well-paid professionals and managers and undereducated workers who struggle with low pay, no benefits, and little job security. U.S. government policies and programs designed to regulate the economy, protect the most vulnerable, and provide opportunities for social

mobility have been reduced, including public education, housing, and investment in infrastructure—roads, bridges, water systems, and power grids.

Goode and Maskovsky warn that as poverty and inequality grow, those most deeply affected—including the one in five U.S. children who live in poverty (U.S. Census Bureau 2014)—remain largely hidden and disappear from national awareness. In response, they encourage a new awareness of the many ways in which poor people engage in collective and individual strategies to survive. They call for anthropologists to engage in ethnographic research that contributes to the grassroots efforts of the poor (Dudley 2000; Anglin 2002). In addition, they call for adequate public investment in affordable housing, health care, education, and nutrition programs to create a framework whereby individual initiative can more readily succeed.

Discussions about the root causes of poverty continue today in both popular conversations and policy circles. Intense debate continues, for instance, on the appropriate role of government in addressing problems of persistent poverty. Arguments often draw on the distinction between seeing its roots in a culture of poverty or in a long-term structural problem of exclusion. Can poverty be addressed through improved housing, provision of health care, education, and the creation of living-wage jobs (the structural causes), or must perceived patterns of dependency on government programs and services be addressed to confront an underlying culture that holds people back? You will encounter these questions in conversations with classmates and coworkers, and you will influence these debates at different points in your life—perhaps as you undertake community service as a college student or later as you participate in the U.S. political process.

How is flexible accumulation shaping U.S. inequality? Laid-off factory workers of the closed Doosan Bobcat plant, Bismarck, North Dakota, symbolically leave behind steel-toed work boots in the parking lot as they exit the plant for the final time.

Why Are Class and Inequality Largely Invisible in U.S. Culture?

The review of economic data in this chapter has revealed the existence of class and inequality in U.S. society as well as the disturbing reality that inequality is increasing. Even with the statistical evidence of class in America, attention to this pattern of stratification is minimal and inequality remains largely invisible. Why?

THE ROLE OF THE MEDIA

Anthropologist Gregory Mantsios (2003) suggests that the media play a significant role in hiding class stratification in the United States by largely ignoring it. In an analysis of news articles, Mantsios found that only one in every five hundred *New York Times* stories addressed poverty. In a broader review, using the *Reader's Guide to Periodic Literature*, Mantsios found that only one article in every one thousand addressed poverty. Instead, the media focus on promoting a narrative of the United States as a meritocracy and an egalitarian society. And at the same time, poverty and class divisions are described as strange and abnormal— as aberrations of true American life, not as a reflection of the structure of the nation's economic system.

Class is particularly invisible in U.S. television programming. Programs rarely portray poverty. Poor people are absent or ignored. Instead the typical television series presents a homogenized version of the upper middle class designed to represent "everyone." Living in a generic upper-middle-class neighborhood, everyone is a cop, a doctor, a lawyer, or a business executive. Even those with blue-collar jobs are portrayed as middle class. Everyone is well off and, if not rich already, aspiring to be so. Among the cool young people who inhabit these communities, difference and stratification arise from beauty and sexuality, not from jobs, income, or wealth (McGrath 2005).

THE CONSUMER CULTURE

The consumer culture provides another explanation for the invisibility of class in the United States. Despite falling incomes over the past thirty years, many families have been able to maintain at least the experience of a middle-class lifestyle. They accomplish this by working more (especially women, who have entered the workforce in increasing numbers), borrowing money in mortgages against the value of their homes, running up credit card debt, and taking out more student loans to pay for their own or their children's college education.

Though income and wealth have not increased for the vast majority of the nation's population, people have been able to consume as if they were upwardly mobile—at least until the collapse of the housing bubble in 2007 and the meltdown of financial markets beginning in late 2008. At that point, banks began to foreclose on homes that were no longer worth as much as the owners had borrowed against them. Credit card interest rates skyrocketed, and credit lines were reduced. Still, total credit card debt in 2014 was $793 billion (Board of Governors of the Federal Reserve System 2015a), a sign of the extent to which the population continues to consume as if it were middle and upper class even when annual income does not support this lifestyle. Fully 56 percent of U.S. households carried a balance on their credit cards, with an average of nearly $16,000 per indebted household. Perhaps more surprising, in 2010 student loan debt surpassed total credit card debt for the first time, climbing to $1.2 trillion in 2015 and revealing the shifting burden of educational expenses into long-term debt (FinAid 2015). Total mortgage debt in 2014 stood at a staggering $13.4 trillion (Board of Governors of the Federal Reserve System 2015b). These sobering statistics reveal the ways consumer spending has been supported by mortgage, credit card, and education debt, thereby masking the growing inequalities of income and wealth in the United States (Williams 2004).

The role of class is rarely discussed but present everywhere in U.S. society, as is the attempt to "consume" class. In *Consuming the Romantic Utopia: Love and Cultural Contradictions of Capitalism* (1997), sociologist Eva Illouz suggests that even love and romance are shaped by class—both by financial capital and by cultural capital. As a college student, you experience this tension all the time. Dating is expensive. Romance takes time and money. How do you show you are in love? The rituals of love—the acts that are expected to show affection and cultivate romance—depend on the ability to shop and buy. You need the right clothes, haircut, makeup, perfume or cologne, shoes, birth control. You need a gym membership to stay fit or diet pills to stay skinny. The rituals of romance, including food, drinks, movies, gifts, and travel, all require money. A romantic dinner out is expensive. Even a romantic dinner at home may require extra expense for wine, candles, and special music to complete the ritual.

Class even shapes our choice of romantic partners. We often think of love as a spontaneous act of emotion, good chemistry—a matter of the heart. But why do we feel that connection? Research shows that people are likely to marry someone of their own race (see Chapter 2). Discounting Hollywood movies, how likely is it that you would marry someone outside your class? Finding someone of a similar background who has the same cultural capital and knows the same language and symbols of romance strongly influences our choices of romantic partners. What has your own experience been in this regard?

As you develop your skills as a budding anthropologist, clearly seeing the outlines of class and its effects on you and the people around you may require extra effort. Media—from movies to television to the press—largely ignore the existence of income inequality and the gaps between wealth and poverty. Consumption patterns, fueled by deep indebtedness through credit cards, home mortgages, and educational loans, mask class differences at least on the level of acquisition of consumer goods. Perhaps this cultural tendency to mask class and inequality—to make them invisible—is one reason the abrupt rise of the Occupy Wall Street movement in the fall of 2011, with its class-revealing slogan "We Are the 99%," surprised many people. But perhaps the same tendency to make class invisible explains why the movement fell so quickly from the media's public eye once protestors were removed from the spaces they physically occupied in parks and town squares. Nonetheless, a careful understanding and analysis of class will prove to be a crucial tool in your toolkit as you attempt to understand the complexities of the global world in which you live.

What Are the Effects of Global Inequality?

Globalization has produced unprecedented opportunities for the creation of wealth, but it has also produced widespread poverty. This uneven development is a central characteristic of the global capitalist system. Because it affects every corner of the world, it will be increasingly important for you as a global citizen to understand its impact.

Statistics reveal the extremes of uneven development. For example, in 2013 the world had 1,426 billionaires, up from 937 billionaires in 2010 (Geromel 2013); yet, with the exception of China, global poverty has increased over the past twenty years. Today 40 percent of the world's population lives in poverty, defined by the United Nations (UN) as income of less than $2 per day. One-sixth of the world's population—877 million people—lives in extreme poverty, surviving on less than $1 each day. The UN has calculated that if household wealth were divided equally on a global basis, using 2000 data each household would have roughly $20,000. Instead the report found that 2 percent of the world's population owns more than half of all wealth on the entire planet. The wealthiest 20 percent of the world's population receives 75 percent of the total global income (Davies et al. 2007).

The Gini index developed by the World Bank provides a global picture of inequality by comparing the per capita gross national income—total income produced by the economic activity of a state—of the world's economies. The World Bank classifies countries as high income ($12,746 or more per person), upper middle income ($4,126 to $12,745), lower middle income ($1,046 to $4,125), or low income ($1,045 or less). According to the Gini index, the gap between rich and poor countries has grown in recent years and continues to widen (Figure 10.2). Although the index provides a comparison of country averages, it does not take into account inequality within countries. Even the poorest countries have an elite organized around political, economic, or military power. The richest countries, as we have seen in the United States, have an increasing number of people living in poverty. What does this mean in concrete terms?

Growing global inequality affects the life chances of the world's population on many fronts, including hunger and malnutrition, health, education, vulnerability to climate change, and access to technology. Hunger is indeed a global problem. Although there is enough food in the world to feed everyone, it is unevenly distributed. Every day 870 million people go hungry—one out of every eight—according to the UN World Food Programme. Two hundred million children under age five are malnourished (World Food Programme 2013).

Health and mortality are also serious problem areas. Preventable infectious diseases such as malaria, measles, and HIV / AIDS kill millions each year in poor countries. People are more likely to die in infancy in low-income countries—and eleven times more likely to die at birth than in wealthy countries. Moreover, people live longer in high-income countries, averaging a seventy-eight-year life span compared to fifty-eight in low-income countries (World Food Programme 2013).

Access to education, a gateway to economic advancement, is also uneven. Basic literacy varies widely between high- and low-income countries. In addition, the digital divide prevents the majority of the world's inhabitants from participating in technological advances that are transforming the world's economy.

Climate change also affects the rich and poor unequally. Those with financial and political resources can buy safety, living outside areas that are vulnerable to natural disasters. A recent example from the United States underscores

FIGURE 10.2
The World by Income, 2014

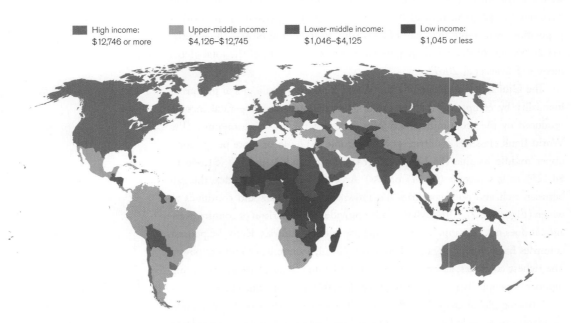

High income: Upper-middle income: Lower-middle income: Low income:
$12,746 or more $4,126–$12,745 $1,046–$4,125 $1,045 or less

Source: The World Bank. 2015. Country and Lending Groups. http://data.worldbank.org/about/country-and-lending-groups (accessed 6/8/15).

this point: anthropologist Neil Smith, when examining the effects of Hurricane Katrina on the people of New Orleans, called it an "unnatural disaster" because the storm's most severe effects were caused by the government's failure to adequately build and maintain the city's levee system, not by the storm itself. New Orleans residents experienced Katrina's effects unevenly along lines of class as well as race and gender (Smith 2006).

Throughout this chapter we have explored the complexity of class stratification and inequality both within the United States and globally. Despite the centrality of class-based stratification in the dynamics of globalization and its powerful effects on individuals' life chances and possibility for social mobility, class arguably remains the most overlooked of the systems of power we have considered in this textbook. Careful attention to the theoretical approaches to class adopted by anthropologists, including ethnographic research and data analysis, will position you to more fully engage issues of income and wealth inequality as you participate in a rapidly globalizing world.

Toolkit

Thinking Like an Anthropologist:
Observing the Dynamics of Class through Baseball and Beyond

In our chapter-opening story, we began to tease out the dynamics of class through the context of a baseball game. Baseball is perhaps the quintessential all-American sport. Millions of kids grow up playing Little League baseball, going to games with their parents, and watching games on television. Kids and adults join fantasy baseball leagues, and adults check the box scores online or talk about the latest games with colleagues at the office. High schools celebrate their teams' exploits. Cities promote the local baseball franchise as central to the community's identity. But what lies underneath the surface in the business of baseball?

Having read this chapter, you are now better prepared to analyze this iconic U.S. cultural activity through the lens of class. For underneath the bright lights, celebrity, and adoring fans of a Major League Baseball game lies a set of unequal relationships. And these differences—starkly revealed by comparing the lives of team owner Peter Angelos and the day laborers who clean the Baltimore Orioles stadium—translate into significantly different access to services, resources, and life chances. Our discussion in this chapter has expanded from the baseball context to explore the following questions:

- **Is inequality a natural part of human culture?**

- **How do anthropologists analyze class and inequality?**

- **How are class and inequality constructed in the United States?**

- **What are the roots of poverty in the United States?**

- **Why are class and inequality largely invisible in U.S. culture?**

- **What are the effects of global inequality?**

As systems of class stratification create widening inequality, your ability to perceive, analyze, and discuss class will become increasingly important. Class affects life chances in almost all realms of culture, including other sports, the restaurant industry, universities and other elements of the education system, health care, religious organizations, housing, government services, and many others that you can identify. How do these systems of class and inequality affect your own life chances and those of the people closest to you? As you consider these issues, you may be motivated to engage in efforts to reshape systems of inequality. Certainly, as you prepare for a career in the global economy and a life in this global age, being able to analyze the effects of class and inequality will be an essential tool in your anthropological toolkit.

Key Terms

class (p. 265)

egalitarian society (p. 266)

reciprocity (p. 266)

ranked society (p. 267)

redistribution (p. 268)

potlatch (p. 268)

bourgeoisie (p. 270)

means of production (p. 270)

proletariat (p. 270)

prestige (p. 271)

life chances (p. 272)

social mobility (p. 272)

social reproduction (p. 272)

habitus (p. 272)

cultural capital (p. 272)

intersectionality (p. 274)

income (p. 276)

wealth (p. 276)

Part 3

The world is changing rapidly in the twenty-first century. People are on the move, spurred by changes in the global economy, political systems, communication and transportation infrastructures, and more. At Tongi Station on the outskirts of Dhaka, Bangladesh, hundreds of people sit on the roof of an overcrowded train to travel homeward for Eid al-Fitr, a Muslim festival marking the end of the fasting month of Ramadan.

Change in the Modern World

বাংলাদে

Chapter 11
The Global Economy

Do you know where your last chocolate bar came from?

Today's global economy is a complex network of exchanges and connections that reach far beyond the candy machine outside your classroom or the store across the street. A piece of chocolate, a cup of coffee, or an iPod link the wealthiest resident of a world capital or a student at an elite college to a subsistence farmer in Africa or a factory worker in China. In today's world we are all deeply connected. Let's use the chocolate bar to illustrate this point.

Côte d'Ivoire, West Africa, exports 40 percent of the world's cocoa, which is used to make chocolate. Much of the country is covered in tropical forest, amid which are plantations carved out by farmers using hand tools. Seven million Côte d'Ivoirians make a living farming cocoa and coffee. Although the global price for cocoa—set on the commodities market in New York City—is relatively high,

Where does your chocolate come from? A young man on an eastern Côte d'Ivoire farm breaks cocoa pods to extract the beans used to make chocolate.

Côte d'Ivoire's farmers see little return for their work. The bulk of the profits go to transnational agricultural corporations, such as U.S.-based Cargill and Archer Daniels Midland (ADM) and the Swiss firm Barry Callebaut. These corporations buy cocoa beans and process them into chocolate products to be eaten worldwide. Few local farmers in Côte d'Ivoire have ever eaten a chocolate bar.

In recent years, Côte d'Ivoire has been riven by poverty, civil war, and conflict over cocoa and coffee revenues. In a fiercely contested election in 2010, Alassane Ouattara defeated incumbent Laurent Gbagbo for the presidency. Gbagbo's corrupt regime had relied on high taxes on cocoa and coffee farmers to subsidize its excesses and to fund Gbagbo's paramilitary hit squads. The election of Ouattara, a former deputy director of the International Monetary Fund (IMF), gave Côte d'Ivoirians hope of a more secure and prosperous future. But Gbagbo refused to acknowledge his loss in the election and remained ensconced in the presidential palace. By clinging to power and stirring ethnic violence, Gbagbo pushed the country toward civil war.

As fighting between Gbagbo's and Ouattara's supporters escalated in 2011, the French military, returning to its colonial role, stormed the airport outside Abidjan, the country's economic capital and primary port. The French had established a colony in Côte d'Ivoire in 1840 to enter the ivory trade and build coffee and cocoa plantations. Even after Côte d'Ivoire's independence in 1960, however, the French maintained a strong economic and military presence there. In the hopes of limiting violence in the civil war, France joined with the United Nations (UN) to create a demilitarized zone stretching across the country. French and UN soldiers then isolated the presidential palace, still occupied by the defeated Gbagbo, until forces loyal to new president Ouattara forced Gbagbo from the

MAP 11.1
Côte d'Ivoire

What role have chocolate revenues played in the recent conflict in Côte d'Ivoire? Here, soldiers loyal to newly installed president Alassane Ouattara patrol after the arrest of former president Gbagbo.

residence and arrested him. Despite continuing hostility between supporters of Gbagbo and Ouattara, in 2012 the country's economy began to recover. Cocoa production began to stabilize in response to the global demand for chocolate (North 2011; Monnier 2013).

The conflict in Côte d'Ivoire reveals many of the complex dynamics of today's global economy: (1) the interconnectedness of farmers in rural West Africa with chocolate eaters and coffee drinkers worldwide; (2) the tension-filled relationship between nation-states and transnational corporations; (3) the strategic military interventions, often by former colonial powers, that serve to police local political affairs and global economic flows; (4) the power of global financial markets to determine the price of coffee and cocoa, and thus the quality of life of small farmers; and (5) the link between consumers and producers through global commodity chains that have shattered notions of distinct national territories.

To fully understand the modern world economy, we must examine the concept of an economy as well as the historical developments that underlie today's global economy. In this chapter we will explore the following questions:

- **What is an economy, and what is its purpose?**
- **What are the roots of today's global economy?**
- **What are the dominant organizing principles of the modern world economic system?**
- **How does today's global economy link workers with consumers worldwide?**
- **How is today's global economy reshaping migration?**
- **Is today's global economic system sustainable?**

By the end of the chapter you should be able to analyze the major economic patterns of the contemporary global economy and assess its underlying principles. Armed with this information, you will be better prepared to make choices about your own lifestyle as a consumer and to engage in debates about how to create a sustainable economic system as the growing human population places increasing pressure on Earth's resources.

What Is an Economy, and What Is Its Purpose?

At the most basic level, an **economy** is a cultural adaptation to the environment— a set of ideas, activities, and technologies that enable a group of humans to use the available land, resources, and labor to satisfy their basic needs and, if organized

economy

A cultural adaptation to the environment that enables a group of humans to use the available resources to satisfy their needs and to thrive.

well, to thrive. Thus an economic system is a pattern of relations and institutions that humans construct to help collectively meet the needs of the community. Of course, today the concept of an economy seems much more complicated. But what is an economy at its core?

Anthropologist Yehudi Cohen (1974) refers to an economy as a set of adaptive strategies that humans have used to provide food, water, and shelter to a group of people through the production, distribution, and consumption of foodstuffs and other goods. In the following sections, we will explore the varied ways humans have produced, distributed, and consumed as part of their economic activity.

Cohen (1974) suggests five primary adaptive strategies that developed at different times and places: food foraging, pastoralism, horticulture, agriculture, and industrialism. By reviewing these strategies, we begin to understand that the current consumption-based global economy—with its emphasis on industrial production (even in agriculture), consumption, and technology—is only one of many possible variations.

FROM FORAGING TO INDUSTRIAL AGRICULTURE: A BRIEF SURVEY OF FOOD PRODUCTION

Food Foraging. Before the domestication of plants and animals around ten thousand years ago, all humans were **food foragers**. We made our living by hunting, fishing, and gathering nuts, fruit, and root crops; in fact, we evolved into our current physical form as food foragers. Mobility was key: small, egalitarian groups followed the movement of large animals and the seasonal growth of

food foragers

Humans who subsist by hunting, fishing, and gathering plants to eat.

!Kung san men forage for food in the Kalahari Desert of northeast Namibia. Stereotypical gender divisions of labor—which assume that men hunt and women both gather food and care for children—do not match the reality of food-foraging communities.

fruits, vegetables, and nuts to secure their survival. Throughout human history, food foragers have ranged over a remarkable variety of habitats, from the most hospitable to the most extreme.

Today fewer than 250,000 people make their primary living from food foraging. Most food foragers now incorporate farming and the domestication of animals. The remaining food foragers often live in the most marginal of Earth's environments—cold places, forests, islands—where other economic activity and other strategies for food production are not sustainable. Recent food foragers include the Inuit (Eskimos) of Canada and Alaska, Native Australian aborigines, and inhabitants of African and South American rainforests (e.g., Lee 1984; Turnbull [1961] 2010).

Pastoralism, Horticulture, and Agriculture.

Cohen identifies three adaptive strategies for food production in nonindustrial societies: pastoralism, horticulture, and agriculture. The earliest evidence of food production can be traced to approximately eleven thousand years ago in the region surrounding the Tigris and Euphrates Rivers (the Fertile Crescent) in what is modern-day Iraq. These strategies for food production led to more permanent human settlements that facilitated the development of tools and pottery and the specialization of human trades.

Pastoralism involves the domestication and herding of animals for food production. **Horticulture** is the cultivation of plants for subsistence through a nonintensive use of land and labor. Horticulturalists use simple tools such as sticks and hoes to cultivate small garden plots. Horticulturalists frequently employ slash and burn agriculture—also called "swidden farming"—to clear land for cultivation, kill insects that may inhibit crop growth, and produce nutrient-rich ash that serves as fertilizer.

In addition to the Fertile Crescent, early evidence of agricultural activity exists in Pakistan's Indus River Valley, China's Yellow River Valley, and the Nile Valley of Egypt, as well as in Mexico and the Andes region of South America. **Agriculture** requires an intensive investment in farming and well-orchestrated land-use strategies. Irrigation, fertilizer, draft animals, and machinery such as plows and tractors provide the technology and labor for successful agriculture. Through agriculture, humans produce enough food on permanently cultivated land to satisfy the immediate needs of the community and to create a surplus that can be sold or traded.

Whereas hunter-gatherer societies tended to be largely egalitarian, the rise of intensive agriculture in nonindustrial cultures led to social stratification. Social distinctions included large landholders, wealthy merchants, and owners of small businesses, as well as small-scale rural farmers and landless tenants working on large farms and estates as wage laborers.

pastoralism

A strategy for food production involving the domestication of animals.

horticulture

The cultivation of plants for subsistence through nonintensive use of land and labor.

agriculture

An intensive farming strategy for food production involving permanently cultivated land.

Industrial Agriculture. Recent years have seen the rise of industrial agriculture, which involves a massive mechanization of farming and the mass production of foodstuffs. In fact, in the twentieth century, agricultural production shifted from individual farms and farmers to large corporate-run farms, or agribusinesses, that rely on the intensive use of machinery (such as tractors and combines), irrigation systems, pesticides, and fertilizers.

Despite increased food production, industrial agriculture and agribusinesses have yielded complicated results. For example, chemical fertilizers and pesticides pose dangers to workers and to local water resources. Antibiotics that keep poultry and livestock healthy in industrial production facilities seep into the human food chain. Genetic engineering reduces crop diversity, making crops more susceptible to harsh weather and pests in the long term. Food irradiation poses potential safety and health hazards. Furthermore, as fewer people work in agriculture, displaced rural populations are moving to urban centers in search of wage labor. And the unequal distribution of global food supplies results in famines and food shortages in portions of the world.

All adaptive strategies are subject to the limitations of the natural environment. **Carrying capacity** is the number of people who can be supported by the resources of the surrounding region. The carrying capacity of land for food foragers, pastoralists, horticulturalists, or lower-intensity agriculturalists is more locally limited. But in most cases, farming generates a higher carrying capacity than food foraging because the labor-intensive activity of farming supports more extensive human settlements.

Given the expansion of industrialism, including industrial agriculture, the impact of economic activity has more global consequences today. What is Earth's carrying capacity? Can the planet support our projected population growth and consumption of natural resources? Can our contemporary economy meet current human needs, given the planet's carrying capacity? We will consider these questions as we explore the modern world economic system over the remainder of this chapter.

DISTRIBUTION AND EXCHANGE

All cultures have developed patterns for the distribution and exchange of goods and information produced by their members. In fact, the exchange of goods and ideas appears to be central to the workings of culture, establishing patterns of interaction and obligation among people. Anthropologists recognize three main patterns of exchange: reciprocity, redistribution, and market exchange. All are embedded in the everyday workings of almost every culture.

Reciprocity. **Reciprocity** involves an exchange of goods and services among people of relatively equal status. Such exchanges create and reinforce social ties between givers and receivers, fulfill social obligations, and often raise the prestige

carrying capacity
The number of people who can be supported by the resources of the surrounding region.

reciprocity
The exchange of resources, goods, and services among people of relatively equal status; meant to create and reinforce social ties.

of the gift giver. For example, the sharing of food resources, whether in earlier hunter-gatherer groups or among contemporary families, builds a sense of community, fulfills social obligations to the group, and raises the prestige of the provider. Anthropologists identify three types of reciprocity defined by the social distance between exchange partners: generalized reciprocity, balanced reciprocity, and negative reciprocity (Sahlins [1974] 2004; Service 1966).

Generalized reciprocity encompasses exchanges in which the value of what is exchanged is not carefully calculated and the timing or amount of repayment is not predetermined. Generalized reciprocity is common among close kin or close friends, serving as an expression of personal connection while reinforcing family and social networks. You may often experience generalized reciprocity without recognizing it: offering to take someone to the airport without expecting exact or timely reciprocity; borrowing a pen or sheets of paper; offering some of your food to a friend. Likewise, parents provide for their children—food, shelter, education, clothes, protection—without calculating the value or expecting repayment on predetermined terms.

Balanced reciprocity occurs between people who are more distantly related. This type of exchange includes norms about giving, accepting, and reciprocating. The giver expects the gift to be accepted and then to receive something in return. The recipient has an obligation to accept the gift (or is otherwise considered rude or ungrateful) and reciprocate promptly with a gift of equal value. The goal of exchanges based on balanced reciprocity is to build and maintain social relationships, often beyond the immediate kin group.

Negative reciprocity refers to a pattern of exchange in which the parties seek to receive more than they give, reaping a material advantage through the exchange. Whereas general and balanced reciprocity are based on relationships of trust and familiarity, negative reciprocity occurs among people who are strangers, antagonists, and enemies with opposing interests. Through hard bargaining, cleverness, deception, or cheating, the parties hope to minimize their cost and maximize their return.

Redistribution. **Redistribution** is a form of exchange in which goods are collected from the members of the group and reallocated in a different pattern. Redistribution requires the collected goods to flow through a central location—a chief, a storehouse, or a central government—where it can be sorted, counted, and redistributed. In small-scale societies, redistribution brings prestige to the community leader as food and goods collected from the leader's supporters are reallocated for supporting the general populace or establishing alliances with outside groups.

You have experienced redistribution directly if in your family those who work outside the home share their wages with those who do not in order to provide

redistribution

A form of exchange in which accumulated wealth is collected from the members of the group and reallocated in a different pattern.

all members with food and shelter. And if you receive a paycheck for a job, your taxes are part of the U.S. government's system of redistribution.

Redistribution may increase or decrease the inequality of wealth and resources within a group. In fact, many cultures have leveling mechanisms—practices and organizations that level out resources within the group. In the United States, for example, as in many other nation-states, redistribution is enacted through local, state, and federal tax codes. The government collects money (more from those with greater resources) and then reallocates and redistributes the nation's wealth to provide services (for example, the military) and infrastructure (for example, roads and bridges). Leveling mechanisms enact a cultural commitment to the collective good that seeks access to safety, health, education, food, and shelter for all group members irrespective of class.

Market Exchange. Finally, today's patterns of distribution and exchange are heavily influenced by economic markets that facilitate the buying and selling of land, natural resources, goods, services, labor, and ideas. Contemporary markets range in size and scope from village markets in India to the New York Stock Exchange on Wall Street. Though some people may barter—that is, exchange goods and services one for the other—most contemporary economic transactions are based on an exchange medium, or some form of money. In recent human history, the medium of exchange has varied. Items such as salt, precious stones, shells, livestock, precious metals such as gold or silver, coins, and most recently paper money and digital transfers of money have served to make payments for goods and services (Davies 2005; Wolf 1982).

What Are the Roots of Today's Global Economy?

Recent centuries have intensified the integration of all humanity into an interconnected global economy. Economic anthropology—the study of human economic activity and relations—views the world through the lens of movement rather than through the perspective of fixed and discrete groups. The key characteristics of today's global economy are mobility and connection. But not all of these connections have been smooth and easy. Many have been—and still are—contentious and unequal.

EARLY LONG-DISTANCE TRADE ROUTES

More than two thousand years ago, long-distance trade routes connected Asia, the Middle East, Africa, and Europe in a dynamic international network of

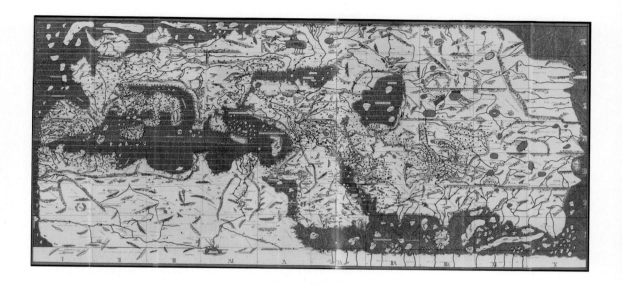

Long-distance trade routes have connected Asia, the Middle East, Europe, and Africa for over two thousand years. Here, the Tabula Rogeriana, a map of trade routes through northern Africa, Europe, the Indian Ocean, and much of Asia, written in Arabic and attributed to the Arab geographer Muhammad al-Idrisi, 1154.

economic exchange (Wolf 1982; Frank 1998; Braudel [1979] 1992; Abu-Lughod 1989; Schneider 1977). Movement was slow, but long-distance trade moved luxury items across vast territory. China led the world in the production and export of silk, porcelain ceramics (china), tea, fruit, drugs, cotton, tobacco, arms and powder, copper and iron products, zinc, and cupronickel (Frank 1998; Aub-Lughod 1989). Before long, Europe's elite were seeking greater access to China's desirable commodities.

By the time Columbus sailed in 1492, Europe's elite needed more than a shorter trade route to Asia to enter the world economy. They needed a way to buy themselves in. Although China wanted or needed very little from the West, Europeans increasingly sought its export commodities. As a result, European trade in Asia created surpluses for China, whose exports constantly surpassed its imports. China demanded payment of all deficits in silver and gold, setting off an intense global competition for these scarce resources.

As a result, acquisition of silver and gold was high on the Europeans' agenda in the Caribbean and the Americas. They systematically plundered the Mayan and Aztec kingdoms as well as the indigenous populations as they conquered the South American continent. Local populations were forced into slave labor to extract precious minerals, as at the lucrative silver mines in Peru (Robbins 2013). The gold and silver plundered from the Americas enabled Europeans to buy a seat on the economic train based in Asia (Frank 1998; Spence 2013).

COLONIALISM

Europe's global economic engagements between 1500 and 1800 relied primarily on extensive maritime trade within the existing global economic system. The drain, for many of the most highly skilled professionals trained in developing (periphery) countries are enticed by wages and other opportunities to relocate to developed (core) countries.

Entrepreneurial immigrants move to new locations to conduct trade and establish businesses as merchants, restaurateurs, and small shopkeepers in countries worldwide. In fact, entrepreneurial migrants have been on the move for thousands of years along local, regional, and long-distance trade routes. Contemporary globalization has only increased the volume of entrepreneurial activity and enhanced entrepreneurs' ability to engage in their trade in places farther from home.

Refugees constitute a fourth type of immigrant. These are people who have been forced to migrate beyond their national borders because of political or religious persecution, armed conflict or other forms of violence, or natural or human-made disasters. The UN estimated a total of 16.7 million refugees worldwide in 2013 (UN High Commissioner for Refugees 2014).

Although refugee status technically applies to those who seek asylum in another nation, the experiences of internally displaced persons can be just as devastating. These migrants' experiences mirror those of international refugees, except they take place in the migrants' own countries (Internal Displacement Monitoring Center 2012).

In another phenomenon of globalization, time-space compression—notably, advances in communication and transportation—has transformed the migration experience by tying migrants more closely to their families and communities back home. Today, many migrants travel back and forth, send money home, talk regularly with family and friends by telephone, and share videos and movies. These *transnational immigrants* actively participate in social, economic, religious, and political spheres across national borders.

Malian Migrants: Reshaping Globalization from the Ground Up.

Though international movements of people between continents and across oceans often capture public and scholarly attention, today significant movement occurs between neighboring countries. In *Migrants and Strangers in an African City* (2012), anthropologist Bruce Whitehouse examines the large-scale migrations happening within Africa as people move in response to poverty and uncertainty. Whitehouse focuses on migrants from Mali, a large West African nation of 16 million people. Though landlocked, Mali's position at the center of regional trade networks crisscrossing West and North Africa has a long history. Today Malians, along with hundreds of thousands of other West Africans, increasingly have been on the move. Some have settled in developed Western countries

---

entrepreneurial immigrant
A person who moves to a new location to conduct trade and establish a business.

refugee
A person who has been forced to move beyond his or her national borders because of persecution, armed conflict, or natural disasters.

American colonies were an important exception. They served as a harbinger of colonial expansion in the rest of the world in the nineteenth and early twentieth centuries. In fact, the European conquest of the New World—the Caribbean and the Americas—launched an era of colonialism that eventually touched every corner of the globe.

Under **colonialism**, colonial powers redrew the map of the world and fundamentally reorganized the political and economic balance of power on a global scale. Europeans' advanced military weaponry and strategies, developed through years of continental warfare and naval battles, gave them an advantage that enabled them to dominate others in the colonial era.

Beginning in the 1500s, European colonialism played a pivotal role in establishing the framework for today's global economic system. Patterns of trade in slaves, sugar, furs, and cotton, enforced through military interventions, drew together the people, politics, economics, and even diseases of Europe, Africa, and the Americas in a triangle of previously unimaginable, highly unequal, and long-lasting relationships of exchange. Even today, we can find traces of many of these connections in the global economy—for example, the French military operating in Côte d'Ivoire in the story that opened this chapter.

colonialism

The practice by which a nation-state extends political, economic, and military power beyond its own borders over an extended period of time to secure access to raw materials, cheap labor, and markets in other countries or regions.

The Triangle Trade. The triangle trade that emerged in the 1500s among Europe, Africa, and the Americas involved an extensive exchange of goods, people, wealth, food, diseases, and ideas that transformed economic, political, and social life on both sides of the Atlantic (Figure 11.1). It also brought western Europeans the resources they needed to grow their national economies and expand their role in international trade.

Europeans established a plantation economy in the Caribbean and South America to produce sugar for export to Europe. Columbus had carried sugar to the Caribbean, which, along with Brazil, offered an ideal climate for sugarcane cultivation. But now, plantation production transformed sugar from a luxury item to a key component of the European diet. Sugar also sweetened three other key commodities in the triangle trade—all stimulants (drugs)—coffee, tea, and cocoa (Mintz 1985).

The expansion of sugarcane plantations by the Spanish and Portuguese could not be sustained by the local populations in the Caribbean and South America because they were decimated by European diseases and the grueling conditions of forced labor. So plantation owners turned to the African slave trade to supply their labor needs. Between the sixteenth and eighteenth centuries, millions of Africans were sold into slavery and transported across the Atlantic to work on sugarcane plantations in the Caribbean and South America. Later, rising demand for cotton for England's textile industry required more laborers for cotton plantations in the southern region of what is now the United States. This pressure further stimulated demand for African slaves. Many Africans—perhaps

FIGURE 11.1
The Triangle Trade

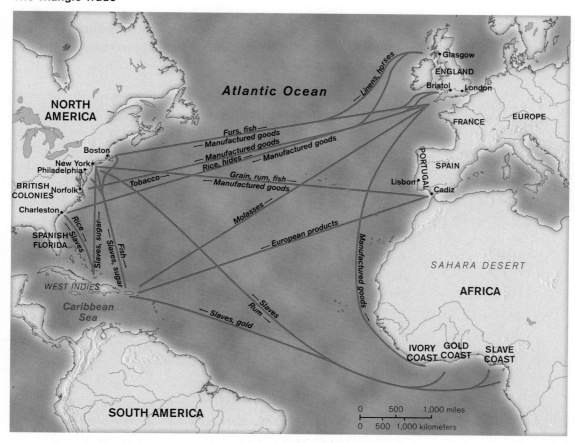

millions—died in the traumatic passage across the Atlantic, and millions more died in inhuman conditions of incarceration and slavery after arriving in the Americas. The uncompensated labor of African slaves, extracted under brutal conditions, subsidized the economic growth and development of Europe and the American colonies for more than 350 years.

In North America, the fur trade, particularly in beaver pelts, pulled the continent into the global economy. The European demand for fur drove the European expansion deeper into the North American continent. Native American settlement patterns were severely disrupted, as were local agricultural practices and economic activities. Conflicts between the British and French drew indigenous populations into colonial wars. European germs devastated a population that had no immunity to European diseases (Wolf 1982).

The decimation of the indigenous populations in North and South America and the Caribbean (estimated by some scholars to be as many as fifteen million people), combined with the relocation of millions of Africans and the arrival of millions of European immigrants, transformed the human population of the New World over a period of a few centuries. Furthermore, the large-scale migration of Europeans and the forced migration of Africans had lasting repercussions on their home communities as well (Wolf 1982; Robbins 2013).

The Industrial Revolution. The Industrial Revolution in the eighteenth and nineteenth centuries drove the next phase of European colonial activities. As European economies, led by Great Britain, shifted toward machine-based manufacturing, the new industries relied heavily on the raw materials, cheap labor, and open markets of the colonies. At the same time, Europe's expanding cities, combined with growing colonies, provided markets for goods produced in Europe's factories. The huge profits from the transatlantic triangle trade provided the capital infusion necessary to fund Europe's industrial transformation.

Industrial expansion of the capitalist economy created intense competition among European countries for raw materials, cheap labor, and markets. Throughout the nineteenth and early twentieth centuries Great Britain, France, the Netherlands, Belgium, Russia, and Japan all raced to divide nonindustrial regions of the world into colonies that would secure their economic growth. In the process, European countries redrew the political map of the world—especially in Asia, Africa, and the Middle East—and restructured the global economy to serve their expanding industrial activities.

ANTICOLONIAL STRUGGLES

Local populations resisted colonialism with mixed success. Independence movements used strategies of rebellion, resistance, and negotiation to achieve their goals. These included nonviolent actions such as those led by Mohandas Ghandi in the Indian struggle against British colonialism, as well as violent uprisings such as those in Algeria. Frequently, external factors such as wars, economic crises, and international pressures aided independence movements by creating conditions for their success.

In the Americas, independence movements on both continents brought changes. The United States declared independence from Great Britain in 1776, eventually winning independence through the Revolutionary War. The people of Haiti, a highly profitable Caribbean French colony known for its sugarcane, coffee, cocoa, indigo, and cotton plantations, declared independence in 1804 and became the first independent former colony to be ruled by people of African descent. In Latin America, Brazil declared independence from Portugal in 1822. By 1825, most of Spain's colonies in South America had achieved independence.

Ultimately, World War II created conditions for the success of national independence movements and the collapse of the colonial system. For example,

Japanese occupation destroyed much of the European colonial infrastructure in Asia and inspired organized national resistance movements. These forces led efforts toward national independence when the war ended. On a global scale, the war-ravaged economies and political institutions of the European colonial powers could no longer sustain their colonial enterprises, especially in the face of organized resistance movements. Between 1945 and 1990, more than one hundred former colonies gained their independence. But as we have seen in the opening story about Côte d'Ivoire, and as we will see throughout the remainder of this chapter, despite the formal end of the colonial era, patterns of relationship established under colonialism—from migration and economics to military involvement—continue to influence both former colonies and colonizers.

THE MODERN WORLD ECONOMIC SYSTEM

With the end of the colonial era, many people believed that the former colonies—wealthy in natural resources and freed from colonial control—would see rapid economic growth. But such growth, as well as diminished poverty and the possibility for income equality, has proved to be elusive. Why have patterns of inequality established under colonialism persisted into the current era?

Conflicting Theories. **Modernization theories,** which became popular following World War II, predicted that with the end of colonialism the less-developed countries would follow the same trajectory as the industrialized countries and achieve improved standards of living. Certainly, the rise of industrial capitalism in Europe beginning in the late eighteenth century had spurred

modernization theories
Post–World War II economic theories that predicted that with the end of colonialism less-developed countries would follow the same trajectory toward modernization as the industrialized countries.

development

Post–World War II strategy of wealthy nations to spur global economic growth, alleviate poverty, and raise living standards through strategic investment in national economies of former colonies.

spectacular advances in production and a sense of optimism in the possibilities for dramatic material progress—in other words, **development** (Larrain 1989). As decolonization approached, politicians and economists in industrialized nations began to strategize about how to develop the economies of the colonies of Britain, France, Portugal, and other European powers (Leys 1996). The modernization model was assumed to be the key. Progress, modernization, and industrialization would be the natural path of economic development throughout the global capitalist economy, though this process would need nurturing through foreign aid and international investment.

After World War II, through an array of new international aid agencies and financial institutions, such as the World Bank, the IMF, and the UN, wealthy nations worked with emerging national governments in former colonies to develop programs they hoped would stimulate growth, alleviate poverty, and raise living standards. Development projects often emphasized state investment in infrastructure as an engine of economic growth, focusing on the construction of ports, roads, dams, and irrigation systems (Cowen and Shenton 1996; Edelman and Haugerud 2005).

But by the 1960s, scholars began to question the Western development model. Despite the end of colonialism, less-developed countries, even those with rich natural resources, did not experience modernization and economic growth. Many local and national economies remained stagnant or lost ground in the international economy. Many countries took on increasing international debt to keep their economies stable in the postcolonial era.

dependency theory

A critique of modernization theory that argued that despite the end of colonialism the underlying economic relations of the modern world economic system had not changed.

underdevelopment

The term used to suggest that poor countries are poor as a result of their relationship to an unbalanced global economic system.

At this time, **dependency theory** emerged as a critique of modernization theory. Scholars from Latin America, in particular, argued that a new kind of colonialism—neocolonialism—had emerged (Cardoso and Faletto 1969; Frank 1969). Dependency theorists argued that despite the end of colonialism, the underlying economic relations of the modern world system had not changed. These scholars introduced the term **underdevelopment** to suggest that poor countries were not poor because of some fundamental structural flaw (such as inadequate natural resources), but because participation in the global economy left them underdeveloped. It was still structured to extract resources from less developed countries and transfer them to developed, industrialized countries. Thus, dependency theorists argued, underdeveloped countries should break their dependency on the global economic system and build up and protect their own self-sufficient national economic activities.

core countries

Industrialized former colonial states that dominate the world economic system.

Core and Periphery. Immanuel Wallerstein (1974) introduced to these debates a *modern world systems* analysis. Wallerstein characterized the nations within the world economic system as occupying core, semiperiphery, and periphery positions (Figure 11.2). The **core countries**—primarily industrialized

FIGURE 11.2
The Core/Periphery Division of the World

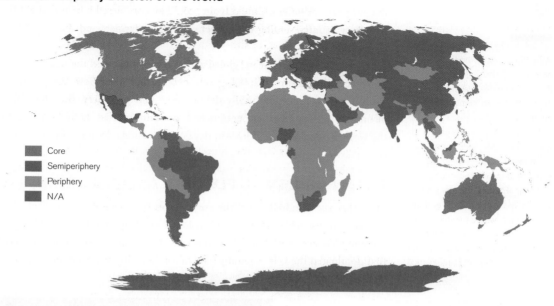

former colonial states—dominate the world system, extracting cheap labor and raw materials from periphery countries and sending them to the industrialized core. Finished products, with value added in the manufacturing process, are then returned to markets in the periphery. Core countries control the most lucrative economic processes, including the financial services sectors.

Periphery countries—among the least developed and least powerful nations—serve primarily as sources of raw materials, agricultural products, cheap labor, and markets for the economic activities of the core. Established patterns of economic, political, and military relationship ensure the steady transfer of wealth, natural resources, and human resources from the periphery to core, contributing to underdevelopment. Semiperiphery countries occupy a middle position. They may have developed some industry, draw resources from the periphery, and export manufactured products to the core and periphery, but they lack the economic and political power of the core.

Core and periphery are not necessarily geographically isolated from one another. Wallerstein suggests that peripheral areas often exist within core countries as pockets of poverty amid generally high standards of living. In the United States, the Appalachian mountain region might be considered a periphery within a core country: it has abundant natural resources of coal, timber, and water but intense poverty, poor education and health care, and limited infrastructure. Core areas also exist within periphery countries. These include urban centers (ports and capital cities), dominated by the economic, military, and political elite, that

periphery countries
The least developed and least powerful nations; often exploited by the core countries as sources of raw materials, cheap labor, and markets.

provide linkages between core countries and the often more rural people in the periphery. Abidjan, Côte d'Ivoire, could be considered a core area within a periphery country, serving to connect rural cocoa farmers and the global chocolate trade.

Over the past forty years, globalization has complicated the neat categories of Wallerstein's theory. Capital, goods, people, and ideas flow less predictably today between a geographically defined core and periphery. But the realities of uneven development and entrenched inequality persist. Fully 80 percent of the world's population still lives in developing nations decades after the end of colonialism.

FROM FORDISM TO FLEXIBLE ACCUMULATION

Over the past hundred years, the corporation has increasingly challenged the nation-state (which dominated the colonial era) for supremacy in the global economy. We can trace this change through the history of two economic models that dominated the U.S. economy (and beyond) during the twentieth century.

Where does your iPhone come from? The journey of an iPhone illustrates Wallerstein's concepts of core, semiperiphery, and periphery. *Clockwise from right:* A worker at a rare earth mine in Inner Mongolia; rare earth elements are vital to the manufacturing of electronics, including iPhones. Factory workers at the Foxconn plant in Shenzhen, south China, where most iPhones, iPads, and other Apple products are made. A woman takes a photo of the Eiffel Tower in Paris, France.

In 1914 Henry Ford, the founder of Ford Motor Company, a U.S. automobile manufacturer, experimented with a new strategy for profit making within the industrializing economy of the United States. Ford is famous for refining the factory assembly line and the division of labor that facilitated efficiency in industrial mass production. Perhaps equally significant, at a time when many U.S. manufacturers were exploiting immigrant workers with low wages and long work hours to maximize profits, Ford introduced a $5, eight-hour workday—a living wage that he hoped would create a worker who was loyal, dependable, and cooperative. Ford also believed that higher wages and shorter hours would turn his workers into a new pool of consumers with the income and leisure to purchase and enjoy a Ford car. Ford sought to form a new social compact between labor and capital that would benefit his corporation. These were the central aspects of **Fordism**.

Fordism took hold firmly after World War II with growing cooperation among corporations, labor, and government. The latter stepped in to regulate corporate responsibility for worker health and safety and, eventually, environmental impact. Wages and benefits, along with corporate profits, rose steadily through a long postwar boom that drove a rapid expansion of the middle class through the early 1970s.

However, industrial economic activity in the late 1960s and 1970s began to shift away from the Fordist model toward what geographer David Harvey (1990) has called "strategies of flexible accumulation" to address shrinking corporate profits brought about by increased global competition and a global recession.

Flexible accumulation refers to the increasingly flexible strategies that corporations use to accumulate profits in an era of globalization. In particular, these strategies include *offshoring* (relocating factories anywhere in the world

Fordism
The dominant model of industrial production for much of the twentieth century, based on a social compact among labor, corporations, and government.

flexible accumulation
The increasingly flexible strategies that corporations use to accumulate profits in an era of globalization, enabled by innovative communication and transportation technologies.

Who answered your last call for tech support? Here, a call center agent in the Philippines talks to a client in the United States, an example of how jobs are being outsourced from core countries to low-wage destinations under flexible accumulation.

that provides optimal production, infrastructure, labor, marketing, and political conditions) and *outsourcing* (hiring low-wage laborers in periphery countries to perform jobs previously done in core countries, such as software design, airplane reservations, data processing, radiology readings, and data analysis). By so doing, corporations could bypass high production costs, organized labor, and environmental laws in the core industrial cities and core countries.

Under flexible accumulation, corporations—even highly profitable ones—began to eliminate jobs in old core industrial centers. Instead they opened factories "offshore" in places such as Mexico, the Caribbean, South Korea, and Taiwan. In the 1980s they began to relocate factories to China to take advantage of even lower wages, lower taxes, and weaker environmental restrictions. Recent strikes by Chinese workers demanding higher wages and better working conditions have led some corporations to relocate again, opening new factories in Thailand, Cambodia, Vietnam, and Bangladesh. Over the past forty years, strategies of flexible accumulation have transformed the local factory assembly line into a global assembly line.

What Are the Dominant Organizing Principles of the Modern World Economic System?

Flows of capital, goods, and services associated with flexible accumulation have built on old colonial patterns and have made use of advances in transportation and communication technologies (time-space compression). But other forces also help integrate all people and nations into one free market with minimal barriers. These forces include powerful international financial institutions such as the World Bank, the IMF, and the World Trade Organization (WTO); international trade agreements such as the former Global Agreement on Trade and Tariffs (GATT); and regional agreements such as the North American Free Trade Agreement (NAFTA) or the Asia-Pacific Trade Agreement (APTA). Drawing on an economic philosophy called "neoliberalism," these institutions and agreements have created a strong international financial and policy framework, one that promotes an even deeper integration of nations and local communities into a modern world economic system.

CAPITALISM, ECONOMIC LIBERALISM, AND THE FREE MARKET

The work of the Scottish economist and philosopher Adam Smith (1723–1790) and the British economist John Maynard Keynes (1883–1946) provided key intellectual counterpoints that have shaped economic debates about the functioning of capitalism in the twentieth century. In *The Wealth of Nations* (1776), Adam Smith promoted economic liberalism through his ideas of laissez-faire ("leave it alone") capitalism. In Smith's view, free markets and free trade, being liberated from government intervention, would provide the best conditions for economic growth: they would unleash competition to maximize profits. In contrast, Keynes later argued that capitalism would work best when the government had a role in moderating the excesses of capitalism and ensuring the basic welfare of all citizens (Keynes [1936] 2007).

After World War II, leading Western governments applied Keynesian economic philosophy in rebuilding their war-torn economies and establishing development projects to stimulate growth in former colonies. Keynesian economics began to lose popularity in the 1970s in the wake of a global recession. But today it maintains a role in certain government policies—those that (1) stimulate economic activity through public investment in infrastructure projects and the employment of civil servants while also (2) seeking to regulate the excesses of corporate and financial activities and moderate the most extreme effects of capitalism on the population through the provision of a social safety net and investment in health, education, and housing.

NEOLIBERALISM

Economic liberalism, building on Smith's philosophy, has reemerged since the 1970s as a guiding philosophy for the global economy. This **neoliberalism**, associated with conservative fiscal and political policies in the United States, views the free market—not the state—as the main mechanism for ensuring economic growth. Neoliberal policies focus on promoting free trade on a global scale, eliminating trade barriers, and reducing taxes, tariffs, and all government intervention in the economy. Neoliberalism promotes the privatization of public assets (such as publicly owned utilities and transportation systems) and an overall reduction, if not privatization, of government spending on health, education, and welfare. Since the 1980s, powerful international financial institutions, such as the IMF, the World Bank, and the WTO, have promoted neoliberal policies, frequently using structural adjustment loans as a key, though controversial, mechanism to address poverty and development in poorer nations. Structural adjustment loans seek to stabilize a country's long-term economic development. They require fiscal austerity measures, a reduced role for the state in the economy, and a restructuring of national trade and tariff policies so as to create freer access to local markets.

neoliberalism
An economic and political worldview that sees the free market as the main mechanism for ensuring economic growth, with a severely restricted role for government.

Pros and Cons of Neoliberal Policies.
Debates continue over the effectiveness of neoliberal policies. In particular, there is skepticism in many countries over the notion that facilitating competition and profit making through free trade, free markets, and privatization promotes improved economic

opportunities for most of the world's people. Much of Latin America has repaid debts to the IMF and has rejected neoliberal economic strategies. The World Social Forum, an annual international meeting of social movements and NGOs, explores alternatives to neoliberal economic policies and the negative aspects of globalization.

But in Europe, several nations (Greece, Spain, Portugal, and Ireland) struggled to adapt to mandates for austerity imposed by the IMF and the European Central Bank in return for loans made to stabilize their national economies. Widespread protests by affected workers, especially in Greece, have threatened the stability of national governing coalitions that agreed to the externally imposed restrictions. Leaders of underdeveloped countries, scholars, and activists have argued that these policies are the centerpiece of an ever-evolving global economic system that promotes uneven development and ensures that wealthy countries remain wealthy and poor countries remain poor (Sachs 2005; Krugman 2009; Stiglitz 2010).

The debate over neoliberal and Keynesian economic strategies continues to rage in the United States after the financial collapse of 2008 led to the so-called Great Recession. Followers of Keynesian economics—often associated with political liberals and moderates—argue for greater regulation of financial markets, increased consumer protections, an expanded health care safety net, and heavy investment in infrastructure projects to put people back to work. Followers of neoliberalism—primarily associated with conservatives—seek lower taxes, smaller government, faster debt repayment, and reduced regulation to stimulate economic activity by businesses. Crucial debates continue over efforts to privatize Social Security, Medicare, and Medicaid and to reduce government support for education.

How Does Today's Global Economy Link Workers with Consumers Worldwide?

Through much of recent human history, markets have been places where farmers and craftsmen, traders and consumers exchange products, ideas, information, and news, linking local communities to one another and to communities at greater distances, enabling all to benefit (Polanyi [1944] 2001). Today local markets are more deeply integrated as social and material commodities often flow across national borders (Hannerz 1996). Although **commodity chains**—the hands an item (commodity) passes through between producer and consumer—used to be primarily local, globalization has extended their span across territories and

commodity chain
The hands an item passes through between producer and consumer.

cultures, intensifying the connection between the local and global in ways previously unimaginable (Haugerud, Stone, and Little 2000). Tsukiji Fish Market, the largest fish market in the world today, is a prime example.

TSUKIJI: FISH MARKET AT THE CENTER OF THE WORLD

Standing in the heart of downtown Tokyo, Japan, Tsukiji Fish Market is the center of a massive global trade in seafood and a cultural icon of Japanese cuisine. Each day sixty thousand traders gather to auction bluefin tuna from Maine, eel from southern China, octopus from West Africa, salmon from Canada, and shellfish from California; these then make their way into the restaurants, supermarkets, and homes of Japanese people across the country. Tsukiji Fish Market feeds the city's 22 million people and many more throughout Japan. But Tokyo and the Tsukiji Market are also command central for an intricate global trade in seafood.

The Japanese people's desire for sushi and sashimi has established Japan as the world's main market for fresh tuna. And Japanese cultural influence has spurred the consumption of sushi in other countries. At the same time, rising demand in Japan has led to overfishing and the decimation of the local tuna fishery. Forty years of time-space compression have facilitated an extension of the tuna commodity chain to previously unconnected places and people. Advances in transportation and communication—refrigerated trucks and cargo jets traveling

MAP 11.2
Tokyo

Where does your fish come from? Here, a tuna fish auction at Tsukiji Fish Market, Tokyo, Japan, 2007.

international routes, along with cell phones, faxes, and the Internet—have promoted an integrated network of fishermen, buyers, and shippers. The search for the perfect tuna has now expanded to the North Atlantic, the Mediterranean, and Australia.

Anthropologist Theodore Bestor's study (2004) of the transnational tuna trade, particularly in Atlantic bluefin tuna, takes him to coastal Maine and the Mediterranean coast of Spain to reveal a complex view of global markets. The stories of these global commodity chains—what Appadurai (1986) calls tracing the "social life of things"—illustrate how the modern world economic system works. Tsukiji Market and the movement of tuna to it enhance our understandings of Wallerstein's ideas of an integrated, but increasingly complicated, world system. Goods, money, ideas, and even people (or, in this case, tuna) flow from periphery to core. But assumptions of a fixed core and periphery, as well as expectations of a predictable flow of raw materials, are called into question. In the story of tuna and sushi, natural resources flow to consumers at the center of the global market and at the end of the global commodity chain. But in this story Japan is the core. The Atlantic seaboards of North America and Europe are the periphery (Bestor 2001, 2004; Stevens 2005; Jacobs 2005).

How Is Today's Global Economy Reshaping Migration?

Just as globalization has expanded the span of commodity chains, the past thirty years have also seen one of the highest rates of global migration in modern history, not only between countries but within them as well. The powerful effects of globalization have stimulated migration from rural areas to urban areas and from less developed countries to more developed countries. At the same time, time-space compression (see Chapter 1) has transformed the migration experience: rapid transportation and instantaneous communication enable some migrants to travel more cheaply and quickly, and to still stay connected with folks back home, in ways that were impossible for earlier migrant generations. Flexible accumulation also stimulates migration by disrupting local economic, political, and social relationships while linking local communities to global economic processes. In 2013 the United Nations (UN) estimated that there were 232 million international migrants, plus hundreds of millions more internal migrants moving within their own national borders (UN Department of Economic and Social Affairs, Population Division 2013). The Chinese government estimates that more than 230 million people migrate internally in that one country alone (Liang 2012). But why do people migrate?

PUSHES AND PULLS

The decision to migrate and the chosen destination are often shaped by **pushes and pulls**. People are *pushed* to migrate from their home community by poverty, famine, natural disasters, war, ethnic conflict, genocide, disease, or political or religious oppression. Those who are forced to migrate are often termed "refugees." The uneven development in the global economy stimulates much of today's global migration. Frustrated by their inability to achieve life aspirations and meet the needs of their families at home, many people seek opportunities elsewhere (Portes and Rumbaut 2006).

Destinations are not chosen randomly, nor are all destinations equal. When considering migration, people are *pulled* to certain places by job opportunities, higher wages, educational opportunities for themselves and their children, access to health care, or investment opportunities. Family and friends who have already migrated provide encouragement and connections. At the same time, media such as television, music, and film, along with powerful advertising, promote the desire to live a Western middle-class, consumer-oriented lifestyle.

BRIDGES AND BARRIERS

Immigrants also encounter bridges and barriers that influence who moves and where they go. Bridges may include family networks, transportation links, government immigration policies, recruitment agencies, and even human smugglers. Barriers range from language difference and geographical distance to tightly regulated borders and expenditures for passports, visas, and transportation.

My own research, published in *God in Chinatown: Religion and Survival in New York's Evolving Immigrant Community* (2003), focuses on migrants from towns and villages near Fuzhou in southeastern China. In recent years, these

Global migration today takes many forms. *Left:* Women line up outside an employment agency in Manila, Philippines, seeking jobs as domestic workers in Middle Eastern countries. *Right:* Croatian Serb refugees flee Bosnia and Herzegovina in 1995.

pushes and pulls

The forces that spur migration from the country of origin and draw immigrants to a particular new destination country.

MAP 11.3
Fuzhou City

individuals have come in large numbers: first to New York to work in Chinese restaurants, garment shops, and construction trades; and now spreading across the United States as they open take-out restaurants and all-you-can-eat buffets. As much as 50 to 70 percent of the population in many towns and villages has migrated out, and hundreds of thousands of them have come to and through New York City.

Of the 1.3 billion people in China, why have people from the Fuzhou City area decided to migrate out of China? And why do so many go to New York City? The pushes are the same for Fuzhounese as they are for many rural people in China—small incomes, difficult farm labor, limited opportunities for upward mobility or education. And the pulls of New York City—in this case, the tremendous need for low-wage workers—exist in many big cities, not only in the United States but also in countries much closer to China.

In the back of a Chinese restaurant in New York City, I interviewed Chen Dawei, age nineteen, who had come from Fuzhou one year earlier and whose story sheds light on the Fuzhounese immigrant experience:

> I didn't really want to go to America. But everyone else my age had already gone. I didn't want to seem stupid. My parents really wanted to send me. They have a little shop on the main street. We aren't poor. But we don't make much money either. Making $1,500 a month as a delivery man for a Chinese restaurant in the United States sounds really good when your family is lucky to make that much in a whole year back home. I really didn't want to go. But people kept calling to say how well they were doing. Both of my uncles were already in

the U.S. Lots of people were sending money back home. And people who got green cards would come back and build a nice home for their family.

So my dad arranged with a snakehead (smuggler) to send me to New York. It cost $65,000. We borrowed some from my uncles. And some from friends who had already gone to New York. The rest we borrowed at really high interest. It will probably take me four or five years to pay it all off.

Can you identify the pushes, pulls, bridges, and barriers in Chen Dawei's migration story?

Chinese Restaurants and the Global Economy. The journey of Fuzhounese immigrants does not end in New York and may, in fact, continue to your college dorm or apartment front door. Have you ever wondered why chicken with broccoli is so cheap in your local Chinese restaurant? The answer lies along a street called East Broadway in Chinatown on the Lower East Side of Manhattan. There, an entire migration industry draws Chinese immigrants from the rural villages of the Fuzhou area of southeastern China to New York City and sets them on the move again to a Chinese restaurant near you.

Located along East Broadway are a cluster of services that facilitate the movement of Chinese immigrants. Offices for immigration lawyers, English language classes, driving schools, and producers of legitimate and illegitimate documents stand alongside doctors' offices, pharmacies, clothing stores, and gambling parlors. East Broadway's human smugglers help undocumented immigrants make their way across national borders. Phone card sales booths help workers keep in touch with family back in China. MoneyGram and Western Union wire transfer offices send money back to family members in the home villages. Key to this migration industry are two dozen employment agencies that match newly arrived workers with Chinese restaurants across the country and another dozen long-distance buses that deliver Fuzhounese to those restaurants.

This global flow of Fuzhounese is fraught with frictions. Chinese human smugglers charge more than $80,000 to bring a person to the United States, leaving immigrants with huge debts that may take years to repay. Restaurant owners rely on vulnerable, underpaid workers to make their profit margins on inexpensive dishes such as chicken with broccoli. Workers often live and work in the restaurants, putting in twelve- to fourteen-hour days, six or seven days a week. Chinatown buses provide the link that moves workers between out-of-town jobs and the support system of the migration industry along East Broadway. As many as fifty thousand individuals are circulating through this Chinese restaurant industry at any given time.

The movement of rural men and women from Chinese villages to the far reaches of the United States illustrates the deep interconnectivity of people in the modern world economic system. The demand for inexpensive Chinese food in Omaha, Nebraska, can pull a young Chinese farmer across an ocean to help fill the demand of a global labor market and pursue her dream of wealth and happiness for herself and her family. That is the story behind your next dish of chicken with broccoli (Guest 2011).

GLOBAL MIGRATION PATTERNS

Globalization has transformed the spatiality of the world economy and has intensified the volume and types of movement occurring within and across political boundaries (Trouillot 2003). But not every country is equally affected by today's global flows of migrants. Some are primarily sending countries; others are primarily receiving countries. Moreover, not all migration occurs across borders. Thus a truly global perspective on migration must include both international and internal migration.

International migrants, or migrants who cross borders, exist across the globe, but they largely relocate to more developed countries. Figure 11.3 shows the primary migration flows for receiving and sending countries. **Internal migration** refers to the movement of people within their own national borders. For example, urban-oriented development programs and the establishment of large-scale export

internal migration

The movement of people within their own national borders.

FIGURE 11.3
Contemporary Global Migration Patterns

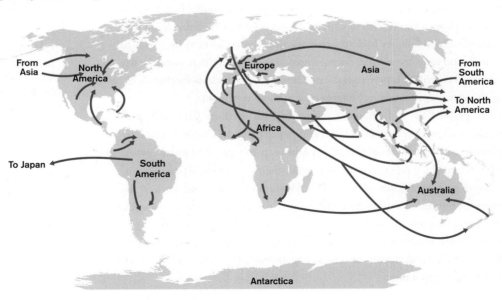

processing zones in developing countries have provided the pulls for significant internal migration from rural to urban areas to fill the new labor needs. Women workers, sought after by factory owners in export processing zones, constitute a high proportion of internal migrants.

TYPES OF IMMIGRANTS

Globally, immigration includes people from a wide variety of class backgrounds, ranging from refugees fleeing war or natural disaster, to unskilled workers with little education, to well-educated doctors and elite corporate businesspeople. Immigration scholars often focus on immigrants' economic roles, whether as laborers, professionals, entrepreneurs, or refugees. Although not applicable to every immigrant journey, these categories delineate certain patterns that constitute a general framework for analysis and comparison.

Labor immigrants move in search of low-skill and low-wage jobs, filling economic niches that native-born workers will not fill. Labor immigrants constitute the majority of migrants in the world today. They may be legal or illegal, but they are drawn by employment opportunities that, though limited, provide jobs at higher wages than are available in their home economies.

Professional immigrants are highly trained individuals who move to fill economic niches in middle-class professions marked by shortages in the receiving country. A key component of the professional immigrant category is university students trained in Western-style professions who lack opportunities to implement their training at home. This migration is often referred to as a brain

labor immigrant
A person who moves in search of a low-skill and low-wage job, often filling an economic niche that native-born workers will not fill.

professional immigrant
A highly trained individual who moves to fill an economic niche in a middle-class profession often marked by shortages in the receiving country.

Why are an increasing number of U.S. health care professionals immigrants from India, the Philippines, and the Caribbean? Here, Dr. Saeid Ahmadpour performs a checkup on a baby at a clinic in Cheyenne Wells, Colorado.

such as France, Spain, and the United States, or in Asian cities such as Dubai, Bangkok, Hong Kong, and Guangzhou. Most, however, have relocated within the African continent—notably to Senegal, Côte d'Ivoire, Burkina Faso, Gabon, Congo, and South Africa.

Whitehouse begins his ethnography with the story of a small town in southern Mali that he calls Togotala. The town lies on an arid plain between desert to the north and forest to the south. With agricultural production being inadequate to meet the immediate needs of the Togotala population, and with no development assistance from the Malian government, the community has a history of producing merchants who enter the regional trade networks in order to send money home to support their families and the community at large. The influence of this money is evident in the larger cinderblock homes that have been constructed in Togotala's central district, a school for children in grades 1 to 9, a water tower run by solar power to pump water to communal faucets throughout the town, a landline phone system, a health clinic, and several modern mosques. These local developments are concrete testimony to Togotala's deep connection to the world beyond its borders, and they hint at the creative individual responses that literally bring home the benefits of the global economy.

Twice daily, battered buses arrive in Togotala carrying goods and passengers and providing the town's primary link to the outside world. A ride south to Mali's capital, Bamako, connects Togotala's merchants to an extensive transport network through which they can reach more distant destinations. Whitehouse traces some of Togotala's residents southward to a large Malian community in Brazzaville, capital of the Republic of Congo. A port city of 1.5 million residents on the northern bank of the Congo River, Brazzaville serves as the country's administrative, manufacturing, and financial center. It is also a transfer point for agricultural products, wood, rubber, and other raw materials coming from upriver onto the Congo-Ocean railroad that links Brazzaville to the seaport of Pointe-Noire. French colonialists originally brought West Africans to Brazzaville in the 1800s to serve as soldiers, porters, laborers, and messengers. But West Africans succeeded in creating parallel economic networks of merchants, traders, laborers, blacksmiths, leatherworkers, and traditional storytellers—economic networks that survived the end of colonialism in 1960. Today a large community of Malians, mostly Muslim, work in Brazzaville as importers, shopkeepers, street vendors, entrepreneurs, and merchants in the diamond and jewelry trades.

Despite their long history in Brazzaville, Malians are treated as outsiders and strangers, segregated by language, social organization, and religion. Under these conditions, a strong connection to home enables the migrant Malians to resist the experience of exclusion from key local spaces, whether political,

MAP 11.4
Mali and Congo

economic, social, or religious. Whitehouse easily portrays why people seek employment outside Togotola. More difficult to understand is why they come back so frequently and continue to be active in Togotala economics, politics, and social life.

From the perspective of Malian life in Brazzaville, the choice to maintain an intense and direct connection to home becomes more understandable. The connection enables them to maintain a sense of place and belonging despite the local marginalization and in the face of increasing mobility and spatial separation from their families and home community.

Migrants, including the merchants of Togotala and other entrepreneurs across Africa, reveal creative individual responses to the intensification of interaction that is occurring worldwide. Actions by migrants such as the Malians in Brazzaville—less powerful people whose stories are often ignored in the grand narrative of globalization—reveal the determined, entrepreneurial strategies that local people employ to bring the benefits of the global economy to their communities and to reshape globalization from the ground up.

Entrepreneurial immigrants from Mali have built a vibrant community in Brazzaville, Republic of Congo.

Is Today's Global Economic System Sustainable?

Today we have an economic system of astounding complexity. Our economic activity surpasses anything we might have imagined even fifty years ago. The global economy integrates all of the world's people to one extent or another into a global system of exchange. But does it work well for everyone? What are the criteria we might use to assess its effectiveness?

SUCCESSES AND FAILURES

The global economy has achieved remarkable success over the past sixty years. For example, gross national income of the global economy rose from around $1 trillion in 1960 to $77.6 trillion in 2014 (International Monetary Fund 2014). The same period saw a 50 percent increase in school enrollments and a drop in infant mortality rates of more than 60 percent. And life expectancy nearly doubled over the last century, reaching 70 years in 2012 (World Health Organization 2015).

But the outlook is not all rosy. In 2013 the world had just over 1 billion people going hungry each day and living in extreme poverty. Another 1.7 billion people live in relative poverty, attempting to survive on the equivalent of $2 a day. Six million children die of malnutrition each year (United Nations Development Programme 2013a). Clearly, global inequality continues to increase. Is the current trajectory of the global economy sustainable? And what can anthropologists contribute to addressing these questions? (Moran 2006).

THE HUMAN ECOLOGICAL FOOTPRINT

Since at least the time of the earliest human settlements and the development of farming and pastoralism, humans have had an impact on their local environments. Human impact increased with an expanding population and was accelerated by the Industrial Revolution. Over the past sixty years, we have transformed our relationship with nature, and now our impact is being felt on a planetary scale.

Can Earth sustain the current global economy? Here, demonstrators in the 2014 New York Climate Change March warn that investments in carbon-generating oil companies may backfire and flood Wall Street.

The UN estimates that the world population, which was 2.5 billion in 1950, will increase from 7.2 billion in 2015 to 10.1 billion by 2100. Each day, we add 220,000 people. Each day, human consumption increases while available natural resources decrease. How will we sustain an almost 50 percent increase in global population when current resources are already overused? As this crisis deepens, how will your life be directly affected? What personal and collective strategies can you imagine for addressing the emerging problems?

Accelerating climate change is already evident, and the human contribution to the environmental crisis is clear. Agricultural yields are being affected by rising temperatures and increased greenhouse gases in the atmosphere. Food shortages are increasing despite intensive farm mechanization, chemical fertilizers, and pesticides. Carbon emissions from burning oil and gas are heating the planet and acidifying the oceans. At the 2009 global climate conference in Copenhagen, Denmark, 167 nations endorsed an agreement that acknowledged the need to cut global emissions drastically to hold the overall increase in global temperatures below 2 degrees Celsius (3.6 degrees Fahrenheit). Meeting this goal was recognized as essential to avoid a global ecological catastrophe. But so far, global temperatures have already risen eight-tenths of a degree Celsius, and humans continue to pour record amounts of carbon into the atmosphere (McKibben 2010, 2012).

The scramble for natural resources—especially freshwater, oil, and coltan (a scarce metal ore used in cell phones and other electronic devices)—pits wealthy nations against poor nations. The ice sheets in the Himalayas that provide drinking water for billions of people in Pakistan, India, Burma, and Indo-China are shrinking from global warming. Underground aquifers that provide freshwater to billions more in China and the Middle East are being depleted faster than nature can replenish them. Environmental trends do not bode well for the global economy using today's technologies.

Humans have a huge ecological footprint. Production, distribution, and consumption have been transformed in the contemporary global economy. And consumerism is driving a dramatic expansion of the human ecological footprint. Studies suggest that as early as 1980 humans began to use more resources than the planet could regenerate. By 2000, our consumption of the world's resources stretched above 50 percent of sustainable levels. In other words, at our current rate of consumption, it would take 1.5 Earths to sustain our rate of resource consumption and absorb our pollution using prevailing technologies. By the year 2030, estimates suggest we would need two planets to sustain our economic activity. This is what scientists call "ecological overshoot," which occurs when human demands on nature exceed the planet's ability to provide. The results are depletion of freshwater systems, the buildup of carbon dioxide in the atmosphere, collapsing fisheries in the oceans, and diminishing forest cover (Global Footprint Network 2013).

WORLD ON THE EDGE

Time is short. Scholars in many fields are asking if we have come to the crisis point where our model of economic growth is leading to ecological collapse. Our current economic system risks pushing us closer to the edge. Although most residents of developed countries have been shielded from the worst effects of these changes, people in poorer countries, particularly in coastal and low-lying regions, are already hard hit. For example, Bangladesh's coastal flood plain has been repeatedly inundated with monsoons, flooding, and devastating erosion. Even the United States is experiencing an increased incidence of droughts, heat waves, and damaging storm fronts.

Perhaps the biggest test of the global economy and its underlying principles will be its sustainability. Can we sustain the current pace of economic growth? Is it within the planet's carrying capacity? Is it reasonable to think that through modernization all people will attain a middle-class lifestyle when we know that if everyone on the planet had the same ecological footprint as an American, the global lifestyle would require five Earths to support?

Toolkit

Thinking Like an Anthropologist: Situating Yourself within the Global Economy

Globalization of the world economy has transformed the way we live. As you analyze the global economy and your connection to it, consider again the questions we raised at the beginning of the chapter:

- **What is an economy, and what is its purpose?**
- **What are the roots of today's global economy?**
- **What are the dominant organizing principles of the modern world economic system?**
- **How does today's global economy link workers with consumers worldwide?**
- **How is today's global economy reshaping migration?**
- **Is today's global economic system sustainable?**

Our opening story of chocolate in Côte d'Ivoire highlighted both the complexities of the global economy and the connections it facilitates among people, states, and corporations worldwide. Chocolate—like coffee, tea, sugar, a laptop, or a smartphone—reveals both (1) the incredible potential of our globalized economy to create connections, and (2) the unwelcome consequences of globalization that lead to imbalances and inequalities.

We have asked whether the global economy works well. Is it sustainable? How can we ensure the adequate distribution of resources necessary for human life—food, clean water, shelter, and health care? These are questions you will have to answer in your lifetime. And you will answer them by the life choices you make. For, with the continuing intensification of globalization, we are all connected in a web of constraints and opportunities. Perhaps your engagement with the global economy is not constrained by poverty, illiteracy, or violence. But it may be constrained by cultural expectations—for instance, group and peer pressure about what you need to fit in, dress well, eat right, and travel from place to place. Do you really have the choice in U.S. culture to not consume? How you address these constraints and opportunities will make a difference.

The good news is that there are many points at which to intervene in the current patterns of the global economy, whether you work to save the forests, recycle, support fair trade, reevaluate your consumption patterns, organize to support the rights of workers around the world, or become an engineer focusing on clean manufacturing or a scientist developing renewable energy sources. Thinking like an anthropologist will help you to analyze your choices in a more informed and responsible way.

Key Terms

economy (p. 299)

food foragers (p. 300)

pastoralism (p. 301)

horticulture (p. 301)

agriculture (p. 301)

carrying capacity (p. 302)

reciprocity (p. 302)

redistribution (p. 303)

colonialism (p. 306)

modernization theories (p. 309)

development (p. 310)

dependency theory (p. 310)

underdevelopment (p. 310)

core countries (p. 310)

periphery countries (p. 311)

Fordism (p. 313)

flexible accumulation (p. 313)

neoliberalism (p. 315)

commodity chain (p. 316)

pushes and pulls (p. 319)

internal migration (p. 322)

labor immigrant (p. 323)

professional immigrant (p. 323)

entrepreneurial immigrant (p. 324)

refugee (p. 324)

Chapter 12
Politics and Power

Throughout 2011 and 2012, the Middle East and North Africa were roiled by antigovernment demonstrations, strikes, marches, and rallies, as well as by sometimes violent responses from police, militaries, and pro-government demonstrators and militias. What has become known as the Arab Spring spread quickly from Tunisia to Egypt, eventually including a civil war in Libya and uprisings in Syria, Bahrain, Yemen, Morocco, Algeria, Iraq, Jordan, and Oman.

The revolution in Egypt caught the world's attention as tens of thousands of young people faced off against the police and soldiers defending the repressive regime of Hosni Mubarak, who had been Egypt's president for thirty-three years. The protestors hurled rocks and paving stones against tear gas and bullets, eventually toppling the Mubarak government and creating an opening for a dramatic shift in the power structure of Egypt, one of the cornerstones of the region's politics.

An Egyptian protestor takes a photo with her mobile phone while chanting slogans in Tahrir Square, Cairo, December 2012.

The movements for social change across the region were marked by new forms of political protest and mobilization. Laptops, the Internet, and search engines enabled a generation separated by national borders to find out about anything going on anywhere, easily bridging the local and the global. Cell phones, flip cameras, Twitter feeds, and Facebook pages brought a new dynamic to the creation of social networks and mass mobilizations as individuals previously separated by geography and political borders found new ways to link together, posting a constantly refreshed stream of YouTube videos of marches, celebrations, violence, and atrocities.

In Egypt, these elements of time-space compression facilitated the cooperation of social networks, student organizations, religious movements, unionized factory workers, and soccer clubs. Global interconnections appeared everywhere. Leaders of the April 6 Youth Movement traveled from Egypt to Europe to learn the nonviolent strategies of the Serbian Youth Brigade, named Otpar, that had helped topple Serbian dictator Slobodan Milosevic in 2000. Egyptian youth also studied the work of American political scientist Gene Sharp (1993), who promoted nonviolence as the most effective means to undermine a police state that might otherwise respond to violent resistance with repressive tactics. An Egyptian executive for Google, Wael Ghonim, established a Facebook group, named We Are All Khaled Said, in honor of a young Egyptian man who had been beaten to death by Egyptian police. The group became the central organizing location for tens of thousands of young Egyptians who were determined to change the life chances and political possibilities of their fellow citizens (Abu-Lughod 2012; Ghannam 2012; Hamdy 2012; Hirschkind 2012).

Power is often described as the ability or potential to bring about change through action or influence—either one's own or that of a group or institution. Indeed, power is embedded in all human relationships, whether that power is openly displayed or carefully avoided—from the most mundane aspects of friendships and family relationships to the myriad ways humans organize institutions and the structural frameworks of whole societies (Wolf 1982).

The presence of politics and relations of power in the ebb and flow of daily life is a central focus of anthropological study. Although uprisings such as the Arab Spring may draw attention to the most public, dramatic, and sometimes violent aspects of politics, anthropologists also consider the multiple local forms of politics—the careful political interactions and activities that occupy much of daily life and are essential in making a community a decent place to live (Gledhill 2000; Kurtz 2001; Lewellen 2003).

Throughout this book we explore power and its intersections with culture. We work to unmask the structures of power built on ideologies of race, gender, ethnicity, and sexuality and the institutions of kinship and religion. We also examine the power dynamics of the world economy and the stratifications of

Who has power? Wael Ghonim, a high-level employee of Google Egypt and one of the leading members of the Egyptian opposition is buoyed by supporters as he leaves his apartment in Cairo.

class. In this chapter, we explore power as it is expressed through political systems and processes: the way humans have organized themselves in small groups, the role of the state in national and international politics, and the ability of people (nonstate actors) to engage in politics and exercise power through individual action and social movements outside the direct control of the state. We consider the historical and contemporary approaches that anthropologists have taken toward these crucial issues and the ways in which globalization is shifting the dynamics of power and politics on local and global levels. In particular, we will examine the following questions:

- **How have anthropologists viewed the origins of human political history?**
- **What is the state?**
- **How is globalization affecting the state?**
- **What is the relationship among politics, the state, violence, and war?**
- **How do people mobilize power outside the state's control?**

While reading this chapter, you will analyze many expressions of politics and the ways in which aspects of power are expressed locally and globally today. You will consider how political anthropology can help you think more deeply about your own expressions as a political creature, including the ways you negotiate human relationships on the interpersonal, group, community, national, and global level. You will examine the changing role of the state in local, national, and global affairs and the ways humans mobilize collectively through social movements to challenge the power of the state and the effects of globalization by advocating for social change and human rights. Finally, you will consider an anthropological debate about the roots of violence in human culture. The skills you acquire in this chapter will be valuable additions to your toolkit for living as a political actor and an engaged citizen in today's global world.

How Have Anthropologists Viewed the Origins of Human Political History?

Over the course of history, humans have organized themselves politically by using flexible strategies to make their groups and communities a better place to live. Our earliest human ancestors appear to have evolved in small, mobile, egalitarian groups of hunter-gatherers. It is in these types of groups that core human characteristics and cultural patterns emerged.

For nearly a century, beginning in the late 1800s, anthropologists studying politics and power focused primarily on the political activities of contemporary hunter-gatherers, pastoralists, and horticulturalists. But beginning in the 1960s, the anthropological gaze shifted to encompass more complex, state-oriented societies and the process by which local settings are politically incorporated into a larger context.

The specialization called *political anthropology* took clear shape after World War II as anthropologists examined the local political systems of Africa (e.g., Meyer Fortes and E. E. Evans-Pritchard 1940; Turner 1957; Gluckman 1954) as well as the Middle East and Asia (Leach 1954; Barth 1959) and the indigenous people of the Americas (Redfield 1941; Wallace 1957).

As they undertook these studies of politics in many cultures, anthropologists attempted to create a common language, a typology that would enable them to communicate across cultural areas and compare and contrast their findings (Gledhill 2000; Lewellen 2003). The political anthropologist Elman Service (1962) famously classified the vast and varied world of political systems into four basic types: bands, tribes, chiefdoms, and states. Although infrequently used today, this framework shaped a generation of anthropological thinking about political systems. Service proposed that political systems develop through a natural, evolutionary progression from simple to complex and from less integrated to more integrated, with patterns of leadership evolving from weaker to stronger. Subsequently, when states emerged as the dominant political actors on the world stage, the examination of bands, tribes, and chiefdoms, anthropologists hoped, might provide insights into the origins and fundamental nature of the state.

BANDS

Anthropologists have used the term **band** to describe small, kinship-based groups of food foragers who move over a particular territory while hunting and gathering. Through archaeological evidence and the study of a few remaining band societies, anthropologists have identified key characteristics of band organization and leadership. A band might range in size from twenty to several hundred people depending on the time of year and the group's hunting and ritual cycles. Bands break up and re-form regularly in response to conflicts among members and the formation of new alliances.

band
A small kinship-based group of foragers who hunt and gather for a living over a particular territory.

Small, close-knit bands served as the primary way of life not only for our modern human ancestors but also for the entire genus *Homo*, including *Homo habilis, Homo erectus,* and early *Homo sapiens.* As a result, evolutionary biologists suggest that life in the band shaped the development of our earliest human characteristics and cultural patterns.

Politically, bands are highly decentralized, with decisions made primarily by consensus. Leaders emerge for a task at hand (organizing the hunt, moving the campsite, negotiating a conflict), with their leadership position resting on their skill, knowledge, generosity toward others, and level of respect within the band. With limited resources to compete for, bands have minimal stratification of wealth and power. But perhaps more important, bands required active cooperation among diverse groups of relatives and nonrelatives in order to successfully adapt to an unpredictable and shifting landscape. In turn, these early patterns may have embedded in humans a tendency toward egalitarian social and political organization rather than hierarchy.

In his book *Hierarchy in the Forest: The Evolution of Egalitarian Behavior* (1999), evolutionary biologist Christopher Boehm explores what life in bands can tell us about whether humans are fundamentally hierarchical or egalitarian. Drawing on ethnographic studies of contemporary and historical hunter-gatherer bands as well as archaeological findings, Boehm argues that the sharing of scarce resources, including food, was for hunter-gatherer bands the most economically efficient—indeed, essential—economic strategy. And this strategy could only be sustained through egalitarianism. Cooperative gathering of foods, coordinated game hunting, and reciprocal sharing went hand in hand with resisting hierarchy and domination as successful adaptations for humans living in hunter-gatherer bands. As a result, over the course of human evolutionary history, hunter-gatherer bands and tribal communities generated an egalitarian ethos that promoted generosity, altruism, and sharing while resisting upstarts, aggression, and egoism.

Despite serving as the predominant economic, social, and political structure over the course of human evolution, by the mid-twentieth century only a few bands of food foragers remained. These groups were living in the most remote areas of the planet: the rain forests of South America, the arctic tundra of North America, and the deserts of Africa and Australia.

TRIBES

The term *tribe* is frequently used in contemporary media when describing conflict among groups within a state. Media coverage of civil wars or internal conflicts—particularly in parts of Africa, the Middle East, Asia, and the Pacific—frequently refers to tribal conflicts, tribal warfare, tribal factions, rifts, and alliances. In these instances, *tribe* is usually a reference to a loosely organized group of people acting together, outside the authority of the state, under unelected leaders and "big men"/"strong men" and drawing on a sense of unity based on a notion of shared ethnicity.

Most popular references to tribes carry connotations of primitive, uncivilized, and violent people who engage in conflict based on "ancient" tribal factions and hatreds. These faulty characterizations reflect the ethnocentric perspectives of observers who operate from inside a state framework. Their characterizations perpetuate the deeply problematic evolutionary assumption that less complex political organizations are naturally less effective, stable, rational, and civilized.

As originally formulated (Service 1962), the term *tribe* referred to a culturally distinct population, often combining several bands, that imagined itself as one people descended from a common ancestor and organized around villages, kin groups, clans, and lineages. Tribes appear to have emerged between ten and twelve thousand years ago as humans began to shift from food foraging to pastoralism and horticulture. Like bands, tribes are largely egalitarian, with a decentralized power structure and consensus decision making. Leaders do emerge, sometimes called "village heads" or "big men" (Sahlins 1971), who garner the support of followers in several villages. But their power is limited. It is built and maintained through the leaders' personal achievements—such as success in war, conflict resolution, group organizing, and generosity of feasts and gifts—rather than awarded through political institutions.

In recent centuries, independent tribal peoples largely have been eliminated; they have been conquered and incorporated into the nation-states that have come to dominate the global political landscape. Today no groups operate totally outside the framework of the state. Even a weak state or a failed state directly influences all those living within its borders. In this context, today we might define a **tribe** more accurately as an indigenous group of people with its own set of loyalties and leaders living to some extent outside the direct control of a centralized, authoritative state. In many cases, current discussions use the term *ethnic group* instead of *tribe* (Ferguson 2011).

CHIEFDOMS

Within Elman Service's evolutionary typology of political systems, the **chiefdom**—an autonomous political unit composed of a number of villages or communities under the permanent control of a paramount chief (Carneiro 1981, 45)—represented a transitional form between the simpler political structures of tribes and the more complex political structures of states. As in bands and tribes, the social relations of the chiefdom were built around extended kinship networks or lineages. The chiefdom might encompass thousands of people spread over many villages.

Unique to chiefdoms, leadership was centralized under a single ruling authority figure—a chief who headed a ranked hierarchy of people, asserted political control over a particular territory, and held the authority to make and enforce decisions. In parts of Polynesia, for instance, chiefs functioned as full-time political specialists, resolving conflicts and organizing collective economic activity. The permanent position of chief endured from generation to generation, often passing through direct descent and inheritance from father to son or through other kinship relationships. Religious rituals and beliefs often served to confirm the chief's authority.

Through feasts and festivals such as the potlatch (see Chapter 10), the chief gathered a portion of the collective bounty of the chiefdom's harvest or hunt and redistributed the communal wealth to the populace, thereby symbolically and practically reinforcing his or her central role among the people. Though group members' access to power and resources depended on one's hierarchical relationship to the chief, the process of redistribution served a central role in moderating inequality and limiting conflict within the chiefdom.

tribe
Originally viewed as a culturally distinct, multiband population that imagined itself as one people descended from a common ancestor; currently used to describe an indigenous group with its own set of loyalties and leaders living to some extent outside the control of a centralized authoritative state.

chiefdom
An autonomous political unit composed of a number of villages or communities under the permanent control of a paramount chief.

Micronesian islanders confront the effects of natural disasters—like this home destroyed by a typhoon (*left*)—with creativity, signs of aesthetic beauty, and flexible kinship structures. In this context, generosity of spirit, duty to one's kin, and the ability to produce food and other goods in quantities that enable gift giving and feasting (*right*) are held in higher esteem than martial skill or the role of the warrior.

PUTTING TYPOLOGIES IN PERSPECTIVE

Though the typology of bands, tribes, chiefdoms, and states provided a basis for cross-cultural comparison, Service's framework has frequently proven too simple to capture the complexity and diversity of political practices and institutions that are reflected in ethnographic studies and the archaeological record. For instance, evidence now clearly suggests that across human history, groups of bands, tribes, and chiefdoms were never as isolated or homogenous as mid-twentieth-century anthropologists proposed. In contrast, today we argue that movement, encounter, exchange, and change have been the hallmarks of human groups, both small and large, throughout human history.

Nor could twentieth-century political systems always be considered trustworthy representations of the human past, recent or distant. Certainly, by the time anthropologists began to enter the field in the late nineteenth century to document and classify people and their political systems, European colonial expansion—including often violent encounters—had transformed peoples and their political structures across the globe. Colonialism, the slave trade, the conquest of indigenous peoples of the Americas, military activity, missionary efforts, and global trade deeply influenced every political arrangement from the most populous urban setting to the most rural village. It is safe to say that anthropologists have not observed a band, tribe, or chiefdom that has not been influenced by colonialism, the power of the state, and the forces of globalization.

Today no political arrangement of band, tribe, or chiefdom can operate outside the pervasive influence of the state. As a result, political anthropology has turned from a primary focus on small-scale, stateless societies to consider both the structures and processes of the state, the ways individuals and local settings are politically incorporated into the larger framework of the state, and the developing position of the state in global affairs.

What Is the State?

As states took on an increasingly central role in shaping the local communities that anthropologists traditionally studied, political anthropologists turned their ethnographic attention to the state itself. Today we typically define the **state** as an autonomous regional structure of political, economic, and military rule with a central government authorized to make laws and use force to maintain order and defend its territory. Some loosely configured states existed as early as five thousand years ago in Mesopotamia and Egypt, and somewhat later in China, Japan, the Indus Valley, and portions of the Americas. Throughout most of human history, however, people organized themselves primarily through less centralized, flexible bands, tribes, and chiefdoms.

The global landscape of contemporary states that now dominates local, regional, and international affairs reflects the impact of Western expansion over the past five hundred years, particularly European imperial and colonial expansion (see Chapter 11). European colonialists deployed economic, political, and military force to redraw the political borders of much of the world to meet colonial economic needs. In this process, the colonial powers carved states and territories out of geographic areas inhabited by indigenous groups who were previously organized along lines based more on local kinship, political, and economic relations.

Few states are older than the United States, which officially formed in 1783. In fact, most of the states in the world today did not exist before World War II—certainly not in their current configurations. Most gained independence from colonial rule only in the decades immediately following World War II. By 2015, there were 196 independent states in the world.

THE MODERN WESTERN-STYLE STATE

The type of state that has emerged since the sixteenth century, built largely on a Western model and expanded through colonization and globalization, developed with certain unique characteristics (Giddens 1985). Unlike earlier forms of the state, such as China's, which had relatively porous borders and loose administration, modern states feature a central administration designed to penetrate the everyday social life of its citizenry. A standing army asserts control over a carefully defined territory. Administrative, communication, and military infrastructures define and enforce the state's borders. The state, rather than a big man or chief, serves as the source of laws and law enforcement. People of all classes within the bounds of the state acquire an identity as citizens who owe allegiance primarily to the state, not to local networks based on kinship, religion, or ethnicity (Asad 1992).

Externally, modern states compete economically and militarily with other states for resources and territory. Internally, each state seeks to establish a

state
An autonomous regional structure of political, economic, and military rule with a central government authorized to make laws and use force to maintain order and defend its territory.

monopoly on the legitimate use of force within a territorial domain (Weber [1919] 1965). For example, it enlists citizens' cooperation and pacifies resistance through expanded administrative power in police forces, the judicial system, tax collection, and regulatory regimes (Giddens 1985). It also accomplishes these objectives via surveillance techniques and institutions such as prisons, hospitals, and asylums, through which individuals classified as deviant from the cultural norm are removed from mainstream society and disciplined (Foucault 1977).

One unique contribution of political anthropologists to the study of the state has been a focus on the processes of the state rather than its institutions and structures. Rather than seeing the state as a completely autonomous, territorially defined entity with fixed institutions, structures, and procedures, political anthropologists have asked how the state came into being, how it was established as the ultimate authority managing all other institutions and social relations, and how each state has been uniquely constructed and organized by people and their cultural norms, values, symbols, and mental maps of reality.

Despite the illusion that the state is fixed, cohesive, and coherent, states are in fact constantly being shaped and reshaped through daily interactions with individuals, communities, nonstate institutions, social movements, and other states. From this perspective, we can see that states are actually quite fluid, contested, and even fragile (Sharma and Gupta 2006).

How does the state become the ultimate authority within a particular territory? Anthropologists suggest that the state becomes real in the imaginations and experiences of people as it is encountered in a particular space. This spatialization of the state (Ferguson and Gupta 2002)—the perception that the state fills a particular space, encompasses all aspects of culture, and stands above all other elements of the society—is produced through mundane bureaucratic state practices. The state is encountered in everyday acts of governance: mail delivery, tax collection, mapping, surveys, issuance of passports, jury duty, voting, notarization, distribution of food to the poor, distribution of pension checks to

the elderly. Through these routine and repetitive acts, the state comes to feel all-encompassing and overarching—a dynamic that Ferguson and Gupta call "vertical encompassment." Representations of the state on the television and radio, as well as in the newspapers or movies, all contribute to the construction of the state as concrete and real. These representations reinforce the conception of the state as the primary institutional form through which people experience social relations—family, community, civil society, economic exchange.

ASPECTS OF STATE POWER

The rituals and routines of the state also include overt practices of coercion. In fact, political philosopher Max Weber argued in 1919 that the fundamental characteristic of a state is its ability to establish a monopoly on the legitimate use of force in a particular territorial domain (Parsons 1964). States exert coercive power not only through military and police forces but also through the guarding and regulating of borders, the determining of criteria for citizenship, and the enforcing of discipline through rules, regulations, taxation, and the judicial system.

State power is also established through **hegemony**, which is the ability of a dominant group to create consent and agreement within a population without the use or threat of force (Gramsci 1971). How is this done? As discussed in Chapter 2, cultural institutions of government, media, schools, and religions shape what group members think is normal, natural, and possible, thereby influencing and limiting the scope of human action and interaction. Group members develop a way of seeing the world—a set of beliefs about what is normal and appropriate—that subconsciously limits their life choices and chances. As discussed in Chapter 6, states reinforce this hegemony by promoting intense feelings of nationalism (a sense of shared history, culture, language, destiny, and purpose, often through invented traditions of holidays, parades, national songs, public ceremonies, and historical reenactments) to promote the perception of the state as a unified entity.

When does the state become real to you? Consider the particular spaces in which you encounter the state. *From left to right:* Passport control at O'Hare Airport, Chicago. A courtroom in Santa Fe, New Mexico. A voting booth in Ciudad Juarez, Mexico. The construction site of a bridge over the Danube River between Romania and Bulgaria. A street in Melbourne, Australia, where firefighters race to an emergency.

hegemony

The ability of a dominant group to create consent and agreement within a population without the use or threat of force.

The hegemonic aspect of power can make group members discipline their own behavior, believing and acting in certain "normal" ways (often against their own interests), even without threat of punishment for misbehavior (Foucault 1977). Within the hegemony of ideas, some thoughts and actions actually become unthinkable and undoable. Others seem reasonable, necessary, and desirable; these include collective actions for the greater good of the "nation," even going so far as killing and being killed. Some modern states, however, are unable to gain the cooperation of their populace through consent and must resort to coercion. Where do you see this dynamic at work in the world today?

How Is Globalization Affecting the State?

Today globalization presents serious challenges to the state, particularly in terms of flexible accumulation, time-space compression, and expanding migration. The boundaries of the state—its influence and control over internal and external affairs—appear to be shrinking in the face of pressures related to globalization and the neoliberalizing global economy.

INTERNATIONAL NONSTATE ACTORS CHALLENGE STATE SOVEREIGNTY

In a global economy with increasing flows of people, money, goods, and ideas, state borders are becoming more porous. As a result, states are increasingly struggling to control who and what enters and leaves their territories. State sovereignty—the right of the state to maintain self-determination within its borders—is being challenged by powerful international nonstate actors.

As discussed in Chapter 11, international financial institutions such as the World Bank, the International Monetary Fund, and the World Trade Organization, backed by the world's most developed economies, are pressuring states to adopt neoliberal economic policies. These policies include free markets; free trade; the free movement of goods, capital, and ideas; and access to local markets for transnational corporations. Furthermore, to receive development loans from international financial institutions, developing countries are required to privatize state-owned infrastructure such as ports, water systems, utilities, and transportation and to reduce state funding for social services, health care, and education. These changes, it is suggested, while lessening the state's ability to control what flows across its borders, will enhance the state's ability to compete in the global economy.

Economic restructuring promoted by international financial institutions and implemented by the state has yielded a flourishing of civil society. This is evident in the phenomenon of people joining together to form local organizations and movements to protest the social upheaval and uneven development that has accompanied the institution of neoliberal economic policies. These nongovernmental organizations (NGOs), sometimes called **civil society organizations**, have become key players in challenging state policies and in creating space through which activists can work together to access resources and opportunities for their local communities.

civil society organization

A local nongovernmental organization that challenges state policies and uneven development, and advocates for resources and opportunities for members of its local communities.

CIVIL SOCIETY ORGANIZATIONS GAIN A GLOBAL REACH

One key strategy of civil society organizations has been to join forces with transnational movements and networks to transform local problems and conflicts into part of a global project for rights and resources. By linking up with groups outside their national borders, local civil society organizations are able to join forces with other activists, networks, and campaigns, such as Amnesty International, Human Rights Watch, Africa Watch, or World Vision and even international agencies like the United Nations. These linkages enable the civil society organizations to advocate for local environmental concerns, women's rights, human rights, and indigenous rights—issues that also transcend the borders of the state.

Communication and transportation advances associated with time-space compression—from cell phones to Facebook, Twitter, and YouTube—facilitate the formation of these transnational networks. This process not only promotes the flow of observers, advisors, and participants in meetings and conferences but also stimulates global information flows of on-the-ground developments and

Activists from an Indonesian civil society organization perform during a protest against the policies of the World Trade Organization, 2008.

organizing strategies. Working together, the international coalitions mobilize international sentiment and bring pressure to bear on nation-states to address problems occurring within their borders. In this way, the coalitions challenge the ultimate claims of state sovereignty over affairs within state borders.

What Is the Relationship among Politics, the State, Violence, and War?

Perhaps no use of power is more troubling and challenging than violence, the "bodily harm that individuals, groups and nations inflict on one another in the course of their conflicts" (Ury 2002, 7). Conflict happens on the playground, in the classroom, in the boardroom, and on the battlefield. As we look globally today, we seem to be experiencing a period during which violent conflict is not sporadic, but permanent—a time of continuous war in one place or another involving extraordinarily sophisticated tools and weaponry (Waterston 2009).

ARE HUMANS NATURALLY VIOLENT OR PEACEFUL?

Underlying many discussions and debates about politics, war, and peace is the question of whether humans are naturally violent or peaceful. Is there something in the human evolutionary past that predisposes modern humans to behave in a particular way when confronted with conflict?

The main arguments can be simplified into three generalizations. First, organized human violence can be seen as a natural expression of the inherent human condition. In this view, human aggression and violence may be attributed to physiological factors such as testosterone, DNA, and neural wiring. Or a natural tendency toward violence may be conceived of as a reasonable adaptation to the frustrations of drives, though an adaptation that only manifests itself when survival is at issue. A second conception of violence considers humans to be inherently peaceful. In this view, violence arises through cultural practices and patterns that overwhelm basic human nature. A third scenario places the roots of human violence in between nature and culture. So, for instance, humans may be naturally prone to violence but culturally capable of avoiding it. Or humans may be naturally peaceful and only culturally provoked into forsaking their nature. Another option posits that these two alternatives are evenly matched.

Challenging the Myth of Killer Apes and Aggressive Humans.

Some who see violence and war as a legacy of our evolutionary past point to a common myth about aggressive primates and killer apes as evidence.

If aggression, competition, and violence are part of our primate relatives' evolutionary development, they argue, then these impulses must be deeply ingrained in human nature as well. According to this view, natural levels of aggression, competition, and violence linked to genes and hormones must be generated internally and instinctively released in social relations. Conflict, then, naturally drives individuals farther apart into competing and warring groups.

Physical anthropologist Frans de Waal (2002), reviewing studies of living primate macaques, chimpanzees, and bonobos, points out patterns of behavior that directly challenge this myth. De Waal notes, for instance, that for social animals such as primates, this pattern of conflict and distancing would lead to everyone living alone, yielding an ineffective pattern of social relationships for individuals who rely on social cooperation for survival. In the primate social groups de Waal has reviewed, a far more complicated dynamic emerges in times of conflict. Rather than increased distance, reconciliation occurs on a regular basis. In fact, increased attraction is regularly observed between opponents after fights. Researchers have identified this reconciliation mechanism in twenty-five separate primate groups, revealing powerful inclinations toward reconciliation among individuals who have a great deal to lose if their relationship deteriorates. Among bonobos, a primate group closely related to humans on a genetic level, sex is used to resolve conflicts. Bonobo conflicts and tensions occur in all combinations of female and male. So do reconciliations. Bonobos have a high rate of reconciliation and a low rate of violence.

De Waal suggests that among primates there are various options for resolving conflicts, including avoidance, tolerance, and aggression. These options are

Are humans naturally violent or peaceful? Despite the myth of killer apes and aggressive humans, primate studies reveal that increased attraction is regularly observed between opponents after a conflict. Here, two female bonobos reconcile after a fight.

What Is the Relationship among Politics, the State, Violence, and War? **347** employed at various times depending on the situation, the partner, and the stakes. According to de Waal, primate studies indicate that "aggression [is] not . . . the product of an inner drive but . . . one of the options that exists when there is a conflict of interest" (24). Ultimately, researchers may find that aggressive primate behavior has a genetic component; but this component does not operate in isolation, nor is it necessarily dominant. Equally natural among primates are mechanisms for cooperation, conflict resolution, rechanneling of aggression, and reconciliation (de Waal 2002).

THE STATE AND WAR

Although genetically controlled impulses for war are hard to isolate and clearly identify, significant contemporary anthropological research has been conducted on the ways in which war and violence are complicated, learned social processes (Besteman 2002; Besteman and Cassanelli 1996; Gusterson 1996, 2004; Farmer 2003; Lutz 2001; Ferguson 2002; Waterston 2009). Over the past one hundred years, war has become far more than waging hand-to-hand combat or pulling a trigger at close range—actions that we might associate with aggression driven by hormones. Instead, modern warfare and violence are considerably more premeditated and calculated, relying on computers, satellites, missiles, GPS tracking, and airborne drone strikes.

Today anthropologists study a highly militarized world in which violence and war seem normalized and permanent. Warfare has become the most visible of all human political institutions that reveals the state's pursuit of power. As we will see in Carolyn Nordstrom's work later in this chapter, warfare can no longer be viewed as a local military phenomenon. Indeed, modern warfare is embedded in a global system of war making. This fact pushes anthropologists to study the intersection of multiple factors that play a role in constructing warfare and violence as a reasonable means for resolving conflicts. These factors may be as disparate as economic stratification, ethnic identity formation, migration, weapons manufacturing and trade, the imbalance between weak states and strong states, and resource shortages involving oil, water, and land (Nugent and Vincent 2004).

Militarization. A growing body of anthropological literature has focused on **militarization**—the contested social process through which a civil society organizes for the production of military violence (Lutz 2004; see also Geyer 1989; Bickford 2011). Catherine Lutz, an anthropologist of militarization, in *Homefront: A Military City and the American Twentieth Century* (2001) describes how the processes of militarization include not only the production of material objects such as bullets, bombs, tanks, planes, and missiles but also the glorification of war and those who make war, as states seek to shape their national histories and political culture.

militarization

The contested social process through which a civil society organizes for the production of military violence.

Lutz warns that left unchecked, militarization threatens to shape other aspects of cultural institutions to its own ends. For example, it influences research in physics, information technology, and psychology; it affects national budget priorities; it impacts discussions and debates about gender and sexuality, race and citizenship, privacy and security; and it limits what can be discussed in the news, online, or in the classroom.

ANTHROPOLOGY ON THE FRONT LINES OF WAR AND GLOBALIZATION

The fact that today's world is rife with conflict presents anthropologists with many opportunities to study current cases of warfare and violence in the context of pressures from globalization. Anthropologist Carolyn Nordstrom's work exemplifies contemporary anthropological contributions to this kind of study. Nordstrom focuses on the real, messy, local experiences of violence, resistance, survival, and creativity in actual communities where war occurs, not in the comfortable offices and remote institutions of military officials and political leaders. At the same time, she turns a spotlight on the complex web of local and foreign interactions and actors that drive war and make warfare a global phenomenon.

How does popular culture glorify war and those who make war?

In Mozambique. Between 1989 and 1996, Nordstrom made multiple visits to war-torn areas of Mozambique, a southeast African country wracked by a fifteen-year civil war after independence from Portugal that claimed a million lives, mostly civilian. To reach rural and forested regions, she traveled with bush pilots making airlifts into war zones. In contrast to typical journalistic war reports, Nordstrom experienced firsthand the low-intensity conflict called "terror warfare," perpetrated by rebel guerrillas and Mozambican government soldiers, that targeted the country's civilian population through military attacks, hunger, and displacement.

These destructive forces of warfare targeted the basic structures of Mozambican community life: hospitals, schools, and government offices, as well as teachers, health care professionals, religious authorities, and community leaders. By destroying and disrupting the institutions, practices, and key practitioners of local culture, the forces of violence sought to destroy the local population's political will.

MAP 12.1
Mozambique

In her ethnography of civil war in Mozambique, *A Different Kind of War Story* (1997), Nordstrom recounts the determined creativity that local populations employed to combat this terror and violence. In one village heavily targeted and frequently overrun by troops of both armies, most community leaders and service providers had fled as refugees to avoid potential assassination. Most resources and infrastructure had been destroyed. During the first severe attack on the village, however, one remaining health care practitioner gathered up as many medical supplies as she could carry and hid in the nearby bush until the soldiers left. Though the soldiers knew her name and searched for her, the villagers kept her secret, kept her safe. On the front lines of battle, soldiers passed through the village regularly in subsequent months. Yet the health worker remained, hiding her medical supplies, living a nomadic life on the outskirts of the area, and being protected by the villagers, who continued to carry their ailing members to her for treatment.

These actions by the health worker and the villagers are emblematic of the creativity that Nordstrom's research finds to be the most potent weapon against war—the determination to survive and resist, to continually refashion and reconstruct one's self, community, and world. Nordstrom concludes her ethnography by suggesting that if, as early political philosophers such as Thomas Hobbes proposed, violence is the "natural state" of human affairs when political institutions collapse, then war-torn regions such as Mozambique should be rife with scenes of aggression, acts of self-preservation, and individual attempts at survival in a dog-eat-dog world. Instead Nordstrom consistently found people who resisted and defeated the political violence of war by attending to the day-to-day matters of their community—sharing food, healing wounds, repairing lives, teaching children, performing rituals, exchanging friendship, rebuilding places, and creatively reconstructing the everyday patterns that constitute a meaningful life (Englund 1999; Honwana 1999; Richards 1999).

A Comparative Study. In a later book, *Shadows of War* (2004), Nordstrom makes the case that standard notions of local wars fought by local actors over local issues are largely fiction. Through a comparative study of war and violence in Mozambique, Sri Lanka, South Africa, and Angola, she instead traces the extensive global networks of individuals and industries that feed and fuel local violence and war. Mercenary soldiers, foreign strategists, arms suppliers, businesspeople, black marketeers, smugglers, humanitarian relief workers, researchers, propagandists, and journalists all circle the globe, moving from one war to the next. Multitrillion-dollar international financial networks support warfare. Illegal drugs, precious gems, weapons, food supplies, military training manuals, and medicines are products moved by international networks of legitimate and illegitimate businesses and agencies that profit from the business of war.

Thanks to globalization, the business of war now operates on a worldwide scale. It influences both the architects of war, who primarily engage the battle from a distance, and the people who suffer the consequences on a war's front lines. Discussing the local people impacted by the business of war, Nordstrom notes that theirs are not the typical war stories recounted in the media. When war is portrayed only through the prism of weapons, soldiers, territory, and strategic interests won or lost, a more significant reality is ignored: the heroic efforts of people on the front lines who resist and maintain life in the face of violence and death (Finnstrom 2005).

With globalization, an extensive network of individuals and industries circles the globe from one war to the next. *From left to right:* United Nations High Commissioner for Refugees workers distribute blankets to Syrian refugees along the Jordanian-Syrian border, 2012. An Australian mercenary trains rebel recruits in Myanmar. Members of the media mark their flak jackets as gunfire rings out near the Tripoli Hotel in Lebanon, 2011.

How Do People Mobilize Power outside the State's Control?

Systems of power, including the state, are never absolute. Their dominance is never complete. Even when a culture's dominant groups and institutions are very powerful in terms of their ability to exercise force or to establish control through hegemony, they do not completely dominate people's lives and thinking. Individuals and groups with less power or no power may still contest the established power relationships and structures through political, economic, religious, or military means and challenge and change cultural norms, values, symbols, and institutions. This power is a potential that anthropologists call **agency**.

In such displays of human agency, we see the way culture becomes the realm in which battles over power are waged; where people contest, negotiate, and enforce what is considered normal and what people can say, do, and even think. Because of human agency, cultures do not remain rigid and static. They change.

agency

The potential power of individuals and groups to contest cultural norms, values, mental maps of reality, symbols, institutions, and structures of power.

Efforts to change cultural patterns take various forms, which we will consider further. Human agency may be expressed through individual strategies of resistance, such as the "weapons of the weak" discussed in Chapter 2, collective efforts such as social movements, and alternative institutions to the state such as those based on religion.

SOCIAL MOVEMENTS

social movement

Collective group actions in response to uneven development, inequality, and injustice that seek to build institutional networks to transform cultural patterns and government policies.

Social movements are collective, group actions in response to uneven development, inequality, and injustice that seek to build institutional networks to transform cultural patterns and government policies. Social movements engage in contentious politics, usually outside the mainstream political process, to address specific social issues, although they usually do not seek to overthrow the social order. The study of social movements is interdisciplinary, engaging not only anthropologists but also sociologists, political scientists, and historians.

Anthropological analysis of social movements emerged forcefully after the turbulent 1960s and 1970s. During that period, the developed countries of Europe and North America had experienced intense grassroots mobilization around civil rights, women's rights, the environment, gay and lesbian rights, and antiwar movements. During the same period, anticolonialist and nationalist movements and insurgencies had erupted in poorer regions of the globe (Edelman 2001).

Recently, the anthropological analysis of social movements has focused on the responses of local communities to the forces of globalization. Factors such as the worldwide movement of capital and production through flexible accumulation, the increasing migration within and across national borders, and rapidly increasing yet uneven rates of development have spurred the emergence of social movements as local communities organize to protect their land, environment, human rights, and cultural identities in a changing economic and political context. Simultaneously, time-space compression has facilitated increased communication and cooperation among individuals, social movements, and NGOs, thus creating opportunities for a "globalization from below" (Falk 1993, 39).

Rural Social Movements. In the last thirty years, rural social movements have drawn anthropologists' attention as farmers engage in creative political struggles to resist the impact of globalization on their land, livelihood, and way of life. As one example, Marc Edelman's *Peasants against Globalization* (1999) examines the activism of the rural poor in Costa Rica, Central America, during the 1980s and 1990s. Edelman recounts a story that reflects the beleaguered experience of rural agricultural workers elsewhere across the globe in recent decades.

Having gained independence from Spain in 1821, Costa Rica is one of the most politically stable countries in the Americas. By the early 1980s, Costa Ricans had built a strong, economically self-sufficient democracy and taken the radical step of abolishing the nation's military in order to invest in programs of national development. Such programs aimed to provide education, health care, tariff protections for local products, and price supports for basic foodstuffs to ensure a basic livelihood for all citizens. The programs also provided government-backed loans to farmers to stabilize agricultural production.

During the mid-1980s, however, Costa Rica was drawn into the civil wars of its neighbors, serving as a key ally of the United States on the Central American peninsula as war and upheaval spread in Nicaragua, Guatemala, and Panama. Simultaneously, a debt crisis affecting most of Latin America shook Costa Rica's economy and spurred rapid inflation. Under the auspices of providing foreign aid to an ally, the U.S.-sponsored Food for Peace program delivered massive quantities of subsidized corn, wheat, and rice—purchased from U.S. farmers—to the Costa Rican market. The subsidized food, however, undercut Costa Rican farm prices, making it increasingly difficult for local farmers to sell their own products at the price needed to break even.

Ultimately, these changes in the Costa Rican food market drove many small-scale farmers out of business, lowered the country's overall food production, and ended its history of food self-sufficiency. Structural adjustment loans offered by the International Monetary Fund and the World Bank to help Costa Rica through the crisis required the government to eliminate price supports, tariff protections, and government-backed loans while drastically reducing investments in health care and education. These measures further deepened the country's crisis.

Edelman retells the stories of local, small-scale farmers—often called "peasants" in the anthropological literature—and their national umbrella group,

MAP 12.2
Costa Rica

A farmer holds a puppet of Costa Rican president Laura Chinchilla during protests in the capital, San José, over new property taxes on agricultural land, 2012.

UPANACIONAL, as they fought these threats to their way of life. The peasants marched, blocked highways, and held street demonstrations. They built alliances with wealthy farmers, lobbied national politicians, and promoted charismatic activist figures into national prominence to speak on their behalf.

The climax of the Costa Rican peasants' collective action and direct pressure tactics came as several dozen farmers and movement leaders occupied government buildings in June 1988. At the conclusion of the standoff, the activists were arrested; however, the negotiated settlement extracted a government commitment to provide access to low-interest credit for Costa Rica's rural farmers. This was a significant victory in response to the peasants' demands. Edelman concludes that the Costa Rican peasants may not have stopped the effects of globalization on their nation's rural population, but through collective action they were able to soften the harshest blows (Gudmundson 2001; Welch 2001).

Occupy Wall Street. Anthropologists seek to understand how social movements arise, mobilize, and sustain themselves. Even though conditions of inequality and injustice are widespread in many parts of the world, the activation of movements for social justice occurs in only certain situations. Anthropologists have investigated the material, human, cognitive, technical, and organizational resources necessary for social movements to succeed (McAdam, McCarthy, and Zald 1996). Recent attention has turned to the **framing process** of movements—specifically, how shared meanings and definitions arise to motivate and justify collective action.

framing process

The creation of shared meanings and definitions that motivate and justify collective action by social movements.

Actions by the Occupy Wall Street movement beginning in September 2011 illustrate the role of the framing process. How did Occupy protestors capture the attention of a nation (and beyond) and build a consensus for social action? What factors led to their success? Anthropologist Jeffrey Juris (2012), who studied Occupy Boston, has noted that social media drew a diverse group of people with shared concerns—in this case, over economic inequality—into shared physical spaces. Listservs, websites, and collaborative networking tools facilitated new patterns of protest that built on and resonated with more traditional forms.

Another key to Occupy's success rested on framing the movement's cause under the banner "We Are the 99%." With this simple phrase, Occupy Wall Street gradually focused public discourse on questions of the fundamental fairness of the U.S. and global economy in light of rapidly growing conditions of inequality over the past forty years that have steadily transferred wealth from 99 percent to 1 percent of the nation's population. Despite growing calls by political leaders and media critics demanding that Occupy Wall Street activists put forward specific policy proposals to address the problems they were decrying, the movement steadfastly refused. Instead its members focused on the underlying issue of inequality framed in their motto, "We Are the 99%."

Writing in the spring of 2012, Juris noted that Occupy Wall Street had already contributed to a shift in public discourse. The framing process of Occupy has successfully highlighted growing inequality and the influence of financial and corporate interests in the economy and politics. At the same time, Occupy has functioned as a laboratory for the production of alternative forms of democracy and community (Juris 2012, 261).

ALTERNATIVE LEGAL STRUCTURES

In addition to overt social movements and subtle, nonovert forms of resistance, it is possible to challenge structures of power in an arena where the state usually holds clear authority: in matters of the law. But how do people organize alternative legal structures outside the direct control of the modern state? What gives authority and legitimacy to alternative structures if they are not enforceable by the state's coercive power? Legal anthropologist Hussein Ali Agrama spent two years conducting ethnographic research on local courts and councils in Cairo, Egypt, to explore these questions (Agrama 2010, 2012).

Islamic Fatwa Councils in Cairo, Egypt. Agrama compared the operations of two key local sources of legal authority: (1) the Personal Status courts operated by the Egyptian state and (2) the Al Azhar Fatwa Council, independently established in 1935 and one of the oldest and most established centers of Islamic authority. In the busy and crowded Personal Status courts, Egyptians of all walks of life appear before a judge, an official of the state, who makes legally binding rulings that draw on the Egyptian Constitution and legal codes that are based on the principles of Islamic Sharia (law). In the equally

MAP 12.3
Cairo

Fatwa council at the Al Azhar Mosque, Cairo, Egypt.

busy and crowded Fatwa Council, held in a spacious room located at the main entrance to the Al Azhar Mosque, seekers approach Islamic legal scholars and interpreters of Islamic law, or muftis, for religious answers about matters of daily life. The muftis respond freely with legally nonbinding answers to anyone who asks. Their decision is called a "fatwa"—a response to a question about how to live ethically and rightly.

In comparing these two court systems, Agrama encounters a startling dynamic. Both deal with an overlapping set of issues heavily focused on matters of marriage, sex, divorce, reconciliation, and inheritance. Both draw their decisions from Islamic Sharia, although the Personal Status courts engage Islamic law through the Egyptian Constitution and legal code, whereas the muftis refer directly to Sharia and other Islamic traditions in their fatwas. What interests Agrama is that despite these basic similarities, the petitioners' responses to the authorities' rulings are markedly different. The legally binding judgments of the Personal Status court are generally looked on with great suspicion. People go to great lengths to avoid the consequences of the court's decisions despite the state's ability to coerce obedience to its judgments. In distinct contrast, the Fatwa Council exercises great authority even though seeking decisions from the Council is not obligatory, a fatwa is not legally binding, and once issued, a fatwa does not have to be obeyed. In fact, petitioners can seek more than one fatwa on the same issue if they wish. But Agrama's research finds that petitioners take fatwas very seriously, following the decisions even if they entail great difficulty or unhappiness—this despite no identifiable institutional enforcement mechanism.

What accounts for the differentiation between Personal Status courts and the Fatwa Council? And how does a given fatwa acquire its authority without the threat of coercive force like that which the state makes available to the Personal Status courts? To understand the authority of the fatwa, Agrama explores the complex interactions and expectations between seekers of fatwas and the muftis that issue them. Contrary to popular impressions, fatwas are not merely designed to dispense points of correct doctrine in obedience to prescriptions found in Islamic Sharia. Rather, the mufti seeks to apply Islamic tradition and law to resolve particular problems, identify an effective solution, and point the seeker toward a path forward. The process includes significant perplexities and uncertainties: the fatwa seeker arrives perplexed by his or her life situation, and at least initially the mufti is uncertain about how to respond. In this context, the mufti typically begins by asking for further information in an attempt to fully understand the context and facts as presented. The fatwa seeker approaches the mufti with the hope that he will have the skills to point the way out of the trouble, to offer a way forward—to discern and speak the right words.

In the end, both seeker and mufti share a collective responsibility for the success of the fatwa: the mufti must be sure to speak the right words, and the seeker must apply them correctly. Although the consequences of an incorrect fatwa may be most damaging for the seeker during his or her lifetime, the mufti is believed to bear responsibility for the outcome in the hereafter. Ultimately, the fatwa is pronounced in order to put the questioner on the right path forward, to offer direction and facilitate a journey on which the seeker can advance within the range of doctrine toward a Muslim ideal. Agrama suggests that it is careful and personal navigation of these complexities that engenders trust and conveys legitimacy on the muftis and their fatwas.

In the opening story of the Arab Spring and in the ethnographic examples presented throughout this chapter, we have seen the remarkable diversity of strategies that humans use to exercise power through the medium of politics. Although the political upheaval in North Africa and the Middle East readily draws the focus of the world media, Agrama's work in Cairo reminds us that human political activity occurs at many different levels during the course of daily life. Whether through the politics of the state, acts of war, social movements, or small-scale resistance that James Scott (1985; see Chapter 2) labeled weapons of the weak, we have considered how anthropologists examine power and politics and the cutting edges of political activism that will continue to draw their interest in the future.

Toolkit

Thinking Like an Anthropologist: Applying Politics to Daily Life and Beyond

In each chapter of this book, we have investigated how human cultures construct, engage, and negotiate systems of power. We have considered the role of influential ideologies and structures of race, gender, ethnicity, class, kinship, and religion. In this chapter, we have explored how power is expressed and organized through political systems and processes. Politics exist in every human relationship and every community, large or small. People are constantly negotiating the interpersonal and institutional balances of power.

As we saw in the chapter-opening story, politics is not necessarily separate from daily life. We don't have to run for political office or start an online petition to be involved in politics. At its most basic level, politics encompasses all of the ways we organize ourselves to achieve what we most desire for our community: our family, friends, classmates, fellow citizens, and fellow inhabitants of planet Earth. As you learn to think like an anthropologist about politics and power, remember the opening questions that we have used to frame our inquiries:

- **How have anthropologists viewed the origins of human political history?**
- **What is the state?**
- **How is globalization affecting the state?**
- **What is the relationship among politics, the state, violence, and war?**
- **How do people mobilize power outside the state's control?**

If, as it appears, humans do not have an overwhelming and uncontrollable biological drive toward aggression and violence, then unlimited avenues open up to explore strategies for addressing problems that confront us today. These strategies include cooperatively engaging the challenging issues of our schools, communities, nations, and world and developing political responses that take into account the unique cultural dynamics of local communities and specific groups.

As a new generation of social activists around the globe develops social networking and social media strategies for expressing their concerns and attempting to influence the systems of power and politics, the networked nature of these movements also means that you, as a college student, have every possibility of becoming an anthropologist who engages the world.

Key Terms

band (p. 337)

tribe (p. 339)

chiefdom (p. 339)

state (p. 341)

hegemony (p. 343)

civil society organization (p. 345)

militarization (p. 348)

agency (p. 351)

social movement (p. 352)

framing process (p. 354)

Chapter 13
Religion

In September 2007 thousands of barefoot, saffron-robed Buddhist monks marched through the streets of Yangon (Rangoon), the capital of Myanmar, leading dramatic demonstrations to protest the repressive policies and abusive practices of Myanmar's military government. A surprise decision to increase fuel prices by as much as 500 percent had sent the cost of everything (from rice and eggs to cooking oil and transportation) skyrocketing—and this in a country where the average annual income is less than $300. Students and workers had launched the earliest protests, but government forces quickly cracked down, searching homes, detaining demonstrators, and arresting movement organizers.

With resistance largely beaten down, dynamics across the country changed when government riot police shot at and beat several monks during protests north of the capital. Suddenly monks took to the streets everywhere.

What is religion? Buddhist monks march through the streets of Yangon, Myanmar, in 2007 to protest actions of the military government.

Because Myanmar's 400,000 Buddhist monks and 75,000 Buddhist nuns are deeply revered, both by civilians and by the military, the arousing of this religious network reignited popular demonstrations. Within weeks thousands of silent monks marched in procession for miles through the streets of Yangon. Cheering crowds created a protective cordon on either side of them, offering water, food, and physical protection as they faced off with government forces.

In one of the most dramatic moments of the demonstrations, one monk marching at the front of the procession held his black wooden begging bowl upside down as the group paraded in front of government military forces. Almsgiving is a religious obligation for Buddhists. In this primarily Buddhist country, giving alms—including food—to Buddhist monks, which they receive daily in their black begging bowls, is one of the most profound acts of religious ritual. By turning over their bowls, the monks symbolically refused to receive alms from the authorities, the military, and their supporters. With this simple gesture they matched their street demonstration with a religious boycott, effectively excommunicating their opponents from the practice of their faith.

Religion plays a central role in human life and human culture. Through the study of religion, anthropologists engage some of the deepest, most difficult, and most enduring human questions—about meaning, difference, power, love, sexuality, mortality, morality, human origins, and kinship. Religion has been a central interest of anthropologists since the beginning of our field. Research about religious beliefs and practices worldwide has explored an amazing diversity of symbols, rituals, myths, institutions, religious experts, groups, deities, and supernatural forces. As you read about diverse religions in this chapter, some beliefs and practices may seem quite familiar. Others may be surprising or unexpected. Many might stretch your basic assumptions of what religion is and does. For example, does the idea of ten thousand Buddhist monks leading protest marches seem strange to you?

Religion offers a rich vein of material for exploring the complexity of human culture, including systems of belief and systems of power. It is perhaps the hottest topic in the world today as globalization brings different traditions, beliefs, and practices into contact. In the United States, immigration over the past five decades has transformed the religious landscape (Figure 13.1). Temples, mosques, gurdwaras, and retreat centers now join churches and synagogues in small towns and big cities across the country. College campuses, too, reflect an expanding religious diversity. As people of different religious traditions encounter one another in neighborhoods, schools, and other public institutions, lively debates take place about education, zoning, health care, public security, and civil rights. These encounters create the potential for tension and misunderstanding on school boards, zoning committees, and town and city councils, as well as in civic associations and even college classrooms. But they also offer opportunities for interfaith encounters,

FIGURE 13.1
Religion in the United States

Extensive public polling in the United States reveals shifts in religious demographics in response to globalization and immigration patterns. In particular, the United States is experiencing a decline in the total percentage of Protestant Christians that parallels a growth in Catholic Christians from Latin America; Muslims from the Middle East, South Asia, and Africa; Orthodox Christians from Eastern Europe and the Middle East; Hindus from India; and Buddhists from China, Southeast Asia, and East Asia.

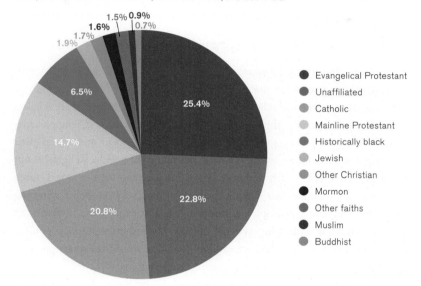

Source: Pew Forum on Religion & Public Life. 2015. "America's Changing Religious Landscape." www.pewforum.org/2015/05/12/americas-changing-religious-landscape/ (accessed 6/8/15).

learning, and engagement. An anthropological understanding of religion can help you to navigate and engage this changing landscape.

In this chapter, we will consider the anthropological approach to understanding the many groups, beliefs, and practices that are called "religion." In particular, we will examine the following questions:

- **What is religion?**
- **What tools do anthropologists use to understand how religion works?**
- **In what ways is religion both a system of meaning and a system of power?**
- **How is globalization changing religion?**

By the end of the chapter you will be able to investigate and analyze religion using the tools of an anthropologist. You will be better able to understand religion in your own life, in the growing religious pluralism of the United States, and in diverse religious expressions around the world. These skills will be increasingly valuable tools for living and working in the twenty-first century.

What Is Religion?

When anthropologists talk about "religion," what are we really talking about? Since the beginning of the discipline, anthropologists have been attempting to create a universal definition that might apply to all religions' local manifestations. But the vast global diversity of unique local expressions makes defining religion a difficult task. Is there something present in all cultures that we can call "religion"?

SEEKING A WORKING DEFINITION

The unique anthropological approach to religion begins with the everyday religious practices of people in their local communities. Through fieldwork, anthropologists focus on the real religious worlds in which humans experience religion physically and express it through their actions. We may study a religion's history, theology, scriptures, and major figures, but we do so to understand their meaning and significance in the life of a community of people. Religion is not theoretical in people's daily activities. People make sense of the world, reach decisions, and organize their lives on the basis of their religious beliefs. Starting from these beginning principles, anthropologists also explore the myriad ways religion intersects with other systems of power, whether economics, politics, race, gender, or sexuality. And we explore how local religious expressions may be connected to larger religious movements or institutions.

Anthropologists have compiled a vast and diverse set of data on religious beliefs and practices worldwide. But are there any common characteristics that

What is religion? At the 600-year-old Prasanna Ganapathi Temple in Bangalore, India, a Hindu priest performs ritual blessings of new cars, auto rickshaws, and motorbikes to bestow divine protections on car and owner.

apply in every situation? In general, we find that all local expressions of religion combine some, but not necessarily all, of the following elements:

- Belief in powers or deities whose abilities transcend those of the natural world and cannot be measured by scientific tools.

- Myths and stories that reflect on the meaning and purpose of life, its origins, and humans' place in the universe.

- Ritual activities that reinforce, recall, instill, and explore collective beliefs.

- Powerful symbols, often used in religious rituals, that represent key aspects of the religion for its followers.

- Specialists who assist the average believer to bridge everyday life experiences and the religion's ideals and supernatural aspects.

- Organizations and institutions that preserve, explore, teach, and implement the religion's key beliefs.

- A community of believers.

As a working definition, we might then say that a **religion** is a set of beliefs based on a unique vision of how the world ought to be, often revealed through insights into a supernatural power, and lived out in community. (For an overview of the distribution of adherents to major world religions today, see Figure 13.2. Considering the range of religions shown there, perhaps you can begin to imagine the challenge inherent in creating a working definition to cover such a broad spectrum.)

As social scientists, anthropologists have largely been uninterested in questions of any religion's ultimate truth or falsity. Instead we understand that religious worlds are real, meaningful, and powerful to those who live in them. Our task is to carefully make those worlds come alive for others by capturing their vivid inner life, sense of moral order, dynamic public expressions, and interactions with other systems of meaning and power—whether those religious expressions occur in a remote Chinese village temple or the most famous Catholic cathedral in Rome (Bowie 2006).

religion

A set of beliefs based on a unique vision of how the world ought to be, often revealed through insights into a supernatural power and lived out in community.

LOCAL EXPRESSIONS AND UNIVERSAL DEFINITIONS

Attention to local religious expressions complicates anthropologists' efforts to create a universal definition of religion. In a religious studies course, you would likely use a textbook that allocates one chapter for each of the largest world religions, including Christianity, Islam, Hinduism, Buddhism, Chinese religion, Sikhism, Judaism, and others. Each chapter might include an overview of the religion's history, theology, scriptures, major figures, and formal institutions. Under such an approach, drawing broad comparisons among the major religions

FIGURE 13.2
Religion in Global Perspective

This chart shows estimated relative distribution of adherents to the major world religions. It is worth noting, however, that few countries collect data on religious beliefs and practices; as we will discuss, local religious expressions may not neatly fit these categories.

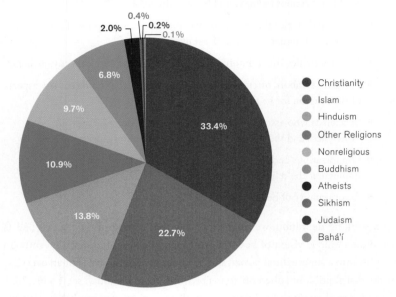

Source: CIA World Factbook, 2014.

can prove helpful in providing a general picture of the world's most established religious traditions and in understanding each religion's ideal expression. At the same time, it may obscure the creative and flexible ways people actually practice their religion that may diverge from the ideal.

Indeed, local expressions and creative adaptations are often at the heart of anthropological research because they reveal how people make a religious tradition come alive in their own context. Let's consider Islam for a moment. Muslims and non-Muslims alike generally regard Islam as highly uniform wherever it is practiced—as a religion that would consistently manifest its core characteristics and definition regardless of location. For example, all Muslims are expected to follow the Five Pillars of Islam: making a declaration of faith, saying prayers five times a day, performing acts of charity, fasting during the holy month of Ramadan, and undertaking a pilgrimage to Mecca. In addition, all Muslims revere the authority of the Quran and the Prophet Muhammad. But on the local level, Muslims frequently expand these formal borders and develop modes of popular expression that may include distinctive devotional practices, life-cycle rituals, marriage customs, ritual clothing, and forms of veiling.

Awareness of the ways in which Muslim life and religious practice vary locally can offer an important insight to an anthropologist conducting research

or to anyone seeking to build relationships across religious boundaries. The example that follows illustrates the possibilities for local variation within a religious tradition that is often assumed to be universal in its expressions.

A Muslim Saint Shrine. Across India, certain popular expressions of Islam push the boundaries of what many people would consider traditional Islam. One example is Husain Tekri, a Muslim saint shrine, or *dargah*, named in memory of the martyred grandson of the Prophet Muhammad. (A **martyr** is a person who sacrifices his or her life for the sake of his or her religion.) Pilgrims from across northern India come to this shrine to remember Husain Tekri, to venerate the Muslim saints, and to participate in healing rituals. (A **saint** is an individual considered exceptionally close to God who is then exalted after death.) Husain Tekri is part of the religious healing circuit of northern India along which both Hindu and Muslim pilgrims travel as they seek the saint or deity with the specific power to cure their ills.

Pilgrims to Husain Tekri may stay for a day or settle in nearby lodges and remain for days, months, or a year. They come in search of healing from suffering, illness, and financial ruin, and relief from the presence of evil spirits (*haziri*). The

Hindu and Muslim pilgrims at the Husain Tekri shrine in northern India breathe in incense to access the healing powers of the shrine.

martyr
A person who sacrifices his or her life for the sake of religion.

saint
An individual who is considered exceptionally close to God and is exalted after death.

main daily ritual activity is the burning and distribution of *loban*—rock-like chunks of incense sold at the shrine and thrown onto red-hot coals eight times a day. As the white smoke of *loban* billows from the braziers, pilgrims—both men and women—are engulfed in the cloud, breathe in the smoke, symbolically consume the *loban,* and absorb its potency. Through pilgrimage and the ritual consumption of *loban*, pilgrims access the healing powers of the shrine. There, they believe, the power and mercy of the martyred Husain and his family enable them to escape their sick bodies, their mental anguish, and the malevolent spirits possessing them.

Surprisingly, pilgrims to the shrine of Husain Tekri are of many religious backgrounds, not only Muslim but also Hindu, Sikh, and Jain. Seeking healing across religious lines is actually a common occurrence in many parts of India, as pilgrims of various faiths try multiple religious systems to find the most successful means of healing, especially for illnesses beyond the powers of mainstream medicine (Bellamy 2011; Flueckiger 2006).

The example above suggests that what are often considered clearly defined, universally uniform, and consistent world religions actually can be flexible and innovative at the local level. From an anthropological perspective, such local expressions of religion are no less complete, meaningful, or true than those taught in the most elite Muslim madrassa, Buddhist monastery, or Christian school of theology.

What Tools Do Anthropologists Use to Understand How Religion Works?

Anthropologists have developed a set of key insights about how religion works that serve as a toolkit for understanding religion as we experience it in our fieldwork. These concepts may prove useful to you in thinking about religion in your own life and in your community, nation, and the world.

Anthropological theories of religion have been deeply influenced by the ideas of nineteenth- and twentieth-century philosophers Émile Durkheim, Karl Marx, and Max Weber. All three examined the connection between religion and the political and economic upheavals of their time: an Industrial Revolution that spurred massive shifts in land relationships throughout western Europe; large-scale rural to urban migration; and high levels of unemployment, poverty, and disease. Through their writing, Durkheim, Marx, and Weber reshaped the study of religion, moving from the theological and cosmological orientation that dominated pre-twentieth-century European and North American thinking to focus on the role of religion in society. These thinkers inspired generations of anthropologists who have expanded and refined their theories.

ÉMILE DURKHEIM: THE SACRED AND THE PROFANE

Émile Durkheim (1858–1917) was a French sociologist who explored ideas of the **sacred** (holy) and the **profane** (unholy), as well as the practical effects of religious **ritual**. His work in these areas has provided key analytical tools for social scientists seeking to understand common elements in different religious movements and the practical application of religious ideas in the social life of religious adherents.

Developing the notion of a fundamental dichotomy between sacred and profane, Durkheim defined religion as "a unified system of beliefs and practices relative to sacred things, that is to say, things set apart and forbidden—beliefs and practices which unite into one single moral community called a Church, all those who adhere to them" ([1912] 1965, 62). Durkheim saw religion as ultimately social—something practiced with others—not private or individual. Through the collective action of religious ritual, group members reaffirm, clarify, and define for one another what is sacred and what is profane. Durkheim's famous study *Elementary Forms of Religious Life* (1912) examined the religious beliefs and practices of Australian aborigines (the indigenous population), which he and others believed to be the most primitive culture of the time and, thus, closest to religion's original forms. The aboriginal "elementary" religious beliefs and practices, he believed, could reveal the most basic elements of religions and shed light on religion's evolution into present forms.

As western European societies experienced radical transformations in the late nineteenth and early twentieth centuries, Durkheim turned to the rising problem of *anomie*—an alienation that individuals experience when faced with physical dislocation and the disruption of social networks and group values. He wondered how society would overcome this crisis and reestablish its essential cohesion. Durkheim argued that religion, particularly religious ritual, plays a crucial role in combating anomie and addressing larger social dynamics of alienation and dislocation by creating social solidarity, cohesion, and stability. He saw religion as the glue that holds together society's many different pieces. Through ritual, Durkheim believed, society is able to regenerate its sense of social solidarity. Ritual defines and reinforces collective ideas of the sacred and profane. Thus, through ritual, the community's sense of cosmic order is reaffirmed, its social solidarity is regenerated, and the group's continued survival and growth are ensured.

Durkheim's work has influenced many anthropologists who have explored the role of ritual in religions and in the wider society. As we will see, the focus on how religion is lived out daily and enacted through ritual has become a cornerstone of the anthropological approach to the study of religion.

French sociologist Émile Durkheim.

sacred

Anything that is considered holy.

profane

Anything that is considered not holy.

ritual

An act or series of acts regularly repeated over years or generations that embody the beliefs of a group of people and create a sense of continuity and belonging.

MAP 13.1
Zambia

Girls kneeling during the *chisungu*, a coming-of-age initiation ceremony among the Bemba people of Zambia.

RELIGION AND RITUAL

Anthropologists of religion have paid particular attention to the role of ritual. Through attention to its central role in religion, anthropologists are aware that religion is not so much talked about as it is *performed* in public displays, rites, and rituals; not so much thought about as it is *danced* and *sung*. Rituals embody the beliefs, passions, and sense of solidarity of a group of people. They make beliefs come alive. When performed repeatedly over years and generations, rituals, as Durkheim suggested, create a sense of continuity and belonging that defines a group and regenerates its sense of solidarity, history, purpose, and meaning.

Rites of Passage. French ethnographer and folklorist Arnold van Gennep (1873–1957) first theorized a category of ritual called **rites of passage** that enacts a change of status from one life stage to another, either for an individual or for a group (van Gennep [1908] 1960). Religious rites of passage are life-transition rituals marking moments of intense change, such as birth, coming of age, marriage, and death.

Audrey Richards (1899–1984), a pioneering British woman in early male-dominated British anthropology, observed and recorded one such rite of passage in 1931 among the Bemba people of Zambia, Central Africa. Their elaborate ritual, called the *chisungu*—a coming-of-age ceremony for young teenage women after first menstruation and in preparation for marriage—was danced in eighteen separate ceremonies over one month in a ritual hut and the surrounding bush. Over fifty special *chisungu* songs and forty different pottery emblems were involved. The *chisungu*, exclusively a women's ritual, was performed to provide magical protection to the girl and her family from the physical dangers of puberty and the magical dangers associated with the first act of intercourse in legal marriage. Within the rituals, older women also passed down the songs, sacred stories, sacred teachings, and secret lore of the Bemba womanhood, marking a clear change of status within the tribe from girl to woman (Richards 1956).

Victor Turner (1920–1983) built on Richards's pioneering work to explore why rituals and rites of passage are so powerful across religions and cultures. Drawing on his own research in Africa and on extensive comparison of cross-cultural data, Turner theorized that the power of ritual comes from the drama contained within it, in which the normal structure of social life is symbolically dissolved and reconstituted. He identified three primary stages in all rites of passage. First, the individual experiences *separation*—physically, psychologically, or symbolically—from the normal, day-to-day activities of the group. This may involve going to a special ritual place, wearing special clothing, or performing actions such as shaving one's head. The second stage, **liminality**, involves a period of outsiderhood during which the ritual participant is set apart from normal society, existing on the margins of everyday life. From this position the individual can gain a new perspective on the past, the present, or the future and thereby experience a new relationship to the community. The final ritual stage, *reaggregation* or *reincorporation*, returns the individual to everyday life and reintegrates him or her into the ritual community, transformed by the experience of liminality and endowed with a deeper sense of meaning, purpose, and connection to the larger group (Turner 1969).

Turner believed that all humans experience these rites of passage and that the experiences shape their perceptions of themselves and their community. Through them, he asserted, humans develop **communitas**: a sense of camaraderie, a common vision of what constitutes the good life, and perhaps most important, a commitment to take social action to move toward achieving this vision. Turner felt that the universal practice and experience of ritual reveals at the root of human existence an underlying desire for community and connection. Based on his cross-cultural investigation of the practice of rituals and rites of passage, Turner suggested that at the center of all human relationships there is a deep longing for shared meaning and connection, not a desire for self-preservation or material gain.

communitas

A sense of camaraderie, a common vision of what constitutes a good life, and a commitment to take social action to move toward achieving this vision that is shaped by the common experience of rites of passage.

Pilgrimage. Turner applied his thinking about rites of passage to the study of religious pilgrimage, which he considered to be a unique form of religious ritual. Pilgrimage rituals, like those to Muslim saint shrines in northern India discussed previously, exist in religions around the world. In a **pilgrimage**, adherents travel to sacred places as a sign of devotion and in search of transformation and enlightenment. For example, all Muslims are obliged to perform, if life

pilgrimage

A religious journey to a sacred place as a sign of devotion and in search of transformation and enlightenment.

Pilgrims circumambulate the Kaaba in Al Masjid al-Haram, the most sacred mosque in Islam, during the *hajj*, in Mecca, Saudi Arabia.

circumstances allow, the *hajj* pilgrimage to Mecca. Jews, Christians, and Muslims all have pilgrimage sites in Jerusalem. Many Hindus travel to the holy city of Varanasi (Benares) to bathe in the Ganges River. Daoists climb Mount Tai in eastern China. The pilgrimage journey, Turner suggested, involves the same process of separation, liminality, and reincorporation associated with other rites of passage. Similarly, pilgrimage creates a shared sense of communitas among those who undertake the journey, even if years or entire generations separate the pilgrimages.

For Turner, life in society is a process of becoming, not being; it is a process of change. He maintained that rituals, pilgrimages, celebrations, and even theatrical performances facilitate this process and have the potential to initiate and foster change, not only in the individual but in the larger culture as well (1969).

KARL MARX: RELIGION AS "THE OPIATE OF THE MASSES"

Karl Marx (1818–1881) was a German political philosopher. He is primarily known for his *Communist Manifesto* (with Friedrich Engels, 1848) and *Capital* (1867), a radical critique of capitalist economics emerging in western Europe in the nineteenth century. However, Marx was also highly critical of the role of religion in society, famously calling religion "the opiate of the masses" (Marx and Engels 1957). What did he mean?

In a time of economic upheaval and intensifying social stratification, Marx warned that religion was like a narcotic: it dulled people's pain so they did not realize how serious the situation was. Religion, Marx argued, played a key role in keeping the proletariat—the working poor—from engaging in the revolutionary social change that he believed was needed to improve their situation.

Marx's statement that religion is "the opiate of the masses" fits within his larger social analysis. He believed that throughout human history, economic realities have formed the foundation of social life and have generated society's primary dynamics, including class stratification and class struggle. He called this economic reality the "base." In his view, the other institutions of culture (including family, government, arts, and religion) arise from and are shaped by economic reality and the deep tensions of economic inequality and class struggle.

The role of these institutions, including religion, according to Marx, is to mask the material conditions and exploitation at the economic base and to contain—or provide a controlled release for—the tensions generated by class difference and class conflict. Religion, which Marx also called "the sigh of the oppressed," could provide to the downtrodden a sense of consolation that the sufferings of this life would end and be rewarded in heaven, thereby offering divine justification for the economic status quo. In Marx's view, religion provided

German political philosopher Karl Marx.

an opiate—a painkiller—to undermine the masses' impulses to resist exploitation and change the social order.

Marx's overall focus on economics and power has pushed anthropologists to consider the relationship between religion and power. Contemporary studies move beyond Marx's idea that religion is merely an illusion that blinds people to economic realities; instead such studies examine how religion can play a complex role in systems of power—both by exercising power through economic resources and the mobilization of religious personnel, and by resisting systems of oppression through alternative ideas, symbols, and resources. The role of the Burmese monks in the chapter-opening story is relevant in this context. As they brought the city of Yangon to a stop in support of human rights activists, they revealed the way religion can exercise its more material power and be a positive force for change in the underlying economic and political order.

Religion and Cultural Materialism. Anthropologist Marvin Harris (1927–2001) built on Marx's analysis of the base, or infrastructure, and the way in which the material conditions of a society shape its other components. Harris's theory of **cultural materialism** argued that material conditions, including technology and the environment, determine patterns of social organization. In this view, human culture is a response to the practical problems of earthly existence. In *Cows, Pigs, Wars, & Witches* (1974), Harris turned this perspective toward many perplexing questions of why humans behave in certain ways—including why Hindus venerate the cow, Jews and Muslims abstain from eating pork, and some people believe in witches. Harris proposed that these practices might have developed in response to very practical problems as people sought to adapt to the natural environment.

Have you ever wondered why cows are considered sacred in India? Harris approached this question not through personal immersion in the worldviews of Indian Hindus, but rather by exploring larger environmental forces—the cultural ecology—that might promote this cultural practice. If you visit India you will find zebu cows—a scrawny, large-humped cattle species found in Africa and Asia—wandering freely about city streets and rural areas. These cows randomly eat food from market stalls, graze on sidewalk shrubs, and defecate indiscriminately. In a country with deep pockets of poverty and malnutrition, why are these cows left to roam and not slaughtered for nutritious, protein-rich dinner beefsteak?

Eating beef is prohibited in Hinduism, as is eating all meat. The cow, in Harris's view, became a symbolic representation of *ahimsa*—the practice of nonviolence and respect for the unity of all life that is key to Hinduism, Buddhism, and Jainism. How this tradition began is unclear, but today the holy mother cow

cultural materialism

A theory that argues that material conditions, including technology, determine patterns of social organization, including religious principles.

MAP 13.2
India

is a symbol of health and abundance, and its image appears throughout Indian culture in media such as posters, movies, and carvings. The symbol also has a literal presence on streets and in fields.

Harris suggests that religious prohibitions protecting the cow have overwhelming practical applications in a culture that relies on agricultural production. Cows, after all, produce calves that grow up to be oxen, which Harris calls the tractor, thresher, and family car of the Indian agricultural system. Without an ox, a family has no way of planting, harvesting, preparing, or transporting its crops. Without an ox, a family loses the capacity to farm and eventually loses its land. Cows also produce vast quantities of dung, almost all of which can be recycled into fertilizer and cooking fuel. Religious dedication to *ahimsa* protects this resource even under the most difficult economic conditions. No matter how hungry the family may be in one season, keeping the cow alive ensures long-term survival.

For Harris, religiously based practices that appear to function in opposition to sound nutritional practices or economic development strategies may in fact be very rational cultural adaptations to the surrounding ecology. In India, the cow is extraordinarily useful. Its protection, especially during difficult economic times, may be essential to the long-term stability and survival of the Indian people and culture.

Think about any other religion, perhaps one you already have an affiliation with. Can you apply the perspectives of Marvin Harris's cultural materialism to any of its practices and beliefs? Can you begin to imagine how certain material conditions of everyday life may have shaped patterns of religious belief and practice?

A sacred cow lies unperturbed and undisturbed in a busy intersection of Varanasi, India. Why is the cow sacred in India?

MAX WEBER: THE PROTESTANT ETHIC AND SECULARIZATION

Max Weber (1864–1920), a German sociologist, philosopher, and economist, considered religious ideas to be a key for understanding the unique development of societies worldwide and the rise of industrial capitalism, particularly in western Europe. Why, he asked, did this highly rationalized, systematized, and industrial form of capitalism emerge in Europe and not in another part of the world?

Unlike Marx, who considered that economics ultimately shapes society, Weber believed that ideas, including religious ideas, can be equally powerful. His book *Sociology of Religion* (1920) was the first sociological attempt to compare the world's religions. In it, Weber suggested that Asian religious beliefs and ethical systems had stood in the way of capitalist economic growth there and had kept Asian economies from developing along the western European path. China, India, and other cultures had developed aspects of modern capitalism even earlier than western Europe did; but without a certain kind of ideological support, a more advanced capitalism had not evolved in Asia. Weber suggested that economic innovations alone could not explain the different paths.

In *The Protestant Ethic and the Spirit of Capitalism* (1905), Weber suggested that the ascetic values of self-denial and self-discipline that developed in western European Protestantism provided the ethic that was necessary for capitalism to flourish. Certain Protestant sects, including Calvinists, felt that it was important to express their religious beliefs and values in a daily lifestyle of thrift, discipline, and hard work. In these ideas, Weber found evidence of the ethical and psychological framework necessary for the success of industrial capitalism. He did not dismiss the role of economics in shaping the social dynamics of western Europe, but he argued that ideas, including religious ideas, may at times equally influence the economic direction of a society.

Also key to the development of Western capitalism, according to Weber, was an increasing systematization and rationalization of religious ideas. As Western Christianity evolved, this increasing rationality brought a decline of practices based on tradition, ritual, and magic. Weber saw these developments echoed in society at large: rationalization led to bureaucracies with clear, intellectual, and systematized rules that replaced tradition, sentiment, and charisma as the operating system in social institutions. Weber imagined an evolution of rationalization in religion that led from (1) traditional religion based on magic and led by shamans; to (2) charismatic religion based on the persuasive power of prophets such as Buddha, Jesus, and Moses; and, finally, to (3) rational religion based on legal codes of conduct, bureaucratic structures, and formally trained religious leaders. He anticipated that this evolutionary process would be almost inevitable. But he warned that as society became more rationalized, it also risked becoming more

German sociologist and philosopher Max Weber.

secular—less religious—and thus losing the very spirit that had driven its success and development.

Scholars have debated Weber's secularization thesis for many years (Stark and Bainbridge 1985; Asad 1993; Casanova 1994; Berger 1999). Certainly in western Europe today, religious identification among native-born residents continues to sink to record lows. In contrast, the United States stands as a striking exception to this pattern in industrialized countries, as religious beliefs and practices remain strong in both the native-born and the immigrant populations. Polls consistently show that nearly 90 percent of the U.S. population believe in God and more than 80 percent identify with a particular religion (Pew Forum on Religion & Public Life 2012). Even the assumed separation of church and state in the United States is far from absolute. Battles continue over the teaching of evolution in the science curriculums of public schools, fans at public high school football games in Texas rise to recite in unison the Christian Lord's Prayer, and crowds at New York's Yankee Stadium stand during the seventh-inning stretch for a moment of silence to remember those serving in the U.S. military and then sing "God Bless America." In these instances, religious sentiments infuse public and political life, and public rituals of civil society take on sacred status (Bellah 1980).

Moreover, widespread revivals of religious ideas, organizations, and movements around the world in the face of increasing modernization—and at times in resistance to the homogenizing influences of globalization and Western culture—provide additional evidence that modernization does not always lead to secularization. The rise of fundamentalist movements in Islam, Hinduism, and Christianity, for instance, suggest that Weber's secularization theory may have limited predictive value.

SHAMANISM

As we saw above, Weber considered the first stage in the evolution of rationalization in religion to involve traditional religion led by shamans. Indeed, more formal religious organizations with trained specialists and elaborate moral rules and ritual practices are fairly recent in human history, spanning two to three thousand years at most with the rise of Hinduism, Buddhism, Judaism, Christianity, and Islam. Throughout much of human history, the religious needs of human communities have been served by **shamans**—part-time religious practitioners with special abilities to connect individuals with supernatural powers or beings. The term *shaman* derives from the name given to healing specialists among the seminomadic people of Siberia, but it has since been applied to healers, spiritualists, witches, and witch doctors in cultures worldwide.

Shamans live as part of the local community, participating in daily activities and work, but are called on at times to perform special rituals and ceremonies.

shaman

A part-time religious practitioner with special abilities to connect individuals with supernatural powers or beings.

They often gain their powers through special training or experience, passing through a journey or test of spirit such as illness, isolation, physical pain, or an emotional ordeal. Through rituals involving prayers, meditation, songs, dance, pain, or drugs, shamans enter a trance, often at will. While entranced, they implore deities and powers to take action or to provide special knowledge and power that may assist individuals or the community at large: healing, medicinal advice, personal guidance, protection from illness or other attack, fortune telling, and control over the weather.

Although the role of the shaman is generally associated with small agricultural or seminomadic societies, shamans today often relocate to contemporary urban settings along with their immigrant communities. A variation of the shaman role also occurs in more formal religious organizations, as trained religious specialists there seek to (1) intervene with their deities on behalf of adherents or (2) assist adherents in practices of prayer and meditation through which they seek healing or guidance.

RELIGION AND MAGIC

Anthropology has a long history of studying cultures where magic is practiced and witches are real. **Magic** involves the use of spells, incantations, words, and actions in an attempt to compel supernatural forces to act in certain ways, whether for good or for evil. Magic is part of cultural practices in every part of the world. And religion, almost everywhere, contains some components of magic.

In *The Golden Bough* (1890), anthropologist James Frazer (1854–1941) distinguishes between imitative magic and contagious magic. **Imitative magic** involves a performance that imitates the desired result, perhaps manipulating a doll or some other representation of the target of magic in the belief that the action will have direct imitative effect. **Contagious magic** centers on the belief that certain materials—perhaps clothing, hair, fingernails, teeth—that have come into contact with one person carry a magical connection that allows power to be transferred from person to person.

In this section we consider the work of E. E. Evans-Pritchard, who sought to understand witchcraft and magic in East Africa; Paul Stoller, who apprenticed with a sorcerer in West Africa; and George Gmelch, who traces the belief in magic in contemporary U.S. society.

E. E. Evans-Pritchard: Rethinking the Logic of Magic.

E. E. Evans-Pritchard (1902–1973), a British anthropologist who conducted extensive fieldwork in Africa's southern Sudan region, challenged Weber's rationalization thesis that assumed modernization and the rise of science would bring increasing rationality in a culture and its religious practices, thereby leading to a decrease in practices of magic. Instead Evans-Pritchard's research among the

magic

The use of spells, incantations, words, and actions in an attempt to compel supernatural forces to act in certain ways, whether for good or for evil.

imitative magic

A ritual performance that achieves efficacy by imitating the desired magical result.

contagious magic

Ritual words or performances that achieve efficacy as certain materials that come into contact with one person carry a magical connection that allows power to be transferred from person to person.

The success of J. R. R. Tolkien's Lord of the Rings trilogy and J. K. Rowling's Harry Potter series has revealed a vast appetite in Western culture for magic, witches, and wizards, at least in their fantastical literary and cinematic form.

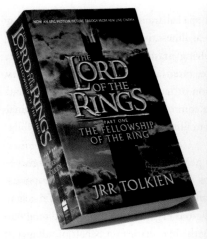

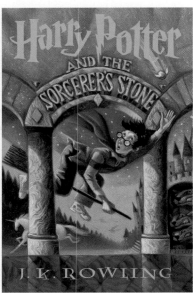

tribal Azande people from 1926 to 1930 found that their use of magic was not an irrational expression but a component of a highly organized, rational, and logical system of thought that complemented science in understanding the way the world works.

In *Witchcraft, Oracles and Magic among the Azande* (1937), Evans-Pritchard describes in careful detail the elaborate religious system of the Azande in which magic, witchcraft, and poison oracles are central elements in daily life and conversation. The Azande trace all misfortunes to witchcraft. Their witchcraft does not involve rituals, spells, or medicines. Instead it is a psychic power that may be used consciously or unconsciously by a witch—a woman or a man—to cause misfortunes or death. Witchcraft is inherited from a parent, and a witch's body contains a witchcraft substance (which the Azande described to Evans-Pritchard as an oval, blackish swelling or bag near the liver of a witch) that cannot be detected during life but can be found during an autopsy.

Magic among the Azande, in contrast to witchcraft, is performed consciously through rites, spells, the preparation of herbal medicines, and other magical techniques. Magic has its own power and can be used to combat witchcraft. If people perceive that magic is being deployed against them, they may consult a witch doctor—almost always a man—who will use magic and medicines to try to thwart the work of the witch.

Witchcraft, Oracles and Magic among the Azande is considered one of the outstanding works of anthropology in the twentieth century. It not only stands as an exquisitely detailed ethnography but also provides the basis for rethinking the

MAP 13.3
Azande region, South Sudan

role of magic in society. Evans-Pritchard challenges the ethnocentric views of Western scholars who dismiss magical practices as irrational and illogical when compared to modern, rational, Western scientific strategies for accumulating knowledge of the external world. He contends instead that Azande ideas that may seem exotic, strange, and irrational to Europeans in actuality formed consistent, comprehensive, and rational systems of thought within the context of the Azande's daily lives and social structures.

Among the Azande, magic explained things that did not make sense otherwise, particularly the experience of misfortune; it provided an alternative theory of causation that supplemented the theory of natural causation. Magic helped explain what could not be explained by scientific study of nature. Evans-Pritchard presented the case of a wooden granary structure that collapsed and injured several people seated underneath it. Science could explain how insects had damaged the wood, which led to the collapse. But science could not explain the misfortune of why the people who were injured were sitting in a particular location at a particular time. For the Azande, witchcraft and magic could explain the misfortune.

Evans-Pritchard argued that the Azande saw no contradiction between witchcraft and empirical knowledge. For them, witchcraft and magic provided a rational and intellectually consistent explanation for what science cannot explain. Belief in witchcraft only appears inconsistent and irrational, Evans-Pritchard chided his Western colleagues, when they are arranged like museum objects on a shelf and examined outside the context of daily life.

Paul Stoller: "In Sorcery's Shadow." In the ethnography *In Sorcery's Shadow* (1987), anthropologist Paul Stoller and his co-author Cherl Olkes extend Evans-Pritchard's commitment to respect and understand others' systems of knowledge, even when they may at first appear irrational, unreasonable, and incomprehensible. Stoller takes Evans-Pritchard's work on magic and sorcery (another term for witchcraft) to a deeper personal level through direct engagement in the beliefs and practices of those he studied.

In the late 1970s Stoller arrived in the Songhay region of the Republic of Niger, West Africa, determined to learn about the role of religion in community life there. Through intensive fieldwork covering five visits over eight years, his deep involvement in a world of magic, spirits, sorcery, and spirit possession prevalent in the Songhay and surrounding regions eventually led him to be initiated as a sorcerer's apprentice. He memorized magical incantations. He ate special foods needed for his initiation. He ingested medicinal powders and wore magical objects to protect himself from antagonistic sorcerers. And he indirectly participated in an attack of sorcery that temporarily paralyzed the intended victim (1987, ix).

MAP 13.4
Songhay region, Niger

A sorcerer preparing a written tablet for a customer in the Songhay region of Niger.

His fieldwork led him to reflect on the transformative and deeply personal experience of conducting research into people's religious worlds:

> Long-term fieldwork and field-language fluency are two important ingredients in the recipe I am compiling. But the most important ingredient, I am convinced, is deep respect for other knowledge, other worlds, and other people. . . . For me, respect means accepting fully beliefs and phenomena which our system of knowledge often holds preposterous. I took my teachers seriously. They *knew* that I used divination in my personal life. They *knew* that I had eaten powders to protect myself. They *knew* I wore objects to demonstrate my respect for the spirits. They *knew* I had an altar in my house over which I recited incantations. They liked the way I carried my knowledge and power and taught me more and more. (1987, 228)

The anthropological commitment to long-term, in-depth participant observation brings many of us into close contact with the beliefs, practices, and emotions of those whom we study, an intimacy that often reveals the vibrant power of religion in their lives that leaves one marked by the encounter.

George Gmelch: Baseball Magic. If reading about the work of Evans-Pritchard and Stoller leaves you relieved that you live in a Western world that relegates belief in magic to children's books and movies, research by anthropologist and former Minor League Baseball player George Gmelch may surprise you. It turns out that beliefs and practices of magic are not so unfamiliar in U.S. culture.

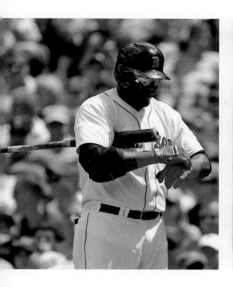

Gmelch's study of baseball in the United States (1992) explores the rituals, taboos, and sacred objects of magic that are in almost constant use. He finds that they reflect the kinds of beliefs and activities that are prevalent in all sports.

Baseball players use charms such as special clothes or jewelry. Moreover, Gmelch found, players believe that good magic is contagious. If it worked before, and if the player uses the same ritual again, perhaps the magical conditions for success can be re-created. Thus players repeat certain actions to help them succeed: Pitchers touch the bill of their cap, wear good-luck charms, or never touch the foul line between home plate and first base when moving between the pitcher's mound and the dugout. Batters wear the same shirt or underwear, or use the same movements over and over again in the batter's box, to capture the magic of previous success.

In baseball, Gmelch found magical thinking to be most prevalent in situations with the most uncertainty. These especially involved pitching and batting, where success rates (the best hitters rarely succeed more than 30 percent of the time) are markedly lower than in fielding (where players successfully complete well over 90 percent of the plays).

Magic rituals, taboos, and sacred objects are used constantly in American sports. *Left:* Boston Red Sox designated hitter David Ortiz adjusts his gloves before every swing, drawing upon a notion of contagious magic to bring him good luck while batting. *Right:* Former New York Mets reliever Turk Wendell's magical practices included always leaping over the baseline when walking to the mound, brushing his teeth between innings, chewing black licorice while pitching, and wearing a necklace decorated with the teeth of wild animals he had hunted and killed.

The study of religion often forces anthropologists to address personal issues of identity, belief, and objectivity in ways that many other areas of study do not. Is it possible to fully understand a religion without being a practitioner? Can someone remain objective if he practices the religion he studies? Anthropologists of religion consider these important questions when conducting fieldwork and writing about their experiences. Through any experience of intensive fieldwork we risk challenging, transforming, and possibly shattering our own worldviews even as we risk influencing those of the people we study. These dynamics are particularly volatile in the study of religion.

In What Ways Is Religion Both a System of Meaning and a System of Power?

Many people in Western cultures think of religion as a system of ideas and beliefs that are primarily a personal matter. In the United States, for instance, doctrines asserting the separation of church and state promote an ideal of the separation of religion from politics. But as we saw in Chapter 2, any analysis of a cultural system that focuses solely on its underlying meanings risks ignoring the ways that power is negotiated within the system and how it engages other systems of power within the culture. This observation applies to our study of religion as well.

RELIGION AND MEANING

Building on the themes of Max Weber's *Protestant Ethic and the Spirit of Capitalism*, anthropologist Clifford Geertz (1926–2006), in his essay "Religion as a Cultural System" (1973b), suggests that religion is essentially a system of ideas surrounding a set of powerful **symbols**. Hindus, for example, consider the cow sacred because by protecting it they symbolically enact the protection of all life. Other widely recognized religious symbols include the cross for Christians, the Torah scroll for Jews, and the holy city of Mecca for Muslims. For Geertz, each symbol has deep meaning and evokes powerful emotions and motivations in the religion's followers. Why?

These symbols acquire significance far beyond the actual material they are made of. Objects made of wood, metal, rock, or paper come to represent influential explanations about what it means to be human and where humans fit in the general order of the universe. Symbols, with their deep pool of meaning, create a sense of order and resist chaos by building and reinforcing a larger worldview—a framework of ideas about what is real, what exists, and what that means.

We can see symbols at work in various religious contexts. For Christians, the bread and wine served at the communion ritual are more than actual bread and wine. They symbolically recall the death and resurrection of Jesus, the power of God to overcome death, and the promise to Jesus's followers of everlasting life beyond the suffering of this world. Communion also recalls the fellowship of all Christian believers who share in the benefits of God's sacrifice, a sense of connection with people around the world. For Jews, the Torah scroll is more than

symbol
Anything that signifies something else.

A Jewish worshiper holds up a Torah scroll to receive a blessing at the Western Wall, Judaism's holiest prayer site, in Jerusalem's Old City. How does an object made of paper and ink become a powerful symbol with deep religious meaning?

a composite of paper and ink. It represents the holy word of God as revealed through the prophets, the story of a covenant between God and the people of Israel, an agreement that in return for faithfulness God will provide liberation from captivity, the establishment of a nation of people, and abundant life. For Hindus, the cow requires veneration because it represents the Hindu practice of *ahimsa*—nonviolence toward all living things. In a practical sense, this means that no leather may enter the temple and all shoes must remain outside the temple door. Even these acts are symbolic of Hindus' belief that all life is sacred and that attention to this fact will transform the practicing individual and lead to his or her reincarnation as a more sentient being.

RELIGION AND POWER

Anthropologist Talal Asad, in his book *Genealogies of Religion* (1993), criticizes Geertz's explanation of religion. Asad bases his inquiry on questions such as these: How did religious symbols get their power? Who or what gave them their authority? What gives religion the power and authority to have meaning in people's lives? After all, Asad asserts, symbols do not have meaning in and of themselves. He suggests that religion and religious symbols are actually produced through complex historical and social developments in which power and meaning are created, contested, and maintained. What historical processes have given the cross, the Torah, the *hajj*, and the cow their symbolic power? Without understanding these particular **authorizing processes**, Asad claims, we cannot understand what really makes religion work.

In the case of Islam, religious beliefs and political power are intricately intertwined in many countries, and national governments may seek to impose

authorizing process

The complex historical and social developments through which symbols are given power and meaning.

a version of Islamic religious law, the Sharia, through mechanisms of the state. Asad suggests that in these cases, Western understandings of the essential nature of religion that assume increasing secularization and separation of church and state may lead scholars and casual observers to dismiss other expressions of religion as irrational and backward. Instead these other religious expressions are simply different—outside the normative definition of religion established in Western scholarship. Asad states that scholars of religion must beware the power of universal definitions to obscure local realities. They must carefully examine local expressions of religion, how those expressions developed over time, and what has given those expressions the power and authority to be so meaningful to believers (Asad 1993).

As you begin to think like an anthropologist of religion, try to examine religious symbols from the perspectives of both Geertz and Asad. As you consider religious symbols in the culture around you—perhaps in your own religious tradition—can you begin to appreciate the power of symbols to evoke intense emotions and motivations that put believers in touch with what feels "really real"? Can you begin to consider the ways in which particular symbols have been constructed, given meaning, and authorized through particular historical and cultural processes?

BLURRING THE BOUNDARIES BETWEEN MEANING AND POWER

The work of both Geertz and Asad has influenced contemporary anthropological research on religion. We now consider a local example of religious activities and organizations in which meaning and power are intertwined and the boundary between religion and other social systems of power is not rigid. As we consider this study, can you begin to see how analyses of both meaning and power are essential in achieving a comprehensive picture of the role of religion in culture?

Religion and Revolution in Mexico. Religion scholar Charlene Floyd's research on the role of the Catholic Church in a revolutionary movement in the Chiapas region of southern Mexico (1996) provides an example of how meaning and power are expressed in religion. Chiapas is one of the poorest states in Mexico, where most children do not finish primary school and many homes have no running water. The people are poor, but the land is rich: it holds large reserves of oil and natural gas, provides most of the country's hydroelectric power, and supports half of its coffee crop. The tension between an impoverished people, on the one hand, and rich natural resources extracted by Mexico's state and corporations, on the other, has not always found a smooth resolution.

In the early hours of January 1, 1994, some of the poor people of Chiapas, calling themselves "Zapatistas" (after the Mexican revolutionary Emiliano

Zapata), covered their faces with bandanas and ski masks, marched into four Chiapas cities, and declared in a dramatic manifesto, "Today we say enough is enough!" Stunned by the uprising, the Mexican government and the economic leaders of Chiapas quickly accused the Catholic Church of inciting the rebellion. In particular, they blamed one of the bishops of Chiapas, Samuel Ruiz García, and his *catequistas*, or lay teachers. But how could a Catholic bishop and a group of lay teachers be accused of inciting a rebellion? Did they actually do so? In considering these questions, we must explore the Church's role in Mexican society.

Today 90 percent of Mexicans identify themselves as Catholic, a faith that has been a key component of Mexican national identity ever since Spanish colonizers forcibly imported it five hundred years ago. In certain periods of Mexican history, religion and politics have been closely aligned. For example, a Catholic priest, Father Miguel Hidalgo y Costilla, is credited with providing the initial spark for the Mexican independence movement in 1810. Calling on the name of Mexico's indigenous saint, the Virgin of Guadalupe, Father Hidalgo challenged his parishioners by asking, "Will you free yourselves?" Despite periods of alignment, Mexican history has seen ongoing tensions between the powerful institution of the Catholic Church (which has been one of Mexico's largest land-holders) and the Mexican state. The Church has been involved in political movements in Mexico before, but did it have a role in the 1994 uprising in Chiapas? A quick look at recent church history may shed light on this question.

In 1959 Pope John XXIII called for a Vatican Council to modernize the Catholic Church. By the end of this conference (1962–65), commonly called Vatican II, the Catholic Church had begun a dramatic revolution in theology and practice. In an attempt to redefine the Church as "the people of God" rather than an institution, Vatican II moved to make local congregations more accessible to the layperson. Congregations were allowed to worship in their own local language rather than Latin. Priests and lay members were encouraged to open the Church more fully to the world, using the Church as an instrument of liberation in people's lives, as a servant to the poor rather than an ally of the politically powerful.

Bishop Samuel Ruiz García, head of the Diocese of San Cristóbal de las Casas in Chiapas, where the Zapatista uprising occurred, attended Vatican II and a subsequent meeting in 1968 of Latin American Catholic leaders. He returned to Mexico determined to implement the new theology of liberation: he would put the Church to work to better the life conditions of the one million primarily indigenous people in his diocese. The diocesan program for training lay teachers, called *catequistas*, transformed its curriculum from a primary focus on Church doctrine, scriptures, law, liturgy, and music to include concerns of community life and social needs. By the time of the Zapatista uprising, the *catequistas* had

Catholic bishop Samuel Ruiz of San Cristóbal in Chiapas, southern Mexico, and the church's network of *catequistas*, or lay teachers, have been accused by the Mexican government of inciting rebellion.

grown from seven hundred to eight thousand. Most were now elected by their local indigenous communities; they were deeply involved not only in traditional Catholic religious education but also in the empowerment of indigenous people in their struggles against poverty. *Catequistas* developed prominent roles as community and political leaders, accompanying their constituents in efforts to eradicate poverty and landlessness in Chiapas and to open the state's political process to greater participation from people at the grassroots.

Were Bishop Ruiz and the *catequistas* responsible for the 1994 Zapatista uprising? No accusations have been proven of a direct role in the Zapatista leadership. But did the *catequistas'* theology of liberation, expressing the Catholic Church's desire for the empowerment of indigenous people and the elimination of poverty, provide moral support and practical training to communities engaged in this struggle? If so, then the Catholic Church of Chiapas provides an instructive example for anthropologists—of how we must consider the role of religious ideas, symbols, and engagements with other systems of power to understand religion in all its fullness (Floyd 1996).

How Is Globalization Changing Religion?

The forces of globalization—especially migration and time-space compression—are stretching and shaping religions and religious practices. Increasing immigration sometimes means that whole communities—their beliefs, religious

How are religious practices crossing national borders in a global age? Every December Mexican Catholic immigrants in New York City march carrying portraits of Our Lady of Guadalupe, patron saint of Mexico.

architecture, religious leaders, and even their gods—relocate across national boundaries. Travel is broadening the encounters of people of different faiths. At the same time, information about religion is more widely available, and communication technologies enable religious institutions to transform their strategies for cultivating and educating participants. Cities, especially those serving as immigrant gateways, are generally the focal point of this increasing encounter. It is here that new immigrants revitalize older religious institutions and construct new ones, often establishing deep ties to home and sophisticated networks of transnational exchange. For example, throughout the United States, Catholic churches are being rejuvenated as immigration from heavily Catholic countries brings new membership, worship styles, social needs, and political engagements. In response, local Catholic churches and key U.S. Catholic leadership have actively supported the reform of U.S. immigration laws. Indeed, the Church saw as a key human rights issue the reuniting of families across the border and eliminating opportunities for the exploitation of vulnerable, low-wage workers. At the same time, today's immigrants are reshaping the Church's future—just as immigrant waves from Ireland, Germany, and Italy did in the nineteenth century.

RELOCATING RITUALS AND DEITIES FROM THE HOME COUNTRY

Globalization is transforming the ritual practices of religious communities large and small as congregations adapt to their members' mobility and the lively flow of ideas, information, and money across borders. These dynamics have rapidly spread the religious practices of a small, local, village Daoist temple in rural

China to New York and beyond through a network of Chinese restaurants opening across the United States. Today, thanks to globalization, the village temple's adherents and their local god have become international border-crossing immigrants.

Immigrant Chinese Gods. A few years ago, I walked into a little temple just off Canal Street in Manhattan's Chinatown as part of a project to map the Chinese religious communities in New York City (Guest 2003). Women and men, young and old, crowded into the noisy and smoky old storefront space, lighting incense, chatting with old friends, and saying prayers at the altar. Most were from the same small village in southeastern China, outside the provincial capital of Fuzhou. They had opened this temple to continue their religious practices in the United States and to serve as a gathering place for fellow immigrant villagers who lived and worked in and around New York City. Here, immigrants can reconnect with friends and relatives from their hometown, participate in rituals of devotion to their deities, and build networks of fellow devotees they may not have known before arriving in New York.

For a highly transient population, the temple serves as a center for exchanging information about jobs, housing, lawyers, doctors, employment agencies, and more. It operates a revolving loan fund for members to pay off smuggling debts or start up a take-out restaurant. Through the temple, members contribute to building their home temple and support other charitable projects in their home community back in China. Despite the undocumented status of many of these immigrants, the temple provides a way to participate in civic activities and express themselves as contributing members of the community.

I later visited the home village temple in China to learn about village life and local religious traditions. One evening as I prepared to leave, the master of the temple expressed disappointment that I had not been able to meet the temple's spirit medium, a young woman who had a special relationship with the village's local god. He explained that on the first and fifteenth day of each lunar month, the local god possesses her and speaks through her to interpret the villagers' dreams and answer their questions: What name should I give my child? What herbal remedy will cure my ill? Will this woman be a good match for my son? When should I try to be smuggled out of China to the United States? I shared the master's disappointment at this missed opportunity and readily accepted his invitation to return on a future visit.

A year later I did return. The spirit medium, however, was gone. She and her husband, the temple master informed me, had moved to the United States and were now working in a restaurant in a place called "Indiana." I was disappointed again, but I expressed my concern that their departure may have disrupted a key element of temple life. The master then told me this story:

> Actually she still does it—only now it's from Indiana. Our believers work in restaurants all over the United States and some are still here in China. When they want to ask the advice of the god, they just pick up their cell phones and call. The spirit medium keeps careful records of their questions and dreams. Then on the first and fifteenth of the lunar month, just as always used to happen when she was here, she goes into a trance. The god leaves our temple here in China and flies to Indiana to possess her. Her husband then asks all the questions and writes down the answers. When the possession is over, the god returns to our village, and the spirit medium and her husband return all the phone calls to report the wisdom of the god.

Perhaps the look on my face and my one raised eyebrow alerted the master to my initial skepticism. "We can feel the god leave here every time," he said. "Really. Why don't you believe that? In America you have lots of Christians who believe the Christian god can be everywhere in the world at the same time. Why can't ours?"

The more I thought about it, the more I wondered why the local god of a village in China couldn't also be in Indiana. As an anthropologist of religion, I was reminded once again that religious practices and beliefs in today's age of globalization continue to be fluid and adaptable. After all, humans are adaptable, and so are their cultural constructions. Religion is a vibrant example of this core anthropological insight.

Toolkit

Thinking Like an Anthropologist: Religion in the Twenty-First Century

After reading this chapter, you should have a deeper understanding of some of the approaches anthropologists take to understanding the role of religion in people's lives and in communities large and small. These insights can serve as a toolkit as you consider expressions of religion in other countries and at home in the United States.

Think again about the Buddhist monks' protest that opened the chapter, and recall the key questions we have asked about religion:

- **What is religion?**
- **What tools do anthropologists use to understand how religion works?**
- **In what ways is religion both a system of meaning and a system of power?**
- **How is globalization changing religion?**

After reading the chapter, can you apply the writings of Durkheim, Marx, Weber, Geertz, and Asad to events in the real world? Can you see concepts of sacred and profane, ritual, rite of passage, communitas, symbol, and power emerge in the actual expressions of religion in Myanmar?

Despite the symbolic power and dramatic physical presence of the Buddhist monks' protests in 2007, a brutal military crackdown put an end to the demonstrations just a few days later. Yet despite the short-term setback, in hindsight one may consider the long-term effects these religious actions may have had on more recent events. The monks' protests demonstrated deep opposition within Myanmar society to the military government—not only by students and workers, but also by 500,000 religious professionals who wielded both symbolic power and a willingness to engage in direct action. In a country where the military government was unaccustomed to organized resistance, the monks demonstrated that through their religious networks they are organized, meet regularly, enjoy an independent communication network, honor their vows of obedience to an authority other than the government, and articulate an alternative vision of a just and peaceful society.

National elections held the following year (2008) were considered by most observers to be rampant with fraud. But shortly afterward, the government began to introduce economic and political reforms that have brought a positive transformation to Myanmar. The changes include dramatic success by the main opposition party in April 2012 elections. What role might the 2007 religious protests have played in creating the environment for political and economic developments in the ensuing years?

Key Terms

religion (p. 365)

martyr (p. 367)

saint (p. 367)

sacred (p. 369)

profane (p. 369)

ritual (p. 369)

rite of passage (p. 370)

liminality (p. 370)

communitas (p. 371)

pilgrimage (p. 371)

cultural materialism (p. 373)

shaman (p. 376)

magic (p. 377)

imitative magic (p. 377)

contagious magic (p. 377)

symbol (p. 382)

authorizing process (p. 383)

Chapter 14
Health and Illness

When we hear about people who live to a ripe old age, such as the twins on the opposite page, we tend to attribute their longevity to good genes or a healthy lifestyle. But is that the whole picture? What is the total range of factors that lead to good health? Let's look at another region of the world to get a broader perspective.

North of the Texas–Mexico border, half a million people live in impoverished communities called *colonias*. Established in the 1950s to house migrant Mexican workers brought to work on America's farms, *colonias* now are permanent settlements. Located largely outside incorporated towns and cities, many lack municipal services of water, sewage, paved roads, and public transport. Fully 64 percent of residents were born in the United States,

---

What makes someone healthy? The oldest twins in the world, sisters Ena Pugh and Lily Millward of Garthbrengy, Wales, turned 100 on January 4, 2010, to much fanfare. The national papers touted the sisters' simple lifestyle, love of laughter, close family ties, exercise, religious faith, and good deeds. "Great-grandmother Lily revealed the secret of their long life is 'laughter and having a joke with each other.' She said 'We used to work on the farm all day, but we would enjoy ourselves.' 'It was a lot of fun and sociable. We've been very lucky and we have always been in good health'" (Daily Mail 2010).

including 85 percent of those under age eighteen. Still, residents of *colonias* struggle to maintain their health. They have limited access to health care, and what they receive lacks continuity between visits. As of 2011, 80 percent had no health insurance. The Texas Department of State Health Services reported incidences of dysentery, cholera, and hepatitis A in the *colonias* far above the state average. Tuberculosis rates were double the state average and four times the U.S. national average. Asthma and bronchitis were common ailments, as were mosquito and tick-borne illnesses such as dengue fever and Lyme disease. Even Hansen's disease, also known as leprosy, continued to occur (Ramshaw 2011).

What accounts for the health disparities between the hundred-year-old British twins and the residents of the *colonias*? Conventional wisdom attributes health and longevity to a combination of "good genes" and good behavioral choices: eating right, not smoking, drinking in moderation, avoiding illegal drugs, exercising, and even flossing. These criteria mesh with core American values of individualism, personal responsibility, and the benefits of hard work and clean living. But are these factors sufficient to explain health and longevity—or the lack of it? Getting sick is a part of life. Everyone experiences colds, fevers, cuts and bruises, perhaps a broken bone. But some people get sick more often than others. Death and dying are part of life; but some people suffer more and die sooner, while others are healthier and live longer. Anthropologists are interested in knowing why.

In this chapter we will explore anthropologists' growing interest in health and illness. Although these concerns have deep roots in our discipline, the specialization of *medical anthropology* has grown immensely since the 1980s as our discipline's key research strategies—intensive fieldwork, extensive participant observation in local communities, and deep immersion in the daily lives of people and their local problems and experiences—have proven profoundly effective in solving pressing public health problems.

Medical anthropologists employ a variety of analytical perspectives to examine the wide range of experiences and practices that humans associate with disease, illness, health, and well-being—both today and in the past. We study the spread of disease and pathogens through the human population (known as epidemiology) by examining the *medical ecology*: the interaction of diseases with the natural environment and human culture. Looking more broadly, medical anthropologists use an *interpretivist approach* to study health systems as systems of meaning: How do humans across cultures make sense of health and illness? How do we think and talk and feel about illness, pain, suffering, birth, and mortality? *Critical medical anthropology* explores the impact of inequality on human health in two important ways. First, it considers how economic and political systems, race, class, gender, and sexuality create and perpetuate unequal access to health care. Second, it examines how health systems themselves are systems of power that promote disparities in health by defining who is sick, who gets treated, and how the treatment is provided.

Medical anthropology's holistic approach to health and illness—examining epidemiology, meaning, and power—assumes that health and illness are more than a result of germs, individual behavior, and genes. Health is also a product of our environment; our access to adequate nutrition, housing, education, and health care; and the absence of poverty, violence, and warfare.

In this chapter we will explore the following questions:

- **How does culture shape our ideas of health and illness?**
- **How can anthropologists help solve health care problems?**
- **Why does the distribution of health and illness mirror that of wealth and power?**
- **How is globalization changing the experience of health and illness and the practice of medicine?**

By the end of the chapter you will understand how anthropologists approach the study of health and illness and how these concepts vary across cultures. You will be able to recognize how your own conceptions of health and illness are a cultural construction. You will be able to critically analyze both the systems of power that shape access to health care and the way in which health systems create and exacerbate inequalities within and between populations.

How Does Culture Shape Our Ideas of Health and Illness?

What does it mean to be healthy? The World Health Organization proposes that **health** includes not merely the absence of disease and infirmity but complete physical, mental, and social well-being. This is a standard that few people in the world currently attain. Perhaps it is enough to be functionally healthy—not perfectly well, but healthy enough to do what you need to do: get up in the morning, go to school, go to work, reproduce the species. What level of health do you expect, hope for, and strive for? What level of health enables your culture to thrive?

Medical anthropologists have dedicated significant effort to document healing practices and health systems around the globe, from indigenous and tribal communities and urban metropolises to farming communities and groups of migrant workers. In the process, medical anthropologists have identified a vast array of healing practices and health systems created by people worldwide—ideas about the causes of health and disease, and varied cultural strategies to address pain, treat illness, and promote health. One key finding is that these beliefs and practices are intricately intertwined with the way local cultures imagine the world works and the relationship of an individual's body to his or her surroundings.

health
The absence of disease and infirmity, as well as the presence of physical, mental, and social well-being.

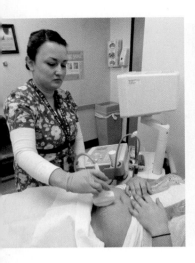

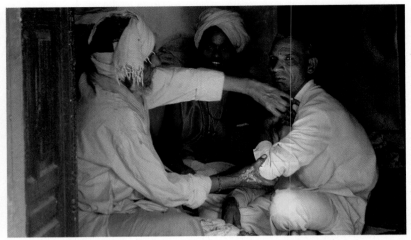

Globally, people have created a vast array of healing practices, all intricately intertwined with local cultural understandings of disease, health, illness, and the body. *Left*: A clinical assistant performs an ultrasound sonogram on a pregnant woman. *Right*: An Indian healer provides a villager with an ayurvedic massage.

disease

A discrete natural entity that can be clinically identified and treated by a health professional.

illness

The individual patient's experience of sickness.

In assessing how disease and health conditions affect specific populations and how specific cultural groups diagnose, manage, and treat health-related problems, medical anthropologists have found it useful to distinguish between disease and illness. A **disease** is a discrete, natural entity that can be clinically identified and treated by a health professional. A disease may be caused genetically or through infection by bacteria, a virus, or parasites. But the bacteria, virus, or parasite are the same regardless of location or cultural context. Illness, however, is more than the biological disease. **Illness** is the individual patient's experience of sickness—the culturally defined understanding of disease. It includes the way he or she feels about it, talks about it, thinks about it, and experiences it within a particular cultural context. Diseases can be observed, measured, and treated by sufferers and healers. But culture gives meaning to disease, shaping the human experience of illness, pain, suffering, dying, and death (Singer and Baer 2007).

People recognize widely different symptoms, illnesses, and causes for health challenges and have developed widely different strategies for achieving and maintaining health. Though the stereotypical Western images of health care often revolve around doctors in white coats, dentists' chairs, hospitals, strong medications, and advanced technology (such as X-rays, MRIs, and CT scans), medical anthropologists have found that these are not the primary points of access to health care for most people in the world. Nor are they even the first point of access for most people in Western countries. Rather, before seeking the assistance of a trained medical professional, people everywhere apply their personal medical knowledge, their own strategies—often handed down within families or communities—for dealing with disease, illness, pain, and discomfort.

THE ANTHROPOLOGY OF CHILDBIRTH

The anthropology of childbirth provides one clear example of the cross-cultural variation of health beliefs and practices. Childbirth is a universal biological event.

Indeed, the physiology of childbirth—the biological process—is the same no matter where the birth occurs. But anthropological research shows that cultures around the world have developed unique practices and beliefs about pregnancy, delivery, and the treatment of newborns and their mothers that shape the way childbirth is understood and experienced.

A Comparative View of Four Cultures. Different cultures conceptualize birth in different ways, and these shared understandings shape women's experiences. For example, a popular view of birth in the United States sees it as a medical procedure—what Robbie Davis-Floyd calls the "technocratic birth" (Davis-Floyd 1992). In this view, women become patients—sick and helpless, seeking the assistance of a medical professional to resolve a dangerous life crisis. In contrast, in Holland birth is perceived as an entirely natural process; in Sweden, as an intensely personal and fulfilling achievement; in Yucatán, Mexico, as a stressful but normal part of life. These differing conceptualizations shape and justify the practices each culture puts into place to support, monitor, and control the birth process. Such practices include the location of the birth, the personnel who attend, the decision-making authority as the birth proceeds, and the expectations of pain and pain management. These differences underlie Brigitte Jordan and Robbie Davis-Floyd's (1993) study *Birth in Four Cultures*.

Birth experiences in Yucatán and the United States contrast sharply. Birth for many Mayan women surveyed in Jordan's study occurred in a small, dimly lit home with a dirt floor, attended by a local midwife using everyday materials, while family life continued around them. Mayan women rested in a hammock, considered the best position for labor, although in the final stages of pushing the women might sit astride a wooden chair turned on its side. The husband and the woman's mother were usually present throughout the entire process. Other women of the extended family, particularly those who had given birth before, might be present as well. During the final stages of labor, the husband and the woman's mother took turns sitting behind the woman, supporting her head and lifting her up toward the ceiling to relieve pressure from the contractions. In a difficult labor, other women would provide emotional and physical support, offering encouragement and participating in "birth talk" by urging, cajoling, and challenging the mother to finish pushing her baby out into the world. There were no drugs and no machines (Jordan and Davis-Floyd 1993).

In contrast, 98 percent of American births today occur in a sterile, brightly lit hospital with sophisticated equipment and the attention of highly trained medical professionals who enforce a strict separation of the laboring mother from family and daily life. The father may be present. Elaborate machinery monitors pregnancy and birth. Sonograms and amniocentesis assess the health of the fetus during pregnancy, and fetal heart monitors track the newborn's heartbeat and stress levels during delivery. Medications are sometimes administered through

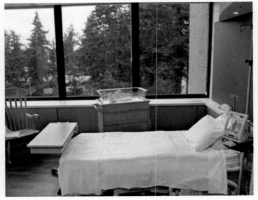

epidural injections near the spinal cord to deaden the mother's pain. To advance childbirth during a difficult delivery, obstetricians may perform episiotomies, surgically widening the opening to the birth canal.

In 2010, one-third of all babies in the United States were delivered by cesarean section, a surgical procedure by which the baby is removed directly from the mother's abdomen rather than through the birth canal. This number was an increase from 20.7 percent in 1996 (U.S. Centers for Disease Control 2012). This rate of C-sections is among the highest in the world, a fact that raises questions about whether these procedures are performed out of necessity or are influenced by cultural understandings of birth and the institutional pressures that shape health care in hospitals. Rates also vary from region to region in the United States, a reflection of the regional cultural variations in the practice of Western medicine rather than an indication of regional variation in rates of complications.

Pain during Childbirth. Can culture shape women's experience of pain during childbirth? Jordan notes that some women in every culture give birth without pain. But a certain amount of pain is expected in almost all cultures. What differs from one medical system to another is the way in which that pain is handled. Jordan's study explores the possibility that cultural expectations of pain during childbirth shape the actual experience and display of pain by laboring mothers.

The introduction of pain medication during childbirth is a recent phenomenon, emerging as part of twentieth-century medicine. Jordan's study found that the use of pain medication during labor was not consistent across cultures. In the United States, pain medication was administered at the discretion of the medical attendants and was often delayed lest the drugs slow the course of labor. Jordan also found that to receive medication, a woman must convince her physician that her pain is severe. Jordan suggests that this dynamic shaped the woman's experience of childbirth, drawing attention away from the delivery and more toward

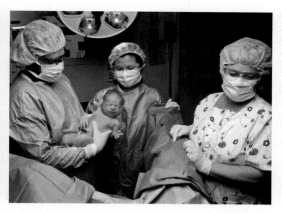

pain—both the experience of pain and the performance of that pain. Obstetric wards in the United States, notes Jordan, as a result of this negotiation between patient and physician, have a relatively high level of noise, anxiety, and vocal despair bordering on panic during the birth process.

In contrast, obstetric wards in Sweden are characterized by quiet, intense concentration on the process of giving birth. Before labor begins, Swedish women are introduced to a variety of pain medicines, their benefits, and side effects. During labor the women themselves make decisions about how much, if any, medication to take and when. Women do not need to convince medical staff of the need for pain medication.

The Dutch view birth as an entirely natural process. They administer no pain medication during the normal course of labor, even in many of the same situations that would lead to the use of pain medication in the United States. The Dutch, like the Maya of Yucatán, are reluctant to interfere with the birth process, waiting for nature to take its course and trusting that women's bodies know best how to handle the process. Birth is not considered a crisis or a medical emergency.

In Yucatán, pain is seen as a natural and expected part of childbirth. It is not frightening. The work of labor is considered a normal part of life. In this view the suffering and pain will pass soon, especially if the mother works hard. Labor is considered a collective process—an experience shared by the woman's husband, mother, and female family members. The pain marks a significant yet normal part of the life experience.

Jordan reflects that the intense experience of childbirth reinforces key Mayan cultural values, particularly local understandings of the importance of hard work, endurance, and the tolerance of difficulty. The Maya view these values and personal qualities as desirable in childbirth as well as in life. During the stress of childbirth, women display these qualities in the public sphere.

The variation of cultural approaches to labor and childbirth—a common human biological activity—suggests the extent to which cultural concepts of the body, health, illness, and pain may shape every aspect of a medical system.

ETHNOMEDICINE

ethnomedicine

Local systems of health and healing rooted in culturally specific norms and values.

Over the years, medical anthropologists have focused extensive research on **ethnomedicine**. This field involves the comparative study of local systems of health and healing rooted in culturally specific norms and values; it includes the ways in which local cultures create unique strategies for identifying and treating disease and conceptualizing the experience of health, illness, and the physical world.

Early research on ethnomedicine focused primarily on non-Western health systems and emphasized natural healing remedies such as herbs, teas, and massage; reliance on religious ritual in health practices; and the role of locally trained healers such as shamans, spirit mediums, and priests as health care professionals. The subdiscipline of **ethnopharmacology** emerged from efforts to document and describe the local use of natural substances, such as herbs, powders, teas, and animal products, in healing remedies and practices. But today, as we will see, even Western biomedicine, which emphasizes science and technology in healing but also reflects a particular system of cultural meanings, is considered through the lens of ethnomedicine. Today medical anthropologists use the concept of ethnomedicine to refer to local health systems everywhere (Saillant and Genest 2007; Green 1999).

ethnopharmacology

The documentation and description of the local use of natural substances in healing remedies and practices.

MAP 14.1
Ladakh

Healing Practices of Tibetan Buddhism Applied in Northern India.
French anthropologist Laurent Pordié (2008) has documented one typical system of ethnomedicine—a variation of Tibetan medicine practiced in the sparsely populated Ladakh region of northern India. Roughly three times the size of Switzerland and straddling the northwestern Himalayas, Ladakh is home to 250,000 villagers, mostly Tibetans, living primarily in remote areas at altitudes up to 5,000 meters (16,400 feet). Their only health care is provided by approximately two hundred *amchis*, traditional healers whose healing practices are deeply rooted in Tibetan Buddhism.

Amchi medicine is based on achieving bodily and spiritual balance between the individual and the surrounding universe. *Amchis* diagnose ailments by asking questions of the patient, examining bodily wastes, and carefully taking the pulse. Recommended treatments include changes in diet and behavior—both social and religious—and the use of natural medicines made from local plants and minerals. Shaped into pills, these remedies are then boiled in water and taken by the patient as an infusion, or drink. Pordié reports that *amchi* treatments are effective for the vast majority of the Ladakhis' health problems, such as respiratory

difficulty from the high altitude and smoke in dwellings, hypertension from high-salt diets, and psychological stress. *Amchis* do not perform surgery. Patients who need surgery are transported, if possible, to an urban area to be treated by a doctor trained in Western biological medicine.

Amchi medicine plays a vital role in the survival of Ladakhis. But the *amchis* and their healing practices are under threat from Westernization, militarization, and economic liberalization. For example, the Indian government strongly favors Western biological medicine over traditional ethnomedicine, though it is still unable to provide care to its dispersed rural population. The pervasive presence of the Indian military in response to civil unrest in the bordering Kashmir region inhibits the movement of *amchis* as they gather plants and minerals for natural medicines. In addition, urbanization and modernization, particularly market-oriented economic activity, have increasingly fragmented community life. In the past, *amchi* healers bartered their services for help in plowing, harvesting, and raising livestock. The *amchis* then had time to forage for medicinal plants. But with the penetration of market-oriented economics even into the rural areas, the barter system has been undermined. *Amchis* must now run their therapeutic practices more like businesses, selling medicines and charging for services rather than bartering. Their time to gather medicines has become limited. And with increasing social mobility, the intergenerational transmission of *amchi* skills has been disrupted.

To address this challenge to the *amchi* system, Pordié and a French non-governmental organization, Nomad RSI, have been working with local *amchis* to establish a coordinated system for growing medicinal plants and distributing them among far-flung villages. *Amchis* from across Ladakh now gather annually to share diagnosis and treatment strategies, and a school has been established to train new practitioners.

Although Tibetan medicine struggles in rural areas where it has been practiced for centuries, it is experiencing unprecedented prominence internationally. Pordié's study also considers how the local *amchi* system of healing is entering the global health arena. Over the last thirty years, as more Tibetans migrate abroad and carry their cultural and religious practices with them, Tibetan medicine has been embraced as an "alternative medicine." The international health market, particularly in Europe and North America, has welcomed Tibetan medicine as natural, spiritual, and holistic, drawing as it does from indigenous, traditional practices, Buddhist moral values, and Tibetan ecological worldviews. *Amchis* and their practices of Tibetan medicine have become quite popular. In this era of globalization, a transnational *amchi* is just as authentic as the *amchi* prescribing healing remedies in a remote village in Ladakh.

From the perspective of medical anthropology, all medical systems constitute a form of ethnomedicine because they develop from and are embedded in a particular local cultural reality. Medical anthropologists have played a significant role in documenting the diverse forms of treatment and care as well as the complex medical epistemologies (ways of knowing) that have been developed by local cultures across the globe. From the perspective of medical anthropology, we might call all healers ethno-healers, practicing local health knowledge about disease, illness, and health. We now turn to consider why this may be true, whether the healer is an *amchi* or a cardiovascular surgeon.

BIOMEDICINE

biomedicine

A practice, often associated with Western medicine, that seeks to apply the principles of biology and the natural sciences to the practice of diagnosing disease and promoting healing.

Biomedicine is the approach to health that has risen to predominance in many Western cultures. **Biomedicine** seeks to apply the principles of biology and the natural sciences (such as physics and chemistry) to the practice of diagnosing diseases and promoting healing. Individual and institutional practitioners of biomedicine—whether doctors, pharmacies, hospitals, medical schools, or pharmaceutical companies—work to clinically identify discrete natural disease entities that can be diagnosed and treated by biomedically trained health professionals. The term *biomedicine* encompasses many local variations and a wide range of treatment practices. But the use of medication, surgery, and other invasive treatments is characteristic of biomedical healing practices (Saillant and Genest 2007; Baer, Singer, and Susser 2003).

Varieties of biomedicine occur across Western industrialized countries, as we considered in our earlier discussion of the anthropology of birth. For example, British doctors are far less concerned about elevated blood pressure and

Western biomedicine or alternative medicines? At a biotech company near Berlin, Germany, researchers develop natural remedies to complement biomedical treatments.

cholesterol counts than are their counterparts in the United States. The German health system, which uses far fewer antibiotics than other Western health systems, recognizes two complementary approaches: *schulmedizin* ("school medicine"), which focuses on typical biomedical treatments, and *naturheilkunde* ("nature cure"), which draws on natural remedies. Biomedicine in the United States emphasizes the most extreme treatments—psychotropic drugs, antibiotics, cholesterol and blood pressure medications, C-section births, hysterectomies, and breast cancer screenings (Payer 1996).

Because biomedicine is closely linked with Western economic and political expansion, it has taken hold well beyond its original local cultural boundaries and increasingly has gained an aura of universality, modernity, and progress. But medical anthropologists have been careful to point out the ways in which, like other ethnomedical systems, the epistemology (ways of knowing) and practice of Western biomedicine are rooted in a particular system of knowledge that draws heavily on European enlightenment values. This system includes ideas of rationality, individualism, and progress—values and ideas that are culturally specific and not universally held. The individual body is the focus of treatment. Diagnosis and treatment are based on rational scientific data. And there is a firm conviction that direct intervention through surgery and medications based on scientific facts will positively affect health.

Biomedical Conceptions of the Body. Nancy Scheper-Hughes and Margaret Lock (1987) recount a now-famous story of a challenging case that illustrates the powerful influence of cultural values on biomedical healing practices. At a teaching hospital, the case of a woman suffering chronic, debilitating headaches was presented to a lecture hall of 250 medical students. When asked about her ailment, the woman recounted that her alcoholic husband beat her, that she had been virtually housebound for five years while caring for her ailing and incontinent mother-in-law, and that she worried about her teenage son, who was failing out of high school. Then one of the medical students raised her hand and asked, "But what is the *real* cause of her headaches?" By this the student meant, What is the real *biomedical* diagnosis; what neurochemical changes created the pain? In the mind of the medical student, the patient's statements were irrelevant to the task of identifying the cause of her pain or determining a treatment. The student's biomedical training, with its focus on the individual body, science, and technology, had not prepared her to recognize that social experiences might produce embodied responses.

The Human Microbiome. Is a typical biomedical notion of the discrete, treatable, individual body really based in science? Recent scientific research suggests that our bodies are not as independent or as self-contained as we have thought. Researchers at the Human Microbiome Project have discovered that the human body, made up of ten trillion cells, is also host to one hundred trillion microbes—microscopic organisms such as bacteria, viruses, and fungi—that live on and within our bodies. Rather than being discrete biological entities, our bodies appear to be more like complex ecosystems (think tropical rainforests), habitats for trillions of different organisms living with us. Thus we can define the **human microbiome** as the complete collection of microorganisms in the body's ecosystem.

These microbes are not random hitchhikers, opportunistic parasites, or dangerous outsider enemies of our bodies. They are deeply integrated into the ways our bodies work. Microbes help us digest food, synthesize vitamins, make natural antibiotics, produce natural moisturizer for the skin, guide the immune system, and spur the development of body parts (such as the intestines). Scientists suggest that we have evolved with these microbes as part of our personal ecosystem for promoting health and combating the pathogens that create disease in our bodies. We not only tolerate these microbes; we need them (Helmreich 2009).

Discoveries of the role of microbes in our bodies' experience of health and illness open the door to rethinking one of the central tenets of Western biomedicine—the notion of the discrete individual body—and offer new pathways for the innovative treatment of both common and rare diseases (Zimmer 2010, 2011).

ARE THERE OTHER GLOBAL HEALTH SYSTEMS?

Although Western biomedicine is intimately tied to Western culture and its values, anthropologists also acknowledge that with the spread of Western cultural influences, biomedicine has crossed beyond its cultural and regional boundaries

human microbiome

The complete collection of microorganisms in the human body's ecosystem.

to become a global health system now used in a wide array of countries as well as in international health agencies that engage in health promotion globally. But are there health systems other than biomedicine that function on a global level? Earlier in this chapter, we discussed the growing popularity of Tibetan medicine, especially in Europe and North America. Now let's consider Chinese medicine today as one health system with a long history, elaborate theories of health and illness, a global reach, and proven effectiveness (e.g., Zhan 2009; Farquhar 1986; Scheid 2002).

Chinese Medicine Today. In very general terms, Chinese medicine conceptualizes health as a harmonious relationship between Heaven and Earth, which are considered the major forces of the universe. An individual's *qi*—translated as "breath" or "air" and referring to an energy found in all living things—must be balanced and flowing in equilibrium with the rest of the universe for a person to be healthy. Illness occurs when the *qi* is blocked and the flow and balance are disrupted. In traditional Chinese medicine, health care practices such as acupuncture, *tuina* (therapeutic massage), acupressure, moxibustion (the burning of herbs near the skin), and the consumption of healing herbs and teas promote health by restoring the free flow of *qi* along the body's meridians, or energy pathways (Farquhar 1986; Scheid 2002).

In her book *Other-Worldly: Making Chinese Medicine through Transnational Frames* (2009), medical anthropologist Mei Zhan challenges many of the stereotypes of Chinese medicine: that it is somehow emblematic of an ancient Chinese culture, regionally limited with fixed healing practices that are the antithesis of, or merely "alternative" to, Western biomedicine. Instead Zhan argues that Chinese medical practices vary widely even within China. Rather than undergoing a regimented and fixed set of health care practices, patients participate in a dynamic health care environment. Patients and doctors carefully negotiate treatments. And no good physician ever writes the same prescription twice because the treatment must meet the needs of each specific patient (Scheid 2002).

Not only does Chinese medical practice vary within China today, but it has varied significantly over time. Zhan notes three key historical moments over the past century that have significantly reshaped modern Chinese medicine. First, the early-twentieth-century expansion of Western biomedicine into China influenced the practice of Chinese medicine. Western biomedicine's emphasis on institution building, laboratory research, clinical and teaching practices, and even insurance policies reshaped Chinese medical thinking and practice. Today the everyday world of Chinese medicine includes interactions with biomedical professionals. Patients move back and forth between biomedicine and Chinese medicine.

Second, upon the founding of the People's Republic of China in 1949, the new Chinese government moved to institutionalize traditional Chinese

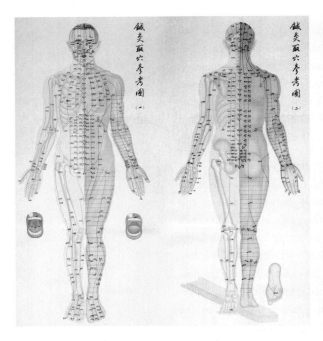 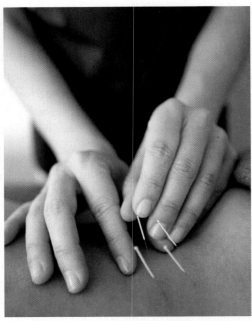

Chinese medicine is a globalized health system with its own internal logic for diagnosing disease and promoting healing. Chinese diagram (*left*) of meridians, or energy pathways, indicates potential sites of blockage that can be restored through treatment with acupuncture (*right*), massage, herbs, and teas.

medicine, subsidize research, formalize teaching, and establish a process for professional certification. The government widely promoted traditional Chinese medicine as a low-tech, low-cost approach to preventive care and trained and deployed "barefoot doctors" to promote health care in every rural Chinese community. The government also exported traditional Chinese medicine—including medicines, doctors, and health-promotion strategies—to the developing world, particularly Africa, to establish international ties of solidarity with other developing nations. This move marked a rapid expansion of Chinese medicine beyond China's national borders into the international arena.

Finally, Zhan documents the shift of Chinese medicine beginning in the 1980s from primarily a developing-world medical practice to one with established niches in developed countries. Traditional Chinese medicine has become popular with cosmopolitan consumers in China, North America, and Europe, both as a preventive medicine and as an alternative treatment for illness when biomedicine proves ineffective. Flows of Chinese medical practitioners and Chinese medical knowledge have increased encounters with Chinese medicine, particularly along routes between Asia and Europe and across the Pacific Ocean.

Zhan carefully demonstrates how Chinese medicine—often viewed as an ancient, culturally specific, fixed ethnomedicine "alternative" to Western biomedicine—has been relocated in both time and space to represent a modern, effective, globally respected body of health care practices (Zhan 2009; Farquhar 1994; Scheid and MacPherson 2012).

How Can Anthropologists Help Solve Health Care Problems?

Anthropologists can apply research strategies and key theoretical concepts of our field to solve pressing public health problems, understand the spread of disease, and improve the delivery of health care. In fact, the work of an anthropologist may be just as crucial to explaining and resolving health challenges as that of a physician, epidemiologist, pathologist, or virologist. The discussion below illustrates this point through the groundbreaking efforts of anthropologist Paul Farmer working in Haiti.

CREATING A PUBLIC HEALTH SYSTEM IN RURAL HAITI

When the American Paul Farmer first visited Cange, Haiti, in 1983, the remote village of one hundred families was one of the poorest places in one of the world's poorest countries. Most people in Haiti lived on $1 a day, but residents of Cange lived on less. Along with intense poverty, Farmer found a village overwhelmed by high levels of infant mortality, childhood malnutrition, typhoid, dysentery, HIV/AIDS, and tuberculosis. Many residents were water refugees, having been pushed off their land by the construction of a hydroelectric dam that flooded their valley to provide power to Haiti's cities and irrigation for large landholders and agribusinesses downstream. With the best farmland taken out of production by the dam's reservoir, the surrounding area suffered from widespread deforestation, soil erosion, and terrible health statistics (Farmer 2006).

MAP 14.2
Cange

Farmer's work in Cange, popularized in the best-selling biography *Mountains beyond Mountains* (Kidder 2003), began with the encouragement of a Haitian Anglican priest, Fritz Lafontant, who had been working in the area for years. In 1984, the year after Farmer's first visit to Haiti, he enrolled in Harvard's medical school and doctoral program in anthropology. He believed that anthropology would be essential to addressing the health needs of poor Haitians. The delivery of medicines and medical procedures would not be enough, he felt. Deeper questions would need to be asked: What made the people sick? How could they stay healthy after being treated? The basic approaches of an anthropologist—understanding the local language, norms, values, classifications of reality, and religious beliefs—would help a trained physician to think about health in the broadest possible sense.

While at Harvard, Farmer immediately began to apply what he was learning, using the research strategies of anthropology and the professional knowledge of medicine to create a public health system for Cange. Living in the community and speaking the local language, Farmer engaged in a process of listening

to the residents' needs and experiences and working with them to identify and treat their public health problems. First he recruited a few villagers to help him conduct a health census. Moving from hut to hut in Cange and two neighboring villages, the census takers identified the breadth of the residents' health problems and established a baseline by which to measure future success. To address the community's needs, Farmer launched Partners in Health, or Zanmi Lasante in the Cange language, with financial support from backers in the United States.

Zanmi Lasante began to create multiple lines of defense to protect the Cange villagers' health. Clean water came first. Because they lived on Haiti's central plateau, the villagers had been climbing down an eight-hundred-foot hillside to draw water from the stagnant reservoir created by the hydroelectric dam. Using old plastic jugs and calabash gourds, they had been carrying water back up the hill to their huts, where it sometimes sat uncovered for days. But now Father Lafontant recruited a construction crew from an Episcopal Church diocese in South Carolina to tap into an underground river to provide fresh water to the families at the top of the hill. Thereafter, Farmer and his associates noticed that the incidence of infant deaths began to drop almost immediately.

Sanitation and hygiene came next. Father LaFontant organized the construction of latrines (outdoor toilets) to improve human waste disposal and protect the water supply. He and Farmer raised money to replace the dirt floors and thatched roofs of the residents' crude lean-to homes with tin roofs and cement floors. An expanded village school provided a place to teach children to read and write and a place to teach the community about basic health practices. Malnourished schoolchildren received free meals with dignity. Childhood vaccinations dramatically improved health in the community.

Perhaps most significant, Zanmi Lasante trained local community members as community health workers. Being familiar with the local language, social structure, values, and religious beliefs, the community health workers were able to identify emerging health care problems, administer vaccinations, and assist people in taking medications. The newly constructed health clinic and hospital of Zanmi Lasante served those who were too sick to be cared for at home. Over time, Zanmi Lasante became one of the largest nongovernmental health care providers in Haiti, serving an area of 1.2 million people with more than four thousand doctors, nurses, and community health workers.

Farmer's research and work in Cange explored how anthropology could tackle the day-to-day challenges of health on the ground—nutrition, clean water, prevention of illness, and promotion of health. Public health work could be guided and greatly improved by the strategies and theoretical concerns of anthropology. However, as Farmer notes, to truly make a difference, anthropology must be used not only to analyze and scrutinize a problem but also to turn research into action (Farmer 1985).

Why Does the Distribution of Health and Illness Mirror That of Wealth and Power?

Writing in the late 1800s, Rudolf Virchow, a renowned pathologist considered to be one of the ancestors of medical anthropology, asked why the distribution of health and illness appeared to mirror the distribution of wealth and power. Although anthropology from its inception has focused on concerns of health and illness, in recent years Virchow's question has become central to the critical medical anthropology approach to health and illness. If the distribution of health and illness cannot be explained solely on the basis of genetic vulnerabilities, individual behaviors, and the random spread of pathogens through a population, then what are the root causes of health disparities?

HEALTH TRANSITION AND CRITICAL MEDICAL ANTHROPOLOGY

Over the twentieth century, much of the human population experienced dramatic improvements in health. Life expectancy rose significantly. Infectious diseases (with the exception of HIV) declined as the primary causes of death and were replaced by chronic diseases such as cancer and heart disease and by syndromes such as stroke. Unfortunately, despite improvements in global health statistics, local populations have not experienced the **health transition** equally. Inequalities of health—sometimes extreme—and unequal access to health care persist between local populations and within them.

Although overall human life expectancy increased from 31 years in 1900 to 65 in 2010 (from 49.2 in 1900 to 78.3 in 2010 in the United States), extreme differences exist among countries. As Table 14.1 shows, in 2012 Japan ranked

health transition

The significant improvements in human health made over the course of the twentieth century that were not, however, distributed evenly across the world's population.

first in overall life expectancy at birth at 82.7 years. Sierra Leone ranked last of 194 countries, with an overall life expectancy at birth of 44.0 years. The United States ranked 40.

These statistics raise crucial questions about health disparities that are central to the concerns of critical medical anthropologists. If the United States is the richest and most technologically advanced country in the world, why is its population's average life expectancy shorter than that of people in thirty-nine other countries? Why is the average life expectancy of the population of Sierra Leone nearly 40 percent below the global average?

critical medical anthropology

An approach to the study of health and illness that analyzes the impact of inequality and stratification within systems of power on individual and group health outcomes.

Critical medical anthropology examines health as a system of power. Specifically, it explores the impact of inequality on human health by examining (1) how economic and political systems, race, class, gender, and sexuality create and perpetuate unequal access to health care, and (2) how health systems themselves are systems of power that generate disparities in health by defining who is sick, who gets treated, and how. Critical medical anthropologists look beyond

TABLE 14.1
Global Life Expectancy

COUNTRY	RANK	LIFE EXPECTANCY AT BIRTH (IN YEARS)
Japan	1	82.7
Hong Kong	2	82.4
Switzerland	3	81.8
Australia	4	81.7
Italy	5	81.5
Iceland	6	81.4
Singapore	7	81.2
Spain	8	81.2
Sweden	9	81.1
France	10	80.9
Netherlands	15	80.2
Germany	20	79.8
United States	40	78.1
World		68.7
India	148	64.9
Haiti	158	60.7
Afghanistan	167	58.4
Mozambique	193	48.4
Swaziland	195	47.4
Sierra Leone	200	44.0

Source: UN Department of Economic and Social Affairs, Population Division. 2013. "World Population Prospects, the 2012 Revision." http://esa.un.org/wpp/index.htm (accessed 5/7/15).

Western biomedicine's traditional focus on individual patients' problems; instead they analyze patterns of health and illness among entire groups. Critical medical anthropologists search for the origins of these health disparities, the mechanisms that perpetuate them, and strategies for overcoming them (Baer, Singer, and Susser 2003; Budrys 2010).

Patterns of inequality in a culture create patterns of inequality in health care. Health practices and policies in turn create and reinforce patterns of inequality. We might actually say that illness can have social origins in poverty, violence, fear of violence, and discrimination based on race, ethnicity, gender, sexuality, and age. Illness and disease can result from cultural patterns of inequality and the distribution of health care resources within a population (Schulz and Mullings 2006).

STAFF ATTITUDES AFFECT HEALTH CARE DELIVERY IN A NEW YORK WOMEN'S CLINIC

Various systems of power—including economics, politics, race, class, gender, and sexuality—shape the distribution and accessibility of health care resources (Chapman and Berggren 2005). In *Reproducing Race* (2011), legal scholar and anthropologist Khiara Bridges examines the ways in which race, class, and gender intersect to shape the delivery of health care in a women's health clinic at a famous trauma hospital on Manhattan's East Side. This facility provides prenatal, delivery, and postpartum checkups and services to pregnant women who are poor. The women's health clinic of Alpha Hospital (a pseudonym), which also serves as a top-tier teaching hospital, treats an incredibly diverse population of patients, including some whites but mostly people of color. Because of their economic status, all patients qualify for the U.S. federal government's Medicaid program.

MAP 14.3
New York City

In contrast to the patient population, physicians working in Alpha's women's health clinic are predominantly white. Most medical staffers are women of color but of immigrant backgrounds. Tensions exist between these groups. During a year and a half of fieldwork, Bridges documented the stereotypes and prejudices expressed by physicians and medical staff about their patients. In a Medicaid-supported women's health clinic, women of color are already treated in ways that non-Medicaid patients would not be. For example, because the government has categorized Medicaid patients as an "at risk" population whose exceptional health issues require special treatment, these women are subjected to interviews, counseling sessions, intrusive procedures, and invasive examinations that non-Medicaid pregnant women do not undergo. In addition to the exceptional institutional requirements, Bridges raises the possibility that physicians' racial attitudes may contribute to the health disparities experienced by patients who are women of color.

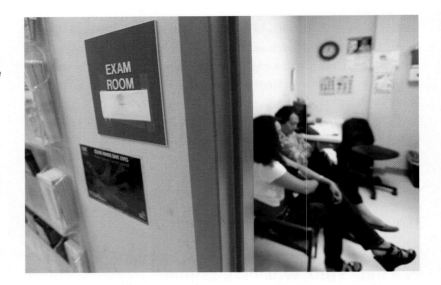

How might dynamics of race, gender, age, and class affect the medical care that patients receive in a hospital, clinic, or doctor's office?

Bridges's research documents a racist oral tradition within the medical profession that features stories and folklore about black women's bodies. One common theme centers on the supposedly unique strength and hardiness of black women and other women of color, who, often referred to as more "primitive" by health workers, were assumed to be able to endure more intense pain and overcome more hardship in medical procedures than other women.

Bridges presents these troubling anecdotes in relationship to statistics that show significant racial disparities in infant and maternal mortality. In the United States, black babies are nearly two and a half times more likely to die as infants than white babies. Black women are three times more likely than white women to die from complications of pregnancy and childbirth. In New York City, they are five times more likely to do so!

Are these women and infants dying because they are poor or because they are black? Bridges suggests that the mortality rates reflect more than poverty. Studies consistently show that racial and ethnic minorities in the United States receive lower-quality health care. But even when ruling out variables such as insurance status, income, age, and severity of medical condition, black women and infants have higher mortality rates than whites with similar profiles.

Bridges notes a deep reluctance within Western medicine to invade physicians' privacy by interrogating their human frailties. Perhaps as a result, the existence of physicians' racism is never addressed in the larger medical literature. But based on the patterns of behavior she observed at Alpha Hospital's women's health clinic, Bridges argues for the need to explore the possibility that physicians' views regarding patients of color may lead to different treatment during pregnancy and childbirth, disparate health outcomes, and higher infant and maternal mortality rates (Bridges 2011; Chapman and Berggren 2005).

How Is Globalization Changing the Experience of Health and Illness and the Practice of Medicine?

Even though globalization is not an exclusively recent phenomenon, the current era of worldwide interconnectedness is bringing profound changes to individuals' experience of health and illness and to the practice of medicine. Various facets of medical migration, as well as encounters among multiple systems of healing, make today's era of globalization unique.

MEDICAL MIGRATION

Globalization today has launched a new and intensified era of **medical migration**—not only of disease but also of health care systems, diagnoses, and treatments (Roberts and Scheper-Hughes 2011), with both positive and negative results. Medical treatments and technologies cross national borders as vaccines have been introduced worldwide to treat previously fatal or debilitating illnesses such as polio, tuberculosis, measles, mumps, rubella, tetanus, typhoid, and diphtheria. Antibiotics treat bacterial infections. Pesticides inhibit the spread of disease-carrying insects. At the same time, diseases migrate on a global scale. HIV/AIDS knows no national boundaries. Medical researchers travel with their scientific knowledge and technology in search of subjects for medical research and experimental clinical trials. Images of youth, health, and beauty (as well as consumer products that purport to provide and prolong them) infuse global media.

Medical travelers cross borders in search of cures and therapies for every condition possible, from heart disease to obesity, failed organs, infertility, and sexual dysfunction. Senior citizens travel from the United States to Canada and Mexico to buy lower-priced generic drugs that are unavailable or unaffordable at home. The wealthy travel on tourist visas to impoverished countries to receive organ transplants. The poor travel without documents to wealthy countries to receive basic health care. Religious pilgrims travel to sacred shrines, holy mountains, and healing waters.

> **medical migration**
> The movement of diseases, medical treatments, and entire health care systems, as well as those seeking medical care, across national borders.

MULTIPLE SYSTEMS OF HEALING

This era of medical migration has spurred the encounter of multiple systems of healing, including ideas of health and illness that overlap and often conflict. The intersection of multiple cultural approaches to healing, called **medical pluralism**, often creates tensions, especially in the encounter between Western biomedicine and other cultural patterns of health and illness. But the engagement also provides opportunities for additional alternative and complementary choices and medical options to emerge (Lock 1993, 2002).

> **medical pluralism**
> The intersection of multiple cultural approaches to healing.

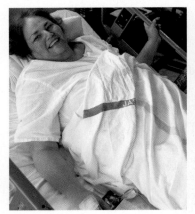

Globalization has spurred many forms of medical migration. *Clockwise from top*: Crowds seek healing at the sacred grotto sanctuary of Our Lady of Lourdes in France. Thousands of Americans cross the border from Arizona to buy prescription drugs at Mexican pharmacies for a fraction of their U.S. cost. A school bus driver, Edna Harsha, from Minnesota, traveled to Bombay, India, for hip replacement surgery.

Colliding Cultures: Hmong Refugees and the U.S. Health Care System. Anne Fadiman's *The Spirit Catches You and You Fall Down* (1997) captures the intensity and danger of cross-cultural medical encounters through the story of the Lees, a Hmong refugee family from Laos in Southeast Asia. The Lees settled in the city of Merced in California's agricultural Central Valley in the 1980s. More than 150,000 Hmong refugees fled Laos in the 1970s and 1980s. Many had fought clandestinely with the United States on the losing side of wars in Vietnam and Laos. More than 12,000 Hmong eventually settled in Merced, a city of only 61,000 people.

The Lees' fourteenth child, Lia Lee, was born on July 9, 1982, apparently a healthy, happy baby. But at three months of age, her seizures began. At first, her family comforted her and cared for her at home. Her uncontrollable convulsions on October 24 led the family to Merced Community Medical Center (MCMC), a small county hospital but also a teaching hospital where first-year residents from the University of California–Davis train in family practice. The October 24 visit began a long and painful encounter—a collision—between the Lee family and the U.S. health care system.

Unbeknownst to the doctors at MCMC, the Lees had already diagnosed Lia's illness as *qaug dab peg*, which translates into English as epilepsy. Familiar with *qaug dab peg* in their own cultural context, the Lees were ambivalent about their daughter's illness. The seizures, they knew, could be dangerous. But among the Hmong, those suffering from *qaug dab peg* were held in high esteem. Many became powerful shamans—traditional healers and community visionaries. The Lees had come to the hospital for their daughter to be healed, but they also wondered about her potentially auspicious future.

Also unbeknownst to the MCMC doctors, the Lees knew what had caused Lia's illness and how to treat it. She suffered from soul loss. Her older sister had allowed the front door of their small home to slam, and the loud noise had scared Lia's soul away. An elaborate ritual of soul-calling conducted by a Hmong shaman could trap the lost soul and return it to Lia's body. But her seizures on that October night were overwhelming, and her parents feared that she would die without immediate care.

By the time the Lees arrived at the hospital, the seizures had stopped. With no clear symptoms to treat, the doctors were at a loss. The hospital had no translator, and the Lees spoke no English. The resident on call misdiagnosed the remaining symptoms as an infection, prescribed medication, and sent the family home. Unfortunately, the prescription and medication instructions were written in English, which the Lees could not understand. Lia Lee was misdiagnosed at the hospital again on November 11. Finally, on March 3, 1983, the family arrived with Lia still convulsing. A young family member who spoke some English translated. The resident on call diagnosed the cause as epilepsy. Then the child was subjected to a battery of invasive tests, including a spinal tap, a CT scan, a chest X-ray, and blood work—none of which the hospital staff could adequately explain to Lia's parents. The child had experienced five months of seizures small and large without proper diagnosis and medication, and now she endured a terrifying night at the hospital.

Between the ages of eight months and four and a half years, Lia Lee was admitted to MCMC seventeen times and made more than one hundred outpatient visits for treatment of her seizures. Over the same period, her doctors prescribed fourteen different medications in different combinations and dosages, changing her prescription twenty-three times—all with a family unfamiliar with English, Western medical practices, or the U.S. system of weights and measures needed to determine the proper dosage.

The collision of cultures escalated when doctors decided that Lia Lee's ongoing seizures were caused by her parents' failure to comply with the medication prescriptions. This, the lead doctor determined, qualified as child neglect and child abuse. Acting on the doctor's concerns, the county courts ordered Lia Lee removed from her parents' custody and placed in foster care so that her medicines could be properly administered. The doctors thought they were acting to protect the child. Her parents, however, unable to understand the medical, legal, or moral logic of removing a child from her family and convinced that they were doing everything in their power to care for their daughter, could only imagine that they were being punished for some unknown reason.

MAP 14.4
Laos

The courts eventually returned Lia Lee to her parents after nearly a year in foster care. Her condition had not improved. Her parents, in fact, felt that her cognitive abilities and social skills had deteriorated during the year away. Despite the parents' efforts to comply with Lia's drug regimen, another series of catastrophic epileptic seizures landed her in MCMC again and finally in a children's hospital in nearby Fresno. Treatment of the seizures was ultimately ineffective. Despite what hospital staff considered heroic measures, Lia was left with the dramatically reduced brain activity that doctors call a "persistent vegetative state." Doctors removed all life support and feeding tubes. She was returned to MCMC and finally to the Lees' home.

Considering her lingering fevers, the medical professionals expected her to die. But Lia's parents bathed her in soothing herbal baths, fed her, carried her with them, slept with her in their bed, and continued the elaborate Hmong rituals of soul-calling to return her to health. Though her brain activity never returned, Lia did not die. Her parents were convinced that all the medicines the doctors had forced on her had left her in this condition. (Indeed, Fadiman found some evidence suggesting that Lia's massive final seizure may have been caused by a hospital-acquired infection.) They hoped that their traditional healing methods might still return her lost soul to her body.

Bridging Cultural Divides via Illness Narratives. Fadiman's interviews found that the parties in this cross-cultural health encounter held vastly different views of what had occurred. Most of the doctors criticized the parents as uncooperative. They debated whether this stemmed from cultural barriers, lack of intelligence, or character flaws that kept them from caring properly for their daughter. Many saw the parents as ungrateful for all the effort and resources that had been expended on their daughter's case. Few made any attempt to ask the Lees how they understood Lia's illness and how they would treat it. In contrast, the Lees considered most of the medical staff to be uncommunicative, arrogant, cold, and punitive; they also described the medical procedures Lia had undergone as invasive, culturally inappropriate, and ineffective. They never understood how the government could take their beloved daughter from them to be put in the care of strangers.

At the conclusion of her research, Fadiman contacted a preeminent medical anthropologist, Arthur Kleinman of Harvard University. Kleinman, a specialist in cross-cultural issues in health and illness, has been instrumental in formulating a concept of collecting illness narratives as a way to bridge cultural divides in treating illness and promoting health (Kleinman 1988). **Illness narratives** are the personal stories that people tell to explain their illness. The narratives reveal the psychological, social, and cultural aspects that give illness its context and meaning. These stories can provide healers with an essential framework for developing treatment strategies that will make sense to the patient and have the greatest chance of success.

illness narratives
The personal stories that people tell to explain their illnesses.

Would Lia Lee's treatment have been effective had the MCMC medical staff asked the family to provide this illness narrative—the cultural framework through which they viewed the cause and potential treatment of her illness? Doing so might have provided an avenue to engage the family in a cooperative treatment process. Through that process, multiple systems of healing and concepts of health and illness might have intersected to create a multifaceted approach to healing for Lia Lee.

Encounters of distinct medical systems like that experienced by Lia Lee and her family in the California health care system will only increase as globalization continues to break down barriers to the flow of ideas, people, diseases, medical treatments, and health practitioners from one world region to another. These encounters will continue to challenge and expand our notions of disease, illness, and health care. As we have seen in this chapter, medical anthropologists are deeply engaged in the analysis and understanding of these transitions and in the articulation of strategies to develop and promote sophisticated, people-centered, and holistic approaches to the challenges of health and illness.

Toolkit

Thinking Like an Anthropologist: Health in the Individual and in the Global Population

The human body is a spectacularly sophisticated organism. Its ten trillion cells constitute complex cardiovascular, pulmonary, and digestive systems made up of muscles, ligaments, organs, veins, and arteries, all shaped and guided by approximately twenty thousand protein-coding genes that form our DNA sequence. The body, which has evolved over millions of years, enables us to interact with one another, reproduce our species, and adapt to the remarkable variety of environments found on Earth.

Healthy bodies are produced through a complex interaction between genetics and culture. The human genetic code provides a basic framework for the body's growth, but culture and the natural environment influence how our bodies actually develop. Nutrition, disease, and exercise, along with our collective human health care practices, impact what we look like, how we feel, how well we live, and how long we live. Even the human mind is not fully formed at birth. Nutrition, stimulation, affection, and trauma after birth continue to shape the contours of our brains.

When medical anthropologists consider issues of health, they think about both the individual body and the social body. As discussed in this chapter, we humans and our individual bodies do not live in isolation. Nor is our health created in isolation. We live in relation to one another as part of a social body—a collection of individuals whose health is tied to the success of the group as well (Scheper-Hughes and Lock 1987). The health of the hundred-year-old twins Ena and Lily and the residents of *colonias* on the Texas–Mexico border discussed in the chapter opener, like the health of Lia Lee, are directly related to the health of those around them and to the system of health care created and shared by the larger culture in which they live.

As you think more about health and illness—perhaps your own personal experiences or those of people around you—remember the big questions we have been exploring:

- How does culture shape our ideas of health and illness?

- How can anthropologists help solve health care problems?

- Why does the distribution of health and illness mirror that of wealth and power?

- How is globalization changing the experience of health and illness and the practice of medicine?

After reading this chapter, are you able to apply these questions to specific situations?

As we have seen, medical anthropologists examine the diverse strategies that cultures have developed to protect and promote the health of the body. And they work to apply the methodological and analytical tools of anthropology to enhance and expand health care in the face of increasing global health inequalities. Debates about health and illness are all around us: Will all 50 U.S. states expand Medicaid eligibility for the poor as envisioned by the 2010 Affordable Care Act? Will the Medicare eligibility age be raised, making it harder for seniors to find health coverage? Will your college or university adequately fund its student health center to provide for all of a student's health needs? Who sets the health center's policies and budget? How will you engage these debates? Thinking like an anthropologist can help you better understand and address these issues, whether they present themselves as your own personal issues of health and illness, those of your friends and family, or the health of the global human population.

Key Terms

health (p. 395)

disease (p. 396)

illness (p. 396)

ethnomedicine (p. 400)

ethnopharmacology (p. 400)

biomedicine (p. 402)

human microbiome (p. 404)

health transition (p. 409)

critical medical anthropology (p. 410)

medical migration (p. 413)

medical pluralism (p. 413)

illness narratives (p. 416)

Glossary

affinal relationship: A kinship relationship established through marriage and/or alliance, not through biology or common descent.

agency: The potential power of individuals and groups to contest cultural norms, values, mental maps of reality, symbols, institutions, and structures of power.

agriculture: An intensive farming strategy for food production involving permanently cultivated land.

anonymity: Protection of the identities of the people involved in a study by changing or omitting their names or other identifying characteristics.

anthropologist's toolkit: The tools needed to conduct fieldwork, including a notebook, pen, camera, voice recorder, and dictionary.

anthropology: The study of the full scope of human diversity, past and present, and the application of that knowledge to help people of different backgrounds better understand one another.

archaeology: The investigation of the human past by means of excavating and analyzing artifacts.

arranged marriage: Marriage orchestrated by the families of the involved parties.

asexuality: A lack of erotic attraction to others.

assimilation: The process through which minorities accept the patterns and norms of the dominant culture and cease to exist as separate groups.

authorizing process: The complex historical and social developments through which symbols are given power and meaning.

band: A small kinship-based group of foragers who hunt and gather for a living over a particular territory.

biomedicine: A practice, often associated with Western medicine, that seeks to apply the principles of biology and the natural sciences to the practice of diagnosing disease and promoting healing.

bisexuality: Attraction to and sexual relations with members of both sexes.

bourgeoisie: Marxist term for the capitalist class that owns the means of production.

bridewealth: The gift of goods or money from the groom's family to the bride's family as part of the marriage process.

built environment: The intentionally designed features of human settlement, including buildings, transportation and public service infrastructure, and public spaces.

carrying capacity: The number of people who can be supported by the resources of the surrounding region.

chiefdom: An autonomous political unit composed of a number of villages or communities under the permanent control of a paramount chief.

civil society organization: A local nongovernmental organization that challenges state policies and uneven development, and advocates for resources and opportunities for members of its local communities.

clan: A type of descent group based on a claim to a founding ancestor but lacking genealogical documentation.

class: A system of power based on wealth, income, and status that creates an unequal distribution of a society's resources.

climate change: Changes to Earth's climate, including global warming produced primarily by increasing concentrations of greenhouse gases created by human activity such as burning fossil fuels and deforestation.

code switching: Switching back and forth between one linguistic variant and another depending on the cultural context.

colonialism: The practice by which a nation-state extends political, economic, and military power beyond its own borders over an extended period of time to secure access to raw materials, cheap labor, and markets in other countries or regions.

commodity chain: The hands an item passes through between producer and consumer.

communitas: A sense of camaraderie, a common vision of what constitutes a good life, and a commitment to take social action to move toward achieving this vision that is shaped by the common experience of rites of passage.

companionate marriage: Marriage built on love, intimacy, and personal choice rather than social obligation.

contagious magic: Ritual words or performances that achieve efficacy as certain materials that come into contact with one person carry a magical connection that allows power to be transferred from person to person.

core countries: Industrialized former colonial states that dominate the world economic system.

cosmopolitanism: A global outlook emerging in response to increasing globalization.

critical medical anthropology: An approach to the study of health and illness that analyzes the impact of inequality and stratification within systems of power on individual and group health outcomes.

cultural anthropology: The study of people's communities, behaviors, beliefs, and institutions, including how people make meaning as they live, work, and play together.

cultural capital: The knowledge, habits, and tastes learned from parents and family that individuals can use to gain access to scarce and valuable resources in society.

cultural construction of gender: The ways humans learn to behave as a man or woman and to recognize behaviors as masculine or feminine within their cultural context.

cultural materialism: A theory that argues that material conditions, including technology, determine patterns of social organization, including religious principles.

cultural relativism: Understanding a group's beliefs and practices within their own cultural context, without making judgments.

culture: A system of knowledge, beliefs, patterns of behavior, artifacts, and institutions that are created, learned, and shared by a group of people.

dependency theory: A critique of modernization theory that argued that despite the end of colonialism the underlying economic relations of the modern world economic system had not changed.

descent group: A kinship group in which primary relationships are traced through consanguineous ("blood") relatives.

descriptive linguistics: The study of the sounds, symbols, and gestures of a language, and their combination into forms that communicate meaning.

descriptive linguists: Those who analyze languages and their component parts.

development: Post–World War II strategy of wealthy nations to spur global economic growth, alleviate poverty, and raise living standards through strategic investment in national economies of former colonies.

dialect: A nonstandard variation of a language.

disease: A discrete natural entity that can be clinically identified and treated by a health professional.

displacement: The ability to use words to refer to objects not immediately present or events occurring in the past or future.

dowry: The gift of goods or money from the bride's family to the groom's family as part of the marriage process.

economy: A cultural adaptation to the environment that enables a group of humans to use the available resources to satisfy their needs and to thrive.

egalitarian society: A group based on the sharing of resources to ensure success with a relative absence of hierarchy and violence.

emic: Involving an approach to gathering data that investigates how local people think and how they understand the world.

enculturation: The process of learning culture.

endogamy: Marriage to someone within the kinship group.

entrepreneurial immigrant: A person who moves to a new location to conduct trade and establish a business.

ethnic boundary marker: A practice or belief, such as food, clothing, language, shared name, or religion, used to signify who is in a group and who is not.

ethnic cleansing: Efforts by representatives of one ethnic or religious group to remove or destroy another group in a particular geographic area.

ethnicity: A sense of historical, cultural, and sometimes ancestral connection to a group of people who are imagined to be distinct from those outside the group.

ethnocentrism: The belief that one's own culture or way of life is normal and natural; using one's own culture to evaluate and judge the practices and ideals of others.

ethnographic fieldwork: A primary research strategy in cultural anthropology involving living with a community of people over an extended period to better understand their lives.

ethnology: The analysis and comparison of ethnographic data across cultures.

ethnomedicine: Local systems of health and healing rooted in culturally specific norms and values.

ethnopharmacology: The documentation and description of the local use of natural substances in healing remedies and practices.

etic: Involving description of local behavior and beliefs from the anthropologist's perspective in ways that can be compared across cultures.

eugenics: A pseudoscience attempting to scientifically prove the existence of separate human races to improve the population's genetic composition by favoring some races over others.

exogamy: Marriage to someone outside the kinship group.

family of orientation: The family group in which one is born, grows up, and develops life skills.

family of procreation: The family group created when one reproduces and within which one rears children.

field notes: The anthropologist's written observations and reflections on places, practices, events, and interviews.

flexible accumulation: The increasingly flexible strategies that corporations use to accumulate profits in an era of globalization, enabled by innovative communication and transportation technologies.

focal vocabulary: The words and terminology that develop with particular sophistication to describe the unique cultural realities experienced by a group of people.

food foragers: Humans who subsist by hunting, fishing, and gathering plants to eat.

Fordism: The dominant model of industrial production for much of the twentieth century, based on a social compact between labor, corporations, and government.

four-field approach: The use of four interrelated disciplines to study humanity: physical anthropology, archaeology, linguistic anthropology, and cultural anthropology.

framing process: The creation of shared meanings and definitions that motivate and justify collective action by social movements.

gender: The expectations of thought and behavior that each culture assigns to people of different sexes.

gender ideology: A set of cultural ideas, usually stereotypical, about the essential character of different genders that functions to promote and justify gender stratification.

gender performance: The way gender identity is expressed through action.

gender stereotype: A preconceived notion about the attributes of, differences between, and proper roles for men and women in a culture.

gender stratification: An unequal distribution of power and access to a group's resources, opportunities, rights, and privileges based on gender.

gender studies: Research into masculinity and femininity as flexible, complex, and historically and culturally constructed categories.

genocide: The deliberate and systematic destruction of an ethnic or religious group.

genotype: The inherited genetic factors that provide the framework for an organism's physical form.

globalization: The worldwide intensification of interactions and increased movement of money, people, goods, and ideas within and across national borders.

grammar: The combined set of observations about the rules governing the formation of morphemes and syntax that guide language use.

habitus: Bourdieu's term to describe the self-perceptions and beliefs that develop as part of one's social identity and shape one's conceptions of the world and where one fits into it.

health: The absence of disease and infirmity, as well as the presence of physical, mental, and social well-being.

health transition: The significant improvements in human health made over the course of the twentieth century that were not, however, distributed evenly across the world's population.

hegemony: The ability of a dominant group to create consent and agreement within a population without the use or threat of force.

heterosexuality: Attraction to and sexual relations between individuals of the opposite sex.

historic archaeology: The exploration of the more recent past through an examination of physical remains and artifacts as well as written or oral records.

historic linguists: Those who study how language changes over time within a culture and how languages travel across cultures.

historical linguistics: The study of the development of language over time, including its changes and variations.

historical particularism: The idea, attributed to Franz Boas, that cultures develop in specific ways because of their unique histories.

holism: The anthropological commitment to consider the full scope of human life, including culture, biology, history, and language, across space and time.

homosexuality: Attraction to and sexual relations between individuals of the same sex.

horticulture: The cultivation of plants for subsistence through non-intensive use of land and labor.

human microbiome: The complete collection of microorganisms in the human body's ecosystem.

hypodescent: Sometimes called the "one drop of blood rule"; the assignment of children of racially "mixed" unions to the subordinate group.

illness: The individual patient's experience of sickness.

illness narratives: The personal stories that people tell to explain their illnesses.

imagined community: The invented sense of connection and shared traditions that underlies identification with a particular ethnic group or nation whose members likely will never all meet.

imitative magic: A ritual performance that achieves efficacy by imitating the desired magical result.

incest taboo: Cultural rules that forbid sexual relations with certain close relatives.

income: What people earn from work, plus dividends and interest on investments, along with rents and royalties.

increasing migration: The accelerated movement of people within and between countries.

individual racism: Personal prejudiced beliefs and discriminatory actions based on race.

informed consent: A key strategy for protecting those being studied by ensuring that they are fully informed of the goals of the project and have clearly indicated their consent to participate.

institutional racism: Patterns by which racial inequality is structured through key cultural institutions, policies, and systems.

internal migration: The movement of people within their own national borders.

interpretivist approach: A conceptual framework that sees culture primarily as a symbolic system of deep meaning.

intersectionality: An analytic framework for assessing how factors such as race, gender, and class interact to shape individual life chances and societal patterns of stratification.

intersexual: An individual who is born with a combination of male and female genitalia, gonads, and/or chromosomes.

interview: A research strategy of gathering data through formal or informal conversation with informants.

Jim Crow: Laws implemented after the U.S. Civil War to legally enforce segregation, particularly in the South, after the end of slavery.

key informant: A community member who advises the anthropologist on community issues, provides feedback, and warns against cultural miscues. Also called "cultural consultant."

kinesics: The study of the relationship between body movements and communication.

kinship: The system of meaning and power that cultures create to determine who is related to whom and to define their mutual expectations, rights, and responsibilities.

kinship analysis: A traditional strategy of examining genealogies to uncover the relationships built upon structures such as marriage and family ties.

labor immigrant: A person who moves in search of a low-skill and low-wage job, often filling an economic niche that native-born workers will not fill.

language: A system of communication organized by rules that uses symbols such as words, sounds, and gestures to convey information.

language continuum: The idea that variation in languages appears gradually over distance so that groups of people who live near one another speak in a way that is mutually intelligible.

language loss: The extinction of languages that have very few speakers.

lexicon: All the words for names, ideas, and events that make up a language's dictionary.

life chances: An individual's opportunities to improve quality of life and achieve life goals.

life history: A form of interview that traces the biography of a person over time, examining changes and illuminating the interlocking network of relationships in the community.

liminality: One stage in a rite of passage during which a ritual participant experiences a period of outsiderhood, set apart from normal society, that is key to achieving a new perspective on the past, future, and current community.

lineage: A type of descent group that traces genealogical connection through generations by linking persons to a founding ancestor.

linguistic anthropology: The study of human language in the past and the present.

literature review: The process of reading all the available published material about a research site and/or research issues, usually done before fieldwork begins.

magic: The use of spells, incantations, words, and actions in an attempt to compel supernatural forces to act in certain ways, whether for good or for evil.

mapping: The analysis of the physical and/or geographic space where fieldwork is being conducted.

marriage: A socially recognized relationship that may involve physical and emotional intimacy as well as legal rights to property and inheritance.

martyr: A person who sacrifices his or her life for the sake of religion.

means of production: The factories, machines, tools, raw materials, land, and financial capital needed to make things.

medical migration: The movement of diseases, medical treatments, and entire health care systems, as well as those seeking medical care, across national borders.

medical pluralism: The intersection of multiple cultural approaches to healing.

melting pot: A metaphor used to describe the process of immigrant assimilation into U.S. dominant culture.

mental maps of reality: Cultural classifications of what kinds of people and things exist, and the assignment of meaning to those classifications.

militarization: The contested social process through which a civil society organizes for the production of military violence.

miscegenation: A demeaning historical term for interracial marriage.

modernization theories: Post–World War II economic theories that predicted that with the end of colonialism less-developed countries would follow the same trajectory toward modernization as the industrialized countries.

monogamy: A relationship between only two partners.

morphemes: The smallest units of sound that carry meaning on their own.

morphology: The study of patterns and rules of how sounds combine to make morphemes.

multiculturalism: A pattern of ethnic relations in which new immigrants and their children enculturate into the dominant national culture and yet retain an ethnic culture.

mutual transformation: The potential for both the anthropologist and the members of the community being studied to be transformed by the interactions of fieldwork.

nation: A term once used to describe a group of people who shared a place of origin; now used interchangeably with *nation-state*.

nation-state: A political entity, located within a geographic territory with enforced borders, where the population shares a sense of culture, ancestry, and destiny as a people.

nationalism: The desire of an ethnic community to create and/or maintain a nation-state.

nativism: The favoring of certain long-term inhabitants over new immigrants.

neoliberalism: An economic and political worldview that sees the free market as the main mechanism for ensuring economic growth, with a severely restricted role for government.

norms: Ideas or rules about how people should behave in particular situations or toward certain other people.

nuclear family: The kinship unit of mother, father, and children.

origin myth: A story told about the founding and history of a particular group to reinforce a sense of common identity.

paleoanthropology: The study of the history of human evolution through the fossil record.

paralanguage: An extensive set of noises (such as cries) and tones of voice that convey significant information about the speaker.

participant observation: A key anthropological research strategy involving both participation in and observation of the daily life of the people being studied.

pastoralism: A strategy for food production involving the domestication of animals.

periphery countries: The least developed and least powerful nations; often exploited by the core countries as sources of raw materials, cheap labor, and markets.

phenotype: The way genes are expressed in an organism's physical form as a result of genotype interaction with environmental factors.

phonemes: The smallest units of sound that can make a difference in meaning.

phonology: The study of what sounds exist and which ones are important for a particular language.

physical anthropology: The study of humans from a biological perspective, particularly focused on human evolution.

pilgrimage: A religious journey to a sacred place as a sign of devotion and in search of transformation and enlightenment.

polyandry: Marriage between one woman and two or more men.

polygyny: Marriage between one man and two or more women.

polyvocality: The practice of using many different voices in ethnographic writing and research question development, allowing the reader to hear more directly from the people in the study.

potlatch: Elaborate redistribution ceremony practiced among the Kwakiutl of the Pacific Northwest.

power: The ability or potential to bring about change through action or influence.

prehistoric archaeology: The reconstruction of human behavior in the distant past (before written records) through the examination of artifacts.

prestige: The reputation, influence, and deference bestowed on certain people because of their membership in certain groups.

prestige language: A particular way of speaking, or language variation, that is associated with wealth, success, education, and power.

primatology: The study of living nonhuman primates as well as primate fossils to better understand human evolution and early human behavior.

productivity: The linguistic ability to use known words to invent new word combinations.

profane: Anything that is considered not holy.

professional immigrant: A highly trained individual who moves to fill an economic niche in a middle-class profession often marked by shortages in the receiving country.

proletariat: Marxist term for the class of laborers who own only their labor.

pushes and pulls: The forces that spur migration from the country of origin and draw immigrants to a particular new destination country.

qualitative data: Descriptive data drawn from nonstatistical sources, including participant observation, personal stories, interviews, and life histories.

quantitative data: Statistical information about a community that can be measured and compared.

race: A flawed system of classification, with no biological basis, that uses certain physical characteristics to divide the human population into supposedly discrete groups.

racial ideology: A set of popular ideas about race that allows the discriminatory behaviors of individuals and institutions to seem reasonable, rational, and normal.

racialization: The process of categorizing, differentiating, and attributing a particular racial character to a person or group of people.

racism: Individual thoughts and actions and institutional patterns and policies that create unequal access to power, privilege, resources, and opportunities based on imagined differences among groups.

ranked society: A group in which wealth is not stratified but prestige and status are.

rapid change: The dramatic transformations of economics, politics, and culture characteristic of contemporary globalization.

rapport: The relationships of trust and familiarity developed with members of the community being studied.

reciprocity: The exchange of resources, goods, and services among people of relatively equal status; meant to create and reinforce social ties.

redistribution: A form of exchange in which accumulated wealth is collected from the members of the group and reallocated in a different pattern.

reflexivity: A critical self-examination of the role the anthropologist plays and an awareness that one's identity affects one's fieldwork and theoretical analyses.

refugee: A person who has been forced to move beyond his or her national borders because of persecution, armed conflict, or natural disasters.

religion: A set of beliefs based on a unique vision of how the world ought to be, often revealed through insights into a supernatural power and lived out in community.

rite of passage: A category of ritual that enacts a change of status from one life stage to another, either for an individual or for a group.

ritual: An act or series of acts regularly repeated over years or generations that embody the beliefs of a group of people and create a sense of continuity and belonging.

sacred: Anything that is considered holy.

saint: An individual who is considered exceptionally close to God and is exalted after death.

salvage ethnography: Fieldwork strategy developed by Franz Boas to rapidly collect cultural, material, linguistic, and biological information about U.S. Native populations being devastated by westward expansion.

Sapir-Whorf hypothesis: The idea that different languages create different ways of thinking.

sex: The observable physical differences between male and female, especially biological differences related to human reproduction.

sexual dimorphism: The phenotypic differences between males and females of the same species.

sexual violence: Violence perpetuated through sexually related physical assaults such as rape.

sexuality: The complex range of desires, beliefs, and behaviors that are related to erotic physical contact and the cultural arena within which people debate about what kinds of physical desires and behaviors are right, appropriate, and natural.

shaman: A part-time religious practitioner with special abilities to connect individuals with supernatural powers or beings.

situational negotiation of identity: An individual's self-identification with a particular group that can shift according to social location.

social mobility: The movement of one's class position, upward or downward, in stratified societies.

social movement: Collective group actions in response to uneven development, inequality, and injustice that seek to build institutional networks to transform cultural patterns and government policies.

social network analysis: A method for examining relationships in a community, often conducted by identifying who people turn to in times of need.

social reproduction: The phenomenon whereby social and class relations of prestige or lack of prestige are passed from one generation to the next.

sociolinguistics: The study of the ways culture shapes language and language shapes culture, particularly the intersection of language with cultural categories and systems of power such as race, gender, class, and age.

sociolinguists: Those who study language in its social and cultural contexts.

species: A group of related organisms that can interbreed and produce fertile, viable offspring.

state: An autonomous regional structure of political, economic, and military rule with a central government authorized to make laws and use force to maintain order and defend its territory.

stratification: The uneven distribution of resources and privileges among participants in a group or culture.

structural functionalism: A conceptual framework positing that each element of society serves a particular function to keep the entire system in equilibrium.

survey: An information-gathering tool for quantitative data analysis.

symbol: Anything that signifies something else.

syntax: The specific patterns and rules for constructing phrases and sentences.

thick description: A research strategy that combines detailed description of cultural activity with an analysis of the layers of deep cultural meaning in which those activities are embedded.

time-space compression: The rapid innovation of communication and transportation technologies associated with globalization that transforms the way people think about space and time.

transgender: A gender identity or performance that does not fit with cultural norms related to one's assigned sex at birth.

tribe: Originally viewed as a culturally distinct, multiband population that imagined itself as one people descended from a common ancestor; currently used to describe an indigenous group with its own set of loyalties and leaders living to some extent outside the control of a centralized authoritative state.

underdevelopment: The term used to suggest that poor countries are poor as a result of their relationship to an unbalanced global economic system.

uneven development: The unequal distribution of the benefits of globalization.

unilineal cultural evolution: The theory proposed by nineteenth-century anthropologists that all cultures naturally evolve through the same sequence of stages from simple to complex.

values: Fundamental beliefs about what is important, true, or beautiful, and what makes a good life.

wealth: The total value of what someone owns, minus any debt.

white supremacy: The belief that whites are biologically different from and superior to people of other races.

whiteness: A culturally constructed concept originating in 1691 Virginia designed to establish clear boundaries of who is white and who is not, a process central to the formation of U.S. racial stratification.

zeros: Elements of a story or a picture that are not told or seen and yet offer key insights into issues that might be too sensitive to discuss or display publicly.

References

Abu-Lughod, Janet L. 1989. *Before European Hegemony: The World System A.D. 1250–1350.* New York: Oxford University Press.

———. 2000. *Veiled Sentiments: Honor and Poetry in a Bedouin Society.* Berkeley: University of California Press.

———. 2005. *Dramas of Nationhood: The Politics of Television in Egypt.* Chicago: University of Chicago Press.

———. 2012. "Living the 'Revolution' in an Egyptian Village: Moral Action in a National Sphere." *American Ethnologist* 39(1): 21–25.

Agrama, Hussein Ali. 2010. "Ethics, Tradition, Authority: Toward an Anthropology of the Fatwa." *American Ethnologist* 37(1): 2–18.

———. 2012. *Questioning Secularism: Islam, Sovereignty and the Rule of Law in Modern Egypt.* Chicago: Chicago University Press.

Aiyer, Ananthakrishnan. 2007. "The Allure of the Transnational: Notes on Some Aspects of the Political Economy of Water in India." *Cultural Anthropology* 22(4): 640–58.

American Academy of Pediatrics. 2000. "Evaluation of the Newborn with Developmental Anomalies of the External Genitalia." *Pediatrics* 106(1): 138–42.

———. 2006. "Children, Adolescents, and Advertising." *Pediatrics* 118(6): 2563–69.

American Anthropological Association. 2004. "Statement on Marriage and the Family." www.aaanet.org/issues/policy-advocacy/Statement-on-Marriage-and-the-family.cfm.

Anderson, Benedict. 1983. *Imagined Communities: Reflections on the Origin and Spread of Nationalism.* London: Verso.

Anglin, Mary K. 2002. *Women, Power, and Dissent in the Hills of Carolina.* Urbana: University of Illinois.

Appadurai, Arjun, ed. 1986. *The Social Life of Things: Commodities in Cultural Perspective.* Cambridge, UK: Cambridge University Press.

Appiah, Kwame Anthony. 2006. *Cosmopolitanism: Ethics in a World of Strangers.* New York: Norton.

Archetti, Eduardo P. 1999. *Masculinities: Football, Polo and the Tango in Argentina.* Oxford, UK: Berg.

Arobba, Biagio, Robert E. McGrath, Joe Futrelle, and Alan B. Craig. 2010. *A Community-Based Social Media Approach for Preserving Endangered Languages and Culture.* www.ideals.illinois.edu/bitstream/handle/2142/17078/lat-comm-info-2-sep-2010.pdf?sequence=2.

Asad, Talal, ed. 1973. *Anthropology and the Colonial Encounter.* London: Ithaca Press.

———. 1992. *Anthropology and the Colonial Encounter.* Atlantic Highlands, NJ: Humanity Books.

———. 1993. *Genealogies of Religion: Discipline and Reasons of Power in Christianity and Islam.* Baltimore: Johns Hopkins University Press.

Baer, Hans A., Merrill Singer, and Ida Susser. 2003. *Medical Anthropology and the World System.* Westport, CT: Praeger.

Baker, Lee D. 1995. "Racism in Professional Settings: Forms of Address as Clues to Power Relations." *Journal of Applied Behavioral Science* 31(2): 186–201.

———. 2004. "Franz Boas Out of the Ivory Tower." *Anthropological Theory* 4(1): 29–51.

Barth, Fredrik. 1959. *Political Leadership among Swat Pathans.* London: Athlone Press.

———. 1969. "Introduction." In *Ethnic Groups and Boundaries*, edited by Fredrik Barth. Boston: Little, Brown.

Basso, Keith. 1996. *Wisdom Sits in Places: Landscape and Language among the Western Apache.* Albuquerque: University of New Mexico Press.

Bellah, Robert. 1980. *Varieties of Civil Religion.* San Francisco: Harper & Row.

Bellamy, Carla. 2011. *The Powerful Ephemeral: Everyday Healing in an Ambiguously Islamic Place.* Berkeley: University of California Press.

Benedict, Ruth. 1934. *Patterns of Culture*. Boston: Houghton Mifflin.

———. 1946. *The Chrysanthemum and the Sword: Patterns of Japanese Culture*. Boston: Houghton Mifflin.

Bennet, R. L., A. G. Motulsky, A. H. Bittles, S. A. Uhrich, D. L. Doyle, K. A. Silvey, E. Cheng, R. A. Steiner, and B. McGillivray. 2002. "Genetic Counseling and Screening of Consanguineous Couples and Their Offspring: Recommendations of the National Society of Genetic Counselors." *Journal of Genetic Counseling* 11(2): 97–119.

Berger, Peter, ed. 1999. *The Desecularization of the World: Resurgent Religion and World Politics*. Grand Rapids, MI: Wm. B. Eerdmans.

Bern, Sandra Lipsitz. 1981. "Gender Schema Theory: A Cognitive Account of Sex Typing." *Psychological Review* 88: 354–64.

———. 1983. "Gender Schema Theory and Its Implications for Child Development: Raising Gender-Aschematic Children in a Gender-Schematic Society." *Signs: Journal of Women in Culture and Society* 8: 598–616.

Besteman, Catherine L., ed. 2002. *Violence: A Reader*. New York: New York University Press.

Besteman, Catherine L., and Lee V. Cassanelli. 1996. *The Struggle for Land in Southern Somalia: The War behind the War*. Boulder, CO: Westview Press.

Bestor, Theodore C. 2001. "Supply-Side Sushi: Commodity, Market, and the Global City." *American Anthropologist* 102(1): 76–95.

———. 2004. *Tsukiji: The Fish Market at the Center of the World*. Berkeley: University of California Press.

Blackless, Melanie, Anthony Charuvastra, Amanda Derryck, Anne Fausto-Sterling, Karl Lauzanne, and Ellen Lee. 2000. "How Sexually Dimorphic Are We? Review and Synthesis." *American Journal of Human Biology* 12: 151–66.

Board of Governors of the Federal Reserve System. 2012. "Changes in U.S. Family Finances from 2007 to 2010: Evidence from the Survey of Consumer Finances." www.federalreserve.gov /pubs/bulletin/2012/pdf/scf12.pdf.

———. 2015a. "Consumer Credit-G.19." www .federalreserve.gov /releases/g19/current/default .htm.

———. 2015b. "Mortgage Debt Outstanding." www.federalreserve.gov/econresdata/releases /mortoutstand/current.htm.

Boas, Franz. 1912. "Changes in the Bodily Form of Descendants of Immigrants." *American Anthropologist* 14(3).

———. 1966. *Kwakiutl Ethnography* (Classics of Anthropology). Helen F. Codere, ed. Chicago: University of Chicago Press.

Boehm, Christopher. 1999. *Hierarchy in the Forest: The Evolution of Egalitarian Behavior*. Cambridge, MA: Harvard University Press.

Bohannan, Laura. 1966. "Shakespeare in the Bush: An American Anthropologist Set Out to Study the Tiv of West Africa and Was Taught the True Meaning of *Hamlet*." *Natural History* 75: 28–33.

Bolin, Anne. 1992. "Families We Choose: Lesbians, Gays, Kinship [Review]." *American Anthropologist* 94(4): 947–48.

Bonilla-Silva, Eduardo. 2010. *Racism without Racists: Color-Blind Racism and Racial Inequality in Contemporary America*, 3rd ed. New York: Rowman and Littlefield.

Bonvillain, Nancy. 2007. *Women and Men: Cultural Constructions of Gender*, 4th ed. Upper Saddle River, NJ: Prentice Hall.

Bourdieu, Pierre. 1982. *Ce que parler veut dire*. Paris: Fayard.

———. 1984. *Distinction: A Social Critique of the Judgment of Taste*. Translated by R. Nice. Cambridge, MA: Harvard University Press.

Bourdieu, Pierre, with Jean-Claude Passeron. (1970) 1990. *Reproduction in Education, Society and Culture*, 2nd ed. (Theory, Culture, and Society Series vol 4). Translated by Lois Wacquant. New York: Sage.

Bourgois, Philippe I. 2003. *In Search of Respect: Selling Crack in El Barrio*, 2nd ed. Cambridge, UK: Cambridge University Press.

Bowen, John R. 2006. *Why the French Don't Like Headscarves: Islam, the State, and Public Space*. Princeton, NJ: Princeton University Press.

Bowie, Fiona. 2006. *The Anthropology of Religion: An Introduction*, 2nd ed. Malden, MA: Blackwell.

Brash, Julian. 2011. *Bloomberg's New York: Class and Governance in the Luxury City*. Athens: University of Georgia.

Braudel, Fernand. (1979) 1992. *Civilization and Capitalism, 15th to 18th Centuries*, vol. 3, *The Perspective of the World*. Translated by Siân Reynolds. Berkeley: University of California Press.

Brettell, Caroline B., and C. F. Sargent, eds. 2009. *Gender in Cross-Cultural Perspective*, 5th ed. Upper Saddle River, NJ: Pearson/Prentice Hall.

Bridges, Khiara M. 2011. *Reproducing Race: An Ethnography of Pregnancy as a Site of Racialization*. Berkeley: University of California Press.

Bridges, Tristan S. 2007. "Dude You're a Fag: Masculinity and Sexuality in High School [Review]." *Gender and Society* 21(5): 776–78.

Bringa, Tone. 1993. *Bosnia: We Are All Neighbors*. Granada Television.

———. 1995. *Being Muslim the Bosnian Way: Identity and Community in a Central Bosnian Village*. Princeton, NJ: Princeton University Press.

Bringa, Tone, and Peter Loizos. 2002. *Returning Home: Revival of a Bosnian Village*. Sage Film and Video (Sarajevo).

Brodkin, Karen. 1998. *How the Jews Became White Folks: And What That Says about Race in America*. New Brunswick, NJ: Rutgers University Press.

———. 2007. "Foreword." In *The Gender of Globalization: Women Navigating Cultural and Economic Marginalities*, edited by Nandini Gunewardena and Ann Kingsolver. Santa Fe, NM: School for Advanced Research Press.

Brown, Jacqueline Nassy. 2007. "Suriname, Sweet Suriname [Review]." *GLQ: A Journal of Lesbian and Gay Studies* 13(2–3): 406–8.

Brubaker, Rogers. 2004. *Ethnicity without Groups*. Cambridge, MA: Harvard University Press.

Brundage, W. Fitzhugh. 1993. *Lynching in the New South: Georgia and Virginia, 1880–1930*. Chicago: University of Illinois Press.

Buck, Pem Davidson. 2001. *Worked to the Bone: Race, Class, Power, and Privilege in Kentucky*. New York: Monthly Review Press.

———. 2009. *In/equality: An Alternative Anthropology*. Redding, CA: CAT Publishing.

Budrys, Grace. 2010. *Unequal Health: How Inequality Contributes to Health or Illness*. Lanham, MD: Rowman and Littlefield.

Butler, Judith. 1990. *Gender Trouble: Feminism and the Subversion of Identity*. New York: Routledge.

Calderwood, Brent. 2008. "Be Butch or Be Bashed." *Gay and Lesbian Review* 155(1): 38–39.

Cameron, Deborah. 1994. "Degrees of Consent: The Antioch College Sexual Offense Policy." In *The Language and Sexuality Reader*, edited by Deborah Cameron and Don Kulick. New York: Routledge, 2006.

———. 2007. *The Myth of Mars and Venus*. Oxford, UK: Oxford University Press.

Cardoso, Fernando Henrique, and Enzo Faletto. 1969. *Dependencia y desarrollo en American Latina: ensayo de interpretación sociologica*. México: Siglo Veintiuno Editores.

Carneiro, Robert. 1981. "The Chiefdom: Precursor of the State." In *The Transition to Statehood in the New World*, edited by Grant Jones and Robert Kautz, 37–79. Cambridge, UK: Cambridge University Press.

Carroll, John B., ed. 1956. *Language, Thought, and Reality: Selected Writings of Benjamin Lee Whorf*. Cambridge, MA: MIT Press.

Carsten, Janet. 1997. *The Heat of the Hearth: The Process of Kinship in a Malay Fishing Community*. Oxford, UK: Clarendon Press.

———. 2004. *After Kinship*. Cambridge, UK: Cambridge University Press.

Casanova, Jose. 1994. *Public Religions in the Modern World*. Chicago: University of Chicago Press.

Cawthon Lang, Kristina. 2005. "Primate Factsheets: Gorilla Taxonomy, Morphology, & Ecology." Primate Info Net. http://pin.primate.wisc.edu/factsheets/entry/gorilla/taxon.

Cazenave, Noel A. 2011. *The Urban Racial State: Managing Race Relations in American Cities*. Lanham, MD: Rowman and Littlefield.

Chagnon, Napoleon A. 1968. *Yąnomamö: The Fierce People*. New York: Holt, Rinehart and Winston.

Chan, Selina Ching. 2006. "Love and Jewelry: Patriarchal Control, Conjugal Ties, and Changing Identities." In *Modern Loves: The Anthropology of Romantic Courtship and Companionate Marriage*, edited by Jennifer S. Hirsch and Holly Wardlow, 35–50. Ann Arbor: University of Michigan Press.

Chapman, Gary. 2010. *The 5 Love Languages: The Secret to Love That Lasts*. Chicago: Northfield Publishing.

Chapman, Rachel R., and Jean R. Berggren. 2005. "Radical Contextualization: Contributions to an Anthropology of Racial/Ethnic Health Disparities." *Health* 9(2): 145–67.

Chio, Jenny. 2014. *A Landscape of Travel: The Work of Tourism in Ethnic China*. Seattle: University of Washington Press.

Chodorow, Nancy. 1974. "Strategies, Cooperation and Conflict among Women in Domestic Groups." In *Woman, Culture and Society*, edited by Michelle Z. Rosaldo and Louise Lamphere, 97–113. Stanford, CA: Stanford University Press.

Chomsky, Noam. 1957. *Syntactic Structures*. The Hague/Paris: Mouton.

Cohen, Yehudi A. 1974. *Man in Adaptation: The Cultural Present*. Chicago: Aldine.

Comaroff, John L., and Jean Comaroff. 2009. *Ethnicity, Inc.* Chicago: University of Chicago Press.

Coontz, Stephanie. 1988. *The Social Origins of Private Life: A History of American Families 1600–1900*. New York: Verso.

———. 1992. *The Way We Never Were: American Families and the Nostalgia Trap*. New York: Basic Books.

Cowen, M. P., and R. W. Shenton. 1996. *Doctrines of Development*. London: Routledge.

Curtis, Debra. 2009. *Pleasures and Perils: Girls' Sexuality in a Caribbean Consumer Culture*. New Brunswick, NJ: Rutgers University Press.

Dahlberg, Frances, ed. 1981. *Woman the Gatherer*. New Haven, CT: Yale University Press.

Daily Mail. 2010. "200 Not Out! Meet Welsh Wonders Lily and Ena, The World's Oldest Twins." *Daily Mail* [London], October 4.

Davies, G. 2005. *A History of Money from the Earliest Times to Present Day*, 3rd ed. Cardiff, UK: University of Wales Press.

Davies, James B., Susanna Sandstrom, Anthony Shorrocks, and Edward N. Wolff. 2007. *Estimating the Level and Distribution of Global Household Wealth*. Helsinki: UNU-WIDER. www.wider.unu.edu/publications /working-papers/research-papers/2007/en_GB /rp2007-77/.

Davis-Floyd, Robbie. 1992. *Birth as an American Rite of Passage*. Berkeley: University of California Press.

Davis-Floyd, Robbie, and Joseph Dumit, eds. 1997. *Cyborg Babies: From Techno-Sex to Techno-Tots*. London: Routledge.

D'Emilio, John, and Estelle B. Freedman. 1998. *Intimate Matters: A History of Sexuality in America*, 2nd ed. Chicago: University of Chicago Press.

de Waal, Frans. 2002. "Primate Behavior and Human Aggression." In *Must We Fight? From the Battlefield to the Schoolyard, a New Perspective on Violent Conflict and Its Prevention*, edited by William L. Ury, 13–25. San Francisco: Jossey-Bass.

Diamond, Jared. 1997. "The Animal with the Weirdest Sex Life." In *Constructing Sexualities: Readings in Sexuality, Gender and Culture*, edited by Suzanne LaFont. Upper Saddle River, NJ: Prentice Hall, 2002.

Dill, Bonnie Thornton. 1983. "Race, Class and Gender: Prospects for an All-Inclusive Sisterhood." *Feminist Studies* 9: 131–50.

Domhoff, G. William. 2012. "Power in America: Wealth, Income, and Power." *Who Rules America?* http://sociology.ucsc.edu/whorulesamerica /power/wealth.html.

Downey, Greg. 2005. *Learning Capoeira: Lessons in Cunning from an Afro-Brazilian Art*. New York: Oxford University Press.

Dudley, Kathryn Marie. 2000. *Debt and Dispossession: Farm Loss in America's Heartland*. Chicago: University of Chicago Press.

Durkheim, Émile. (1912) 1965. *The Elementary Forms of Religious Life*. New York: Free Press.

Durrenberger, E. Paul. 2001. "No Shame in My Game: The Working Poor in the Inner City [Review]." *American Anthropologist* 103(4): 1210–11.

Durrenberger, E. Paul, and Suzan Erem. 2010. *Anthropology Unbound: A Field Guide to the 21st Century*, 2nd ed. Boulder, CO: Paradigm.

Economic Policy Institute. 2011. "Wealth Holdings Remain Unequal in Good and Bad Times." *The State of Working America*. Washington, DC: Economic Policy Institute.

Edelman, Marc. 1999. *Peasants against Globalization: Rural Social Movements in Costa Rica*. Stanford, CA: Stanford University Press.

———. 2001. "Social Movements: Changing Paradigms and Forms of Politics." *Annual Review of Anthropology* 30: 285–317.

Edelman, Marc, and Angelique Haugerud. 2005. *The Anthropology of Development and Globalization: From Classical Political Economy to Contemporary Neoliberalism*. Malden, MA: Blackwell.

Eller, Jack David. 1999. *From Culture to Ethnicity to Conflict: An Anthropological Perspective on Ethnic Conflict*. Ann Arbor: University of Michigan Press.

Elliot, Diana B. 2009. "Understanding Changes in Families and Households Pre- and Post-Katrina." Lecture. American Sociological Association Meeting, San Francisco, August 10. www.census .gov/hhes/families/files/katrina-asa.pdf.

England, Sarah. 2002. "The Production and Consumption of Pink-Collar Identities in the Caribbean." *Current Anthropology* 43(3): 522–23.

Englund, Harri. 1999. "A Different Kind of War Story [Review]." *Journal of the Royal Anthropological Institute* 5(1): 141–42.

Ericksen, Thomas Hylland. 2010. *Ethnicity and Nationalism*, 3rd ed. Boulder, CO: Pluto Press.

Evans-Pritchard, E. E. 1937. *Witchcraft, Oracles and Magic among the Azande*. Oxford, UK: Clarendon Press.

———. 1940. *The Nuer: A Description of the Modes of Livelihood and Political Institutions of a Nilotic People*. Oxford, UK: Clarendon Press.

———. 1951. *Kinship and Marriage among the Nuer*. Oxford, UK: Clarendon Press.

Fadiman, Anne. 1997. *The Spirit Catches You and You Fall Down: A Hmong Child, Her American Doctors, and the Collision of Two Cultures*. New York: Farrar, Straus, and Giroux.

Falk, R. 1993. "The Making of Global Citizenship." In *Global Visions: Beyond the New World Order*, edited by Jeremy Brecher, John B. Childs, and Jill Cutler, 39–50. Boston: South End.

Farmer, Paul. 1985. "The Anthropologist Within." *Harvard Medical Alumni Bulletin* 59(1): 23–28.

———. 2003. *Pathologies of Power: Health, Human Rights and the New War on the Poor*. Berkeley: University of California Press.

———. 2006. *AIDS and Accusation: Haiti and the Geography of Blame*. Berkeley: University of California Press.

Farquhar, Judith Brooke. 1986. "Knowledge and Practice in Chinese Medicine." PhD diss., University of Chicago, Department of Anthropology.

———. 1994. *Knowing Practice: The Clinical Encounter of Chinese Medicine*. Boulder, CO: Westview Press.

Fausto-Sterling, Anne. 1993. "The Five Sexes: Why Male and Female Are Not Enough." *The Sciences* May/April: 20–24.

Feagin, Joe R., and Clairece Booher Feagin. 2011. *Racial and Ethnic Relations*, 9th ed. New York: Pearson.

Feagin, Joe R., and Melvin P. Sikes. 1994. *Living with Racism: The Black Middle-Class Experience*. Boston: Beacon Press.

Fedigan, Linda. 1982. *Primate Paradigms: Sex Roles and Social Bonds*. Montreal: Eden Press.

———. 1986. "The Changing Role of Women in Models of Human Evolution." *Annual Reviews of Anthropology* 15: 25–66.

Feldman, Jeffrey D. 2001. "Reproducing Jews: A Cultural Account of Assisted Conception in Israel [Review]." *American Ethnologist* 28(4): 924–25.

Ferguson, Brian R. 2002. "The History of War: Fact vs. Fiction." In *Must We Fight? From the Battlefield to the Schoolyard, a New Perspective on Violent Conflict and Its Prevention*, edited by William L. Ury, 26–37. San Francisco: Jossey-Bass.

———. 2011. "Tribal Warfare." In *Encyclopedia of War*, 1st ed., 1–13. Malden, MA: Blackwell.

Ferguson, James, and Akhil Gupta. 2002. "Spatializing States: Toward an Ethnography of Neoliberal Governmentality." *American Ethnologist* 29(4): 981–1002.

FinAid. 2015. "Student Loan Debt Clock." www .finaid.org/loans/studentloandebtclock.phtml.

Finkler, Kaja. 2002. "Reproducing Jews: A Cultural Account of Assisted Conception in Israel [Review]." *Journal of Anthropological Research* 58(2): 299–301.

Finnstrom, Sverker. 2005. "Shadows of War: Violence, Power and International Profiteering in the Twenty-First Century [Review]." *Anthropological Quarterly* 78(2): 491–96.

Fisher, Bonnie, Leah E. Daigle, and Francis T. Cullen. 2010. *Unsafe in the Ivory Tower: The Sexual Victimization of College Women*. Los Angeles: Sage Publications.

Fisher, Helen. 2004. *Why We Love: The Nature and Chemistry of Romantic Love*. New York: Henry Holt.

Floyd, Charlene J. 1996. "A Theology of Insurrection? Religion and Politics in Mexico." *Journal of International Affairs* 50(1): 142–65.

Flueckiger, Joyce. 2006. *In Amma's Healing Room: Gender and Vernacular Islam in South India*. Bloomington: Indiana University Press.

Fluehr-Lobban, Carolyn. 2006. *Race and Racism: An Introduction*. Lanham, MD: Altamira Press.

Fortes, Meyer. 1949. "Time and Social Structure: An Ashanti Case Study." In *Social Structure: Studies Presented to A. R. Radcliffe-Brown*, edited by Meyer Fortes. Oxford, UK: Clarendon Press.

Fortes, Meyer, and E. E. Evans-Pritchard. 1940. *African Political Systems*. London: Published for the International Institute of African Languages & Cultures by the Oxford University Press.

Foucault, Michel. (1976) 1990. *The History of Sexuality*, vol. 1, *An Introduction*. New York: Vintage Books.

———. 1977. *Discipline and Punish: The Birth of the Prison*. New York: Pantheon.

———. 1978. *The History of Sexuality*. New York: Pantheon.

Fouts, Roger. 1997. *Next of Kin: What Chimpanzees Have Taught Me about Who We Are*. New York: William Morrow.

Frank, Andre Gunder. 1969. *Latin America: Underdevelopment or Revolution. Essays on the Development of Underdevelopment and the Immediate Enemy*. New York: Monthly Review Press.

———. 1998. *ReORIENT: Global Economy in the Asian Age*. Berkeley: University of California Press.

Franklin, Sarah. 1997. *Embodied Progress: A Cultural Account of Assisted Conception*. London: Routledge.

Frazer, James George. 1890. *The Golden Bough: A Study in Magic and Religion.* Reprint, New York: Macmillan, 1951.

Freeman, Carla. 2000. *High Tech and High Heels in the Global Economy: Women, Work, and Pink-Collar Identities in the Caribbean*. Durham, NC: Duke University Press.

Freud, Sigmund. 1952. *Totem and Taboo: Some Points of Agreement between the Mental Lives of Savages and Neurotics.* New York: Norton.

Freyre, Gilberto. (1933) 1944. *The Masters and the Slaves: A Study in the Development of Brazilian Civilization*. New York: Knopf.

Friedman, Jaclyn, and Jessica Valenti. 2008. *Yes Means Yes! Visions of Female Sexual Power and a World without Rape*. Berkeley, CA: Seal Press.

Gaudio, Rudolf. 2009. *Allah Made Us: Sexual Outlaws in an Islamic African City*. Malden, MA: Wiley-Blackwell.

Geertz, Clifford. 1973a. "Deep Play: Notes on a Balinese Cockfight." In *The Interpretation of Cultures*. New York: Basic Books.

———. 1973b. "Religion as a Cultural System." In *The Interpretation of Cultures*. New York: Basic Books.

Gellner, Ernest. 1983. *Nations and Nationalism*. Ithaca, NY: Cornell University Press.

Geromel, Ricardo. 2013. "Forbes' Billionaires World Map." *Forbes*, March 22. www.forbes.com/sites/ricardogeromel/2013/03/22/forbes-billionaires-map/.

Geyer, Michael. 1989. "The Militarization of Europe, 1914–1945." In *The Militarization of the Western World*, edited by John Gillis, 65–102. New Brunswick, NJ: Rutgers University Press.

Ghannam, Farha. 2012. "Meanings and Feelings: Local Interpretations of the Use of Violence in the Egyptian Revolution." *American Ethnologist* 39(1): 32–36.

Gibson, Jane. 1996. "The Social Construction of Whiteness in Shellcracker Haven, Florida." *Human Organization* 55(4): 379–89.

Giddens, Anthony. 1985. *The Nation-State and Violence*. Cambridge, UK: Polity.

Glazer, Nathan, and Daniel Patrick Moynihan. 1970. *Beyond the Melting Pot*, 2nd ed. Cambridge, MA: MIT Press.

Gledhill, John. 2000. *Power and Its Disguises: Anthropological Perspectives on Politics*. London: Pluto.

Global Footprint Network. 2013. http://footprintnetwork.org.

Gluckman, Max. 1954. *Rituals of Rebellion in South-East Africa.* Manchester, UK: Manchester University Press.

Gmelch, George. 1992. "Superstition and Ritual in American Baseball." *Elysian Fields Quarterly* 11(3): 25–36.

Goldstein, Donna M. 2003. *Laughter Out of Place: Race, Class, Violence, and Sexuality in a Rio Shantytown*. Berkeley: University of California Press.

Goode, Judith, and Jeff Maskovsky, eds. 2001. *The New Poverty Studies: The Ethnography of Power, Politics, and Impoverished People in the United States*. New York: New York University Press.

Gough, Kathleen. (1971) 2001. "Nuer Kinship: A Reexamination." In *The Translation of Culture: Essays to E. E. Evans-Pritchard*, edited by Thomas O. Beidelman, 79–121. London: Tavistock Publications.

Graeber, David. 2011. *Debt: The First Five Thousand Years*. Brooklyn, NY: Melville House.

Gramsci, Antonio. 1971. *Selections from the Prison Notebooks*. Quintin Hoare and Geoffrey Nowell Smith, translators and editors. New York: International Publishers.

Gray, John. 2004. *Men Are from Mars, Women Are from Venus: The Classic Guide to Understanding the Opposite Sex*. New York: Harper.

Green, Edward C. 1999. *Indigenous Theories of Contagious Disease*. Walnut Creek, CA: AltaMira.

Gregg, Jessica L. 2003. *Virtually Virgins: Sexual Strategies and Cervical Cancer in Recife, Brazil.* Stanford, CA: Stanford University Press.

Gregory, Steven. 1998. *Black Corona: Race and the Politics of Place in an Urban Community.* Princeton, NJ: Princeton University Press.

———. 2006. *The Devil behind the Mirror: Globalization and Politics in the Dominican Republic.* Berkeley: University of California Press.

Gregory, Steven, and Roger Sanjek, eds. 1994. *Race.* New Brunswick, NJ: Rutgers University Press.

Gudmundson, Lowell. 2001. "Peasants against Globalization: Rural Social Movement in Costa Rica [Review]." *Agricultural History* 75(4): 504–6.

Guest, Kenneth J. 2003. *God in Chinatown: Religion and Survival in New York's Evolving Immigrant Community.* New York: New York University Press.

———. 2011. "From Mott Street to East Broadway: Fuzhounese Immigrants and the Revitalization of New York's Chinatown." *Journal of Chinese Overseas* 2011(7): 24–44.

Gupta, Akhil, and James Ferguson, eds. 1997. *Culture, Power, Place: Explorations in Critical Anthropology.* Durham, NC: Duke University Press.

Gusterson, Hugh. 1996. *Nuclear Rites: A Weapons Laboratory at the End of the Cold War.* Berkeley: University of California Press.

———. 2004. *People of the Bomb: Portraits of America's Nuclear Complex.* Minneapolis: University of Minnesota Press.

Gutmann, Matthew C. 2007. *The Meanings of Macho: Being a Man in Mexico City.* Berkeley: University of California Press. First published 1996.

Hall, Edward T. 1966. *The Hidden Dimension.* New York: Anchor Books.

Hamdy, Sherine F. 2012. "Strength and Vulnerability after Egypt's Arab Spring Uprisings." *American Ethnologist* 39(1): 43–48.

Hannerz, Ulf. 1996. *Transnational Connections: Culture, People, Places.* London: Routledge.

Harding, Jennifer. 1998. "Investigating Sex: Essentialism and Constructionism." In *Sex Acts*, 8–22. London: Sage Publications.

Hargrove, Melissa D. 2009. "Mapping the 'Social Field of Whiteness': White Racism as Habitus in the City Where History Lives." *Transforming Anthropology* 17(2): 93–104.

Harris, Marvin. 1964. *Patterns of Race in the Americas.* New York: Walker.

———. 1970. "Referential Ambiguity in the Calculus of Brazilian Racial Identity." *Southwestern Journal of Anthropology* 21(1): 1–14.

———. 1974. *Cows, Pigs, Wars & Witches: The Riddles of Culture.* New York: Random House.

Harris, Reginald. 2009. "Allah Made Us [Review]." *Gay and Lesbian Review Worldwide* 16(6): 42.

Harrison, Faye V. 1998. "Introduction: Expanding the Discourse on 'Race.'" *American Anthropologist* 100(3): 609–31.

———. 2002a. "Subverting the Cultural Logics of Marked and Unmarked Racisms in the Global Era." In *Discrimination and Tolerations*, edited by K. Hastrup and G. Ulrich, 97–125. London: Kluwer Law International.

———. 2002b. "Unraveling 'Race' for the 21st Century." In *Exotic No More: Anthropology on the Front Lines*, edited by Jeremy MacClancy. Chicago: University of Chicago Press.

Harrison, K. David. 2007. *When Languages Die: The Extinction of the World's Languages and the Erosion of Human Knowledge.* New York: Oxford University Press.

Hartigan, John Jr. 1999. *Racial Situations: Class Predicaments of Whiteness in Detroit.* Princeton, NJ: Princeton University Press.

———. 2005. *Odd Tribes: Toward a Cultural Analysis of White People.* Durham, NC: Duke University Press.

Harvey, David. 1990. *The Condition of Postmodernity: An Enquiry into the Origins of Cultural Change.* Malden, MA: Blackwell.

Haugerud, Angelique, Margaret Priscilla Stone, and Peter D. Little. 2000. *Commodities and Globalization: Anthropological Perspectives.* Lanham, MD: Rowman and Littlefield.

Hearn, Jonathan. 2006. *Rethinking Nationalism: A Critical Introduction.* New York: Palgrave Macmillan.

Helmreich, Stefan. 2009. *Alien Ocean: Anthropological Voyages in Microbial Seas.* Berkeley: University of California Press.

Higgenbotham, Evelyn Brooks. 1992. "African-American Women's History and the Metalanguage of Race." *Signs: Journal of Women in Culture and Society* 17: 251–74.

Hirschkind, Charles. 2012. "Beyond Secular and Religious: An Intellectual Genealogy of Tahrir Square." *American Ethnologist* 39(1): 49–53.

Ho, Karen. 2008. *Liquidated: An Ethnography of Wall Street*. Durham, NC: Duke University Press.

Hobhouse, L. T. 1915. *Morals in Evolution; A Study in Comparative Ethics*. New York: Holt.

Hobsbawm, Eric, and Terence Ranger. 1983. *Invented Traditions*. Cambridge, UK: Cambridge University Press.

Hockings, Paul Edward, ed. 2003. *Principles of Visual Anthropology*, 3rd ed. Berlin: Mouton De Gruyter.

Holmes, Janet. 1998. "Women's Talk: The Question of Sociolinguistic Universals." In *Language and Gender: A Reader*, edited by Jennifer Coates, 461–83. Oxford, UK: Blackwell.

Honwana, Alcinda. 1999. "A Different Kind of War Story [Review]." *American Ethnologist* 26(2): 504–5.

Hopkins, Nancy. 1999. "A Study on the Status of Women Faculty in Science at MIT." *MIT Faculty Newsletter*, 11(4): 1–15. http://web.mit.edu/fnl/women/fnl114x.pdf.

Hostetler, John A. 1993. *Amish Society*, 4th ed. Baltimore: Johns Hopkins University Press.

———. 1997. *Hutterite Society*, 2nd ed. Baltimore: Johns Hopkins University Press.

Hubbard, Ruth. 1990. "The Social Construction of Sexuality." In *The Politics of Women's Biology*. New Brunswick, NJ: Rutgers University Press.

Ignatiev, Noel. 1995. *How the Irish Became White*. New York: Routledge Press.

Illouz, Eva. 1997. *Consuming the Romantic Utopia: Love and Cultural Contradictions of Capitalism*. Berkeley: University of California Press.

Inda, Jonathan Xavier, and Renato Rosaldo. 2002. *The Anthropology of Globalization: A Reader*. Malden, MA: Blackwell.

Ingraham, Chrys. 2008. *White Weddings: Romancing Heterosexuality in Popular Culture*, rev. ed. New York: Routledge. First published 1999.

Inhorn, Marcia. 1996. *Infertility and Patriarchy: The Cultural Politics of Gender and Family Life in Egypt*. Philadelphia: University of Pennsylvania Press.

International Monetary Fund. 2014. "World Economic Outlook Database." https://www.imf.org/external/pubs/ft/weo/2014/02/weodata/index.aspx.

International Organization for Migration. 2012. "Global Trends." www.iom.int/cms/en/sites/iom/home/about-migration/facts—figures-1.html.

Jacobs, A. J. 2005. "Tsukiji: The Fish Market at the Center of the World [Review]." *Contemporary Sociology* 34(4): 373–75.

Jankowiak, William, and Edward Fisher. 1992. "A Cross-Cultural Perspective on Romantic Love." *Ethnology* 31(2): 149–55.

Jaynes, Gregory. 1982. "A Louisiana Lawsuit Asks What It Means to Be Black, White, or 'Colored' in America." *Providence Sunday Journal*, October 14, A-19.

Jenkins, Richard. 1996. *Social Identity*. New York: Routledge.

———. 2008. *Rethinking Ethnicity*, 2nd ed. Thousand Oaks, CA: Sage.

Jones, Camara Phyllis. 2000. "Levels of Racism: A Theoretic Framework and a Gardener's Tale." *American Journal of Public Health* 90(8): 1212–15.

Jordan, Brigitte. 1993. *Birth in Four Cultures: A Crosscultural Investigation of Childbirth in Yucatan, Holland, Sweden, and the United States*. Rev. and expanded by Robbie Davis-Floyd. Prospect Heights, IL: Waveland Press.

Jordan, Miriam. 2010. "Arizona Grades Teachers on Fluency: State Pushes School Districts to Reassign Instructors with Heavy Accents or Other Shortcomings in Their English." *Wall Street Journal*, April 30.

Juris, Jeffrey S. 2012. "Reflections on #Occupy Everywhere: Social Media, Public Space, and Emerging Logics of Aggregation." *American Ethnologist* 39(2): 259–79.

Juris, Jeffrey S., and Alex Khasnabish. 2013. *Insurgent Encounters: Transnational Activism, Ethnography, and the Political*. Durham, NC: Duke University Press.

Kahn, Susan Martha. 2000. *Reproducing Jews: A Cultural Account of Assisted Conception in Israel*. Durham, NC: Duke University Press.

Katz, Jonathan Ned. 2007. *The Invention of Heterosexuality*, with a new preface. Chicago: University of Chicago Press. First published 1995.

Kennedy, Elizabeth Lapovsky. 1999. "Recognizing Ourselves [Review]." *American Ethnologist* 26(4): 1020–21.

Keynes, John Maynard. (1936) 2007. *The General Theory of Employment Interest and Money*. Houndmills, UK: Palgrave Macmillan.

Kidder, Tracy. 2003. *Mountains beyond Mountains: The Quest of Dr. Paul Farmer, A Man Who Would Cure the World*. New York: Random House.

Kingfisher, Catherine. 2001. "Poverty and Downward Mobility in the Land of Opportunity." *American Anthropologist* 103(3): 824–27.

Kinsey, Alfred C. 1953. *Sexual Behavior in the Human Female*. Philadelphia: W. B. Saunders.

Kinsey, Alfred C., Wardell Baxter Pomeroy, and Clyde E. Martin. 1948. *Sexual Behavior in the Human Male*. Philadelphia: W. B. Saunders.

Kleinman, Arthur. 1988. *The Illness Narratives: Suffering, Healing, and the Human Condition*. New York: Basic Books.

Knauft, Bruce M. 1991. "Violence and Sociality in Human Evolution." *Current Anthropology* 32(4): 391–408.

Kottak, Conrad P. 2006. *Assault on Paradise: The Globalization of a Little Community in Brazil*, 4th ed. New York: McGraw-Hill.

Kromidas, Maria. 2004. "Learning War/Learning Race: Fourth-Grade Students in the Aftermath of September 11th in New York City." *Critique of Anthropology* 24(1).

Krugman, Paul R. 2009. *The Return of Depression Economics and the Crisis of 2008*. New York: Norton.

Kuper, Adam. 1983. *Anthropology and Anthropologists: The Modern British School*. London: Routledge & Kegan Paul.

Kurtz, Donald V. 2001. *Political Anthropology: Power and Paradigms*. Boulder, CO: Westview Press.

Labov, William. 1972. *Language in the Inner City: Studies in the Black English Vernacular*. Philadelphia: University of Pennsylvania Press.

Lakoff, Robin T. 2004. *Language and Woman's Place: Text and Commentaries.* Edited by Mary Bucholtz. New York: Oxford University Press.

Lancaster, Roger N. 1994. *Life Is Hard: Machismo, Danger, and the Intimacy of Power in Nicaragua*. Berkeley: University of California Press.

———. 2003. *The Trouble with Nature: Sex in Science and Popular Culture*. Berkeley: University of California Press.

Landers, Melissa A., and Gary Alan Fine. 1996. "Learning Life's Lessons in Tee Ball: The Reinforcement of Gender and Status in Kindergarten Sport." *Sociology of Sport Journal* 13(1).

Larrain, Jorge, 1989. *Theories of Development: Capitalism, Colonialism and Dependency*. London: Polity Press.

Larsen, Clark Spencer. 2014. *Our Origins: Discovering Physical Anthropology*, 3rd ed. New York: Norton.

Leach, Edmund. 1954. *Political Systems of Highland Burma: A Study of Kachin Social Structure*. Cambridge, MA: Harvard University Press.

Leacock, Eleanor Burke. 1971. *The Culture of Poverty: A Critique*. New York: Simon & Schuster.

———. 1981. *Myths of Male Dominance: Collected Articles on Women Cross-Culturally*. New York: Monthly Review Press.

Leap, William L. 2010. "Allah Made Us [Review]." *Journal of the Royal Anthropological Institute* 16: 938–39.

Lee, Richard B. 1984. *The Dobe !Kung*. New York: Holt, Rinehart and Winston.

———. 2003. *The Dobe JuHoansi*, 3rd ed. (Case Studies in Cultural Anthropology). Belmont, CA: Wadsworth Publishing.

Lee, Richard B., and Irven Devore, eds. 1968. *Man the Hunter: The First Intensive Survey of a Single Crucial Stage of Human Development—Man's Once Universal Hunting Way of Life*. New York: The Wenner-Gren Foundation for Anthropological Research.

Lessinger, Johanna. 1995. *From the Ganges to the Hudson: Indian Immigrants in New York City*. Boston: Allyn & Bacon.

Lewellen, Ted C. 2002. *The Anthropology of Globalization: Cultural Anthropology Enters the 21st Century*. Westport, CT: Praeger.

———. 2003. *Political Anthropology: An Introduction*. Westport, CT: Praeger.

Lewin, Ellen. 1992. "Families We Choose: Lesbians, Gays, Kinship [Review]." *American Ethnologist* 19(4): 825–26.

———. 1995. "Life Is Hard [Review]." *American Ethnologist* 22(2): 441–42.

———. 1998. *Recognizing Ourselves: Ceremonies of Lesbian and Gay Commitment*. New York: Columbia University Press.

Lewis, M. Paul, Gary F. Simonds, and Charles D. Fennig, eds. 2014. *Ethnologue: Languages of the World*, 17th ed. Dallas: SIL International. www.ethnologue.org/17/.

Lewis, Oscar. 1959. *Five Families: Mexican Case Studies in the Culture of Poverty*. New York: Basic Books.

———. 1966. *La Vida: A Puerto Rican Family in the Culture of Poverty—San Juan and New York*. New York: Random House.

Leys, Colin. 1996. *The Rise and Fall of Development Theory*. Oxford, UK: James Currey.

Liang, Zai. 2012. "Recent Migration Trends in China: Geographic and Demographic Aspects of Development Implications." Presentation for UN Expert Group Meeting on New Trends in Migration: Demographic Aspects, New York, December 3. www.un.org/esa/population /meetings/EGM_MigrationTrends/UN _presentation_Dec_2012_FINAL_SH.pdf.

Limon, Jose E. 1997. "The Meanings of Macho: Being a Man in Mexico City [Review]." *American Anthropologist* 99(1): 185.

Lock, Margaret M. 1993. *Encounters with Aging: Mythologies of Menopause in Japan and North America.* Berkeley: University of California Press.

———. 2002. *Twice Dead: Organ Transplants and the Reinvention of Death.* Berkeley: University of California Press.

Lopez, Ian Haney. 2006. *White by Law: The Legal Construction of Race,* 2nd ed. New York: New York University Press.

Lorber, Judith. 1994. *Paradoxes of Gender.* New Haven, CT: Yale University Press.

Lowie, Robert Harry. (1920) 1961. *Primitive Society.* Reprint, New York: Harper & Brothers.

Lutz, Catherine. 2001. *Homefront: A Military City and the American Twentieth Century.* Boston: Beacon.

MacClancy, Jeremy, ed. 1996. *Sport, Identity and Ethnicity.* Oxford, UK: Berg.

Malinowski, Bronislaw. (1922) 2002. *Argonauts of the Western Pacific.* Reprint, London: Routledge.

———. 1927. *Sex and Repression in Savage Society.* London: Kegan Paul, Trench, Trübner & Co.

———. 1929. *The Sexual Life of Savages in North Western Melanesia: An Ethnographic Account of Courtship, Marriage and Family Life among the Natives of the Trobriand Islands, British New Guinea.* London: Kegan Paul, Trench, Trübner & Co.

———. 1930. "Parenthood—The Basis of Social Structure." In *The New Generation: The Intimate Problems of Modern Parents and Children,* edited by Victor F. Calverton and Samuel D. Schmalhausen. London: George Allen & Unwin.

Mallory, J. P., and D. Q. Adams. 2006. *The Oxford Introduction to Proto-Indo-European and the Proto-Indo-European World.* Oxford, UK: Oxford University Press.

Mamdani, Mahmood. 2002. *When Victims Become Killers: Colonialism, Nativism, and the Genocide in Rwanda.* Princeton, NJ: Princeton University Press.

Mantsios, Gregory. 2003. "Media Magic: Making Class Invisible." In *Race, Class, and Gender in the United States,* 6th ed., edited by Paula Rothenberg. New York: Worth Publishers.

Marable, Manning. 2002. "Whither Whiteness." *Souls: A Critical Journal of Black Politics, Culture and Society* 4(4): 45–73.

———. 2006. "Katrina's Unnatural Disaster: A Tragedy of Black Suffering and White Denial." *Souls: A Critical Journal of Black Politics, Culture and Society* 8(1): 1–8.

Marks, Jonathan. 1995. *Human Biodiversity: Genes, Race, and History.* New York: Aldine de Gruyter.

Marlowe, Frank. 2010. *The Hadza: Hunter-Gatherers of Tanzania.* Berkeley: University of California Press.

Martin, Emily. 1991. "The Egg and the Sperm: How Science Has Constructed a Romance Based on Stereotypical Male-Female Roles." *Signs: Journal of Women in Culture and Society* 16(3): 485–501.

Martin, Joann. 1999. "Women and Social Movements in Latin America: Power from Below [Review]." *American Ethnologist* 26(2): 482–83.

Marx, Karl. 1867. *Capital.* Reprint, London: Penguin, 1986.

Marx, Karl, and Friedrich Engels. 1848. *The Communist Manifesto.* Reprint, London: Penguin, 1967.

———. 1957. *On Religion.* Moscow: Foreign Languages Publishing House.

Mascia-Lees, Frances E. 2009. *Gender and Difference in a Globalizing World: Twenty-First Century Anthropology.* Prospect Heights, IL: Waveland Press.

Mauss, Marcel. 1979. "Body Techniques." In *Sociology and Psychology: Essays by Marcel Mauss.* Translated by Ben Brewster. London: Routledge and Kegan Paul.

McAdam, Doug, John D. McCarthy, and Mayer N. Zald. 1996. *Comparative Perspectives on Social Movements: Political Opportunities, Mobilizing Structures, and Cultural Framings.* Cambridge, UK: Cambridge University Press.

McAdoo, Harriette Pipes. 2000. "All Our Kin: Strategies for Survival in a Black Community [Review]." *Journal of Marriage and Family* 62(3): 864–65.

McCracken, Grant. 1991. *Culture and Consumption: New Approaches to the Symbolic Character of Consumer Goods and Activities*. Bloomington: Indiana University Press.

———. 2005. *Culture and Consumption II: Markets, Meaning, and Brand Management*. Bloomington: Indiana University Press.

McFate, Montgomery. 2005. "Anthropology and Counterinsurgency: The Strange Story of Their Curious Relationship." *Military Review* (March-April): 24–38.

McGrath, Charles. 2005. "In Fiction, a Long History of Fixation on the Social Gap." *New York Times*, June 8.

McIntosh, Peggy. 1989. "White Privilege: Unpacking the Invisible Knapsack." *Peace and Freedom* (July–August): 10–12.

McKibben, William. 2010. *Eaarth: Making a Life on a Tough New Planet*. New York: Henry Holt.

———. 2012. "Global Warming's Terrifying New Math." *Rolling Stone*, July 19. www.rollingstone.com/politics/news/global-warmings-terrifying-new-math-20120719.

McWhorter, John H. 2001. *The Power of Babel: A Natural History of Language*. New York: HarperCollins.

Mead, Margaret. 1928. *Coming of Age in Samoa: A Psychological Study of Primitive Youth for Western Civilization*. New York: William Morrow.

———. 1935. *Sex and Temperament in Three Primitive Societies*. New York: William Morrow.

Miles, H. Lyn White. 1993. "Language and the Orangutan: The Old 'Person of the Forest.'" In *The Great Ape Project*, edited by Paola Cavalieri and Peter Singer, 45–50. New York: St. Martin's Press.

Milkie, Melissa A. 2000. "White Weddings [Review]." *Gender and Society* 14(6): 824–26.

Miller, Raegen, and Diana Epstein. 2011. "There Still Be Dragons: Racial Disparity in School Funding Is No Myth." Center for American Progress. www.americanprogress.org/issues/education/report/2011/07/05/9943/there-still-be-dragons/.

Mills, Mary Beth. 2003. "Gender and Inequality in the Global Labor Force." *Annual Review of Anthropology* 32: 41–62.

Miner, Horace. 1956. "Body Ritual among the Nacirema." *American Anthropologist* 58(3): 503–7.

Mintz, Sidney W. 1985. *Sweetness and Power: The Place of Sugar in Modern History*. New York: Viking Penguin.

Molyneux, Maxine. 1999. "Women and Social Movements in Latin America: Power from Below [Review]." *Journal of Latin American Studies* 31(2): 535–37.

Monnier, Oliver. 2013. "Agribusiness: Smoothing Out the Bumps in Côte d'Ivoire." *The Africa Report*. July 25. www.theafricareport.com/West-Africa/agribusiness-smoothing-out-the-bumps-in-Cote-divoire.html.

Moore, Mignon R. 2011. *Invisible Families: Gay Identities, Relationships, and Motherhood among Black Women*. Berkeley: University of California Press.

———. 2012. "Intersectionality and the Study of Black, Sexual Minority Women." *Gender and Society* 26: 33–39.

Moran, Emilio F. 2006. *People and Nature: An Introduction to Human Ecological Relations*. Malden, MA: Blackwell.

Morgan, Lewis Henry. (1877) 1964. *Ancient Society*. Reprint, Cambridge, MA: Belknap Press.

Morrell, Virginia. 2008. "Inside Animal Minds: Birds, Apes, Dolphins and a Dog with a World-Class Vocabulary." *National Geographic*, March.

Moynihan, Daniel Patrick. 1965. *The Negro Family: The Case for National Action*. Washington, DC: U.S. Department of Labor.

Mukhopadhyay, Carol C., Rosemary Henze, and Yolanda T. Moses. 2007. *How Real Is Race? A Sourcebook on Race, Culture, and Biology*. Lanham, MD: Rowman and Littlefield.

Mullings, Leith. 2005a. "Interrogating Racism: Toward an Anti-Racist Anthropology." *Annual Review of Anthropology* 34: 667–93.

———. 2005b. "Resistance and Resilience: The Sojourner Syndrome and the Social Context of Reproduction in Central Harlem." *Transforming Anthropology* 13(2): 79–91.

Mullings, Leith, and Alaka Wali. 2001. *Stress and Resilience: The Social Context of Reproduction in Central Harlem*. New York: Kluwer Academic/Plenum Publishers.

Myerhoff, Barbara G. 1974. *Peyote Hunt: The Sacred Journey of the Huichol Indians*. Ithaca, NY: Cornell University Press.

———. 1978. *Number Our Days*. New York: Dutton.

Nader, Laura. 1972. "Up the Anthropologist: Perspectives Gained from Studying Up." In *Reinventing Anthropology*, edited by Dell H. Hymes, 284–311. New York: Pantheon.

Nahman, Michal Rachel. 2002. "Reproducing Jews: A Cultural Account of Assisted Conception in Israel [Review]." *Canadian Review of Sociology and Anthropology* 39(3): 359–61.

Nanda, Serena. 1998. *Neither Man nor Woman: The Hijras of India*, 2nd ed. Florence, KY: Wadsworth.

National Center for Women and Information Technology. 2015. "By the Numbers." www.ncwit.org/sites/default/files/resources/btn_04032015_web.pdf.

Neubeck, Kenneth J., and Noel A. Cazenave. 2001. *Welfare Racism: Playing the Race Card against America's Poor*. New York: Routledge.

Newman, Katherine S. (1988) 1999. *Falling from Grace: Downward Mobility in the Age of Affluence*. Reprint, Berkeley: University of California Press.

———. 1993. *Declining Fortunes: The Withering of the American Dream*. New York: Basic Books.

———. 1999. *No Shame in My Game: The Working Poor in the Inner City*. New York: Vintage.

Nordstrom, Carolyn. 1997. *A Different Kind of War Story*. Philadelphia: University of Pennsylvania Press.

———. 2004. *Shadows of War: Violence, Power, and International Profiteering in the Twenty-First Century*. Berkeley: University of California Press.

North, James. 2011. "The Roots of the Côte d'Ivoire Crisis: How the Demand for Chocolate—Yes, Chocolate!—Helped Fuel the Country's Civil War." *The Nation*, April 25.

Norton, M. I., and D. Ariely. 2011. "Building a Better America—One Wealth Quintile at a Time." *Perspectives on Psychological Science* 6(1): 9–12.

Nugent, David, and Joan Vincent, eds. 2004. *A Companion to the Anthropology of Politics*. Malden, MA: Blackwell.

Ogden, Cynthia L., Cheryl D. Fryar, Margaret D. Carroll, and Katherine M. Flegal. 2004. "Mean Body Weight, Height, and Body Mass Index, United States 1960–2002." *Advance Data from Vital and Health Statistics* 347(October 27).

Omi, Michael, and Howard Winant. 1994. *Racial Formation in the United States from the 1960s to the 1990s*, 2nd ed. New York: Routledge.

Ore, Tracy. 2010. *The Social Construction of Difference and Inequality: Race, Class, Gender, and Sexuality*. New York: McGraw-Hill.

Ortner, Sherri. 1974. "Is Female to Male as Nature Is to Culture?" In *Woman, Culture and Society*, edited by Michelle Z. Rosaldo and Louise Lamphere. Stanford, CA: Stanford University Press.

Parker, Richard. 1999. "The Meanings of Macho [Review]." *American Ethnologist* 26(2): 497–98.

Parsons, Talcott. 1964. *Theory of Social and Economic Organization*. New York: Simon & Schuster.

Pascoe, C. J. 2007. *Dude, You're a Fag: Masculinity and Sexuality in High School*. Berkeley: University of California Press.

Payer, Lynn. 1996. *Medicine and Culture: Varieties of Treatment in the United States, England, West Germany, and France*. New York: Henry Holt.

PayScale. 2015. www.payscale.com.

Peletz, Michael G. 1999. "The Heat of the Hearth [Review]." *American Ethnologist* 26(1): 251–52.

Pérez-Alemán, Paola. 1994. "Life Is Hard [Review]." *American Journal of Sociology* 99(5): 1393–95.

Perlroth, Nicole. 2012. "Venture Capital Partner Claims Sexual Harassment." *New York Times*, May 22. http://bits.blogs.nytimes.com/2012/05/22/kleiner-perkins-accused-of-sexual-harassment/.

Petersen, Glenn. 2009. *Traditional Micronesian Societies: Adaptation, Integration, and Political Organization*. Honolulu: University of Hawaii Press.

Pew Forum on Religion and Public Life. 2012. "'Nones' on the Rise." Poll, October 9. www.pewforum.org/Unaffiliated/nones-on-the-rise.aspx.

Pietsch, Theodore W. 1975. "Precocious Sexual Parasitism in the Deep Sea Ceratioid Anglerfish, *Cryptopsaras couesi* Gill." *Nature* 256(July 3): 38–40.

Pollitt, Katha. 2005. "Summers of Our Discontent." *The Nation*, February 21.

Polanyi, Karl. (1944) 2001. *The Great Transformation*. Reprint, Boston: Beacon.

Pordié, Laurent. 2008. *Tibetan Medicine in the Contemporary World: Global Politics of Medical Knowledge and Practice*. London: Routledge.

Portes, Alejandro, Patricia Fernández-Kelly, and William Haller. 2009. "The Adaptation of the Immigrant Second Generation in America: Theoretical Overview and Recent Evidence." *Journal of Ethnic and Migration Studies* 35(7): 1077–1104.

Portes, Alejandro, and Rubén G. Rumbaut. 2006. *Immigrant America: A Portrait*. Berkeley: University of California Press.

Price, David H. 2011. *Weaponizing Anthropology: Social Science in Service of the Militarized State*. Oakland, CA: AK Distribution.

Quinn, Naomi. 1977. "Anthropological Studies on Women's Status." *Annual Review of Anthropology* 6: 181–222.

Radcliffe-Brown, A. R. 1950. "Introduction." In *African Systems of Kinship and Marriage*, edited by A. R. Radcliffe-Brown and Daryll Forde. London: Oxford University Press.

Ramshaw, Emily. 2011. "Major Health Problems Linked to Poverty." *New York Times*, July 9. www.nytimes.com/2011/07/10/us/10tthealth.html.

Rathje, William, and Cullen Murphy. 2001. *Rubbish!: The Archaeology of Garbage*. Tucson: University of Arizona Press.

Rebhun, L. A., 1999. *The Heart Is Unknown Country: Love in the Changing Economy of Northeast Brazil*. Stanford, CA: Stanford University Press.

Redfield, Robert. 1941. *The Folk Culture of the Yucatan*. Chicago: University of Chicago Press.

Richards, Audrey. 1956. *Chisungu: A Girl's Initiation Ceremony among the Bemba of Northern Rhodesia*. London: Faber.

Richards, Paul. 1999. "A Different Kind of War Story [Review]." *American Anthropologist* 101(1): 214–15.

Richman, Karen. 2001. "High Tech and High Heels in the Global Economy [Review]." *American Ethnologist* 28(4): 954–55.

Richtel, Matt. 2006. "The Long-Distance Journey of a Fast Food Order." *New York Times*, April 11.

Rickford, John R., and Russell J. Rickford. 2000. *Spoken Soul: The Story of Black English*. New York: Wiley.

Robbins, Richard H. 2013. *Global Problems and the Culture of Capitalism*, 6th ed. Boston: Pearson.

Roberts, Elizabeth F. S., and Nancy Scheper-Hughes. 2011. "Introduction: Medical Migrations." *Body and Society* 17(2&3): 1–30.

Rodriquez, Clara. 2000. *Changing Race: Latinos, the Census, and the History of Ethnicity*. New York: New York University Press.

Rodseth, L., R. W. Wrangham, A. M. Harrigan, and B. Smuts. 1991. "The Human Community as a Primate Society." *Current Anthropology* 32: 221–54.

Roediger, David. 1992. *The Wages of Whiteness: Race and the Making of the American Working Class*. New York: Verso.

Rosaldo, Michelle Z. 1974. "Women, Culture and Society: A Theoretical Overview." In *Woman, Culture and Society*, edited by Michelle Z. Rosaldo and Louise Lamphere. Stanford, CA: Stanford University Press.

———. 1980. "The Use and Abuse of Anthropology: Reflections on Feminism and Cross-Cultural Understanding." *Signs: Journal of Women in Culture and Society* 5(3): 389–417.

Rouse, Roger. 1994. "Life Is Hard [Review]." *Contemporary Sociology* 23(1): 57–59.

Rubin, Gayle. 1975. "The Traffic in Women: Notes on the 'Political Economy' of Sex." In *Toward an Anthropology of Women*, edited by Rayna Reiter. New York: Monthly Review Press.

Rumbaut, Ruben G., and Alejandro Portes, eds. 2001. *Ethnicities: Children of Immigrants in America*. Berkeley: University of California Press.

Sachs, Jeffrey. 2005. *The End of Poverty: Economic Possibilities for Our Time*. New York: Penguin.

Sadker, Myra, and David Sadker. 1985. "Sexism in the Schoolroom of the 80s." *Psychology Today* (March): 54–57.

Sahlins, Marshall D. 1971. *Social Stratification in Polynesia*. Seattle: University of Washington Press.

———. (1974) 2004. *Stone Age Economics*. New York: Routledge.

Saillant, Francine, and Serge Genest, eds. 2007. *Medical Anthropology: Regional Perspectives and Shared Concerns*. Malden, MA: Blackwell.

Sanday, Peggy. 1990. *Fraternity Gang Rape: Sex, Brotherhood, and Privilege on Campus*. New York: New York University Press.

Sanders, Stephanie A., and June Machover Reinisch. 2006. "Would You Say You 'Had Sex' If . . . ?" In *The Language and Sexuality Reader*, edited by Deborah Cameron and Don Kulick. New York: Routledge.

Sanjek, Roger. 1994. "The Enduring Inequalities of Race." In *Race*, edited by Steven Gregory and Roger Sanjek, 1–17. New Brunswick, NJ: Rutgers University Press.

Sapir, Edward, and Morris Swadesh. 1946. "Word 2." In *American Indian Grammatical Categories*, 103–12. Reedited for Dell Hymes in *Language in Culture and Society*, 100–7. New York: Harper and Row, 1964.

Savage, Michael. 2003. *The Savage Nation: Saving America from the Liberal Assault on Our Borders, Language, and Culture*. Washington, DC: WND Books.

Savage, Michael, and Karel Williams, eds. 2008. *Remembering Elites*. Malden, MA: Blackwell.

Scheid, Volker. 2002. *Chinese Medicine in Contemporary China: Plurality and Synthesis.* Durham, NC: Duke University Press.

Scheid, Volker, and Hugh MacPherson. 2012. *Integrating East Asian Medicine into Contemporary Healthcare.* Edinburgh, UK: Churchill Livingstone Elsevier.

Scheper-Hughes, Nancy. 1992. *Death without Weeping: The Violence of Everyday Life in Brazil.* Berkeley: University of California Press.

———. 2002. "Min(d)ing the Body: On the Trail of Organ-Stealing Rumors." In *Exotic No More: Anthropology on the Front Lines*, edited by Jeremy MacClancy, 33–63. Chicago: University of Chicago Press.

———. 2013. "No More Angel Babies on the Alto do Cruzeiro: A Dispatch from Brazil's Revolution in Child Survival." *Natural History.* www.naturalhistorymag.com/features/282558 /no-more-angel-babies-on-the-alto-do-cruzeiro.

Scheper-Hughes, Nancy, and Margaret M. Lock. 1987. "The Mindful Body: A Prolegomenon to Future Work in Medical Anthropology." *Medical Anthropology Quarterly* 1(1): 6–41.

Schneider, David M. 1980. *American Kinship: A Cultural Account*, 2nd ed. Chicago: University of Chicago Press.

Schneider, Jane. 1977. "Was There a Pre-Capitalist World System?" *Peasant Studies* 6(1): 20–29.

Schoendorf, Kenneth C., Carol J. R. Hogue, and Joel C. Kleinman. 1992. "Mortality among Infants of Blacks as Compared to White College-Educated Parents." *New England Journal of Medicine* 326(23): 1522–26.

Schulz, Amy J., and Leith Mullings. 2006. *Gender, Race, Class, and Health: Intersectional Approaches.* San Francisco: Jossey-Bass.

Scott, James C. 1985. *Weapons of the Weak: Everyday Forms of Peasant Resistance.* New Haven, CT: Yale University Press.

Sebeok, Thomas A., and Donna J. Umiker-Sebeok, eds. 1980. *Speaking of Apes: A Critical Anthology of Two-Way Communication with Man*, 407–27. New York: Plenum Press.

Service, Elman R. 1962. *Primitive Social Organization: An Evolutionary Perspective.* New York: Random House.

———. 1966. *The Hunters.* Englewood Cliffs, NJ: Prentice Hall.

Severson, Kim. 2011. "Race-Based Names Dot the Landscape." *New York Times*, October 6.

Shanklin, Eugenia. 1998. "The Profession of the Color Blind: Sociocultural Anthropology and Racism in the 21st Century." *American Anthropologist* 100(3): 669–79.

Sharma, Aradhana, and Akhil Gupta, eds. 2006. *The Anthropology of the State: A Reader.* Malden, MA: Blackwell.

Sharp, Gene. 1993. *From Dictatorship to Democracy: A Conceptual Framework for Liberation.* East Boston: Albert Einstein Institution.

Shaw, Stephanie. 1996. *What a Woman Ought to Be and to Do: Black Professional Women Workers during the Jim Crow Era.* Chicago: University of Chicago Press.

Shiva, Vandana. 2006. "Building Water Democracy: People's Victory against Coca-Cola in Plachimada." In *Beyond Borders: Thinking Critically about Global Issues*, edited by Paula S. Rothenberg, 580–83. New York: Worth Publishers.

Siebel, Catherine. 2000. "White Weddings [Review]." *Teaching Sociology* 28(2): 175–76.

Singer, Merrill, and Hans A. Baer. 2007. *Introducing Medical Anthropology: A Discipline in Action.* Lanham, MD: AltaMira.

Smedley, Audrey. 1993. *Race in North America: Origins and Evolution of a Worldview.* Boulder, CO: Westview Press.

Smith, Adam. 1776. *Wealth of Nations.* Reprint, New York: Simon & Brown, 2010.

Smith, Neil. 2006. "There's No Such Thing as a Natural Disaster." In *Understanding Katrina: Perspectives from the Social Sciences.* Social Science Research Council. http://understandingkatrina .ssrc.org/Smith.

Smith, Robert C. 2006. *Mexican New York: Transnational Lives of New Immigrants.* Berkeley: University of California Press.

Spence, Jonathan D. 2013. *The Search for Modern China*, 3rd ed. New York: Norton.

Stack, Carol B. 1974. *All Our Kin: Strategies for Survival in a Black Community.* New York: Harper & Row.

Stange, Mary Zeiss. 1997. *Woman the Hunter.* Boston: Beacon Press.

Stark, Rodney, and William Sims Bainbridge. 1985. *The Future of Religion: Secularization, Revival, and Cult Formation.* Berkeley: University of California Press.

StatisticBrain.com. 2014. "Credit Card Debt Statistics – Statistic Brain." Statistic Brain

Research Institute, publishing as Statistic Brain. July 12. www.statisticbrain.com/credit-card -debt-statistics/.

Stephen, Lynn. 1995. "Women's Rights Are Human Rights: The Merging of Feminine and Feminist Interests among El Salvador's Mothers of the Disappeared (CO-MADRES)." *American Ethnologist* 22(4): 807–27.

Sterk, Claire E. 2000. *Tricking and Tripping: Prostitution in the Era of AIDS*. Putnam Valley, NY: Social Change.

Stevens, Carolyn S. 2005. "Tsukiji: The Fish Market at the Center of the World [Review]." *Journal of Asian Studies*, 64(4): 1022–23.

Steward, Julian H. 1956. *The People of Puerto Rico: A Study in Social Anthropology*. Urbana: University of Illinois Press.

Stiglitz, Joseph E. 2010. *Freefall: America, Free Markets, and the Sinking of the World Economy*. New York: Norton.

———. 2012. *The Price of Inequality: How Today's Divided Society Endangers Our Future*. New York: Norton.

Stocking, George W. 1983. *Observers Observed: Essays on Ethnographic Fieldwork*. Madison: University of Wisconsin Press.

———, ed. 1989. *A Franz Boas Reader: The Shaping of American Anthropology, 1883–1911*. Chicago: University of Chicago Press.

Stoller, Paul, and Cheryl Olkes. 1987. *In Sorcery's Shadow: A Memoir of Apprenticeship among the Songhay of Niger*. Chicago: University of Chicago Press.

Stone, Amy L. 2007. "Sexuality and Social Change: Sexual Relations in a Capitalist System." *American Anthropologist* 109(4): 753–55.

Stone, Linda. 2009. *Kinship and Gender: An Introduction*, 4th ed. Boulder, CO: Westview Press.

Swann, Joan. 2007. "Talk Control: An Illustration from the Classroom of Problems in Analysing Male Dominance of Conversation." In *Language and Gender: A Reader*, edited by Jennifer Coates, 185–96. London: Blackwell.

Tannen, Deborah. 2001. *You Just Don't Understand: Women and Men in Conversation*, 2nd ed. New York: Ballantine.

Tax Policy Center. 2015. Tax Facts. www .taxpolicycenter.org/taxfacts/displayafact .cfm?Docid=474.

Taylor, Robert Joseph. 2000. "All Our Kin: Strategies for Survival in a Black Community [Review]." *Journal of Marriage and Family* 62(3): 865–67.

Terrace, Herbert S., L. A. Petitto, R. J. Sanders, and T. G. Bever. 1979. "Can an Ape Create a Sentence?" *Science* 206(4421): 891–902.

Tett, Gillian. 2010. *Fool's Gold: The Inside Story of J.P. Morgan and How Wall Street Greed Corrupted Its Bold Dream and Created a Financial Catastrophe*. New York: Free Press.

Tierney, Patrick. 2000. *Darkness in El Dorado: How Scientists and Journalists Devastated the Amazon*. New York: Norton.

Trivedi, Bijal P. 2001. "Scientists Identify a Language Gene." *National Geographic News*, October 4. http://news.nationalgeographic.com /news/2001/10/1004_TVlanguagegene.html.

Trouillot, Michel-Rolph. 1994. "Culture, Color, and Politics in Haiti." In *Race*, edited by Steven Gregory and Roger Sanjek, 146–74. New Brunswick, NJ: Rutgers University Press.

———. 2003. *Global Transformations: Anthropology and the Modern World*. New York: Palgrave Macmillan.

Turnbull, Colin M. (1961) 2010. *The Forest People*. New York: Simon & Schuster.

Turner, Victor. 1957. *Schism and Continuity in an African Society: A Study of Ndembu Village Life*. Manchester, UK: Manchester University Press.

———. 1969. *The Ritual Process: Structure and Anti-Structure*. Chicago: Aldine.

Tylor, Edward Burnett. 1871. *Primitive Culture*. London: Murray.

United Nations Department of Economic and Social Affairs, Population Division. 2013. International Migrant Stock: the 2013 revision. www.un.org/en/development/desa /population/migration/data/estimates2/index .shtml.

United Nations Development Programme. 2013a. "Fast Facts: Poverty Reduction." www .fj.undp.org/content/undp/en/home/librarypage /results/fast_facts/poverty-reduction.html.

———. 2013b. "The Millennium Development Goals: Eight Goals for 2015." www.undp.org /mdg/.

United Nations High Commissioner for Refugees. 2014. "UNHCR Global Trends 2013." www. unhcr.org/5399a14f9.html.

Ury, William, ed. 2002. *Must We Fight? From the Battlefield to the Schoolyard—A New Perspective on Violent Conflict and Its Prevention*. San Francisco: Jossey-Bass.

Useem, Elizabeth. 1992. "Middle Schools and Math Groups: Parents' Involvement in Children's Math Placement." *Sociology of Education* 65: 263–79.

U.S. Census Bureau. 2010. "America's Families and Living Arrangements: 2010," Table FG3. www .census.gov/hhes/families/files/cps2010/tabFG4 -all.xls.

———. 2013. "New Orleans (city), Louisiana." State & County QuickFacts. http://quickfacts .census.gov/qfd/states/22/2255000.html.

———. 2014. "Income and Poverty, in the United States: 2013." www.census.gov/content/dam /Census/library/publications/2014/demo /p60-249.pdf.

U.S. Centers for Disease Control. 2012. "Births: Final Data for 2010." *National Vital Statistics Reports*, August 28. www.cdc.gov/nchs/data /nvsr/nvsr61/nvsr61_01.pdf#table02.

Valentine, David. 2007. *Imagining Transgender: An Ethnography of a Category*. Durham, NC: Duke University Press.

Van Gennep, Arnold. (1908) 1960. *The Rites of Passage*. Reprint, Chicago: University of Chicago Press.

Wacquant, Loic. 2002. "Scrutinizing the Street: Poverty, Morality, and the Pitfalls of Urban Ethnography." *American Journal of Sociology* 107(6): 1468–1532.

Wakin, Eric. 1992. *Anthropology Goes to War: Professional Ethics & Counterinsurgency in Thailand*. Madison: University of Wisconsin, Center for Southeast Asian Studies.

Walker, Sheila S. 2002. "Africanity vs Blackness: Race, Class and Culture in Brazil." *NACLA Report on the Americas* 35(6): 16–20.

Wallace, Anthony F. C. 1957. "Political Organization and Land Tenure among the Northwestern Indians, 1600–1830." *Southwest Journal of Anthropology* 13: 301–21.

Wallerstein, Immanuel Maurice. 1974. *World-Systems Analysis: An Introduction*. Durham, NC: Duke University Press.

Wardhaugh, Ronald. 2009. *An Introduction to Sociolinguistics*, 6th ed. London: Blackwell.

Wardlow, Holly. 2006. *Wayward Women: Sexuality and Agency in a New Guinea Society*. Berkeley: University of California Press.

Waterston, Alisse. 2009. *An Anthropology of War: Views from War Zones*. New York: Berghahn.

Watson, James L., ed. 1998. *Golden Arches East: McDonald's in East Asia*. Stanford, CA: Stanford University Press.

Weber, Eugen. 1976. *Peasants into Frenchmen: The Modernization of Rural France, 1870–1914*. Stanford, CA: Stanford University Press.

Weber, Max. (1905) 2002. *The Protestant Ethic and the Spirit of Capitalism*. Reprint, London: Routledge.

———. (1919) 1965. *Politics as a Vocation*. Reprint, Philadelphia: Fortress.

———. (1920) 1946. "Class, Status and Party." In *From Max Weber: Essays in Sociology*, edited and translated by Hans Gerth and C. Wright Mills. Reprint, New York: Free Press.

———. 1920. *Sociology of Religion*. Reprint, Boston: Beacon Press, 1993.

Weiner, Annette. 1976. *Women of Value, Men of Renown: New Perspectives in Trobriand Exchange*. Austin: University of Texas Press.

———. 1988. *The Trobrianders of Papua New Guinea*. New York: Holt, Rinehart and Winston.

Wekker, Gloria. 1999. "What's Identity Got to Do with It? Rethinking Identity in Light of the Mati Work in Suriname." In *Female Desires: Same-Sex and Transgender Practices across Cultures*, edited by Evelyn Blackwood and Saskia E. Wieringa, 119–38. New York: Columbia University Press.

———. 2006. *The Politics of Passion: Women's Sexual Culture in Afro-Surinamese Diaspora*. New York: Columbia University Press.

Welch, Cliff. 2001. "Peasants against Globalization: Rural Social Movement in Costa Rica [Review]." *Latin American Politics and Society* 43(4): 166–68.

West, Candace. 1998. "When the Doctor Is a 'Lady': Power, Status and Gender in Physician-Patient Encounters." In *Language and Gender: A Reader*, edited by Jennifer Coates, 396–412. London: Blackwell.

Weston, Kath. 1991. *Families We Choose: Lesbians, Gays, Kinship*. New York: Columbia University Press.

———. 1993. "Lesbian/Gay Studies in the House of Anthropology." *Annual Review of Anthropology* 22: 339–67.

Whitehouse, Bruce. 2012. *Migrants and Strangers in an African City: Exile, Dignity, Belonging*. Bloomington: Indiana University Press.

Wilkins, Amy C. 2008. "Dude You're a Fag: Masculinity and Sexuality in High School [Review]." *Contemporary Sociology* 37(3): 242–43.

Williams, Brackette F. 1995. "The Public I/Eye: Conducting Fieldwork to Do Homework on Homelessness and Begging in Two U.S. Cities." *Current Anthropology* 36(1): 25–51.

Williams, Brett. 2004. *Debt for Sale: A Social History of the Credit Trap*. Philadelphia: University of Pennsylvania Press.

Wilson, William Julius. 1987. *The Truly Disadvantaged: The Inner City, the Underclass, and Public Policy*. Chicago: University of Chicago Press.

Wolcott, Victoria W. 2001. *Remaking Respectability: African American Women in Interwar Detroit*. Chapel Hill: University of North Carolina Press.

Wolf, Eric R. 1982. *Europe and the People without History*. Berkeley: University of California Press.

———. 1990. "Distinguished Lecture: Facing Power—Old Insights, New Questions." *American Anthropologist* 92: 586–96.

———. 1999. *Envisioning Power: Ideologies of Dominance and Crisis*. Berkeley: University of California Press.

———. 2001. "Ethnicity and Nationhood." In *Pathways of Power: Building an Anthropology of the Modern World*. Berkeley: University of California Press.

Wolf-Meyer, Matthew J. 2012. *The Slumbering Masses: Sleep, Medicine, and Modern American Life*. Minneapolis: University of Minnesota Press.

World Food Programme. 2013. www.wfp.org.

World Health Organization. 2015. "Life expectancy." http://who.int/gho/mortality_burden_disease /life_tables/en/.

Wray, Matt, and Annalee Newitz, eds. 1996. *White Trash: Class, Race and the Construction of American Identity*. London: Routledge.

Yan, Yunxiang. 2003. *Private Life under Socialism: Love, Intimacy, and Family Change in a Chinese Village, 1949-1999*. Stanford, CA: Stanford University Press.

Younge, Gary. 2010. "What Soccer Says about Us." *The Nation,* July 19.

Zhan, Mei. 2009. *Other-Worldly: Making Chinese Medicine through Transnational Frames*. Durham, NC: Duke University Press.

Zimmer, Carl. 2010. "How Microbes Defend and Define Us." *New York Times,* July 13.

———. 2011. "Bacterial Ecosystems Divide People into 3 Groups, Scientists Say." *New York Times,* April 20.

Zinn, Howard. 2005. *A People's History of the United States: 1492–Present*, rev. ed. New York: HarperPerennial.

Credits

Index

Page numbers in *italics* refer to figures, illustrations, and tables.

A

AAA, *see* American Anthropological Association (AAA)

Abu-Lughod, Lila, 58, 59

academia, code switching in, 107

Accord Alliance, 187

adaptations in skin color, 127

adaptive strategies, *300,* 300–302

Admiralty Islands, 74

advertising

consumerism and, 56

sexuality in, *204, 205, 211,* 232

affinal relationships, 246–51, *250*

Afghanistan, 85, *85,* 180

Africa, 11

bridewealth agreements in, 250

evolution and, 13, *14,* 127

globalization and uneven development in, 21–22

Ju / Hoansi of, 267

Ku Klux Klan and, 134

marriage in, 248, 250

trade routes through, 304, *305*

see also specific countries

African Americans

Black English and, *108,* 108–9, *109*

Hurricane Katrina and, 122

intersectionality and, 147, 224–26, *225*

Jena High School incident and, 50–52, *51*

lynching of, 51

political activism of, in Corona, *143,* 143–45

poverty and, 252–53, 283, *284,* 285

use of the "N-word," *103,* 103–4

women

in computing workforce, 178

gay, intersection of race and sexuality for, 224–26, *225*

Harlem Birth Right Project and, 274–75, *275*

health care and, 411–12, *412*

see also race; racism

Africa Watch, 345

agency, 48–49, *50,* 351–52

aggression among primates, 347–48

Agrama, Hussein Ali, 355, 356, 357

agriculture, 300, 301, 302

ahimsa, 373–74

Algeria, 308, *309,* 333

Aliyah Senior Center, 75, 76

***Allah Made Us* (Gaudio),** 229

***All Our Kin* (Stack),** 252

Al Masjid al-Haram, *371*

Alto do Cruzeiro, 63–64, *64,* 87

ambilineal descent groups, 239

amchis, 400–402, *401*

American Academy of Pediatrics, 187

American Anthropological Association (AAA)

ethical guidelines of, 84

on same-sex partnerships, 259

American origin myth, 157–58, *158*

American Revolution, 134, 308

Amish, 267, *267*

Amnesty International, 345

analysis in ethnographic fieldwork, 80–81, *81*

Anderson, Benedict, 169–70, 253

Angelos, Peter, 264, 266, 292

anomie, 369

anonymity in research notes and publications, 86

anthropologist's toolkit, 77

anthropology

applied, 9

of childbirth, 396–400, *398, 399*

critical medical, 410–11

culture concept in, development of, *42,* 42–45, *43, 44, 45*

definition of, 8

four-field approach of, 12–18

archaeology in, 12, 15–17, *16*

cultural anthropology in, 12, 18

linguistic anthropology in, 12, 17–18

physical anthropology in, 12, *13,* 13–15, *14*

globalization and, 19–20, 24–27, *25, 26,* 70

medical, 394–95

overview of, 8–12

political, 336, 340

study of human sexuality, history of, 206

weaponizing of, 85

anticolonial struggles, 308–9, *310,* 352

Antioch College's sexual conduct policy, 226–28, *227*

antiwar movements, 352

ants, 95

apartheid, 36, 129

apes, 34, 209

applied anthropology, 9

April 6 Youth Movement, 334

APTA (Asia-Pacific Trade Agreement), 314

Arab Spring, 333–34, 357

archaeology, 12, 15–17, *16*

archaic *Homo sapiens,* 97

Ardhanari, *189*

Argentina, 249

***Argonauts of the Western Pacific* (Malinowski),** 44, 71–72

Arizona, 93–94, 116–17

arranged marriages, 246, 249
artificial insemination
    in Israel, 253–55, *254*
    via sperm donor, 235
Asad, Talal, 383
asexuality, 215
Asia, 304–5, *305*
    see also specific countries
Asian American women, 178
Asia-Pacific Trade Agreement
    (APTA), 314
assimilation vs.
    multiculturalism, 168–69
assisted reproductive
    technologies, 235,
    253–55, *254*, 257–58
asthma, 394
Australia
    aborigines of, 301, 369
    language loss in, 113
authorizing process for
    symbols, 383–84
Aymar Indians, 102
Azande, 378–79
Azhar Fatwa Council, 355
Aztec kingdom, 305

B
Bafokeng, 165–66
Bafokeng, Inc., 165–67, *166, 167*
Bahrain, 333
Bahuchara Mata, 188
balanced reciprocity, 303
Bali, 45, *45*
Baltimore Orioles, 263–64, 292
bands, *337,* 337–38, 340
Bangalore, *364*
Bangladesh, *7, 294,* 314
Barbados, 199–200, *200*
Barth, Fredrik, 157
baseball
    class and, 263–65, 292
    magic and, 380–81, *381*
bees, 95
behavior and culture, 52–54
Being Muslim the Bosnian Way
    (Bringa), 164
Belgium
    colonial rule in Rwanda, 162
    same-sex marriage in, 249
Bemba people, 8–9, 370, *370*

Benedict, Ruth, 43, *43*
Bestor, Theodore, 318
Beyond the Melting (Glazer
    and Moynihan), 168
Bharatiya Janata Party, 32
bilateral descent groups, 239
bilingual educational
    programs, 116–17
biological anthropology, *see*
    physical anthropology
biological needs vs. cultural
    patterns, 52–53
biomedicine, 402–4, *403,* 405
biopower, 187
birth, 396–400, *398, 399*
Birth in Four Cultures
    (Davis-Floyd), 397
bisexuality, 215
Bissessar, Kamla Persad, *160*
Black Corona (Gregory), 143
Black English, *108,* 108–9, *109*
blood relatives, 238
Board of Education, Brown v.,
    142, *142*
Boas, Franz, 8, 42, 43, 70–71, *71*
Boateng, Jerome, *153,* 154
Boateng, Kevin-Prince, *153,* 154
body, biomedical conceptions
    of, 403–4
body weight, 180
Boehm, Christopher, 338
Bohannan, Laura, 101
Bolivia, 102
Bonilla-Silva, Eduardo, 143
bonobos, sexuality of, 209, *209,*
    347, *347*
Bosnia, 163–64, *164, 165*
Bosnia: We Are All Neighbors,
    164
Bourdieu, Pierre, 106, 269, *272,*
    272–73
bourgeoisie, 270
Bourgois, Philippe, 86
Brahmans of Nepal, 247
Brazil
    Alto do Cruzeiro, 63–64, *64,* 87
    independence of, 308
    infant mortality rates in, 87
    kissing in, 32, *32*
    race, class, and gender in, 40,
    129–31, 130

    same-sex marriage in, 249
    Yanomami people of, 84
bridewealth, 250
Bridges, Khiara, 411, 412
Bringa, Tone, 163–64
Brodkin, Karen, 138–39
bronchitis, 394
Brown, Linda, *142*
Brown, Terry Lynn, *142*
Brown v. Board of Education,
    142, *142*
Brubaker, Rogers, 161
Buck, Pem, 134, 278, 279–80
Buddhism, 373–74, *400,*
    400–402, *401*
Buddhist monks in Myanmar,
    360, 361–62, 390–91
built environment, 79

C
Cairo, *50,* 355–57, *356*
calendars, 40
Cambodia, 314
Camden Yards Stadium, *262,*
    264
Cameron, Deborah, 228
Capital (Marx), 372
capitalism
    consumerism and, 55–56, *56*
    global economy and, 314–15
    Weber on, 375
Caribbean
    indigenous populations' lack of
    immunity to European
    diseases, 307–8
    offshoring in, 314
    plantation economy in, 306
carrying capacity, 302
Carsten, Janet, 251, 253
Catalan Atlas, *69*
catequistas, 385–86, *386*
Catholic Church
    Gregorian calendar and, 40
    revolutionary movement in
    Mexico and, 384, 385–86,
    386
    in the United States, 387, *387*
cattle, 239, 373–74, *374,* 382, 383
CCA (Concerned Community
    Adults), 144
Census, U.S., *132,* 132–33, 283

cesarean sections, 398
Chagnon, Napolean, 84
change, rapid, 22
Chantek (orangutan), 96
chemical waste, 6
Chiapas, 384–86, *386*
Chicago, 252–53
chiefdoms, 339, 340
childbirth, 396–400, *398, 399*
child labor, 41, *41*
children and poverty, 283
chimpanzees, 34, 97
China, 169, 341
   consumerism in, 55
   Cultural Revolution in, 244
   Dai Minority Park in, *167*
   economic growth in, 22
   globalization and, 21, 27,
      244–45
   kinship in, *244,* 244–46, *245*
   language continuum in, 110
   lunar calendar and, 40
   marriage in, 248
   migration and, 21, 27, 244–45,
      318, 319–20, *320,* 387–89
   offshoring in, 314
   termination of female fetuses
      in, 258
   time zone of, 40
   trade routes through, 304–5,
      305
   Yellow River Valley, 301
Chinchilla, Laura, 353
Chinese Americans, 136
Chinese medicine, 405–6, *406*
chisungu, 370, *370*
Chisungu (Richards), 8
Chomsky, Noam, 100
Christianity and symbols,
   382–83
chromosomes, 179
*Chrysanthemum and the
   Sword, The* (Benedict),
   43
civil rights movement, 129
civil society organizations, *345,*
   345–46
Civil War, American, 134
clans, 238
class, 263–93
   in Brazil, *130,* 130–31

definition of, 265
egalitarian societies and,
   266–67, *267*
health care and, 411–12, *412*
Hurricane Katrina and, 291
ranked societies and, 267–69,
   268
theories of, 269–75
   Bourdieu, *272,* 272–73
   Marx, 269–71, *271*
   Mullings, 273–75, *275*
   Weber, 271–72
   in the United States, 263–65,
      275–83
   consumer culture and,
      287–89
   income inequality and, 276,
      277
   media and, 287, 288
   middle class and working
      poor, 280–81
   poor whites in rural
      Kentucky, 278–80, *279*
   poverty and, 283–86, *284,*
      286
   wealth, Wall Street, and,
      281–82, *282*
   wealth inequality and,
      276–78, *277*
   whiteness and, intersections of,
      147, 147–49, *148*
climate change
   accelerating, 328
   globalization and, 24
   inequality and, 290–91
   tracking, 16
Clinton, Bill, 207
CNN, 25, 57
coal miners, *279*
Coca-Cola Company, 5–6,
   25, 57
cockfights, 45, *45*
cocoa, *296,* 297–98, *298*
code switching, 107
cognatic descent groups, 239
Cohen, Yehudi, 300
college campuses, U.S.
   religion on, 362
   sexuality and power on, 226–28,
      227
colonialism, 340

anthropology and, 8, 42, 70
definition of, 128, 306
France and, 155
global economy and, 305–8, *307*
impact on local people, 11, 75
language and, 94, 108, 111
nationalism and, 171
race and, 122, 128–31, *129,*
   130, 133
resistance to, 308–9, *310*
role of anthropologists in, 84, 85
in Rwanda, 162
in Tahiti, 32
triangle trade and, 306–8, *307*
colonias, 393–94
color, differences in
   descriptions and
   perceptions of, 102
color-blind ideology, 143
Columbus, Christopher, 70,
   305, 306
CO-MADRES, *197,* 197–99
Comaroff, Jean, 165
Comaroff, John, 165
Coming of Age in Samoa
   (Mead), 43, 74
commitment ceremonies,
   221–23
commodity chains, 316–18, *317*
communication, *see* language
communication technologies,
   6–7
Communion, 382
Communist Manifesto (Marx
   and Engels), 271, 372
communitas, 371
communities
   globalization and change in, 25
   imagined, 169–70
companionate marriage, 246,
   247
Concerned Community Adults
   (CCA), 144
consanguineal relatives, 238
consanguineous unions, 249
Constitution, U.S., 134, 174
consumer culture, 287–89
consumerism, 55–56, *56*
*Consuming the Romantic
   Utopia* (Illouz), 288
contagious magic, 377

core countries, 310–12, *311, 312*
Corona, Queens (New York City), 143–45
Coronado, Francisco Vásquez de, 94
corporate culture, 281–82, *282*
Cortéz, Hernando, 94
cosmopolitanism, *58,* 58–59, *59*
Costa Rica, 352–54, *353*
Côte d'Ivoire, 297–99, *298, 306,* 309, 312, 325
cows, 373–74, *374,* 382, 383
Cows, Pigs, Wars, & Witches (Harris), 373
credit cards, 56, 287–88
critical medical anthropology, 410–11
cross-cultural analysis, 81
Crow kinship system, 241, *241*
cultural anthropology, 12, 18
cultural capital, 272–73, *273*
cultural institutions, 46–48, *47*
cultural materialism, 373–74, *374*
cultural patterns vs. biological needs, 52–53
cultural relativism, 71
Cultural Revolution, 244
culture, 31–61
    behavior and, 52–54
    of consumerism, 55–56, *56,* 287–89
    corporate, 281–82, *282*
    creation of, 55–56, *56*
    definition of, 33
    development of concept of, *42,* 42–45, *43, 44, 45*
    elements of, 35–41
        mental maps of reality, 35, 39–41, *41*
        norms, 35–36
        symbols, 35, 37–39, *38*
        values, 35, 37
    four-field approach to, 12–18
        archaeology in, 12, 15–17, *16*
        cultural anthropology in, 12, 18
        linguistic anthropology in, 12, 17–18
        physical anthropology in, 12, *13,* 13–15, *14*

globalization and, 56–59, *58, 59*
influence on health and illness, 395–96, *396,* 414–17, *417*
    biomedicine, 402–4, *403*
    childbirth, 396–400, *398, 399*
    ethnomedicine, 400–402, *401*
kissing and, 31–32, *32,* 36, 41, 60–61
language and, 94
    debates on bilingual educational programs and, 116–17
    dialect and, 106
    gender and, 104–6, *105*
    historical linguistics, 109–11
    "N-word," 17–18, *103,* 103–4
    thinking and, 100–102
    variation in the United States, 107–9, *108, 109*
of poverty, *284,* 284–85
power and, 46–52, *47, 49, 50, 51,* 80–81
    agency in, 48–49, *50*
    cultural institutions and, 46–48, *47*
    hegemony in, 48, *49*
    meaning in, 50–52, *51*
process of learning, 34, *34*
sexuality and, *211,* 211–12, 231
as shared yet contested, 35
in the United States, 107–9, *108, 109, 284,* 284–85
wedding, 219–21, *221*

D
Dai Minority Park, *167*
dargah, 367
Darkness in El Dorado (Tierney), 84
Darwin, Charles, 42
data
    analysis of, 80–81, *81*
    strategies for gathering, 77–78
date rape, 226
Davis-Floyd, Robbie, 397
Dawei, Chen, 320–21
death squads in El Salvador, 197, *197*

Death without Weeping (Scheper-Hughes), 63
Defense of Marriage Act (DOMA), 223, 259
Denmark, 249
dependency theory, 310
descent groups, 238–46
    in a Chinese village, *244,* 244–46, *245*
    definition of, 238
    patterns in, searching for, 240–41, *240–41,* 243
    types of, 238–40, *239, 242,* 243
descriptive linguistics, 98–99, *99*
descriptive linguists, 17
development and industrial capitalism, 310
de Waal, Frans, 347–48
Dhaka, *7, 294*
dialect, 106
Diamond, Jared, 208, 210
Dibble, Scott, *211*
Dick, Ramona, *113*
difference model, 104–5
Different Kind of War Story, A (Nordstrom), 350
dimorphism, sexual, *see* sexual dimorphism
Dinka ethnic group, 243
Discipline and Punish (Foucault), 48
discrimination
    racial
        against immigrants to the United States, 136–37, *137*
        in individual racism, 141
        resistance to, *143,* 143–44
        white privilege and, 146–47
    sexual, 177
disease, 396
    illness vs., 396
    indigenous populations and, 84, 307–8
Disney, 25, 27
displacement, 97
distribution and exchange, 302–4
diversity

human, 6, 126–28
language, 111–12, *114*
DNA, 237
   race and, 125
   sequencing of, 13–14, 418
   testing, 258
dogs, 95, *95*
dolphins, 95, 209, *209*
DOMA (Defense of Marriage Act), 223, 259
domestic violence, 226
dominance model, 104, 105–6
"Do no harm" mandate, 84–85, *85*
Donor Sibling Registry, 235
dopamine, 210
dowries, 250–51
Dramas of Nationhood (Abu-Lughod), 58
drug dealers, 86
Dude, You're a Fag (Pascoe), 183
Durkheim, Émile, 369, *369*
dysentery, 394

E
Ebonics, 109
ecological footprint, human, *327*, 327–29
ecological overshoot, 328
economic liberalism, 314–15
economy, 299–300
   adaptive strategies and, *300*, 300–302
   definition of, 299
   distribution and exchange in, 302–4
   gender and, 192, *192*
   global, *see* global economy
   plantation, 306
   purpose of, 299–300
Edelman, Marc, 352, 353
education
   Bourdieu on, 272–73
   cultural capital and, 273, *273*
   debates over language instruction in Arizona, 116–17
   evolution and, 376
   inequality in, 290
   meritocracy of, 272

racial segregation in, 141–42, *142*
   sex education curriculums, 205, *211*
   social reproduction in, 272
egalitarian societies, 266–67, *267*, 301
egg, *193*, 193–94
Egypt, 341
   ancient stele with hieroglyphs from, *99*
   Arab Spring and, 333–34
   cosmopolitanism among rural poor in, *58*, 58–59, *59*
   Islamic Fatwa Councils in, 355–57, *356*
   marriage among ancient royalty in, 248
   Nile Valley of, 301
   protesters in Tahrir Square, *50*
Eid al-Fitr, *7*, *294*
Elementary Forms of Religious Life (Durkheim), 369
El Salvador
   mothers of "The Disappeared" in, *197*, 197–98
   rape as a weapon of state-sponsored torture, 198–99
e-mails, 100, *100*, 107
Emancipation Proclamation, 134
emic perspective, 81
emojis, 100
emoticons, 100, *100*
enculturation, 35
   definition of, 34
   families and, 237
   gender, 183
endangered languages, preserving, 113, 115
endogamy, 36, 249
Engels, Friedrich, 271, 372
England, 154
   see also United Kingdom
English-only laws, 94
entrepreneurial immigrants, 324
environment, 22–24, *23*, 352
epilepsy, 414–15
Episcopal Church, 258
Eskimo, *see* Inuit
ethics code, 83–86, *85*

ethnic boundary markers, 158
ethnic cleansing, 164, *165*
ethnicity, 153–75
   as a cultural construction, 157–60, *158*, *160*, 174
   definition of, 156
   as identity, 156–57
   nationalism and, 169–73, *170*, 174, 253
   race vs., 156
   as a source of conflict, 161–64
      in the former Yugoslavia, 161, 163–64, *164*, *165*
      in Rwanda, 161–63, *162*, *163*
   as a source of opportunity, 165–67, *167*
   in the United States, 168–69
   Ethnicity, Inc. (Comaroff and Comaroff), 165
Ethnicity without Groups (Brubaker), 161
ethnic vs. minority, 156
ethnocentrism, 9
ethnographic authority, 83
ethnographic fieldwork, 63–81
   as an essential part of anthropologist's training, 66–68, *67*
   definition of, 10, 63, 64
   development of idea of, 69–76, *71*, *72*, *73*, *74*, *76*
   globalization and changes in, 86–89, *88*
   as informing daily life, 69, *69*
   moral and ethical concerns in, 83–86, *85*
   multi-sited, *25*, 25–27, *26*
   reflexivity in conducting, 75
   as social science and art, 68–69
   synchronic approach to, 72–73
   techniques in
      analysis, 80–81, *81*
      mapping, 78–79
      preparation for fieldwork, 76–77
      skills and perspectives, 79–80
      strategies for gathering data, 77–78

ethnographies, writing
    ethnographic authority in, 83
    moral and ethical concerns in,
        83–86, *85*
    polyvocality in, 82–83
    reflexivity in, 83
Ethnologue, 113, *114*
ethnology, 18, 81
ethnomedicine, 400–402, *401*
ethnopharmacology, 400
etic perspective, 81
eugenics, 136
Europe
    emergence of social movements
        in, 352
    kissing in, 32
    trade routes through, 304–5,
        305
    see also specific countries
European Central Bank, 316
*Europe and the People without
    History* (Wolf), 75
Evans-Pritchard, E. E., 81, 83
    study of the Azande, 378–79
    study of the Nuer, 44, 73, *73,*
        102, 239, 243
evolution, 13, 14
    Darwin on, 42
    debates over teaching of, 376
    egalitarian societies and, 266
    gender ideologies on gender
        roles and, 194–96, *195*
    of human language capacity,
        97–98
    sexuality and, 210
    unilineal cultural, 42, 70
    violence and, 347
exchange of goods, 302–4
exogamy, 36, 249
export-processing factories,
    199–200, *200*

F
Facebook, 7
    Arab Spring and, 334
    civil society organizations' use
        of, 345
    code switching in, 107
Fadiman, Anne, 414, 415
Falling from Grace (Newman),
    281

Families We Choose (Weston),
    257
families, 236, 237
    of choice, 256–57, *257,* 259
    nuclear, 236, *240,* 255–56, *256*
    of same-sex partners, *258,*
        258–59
    see also descent groups
family of orientation, 255
family of procreation, 255
Farmer, Paul, 407, 408, 409
Fausto-Sterling, Anne, 187
Feagin, Joe, 147
feminism and reflexivity, 75
Ferguson, Plessy v., 141
Fertile Crescent, 301
fictive kin, 253
field notes, 78
fieldwork, ethnographic, *see*
    ethnographic fieldwork
FIFA, 154
financial services industry, 56
Fisher, Edward, 247
Fisher, Helen, 210
flexible accumulation, 20–21,
    313, 313–14, 318
Flickr, 115
Floyd, Charlene, 384
focal vocabulary, 101–2
food foragers, 300–301, *301,*
    337, 337–38
food foraging, *300,* 300–301
Food for Peace program, 353
Ford, Henry, 313
Fordism, 313
Ford Motor Company, 313
Fortes, Meyer, 336
Foucault, Michel, 48
    on biopower, 187
    on sexuality, 224
four-field approach, 12–18
    archaeology in, 12, 15–17, *16*
    Boas and, 70–71
    cultural anthropology in, 12, 18
    linguistic anthropology in, 12,
        17–18
    physical anthropology in, 12,
        13, 13–15, *14*
Fourteenth Amendment, 134,
    174
FOXP2 gene, 97

framing process, 354–55, *355*
France
    Algeria and, 308, *309*
    ban on religious symbols in
        public schools, *47,* 47–48,
        155
    colonial wars and, 307
    Côte d'Ivoire and, 298
    creation of common sense of
        nationality, *170,* 170–71
    ethnicity and nationalism in,
        155
    Haiti and, 308
    kissing in, 32, *32*
    language continuum between
        Italy and, 110
    Our Lady of Lourdes in, *414*
    same-sex marriage in, 249
    Sykes-Picot Agreement and,
        172
    World Cup and, 154–55, *155*
Frazer, James, 42, 43, 377
Freeman, Carla, 199, 200, 201
free market, 314–15
Freud, Sigmund, 248
*From the Ganges to the
    Hudson* (Lessinger),
    159
fur trade, 307
Fuzhou City, 244–45, 318,
    319–20, *320,* 388

G
Garbage Project, *16,* 16–17
Garner, Tyron, *250*
gatherers/gathering, *see*
    hunting and gathering
GATT, *see* Global Agreement
    on Trade and Tariffs
    (GATT)
Gaudio, Rudolf, 229, 231
gays and lesbians
    commitment ceremonies and,
        221–23
    emergence of grassroots rights
        movement for, 352
    families of same-sex partners,
        258, 258–59
    intersection of race and
        sexuality for black gay
        women, 224–26, *225*

marriage and, 211, 223, *223*, *258*, 258–59
in Nigeria, 229–31, *230*
as parents, 257, *257*
in South Africa, 230
Gbagbo, Laurent, 298–99
Geertz, Clifford, 44, 45, 83, 382, 384
gender, 177–202
  alternate, 188–90, *189*
  in Brazil, *130*, 130–31
  color vocabulary and, 102
  cultural construction of, 181–85, *182, 185*
  definition of, 179
  focal vocabulary and, 102
  globalization and, 199–201, *200*
  health care and, 411–12, *412*
  information technology industry and, 177–78, 202
  language and, 104–6, *105*
  Mullings on, 273–75, *275*
  performance of, 185–86
  power and, 191–92
  race, sexuality, and, 224–26, *225*
  sex vs., 179–81
gender ideologies
  challenging, 196–99, *197*
  definition of, 193
  on gender roles and evolution, 194–96, *195*
  on human reproduction, *193*, 193–94
gender inequality
  heterosexual marriage and, 220
  origins of, 53–54
gender performance, 185–86
gender roles
  early research on, 191–92, *192*
  as in flux, *180*
  gender ideologies on evolution and, 194–96, *195*
gender stereotypes, 193
gender stratification
  challenging, 196–99, *197*
  definition of, 193
  language and, 104–5, *105*
gender studies
  definition of, 178
  on male dominance, 191–92, *192*

genealogical descent, *see* descent groups
***Genealogies of Religion* (Asad),** 383
generalized reciprocity, 303
General Motors, 21
genetic variation, 125–28
genocide and ethnicity, 158, 161–63, *162, 163*
genotype, 126–28
Gere, Richard, *30*, 31, 32, 36, 41
Ghandi, Mohandas, 308
Ghonim, Wael, 334, *335*
GI Bill of Rights, 138
Gibson, Jane, 147, 148
Gini index, 289
Girls Who Code, 177
Giuliani, Rudy, 248
Glazer, Nathan, 168
Global Agreement on Trade and Tariffs (GATT), 314
global economy, 297–331
  commodity chains and, 316–18, *317*
  Côte d'Ivoire and, 297–99, *298*, 306, 309, 312, 325
  distribution and exchange in, 302–4
  gross national income of, 326
  organizing principles of, 314–16, 344
  purpose of, 299–300
  as reshaping migration, 318–26, *319, 320, 322, 323, 326*
  roots of, 304–14
    anticolonial struggles, 308–9, *310*
    colonialism, 305–8, *307*
    early long-distance trade routes, 304–5, *305*
    from Fordism to flexible accumulation, 312–14, *313*
    modern world economic system, 309–12, *311, 312*
  sustainability of, 326–29, *327*
  see also economy
global inequality, 289–91, *290*
globalization, 12, 18–27, 340
  anthropology and, 19–20, 24–27, *25, 26*, 70

  characteristics of, 20–24
    adapting to the natural world, 22
    climate change, 24
    flexible accumulation, 20–21, *313*, 313–14
    increasing migration, 19, *19*, 21, 57–58, *58*
    rapid change, 22
    shaping the natural world, *23*, 23–24
    time-space compression, 20
    uneven development, 21–22
  commodity chains and, 316–18
  culture and, 56–59, *58, 59*
  definition of, 18
  ethnographic fieldwork and, 86–89, *88*
  health and illness and, 413–17, *414, 417*
  impact on women in the labor force, 199–201, *200*
  language and, 111–13, *112, 113, 114*, 115
  poverty and, 285, 289
  racism and, 129
  religion and, 386–89, *387*
  sexuality and, 228–31, *230*
  states and, 344–46, *345*
  war and, 349–51, *351*
global migration patterns, *322*, 322–23
global warming, 16, 24
Gluckman, Max, 44
Gmelch, George, 380–81
***God in Chinatown* (Guest),** 82, 319
***Golden Arches East* (Watson),** 57
***Golden Bough, The* (Frazer),** 377
Goldstein, Donna, 130, 131
gonads, 179
Goodall, Jane, *14*
Goode, Judith, 285, 286
gorillas, *96*, 97, 180
Gough, Kathleen, 75, 243, 244
grammar, 99
Gramsci, Antonio, 48

Great Britain
    colonial wars and, 307
    FOXP2 gene in, 97
    Iraq and, 172, 173
    Sykes-Picot Agreement and,
       172
Greece, 316
greenhouse gases, 24
Gregorian calendar, 40
Gregory, Steven, 143, 145
gross national income of
    global economy, 326
Gutmann, Matthew, 184–85

H
habitus, 272
Hadza of Tanzania, 257
Haiti, 308, *407,* 407–9, *408*
hajj, 372
Hamlet, 101
Hansen's disease, 394
Harlem Birth Right Project,
    274–75, *275*
Harris, Marvin, 373
Harrison, Jeffrey, *235,* 236
Harry Potter series (Rowling),
    378
Harsha, Edna, *414*
harvested human organ
    trafficking, 87–89, *88*
Hawaii, 248
Hawaiian kinship system,
    240, 241
healing
    in India, 368, *400,* 400–402,
       401
    multiple systems of, 413–17,
       414, 417
health, 393–419
    Chinese medicine and, 405–6,
       406
    in *colonias,* 393–94
    cultural influences on, 395–96,
       396, 414–17, *417*
       biomedicine, 402–4, *403*
       childbirth, 396–400, *398,*
         399
       ethnomedicine, 400–402,
         401
    definition of, 395
    disparities, 409–12, *410, 412*

globalization and, 413–17,
    414, 417
    inequality, 290
    in rural Haiti, creating public
       health system, *407,* 407–9,
       408
    of women, 274–75, *275*
health care
    colliding cultures and, 414–16
    staff attitudes and delivery of
       in a New York women's
       clinic, 411–12, *412*
health transition, 409
hegemony, 48, *49,* 343–44
hepatitis A, 394
hermaphrodites, *see*
    intersexuals
Herodotus, 69
heterosexuality
    constructing, 219–21, *221*
    definition of, 215
    invention of, 216–18, *218*
Heurtelou, Luz, *258*
Heurtelou, Nastassia, *258*
Hidalgo y Costilla, Miguel, 385
Hierarchy in the Forest
    (Boehm), 338
High Tech, High Heels
    (Freeman), 199
hijras in Hinduism, 188–90, *189*
Hinduism
    alternate sexes and genders in,
       188–90, *189*
    cow as sacred in, 373–74, 382,
       383
    pilgrimage and, 372
    priest performing ritual
       blessings, *364*
hip-hop music, *103*
Hispanic American women,
    178
historical linguistics, 109–11
historical particularism, 43
historic archaeology, 16
historic linguists, 17
Hite, Shere, 217
Hmong refugees, 414–16
Ho, Karen, 281, 282
Hobbes, Thomas, 350
Hobsbawm, Eric, 170
holism, 12

Holland, 397
Hollywood, 25, 57
Homefront (Lutz), 348
homelessness, 69, *69*
Homo sapiens, archaic, 97
homosexuality, 215, 217
    see also gays and lesbians
Hopi language, 101
hormones, 210, 347
horticulture, 301
How the Jews Became White
    Folks (Brodkin), 138
Huichol Indians, 75
human agency, *see* agency
human ecological footprint,
    327, 327–29
human microbiome, 404
Human Microbiome Project,
    404
human organ trafficking,
    87–89, *88*
Human Relations Area Files, 81
Human Rights Watch, 345
Human Terrain Systems
    program, 85
hunger, global, 289–90
hunting and gathering
    bands and, 337, *337,* 338
    egalitarian societies and, 265,
       301
    gender ideologies on, 194–96,
       195, 300
    Ju / Hoansi of Kalahari region,
       267
    tribes and, 338
Hurricane Katrina, *120,* 121–22,
    150, 291
Husain Tekri shrine, *367,*
    367–68
Hussein, Saddam, 173
Hutterites, 267
Hutu, 161–63, *162, 163*
hypodescent, 135–36

I
Iceland, 249
identity
    ethnic, creating, 157–60, *158,*
       160
    ethnicity as, 156–57
    situational negotiation of, 159

illness
cultural influences on, 395–96,
    396, 414–17, *417*
definition of, 396
disease vs., 396
disparities, 409–12, *410*, *412*
globalization and, 413–17, *414*,
    417
see also health
illness narratives, 416–17, *417*
Illouz, Eva, 288
imagined communities,
    169–70
Imagined Communities
    (Anderson), 253
IMF, *see* International
    Monetary Fund (IMF)
imitative magic, 377
immigrants
children of, 116, 174–75
in France, 155
health care and, 411–12, *412*
Indian, 159–60, *160*
from Mali, 324–26, *325*, *326*
types of, *323*, 323–26, *326*
undocumented, 93–94, 174–75
see also migration
immigration
Boas' studies of U.S. policies on, 8
debates over Arizona's new law
    on, 116
race and, 136–40, *137*
religion and, 362, *363*, *387*,
    387–89
see also migration
Immorality Act, 36
Inca, 248
incest taboos, 247–49
income
definition of, 276
inequality
    global, 289, *290*, *290*
    increase in, 6
    in the United States, 276,
        277, 288
increasing migration, 19, *19*, 21
indentured workers, 133
India, 169
consumerism in, 55
dowries in, 250–51
healing in, *400*, 400–402, *401*

Husain Tekri shrine in, *367*,
    367–68
kissing in, 31–32, 36, 41
marriage in, 247, 248, 250–51
Prasanna Ganapathi Temple in
    Bangalore, *364*
resistance to British colonialism,
    308
termination of female fetuses
    in, 258
water scarcity in, 5–6, *6*, 23
Indian immigrants, 159–60, *160*
individual racism, 141
industrial agriculture, 300, 302
industrialism, 302
industrial mass production,
    313
Industrial Revolution, 270, 308,
    327
inequality, 263–93
egalitarian societies and,
    266–67, *267*
gender, 53–54, 220
global, effects of, 289–91, *290*
of health, 409–12, *410*, *412*
income, 6, 276, *277*, 288, 289,
    290, *290*
Millennial Development Goals
    to eliminate, 190
ranked societies and, 267–69, *268*
theories of class and, 269–75
    Bourdieu, *272*, 272–73
    Marx, 269–71, *271*
    Mullings, 273–75, *275*
    Weber, 271–72
in the United States, 263–65,
    275–83
    consumer culture and,
        287–89
    in income distribution, 276,
        277
    media and, 287, 288
    middle class and working
        poor and, 280–81
    poor whites in rural
        Kentucky and, 278–80,
        279
    poverty and, 283–86, *284*,
        286
    wealth, Wall Street, and,
        281–82, *282*

in wealth distribution,
    276–78, *277*, 304
infant mortality
in Brazil, 87
global economy and, 326
Harlem Birth Right Project
    and, 274
race and, 412
infectious disease, 84, 409
information technology
    industry, 177–78, 202
informed consent, 85–86
Ingraham, Chrys, 219, 220, 221
In Sorcery's Shadow (Stoller
    and Olkes), 379
institutional racism, 141–42, *143*
internal migration, *322*, 322–23
International Monetary Fund
    (IMF), 310
Costa Rica and, 353
free market and, 314
neoliberal policies and, 315,
    316, 344
Ouattara and, 298
interpretivist approach, 44–45,
    45, 394
interracial marriage, 48, *49*, 130
U.S. laws outlawing, 36, 134,
    249, *250*
intersectionality
among race, gender, and class
    Harlem Birth Right Project,
        273–75, *275*
    poor whites in rural
        Kentucky, 278–80, *279*
definition of, 147, 274
of whiteness and class, *147*,
    147–49, *148*
Intersex Society of North
    America, 187
intersexuals, 187–88
interviews, 78
Inuit, 257, 301
hunting and, *337*
kinship system, *240*, 241
Invisible Families (Moore),
    224
iPhone, *312*
Iraq, 85, 169, *172*, 172–73, 333
Ireland, 156
Irish Americans, 136–38

Iroquois kinship system, 241, *241*

ISIL (the Islamic State in Iraq and the Levant), 172

ISIS, *see* ISIL (the Islamic State in Iraq and the Levant)

Islam
Five Pillars of, 366
local expressions and creative adaptations of, 366–68, *367*
sharia law, 229, 355–56, 357
see also Muslims

Islamic Fatwa Councils, 355–57, *356*

Israel, 253–55, *254*

Italy, 110

J

Jackson Heights, Queens (New York City), 159–60, *160*

Jainism, 373–74

Jankowiak, William, 247

Japan, 341
global trade in seafood in, *317*, 317–18
life expectancy in, 409–10, *410*
racial categories of, 40
World War II and, 309

Jay-Z, *103*

Jena High School, 50–52, *51*

Jerusalem, 372

Jewish immigrants, 75, *76*

Jim Crow laws, 134, 141
definition of, 134
in Kentucky, 279
poverty and, 285

Johnson, Virginia, 217

John XXIII, 385

Jones, Adam, 263

Jordan, 333

Judaism and symbols, 382–83, *383*

Judge, *137*

Ju / Hoansi, 267

Juris, Jeffrey, 354, 355

K

Kaaba, *371*

Kahn, Susan, 253

Kano, *229*, 229–31, *230*

Katz, Jonathan, 216

Kennedy, John F., *239*

Kennedy, Joseph, Sr., 238, *239*

Kennedy, Robert, *239*

Kentucky, 278–80, *279*

Kenya, 21, 249

key informants, 77

Keynes, John Maynard, 314, 315, 316

kidneys, trafficking of, *88*, 88–89

kindred exogamy, 249

kinesics, 99, 100

Kinsey, Alfred, 217–18, *218*

kinship, 235–60
among the Langkawi, 251–52, *252*
artificial insemination in Israel and, 253–55, *254*
bands, *337*, 337–38
definition of, 236
by descent, 238–46
in a Chinese village, *244*, 244–46, *245*
patterns in, searching for, 240–41, *240–41*, 243
types of, 238–40, *239*, *242*, 243
fictive, 253
as a means to survive poverty, 252–53
through marriage and affinal ties, 246–51, *250*
in the United States
familes of same-sex partners, *258*, 258–59
impact of assisted reproductive technologies on, 257–58
nuclear family, 255–56, *256*
through choice, 256–57, *257, 259*

kinship analysis, 78

kissing, 31–32, *32*, 36, 41, 60–61

Kleiner Perkins Caufield & Byers, 177

Kleinman, Arthur, 416

Koko (gorilla), *96*

Krafft-Ebings, Richard von, 216

Kromidas, Maria, 138, 140

Ku Klux Klan, 134

Kula ring, 72

!Kung san men, *300*

Kurds, 172–73

Kwakiutl, 268–69

Kwakiutl indigenous people, 43, 71

L

labor immigrants, 323

Lakoff, Robin, 102

Lakota language, 113, 115

Lancaster, Roger, 214

Langkawi, 251–52, *252*

language, 93–117
of Arizona's law on undocumented immigrants, 93–94
of children of immigrants, 116
culture and, 94
dialect and, 106
gender and, 104–6, *105*
historical linguistics, 109–11
"N-word," 17–18, *103*, 103–4
thinking and, 100–102
variation in the United States, 107–9, *108, 109*
debates on bilingual educational programs in Arizona and, 116–17
definition of, 95
globalization and, 111–15, *112*
diminishing language diversity, 111–12
hastening language loss, 112–13, *113, 114,* 115
sexuality and, in Nigeria, *229*, 229–31, *230*
origins of, 95–100, *99*
revitalization, 113
top twenty world languages, *112*
world languages by country, *114*

language continuum, 110

language loss, 112–13, *113, 114,* 115

Laos, *32*

Latin America
debt crisis in, 353
debts to IMF, 316
see also specific countries

Laughter Out of Place (Goldstein), 130
Lawrence, John, *250*
Lawrence v. Texas, 250
Leacock, Eleanor Burke, 285
League of Nations, 172
Lee, Lia, 414–16, 417, *417,* 418
LeFrak City, 144
leprosy, 394
lesbians, *see* gays and lesbians
Lessinger, Johanna, 159
Levi's, 25, 57
Levi-Strauss, Claude, 100
Lewin, Ellen, 221, 222
Lewinsky, Monica, 207
Lewis, Oscar, 284
lexicon, 101
Libya, 333
life chances, 272
life expectancy, 326.409, *410*
life histories, 78
Life Is Hard (Lancaster), 214
liminality, 370–71
Lincoln, Abraham, 134
lineages, 238
linguistic anthropology, 12, 17–18
    focal vocabulary and, 101–2
    historical linguistics and, 109–11
    language and gender in, 104–6, *105*
    see also language; sociolinguistics
Linnaeus, Carolus, 39
Liquidated (Ho), 281
literature review, 76–77
LiveAndTell, 115
Living with Racism (Feagin and Sikes), 147
loban, 368
Lock, Margaret, 403
London, *10*
Lord of the Rings (Tolkien), *378*
Louisiana
    Hurricane Katrina and, *120,* 121–22, 150, 291
    Jena High School in, 50–52, *51*
love, 210, 247
Loving, Mildred, *250*
Loving, Richard, *250*

Loving v. Virginia, 36, *250*
lunar calendar, 40
lust, 210
Lutz, Catherine, 348, 349
lynching of African Americans, 51
Lyndon, Johnson, 284–85

M
machismo
    in Mexico, 184–85, *185*
    in Nicaragua, 214–15
magic
    baseball and, 380–81, *381*
    contagious, 377
    definition of, 377
    imitative, 377
    religion and, 377–80, *378, 380,* 381–82
Makah Nation, *268*
Malaysia, *50,* 251–52, *252*
Mali
    King of (in 1375), *11*
    migrants from, 324–26, *325, 326*
Malinowski, Bronislaw, 42, 44, *72,* 75, 192, *192, 239*
    as the father of fieldwork, 71–72
    on human sexuality, 206
    on incest taboos, 248
Managua, alternate constructions of sexuality in, 214–15
Mandarin, 110
Mantsios, Gregory, 287
mapping, 78–79
Mardi Gras (film), 81
Mardi Gras beads, 81, *81*
market exchange, 304
Marks, Jonathan, 127
marriage
    among the Nuer, *242,* 247, 249
    arranged, 246, 249
    companionate, 246, 247
    culture and, 36
    definition of, 246
    heterosexuality and, 220–21
    between Hutu and Tutsi, 162
    incest taboos and, 247–49
    interracial, 36, 48, *49,* 130, 134, 249, *250*

kinship through, 246–51, *250*
    same-sex, 211, 223, *223,* 249, *258,* 258–59
Martin, Emily, 193, 194
martyrs, 367
Marx, Karl, 269, *372*
    on religion, 372–73
    theory on class, 269–71, *271*
Maryland Stadium Authority, 264
masculinity
    in Mexico, 184–85, *185*
    in a U.S. high school, 183–84
Maskovsky, Jeff, 285, 286
mass production, industrial, 313
Masters, William, 217
masturbation, 216
masu harka, 229, 231
maternal mortality, 412
mati work, 212–14, *213*
matrilineal descent groups, 238, 239
Mayan kingdom, 305
McDonald's, 25, 27, 57, *58*
McIntosh, Peggy, 146, 147
Mead, Margaret, 43, 74, *74,* 178, 206
meaning, religion as a system of, 382–83, *383,* 384–86, *386*
Meanings of Macho, The (Gutmann), 184
means of production, 270
Mecca, 366, 372
media
    role in class and inequality in the United States, 287, 288
    on tribes, 338
Medicaid, 411
medical anthropology, 394–95
medical ecology, 394
medical migration, 413, *414*
medical pluralism, 413–17, *414, 417*
medicine, practice of
    colliding cultures and, 414–16
    globalization and, 413–17, *414, 417*
    staff attitudes and, 411–12, *412*
    see also health

melting pot, 168
mental maps of reality, 35,
    39–41, *41*
meritocracy, 143, 272
Mesopotamia, 341
Metropolitan Museum of Art,
    273
Mexican independence
    movement, 385–86
Mexican New York (Smith), 57
Mexico
    childbirth in, 397, *398*, 399
    machismo in, 184–85, *185*
    offshoring in, 314
    religion and revolution in,
        384–86, *386*
microbes, 404
Microsoft, 25
middle class, U.S., 280–81
Middle East
    Arab Spring in, 333–34, 357
    consumerism in, 55
    early long-distance trade routes
        through, 304, *305*
    marriage in, 248
    migration in, *319*
Middle Easterners,
    racialization of,
    138–40
middle sexes, see intersexuals
Midwestern accent, 107
*Migrants and Strangers in
    an African City*
    (Whitehouse), 324
migration
    global economy and, 318–26,
        323, 326
    bridges and barriers in,
        319–22, *320*
    global migration patterns,
        322, 322–23
    pushes and pulls in, 319, *319*
    types of immigrants, *323,*
        323–26, *326*
    globalization and, 19, *19,* 21,
        57–58, *58*
    internal, *322,* 322–23
    medical, 413, *414*
Miles, Lyn, 96
militarization, 348–49, *349*
military

intervention, 297–99
    U.S., 84, 85, *85, 180,* 206
Millennial Development Goals,
    190
Millward, Lily, *392,* 393
Milosevic, Slobodan, 334
Miner, Horace, 67–68
miners, *279*
minority vs. ethnic, 156
Mintz, Sydney, 74, 75
miscegenation, 36, 48, *49,*
    130, 249
missionaries in Summer
    Institute of Linguistics,
    113
modernization theories, 309–10
modern world systems
    analysis, 310–12, *311,*
    312
monkeys, 34
monogamy, 247
Moore, Mignon, 224, 226
moral code, 83–86, 85
Morgan, Lewis Henry, 42, 43, 70
Morocco, 333
morphemes, 98–99
morphology, 98
mortgage foreclosures, protest
    against, *145*
mothers of "The Disappeared"
    in El Salvador, *197,*
    197–98
Mountains beyond Mountains
    (Farmer), 407
movies, sexuality in, 205
Moynihan, Daniel Patrick, 168,
    284, 285
Moynihan Report, 252
Mozambique, 349–50
Mubarak, Hosni, 333
Muhammad (Prophet), 366, 367
Mullings, Leith, 269, 273–75,
    275, 285
multiculturalism vs.
    assimilation, 168–69
multi-sited ethnography, *25,*
    25–27, *26*
Muslims
    in Bosnia, 163–64, *165*
    in France, *47,* 47–48
    in Nigeria, 229

see also Islam
mutual transformation, 80
Myanmar, *360,* 361–62, 390–91
Myerhoff, Barbara, 75–76, *76*

N
Nacirema, 67–68, *68*
NAFTA (North American Free
    Trade Agreement), 314
Nanda, Serena, 188
Nandi, 249
National Center for Women
    and Information
    Technology, 178
nationalism, 153–56, 169–75
    anticolonialism and, 171
    definition of, 169
    ethnicity and, 169–73, *170,*
        174, 253
    kinship and, 253, 254–55
nationality, 154
nations
    definition of, 169
    as imagined communities,
        169–70
    as invented traditions, 170–71
nation-states, 169, 297–99
Native Americans
    dispossession from lands, 279
    fur trade and, 307
    Hopi language, 101
    kinship systems among, 241,
        241
    lack of immunity to European
        diseases, 307–8
    language loss among, 113
    Morgan's fieldwork among, 70
    potlatch among, *268,* 268–69
nativism, 136, 137
nature vs. nurture, 12, 53–54
Nazi Germany, 36
Neandertals, 97
Neel, James, 84
negative reciprocity, 303
Neither Man nor Woman
    (Nanda), 188
neocolonialism, 310
neoliberalism
    definition of, 315
    global economy and, 314,
        315–16, 344

pros and cons of neoliberal policies, 315–16
Nepal, 247
Netherlands, 32, 249
New Guinea, 74
Newman, Katherine S., 281
New Orleans, *120*, 121–22, 150, 291
New York City
    funding of public schools in, 142
    Indian immigrants in, 159–60, *160*
    Islamic community center in, 175
    political activism of community in, *143*, 143–45
New York Climate Change March, *327*
New York Times, 235, 287
New Zealand, 249
NGOs, *see* civil society organizations
Nicaragua, 214–15
Niger, 379–80, *380*
Nigeria
    Bohannan's fieldwork in, 101
    sexuality, language, and the effects of globalization in, *229*, 229–31, *230*
Nile Valley, 301
nongovernmental organizations (NGOs), *see* civil society organizations
nonviolence
    as political resistance, 334
    religion and, 373–74
Nordstrom, Carolyn, 349, 350, 351
norepinephrine, 210
norms, 35–36
North American Free Trade Agreement (NAFTA), 314
North Atlantic Biocultural Organisation international field school, 16
Northern Ireland, 154
    see also United Kingdom

Norway, 249
No Shame in My Game (Newman), 281
nuclear family
    definition of, 236
    Hawaiian, *240*
    the ideal vs. the reality, 255–56, *256*
    incest taboos and, 247–48
Nuer, The (Evans-Pritchard), 44, 73
Nuer of Southern Sudan
    Evans-Pritchard fieldwork with, 44, 73, *73*, 102
    Gough fieldwork with, 75
    kinship relations of, 239–40, *242*, 243
    marriage and, *242*, 247, 249
Number Our Days (Myerhoff), 75–76, *76*
Nuremburg Laws, 36
nurture, nature vs., 12, 53–54
"N-word," 17–18, *103*, 103–4
Nyar of India, 247
Nyimba of Tibet, 247

O
Oakland Unified School District, 109
Obama, Barack, 136, 174
Occupy Boston, 354
Occupy Wall Street movement, 288, 354–55, *355*
ocytocin, 210
O'Donnell, Rosie, 258
offshoring, 21, *313*, 313–14
Oklahoma, 113
Olkes, Cherl, 379
Omaha kinship system, 241, *241*
Oman, 333
"one drop of blood rule," 135–36
open-mindedness in ethnographic fieldwork, 79–80
orangutans, 96, 97
Organs Watch, 88
organ trafficking, human, 87–89, *88*
origin myths, 157–58, *158*

Ortiz, David, *381*
Ortner, Sherri, 191
Other-Worldly (Zhan), 405
Otpar, 334
Ottoman Empire, 172
Ouattara, Alassane, 298–99
Our Lady of Lourdes, *414*
outsourcing, *313*, 314
Oxford English Dictionary Supplement, 216

P
pain during childbirth, 398–400, *399*
Pakistan, 21, 301
paleoanthropology, *13*, 13–14
Panameno de Garcia, Alicia, 198
Pao, Ellen, 177
paralanguage, 99–100
Paramaribo, Suriname, 212–14, *213*
participant observation, 18, 72
Partners in Health, 408–9
Pascoe, C. J., 183–84
pastoralism, 301, 338
Patrick, Neil, 258
patrilineal descent groups, 238–40, *239*, *242*, 243
Patterns of Culture (Benedict), 43
Patterson, Francine, *96*
Peasants against Globalization (Edelman), 352
Pediatrics, 188
People of Puerto Rico, The (Steward), 74
People's History of the United States, A (Zinn), 158
periphery countries, *311*, 311–12, *312*
Peru, 21, 248
petroglyphs, ancient, *195*
Peyote Hunt (Myerhoff), 75
phenotype
    classification based on, 128–29
    (*see also* racism)
    definition of, 127
    linking genotype and, 126–28
Phipps, Susie, 135
phonemes, 98

phonology, 98
physical anthropology, 12, *13*,
 13–15, *14*
pilgrimage, *371*, 371–72
Plachimada, 5–6, *6*, 23, 25
plantation economy, 306
Plessy v. Ferguson, 141
political anthropology,
 336, 340
politics and power, 333–59
 origins of history of, 336–40,
  337, 340
 sexuality and, 205
 states and, 341–44
  alternative legal structures
   and, 355–57, *356*
  civil society organizations
   and, *345*, 345–46
  international nonstate actors
   as challenging sovereignty
   of, 344–45
  mobilizing power outside the
   control of, 352–57, *353,
   355, 356*
  social movements and,
   352–55, *353, 355*
  violence and, 346–51,
   349, 351
Politics of Passion (Wekker),
 212
pollution, 23, *23*
Polo, Marco, 69–70
polyandry, 247
polygyny, 247
Polynesia, 339
polyvocality, 82–83
poor in the United states,
 278–81, *279*
population, world, 328
Pordié, Laurent, 400
pornography, 205
Port Authority of New York and
 New Jersey, 144–45
Portugal
 Brazil as colony of, 129, 308
 Mozambique's independence
  from, 349
 same-sex marriage in, 249
potlatch, *268*, 268–69, 339
poverty
 in Côte d'Ivoire, 298

globalization and, 285, 289
kinship as a means to survive,
 252–53
Millennial Development Goals
 to eliminate, 190
in the United states, 265, 283
 roots of, 283–86, *284,
  286*
 urban, 281
of world's population, 22
power
 culture and, 46–52, 80–81,
  116–17
  agency in, 48–49, *50*
  cultural institutions and,
   46–48, *47*
  hegemony in, 48, *49*
  meaning in, 50–52, *51*
 definition of, 46
 gender and, 191–92
 health care and systems of,
  411–12, *412*
 income and distribution of,
  276, *277*
 language and systems of, *see*
  sociolinguistics
 politics and, *see* politics and
  power
 religion as a system of, 383–86,
  386
 sexuality and relations of,
  224–28
  intersection of race and
   sexuality for black gay
   women, 224–26, *225*
  on U.S. college campuses,
   226–28, *227*
 wealth and distribution of,
  276–78, *277*
Prasanna Ganapathi Temple,
 364
prehistoric archaeology, 15
preserving endangered
 languages, 113, 115
prestige, 271
prestige language, 106
primates
 communication of, *96*, 96–97
 humans and, 13–14
 study of, 14
 violence and, *347*, 347–48

primatology, 14
Primitive Culture (Tylor), 42
privacy, 37
productivity, 97
profane, 369
professional immigrants, *323*,
 323–24
Prohibition of Mixed Marriages
 Act, 36
proletariat, 270
proto-Latin language, 110
prostitution, 86
*Protestant Ethic and the Spirit
 of Capitalism, The*
 (Weber), 375, 382
Psychopathia Sexualis (Krafft-
 Ebings), 216
Puerto Rico, 74–75
Pugh, Ena, *392*, 393
Purvis, Kenneth, 50
pushes and pulls, 319

Q
Qaanaaq, Greenland, dog
 teams, *337*
qi, 405
qualitative data, 77–78
quantitative data, 77–78
Queens (New York City)
 Indian immigrants in, 159–60,
  160
 political activism in, *143*,
  143–45
Quran, 366

R
race, 121–51
 in Brazil, 129–31, *130*
 colonialism and, 122, 128–31,
  129, 133
 definition of, 123
 ethnicity vs., 156
 health care and, 411–12, *412*
 Hurricane Katrina and, 122, 291
 lack of biological basis for
  classifications of, 40,
  122–23, 124–28
 Mullings on, 273–75, *275*
 segregation and, 134, *135*,
  141–42, *142*
 in the United States, 131–40

history of racial categories,
133, 133–34, *135*
immigration and, 136–40,
137
poverty and, 283, *284*, 285
rule of hypodescent and,
135–36
U.S. Census and, *132*,
132–33
see also African Americans;
intersectionality; racism;
whiteness
racial endogamy, 249
racial ideology, 142–43
racialization, 138–40
racial profiling, *92*, 93–94
racism
in Brazil, *130*, 130–31
colonialism and, 128–29, 131
definition of, 124
against immigrants, 136–37,
137
individual, 141
institutional, 141–42, *143*
Jena High School incident and,
50–52, *51*
"N-word" and, 17–18, *103*,
103–4
race, whiteness, and, 146–49,
148
racial ideology and, 142–43
resisting, 143–46, *145*
types of, 140–43, *142*
see also African Americans; race
Racism without Racists
(Bonilla-Silva), 143
Ramadan, 366
Ranger, Terence, 170
ranked societies, 267–69, *268*
rape
date, 226
in El Salvador, 198–99
on U.S. college campuses,
226–28, *227*
in the U.S military, 206
rapid change, 22
rap music, 103, *103*
rapport, 77
Rathje, William, 16
RBN (Royal Bafokeng Nation),
166–67

Reader's Guide to Periodic
Literature, 287
reciprocity
in an Amish community, *267*
balanced, 303
definition of, 266, 302
in distribution and exchange,
302–3
egalitarian societies and, 265–66
generalized, 303
negative, 303
Recognizing Ourselves **(Lewin)**,
221
redistribution
definition of, 268, 303
in distribution and exchange,
303–4
in ranked societies, *268*, 268–69
Redmon, David, 81
reflexivity, 75, 83
refugees, 324, 414–16
religion, 361–91
alternate sexes and genders in
Hinduism, 188–90, *189*
blurring of boundaries between
meaning and power,
384–86, *386*
cultural materialism and,
373–74, *374*
debates on gay and lesbian
minsters/rabbis, 206
defining, 364–68, *366*, *367*
distribution of adherents to
major world religions,
366
Durkheim on, 369
Evans-Pritchard on, 378–79
globalization and, 386–89, *387*
local expressions and creative
adaptations of, 365–68,
367
magic and, 377–80, *378*, *380*,
381–82
Marx on, *372*, 372–73
rituals and, 370–72
Durkheim on, 369
pilgrimage, 371–72
rites of passage, *370*, 370–71
shamanism, 376–77
symbols and, 37–38, 373–74,
374, 382

as a system of meaning, 382–83,
383
as a system of power, 383–84
in the United States, 362, *363*,
387, 387–89
Weber on, *375*, 375–76
see also specific religions
Reproducing Jews **(Kahn)**,
253–54
Reproducing Race **(Bridges)**,
411
reproduction, human, *193*,
193–94
research, *see* ethnographic
fieldwork
Returning Home, 164
revitalization of language, 113
Richards, Audrey, 8–9, 370
rites of passage, *370*, 370–71
rituals
in baseball, 381, *381*
definition of, 369
religion and, 370–72
Durkheim on, 369
pilgrimage, *371*, 371–72
rites of passage, *370*,
370–71
Robinson, Eugene, 258
rock carvings in Saudi Arabia,
195
Rockefeller, John D., 238
romantic love, 247
Rosaldo, Michelle, 191
Rowling, J. K., *378*
Royal Bafokeng Nation (RBN),
166–67
Ruiz García, Samuel, 385, *386*
rule of hypodescent, 135–36
rune stone, 99
rural social movements,
352–54, *353*
Russia, 40, 55, 172
Rwanda, 156, 161–63, *162*, *163*

S
Sabin, Ashley, 81
sacred, 369
saints, 367
salvage ethnography, 71
same-sex marriage, 211, 223,
223, 249, *258*, 258–59

Samoa, 43, 74
Sapir, Edward, 100
Sapir-Whorf hypothesis,
    100–101
Saussure, Ferdinand de, 100
Savage, Michael, 93
Scheper-Hughes, Nancy,
    63–64, 86, 87–88,
    89, 403
Scotland, 154
    see also United Kingdom
Scott, James, 49, 357
secularization theory of Weber,
    375–76
security, 37
segregation, racial, 134, *135,*
    141–42, *142*
semiperiphery countries, 311,
    311, 312
September 11, 2001, attacks
    controversy in France on
        headscarves after, 47, *47*
    racialization of Middle
        Easterners after, 138–40
    security after, 37
Serbian Youth Brigade, 334
serotonin, 210
Service, Elman, 336
sex
    alternate, 188–90, *189*
    definition of, 179
    gender vs., 179–81
    intersexuals, 187–88
sexology, 217–18, *218*
*Sexual Behavior in the Human
    Female* (Kinsey,
    Pomeroy, and Martin),
    217
*Sexual Behavior in the Human
    Male* (Kinsey, Pomeroy,
    and Martin), 217
sexual dimorphism, 179–80
sexual harassment, 177, 226
sexuality, 205–32
    in advertising, *204,* 205, *211,*
        232
    alternate constructions of
        in Nicaragua, 214–15
        in Suriname, 212–14, *213*
        among bonobos, 209, *209,*
            347, *347*

biology and, intersection of,
        208–11, *209*
    culture and, *211,* 211–12, 231
    definition of, 208
    globalization's influence on,
        228–31, *230*
    intersection of race and, 224–26,
        225
    power and, relations of, 224–28,
        225, 227
    in the United States, 205–6,
        215–23
        gay and lesbian commitment
            ceremonies, 221–23
        intersection of race and
            sexuality for black gay
            women, 224–26, *225*
        invention of heterosexuality,
            216–18, *218*
        wedding culture
            and constructing
            heterosexuality, 219–21,
            221
    Victorian ideal of, 216
sexual violence, 226–28, *227*
    see also rape
Shadows of War (Nordstrom),
    350
Shakti, *189*
shamanism, 376–77
shamans, 376–77, 415
sharecropping, 279
sharia law
    in Egypt, 355–56, 357
    in Nigeria, 229
Sharp, Gene, 334
Shetty, Shilpa, *30,* 31, 32, 36, 41
Shia, 172–73
Shiva, *189*
Showalter, Buck, 263–64
Siberia, 113
Sierra Leone, 410, *410*
sign language, primates and,
    96, *96*
Sikes, Melvin, 147
SIL (Summer Institute of
    Linguistics), 113, *114*
situational negotiation of
    identity, 159
skin color, 126, 127, 128–29
slavery

in Brazil, 129
    of indigenous populations,
        Europeans and, 305
    influence on U.S. racial system,
        133
    triangle trade and, 306–7, *307,*
        308
slaves
    construction of race in
        Kentucky through, 279
    imported to the United States,
        133, 133–34
    insight into lives of, 16
    at slave auctions, *133*
    as source of Black English,
        108
slave ships, 129, *129*
slave trade, 11, 129, *129*
smiling, 54
Smith, Adam, 314, 315
Smith, Neil, 122, 291
Smith, Robert, 57
soccer, *152,* 153—154, 155, *155*
social class, *see* class
social media, 7
    Arab Spring and, 334
    civil society organizations' use
        of, 345
    code switching in, 107
    language preservation through,
        115
social mobility, 272, 281, 291
social movements, 352–55,
    353, 355
    definition of, 352
    Occupy Wall Street, 288,
        354–55
    rural, 352–54, *353*
social network analysis, 78
social reproduction, 272
sociolinguistics, 102–11
    definition of, 102
    dialect and language, 106
    gender and language, 104–6,
        105
    historical linguistics, 109–11
    language variation in the United
        States, 107–9, *108, 109*
    "N-word," 17–18, *103,* 103–4
    see also language
sociolinguists, 17–18

Sociology of Religion (Weber), 375

sorcery, 379–80, *380*

soul-calling, 415, 416

South Africa

Bafokeng, Inc. in, 165–67, *166, 167*

gay rights in, 230, 249

marriage in, 36

South America

independence of, 308

indigenous populations' lack of immunity to European diseases, 307–8

language loss in, 113

plantation economy in, 306

see also specific countries

South Korea, 314

Spain, 249, 308, 352

spatial comfort zones, 36–37

sperm, *193,* 193–94

sperm donors, *234,* 235

Spirit Catches You and You Fall Down, The (Fadiman), 414

"Spoken Soul," *see* Black English

sports, youth, *182,* 182–83

Sri Lanka, 156

SSAE (Standard Spoken American English), 107, *108*

Stack, Carol, 252

Standard Spoken American English (SSAE), 107, *108*

states, 169, 341–44

aspects of power of, 343–44

challenge to sovereignty of, by international nonstate actors, 344–45

civil society organizations and, *345,* 345–46

definition of, 169, 341

globalization and, 344–46, *345*

mobilizing power outside the control of, 352–57, *353, 355, 356*

modern western-style, 341–43, *342–43*

war and, 348–49, *349*

Stephen, Lynn, 198

stereotypes

gender, 193

of poor whites, 148

Sterk, Claire, 86

Steward, Julian, 74

Stoller, Paul, 379, 380

Stone, Linda, 259

stone tools, 54

stratification, 46

agriculture in nonindustrial cultures and, 301

class, *see* class

definition of, 46

gender

challenging, 196–99, *197*

definition of, 193

language and, 104–5, *105*

structural functionalism, 44

structural racism, *see* institutional racism

Sudan

kinship system in, *240,* 241

Nuer in, *see* Nuer of Southern Sudan

witchcraft among the Azande of, 378–79

sugar, export of, 306

Summer Institute of Linguistics (SIL), 113, *114*

Summers, Lawrence, 53

Sunni, 172–73

Supreme Court, U.S.

Brown v. Board of Education, 142

on hypodescent rules, 135

on interracial marriage, 134, 249, *250*

Lawrence v. Texas, 250

Loving v. Virginia, 36, *250*

Plessy v. Ferguson, 141

on same-sex marriage, 223, *250*

Suriname, 212–14, *213*

surveys in ethnographic fieldwork, 78

Sweden

childbirth in, 397, *398,* 399

same-sex marriage in, 249

Sweetness and Power (Mintz), 75

Sykes-Picot Agreement, 172

symbols, 35, 37–39, *38*

authorizing process for, 383–84

collective understandings of, 45

definition of, 37, 382

religion and, 37–38, 373–74, *374,* 382

synchronic approach to ethnographic fieldwork, 72–73

syntax, 99

Syria, 333

T

Tabula Rogeriana, *305*

Tahiti, 32

Taiwan, 314

Tannen, Deborah, 104–5

Tanzania, 257

Task Force on the Education of African American Students, *109*

technocratic birth, 397

teeth of early hominids, 195

television

globalization and, 58–59, *59*

programs on poverty, 287

sexuality on, 205, 232

testosterone, 210, 211

Texas, 393–94

Texas, Lawrence v., 250

text messages, 100, *100,* 107

Thailand, 314

thick description, 45

Thind, Bhagat Singh, 137

thinking, 100–102

Tibet, 247

Tibetan Buddhism, *400,* 400–402, *401*

tick-borne illnesses, 394

Tierney, Patrick, 84

time-space compression theory, 20

time zones, 40

Timo, Don, 184

Tokyo, *317,* 317–18

Tolkien, J. R. R., *378*

Tongi Station, *294*

toolkit, anthropologist's, 77

tools, stone, 54

Torah, 382–83, *383*
trade routes, *11*, 304–5, *305*, 306–8, *307*
transgender, 188–90, *189*, 215
transnational agricultural corporations, 298
transnational corporations, 297–99
triangle trade, 306–8, *307*
tribes, 338–39, 340
Trobriand Islands
    Malinowski's ethnography of, 44, *44*, 192, *192*, *239*
    Weiner's ethnography of, 75, 192, *192*
Tsukiji Fish Market, *317*, 317–18
tuberculosis, 394
Tunisia, 333
Turner, Victor, 44, 76, 370, 371, 372
Tutsi, 161–63, *162*, *163*
Twa, 162
twins, *392*, 393, 418
Twitter, 334, 345
Tylor, Edward Burnett, 42, 43, 70

U
underdevelopment, 310
undocumented immigrants, 93–94, 174–75
uneven development, 21–22
unfair lending practices, protests against, *145*
unilineal cultural evolution, 42, 70
United Kingdom
    colonial wars and, 307
    FOXP2 gene in, 97
    Iraq and, 172, 173
    kissing in, 32
    on migrants, 318
    same-sex marriage in, 249
    Sykes-Picot Agreement and, 172
United Nations, 310, 345
    Côte d'Ivoire and, 298
    High Commissioner for Refugees, *351*
    Millennial Development Goals of, 190
    on poverty, 289
    on refugees, 324

Rwanda and, 162
on world population, 328
United States
    American origin myth in, 157–58, *158*
    biomedicine in, *403*, 403–4
    childbirth in, 397, 398, *398*, 399
    class and inequality in, 263–65, 275–83
        consumer culture and, 287–89
        income distribution and, 276, *277*
        media and, 287, 288
        middle class and working poor, 280–81
        poor whites in rural Kentucky, 278–80, *279*
        poverty and, 265, 283–86, *284*, *286*
        wealth, Wall Street, and, 281–82, *282*
        wealth distribution and, 276–78, *277*, 304
    consumerism in, 55
    cultural capital and, 273, *273*
    English-only laws in, 94
    ethnic interaction in, 168–69
    gender in, *182*, 182–84
    globalization and, 21
    independence from Great Britain, 134, 308
    interracial marriage in, 36, 48, *49*, 134, *250*
    kinship in
        familes of same-sex partners, *258*, 258–59
        impact of assisted reproductive technologies on, 257–58
        nuclear family, 255–56, *256*
        through choice, 256–57, *257*, 259
    language loss in, 113
    language variation in, 107–9, *108*, *109*
    life expectancy in, 410, *410*
    military, 84, 85, *85*, *180*, 206
    occupation of Iraq, 172, 1733
    race in, 131–40

    history of racial categories, *133*, 133–34, *135*
    immigration and, 136–40, *137*
    rule of hypodescent and, 135–36
    U.S. Census and, *132*, 132–33
    see also African Americans; racism
    same-sex marriage in, 211, 223, *223*, 249, *258*, 258–59
    sexuality in, 205–6, 215–23
        on college campuses, 226–28, 227
        gay and lesbian commitment ceremonies, 221–23
        intersection of race and sexuality for black gay women, 224–26, *225*
        invention of heterosexuality, 216–18, *218*
        same-sex marriage, 223, *223*
        wedding culture and constructing heterosexuality, 219–21, *221*
    spatial comfort zones, 36
    welfare in, 22
United Workers Association (UWA), 264–65
UPANACIONAL, 354
Uruguay, 249
U.S. Census, *132*, 132–33, 283
USA PATRIOT Acts, 37
UWA (United Workers Association), 264–65

V
values, 35, 37
van Gennep, Arnold, 370
vasopressin, 210
Vatican II, 385
Victoria, Queen, 216
Vietnam, 314
Vietnam War, 84, 85
violence
    humans and, 346–48
    war and
        globalization and, 349–51, *351*
        militarization and, 348–49

in Mozambique, 349–50
see also rape
Virchow, Rudolf, 409
Virginia, Loving v., 36, *250*
Virgin of Guadalupe, 385

W
Wales, 154
see also United Kingdom
Wallerstein, Immanuel, 310, 311, 312, 318
Wall Street executives, 281–82, *282*
Walmart, 25
war
anthropology as a tool of, 84–85, *85*
globalization and, 349–51, *351*
nationalism and, 171
states and, 348–49, *349*
Washoe tribe, *113*
water scarcity in India, 5–6, *6,* 23
Watson, James, 57
wealth
definition of, 276
inequality in the United States, 276–78, *277,* 281–82, *282,* 304
Wealth of Nations, The (Smith), 315
weaponizing of anthropology, 85
Weapons of the Weak (Scott), 49
We Are All Khaled Said, 334
Weber, Max, 269, *375*
on religion, 375–76, 382
on states' use of force, 343
theory on class, 271–72
wedding culture, 219–21, *221,* 242
weight, 180
Weiner, Annette, 75, 192, *192*
Weinreich, Max, 106
Wekker, Gloria, 212, 213
welfare, 22
Wendell, Turk, *381*
West, Kanye, *103*
West Africa
Côte d'Ivoire, 297–99, *298,* 306, 309, 312, 325

King of Mali (in 1375), *11*
Weston, Kath, 257
whales, 34, 95
Whitehouse, Bruce, 324, 325
whiteness
class and, intersections of, *147,* 147–49, *148,* 278–80, *279*
construction of, 134
definition of, 134
European immigrants and, 137–38
race, racism, and, 146–49, *148*
white privilege, 146–47
white supremacy, 133–34
White Weddings (Ingraham), 219, 220
Whorf, Benjamin Lee, 100–101
Why We Love (Fisher), 210
Williams, Brackette, 69
Wiradyana, Ketut, *13*
witchcraft, 378–79
Witchcraft, Oracles and Magic among the Azande (Evans-Pritchard), 378–79
Wolf, Eric
fieldwork in Puerto Rico, 74, 75
on power, 46, 80–81, 226
wolves, 34
women
black gay, 224–26, *225*
globalization's impact on, 199–201, *200*
health of, 274–75, *275,* 411–12, *412*
in information technology industry, 177–78
mati work in Suriname and, 212–14, *213*
in the military, *180,* 206
mothers of "The Disappeared" in El Salvador, *197,* 197–98
see also gender
Worked to the Bone (Buck), 134, 278
working poor, U.S., 280–81
World Bank, 310
Costa Rica and, 353
free market and, 314
Gini index of, 289
neoliberal policies and, 315, 344

World Cup in 2010, *152,* 153—154, 155, *155,* 174
World Health Organization, 395
World Social Forum, 316
World Trade Organization (WTO), 314, 315, 344, *3145*
World Vision, 345
World War II, colonialism and, 171, 308–9, *309*
WTO (World Trade Organization), 314, 315, 344, *3145*
Wycliff Bible Translators, *see* Summer Institute of Linguistics (SIL)

X
X chromosomes, 179

Y
'yan daudu, 229, *230,* 231
Yang, Foua, *417*
Yangon, Myanmar, *360,* 361–62
Yanomami people, 84
Y chromosomes, 179
Yemen, 333
You Just Don't Understand (Tannen), 104
youth sports, *182,* 182–83
YouTube, 7
Arab Spring and, 334
civil society organizations' use of, 345
language preservation through, 115
Yucatán, 397, *398,* 399
Yugoslavia, 161, 163–64, *164,* 165

Z
Zambia, 370, *370*
Zanmi Lasante, 408–9
Zapata, Emiliano, 384–85
Zapatistas, 384–86
zeros, 80
Zhan, Mei, 405, 406
Zheng, He, 70
Zinn, Howard, 158
Zinta, Preity, *160*